Your Office

Microsoft® Excel® 2010

COMPREHENSIVE

Amy Kinser

O'KEEFE | STOUT | NIGHTINGALE

WAGNER | MORIARITY

PEARSON

Boston   Columbus   Indianapolis   New York   San Francisco   Upper Saddle River
Amsterdam   Cape Town   Dubai   London   Madrid   Milan   Munich   Paris   Montreal   Toronto
Delhi   Mexico City   Sao Paulo   Sydney   Hong Kong   Seoul   Singapore   Taipei   Tokyo

Editor in Chief: Michael Payne
Acquisitions Editor: Samantha McAfee
Product Development Manager: Laura Burgess
Development Editor: Linda Harrison
Editorial Assistant: Erin Clark
Director of Digital Development: Zara Wanlass
Executive Editor, Digital Learning & Assessment: Paul Gentile
Director, Media Development: Cathi Profitko
Senior Editorial Media Project Manager: Alana Coles
Production Media Project Manager: John Cassar
VP/Director of IT Marketing & Customer Experience: Kate Valentine
Senior Marketing Manager: Tori Olson Alves
Marketing Coordinator: Susan Osterlitz
Marketing Assistant: Darshika Vyas
Senior Managing Editor: Cynthia Zonneveld
Associate Managing Editor: Camille Trentacoste
Operations Director: Nick Sklitsis
Senior Operations Specialist: Natacha Moore
Senior Art Director: Jonathan Boylan
Interior Design: Anthony Gemmellaro
Cover Design: Anthony Gemmellaro
Composition: GEX Publishing Services
Full-Service Project Management: GEX Publishing Services

Credits and acknowledgments borrowed from other sources and reproduced, with permission, in this textbook appear on appropriate page within text.

Microsoft, Windows, Word, PowerPoint, Outlook, FrontPage, Visual Basic, MSN, The Microsoft Network, and/or other Microsoft products referenced herein are either registered trademarks or registered trademarks of the Microsoft Corporation in the U.S.A. and other countries. Screen shots and icons reprinted with permission from the Microsoft Corporation. This book is not sponsored or endorsed by or affiliated with the Microsoft Corporation.

Pearson Education Ltd., London
Pearson Education Singapore, Pte. Ltd
Pearson Education, Canada, Inc.
Pearson Education–Japan
Pearson Education Australia PTY, Limited

Pearson Education North Asia Ltd., Hong Kong
Pearson Educación de Mexico, S.A. de C.V.
Pearson Education Malaysia, Pte. Ltd.
Pearson Education, Upper Saddle River, New Jersey

Library of Congress Cataloging-in-Publication Data

Kinser, Amy.
  Microsoft Excel 2010 : comprehensive / Amy Kinser.
    p. cm. -- (Your office)
  Includes index.
  ISBN 978-0-13-261044-5 (0-13-261044-2)
  1. Microsoft Excel (Computer file) 2. Business--Computer programs. 3.
Electronic spreadsheets. I. Title.
  HF5548.4.M523K565 2012
  005.54--dc23

2011030731
3 4 5 6 7 8 9 10 V064 16 15 14 13 12
ISBN-13: 978-0-13-261044-5
ISBN-10: 0-13-261044-2

Dedications

I dedicate this series to my Kinser Boyz for their unwavering love, support, and patience; to my parents and sister for their love; to my students for inspiring me; to Sam for believing in me; and to the instructors I hope this series will inspire!

Amy Kinser

I dedicate this book to my amazing wife, April. Without her support and understanding this would not have been possible.

Brant Moriarity

To my parents, who always believed in and encouraged me. To my husband and best friend, who gave me support, patience, and love. To my brother and my hero—may you be watching from Heaven with joy in your heart.

Jennifer Nightingale

I dedicate this work to my beautiful wife, Jackie. She is the spark to my plug, the sugar on my crème brulee, the lime in my Corona. She is the universe in which I exist.

Nathan Stout

This book is a product of the unselfish support and patience of my wife and daughters, Bonnie, Kelsie and Maggie, and of the values instilled by my parents, Paul and Carol. They are the authors—I am just a writer.

Timothy O'Keefe

I would like to dedicate this book to my brothers, Larry, David, and Peter. They have affected my life in countless ways and are continually inspiring me with their many examples of hard work, skillfulness, and creativity.

William Wagner

I dedicate this to my husband, Jim. He is my support and my rock.

Joyce Thompson

About the Authors

Amy S. Kinser, Esq., Series Editor

Amy Kinser holds a B.A. degree in Chemistry with a Business minor and a J.D. from the Maurer School of Law, both at Indiana University. After working as an environmental chemist, starting her own technology consulting company, and practicing intellectual property law, she has spent the past 11 years teaching technology at the Kelley School of Business in Bloomington, Indiana. Currently, she serves as the Director of Computer Skills and Senior Lecturer at the Kelley School of Business at Indiana University. She also loves spending time with her two sons, Aidan and J. Matthew, and her husband J. Eric.

Brant Moriarity

Brant Moriarity earned his B.A. in Religious Studies/Philosophy at the Indiana University College of Arts and Sciences and an M.S. in Information Systems at the Indiana University Kelley School of Business. He is currently teaching at the Kelley School of Business.

Dr. Jennifer Paige Nightingale

Jennifer Nightingale, assistant professor at Duquesne University, has taught Information Systems Management since 2000. Before joining Duquesne University, she spent 15 years in industry with a focus in management and training. Her research expertise is in instructional technology, using technology as a teaching tool, and the impact of instructional technologies on student learning. She has earned numerous teaching and research honors and awards, holds an Ed.D. (instructional technology) and two M.S. degrees (information systems management and education) from Duquesne University, and a B.A. from the University of Pittsburgh.

Dr. Nathan Stout

Nathan Stout received an M.B.A. in Organizational Behavior and Human Resources and a Ph.D. in MIS from Indiana University. He has been teaching Information Systems courses for more than 15 years, primarily teaching large introductory courses. He enjoys developing materials in a variety of media to enhance the learning of students. He has received teaching excellence awards as well as recognition for innovative teaching. When not teaching, he enjoys the hiking, canoeing, and landscaping during the day and relaxing with his wife in the evenings.

Dr. Timothy P. O'Keefe

Tim O'Keefe is a professor of Information Systems and Entrepreneurship, Chairman of the Department of Information Systems and Business Education, and M.B.A. Director at the University of North Dakota. He is an Information Technology consultant, co-founder of a successful Internet services company, and has taught in higher education for 28 years.

Tim is married to his high-school sweetheart, Bonnie; they have two beautiful daughters, Kelsie and Maggie. In his spare time he enjoys family, cherished friends and colleagues, his dogs, travelling, and archery.

Dr. William (Bill) P. Wagner

Bill Wagner has been teaching, consulting, and conducting research in Information Systems since 1988. He received a Ph.D. in Information Systems from the University of Kentucky, and has been on the faculty of Villanova University for the past 20 years. Dr. Wagner has developed over 20 innovative IT courses, including new courses on Enterprise Resource Planning, Business Intelligence, and most recently, Mobile Application Development. His research has appeared in many internationally known journals. He also co-authored the first college textbooks on Extensible Markup Language (2003), and customer relationship management (2007).

Joyce Thompson, Common Features Author

Joyce Thompson is an Associate Professor at Lehigh Carbon Community College where she has facilitated learning in Computer Literacy and Computer Applications, Cisco, and Geographic Information Systems since 2002. She has been teaching computer applications for over 20 years. She received her M.Ed. in Instructional Design and Technology. Joyce resides in Pennsylvania with her husband and two cats.

Brief Contents

Contents

EXCEL MODULE 3

EXCEL MODULE 4

EXCEL MODULE 5

Acknowledgments

The *Your Office* team would like to thank the following reviewers who have invested time and energy to help shape this series from the very beginning, providing us with invaluable feedback through their comments, suggestions, and constructive criticism.

We'd like to thank our Editorial Board:

Marni Ferner
University of North Carolina, Wilmington

Jan Hime
University of Nebraska, Lincoln

Linda Kavanaugh
Robert Morris University

Mike Kelly
Community College of Rhode Island

Suhong Li
Bryant University

Sebena Masline
Florida State College of Jacksonville

Candace Ryder
Colorado State University

Cindi Smatt
Texas A&M University

Jill Weiss
Florida International University

We'd like to thank our class testers:

Melody Alexander
Ball State University

Karen Allen
Community College of Rhode Island

Charmayne Cullom
University of Northern Colorado

Christy Culver
Marion Technical College

Marni Ferner
University of North Carolina, Wilmington

Linda Fried
University of Colorado, Denver

Darren Hayes
Pace University

Jan Hime
University of Nebraska, Lincoln

Emily Holliday
Campbell University

Carla Jones
Middle Tennessee State Unversity

Mike Kelly
Community College of Rhode Island

David Largent
Ball State University

Freda Leonard
Delgado Community College

Suhong Li
Bryant University

Sabina Masline
Florida State College of Jacksonville

Sandra McCormack
Monroe Community College

Sue McCrory
Missouri State University

Patsy Parker
Southwest Oklahoma State University

Alicia Pearlman
Baker College, Allen Park

Vickie Pickett
Midland College

Rose Pollard
Southeast Community College

Leonard Presby
William Paterson University

Amy Rutledge
Oakland University

Cindi Smatt
Texas A&M University

Jill Weiss
Florida International University

We'd like to thank our reviewers and focus group attendees:

Sven Aelterman
Troy University

Angel Alexander
Piedmont Technical College

Melody Alexander
Ball State University

Karen Allen
Community College of Rhode Island

Maureen Allen
Elon University

Wilma Andrews
Virginia Commonwealth University

Mazhar Anik
Owens Community College

David Antol
Harford Community College

Kirk Atkinson
Western Kentucky University

Barbara Baker
Indiana Wesleyan University

Kristi Berg
Minot State University

Kavuri Bharath
Old Dominion University

Ann Blackman
Parkland College

Jeanann Boyce
Montgomery College

Cheryl Brown
Delgado Community College West
Bank Campus

Bonnie Buchanan
Central Ohio Technical College

Peggy Burrus
Red Rocks Community College

Richard Cacace
Pensacola State College

Margo Chaney
Carroll Community College

Shanan Chappell
College of the Albemarle, North Carolina

Kuan-Chou Chen
Purdue University, Calumet

David Childress
Ashland Community and Technical College

Keh-Wen Chuang
Purdue University North Central

Amy Clubb
Portland Community College

Bruce Collins
Davenport University

Charmayne Cullom
University of Northern Colorado

Juliana Cypert
Tarrant County College

Harold Davis
Southeastern Louisiana University

Jeff Davis
Jamestown Community College

Jennifer Day
Sinclair Community College

Anna Degtyareva
Mt. San Antonio College

Beth Deinert
Southeast Community College

Kathleen DeNisco
Erie Community College

Donald Dershem
Mountain View College

Bambi Edwards
Craven Community College

Elaine Emanuel
Mt. San Antonio College

Diane Endres
Ancilla College

Nancy Evans
Indiana University, Purdue University,
Indianapolis

Linda Fried
University of Colorado, Denver

Diana Friedman
Riverside Community College

Susan Fry
Boise State University

Virginia Fullwood
Texas A&M University, Commerce

Janos Fustos
Metropolitan State College of Denver

Saiid Ganjalizadeh
The Catholic University of America

Randolph Garvin
Tyler Junior College

Diane Glowacki
Tarrant County College

Jerome Gonnella
Northern Kentucky University

Connie Grimes
Morehead State University

Babita Gupta
California State University, Monterey Bay

Lewis Hall
Riverside City College

Jane Hammer
Valley City State University

Marie Hartlein
Montgomery County Community
College

Darren Hayes
Pace Unversity

Paul Hayes
Eastern New Mexico University

Mary Hedberg
Johnson County Community College

Lynda Henrie
LDS Business College

Deedee Herrera
Dodge City Community College

Cheryl Hinds
Norfolk State University

Mary Kay Hinkson
Fox Valley Technical College

Margaret Hohly
Cerritos College

Brian Holbert
Spring Hill College

Susan Holland
Southeast Community College

Anita Hollander
University of Tennessee, Knoxville

Emily Holliday
Campbell University

Stacy Hollins
St. Louis Community College
Florissant Valley

Mike Horn
State University of New York, Geneseo

Christie Hovey
Lincoln Land Community College

Margaret Hvatum
St. Louis Community College Meramec

Jean Insinga
Middlesex Community College

Jon (Sean) Jasperson
Texas A&M University

Glen Jenewein
Kaplan University

Gina Jerry
Santa Monica College

Dana Johnson
North Dakota State University

Mary Johnson
Mt. San Antonio College

Linda Johnsonius
Murray State University

Carla Jones
Middle Tennessee State Unversity

Susan Jones
Utah State University

Nenad Jukic
Loyola University, Chicago

Sali Kaceli
Philadelphia Biblical University

Sue Kanda
Baker College of Auburn Hills

Robert Kansa
Macomb Community College

Susumu Kasai
Salt Lake Community College

Debby Keen
University of Kentucky

Melody Kiang
California State University, Long Beach

Lori Kielty
College of Central Florida

Richard Kirk
Pensacola State College

Dawn Konicek
Blackhawk Tech

John Kucharczuk
Centennial College

David Largent
Ball State University

Frank Lee
Fairmont State University

Luis Leon
The University of Tennessee at Chattanooga

Freda Leonard
Delgado Community College

Julie Lewis
Baker College, Allen Park

Renee Lightner
Florida State College

John Lombardi
South University

Rhonda Lucas
Spring Hill College

Adriana Lumpkin
Midland College

Lynne Lyon
Durham College

Nicole Lytle
California State University, San Bernardino

Donna Madsen
Kirkwood Community College

Paul Martin
Harrisburg Area Community College

Cheryl Martucci
Diablo Valley College

Sherry Massoni
Harford Community College

Lee McClain
Western Washington University

Sandra McCormack
Monroe Community College

Sue McCrory
Missouri State University

Barbara Miller
University of Notre Dame

Michael O. Moorman
Saint Leo University

Alysse Morton
Westminster College

Elobaid Muna
University of Maryland Eastern Shore

Jackie Myers
Sinclair Community College

Bernie Negrete
Cerritos College

Melissa Nemeth
Indiana University–Purdue University, Indianapolis

Kathie O'Brien
North Idaho College

Patsy Parker
Southwestern Oklahoma State University

Laurie Patterson
University of North Carolina, Wilmington

Alicia Pearlman
Baker College

Diane Perreault
Sierra College and California State University, Sacramento

Vickie Pickett
Midland College

Marcia Polanis
Forsyth Technical Community College

Rose Pollard
Southeast Community College

Stephen Pomeroy
Norwich University

Leonard Presby
William Paterson University

Donna Reavis
Delta Career Education

Eris Reddoch
Pensacola State College

James Reddoch
Pensacola State College

Michael Redmond
La Salle University

Terri Rentfro
John A. Logan College

Vicki Robertson
Southwest Tennessee Community College

Dianne Ross
University of Louisiana at Lafayette

Ann Rowlette
Liberty University

Amy Rutledge
Oakland University

Joann Segovia
Winona State University

Eileen Shifflett
James Madison University

Sandeep Shiva
Old Dominion University

Robert Sindt
Johnson County Community College

Edward Souza
Hawaii Pacific University

Nora Spencer
Fullerton College

Alicia Stonesifer
La Salle University

Cheryl Sypniewski
Macomb Community College

Arta Szathmary
Bucks County Community College

Nasser Tadayon
Southern Utah University

Asela Thomason
California State University Long Beach

Joyce Thompson
Lehigh Carbon Community College

Terri Tiedeman
Southeast Community College, Nebraska

Lewis Todd
Belhaven University

Barb Tollinger
Sinclair Community College

Allen Truell
Ball State University

Erhan Uskup
Houston Community College

Michelle Vlaich-Lee
Greenville Technical College

Barry Walker
Monroe Community College

Rosalyn Warren
Enterprise State Community College

Eric Weinstein
Suffolk County Community College

Lorna Wells
Salt Lake Community College

Rosalie Westerberg
Clover Park Technical College

Clemetee Whaley
Southwest Tennessee Community College

MaryLou Wilson
Piedmont Technical College

John Windsor
University of North Texas

Kathy Winters
University of Tennessee, Chattanooga

Nancy Woolridge
Fullerton College

Jensen Zhao
Ball State University

Martha Zimmer
University of Evansville

Molly Zimmer
University of Evansville

Matthew Zullo
Wake Technical Community College

Additionally, we'd like to thank our my**it**lab team for their tireless work:

Jerri Williams
my**it**lab content author

Ralph Moore
my**it**lab content author

LeeAnn Bates
my**it**lab content author

Jennifer Hurley
my**it**lab content author

Jessica Brandi
Associate Media Project Manager

Jaimie Howard
Media Producer

Cathi Profitko
Director, Media Development

Preface

The **Your Office** series is built upon the discovery that both instructors and students need a modern approach to teaching and learning Microsoft Office applications, an approach that weaves in a business context and focuses on using Office as a decision-making tool.

The process of developing this unique series for you, the modern student or instructor, required innovative ideas regarding the pedagogy and organization of the text. You learn best when doing—so you will be active from Page 1. Your learning goes to the next level when you are challenged to do more with less—your hand will be held at first, but progressively the cases require more from you. Since you care about how things work in the real world—in your classes, your future jobs, your personal life—these innovative features will help you progress from a basic understanding of Office to mastering each application, empowering you to perform with confidence in Excel.

No matter what career you may choose to pursue in life, this series will give you the foundation to succeed. **Your Office** uses cases that will enable you to be immersed in a realistic business as you learn Office in the context of a running business scenario—the Painted Paradise Resort and Spa. You will immediately delve into the many interesting, smaller businesses in this resort (golf course, spa, restaurants, hotel, etc.) to learn how a business or organization uses Office. You will learn how to make Office work for you now as a student and in your future career.

Today, the experience of working with Office is not isolated to working in a job in a cubicle. Your physical office is wherever you are with a laptop or a mobile device. Office has changed. It's modern. It's mobile. It's personal. And when you learn these valuable skills and master Office, you are able to make Office your own. The title of this series is a promise to you, the student: Our goal is to make Microsoft Office **Your Office**.

Key Features

- **Starting and Ending Files:** Before every case, the Starting and Ending Files are identified for students. Starting Files identify exactly which Student Data Files are needed to complete each case. Ending Files are provided to show students the naming conventions they should use when saving their files.

- **Workshop Objectives List:** The learning objectives to be achieved as students work through the workshop. Page numbers are included for easy reference.

- **Active Text:** Appears throughout the workshop and is easily distinguishable from explanatory text by the shaded background. Active Text helps students quickly identify what steps they need to follow to complete the workshop Prepare Case.

- **Quick Reference Box:** A boxed feature that appears throughout the workshop where applicable, summarizing generic or alternative instructions on how to accomplish a task. This feature enables students to quickly find important skills.

- **Real World Advice Box:** A boxed feature that appears throughout the workshop where applicable, offering advice and best practices for general use of important Office skills. The goal is to instruct students as a manager might in a future job.

- **Side Note:** A brief tip or piece of information that is aligned with a step in the workshop quickly advising students completing that particular step.

- **Consider This:** In-text questions or topics for discussion set apart from the main explanatory text, that allow students to step back from the project and think about the skills and the applications of what they are learning and how they might be used in the future.

- **Troubleshooting:** A note related to a step in the active text that helps students work around common pitfalls or errors that might occur.

- **Concept Check:** A section at the end of each workshop made up of approximately five concept-related questions that are short answer or open ended for students to review.

- **Visual Summary:** A visual representation of the important skills learned in the workshop. Call-outs and brief explanations illustrate important buttons or skills demonstrated in a screenshot of the final solution for the Workshop Prepare Case. Intended as a visual review of the objectives learned in the workshop; it is mapped to the objectives using page numbers so students can easily find the section of text to refer to for a refresher.

Instructor Resources

The Instructor's Resource Center, available at www.pearsonhighered.com includes the following:

- Annotated Solution Files with Scorecards assist with grading the Prepare, Practice, Problem Solve, and Perform Cases.

- Data and Solution Files

- Rubrics for Perform Cases in Microsoft Word format enable instructors to easily grade open-ended assignments with no definite solution.

- PowerPoint Presentations with notes for each chapter are included for out-of-class study or review.

- Lesson Plans that provide a detailed blueprint to achieve workshop learning objectives and outcomes and best use the unique structure of the modules.

- Complete Test Bank, also available in TestGen format

- Syllabus templates for 8-week, 12-week, and 16-week courses
- Additional Perform Cases for more exercises where you have to "start from scratch."
- Workshop-level Problem Solve Cases for more assessment on the objectives on an individual workshop level.
- Scripted Lectures that provide instructors with a lecture outline that mirrors the Workshop Prepare Case.
- Online Course Cartridges
- Flexible, robust, and customizable content is available for all major online course platforms that include everything instructors need in one place. Please contact your sales representative for information on accessing course cartridges for WebCT, Blackboard, or CourseCompass.

Student Resources

- Student Data CD
- Student Data Files
- Workshop Prepare Case videos walk students through a case similar to the Workshop Prepare Case, which follows the click path and individual skills students learn in the workshop. There is one video per workshop.
- Real World Interview videos introduce students to real professionals talking about how they use Microsoft Office on a daily basis in their work. These videos provide the relevance students seek while learning this material. There is one video per workshop.

Pearson's Companion Website

www.pearsonhighered.com/youroffice offers expanded IT resources and downloadable supplements. Students can find the following self-study tools for each workshop:

- Online Study Guide
- Workshop Objectives
- Glossary
- Workshop Objectives Review
- Web Resources
- Student Data Files

myitlab for Office 2010 is a solution designed by professors for professors that allows easy delivery of Office courses with defensible assessment and outcomes-based training. The new **Your Office 2010** system will seamlessly integrate online assessment, training, and projects with myitlab for Microsoft Office 2010!

myitlab for Office 2010 Features…

- **Assessment and training built to match *Your Office 2010*** instructional content so that myitlab works with Your Office to help students make Office their own.
- **Both project-based and skill-based assessment and training** allow instructors to test and train students on complete exercises or individual Office application skills.
- **Full course management functionality** which includes all instructor and student resources, a complete Gradebook, and the ability to run a variety of reports including detailed student clickstream data.
- **The most open, realistic, high-fidelity simulation** of Office 2010 makes students feel like they are learning Office, not just a simulation.
- **Grader, a live-in-the-application project-grading tool,** enables instructors to assign projects taken from the end-of-chapter material and additional projects included in the instructor resources. These are graded automatically, with detailed feedback provided to both instructors and students.

Common Features workshop efficiently covers skills most common among all applications, reducing repetition and allowing instructors to move faster over such topics as save, print, and bold.

Common Features of Microsoft Office 2010

WORKSHOP 1

Objectives

1. Starting and exploring Office programs and common window elements. p. 59
2. Using the Ribbon. p. 66
3. Using contextual tools. p. 73
4. Working with files. p. 76
5. Sharing files using Windows Live SkyDrive. p. 81
6. Getting help. p. 85
7. Printing a file. p. 87
8. Exiting programs. p. 87

Understanding the Common Features of Microsoft Office

PREPARE CASE
Working with the Common Features

The gift shop at the Red Bluff Golf Club has an array of items available for purchase from toiletries to clothes to presents for loved ones back home. There are numerous part-time employees including students from the local college. Frequently, the gift shop holds training luncheons for new employees. Susan Brock, the manager, is worried about the expense of providing lunch at the trainings. Your first assignment will be to start two documents for a meeting with Susan. You will begin a Word document for meeting minutes and an Excel spreadsheet to add and analyze expenses during the meeting. To complete this task, you need to understand and work with the common features from the Microsoft Office Suite.

Courtesy of www.Shutterstock.com

Student data files needed for this workshop:

 New, blank Word document

 New, blank Excel workbook

You will save your files as:

 Lastname_Firstname_cf01_ws01_Minutes

 Lastname_Firstname_cf01_ws01_Budget

57

Unique Structure Providing for Customizability for Each Course: Instructors can choose to teach with Modules to have students achieve a higher level of understanding of the skills, or they can go more basic and traditional with the Workshops alone.

Workshops: An organizational element of the text that, similar to a chapter, introduces concepts through explanatory text and hands-on projects through Active Text, but in an integrated manner so students are working along with the Workshop Prepare Case the entire time.

Modules: An organizational structure that provides for the synthesis of skills and concepts introduced over two grouped Workshops. Requires students to successfully retain and use skills they have learned over multiple Workshops in new contexts.

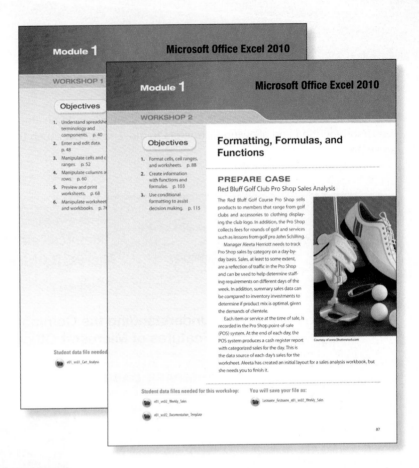

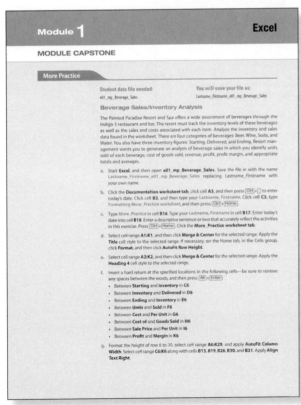

Module Capstone: An organizational section of the text that appears once per Module. The Module Capstone comprises Practice, Problem Solve, and Perform Cases that require students to use learned skills over two Workshops to complete projects.

Clear Objectives with page numbers identify the learning objectives to be achieved as students work through the Workshop. Page numbers are included for students for easy reference. Students are introduced to them at the Workshop opener. Students see these again at the Visual Summary, where students see how each Objective was put into action in a final solution from the Prepare Case.

The **Visual Summary** is intended as a quick visual review of the objectives learned in the Workshop and is mapped to the Objectives using page numbers so students can easily find the section of text to refer to for a refresher.

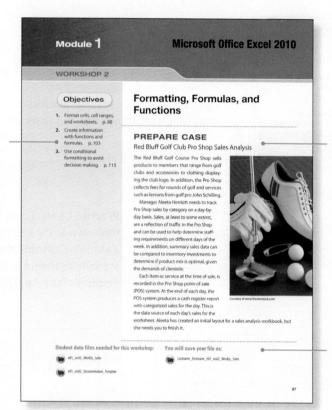

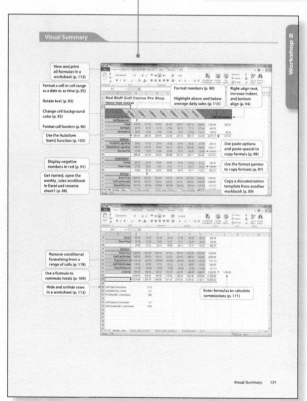

Global Scenario is the basis of the Prepare Cases and is used to help students see the connections between businesses and how they use Microsoft Office in more than just a single case.

Starting and Ending Data Files clearly list the file names of starting data files and naming conventions for the ending data files prior to each Case.

Throughout the Module we use four different kinds of cases that are characterized by the level of instruction or guidance that students receive. The goal of the progression of these cases is to take students from a potentially very introductory level all the way to mastery, so students can learn to make Office their own.

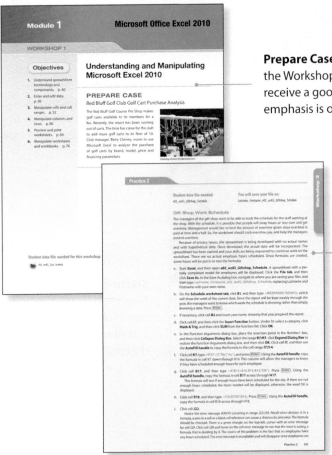

Prepare Cases: Cases that students are guided through via the Workshop. Students work along with the instruction and receive a good deal of hand-holding or cueing. The learning emphasis is on Knowledge and Comprehension of new skills.

Practice Cases: Cases that students complete on their own at the end of a Workshop and beginning of a Module Capstone. Often maintain same or similar scenario or theme as Prepare Case. The learning emphasis is on Applying previously learned skills.

Problem Solve Cases: Cases that students complete on their own at the end of a Module in the Module Capstone. These Cases cover skills learned over the two previous Workshops. The learning emphasis is on Analyzing and Synthesizing of previously learned skills.

Perform Cases: Cases that students complete entirely on their own at the end of a Module in a Module Capstone. Most of these cases require students to work completely from scratch to solve business problems in a variety of scenarios: typical student lives, future careers, and by evaluating how others have performed. The learning emphasis is on Synthesizing, Creating with, and Evaluating projects using previously learned skills.

Troubleshooting identifies a note related to a step in the Active Text that helps students work around common pitfalls or errors that might occur.

Active Text boxes appear throughout the workshop and are easily distinguishable from explanatory text by the shaded background. These boxes help students easily identify what steps they need to follow to complete the Workshop Prepare Case and gets them working hands-on from the first pages of the Workshop all the way through to the end.

Side Note identifies a very brief tip or piece of information that is aligned with a step in the Workshop. This gives a quick piece of help or advice for students completing that particular step.

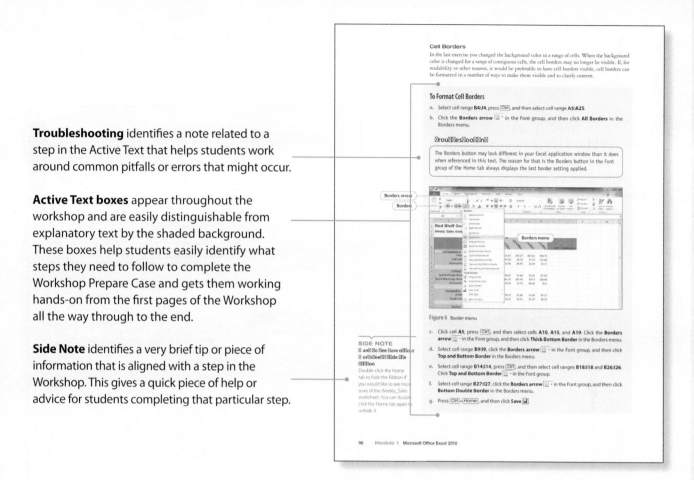

Real World Advice boxes appear throughout the Workshop where applicable, offering advice and best practices for general use of important Office skills. The goal is to instruct students as a manager might in a future career.

Consider This is an in-text question or topic for discussion set apart from the main explanatory text that allow students to step back from the project and think about the skills and the applications of what they are learning and how they might be used in the future.

Quick Reference boxes appear throughout the Workshop where applicable, summarizing generic or alternative instructions for accomplishing a task. The goal is to give students a quick place to find important skills.

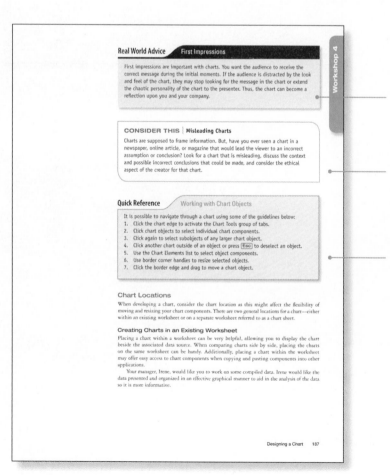

Concept Check is a section at the end of each Workshop that is made up of approximately five concept-related questions that are short answer or open-ended for students to quickly review.

Concept Check

1. You are the manager of the production department and need to create a spreadsheet to track projections. What differences would exist if this spreadsheet were to be used only by you versus being accessed by other staff employees?

2. You have a spreadsheet that contains performance data for the staff. How would you organize this data considering that it would be data used for annual performance reviews for each staff member? What are some of the ethical considerations to keep in mind when using this data?

3. You are reviewing a spreadsheet for your employee and notice the formula that calculates production costs as =B25*10000, where B25 is the unit cost and 10000 is the estimated production. What is wrong with how this formula has been structured and what suggestions would you offer to correct the formula to make it more efficient?

4. You have a range C4:C8 that are the number of transactions for each division of your company. The sum of the transactions is in C9. You want a formula in D4:D8 that will figure the percent of transactions for each division. The formula in D4 is =C4/C9, which works for the first division, but when that formula is copied down through D8, errors occur for the other divisions. Why? How would you fix the formula so it could be copied to other cells and work correctly?

5. You are creating a PMT function and you see PMT(rate, nper,pv,[fv],[type]) just below where you are typing. Why is the nper bold? Why are there [] brackets around the fv and type?

Key Terms

Absolute cell reference 145	Mixed cell reference 146	Rate 168
Argument 154	Named range 149	Relative cell reference 142
Cell reference 140	Nper 168	Show Formulas view 144
Function 154	Pseudocode 172	Syntax 154
Hard-coding 140	PV 168	

Dear Students,

If you want an edge over the competition, make it personal. Whether you love sports, travel, the stock market, or ballet, your passion is personal to you. Capitalizing on your passion leads to success. You live in a global marketplace, and your competition is global. The honors students in China exceed the total number of students in North America. Skills can help set you apart, but passion will make you stand above. *Your Office* is the tool to harness your passion's true potential.

In prior generations, personalization in a professional setting was discouraged. You had a "work" life and a "home" life. As the Series Editor, I write to you about the vision for *Your Office* from my laptop, on my couch, in the middle of the night when inspiration struck me. My classroom and living room are my office. Life has changed from generations before us.

So, let's get personal. My degrees are not in technology, but chemistry and law. I helped put myself through school by working full time in various jobs, including a successful technology consulting business that continues today. My generation did not grow up with computers, but I did. My father was a network administrator for the military. So, I was learning to program in Basic before anyone had played Nintendo's Duck Hunt or Tetris. Technology has always been one of my passions from a young age. In fact, I now tell my husband: don't buy me jewelry for my birthday, buy me the latest gadget on the market!

In my first law position, I was known as the Office guru to the extent that no one gave me a law assignment for the first two months. Once I submitted the assignment, my supervisor remarked, "Wow, you don't just know how to leverage technology, but you really know the law too." I can tell you novel-sized stories from countless prior students in countless industries who gained an edge from using Office as a tool. Bringing technology to your passion makes you well rounded and a cut above the rest, no matter the industry or position.

I am most passionate about teaching, in particular teaching technology. I come from many generations of teachers, including my mother who is a kindergarten teacher. For over 12 years, I have found my dream job passing on my passion for teaching, technology, law, science, music, and life in general at the Kelley School of Business at Indiana University. I have tried to pass on the key to engaging passion to my students. I have helped them see what differentiates them from all the other bright students vying for the same jobs.

Microsoft Office is a tool. All of your competition will have learned Microsoft Office to some degree or another. Some will have learned it to an advanced level. Knowing Microsoft Office is important, but it is also fundamental. Without it, you will not be considered for a position.

Today, you step into your first of many future roles bringing Microsoft Office to your dream job working for Painted Paradise Resort and Spa. You will delve into the business side of the resort and learn how to use *Your Office* to maximum benefit.

Don't let the context of a business fool you. If you don't think of yourself as a business person, you have no need to worry. Whether you realize it or not, everything is business. If you want to be a nurse, you are entering the health care industry. If you want to be a football player in the NFL, you are entering the business of sports as entertainment. In fact, if you want to be a stay-at-home parent, you are entering the business of a family household where *Your Office* still gives you an advantage. For example, you will be able to prepare a budget in Excel and analyze what you need to do to afford a trip to Disney World!

At Painted Paradise Resort and Spa, you will learn how to make Office yours through four learning levels designed to maximize your understanding. You will Prepare, Practice, and Problem Solve your tasks. Then, you will astound when you Perform your new talents. You will be challenged through Consider This questions and gain insight through Real World Advice.

There is something more. You want success in what you are passionate about in your life. It is personal for you. In this position at Painted Paradise Resort and Spa, you will gain your personal competitive advantage that will stay with you for the rest of your life—*Your Office*.

Sincerely,

Amy Kinser

Series Editor

Welcome to the Painted Paradise Resort and Spa Team!

Welcome to your new office at Painted Paradise Resort and Spa, where we specialize in painting perfect getaways. As the Chief Technology Officer, I am excited to have staff dedicated to the Microsoft Office integration between all the areas of the resort. Our team is passionate about our paradise, and I hope you find this to be your dream position here!

Painted Paradise is a resort and spa in New Mexico catering to business people, romantics, families, and anyone who just needs to get away. Inside our resort are many distinct areas. Many of these areas operate as businesses in their own right but must integrate with the other areas of the resort. The main areas of the resort are as follows.

- The **Hotel** is overseen by our Chief Executive Officer, William Mattingly, and is at the core of our business. The hotel offers a variety of accommodations, ranging from individual rooms to a grand villa suite. Further, the hotel offers packages including spa, golf, and special events.

   Room rates vary according to size, season, demand, and discount. The hotel has discounts for typical groups, such as AARP. The hotel also has a loyalty program where guests can earn free nights based on frequency of visits. Guests may charge anything from the resort to the room.

- **Red Bluff Golf Course** is a private world-class golf course and pro shop. The golf course has services such as golf lessons from the famous golf pro John Schilling and playing packages. Also, the golf course attracts local residents. This requires variety in pricing schemes to accommodate both local and hotel guests. The pro shop sells many retail items online.

   The golf course can also be reserved for special events and tournaments. These special events can be in conjunction with a wedding, conference, meetings, or other event covered by the event planning and catering area of the resort.

- **Turquoise Oasis Spa** is a full-service spa. Spa services include haircuts, pedicures, massages, facials, body wraps, waxing, and various other spa services—typical to exotic. Further, the spa offers private consultation, weight training (in the fitness center), a water bar, meditation areas, and steam rooms. Spa services are offered both in the spa and in the resort guest's room.

   Turquoise Oasis Spa uses top-of-the-line products and some house-brand products. The retail side offers products ranging from candles to age-defying home treatments. These products can also be purchased online. Many of the hotel guests who fall in love with the house-brand soaps, lotions, candles, and other items appreciate being able to buy more at any time.

   The spa offers a multitude of packages including special hotel room packages that include spa treatments. Local residents also use the spa. So, the spa guests are not limited to hotel guests. Thus, the packages also include pricing attractive to the local community.

- **Painted Treasures Gift Shop** has an array of items available for purchase, from toiletries to clothes to presents for loved ones back home, including a healthy selection of kids' toys for traveling business people. The gift shop sells a small sampling from the spa, golf course pro shop, and local New Mexico culture. The gift shop also has a small section of snacks and drinks. The gift shop has numerous part-time employees including students from the local college.

- The **Event Planning & Catering** area is central to attracting customers to the resort. From weddings to conferences, the resort is a popular destination. The resort has a substantial number of staff dedicated to planning, coordinating, setting up, catering, and maintaining these events. The resort has several facilities that can accommodate large groups. Packages and prices vary by size, room, and other services such as catering. Further, the Event Planning & Catering team works closely with local vendors for floral decorations, photography, and other event or wedding typical needs. However, all catering must go through the resort (no outside catering permitted). Lastly, the resort stocks several choices of decorations, table arrangements, and centerpieces. These range from professional, simple, themed, and luxurious.

- **Indigo5** and the **Silver Moon Lounge**, a world-class restaurant and lounge, are overseen by the well-known Chef Robin Sanchez. The cuisine is balanced and modern. From steaks to pasta to local southwestern meals, Indigo5 attracts local patrons in addition to resort guests. While the catering function is separate from the restaurant—though menu items may be shared—the restaurant does support all room service for the resort. The resort also has smaller food venues onsite such as the Terra Cotta Brew coffee shop in the lobby.

Currently, these areas are using Office to various degrees. In some areas, paper and pencil are still used for most business functions. Others have been lucky enough to have some technology savvy team members start Microsoft Office Solutions.

Using your skills, I am confident that you can help us integrate and use Microsoft Office on a whole new level! I hope you are excited to call Painted Paradise Resort and Spa *Your Office*.

Looking forward to working with you more closely!

Aidan Matthews

Aidan Matthews
Chief Technology Officer

Common Features of Microsoft Office 2010

Objectives

Understanding the Common Features of Microsoft Office

PREPARE CASE
Working with the Common Features

The gift shop at the Red Bluff Golf Club has an array of items available for purchase from toiletries to clothes to presents for loved ones back home. There are numerous part-time employees including students from the local college. Frequently, the gift shop holds training luncheons for new employees. Susan Brock, the manager, is worried about the expense of providing lunch at the trainings. Your first assignment will be to start two documents for a meeting with Susan. You will begin a Word document for meeting minutes and an Excel spreadsheet

Courtesy of www.Shutterstock.com

to add and analyze expenses during the meeting. To complete this task, you need to understand and work with the common features from the Microsoft Office Suite.

Student data files needed for this workshop:

 New, blank Word document

 New, blank Excel workbook

You will save your files as:

 Lastname_Firstname_cf01_ws01_Minutes

 Lastname_Firstname_cf01_ws01_Budget

Working with the Office Interface and the Ribbon

When you walk into a grocery store, you usually know what you are going to find and that items will be in approximately the same location, regardless of which store you are visiting. The first items you usually see are the fruits and fresh vegetables while the frozen foods are near the end of the store. This similarity among stores creates a level of comfort for the shopper. The brands may be different, but the food types are the same. That is, canned corn is canned corn.

Microsoft Office 2010 creates that same level of comfort with its Ribbons, features, and functions. Each application has a similar appearance or user interface. Microsoft Office 2010 is a suite of productivity applications or programs. Office is available in different suites for PCs and Macs. Office Home and Student includes Word, Excel, PowerPoint, and OneNote 2010. Office Home and Business includes Word, Excel, PowerPoint, OneNote, and Outlook 2010. Office Professional includes Word, Excel, PowerPoint, OneNote, Outlook, Access, and Publisher 2010. Other suites include Office Standard, Office Professional Plus, Office Professional Academic, and Office for Mac 2011. Each of the applications in these suites can be used individually or in combination with other Office applications. Figure 1 shows the interface for Word 2010.

Figure 1 Overview of Office Word 2010 program interface

Microsoft Word is a word processing program. This application can be used to create, edit, and format **documents** such as letters, memos, reports, brochures, resumes, and flyers. Word also provides tools for creating **tables,** which organize information into rows and columns. Using Word, you can add **graphics,** which consist of pictures, clip art, SmartArt, shapes, and charts, that can enhance the look of your documents.

Microsoft Excel is a spreadsheet program. Excel is a two-dimensional database program that can be used to model quantitative data and perform accurate and rapid calculations with results ranging from simple budgets to financial and statistical analyses. Data entered into Excel can be used to generate a variety of charts such as pie charts, bar charts, line charts, or scatter charts, to name a few, to enhance spreadsheet data. The Excel files created are known as **workbooks,** which contain one or more worksheets. Excel makes it possible to analyze, manage, and share information, which can also help you make better and smarter decisions. New analysis and visualization tools help you track and highlight important data trends.

Microsoft PowerPoint is a presentation and slide program. This application can be used to create slide shows for a presentation, as part of a website, or as a stand-alone application on a computer kiosk. These presentations can also be printed as handouts.

Microsoft OneNote is a planner and note-taking program. OneNote can be used to collect information in one easy-to-find place. With OneNote, you can capture text and images, as well as video and audio. By sharing your notebooks, you can simultaneously take and edit notes with other people in other locations, or just keep everyone in sync and up to date. You can also take your OneNote notebooks with you and then view and edit your notes from virtually any computer with an Internet connection or your Windows 7 phone device.

Microsoft Outlook is an e-mail, contact, and information management program. Outlook allows you to stay connected to the world with the most up-to-date e-mail and calendar tools. You can manage and print schedules, task lists, phone directories, and other documents. Outlook's ability to manage scheduled events and contact information is why Outlook is sometimes referred to as an **information management program**.

Microsoft Access is a relational database management program. Access is a three-dimensional database program that allows you to make the most of your data. Access is known as **relational database** software (or three-dimensional database software) because it is able to connect data in separate tables to form a relationship when common fields exist—to offer reassembled information from multiple tables. For example, a business might have one table that lists all the supervisors, their shifts, and which area they supervise. Another table might accumulate data for employees and track which shift they are working. Since the common field in this example, for both database tables are shift hours, a business could use Access to query which employees are working the second shift, who the supervisor is, and produce a report with all their names. Thus, Access is used primarily for decision making by businesses that compile data from multiple records stored in tables to produce informative reports. Many businesses use Access to store data and Excel to model and analyze data by creating charts.

Microsoft Publisher is a desktop publishing program that offers professional tools and templates to help easily communicate a message in a variety of publication types, saving time and money while creating a more polished finished look. Whether you are designing brochures, newsletters, postcards, greeting cards, or e-mail newsletters, Publisher aids in delivering high-quality results without the user having graphic design experience. Publisher helps you to create, personalize, and share a wide range of professional-quality publications and marketing materials with ease.

Starting and Exploring Office Programs and Common Window Elements

There is more than one way to start Office programs. As you become familiar with the various options, you will be able to decide which method is more comfortable and efficient for your personal needs and workflow. Once you start working with these applications, also notice that it is possible to have more than one application open at a time. This is a valuable tool for users. One method for opening any Office program is from the Start menu on the taskbar.

To Start Office Programs

a. Click the **Start** button.

b. Click **All Programs**, scroll if necessary, and then click the **Microsoft Office** folder.

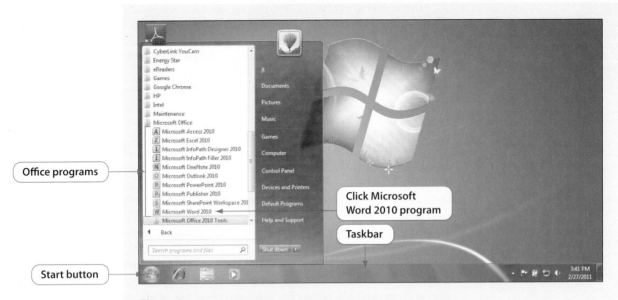

Office programs

Click Microsoft
Word 2010 program

Taskbar

Start button

Figure 2 Starting Word from the Start menu

Troubleshooting

If Microsoft Office is not listed on your menu, you can use the Search programs and files input box at the bottom of the Start menu to type keywords to help find items quickly. Type in the application name desired and a list of options will appear. Notice when "word" is the keyword typed, "Microsoft Word 2010" appears at the top of the list.

Starting Word and Opening a New Blank Document
A blank document is like a blank piece of paper. The insertion point is at the first character of the first line. This provides a clean slate for your document.

To Start Word

a. Click the **Start** button 🌀, and then click **All Programs** to display the All Programs list.

b. Click the **Microsoft Office** folder, and then point to **Microsoft Word 2010**.

c. Click **Microsoft Word 2010**. Word will start with a new blank document.

Quick Access Toolbar

Ribbon

Blank document

Word program icon is displayed on the taskbar

Title bar

View icons

Zoom slider

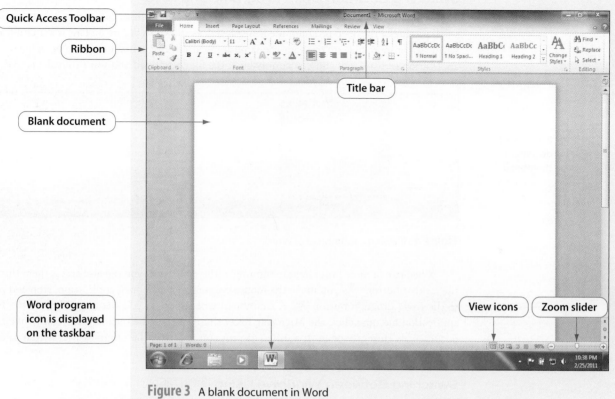

Figure 3 A blank document in Word

Starting Excel and Opening a New Blank Document

A blank spreadsheet is like a blank sheet of columnar paper. The active cell is at the first cell of the first row. This provides a clean slate for your spreadsheet.

To Start Excel

a. Click the **Start** button 🌐, and then click **All Programs** to display the All Programs list.

b. Click **Microsoft Office**, and then point to **Microsoft Excel 2010**.

c. Click **Microsoft Excel 2010**. Excel will start with a new blank workbook.

The other Office programs can be opened using the same method. As previously mentioned, more than one application can be opened at the same time. It is possible to switch between any open applications to view their contents. The taskbar contains icons for open applications, as well as any program icons that have been pinned to the taskbar to allow for quick access when starting a program.

Switching Between Open Programs and Files

When moving your mouse pointer over a taskbar icon for an open program, a **thumbnail** or small picture of the open program file is displayed, as shown in Figure 4. This is a useful feature when two or more files are open for the same application. A thumbnail of each open file for that application is displayed, and you simply click the file thumbnail you want to make active.

Blank Word document thumbnail

Figure 4 Viewing a thumbnail of Word

When two or more programs are running at the same time, you can also access them through the taskbar buttons. As you move the mouse pointer over each open application, stop and point to the Excel program button ▓. A thumbnail will appear. If you want to switch to the Excel application file, just click the Microsoft Excel thumbnail or the button—since only one Excel document is currently open. If a different program is active, the program will switch to make Excel the active program.

Switching Between Windows Using Alt + Tab

As an alternative to using the thumbnails, you can use the keyboard shortcut to move between applications by holding down Alt and pressing Tab. A small window appears in the center of the screen with thumbnails representing each of the open programs. There is also a thumbnail for the desktop. The program name at the top of the window indicates the program that will be active when you release Alt.

To Switch Between Applications

a. On the taskbar, point to **Excel** ▓ and observe the thumbnail of the Excel file.

b. Click the **Microsoft Excel - Book1** thumbnail to make sure the Book1 Excel document is the current active program.

c. In the current active cell **A1**, type Budget, and then press Enter. In the new cell A2, type 1234, and then press Enter.

Resizing Windows and Workspaces

Office has a consistent design and layout as shown in Figure 5. This is beneficial because once you learn to use one Office program; you can use many of those skills when working with the other Office programs.

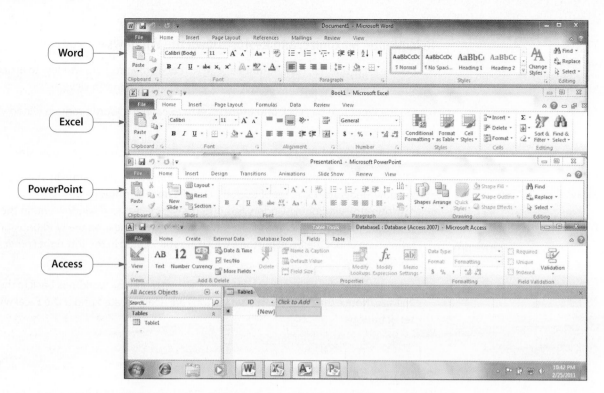

Figure 5 The Ribbons of Word, Excel, PowerPoint, and Access

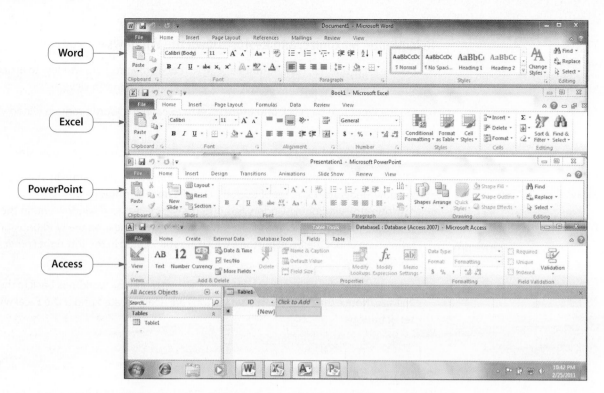

One feature common among all of the applications is the three buttons that appear in the top-right corner of an application's title bar. The left button is the Minimize button. This button hides a window so it is only visible on the taskbar. The middle button is a toggle button between Restore Down and Maximize, depending on the status of the window. If the window is at its maximum size, the button will act in a Restore Down capacity by restoring the window to a previous, smaller size. Once a window is in the Restore Down mode, the button toggles to a Maximize button, which expands the window to its full size. Finally, the button on the right is the Close button, which will close a file or exit the program.

These buttons offer another layer of flexibility in the ability to size and arrange the windows to suit your purpose or to minimize a window and remove it from view. The **Maximize** button might be used most often, since it offers the largest workspace. If several applications are opened, the windows can be arranged using the **Restore Down** button so several windows can be viewed at the same time. If you are not working on an application and want to have it remain open, the **Minimize** button will hide the application on the taskbar.

Excel has two sets of buttons in the top-right corner: the set on the program title bar is for the Excel program, and the set just below that represents the workbook currently open as shown in Figure 6.

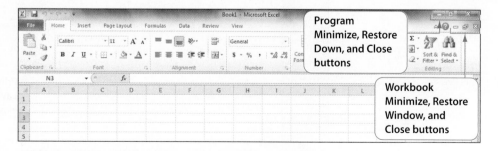

Figure 6 Program and workbook Minimize, Restore Window and Close buttons

To Minimize, Maximize, and Restore Down the Windows

a. On the Excel title bar, click **Minimize** ▭ to reduce the program window to an icon on the taskbar. The Word window will now be the active window in view.

b. On the Word title bar, click **Maximize** ▭ to expand the Word program window to fill the screen.

c. Click the **Restore Down** button ▭ to return Word to its previous window size.

d. Click Excel ▭ on the taskbar to make Excel the active program. On the workbook window, under the Excel set of buttons, click **Restore Window** ▭.

   Notice the workbook window is reduced to a smaller sized window within the Excel window and the three buttons for the workbook now appear on the workbook title bar rather than under the Excel buttons, which are still located in the top-right corner of the Excel window.

e. On the workbook title bar, click **Maximize** ▭ to expand the workbook back to the original size. Notice the workbook set of buttons are again located under the Excel window set of buttons.

Switching Views

There are a variety of views in each program. The views provide different ways to display the file within the program. There are five views in Word: Print Layout, Full Screen Reading, Web Layout, Outline, and Draft. The content or file information is the same in the different views; it is merely the presentation of the document information that appears different. For example, in Word, Print Layout shows how the document appears as a printed page. Web Layout shows how the document appears as a web page. Print Layout is the most commonly used view when creating a draft of a document as shown in Figure 7.

SIDE NOTE
Switching Between Views

You can quickly switch between views using the options located on the View tab in the Document Views group, or you can use the View buttons located on the status bar at the bottom-right side of the window.

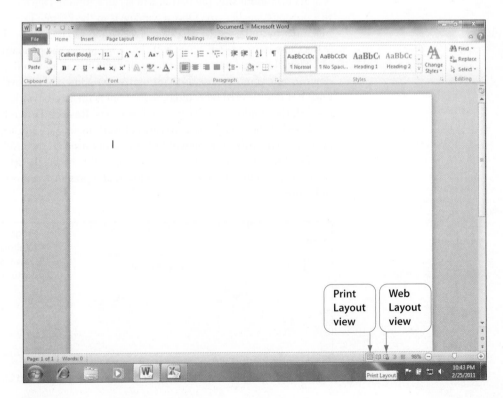

Figure 7 Print and Web Layout views

Zooming and Scrolling

To get a closer look at the content within the program, you can zoom in. Alternatively, if you would like to see more of the contents, you can zoom out. Keep in mind that the Zoom level only affects your view of the document on the monitor and does not affect the printed output of the document, similar to using a magnifying glass to see something bigger—the print on the page is still the same size. Therefore, the zoom level should not be confused with how big the text will print—it only affects your view of the document on the screen. On the right side of the status bar is a slide control that permits zooming in Word from 10% to 500%. The plus and minus propose an easy method, or you can drag the Zoom Slider. In Excel and PowerPoint, the zoom range is from 10% to 400%. When using zoom, sometimes text is shifted off the viewing screen. Depending on the program and the zoom level, you might see the vertical or horizontal scroll bars, or both scroll bars, which can be used to adjust what is displayed in the window. The scroll bars have arrows that can be clicked to shift the workspace in small increments in a specified direction and a scroll box that can be dragged to move a workspace in larger increments.

SIDE NOTE

Using Zoom to Increase or Decrease a Document View

In addition to the Zoom Slider, Zoom is located on the View tab in the Zoom group. Click the Zoom button on the Ribbon to launch the Zoom dialog box, which contains preset zoom selections, or you can type in a custom zoom level in the Percent input box. The Zoom dialog box can also be opened by clicking the Zoom level amount next to the Zoom Slider on the status bar.

To Zoom and Scroll in Office Applications

a. On the taskbar, click **Word**. On the Word title bar, if necessary, click **Maximize** to expand the Word program window to fill the screen.

b. The insertion point should be blinking on the blank document. Type Word.

c. On the Word status bar, drag the **Zoom Slider** to the right until the percentage is **500%**. The document is enlarged to its largest size. This makes the text appear larger.

d. On the Word status bar, click the **Zoom level** button, currently displaying 500%. The Zoom dialog box opens. You can set a customer Zoom level or use one of the preset options.

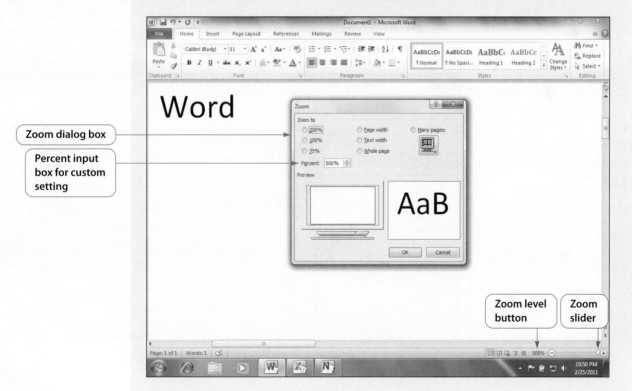

Zoom dialog box

Percent input box for custom setting

Zoom level button

Zoom slider

Figure 8 Zoom dialog box

e. Click **Page width**, and then click **OK**. The Word document is zoomed to its page width.

f. On the taskbar, click **Excel**. The Excel program should now be displayed as the active window.

g. Click cell **B1** (which is the first row cell under Column B on the worksheet).

h. Type Firstname Lastname, replacing Firstname Lastname with your own name.

i. Press Enter. Text has been entered in cell B1, and cell B2 is now the active cell.

j. On the status bar, notice the Zoom level and click **Zoom Out** ⊖ three times. The Zoom level magnification is now 70% (if you started at 100%).

k. On the horizontal scroll bar, click the **right scroll arrow** ▶ two times and the text is shifted to the left. Some columns may not be visible now.

l. On the horizontal scroll bar, drag the scroll box all the way to the left. The columns should be visible again.

m. Drag the **Zoom Slider** to the right to return the Zoom level to **100%**.

n. On the taskbar, click **Word** W. The Word program window is displayed as the active window.

Using the Ribbon

While the tabs, which contain groups of commands on the **Ribbon**, differ from program to program, each program has two tabs in common: the File tab and the Home tab. The File tab is the first tab on the Ribbon and is used for file management needs. When clicked, it opens **Backstage view**, which provides access to the file level features, such as saving a file, creating a new file, opening an existing file, printing a file, and closing a file, as well as program options, as shown in Figure 9. The Home tab is the second tab in each program Ribbon. It contains the commands for the most frequently performed activities, including copying, cutting, and pasting; changing fonts and styles; and other various editing and formatting tools. The commands on these tabs may differ from program to program. Other tabs are program specific, such as the Formulas tab in Excel, the Design tab in PowerPoint, and the Database Tools tab in Access.

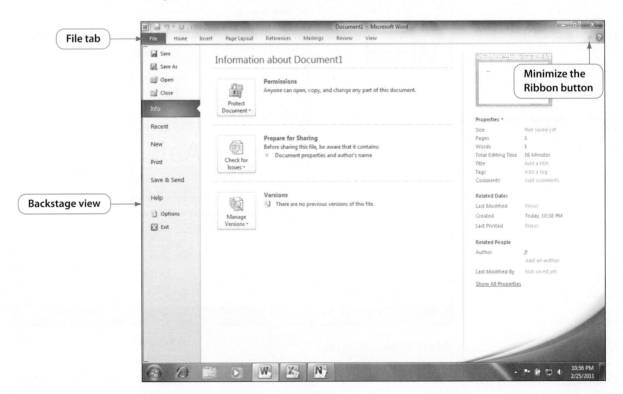

Figure 9 File tab to display Backstage view

Using the Ribbon Tabs

It is possible to enlarge your workspace by minimizing the Ribbon. The Minimize the **Ribbon button**, shown in Figure 9, is located just below the Close button in the top-right corner of the window and directly next to the Help, question mark, button. The Minimize the Ribbon button reduces the Ribbon to a single line and toggles to the Expand the Ribbon button. Click the Expand the Ribbon button to display the full Ribbon again.

To Use Ribbon Tabs

a. Word should be the active application. Click **Maximize** 🔲 to expand the Word program space so the document within the program window fills all of the screen.

b. Click **Minimize the Ribbon** 🔼, and then point to the **Page Layout tab** on the Ribbon. Notice that the Page Layout tab is highlighted but the current tab is still the active tab.

c. Click the **Page Layout tab**. The Page Layout tab Ribbon options are displayed. This tab provides easy access to the page formatting and printing options.

d. Click the **Home tab**. This displays the Home tab options on the Ribbon. If you click in the document again, notice the Ribbon options toggle out of view again. Click **Expand the Ribbon** 🔽 to toggle the Ribbon options into constant view (or alternatively, double-click any of the tab names).

Clicking Buttons

Clicking a button will produce an action. For example, the Font group on the Home tab includes buttons for Bold and Italic. Clicking any of these buttons will produce an intended action. So, if you have selected text that you want to apply bold formatting to, simply click the Bold button and bold formatting is applied to the selected text.

Some buttons are toggle buttons: one click turns a feature on and a second click turns the feature off. When a feature is toggled on, the button remains highlighted. For example, in Word, on the Home tab in the Paragraph group, click the Show/Hide button ¶. Notice paragraph marks appear in your document, and the button is highlighted to show that the feature is turned on. This feature displays characters that do not print. This allows you to see items in the document that can help to troubleshoot a document's formatting, such as when Tab was pressed an arrow is displayed, or when the spacebar was pressed dots appear between words. Click the Show/Hide button again, and the feature is turned off. The button is no longer highlighted, and the paragraph characters, as well as any other nonprinting characters, in the document are no longer displayed.

Also notice that some buttons have two parts: a button that accesses the most commonly used setting or command, and an arrow that opens a gallery menu of all related commands or options for that particular task or button. For example, the Font Color button 🅰 on the Home tab in the Font group includes the different colors that are available for fonts. If you click the button, the last color used will be the default color applied to selected text. Notice this color is also displayed on the icon and will change when a different color is applied in the document. To access the gallery menu for other color options, click the arrow next to the Font Color button, and then click the alternate color or command option. Whenever you see an arrow next to a button, this is an indicator that more options are available.

It should also be said that the two buttons on your mouse operate in a similar fashion. The left mouse click can also be thought of as performing an action, whether it is to click a Ribbon button, menu option, or to open a document. The right-click (or right mouse button) will never perform an action, but rather it provides more options. The options that appear on the shortcut menu when you right-click change depending on the location of the mouse pointer. For example, right-click an empty area of the status bar and you will see options available for status bar features. All of these status bar options are toggles, meaning you can toggle them on or off—a check mark is displayed for the features currently on. By contrast, if you hover the

---

SIDE NOTE

How Buttons and Groups Appear on the Ribbon

If you notice that your Ribbon appears differently from one computer to the next—the buttons and groups might seem condensed in size—there could be a few factors at play. The most common causes could be monitor size, the screen resolution, or the size of the program window. With smaller monitors, lower screen resolutions, or a reduced program window, buttons can appear as icons without labels, and a group can sometimes be condensed into a button that must be clicked to display the group options.

mouse pointer over text in the Word document and right-click, you will see menu options that apply to text—many of the same options found in the Font group on the Home tab. When a desired option is found on a shortcut menu, simply click the option to apply it. If none of the options meets your needs, click in empty space outside the menu to cancel the shortcut menu.

CONSIDER THIS | **Changes Among Versions of Microsoft Office**

A consistent user interface helps users feel comfortable. In Office 2010, Microsoft removed the Office Button used in Office 2007 and created the File tab and Backstage view. Why do you think the company made this change? Which do you prefer? Are there any future changes you would recommend?

To Work with Buttons

a. If necessary, click **Word** 📄 on the taskbar to make it the active window, and then click **Maximize** ▭.

b. Place the mouse pointer over the typed text **Word**, and then double-click to select the text. With the text selected, click the **Home tab**, and then click **Bold** B in the Font group. This will toggle on the Bold command. Notice that the Bold button is now highlighted and the selected text is displayed in bold format.

Bold button toggled on and highlighted

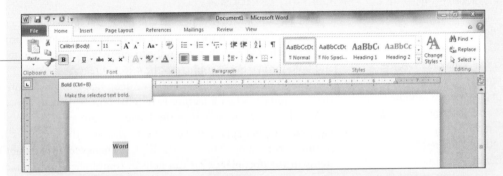

Figure 10 Bold toggled on with text highlighted

c. With the text still selected, press [Backspace] once to delete the text Word. Notice that the Bold button is still highlighted, which means any new text typed will be bold.

d. Type Meeting Minutes, and then press [Enter]. The insertion point moves to the next line of the document. If you made any typing errors, you can press [Backspace] to remove the typing errors and then retype the text.

e. With the insertion point on the second line, click **Bold** B again to toggle it off.

f. Position the insertion point to the left of the word **Meeting**, press and hold the left mouse button, drag the mouse until the text in the first line of text is selected, and then release the mouse button when all the text in Meeting Minutes is highlighted.

g. Click the **Home tab**, and then click the **Font Color arrow** A ⌄ in the Font group. Under **Standard Colors**, point to, but do not click, **Dark Red**. Notice a Live Preview feature that shows how the selected document text will change color. As the mouse pointer hovers over a color, a ScreenTip appears to show the color name.

h. Click **Dark Red**. The selected text should now be bold and dark red.

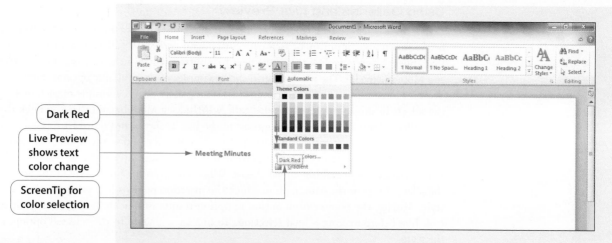

Dark Red

Live Preview shows text color change

ScreenTip for color selection

→ Meeting Minutes

Figure 11 Live Preview of font color

SIDE NOTE

Live Preview Feature

Live Preview, which allows you to see how formatting looks before you apply it, is available for many of the gallery libraries.

i. Click below **Meeting Minutes** to move the insertion point to the next line.

Real World Advice   Using Keyboard Shortcuts and Key Tips

Keyboard shortcuts are extremely useful because they allow you to keep your hands on the keyboard instead of reaching for the mouse to make Ribbon selections. **Key Tips** are also a form of keyboard shortcuts. Pressing Alt will display Key Tips (or keyboard shortcuts) for items on the Ribbon and Quick Access Toolbar. The **Quick Access Toolbar** is located at the top left of the application window and can be customized to offer commonly used buttons. After displaying the Key Tips, you can press the letter or number corresponding to the Ribbon item to request the action from the keyboard. Pressing Alt again will toggle the Key Tips off.

Many keyboard shortcuts are universal to all Windows programs; you will find they work not only in past versions of Office, but they also work in other Windows software. Keyboard shortcuts usually involve two or more keys, in which case you hold down the first key listed, and press the second key once. Some of the more common keyboard shortcuts are shown in Figure 12.

Keyboard Shortcut	To Do This:
Ctrl + C	Copy the selected item
Ctrl + V	Paste a copied item
Ctrl + A	Select all the items in a document or window
Ctrl + B	Bold selected text
Ctrl + Z	Undo an action
Ctrl + Home	Move to the top of the document
Ctrl + End	Move to the end of the document

Figure 12 Common keyboard shortcuts

Using Galleries and Live Preview

Live Preview lets you see the effects of menu selections on your document file or selected item before making a commitment to a particular menu choice. A gallery is a set of menu options that appear when you click the arrow next to a button which, in some cases, may be referred to as a More button ⬇. The menu or grid shows samples of the available options. For example, on Word's Home tab in the Styles group, the Styles gallery shows a sample of each text style you can select. In this example, the Styles gallery includes a More button that you click to expand the gallery to see all the available options in the list, as shown in Figure 13.

When you point to an option in a gallery, Live Preview shows the results that would occur in your file if you were to click that particular option. Using Live Preview, you can experiment with settings before making a final choice. When you point to a text style in the Styles gallery, the selected text or the paragraph in which the insertion point is located appears with that text style. Moving the pointer from option to option results in quickly seeing what your text will look like before making a final selection. To finalize a change to the selected option, click on the style.

SIDE NOTE
Closing a Gallery
[Esc] can be used to close a gallery without making a selection, or, alternatively, you can click an empty area, such as the title bar, outside the gallery menu.

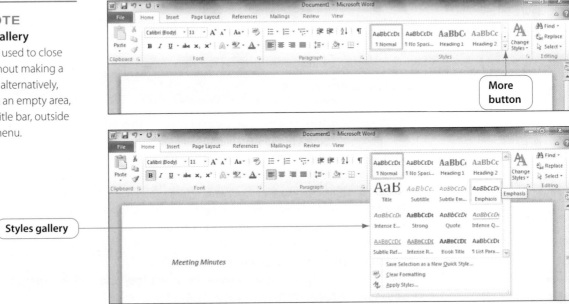

Figure 13 The More button and the Styles gallery

To Use the Numbering Library

a. Click the Home tab, and then click the **Numbering arrow** ≡⬇ in the Paragraph group. The Numbering Library gallery opens.

b. Point to, but do not click, the third option in the first row, the number followed by a closing parenthesis.

c. Place the pointer over each of the remaining number styles, and then preview them in your document.

d. Click the number style with the **1)**.

The Numbering Library gallery closes, and the number 1) is added to the current line of text, which is now indented. The Numbering button remains toggled on when the insertion point is located in a paragraph line where numbering has been applied.

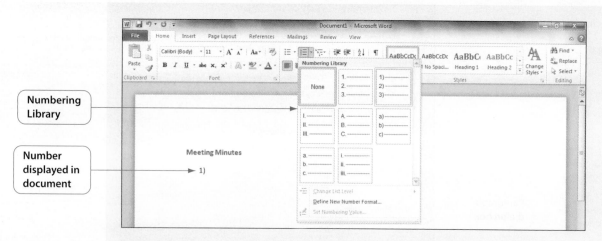

Numbering Library

Number displayed in document

Figure 14 Numbering Library

e. With the insertion point located after the number, type Meeting was called to order at 2:15 pm.

f. Press Enter twice to end the numbered list.

Opening Dialog Boxes and Task Panes

Some Ribbon groups include a diagonal arrow in the bottom-right corner of the group section, called a **Dialog Box Launcher** that opens a corresponding dialog box or task pane. Hovering the mouse pointer near the Dialog Box Launcher will display a ScreenTip to indicate more information. Click the Dialog Box Launcher to open a **dialog box**, which is a window that provides more options or settings beyond those provided on the Ribbon. It often provides access to more precise or less frequently used commands along with the commands offered on the Ribbon; thus using a dialog box offers the ability to apply many related options at the same time and located in one place. As you can see in Figure 15, many dialog boxes organize related information into tabs. In the Paragraph dialog box shown in the figure, the active Indents and Spacing tab shows options to change alignment, indentation, and spacing, with another tab that offers options and settings for Line and Page Breaks. A **task pane** is a smaller window pane that often appears to the side of the program window and offers options or helps you to navigate through completing a task or feature.

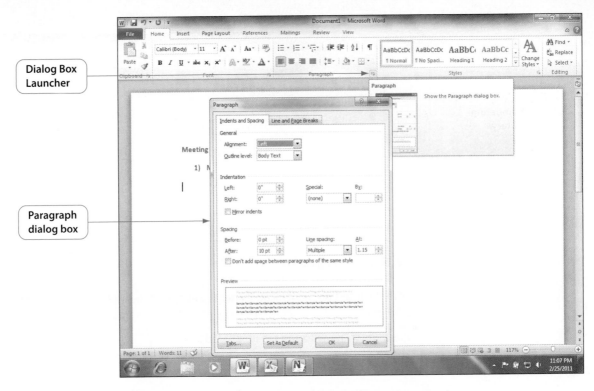

Figure 15 Paragraph Dialog Box Launcher with dialog box overlay

To Open the Format Cells Dialog Box

a. On the taskbar, click **Excel** to make Excel the active program.

b. Click cell **A2**, the first cell in the second row.

c. Click the Home tab, if necessary. The Number group options appear on the Ribbon.

d. Click the **Dialog Box Launcher** in the Number group. The Format Cells dialog box opens with the Number tab displayed.

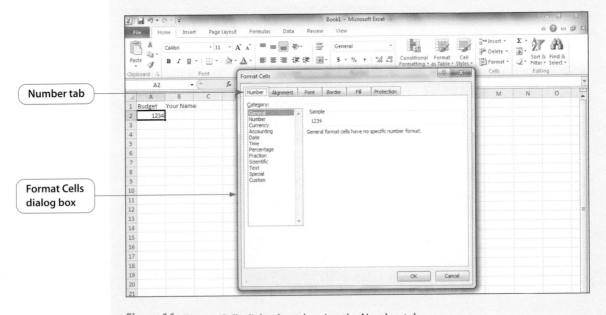

Figure 16 Format Cells dialog box showing the Number tab

SIDE NOTE
Check Box and Radio Options

What is the difference between check box and radio options? When check box options are offered, you can check more than one check box ☑ option in a group of options, but when radio button options are offered, you can select only one radio button option in a group.

e. Under Category, click **Number**. Click the **Use 1000 Separator (,)** check box.

f. Click the **Alignment tab**. Notice, the dialog box displays options that are related to alignment of the text. If you needed to make changes, you could use the check box options or the arrows to display a list of options when appropriate to do so.

g. Click the **Fill tab**, and then click to select **Purple, Accent 4, Lighter 60%**, third row in the eighth column, which will show in the Sample box. Click **OK**. The format changes are made to the number, and the fill color is applied.

Using Contextual Tools

Whenever you see the term "contextual tools," this usually refers to tools that only appear when needed for specific tasks. Some tabs, toolbars, and menus are displayed as you work and only appear if a particular object is selected. Because these tools become available only as you need them, the workspace remains less cluttered.

A **contextual tab** is a Ribbon tab that contains commands related to selected objects so you can manipulate, edit, and format the objects. Examples of objects that can be selected to produce contextual tabs include a table, a picture, a shape, or a chart. A contextual tab appears to the right of the standard Ribbon tabs. For example, Figure 17 shows the Picture Tools Format tab that displays when a picture is selected. The contextual tabs function in the same way as a standard tab on the Ribbon. The contextual tab disappears when you click outside the target object (in the file) to deselect the object. In some instances, contextual tabs can also appear as you switch views.

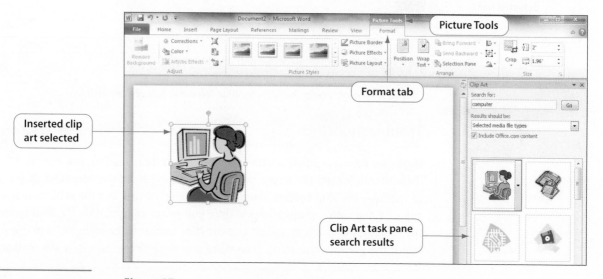

Figure 17 Contextual tab for Picture Tools in Word

SIDE NOTE
Turning Off Mini Toolbar and Live Preview

The Mini toolbar and Live Preview can be turned off in Word, Excel, and PowerPoint. Click the File tab, click the Options command in the General options uncheck the top two appropriate check boxes in the Options dialog box, and then click the OK button.

Accessing the Mini Toolbar

The **Mini toolbar** appears after text is selected and contains buttons for the most commonly used formatting commands, such as font, font size, font color, center alignment, indents, bold, italic, and underline. The Mini toolbar button commands vary for each Office program. The toolbar appears transparent whenever text is selected and comes into clearer view as you move the pointer towards the toolbar. When you move the pointer over the Mini toolbar, it comes into full view, allowing you to click the formatting button or buttons. It disappears if you move the pointer away from the toolbar, press a key, or click in the workspace. All the commands on the Mini toolbar are available on the Ribbon; however, the Mini toolbar offers quicker access to common commands since you do not have to move the mouse pointer far away from selected text for these commands.

To Access the Mini Toolbar

a. If necessary, on the taskbar, click **Excel** 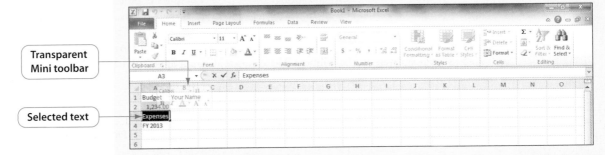. Click cell **A3**, the first cell in the third row of the worksheet.

b. Type Expenses.

c. Press Enter. Text has been entered in cell A3, and cell A4 is selected.

d. Type FY 2013, and then press Enter. The year has been entered in cell A4, and cell A5 is selected.

e. Double-click cell **A3** to place the insertion point in the cell. Double-clicking a cell enables you to enter edit mode for the cell text.

f. Double-click cell **A3** again to select the text. The text appears to be opposite when selected (white text on a black background), and as you move the pointer upwards, the transparent Mini toolbar starts to appear and come into view directly above the selected text.

Figure 18 Transparent Mini toolbar and selected text

g. Move the pointer over the Mini toolbar. Now it is completely visible.

Troubleshooting

If you are having a problem with the Mini toolbar disappearing, you may have inadvertently moved the mouse pointer to another part of the document. If you need to redisplay the Mini toolbar, right-click the selected text and the Mini toolbar will appear along with a shortcut menu. Once you select an option on the Mini toolbar, the shortcut menu will disappear and the Mini toolbar will remain while in use (or repeat the previous two steps, then make sure the pointer stays over the toolbar).

h. On the Mini toolbar, click **Italic** *I*.

The text in cell A3 is now italicized. The Mini toolbar remains visible allowing you to click other buttons.

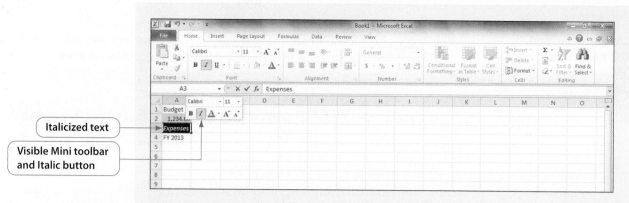

Italicized text

Visible Mini toolbar and Italic button

Figure 19 Cell A3 is now formatted with Italic from the Mini toolbar

i. Press Enter. Cell A4 is selected, and the Mini toolbar disappears.

Opening Shortcut Menus

Shortcut menus are also context sensitive and enable you to quickly access commands that are most likely needed in the context of the task being performed. A **shortcut menu** is a list of commands related to a selection that appears when you right-click (click the right mouse button). This means you can access popular commands without using the Ribbon. Included are commands that perform actions, commands that open dialog boxes, and galleries of options that provide Live Preview. As noted previously, the Mini toolbar opens when you click the right mouse button. If you click a button on the Mini toolbar, the shortcut menu closes, and the Mini toolbar remains open allowing you to continue formatting your selection. For example, right-click selected text to open the shortcut menu *and* the Mini toolbar; the menu contains text-related commands such as Font, Paragraph, Bullets, Numbering, and Styles, as well as other program specific commands related to text.

To Use the Shortcut Menu to Delete Content

a. Right-click cell **A1**. A shortcut menu opens with commands related to common tasks you can perform in a cell, along with the Mini toolbar.

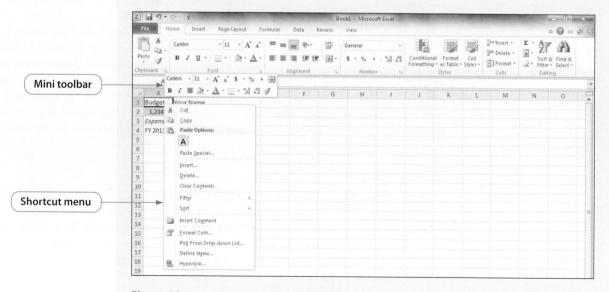

Mini toolbar

Shortcut menu

Figure 20 Shortcut menu and Mini toolbar

Closing Menus and Galleries Using Escape

Esc can be used to cancel or close an unwanted short-cut menu, gallery menu, or Mini toolbar without making a selection.

b. On the shortcut menu, click **Clear Contents**.

The shortcut menu closes, the Mini toolbar disappears, and the text in cell A1 is removed. This is one method that can be used to clear the contents of a cell.

Manipulating Files in the Office Environment

Creating, opening, saving, and closing files are the most common tasks performed in any Office program. These tasks can all be completed in Backstage view, which is accessed from the File tab shown in Figure 21. These processes are basically the same for all the Office programs. When you start a program, you either have to create a new file or open an existing one. When you start Word, Excel, or PowerPoint, the program opens a blank file, which is ready for you to begin working on a new document, workbook, or presentation. When you start Access, the New tab in Backstage view opens, displaying options for creating a new database or opening an existing one.

File tab

Common tasks

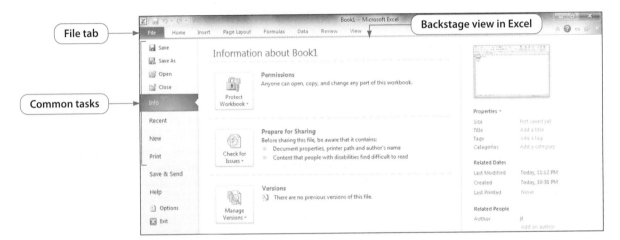

Figure 21 Backstage view in Excel

Working with Files

While working on an Office file, whether creating a new file or modifying an existing file, your work is stored in the temporary memory on your computer, not on the hard drive or your USB Flash drive. Any work done will be lost if you were to exit the program, turn off the computer, or experience a power failure without saving your work. To prevent losing your work, you need to save your work and remember to save frequently—at least every 10 minutes or after adding many changes. That saves you from having to recreate any work you did prior to the last save. You can save files to the hard drive, which is located inside the computer; to an external drive, such as a USB Flash drive; or to a network storage device. Office has an AutoRecovery feature (previously called AutoSave) that will attempt to recover any changes made to a document if something goes wrong, but this should not be relied upon as a substitute for saving your work manually.

Saving a File

To quickly save a file, simply click the Save 🖫 on the Quick Access Toolbar or use the keyboard shortcut Ctrl + S. Backstage view also provides access to the Save command and the Save As command. The first time you save a new file, it behaves the same as the Save As command and the Save As dialog box opens. This allows you to specify the save options. You can also click the Save As command in Backstage view to open the Save As dialog box when saving for the first time, or use the Save As command when you want to save an existing file as a copy or separate version—possibly with a different name. In the Save As dialog box, you name the file and specify the location in which to save it, similar to the first time you save a file. Once you save a file, the simple shortcut methods to save any changes to the file work fine to update the existing file.

No dialog box will open to save after the first time—as long as you do not need to change the file name or location as with the Save As command.

The first time a file is saved, it needs to be named. The file name includes the name you specify and a file extension assigned by the Office program to indicate the file type. The file extension may or may not be visible depending on your computer settings. By default, most computers do not display the file extension (only the file name). Use a descriptive name that accurately reflects the content of the document, workbook, presentation, or database, such as "January 2013 Budget" or "012013 Minutes." The descriptive name can include uppercase and lowercase letters, numbers, hyphens, spaces, and some special characters (excluding ? " / | < > * :) in any combination. Each Office program adds a period and a file extension after the file name to identify the program in which that file was created. Figure 22 shows the common default file extensions for Office 2010. File names can include a maximum of 255 characters including the extension (this includes the number of characters for the file path—the folder names to get to the file location). As a reminder, depending on how your computer is set up, you may or may not see the file extensions.

Application	Extension
Microsoft Word 2010	.docx
Microsoft Excel 2010	.xlsx
Microsoft PowerPoint 2010	.pptx
Microsoft Access 2010	.accdb

Figure 22 Default file extensions for Microsoft Office 2010

Real World Advice — Sharing Files Between Office Versions

Different Office versions are not always compatible. The general rule is that files created in an older version can always be opened in a newer version, but not the other way around (a 2010 Office file is not easily opened in an older version of Office). With this in mind, maybe the company you work for is using Office 2010 and another company you need to share files with is using Office 2003. The concern is, prior to Office 2007 different file extensions were used. For example, .doc was used for Word files instead of docx., .xls instead of .xlsx for Excel, and so on. It is still possible to save the Office 2010 files in a previous format version. To save in one of these formats, use the Save As command, and in the Save As dialog box, click the Save as type option near the bottom of the dialog box. From the list, click the 97-2003 format option. If the file is already in the previous format, it will open in Office 2010 and save with the same format in which it was created.

To Save a File

a. On the taskbar, click **Word** [W] to make Word the active program.

b. Click the **File tab**. Backstage view opens with command options and tabs for managing files, opening existing files, saving, printing, and exiting Word.

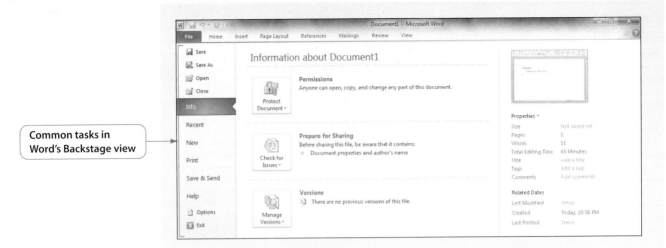

Common tasks in Word's Backstage view

Figure 23 Backstage view in Word

c. Click **Save As**.

The Save As dialog box opens. This provides the opportunity to enter a file name and a storage location. The default storage location is the Documents folder, and the suggested file name is the first few words of the first line of the document.

d. Click the **File name** box, and if necessary, highlight the current suggested file name. Navigate to where you are storing your files, and then type Lastname_Firstname_cf01_ ws01_Minutes in the File name box. This descriptive file name will help you more easily identify the file.

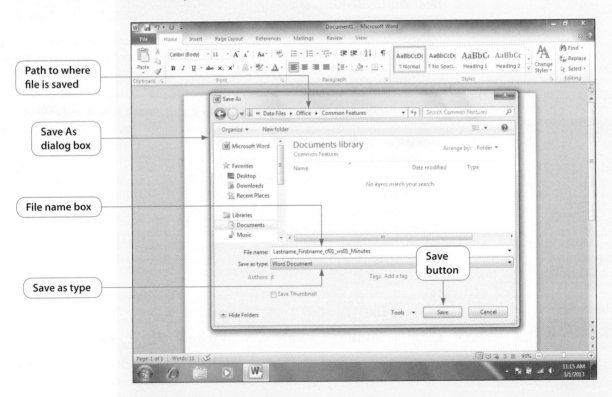

Path to where file is saved

Save As dialog box

File name box

Save as type

Save button

Figure 24 Save As dialog box

e. Click the **Save** button. The Save As dialog box closes, and the name of your file appears in the Word window title bar.

f. Click **Excel** on the taskbar to make Excel the active file, repeat steps b through e and then save the file you created as Lastname_Firstname_cf01_ws01_Budget.

Modifying Saved Files

Saved files only contain what was in the file the last time it was saved. Any changes made after the file was saved are only stored in the computer's memory and are not saved with the file. It is important to remember to save often—after making changes—so the file is updated to reflect its current contents.

Remember, it is not necessary to use the Save As dialog box once a file has been saved unless you want a copy of the file with a different name or you want to store it in a different location.

To Modify a Saved File

a. Click **Word** on the taskbar to make the Word document the active window.

b. Make sure the insertion point is in the last line, below the numbered text. Type Today's date (the date you are doing this exercise), and then press Enter.

c. On the Quick Access Toolbar, click **Save** . The changes you made to the document have just been saved to the file stored in the location you selected earlier. Recall that no dialog boxes will open for the Save command after the first time it has been saved.

SIDE NOTE
Quick Access Toolbar
The Quick Access Toolbar provides one-click access to commonly used commands, such as saving a file and undoing recent actions.

Real World Advice   Saving Files Before Closing

It is recommended that files be saved before closing them or exiting a program. However, most programs have an added safeguard or warning dialog box to remind you to save if you attempt to close a file without saving your changes first. The warning dialog box offers three options. Click Save, and the file will be saved with any new changes. Click Don't Save if you do not want any of the changes added to the file, and the file will close without saving or adding any changes since the last Save command was applied. Click Cancel if you changed your mind about closing the program and want to get back into the file before you close the program. This warning feature helps to ensure that you have the most current version of the file saved.

Closing a File

When you are ready to close a file, you can click the Close command on the File tab in Backstage view. If the file you close is the only file open for that particular program, the program window remains open with no file in the window. You can also close a file by using the Close button in the top-right corner of the window. However, if that is the only file open, the file and program will close.

To Modify and Close a Document

a. With the insertion point on the line under the date, type your course number and section, replacing course number and section with the course and section you are in, on this line and press ⌴Enter⌴. The text you typed should appear below the date.

b. Click the **File tab** to open Backstage view.

c. Click **Close**. A warning dialog box opens, asking if you want to save the changes made to the document.

d. Click **Save**.

    The document closes after saving changes, but the Word program window remains open. You are able to create new files or open previously saved files. If multiple Word documents are open, the document window of the file you just closed will remain open with the other documents that are currently still open in the window.

Opening a File

You create a new file when you open a blank document, workbook, presentation, or database. If you want to work on a previously created file, you must first open it. When you open a file, it transfers a copy of the file from the file's storage location to the computer's temporary memory and displays it on the monitor's screen. There is a copy on the drive and in your computer's memory.

    When opening files downloaded from the Internet, accessed from a shared network, or received as an attachment in e-mail, you may sometimes run across a file in a read-only format called Protected View, as shown in Figure 25. In **Protected View**, the file contents can be seen and read, but you are not able to edit, save, or print the contents until you enable editing. If you were to see the information bar shown in Figure 25, and you trust the source of the file, simply click the Enable Editing button on the information bar.

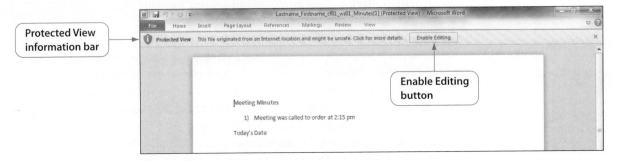

Figure 25 Open document in Protected View

To Reopen a Document

a. In Word, click the **File tab** to display Backstage view.

b. Click **Open**. The Open dialog box is displayed.

c. In the Open dialog box, click the disk drive in the left pane where your student data files are located. Navigate through the folder structure, and then click **Lastname_Firstname_cf01_ws01_Minutes**.

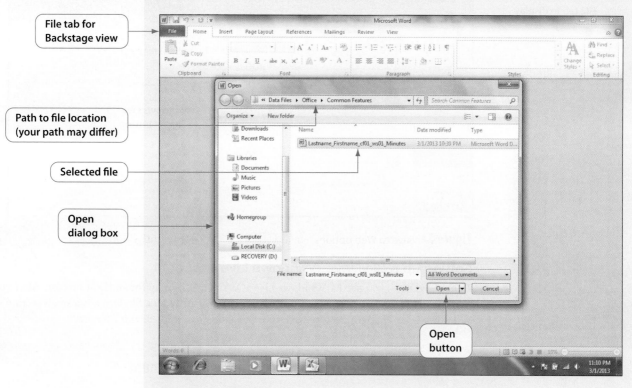

File tab for Backstage view

Path to file location (your path may differ)

Selected file

Open dialog box

Open button

Figure 26 Open dialog box

d. Click **Open**. The file opens in the Word program window.

Sharing Files Using Windows Live SkyDrive

Many times you create files in order to share them with other people. You can share files by attaching the file to an e-mail to send to someone else to read or use. Sometimes you collaborate with others by posting files on a blog. Tools for this can be found on the File tab in Backstage view, on the Save & Send tab.

When a file is sent via e-mail, a copy of the file can be attached, a link can be sent, or you can include a copy of the file in a PDF, RTF, or other file format. The file can also be saved to an online workspace where it can be made available to others for collaboration and review. The Save to Web option on the Save & Send tab in Backstage view gives you access to Windows Live **SkyDrive**, which is an online workspace provided by Microsoft. SkyDrive's online filing cabinet is a free Windows Live service. As of this writing, you are provided with 25 GB of password-protected online file storage. This makes it possible for you to store, access, and share files online from almost anywhere. This personal workspace comes with a Public folder for saving files to share, as well as a My Documents folder for saving files you want to keep private. (As of this writing, SkyDrive is not available for Access.) Figure 27 shows the Save to Web options on the Save & Send tab in Backstage view of Word.

Files saved to an online workspace can be edited by more than one person at the same time. The changes are recorded in the file with each author's name and the date of the change. A web browser is used to access and edit the files, and you can choose who can have access to the files.

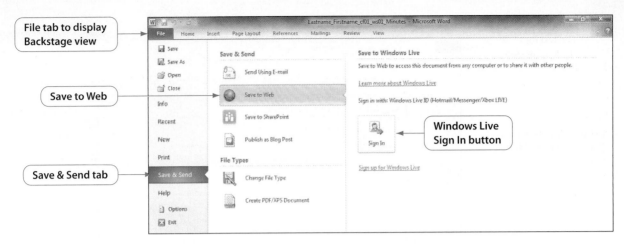

File tab to display Backstage view

Save to Web

Save & Send tab

Windows Live Sign In button

Figure 27 Save to Web options

Setting up a SkyDrive (Windows Live) Account

To use SkyDrive, you need a Windows Live ID. You can sign up for an ID at no cost. After you sign in, you can create new folders and save files into the folders. SkyDrive is a small section of Windows Live. You will need to have Internet access to complete this exercise.

To Set Up and Create a New Document in SkyDrive Account

a. On the taskbar, click **Internet Explorer** 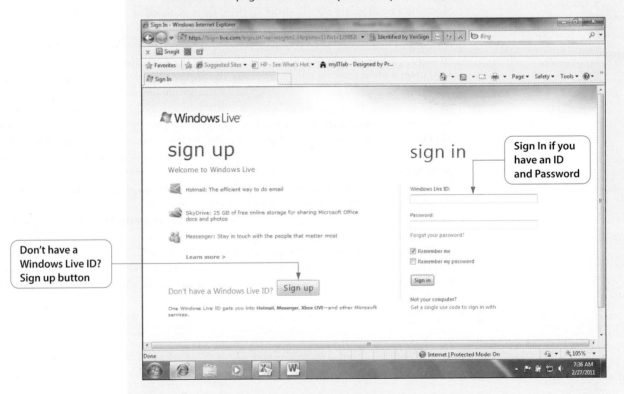 to open Internet Explorer; or alternatively, click the Start button, point to All Programs, and then click Internet Explorer to open the program.

b. In the address bar type skydrive.live.com.

c. If you already have a Windows Live account, login. If not, click the **Sign Up** button on the left side of the page. Follow the steps to set up an account.

Don't have a Windows Live ID? Sign up button

Sign In if you have an ID and Password

Figure 28 Windows Live sign in or Sign up page

SIDE NOTE
**Making SkyDrive the
Active Screen**
If SkyDrive is not the active
screen, you can point to
Windows Live in the upper-
left corner of the window
and then click SkyDrive from
the menu.

d. Once your ID is created, you can log in. Once you log in you will see your SkyDrive with three areas: Documents, Favorites, and Photos.

e. To create a new document, presentation, or workbook, click the **New arrow**. Click **Word document**. Name your document Lastname_Firstname_cf01_ws01_SkyDrive. If you want to share with others, click **Change**. To add people to share with, you need to know their SkyDrive name or e-mail address.

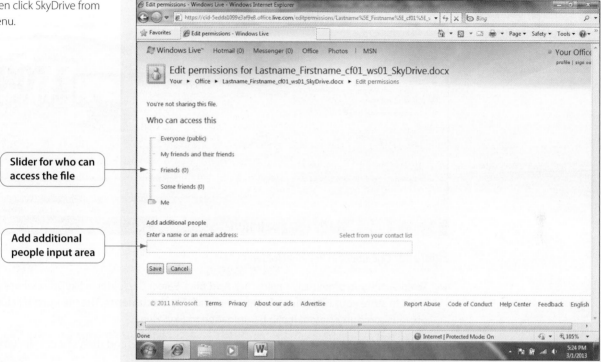

Slider for who can access the file

Add additional people input area

Figure 29 Sharing a document in SkyDrive

f. Click **Save** to save the document and to start typing the content of the file.

g. Type Firstname Lastname replacing Firstname and Lastname with your own name, click the **File tab,** and then click **Save**.

h. To return to your folders, click the Close button in the top-right corner of the document. Your document should appear in the Personal folder list because it was not shared.

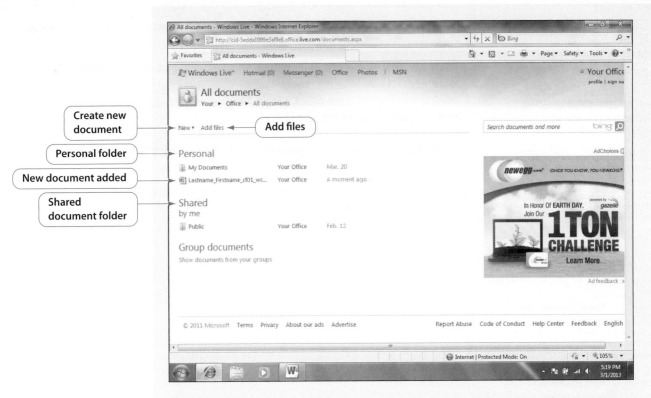

Figure 30 Document in Personal folder

i. To add a file you previously saved, click **Add files**. Select the folder in SkyDrive where you want to store your document. In this case, click **My Documents**. The file must be closed on your computer before it can be uploaded to SkyDrive.

j. Click **select documents from your computer** to navigate, and then select a document from your computer.

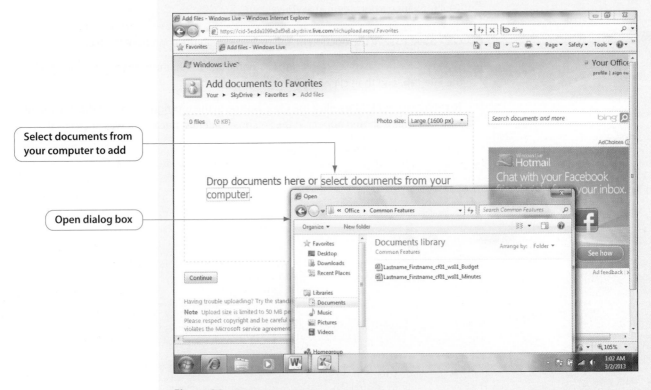

Figure 31 Uploading a file from your computer

k. Navigate to the location where your student files are stored. Select the file **Lastname_ Firstname_cf01_ws01_Minutes**, and then click **Open**. The file will upload to your SkyDrive. If necessary, click **Upload**, and then click **Continue** and you will be returned to the My Documents folder with your newly uploaded file.

l. To delete a file from the folder, hover the mouse pointer near the file name, and then click the **x** at the far right near the file name. Click **OK** to confirm that you wish to delete the file or **Cancel** if you wish to keep the file on SkyDrive. Click **sign out** to exit SkyDrive, located in the top-right corner under your sign in name.

Getting Help

If you require additional information about a feature or are not sure how to perform a task, make sure you acquaint yourself with the Office Help button and how to use it. In addition, do not overlook the ScreenTips within the program, which can also offer guidance along the way.

Viewing ScreenTips

ScreenTips are small windows that display descriptive text when you rest the mouse pointer over an object or button. You just need to point to a button or object in one of the Office applications to display its ScreenTip. In addition to the button's name, a ScreenTip might include the keyboard shortcut if one is available, a description of the command's function, and possibly more information. If you press F1 while displaying some ScreenTips it will open the Help file to the relevant topic displayed.

To Open Help

a. If necessary, on the taskbar, click **Word** W to make Word the active program.

b. Point to **Microsoft Word Help** in the top-right corner of the window. The ScreenTip is displayed with the button's name, its keyboard shortcut, and a brief description.

c. Click the **Home tab**, and then point to the **Format Painter** button in the Clipboard group to display the ScreenTip. With the mouse pointer still over the Format Painter button and the ScreenTip showing, press the F1 key and notice that the Help window opens with information on how to use the Format Painter. Scroll down and read through the information. When you are done, click the **Close** button in the top-right corner of the Word Help window.

Using the Help Window

The Help window provides detailed information on a multitude of topics, as well as access to templates, training videos installed on your computer, and content available on Office.com, the website maintained by Microsoft that provides access to the latest information and additional Help resources. To access the contents at Office.com you must have access to the Internet from the computer. If there is no Internet access, only the files installed on the computer will be displayed in the Help window.

Each program has its own Help window. From each program's Help window you can find information about the Office commands and features as well as step-by-step instructions for using them. There are two ways to locate Help topics—the search function and the topic list.

To search the Help system on a desired topic, type the topic in the search box and click Search. Once a topic is located, you can click a link to open it. Explanations and step-by-step instructions for specific procedures will be presented. There is also a Table of Contents pane, which displays a variety of topics to choose from when exploring various Help subjects and topics. It is organized similar to a book's table of contents. To access a subject or topic, click the subject links to display the subtopic links, and then click a subtopic link to display Help information for that topic.

To Search Help for Information about the Ribbon in Excel

a. On the taskbar, click **Excel** 📊 to make Excel the active program.

b. Click **Microsoft Excel Help** ❓. The Excel Help window opens.

c. If the Table of Contents is not displayed on the left side of the Help window, click the **Show Table of Contents** button 📖 on the toolbar of the Help window. Scroll down and notice the list of topics. Click the **Charts** topic and notice the subtopics displayed. Click **Charts** again to close the topic.

d. Click in the **Type words to search for** box if necessary, and then type ribbon.

e. Click the **Search arrow**. On the displayed Search menu, notice that options for both the online content—if you are connected to the Internet—and local content from your computer are available in the list.

f. If the computer has Internet access, verify there is a check mark next to **All Excel** in the Content from Office.com list. If you are not connected to the Internet, click **Excel Help** in the Content from this computer list.

g. Click the **Search** button. The Help window displays a list of the topics related to the keyword "ribbon" in the right pane.

Figure 32 Excel Help

h. Scroll through the list to review the Help topics.

i. Click the **Minimize the ribbon** link from the list of results.

j. Read the information, and then click the links within this topic to explore how Help links work.

k. On the Help window title bar, click **Close** ❎ to close the window.

Printing a File

There are times you will need a paper copy, also known as a hard copy, of an Office document, spreadsheet, or presentation. Before printing, review and preview the file and adjust the print settings as needed. Many options are available to fit various printing needs, such as the number of copies to print, the printing device to use, and the portion of the file to print. The print settings vary slightly from program to program. It is advisable that you check the file's print preview to ensure the file will print as you intended. Doing a simple print preview will help to avoid having to reprint your document, workbook, or presentation, which requires additional paper, ink, and energy resources.

To Print a File

a. On the taskbar, click **Word** W to make Word the active program.

b. If necessary, open the **Lastname_Firstname_cf01_ws01_Minutes** file.

c. Click the **File tab** to open Backstage view.

d. Click the **Print tab**. The Print settings and Print Preview appears.

e. Verify that the Copies box displays **1**.

f. Verify that the correct printer (as directed by your instructor) appears on the Printer button (your printer choices may vary). If the correct printer is not displayed, click the Printer button arrow, and click to choose the correct or preferred printer from the list of available printers.

g. If your instructor asks you to print the document, click the Print button.

Exiting Programs

When you have completed your work with the Office program, you should exit it. You can exit the program with either a button or a command. You can use the Exit command from Backstage view or the Close button on the top-right side of the title bar. Recall that if you have not saved the final version of the file, a dialog box opens, asking whether you want to save your changes. Clicking the Save button saves the file, closes the file, and then exits the program as long as other files are not open within the same program.

Exiting programs when you are finished with them helps save system resources and keeps your Windows desktop and taskbar uncluttered, as well as prevents data from being accidentally lost.

To Exit Office Applications

a. On the Word title bar, click **Close** [x].
   Both the Word document and the Word program close. Excel should be visible again.

b. Click the **File tab** to open Backstage view, and then click **Exit**. If a dialog box opens asking if you want to save the changes made to the workbook, click Don't Save since no changes need to be saved.

c. The workbook closes without saving a copy, and the Excel program closes.

Concept Check

1. Which application would you use to write a memo?

2. Explain the main purpose for using Backstage view.

3. What is the Quick Access Toolbar?

4. Which tab on the Ribbon would you use to change the font settings?

5. What are the advantages of using SkyDrive instead of a USB Flash drive?

Key Terms

Backstage view 10
Contextual tab 17
Dialog box 15
Dialog Box Launcher 15
Document 2
Graphic 2
Information management program 3
Key Tip 13
Keyboard shortcut 13

Live Preview 14
Maximize 7
Mini toolbar 17
Minimize 7
Protected View 24
Quick Access Toolbar 13
Relational database 3
Restore Down 7
Ribbon 10

Ribbon button 11
ScreenTip 29
Shortcut menu 19
SkyDrive 25
Table 2
Task pane 15
Thumbnail 6
Workbook 2

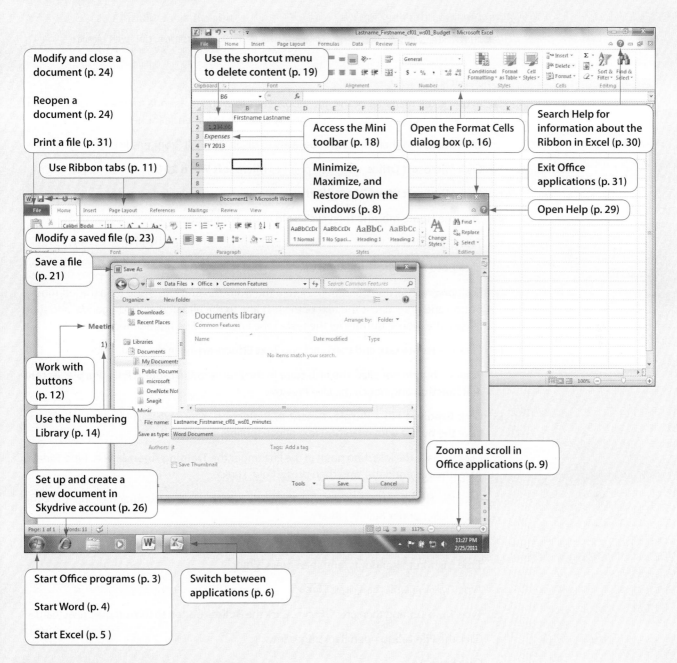

Modify and close a document (p. 24)

Reopen a document (p. 24)

Print a file (p. 31)

Use the shortcut menu to delete content (p. 19)

Use Ribbon tabs (p. 11)

Access the Mini toolbar (p. 18)

Open the Format Cells dialog box (p. 16)

Search Help for information about the Ribbon in Excel (p. 30)

Exit Office applications (p. 31)

Minimize, Maximize, and Restore Down the windows (p. 8)

Open Help (p. 29)

Modify a saved file (p. 23)

Save a file (p. 21)

Work with buttons (p. 12)

Use the Numbering Library (p. 14)

Set up and create a new document in Skydrive account (p. 26)

Zoom and scroll in Office applications (p. 9)

Start Office programs (p. 3)

Start Word (p. 4)

Start Excel (p. 5)

Switch between applications (p. 6)

Figure 33 Working with the Common Features Final

Student data file needed:

New, blank Word document

You will save your file as:

Lastname_Firstname_cf01_ws01_Agenda

Creating an Agenda

Susan Brock, the manager of the gift shop, needs to write an agenda for the upcoming training she will be holding. You will assist her by creating the agenda for her.

a. Click **Start**, and then click **All Programs** to display the All Programs list.

b. Click **Microsoft Office**, and then point to **Microsoft Word 2010**.

c. Click **Microsoft Word 2010**. Word will open with a new blank document.

d. Click the **Home** tab, and then click **Bold** in the Font group.

e. Type TRAINING AGENDA, and then press [Enter].

f. Click **Bold** to toggle the feature off.

g. Position the insertion point to the left of the word Training, press and hold the left mouse button and drag across the text of the first line to the end of the word Agenda, and then release the mouse button. All the text in the line should be highlighted.

h. Click the **Home tab**, and then click the **Text Effects arrow** in the Font group.

i. Point to, but do not click, the fifth color in the fourth row, **Gradient Fill – Purple, Accent 4, Reflection** and notice the Live Preview.

j. Click **Gradient Fill – Purple, Accent 4, Reflection**. Your text should now be bold and have the purple with reflection text effect applied.

k. Click to place the insertion point in the line under the **Training Agenda** text. Type Today's date (the current date), and then press [Enter] twice.

l. Click the **Home tab**, and then click the **Bullets arrow** in the Paragraph group. Click the circle bullet under Bullets Library.

m. Type Welcome trainees 2:00 pm, and then press [Enter].

n. Type Distribute handouts, and then press [Enter].

o. Type Training, and then press [Enter].

p. Type Wrap-Up, and then press [Enter]. Click the **Bullets** button to turn off the bullet feature.

q. Click the **File tab** to open Backstage view.

r. Click **Save As**.

s. In the Navigation Pane, navigate to where you are saving your files. In the File name box, delete the existing file name, and then type Lastname_Firstname_cf01_ws01_Agenda.

t. Click **Save**.

u. Click **Close** in the top-right corner of the title bar to close the document and exit Word.

Practice 2

Student data file needed:
cf01_ws01_Budget

You will save your file as:
Lastname_Firstname_cf01_ws01_Budget_Update

Using the Ribbon for Event Planning

You have been asked to make some changes to the budget spreadsheet for the upcoming book publisher's conference. The publishers will be at the resort for the weekend and will be renting rooms and having a banquet dinner Saturday night. You will be working on a small portion of the banquet budget for the event planning and catering manager. You will need to apply some formatting so the document is not plain.

a. Click **Start**, and then click **All Programs** to display the All Programs list.

b. Click **Microsoft Office**, and then point to **Microsoft Excel 2010**.

c. Click **Microsoft Excel 2010**. Excel starts with a new blank workbook.

d. Click the **File tab** to open Backstage view.

e. Click **Open**.

f. In the Open dialog box, click the disk drive in the left pane where your student data files are located. Navigate through the folder structure, click **cf01_ws01_Budget**, and then click **Open**.

g. If necessary, click the **Home tab**.

h. Click cell **A1** to make it the active cell. Click **Bold** in the Font group to make the text Banquet Budget bold.

i. Highlight column **B** by placing the mouse pointer over column letter B and clicking when the mouse pointer displays a down arrow over the B. Click the **Accounting Number Format** in the Number group.

j. Click the **File tab**, and then click **Save As**. In the Save As dialog box, navigate to where you are saving your files, and then type Lastname_Firstname_cf01_ws01_Budget_Update in the File name box. This descriptive file name will help you more easily identify the file.

k. Click **Save**.

l. Click the **File tab**, and then click **Exit**.

Problem Solve 1

Student data file needed:
cf01_ps01_Agenda

You will save your file as:
Lastname_Firstname_cf01_ps01_Agenda_Updated

Adding More Formatting to a Document

Susan Brock, the manager of the gift shop, was very pleased with the training agenda you created. She decided she would like it a little more stylized. You have been asked to add some more custom formatting to the document.

a. Start **Word**, and then open **cf_ps01_Agenda**.

b. Click the **Page Layout tab**, and then click **Margins** in the Page Setup group.

c. Change the Margins to **Wide**. This will provide space to take notes.

d. Position the insertion point to the left of the words **Training Agenda**, and then drag across the text of the first line to the end of the word **Agenda** to select the text. All the text in the line should be highlighted.

e. Click the **Home tab**, and then click the **Text Highlight Color arrow** in the Font group. Use Live Preview to view the available colors. Select **Turquoise**.

f. Click the **File tab**. Click **Save As** in Backstage view. Navigate to the location where your student files are stored. Save the updated file as Lastname_Firstname_cf01_ps01_Agenda_Updated.

g. Close the document. Close Word.

Perform 1: Perform in Your Career

Student data file needed:

New, blank Excel workbook

You will save your file as:

Lastname_Firstname_cf01_pf01_Training_Schedule

Creating a Training Schedule

One of the managers you worked for recommended you to Aidan Matthews, chief technology officer of the Red Bluff Golf Club. Aidan has asked you to create a training schedule in Excel for several of the trainings he is planning to schedule. The trainings include Windows 7, Word 2010, Excel 2010, and PowerPoint 2010. The trainings will be offered on Mondays, January 14, January 28, February 4, and February 11, 2013. Each training is three hours in length, with one hour between sessions. The first session starts at 9:00 am. There are two trainings per day. You will create an attractive schedule using features you worked with in this workshop.

a. Start **Excel**. Using the features of Excel, create a training spreadsheet that is attractive and easy to read. Some suggestions follow: Create column headings for the application and the date. Fill in the times in the cells where the application and date meet. Format the date (under the Number group use the drop-down list to select long date), format the column headings, format a title for the workbook, use bold, colors, etc.

b. Save the file in your folder as Lastname_Firstname_cf01_pf01_Training_Schedule. Close Excel.

Student data file needed:

New, blank Word document

You will save your file as:

Lastname_Firstname_cf01_pf02_Critique

Improving the Look of Files

Prior to your tenure at the Red Bluff Golf Club, many different students passed through the doors as interns. You have been touted as an expert in how to format documents and spreadsheets. You have been asked to review a spreadsheet and a document and make suggestions on what to do to improve their look. Examine the following figures and answer the statements.

a. Open a new Word 2010 blank document.

b. List five items you would change in the document and why.

c. List five items you would change in the worksheet and why.

d. Save the file as Lastname_Firstname_cf01_pf02_Critique. Submit the file as directed.

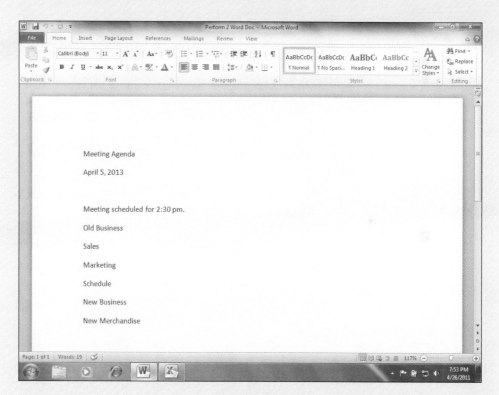

Figure 34 Word document

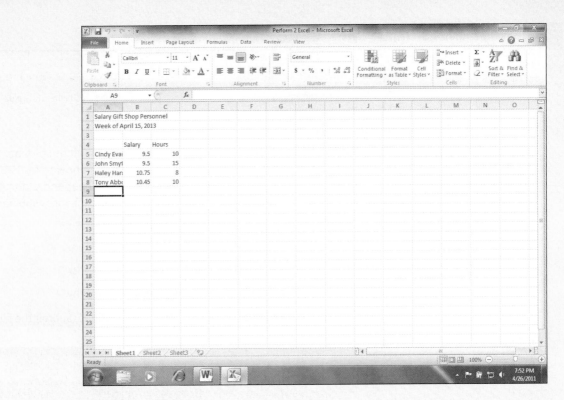

Figure 35 Excel worksheet

WORKSHOP 1

Objectives

1. Understand spreadsheet terminology and components.   p. 40

2. Enter and edit data. p. 48

3. Manipulate cells and cell ranges.   p. 52

4. Manipulate columns and rows.   p. 60

5. Preview and print worksheets.   p. 68

6. Manipulate worksheets and workbooks.   p. 76

Understanding and Manipulating Microsoft Excel 2010

PREPARE CASE

Red Bluff Golf Club Golf Cart Purchase Analysis

The Red Bluff Golf Course Pro Shop makes golf carts available to its members for a fee. Recently, the resort has been running out of carts. The time has come for the club to add more golf carts to its fleet of 10. Club manager, Barry Cheney, wants to use Microsoft Excel to analyze the purchase of golf carts by brand, model, price and financing parameters.

Courtesy of www.Shutterstock.com

Student data file needed for this workshop: **You will save your file as:**

 e01_ws01_Cart_Analysis

 Lastname_Firstname_e01_ws01_Cart_Analysis

Excel Worksheets—What If Data and Information Could Speak?

Data plays an integral part in supporting businesses. Without data, businesses are not able to determine their effectiveness in the market, let alone their profit or loss performance. In addition, as businesses grow or change, the types of data collected by a particular business is one of the few things that remain relatively static over time. Jobs change, products change, and businesses grow or evolve into different organizations (or even lines of business) based on customer and market demands. However, the data gathered and analyzed is constant. That is, much of the same information is required about customers, vendors, products, services, materials, transactions, etc. The values may change, but the type of information remains the same.

The problem is that in all that data, there is so much information to decipher. Thus, the data requires processing—categorization, counting, averaging, summarization, statistical analysis, formatting for effective communication—to reveal information that the data can't tell you itself. With an application like Excel, it is possible to structure data and to process it in a manner that creates information for decision-making purposes. With the help of Excel, you give the data a voice, a medium through which underlying trends, calculated values, predictions, decision recommendations, and other information can be revealed.

In this section, you will be introduced to spreadsheets, otherwise called **worksheets**. You will learn to create worksheets and to manipulate rows and columns, as well as to navigate in and among worksheets within a workbook. You will learn how to enter data—text, numbers, dates, and times—into a worksheet, and how to use powerful analysis features that enable you to work intelligently in the worksheet environment.

Understanding Spreadsheet Terminology and Components

A **spreadsheet** is a powerful computer program with a user interface that is a grid of rows and columns. The intersection of each row and column is called a **cell**. Each cell can contain text, numbers, formulas, and/or functions. A **formula** is an equation that produces a result and may contain numbers, operators, text, and/or functions. A **function** is a built-in program that performs a task such as SUM or AVERAGE. Both formulas and functions must always start with the equal sign (=).

From balancing an accounting ledger to creating a financial report, many business documents are Excel spreadsheets. Excel spreadsheets are designed to support analyzing business data, representing data through charts, and modeling real world situations.

Spreadsheets are also commonly used to perform **what-if analysis**. In what-if analysis, you change values in spreadsheet cells to investigate the effects on calculated values of interest.

Spreadsheets are used for much more than what-if analysis, however. A spreadsheet can be used as a basic collection of data where each row is a **record** and each column is a **field** in the record. Spreadsheets can be built to act as a simple accounting system. Businesses often use spreadsheets to analyze complex financial statements and information. Excel has built-in statistical analysis capabilities. Excel can calculate statistical values such as mean, variance, and standard deviation to name a few. Excel can even be used for advanced statistical models such as forecasting and regression analysis. Spreadsheet applications *excel* at calculations of most any kind.

Starting Excel

Starting Microsoft Excel 2010 can be accomplished in several ways. In this section we will cover how to start Excel from the Start menu.

To Start Excel Using the Menu Shortcut

a. Click the **Start** button 🌐.

b. From the Start Menu, locate and then start **Microsoft Excel 2010**.

c. If you do not see Microsoft Excel 2010 in the Start menu, click **All Programs**, click **Microsoft Office**, and then click **Microsoft Excel 2010**.

Figure 1 Microsoft Excel 2010 in the Start menu

CONSIDER THIS | **Excel Can Store a Vast Amount of Data**

There are 1,048,576 rows x 16,384 columns = 17,179,869,184 cells in an Excel 2010 worksheet. With so much capacity, some are tempted to use Excel as a database. What other Office application would be better for storing vast amounts of data?

What Is a Workbook?

A **workbook** is a file that contains at least one worksheet. In Microsoft Excel, workbooks have a file extension of .xlsx. By default a new, blank workbook contains three worksheets, identified by tabs at the bottom of the Excel window titled *Sheet1*, *Sheet2*, and *Sheet3*. The active worksheet is *Sheet1* by default and is denoted by a white tab with bold letters. Worksheets that are not active are denoted by gray tabs with normal letters. The number of worksheets that can be contained in a workbook is a function of the amount of available memory. The next exercise will show you how to create a blank workbook.

To Create a Blank Workbook

a. Click the **File tab** to enter Backstage view.

b. Click **New** in the menu on the left. Available Templates will appear to the right of the menu. Blank workbook is the default, and is shown in the workbook preview pane.

c. Double-click **Blank workbook**. Alternatively, you can click **Create**.

   You will leave Backstage view and see the blank workbook. As previously mentioned, by default, Excel opens with a blank workbook, so you should now have two blank workbooks opened.

d. You are not going to need this workbook, so there is no need to save it. Click **Close** to exit Excel.

Opening a Workbook

As with many tasks in the Windows operating system, there are a number of ways to open an Excel workbook. For the purposes of this text, we will focus on how workbooks are opened using the Ribbon menu, and dialogs in Excel itself. Now you will open the workbook that you will use for all of the remaining exercises in this workshop.

To Open an Existing Workbook

a. Click the **Start** button.

b. From the Start Menu, locate and then start **Microsoft Excel 2010**.

c. Click the **File tab**, and then click **Open**.

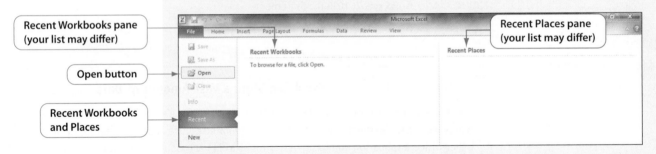

Recent Workbooks pane (your list may differ)

Open button

Recent Workbooks and Places

Recent Places pane (your list may differ)

Figure 2 Open an existing workbook in Backstage view

SIDE NOTE
Recent Workbooks vs. Recent Places

Figure 2 shows the Recent pane in Backstage view. Files recently opened or saved, and the folders where those files are stored, are listed in the Recent Workbooks and Recent Places panes respectively. Double-click an item in either pane to open it.

d. Click the disk drive in the left pane where your student data files are located, navigate through the folder structure, click **e01_ws01_Cart_Analysis**, and then click **Open**.

Saving and Renaming a Workbook

Once a workbook has been created or opened, any changes to the workbook will need to be saved. Save and Save As accomplish the same task, however Save As is useful for saving a copy of a file with a new name. It is useful for creating a backup of a file or for creating a copy of a workbook when you want to use that workbook as the starting point for another workbook.

Save vs. Save As
Click Save 🔲 and your file is saved in its current location with its current filename. Select Save As. Excel shows the Save As dialog box with the current filename and location, both of which you can change to save a new file.

To Save and Rename a Workbook

a. Click the **File tab**. Backstage view of the Info menu pane is displayed. The Info pane displays document properties such as file size, create and modified dates, and author.

b. Click **Save As**. In the Save As dialog box, navigate to the location where you are saving your files. In the File name box, type Lastname_Firstname_e01_ws01_Cart_Analysis replacing Lastname and Firstname with your own name.

c. Click **Save** 🔲.

Real World Advice   AutoRecover and Quick Save—Outsmart Mr. Murphy!

Computers are not perfect. While life's imperfections often make things interesting, they are also an opportunity for Murphy's Law: *Anything that can go wrong, will go wrong*. However, never fear, AutoRecover and Quick Save are here!

1. Excel automatically saves your work at regular intervals. The default is 10 minutes, but you can change it in the Options menu on the File tab, in the Save category of the Excel Options dialog box. The automatically saved copies of your work are called AutoRecover files. If your computer shuts down unexpectedly, Office will recognize that the file you were working on wasn't closed properly and will give you the option of opening the most recent AutoRecover file.

2. The Ctrl+S shortcut quickly saves your file to the same location as the last save. Whenever you make a significant change to your file, save it right away using the "quick save" keyboard shortcut.

Cells, Rows, and Columns

A worksheet consists of rows and columns. Each **row** is numbered in ascending sequence from top to bottom. Each **column** is lettered in ascending sequence from left to right. The intersection of each row and column is called a cell. Each cell has a default name, generally referred to as a **cell reference**—the combination of its column and row. For example, the intersection of column *A* and row *1* has a cell reference of A1 and the intersection of column *D* and row *20* is cell D20.

Worksheet Navigation

Whether a worksheet is small or extremely large, navigation from one cell to another is necessary to enter or to edit numbers, formulas, functions, or text.

Navigating in a small worksheet is simple—move the mouse pointer over the target cell and click. The border around the cell changes to a thick, black line. That is now the **active cell**. Any information you enter via the keyboard is placed into the active cell. **Worksheet navigation** is simply defined as moving the location of the active cell.

Scrolling

When part of a document (or in the case of Excel, a worksheet) is out of view because it is too large to display in the visible application window, use the vertical and horizontal scroll bars to shift other parts of the document into view. The vertical scroll bar is on the right side of the application window, and the horizontal scroll bar is at the bottom of the application window, on the right. *It is important to note that scrolling does not move the active cell, only your view in the document.*

Keyboard Navigation

There are several keyboard shortcuts that may be used to navigate a worksheet in order to change the scope and direction the active cell is moved. Figure 3 contains a description for each of these shortcuts.

Keyboard Navigation	Moves the Active Cell
Enter	Down one row
Shift + Enter	Up one row
→ ← ↓ ↑	One cell in the direction of the arrow key
Home	To column A of the current row
Ctrl + Home	To column A, row 1 (cell A1)
Ctrl + End	To the last cell, highest number row and far-right column, that contains information
End + → End + ← End + ↓ End + ↑	If the first cell in the direction of the arrow beyond the active cell contains data, to the last data containing cell in the arrow direction before an empty cell. If the first cell in the direction of the arrow beyond the active cell is empty, to the next cell in the arrow direction that contains information.
Page Up Page Down	Up one screen, down one screen
Ctrl + Page Up Ctrl + Page Down	One worksheet left One worksheet right
Tab, Shift + Tab	One column right One column left

Figure 3   Navigation using the keyboard

To Navigate Using the Keyboard

a. Click **Sheet 1** to make it the active worksheet, if necessary. Press End + →.
    The active cell should be XFD1. Be sure to release End between keystroke combinations. End does not work like Shift; its effect on other key functions is turned off once another key is pressed. End must then be pressed again to change the function to another key.

b. Press End + ↓. The active cell should be XFD1048576.

c. Press End + ←. The active cell should be A1048576.

d. Press End + ↑. The active cell should be A13, the first nonblank cell in direction of the pressed arrow key.

e. Press End + ↑. The active cell should be A5. Since the active cell was nonblank when you pressed End + ↑, the active cell is shifted to the cell before the next nonblank cell in the direction of the pressed arrow key.

f. Press End + ↑. The active cell should be A1. Excel searches for the next nonblank cell, and stops at row 1.

g. Press → three times. The active cell is D1.

h. Press ↓ five times. The active cell is D6.

i. Press Home. This keystroke takes you to column A of whatever row contains the active cell at the time of the keystroke. The active cell is now A6.

j.   Press ⌈End⌉+⌈→⌉. The active cell is the next nonblank cell—D6.

k.   To finish, press ⌈Ctrl⌉+⌈Home⌉ to return to cell A1.

Troubleshooting

The active cell is repositioned using the mouse pointer, arrows, and Page Up and Page Down. Even experienced users often scroll through a worksheet and press an arrow only to be returned to the active cell where they began scrolling.

Go To

For large worksheets in particular, Go To allows rapid navigation to a specific location. Although the worksheet you are currently working with isn't large, knowledge of how to use the Go To dialog box to navigate directly to any cell in the worksheet by specifying a cell reference is a skill that you will find useful.

To Navigate Using the Go To Dialog Box

SIDE NOTE
Quick Access to the Go To Dialog Box
The Go To dialog box can be accessed very quickly using the keyboard shortcut ⌈Ctrl⌉+⌈G⌉.

a.   Click the **Home tab**, click **Find & Select** in the Editing Group, and then click **Go To**. The Go To dialog box will appear.

b.   In the Reference box, type **B25**, and then click **OK**. The active cell is now B25.

c.   Click **Find & Select** in the Editing Group on the Home tab, and then click **Go To**. Notice that $A$1 is listed in the Go To box. Excel stores the cell reference of the active cell when Go To was invoked in order to make returning to your original location easier.

d.   Select **$A$1** in the Go To box, and then click **OK**.

Navigating Among Worksheets

Workbooks often contain more than one worksheet. In the bottom-left corner of the Excel worksheet window are worksheet tabs. Each tab represents a single worksheet in the workbook. Recall that by default, a new workbook contains three worksheets: Sheet1, Sheet2, and Sheet3.

The **active worksheet**, by default, is Sheet1. Recall, the active sheet is readily identifiable because the background color of its worksheet tab is white. To make a different worksheet active, click its worksheet tab. The following exercise shows you how to change the active worksheet.

To Change the Active Worksheet

a.   Click the **Sheet2 worksheet tab** in the bottom-left corner of the worksheet window. Sheet2 is now the active worksheet.

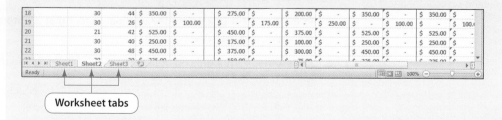

Worksheet tabs

Figure 4   Change the active worksheet

b. Click the **Sheet3 worksheet tab**. Sheet3 is now the active worksheet.

c. Click the **Sheet1 worksheet tab**. Sheet1 is now the active worksheet.

Troubleshooting

All the figures in this text were taken at a monitor resolution of 1024 X 768. Higher or lower resolution will affect the way Excel displays Ribbon options. The order in which groups in the Ribbon are displayed is not affected however.

Documentation

Worksheets are often used by people who did not develop them. Even if a worksheet will never be used by anyone other than its builder, best practice dictates that you document a workbook and its worksheets.

A well-documented worksheet is much easier to use and maintain, particularly for a user who did not develop the worksheet. Documentation also helps the developer return to and use the workbook after a long period of time. You may use a worksheet on a regular basis, but over time you may forget how the worksheet actually operates.

Documentation is vital to ensure that a worksheet remains usable. Documentation can take several forms such as file and worksheet names, worksheet titles, column and/or row titles, cell labels, cell comments, or a dedicated documentation worksheet. Many people do not take the time to document adequately because they don't feel it is time spent productively. Some don't feel it is necessary or don't think anyone else will ever use the workbook. For a workbook to be useful, it must be accurate, easily understood, flexible, efficient, *and* documented. While accuracy is most important, an undocumented workbook can later create inaccurate data. Where documentation is concerned, less is *not* more—more is more and is better. A well-structured worksheet is somewhat self-documented in that there are ample titles, column headings, and cell labels. However, a documentation worksheet and comments are created specifically to add documentation to a worksheet and/or workbook.

SIDE NOTE

Insert the System Date with Ctrl + ;

Ctrl + ; is a keyboard short-cut that inserts the computer system date into the active cell. Rather than type the current date, assuming the system date is set properly, use this keyboard shortcut to insert it.

To Document a Workbook Using a Documentation Worksheet and/or Comments

a. Click the **Sheet3 worksheet tab**. Click cell **A5**. Type today's date in mm/dd/yyyy format or alternatively press Ctrl + ; .

b. Click cell **B5**, and then type Lastname, Firstname replacing Lastname, Firstname with your last name and first name.

c. Click cell **C5**, and then type Added comments to key cells.

d. Click the **Sheet1 worksheet tab**.

e. Click the **Review tab**, click cell **A7**, and then click **New Comment** in the Comments group to create a comment.

f. In the comment box, select the user name text that is automatically inserted into the comment, and then press Delete .

g. Press Ctrl + B to toggle on bold text, type Retail Price, and then press Ctrl + B to toggle off bold text.

h. Press [Enter], and then type Commonly known as Manufacturer's Suggested Retail Price, or MSRP. Click on any worksheet cell. Cell A7 now has a red triangle in the top-right corner to indicate the presence of a comment.

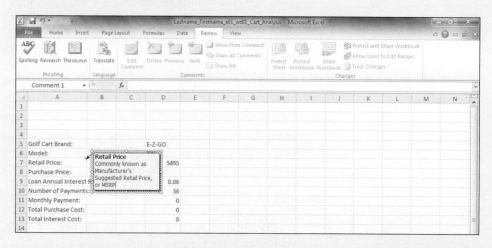

Figure 5 Documenting Retail Price using a Comment

i. Click cell **A8**, and then click **New Comment**. Notice cell A8 now has a red triangle in the top-right corner to indicate the presence of a comment.

j. In the comment box, select the user name that is automatically inserted into the comment, and then press [Delete].

k. Press [Ctrl]+[B] to toggle on bold text. Type Purchase Price, and then press [Ctrl]+[B] to toggle off bold text.

l. Press [Enter], and then type What must you actually pay to purchase the golf cart?

m. Click cell **A9**, and then click **New Comment**. In the comment box, select the user name text that is automatically inserted into the comment, and then press [Delete].

n. Press [Ctrl]+[B] to toggle on bold text, type Annual Interest Rate, and then press [Ctrl]+[B] to toggle off bold text.

o. Press [Enter], and then type Annual rate of interest in decimal or percentage format, e.g., 5% is entered as 0.05 or 5%.

p. Click cell **A10**, and then click **New Comment**.

q. In the Comment box, select the user name text that is automatically inserted into the comment, and then press [Delete].

r. Press [Ctrl]+[B] to toggle on bold text, and then type # of Payments. Press [Ctrl]+[B] to toggle off bold text.

s. Press [Enter], type Total number of payments over the term of the loan and then click any cell in the worksheet.

t. Click **Save** 🔲.

SIDE NOTE

Don't give Mr. Murphy an opportunity!

Don't get caught by Murphy's Law for computer users: *The probability your program or application will crash is directly proportional to the amount of time since you last saved your file.* Press [Ctrl]+[S] often.

Real World Advice — Back Up Your Workbook!

It is a good idea to back up your workbook when you are about to make significant changes to it, when those changes have been made, and/or when you have finished working for the moment.

To make a backup of your workbook:

1. Click the **File tab**. Click **Save As**.

   You may want to create a separate folder for your backup files. If possible, it is best practice to store backup files on an entirely different drive. A USB drive is a great option since you can take it with you as an "off site" backup.

   In the Save As dialog box, navigate to the location where you are saving your files. In the File name box, type the name of your file, for example Your_File_yyyy-mm-dd where yyyy-mm-dd is today's date. Click **Save**.

   Save As not only saves a copy of your file, it changes the file Excel has open. Your_File_yyyy-mm-dd will be the open file, and the title bar at the top of the Excel application window will display the new file name. Click **Close** ⊠ and open your original file before continuing your work.

2. Enter the location and name of the backup in a documentation worksheet in the original file so others (and you) will know the name of backup files and where they are stored.

Failing to Plan is Planning to Fail

Winston Churchill said, "He who fails to plan, plans to fail." The first step in building a worksheet should be planning. There are several questions that should be considered before you begin actually entering information:

- What is the objective of the worksheet? Is it to solve a problem? Is it to analyze data and recommend a course of action? Is it to summarize data and present usable information? Is it to store information for use by another application?

- Do you have all of the data necessary to build this worksheet?

- What information does your worksheet need to generate?

- How should the information in your worksheet be presented? Who is the audience? What form will best present the worksheet information?

A well-designed worksheet presents information in a clear and understandable way and allows for efficiency in the workbook development process.

Enter and Edit Data

In building and maintaining worksheets, the ability to enter and format data is fundamental. As data is entered via keyboard, the data simultaneously appears in the active cell and in the formula bar. Figure 6 shows the result when a cell is double-clicked to place the insertion point into cell contents. Alternatively, if you click in the formula bar, the insertion point is displayed in the formula bar.

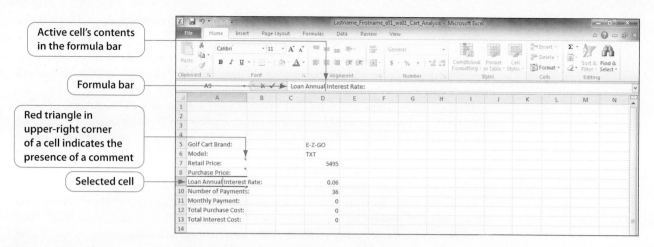

Active cell's contents in the formula bar

Formula bar

Red triangle in upper-right corner of a cell indicates the presence of a comment

Selected cell

Figure 6 Editing data in a cell

Text, Numbers, Dates, and Times

Text data consists of any combination of printable characters including letters, numbers, and special characters available on any standard keyboard.

Numeric data consists of numbers in any form not combined with letters and special characters other than possibly the period (decimal) and/or hyphen (to indicate negativity). Technically, special characters such as the dollar sign ($) or comma (,) are not considered numeric. They are only displayed for contextual and readability purposes and are not stored as part of a numeric cell value.

In Excel, date and time are a special form of numeric data. Information entered in a recognized date and/or time format will be converted automatically to an Excel date and/or time value. Figure 7 includes examples of valid dates and times that can be entered into Excel and how they will be displayed:

Enter	Excel Displays	Enter	Excel Displays
December 21, 2012	21-Dec-12	12/21/2012	12/21/2012
December 21, 2012 10 p	12/21/2012 22:00	2012/12/21	12/21/2012
Dec 21, 2012	21-Dec-12	13:00	13:00
21 Dec 2012 10:30	12/21/2012 10:30	1:00 p	1:00 PM

Figure 7 Date entry and how Excel displays dates

If Excel recognizes a value as a date/time, it will right-align displayed values. If you enter a date or time that is not recognized, Excel treats the information as text and left-aligns it in the cell. By default, Excel left-aligns text data and right-aligns numeric, date and time data.

How Excel Really Stores Date and Time Data

Date and time information is automatically displayed in a format easily understood by the user, but in Excel, dates and times are actually a real number where the value to the left of the decimal place is the number of days since December 31, 1899 (1 = January 1, 1900) and the value to the right of the decimal place is the proportion of 1 day that represents a time value (1.1 = January 1, 1900 + 144 minutes = January 1, 1900 2:24 AM). The advantages of storing date and time in what is commonly referred to as the 1900 date system are many:

- Sorting a list of dates and/or times is as simple as putting the list in ascending or descending numerical order.
- Since date and time are real numbers, mathematical manipulation to add to, or subtract from, date and time is greatly simplified.

- Determining a time span is simply a function of subtracting one date from another, a single calculation.

The vast majority of applications and systems now store date and time in this manner. The main difference between and among them is the base date. For example in DOS, Microsoft's precursor operating system to Windows, the base date is January 1, 1980.

Had all applications and computer systems stored dates as serial numbers, or serial dates, the Y2K bug never would have been an issue when the Western calendar progressed from December 31, 1999, to January 1, 2000. The Y2K bug was the result of a widespread practice in computer industry, that dated as far back as the 1950s, of storing date values with the four-digit year abbreviated to two digits—1999 was stored as 99, and 2000 would have been stored as 00. The purpose was to save expensive disk space—unlike today, digital media was very expensive, every character consumed precious space. Many information systems sort and process information by date, and since 1999 is greater than 2000 when stored as a 2-digit year, many systems would output incorrect information; it was feared that many systems would fail to operate at all as of January 1, 2000 because date data would not sort properly.

Real World Advice   Don't Confuse Formatting with Value

Formatting only changes the way a value is displayed. It does not change the actual value stored in the cell. Special formatting characters such as the dollar sign ($) and the comma (,) are not part of the stored value.

Dates and times may be entered in standard format: mm/dd/yy and hours:minutes: seconds. Excel recognizes information entered in date and/or time format and converts it to a serial value in the 1900 date system. What is stored is a serial real number, what is displayed is determined by the default or selected date/time format.

To Enter Information in a Worksheet

a. Click the **Sheet1 worksheet tab**.

b. Make sure cell **A1** is the active cell. If it is not, press Ctrl+Home.

c. Type Red Bluff Golf Course in cell A1, and then press Enter. The active cell is now A2.

d. Type Golf Cart Purchase Analysis in cell A2, and then press Enter.

e. Click cell A3, and then type 12/15/2013. Use the format mm/dd/yyyy.

f. Click cell **D8** to make it the active cell, type 5295 and then press ↓ and notice how the ↓ performs the same function as Enter. The values in cells D11, D12, and D13 are automatically recalculated.

g. Click cell **D10**, type 48, and then press Enter. Notice the monthly payment changed from 161.084159 to 124.353229.

h. Click cell **D9**, type 7.77%, and then press Enter. Notice the monthly payment changed from 124.353229 to 128.695525.

SIDE NOTE
Undo Keyboard Shortcut

The keyboard shortcut Ctrl+Z is a fast and efficient method of performing an Undo 🔄.

SIDE NOTE
Use Undo History
If you need to Undo a change in the recent past, but have made other changes since, click the arrow next to Undo 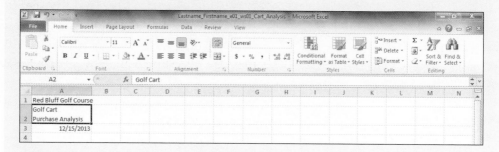 to see a history of changes you've made to your worksheet. Pick the change you would like to Undo from the list.

Troubleshooting

> If the monthly payment is thousands of dollars you probably entered 7.77. That is actually 777% for calculation purposes. You must enter the percentage, 7.77%, or enter .0777—the decimal equivalent for 7.77%.

i. Click **Undo** to return the Loan Annual Interest Rate to 0.06.

j. Click the **Sheet3 worksheet tab**, click cell **A6**, and then type today's date in mm/dd/yyyy format. Click cell **C6**, and then type Entered titles and updated data.

k. Click the **Sheet1 worksheet tab**.

l. Click **Save** .

Text Wrapping and Hard Returns

Excel, by default, places all information in a single line in a cell. Text that is too long to fit in a cell is displayed over contiguous cells to the right, unless contiguous cells contain information. If contiguous cells contain information, then lengthy text from cells to the left is truncated—essentially cut off, at least for display purposes.

A couple of ways to avoid text truncation can be through changing the alignment of a cell in order to wrap words or hard returns can be placed into text to force wrapping at a particular location.

To Wrap or Unwrap Text in a Cell

a. Click the **Home tab**, click cell **A2**, and then click **Wrap Text** in the Alignment group.

The text in cell A2 now wraps so you can see all the text in one cell. Wrap Text has its place, but this sheet title might be better formatted in a manner that allows you more control over the result.

b. Click **Wrap Text** again to unwrap the text in cell A2.

c. Double-click cell **A2**. Either use ← or → to move the cursor or click to position the cursor immediately after Cart.

d. Press Delete to remove the space between **Cart** and **Purchase**.

e. Press Alt + Enter to insert a hard return.

Figure 8 Insert a hard return to control wrap location

f. Click the **Sheet3 worksheet tab**.

g. Click cell **A7**, type today's date in mm/dd/yyyy format, click cell **C7**, and then type Modified titles.

h. Click the **Sheet1 worksheet tab**.

i. Click **Save** 🖫.

Manipulate Cells and Cell Ranges

Part of what makes a worksheet an efficient tool is the ability to perform actions that affect many cells at once. Knowing how to manipulate cells and cell **ranges** is a vital part of maximizing the efficacy of worksheet usage.

Selecting Cells and Cell Ranges

Using the mouse, multiple cells can be selected simultaneously. Selected cells can be contiguous to each other or they can be noncontiguous. Once multiple cells are selected, they can be affected by actions such as clear, delete, copy, paste, formatting, and many other actions while offering the convenience of performing the desired task only once for the selected cells.

To Select Contiguous and Noncontiguous Cell Ranges

a. Click and hold on cell **D5**. Drag down until cells **D5:D13** are selected—the active cell border expands to include D5:D13, and the background color of selected cells also changes.

b. Press Ctrl + Home . Click and hold cell **A5**. Drag down until cells **A5:A13** are selected.

c. Press and hold Ctrl , click and hold cell **C5**, and then drag to select cells **C5:C13**.

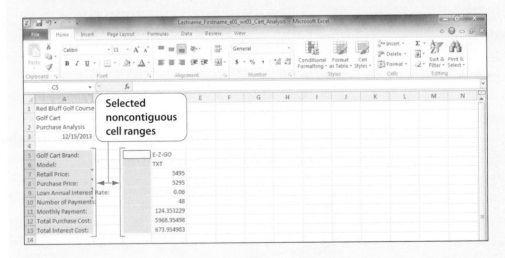

Figure 9 Selecting noncontiguous cell ranges

Quick Reference — Selecting Cell Ranges

There are several ways to select a contiguous range of cells:

1. Expand the active cell by dragging the mouse.
2. Select the first cell in the range, press [Shift], and click the last cell in the desired range.

A contiguous range of rows or columns can be selected in the following ways:

1. Click a row or column heading. Drag the mouse pointer across the headings to select contiguous rows or columns.
2. Click a row or column heading. Press [Shift] and click the last row or column you wish to select.

Once a cell or contiguous range of cells has been selected, you can add noncontiguous cells and ranges by pressing [Ctrl] and using any of the above methods for selecting ranges that do not involve [Shift].

Drag and Drop

As worksheets are designed, built, and modified, it is often necessary to move information from one cell or range of cells to another. One of the most efficient ways to do this is called "drag and drop" and is accomplished entirely with the mouse pointer as shown in the following exercise.

To Drag and Drop Cells

a. Select cell range **D5:D13**. Point to the border of the selected range. The cell pointer changes to a move pointer.

b. Click and hold the left mouse button, and then drag the selected cells to the right one column (column E). A *ghost* range, also referred to as a target range, and range callout are displayed as the pointer is moved to show exactly where the moved cells will be placed.

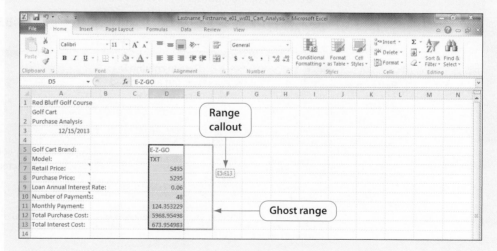

Figure 10 Drag and drop to move a cell range

c. Drop the dragged cells into **column E** by releasing the left mouse button. Be careful to drop the range onto the same rows occupied in column D.

d. Move the cell pointer until it is over the border of the selected range in column E. The cell pointer will change to a move pointer.

e. Press and hold Ctrl. The move pointer changes to a copy pointer.

f. Drag the selected range until the ghost range is directly to the left in column D to copy the cells from range **E5:E13** to the range **D5:D13**. Release the left mouse button and then release Ctrl. Press Ctrl+Home.

g. Click the **Sheet3 worksheet tab**.

h. Click cell **A8**, type today's date in mm/dd/yyyy format, click cell **C8**, and then type Added Column E of data.

i. Click the **Sheet1 worksheet tab**.

j. Press Ctrl+Home, and then click **Save**.

Cut/Copy and Paste

The same copy and/or move results can be obtained with the copy and paste or cut and paste features. The paste feature presents more options than drag and drop through Paste Options and Paste Special to give you more control of exactly what is placed into the target cells. Drag and Drop moves or copies everything in a cell, including formatting. In the next exercise you will learn to use Cut, Copy, and Paste in Excel. Later in this workshop we will learn the advantages of Paste Options and Paste Special.

To Use Cut, Copy, and Paste

a. Select cell range **D5:D13**, and then click **Cut** in the Clipboard group. The solid border around cell range D5:D13 changes to a moving dashed border.

b. Click cell **F5**, and then click **Paste** in the Clipboard group.

c. Click **Copy** in the Clipboard group. The solid border around cell range F5:F13 changes to a moving dashed border.

d. Click cell **D5**, press and hold Ctrl, and then select cells **G5:H5**.

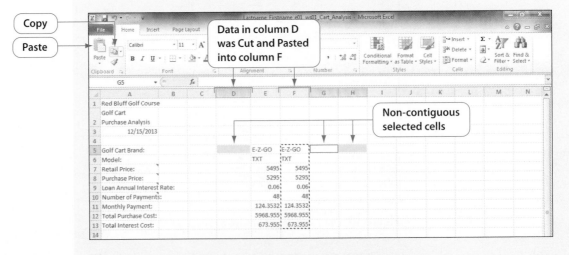

Figure 11 Selection of multiple locations to paste a copied cell range

e. Click **Paste** in the Clipboard group.

f. Press Esc to clear the clipboard and remove the dashed border from around cell range F5:F13.

g. Click the **Sheet3 worksheet tab**.

h. Click cell **A9**, type today's date in mm/dd/yyyy format, click cell **C9**, and then type Added Columns F:H of data.

i. Click the **Sheet1 worksheet tab**.

j. Press Ctrl+Home, and then click **Save** 💾.

Series (AutoFill)

The **AutoFill** feature is a powerful way to minimize the effort required to enter certain types of data. AutoFill copies information from one cell, or a series in contiguous cells, into contiguous cells in the direction the fill handle is dragged. AutoFill is a smart copy that will try to guess how you want values or formulas changed as you copy. Sometimes, AutoFill will save significant time by changing the contents correctly. Other times, AutoFill changes the contents in a way you did not intend—when that happens, the AutoFill Options button makes options available that may be helpful.

The fill handle is a small black square in the bottom-right corner of the active cell or selected cells border. To engage the AutoFill feature, click and drag the fill handle in the direction you wish to expand the active cell.

To Quickly Generate Data Using AutoFill

a. Select cell **D4**, type Option 1, and then press Enter. You need to add titles to the cart option columns you just created.

b. Select cell **D4**. Point to the fill handle—the tiny square in the bottom-right corner of the active cell—and then click and hold the handle once the mouse pointer changes to ➕. Drag the fill handle right until the border around the active cell expands to include cells **D4:H4**, and then release the left mouse button. Sheet1 will have column titles Option1–Option 5.

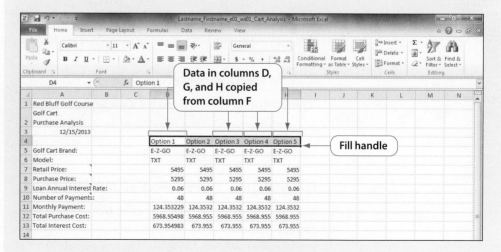

Figure 12 Using AutoFill to generate a series of headings

c. Click the **Sheet2 worksheet tab**. The Analysis of Cart Usage has some data missing that can be supplied using AutoFill.

d. Select cell **A11**. Click the fill handle, drag it down until the border around the cell range expands to include cells **A11:A41**, and then release the left mouse button.

e. Click **AutoFill Options** that has appeared at the bottom right of cell A41. Select **Fill Without Formatting**.

Barry Cheney filled the background color for the first of May because the demand was abnormally high that day. The pink background is specific to May 1st, so you do not want that formatting to be on all the dates. Fill Without Formatting displays all the filled dates as 1900 date system values.

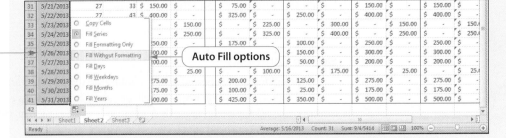

Formatted dates from default "Fill Series"

Figure 13 AutoFill and Fill Without Formatting

f. If necessary, select range **A11:A41**. Click the **Home tab**, click the **Number Format arrow** General ▾ , and then select **Short Date** in the menu.

g. Select cell range **I3:J3**. Selecting more than one cell sets a pattern—in this case increments of one—for the AutoFill to follow.

h. Click and hold the **fill handle**, drag the fill handle to the right until the border around the cell range expands to include cells **I3:M3**, and then release the left mouse button. Notice the AutoFill callout that shows the filled value of each cell as you move the fill handle to the right.

i. Select cell **G9**. Click the fill handle, and then drag it right until you have selected cell range **G9:P9**. If you click the AutoFill Options button, notice you will see the default option currently displays Fill Series, which is why the cells correctly filled by increments of 1.

j. Click the **Sheet3 worksheet tab**.

k. Click cell **A10**, type today's date in mm/dd/yyyy format, click cell **C10**, and then type Filled Series.

l. Click the **Sheet1 worksheet tab**.

m. Press Ctrl + Home , and then click **Save** .

CONSIDER THIS | **More on AutoFill, Anyone?**

You just met Aidan Matthews, the chief technology officer at Painted Paradise Resort and Spa. You explained to him the work you have been completing for Barry. He urged you to explore AutoFill further as it is very flexible and can assist you in many ways. As he reminisced on his time conducting Excel training sessions earlier in his career, he remembered a file he gave trainees to practice AutoFill. If you would like to try some more AutoFill activities, open Aidan's file e01_ws01_Autofill_Practice, and follow the instructions provided in cell comments. When you finish, save the file as Lastname_ Firstname_e01_ws01_Autofill_Practice.

Modifying Cell Information

Copying and pasting content from one range of cells to another range or more is a highly efficient way to reuse parts of a worksheet. The ranges you just pasted into columns D, F, G, and H contain a lot of information that is calculated using formulas you do not want to type more than once. However, you don't need five copies of a purchase analysis of an E-Z-GO TXT golf cart.

Changing the contents of cells is as simple as double-clicking on the cell to invoke edit mode. The active cell will contain an insertion point. If you want to change part of the content, use the arrow keys or click to position the insertion point at the desired location. If all the cell content is to be replaced, click the cell once to make it the active cell. All cell content will be replaced when you begin typing to enter the new content for the selected cell.

To Modify Worksheet Contents by Changing Copied Information

a. Click cell **E6**, type RXV, and then double-click cell **F6**. Press ⎡Home⎤ to go to the left margin of the cell, type Freedom, and then press ⎡Spacebar⎤ once so the formula bar displays **Freedom TXT**. Press ⎡Enter⎤. Click cell **G6**, type Freedom RXV. Press ⎡Enter⎤. Click cell **H6**, and then type The Drive.

b. Click cell **E7**, and then type 5995. Press ⎡Tab⎤ to move to cell **F7**, and then type 6495. Press ⎡Tab⎤ to move to cell **G7**, and then type 7135.

c. Click cell **E8**, and then type 5695. Press ⎡Tab⎤ to move to cell **F8**, and then type 5995. Press ⎡Tab⎤ to move to cell **G8**, and then type 6125. Click cell **H8**, and then type 5150. Notice that as you change the values in each of the cells in row 8 that Monthly Payment, Total Purchase Cost, and Total Interest Cost are recalculated.

d. Click cell **H5**, type Yamaha, and then press ⎡Enter⎤.

e. Select cell range **F6:G6**, and then click **Wrap Text** in the Alignment group.

f. Click the **Sheet3 worksheet tab**.

g. Click cell **A11**, type today's date in mm/dd/yyyy format, click cell **C11**, and then type Updated cart data.

h. Click the **Sheet1 worksheet tab**.

i. Press ⎡Ctrl⎤+⎡Home⎤, and then click **Save** 🖫.

Inserting Cells

You want to make the golf cart analysis worksheet easier to read and use by adding some white space. **White space** is part of a document that does not contain data or documentation. While white space does not need to be the color white, the lack of data gives a document visual structure and creates a sense of order in the mind of the worksheet user. For example, white space above and below Loan Annual Interest Rate and Number of Payments visually creates a group of information associated with financing the golf carts.

To Insert Rows in a Worksheet

a. Click cell **A7**, click the **Insert arrow** in the Cells group, and then click **Insert Sheet Rows**. Excel inserts a row above the active cell location and moves all cells at A7 and below down to make room.

Figure 14 Home Tab, Insert to insert sheet rows

b. Select cell range **A10:A11**, click the **Insert arrow** in the Cells group, and then click **Insert Sheet Rows**. If you have more than one cell (or row) selected, Excel will interpret the number of rows selected as the number of rows you want inserted.

c. Select cell range **A14:A15**, click the **Insert arrow** in the Cells group, and then click **Insert Sheet Rows**. Press Ctrl+Home.

Troubleshooting

White space was only inserted in column A!
If you click the Insert button instead of the Insert arrow, Excel will default to inserting extra cells only, instead of a row. Inserting rows is often more efficient and less error prone than inserting cells. When inserting white space throughout your data, insert rows.

d. Click the **Sheet3 worksheet tab**.

e. Click cell **A12**, type today's date in mm/dd/yyyy format, click cell **C12**, and then type Created white space.

f. You need more rows in the modifications section of the documentation worksheet. Select rows **14:29** using the row headings, and then click **Insert** in the Cells group.

g. Click the **Sheet1 worksheet tab**.

h. Press Ctrl+Home, and then click **Save**.

Deleting Cells

White space is a good way to visually separate and logically categorize information in a worksheet. However, the old saying, "You can't have too much of a good thing" definitely is not true where white space is concerned. There is too much white space between the headings in column A and the numbers in column D. One way to move the columns of cart information to the left is to delete a few cells.

To Delete Cells, Cell Ranges, and Rows

a. Click cell **B4**, and then click **Delete** in the Cells group. Notice that only the Option numbers in row 5 moved left.

b. Select cell range **B5:B18**, and click **Delete** in the Cells group. The remaining data cell values in rows 5:18 moved left.

c. Click a cell in row **10**. Press and hold $\boxed{\text{Ctrl}}$, and then click a cell in row **15**. Click the **Delete arrow** in the Cells group.

d. Click **Delete Sheet Rows**, and then press $\boxed{\text{Ctrl}}+\boxed{\text{Home}}$.

e. Click the **Sheet3 worksheet tab**.

f. Click cell **A13**, type today's date in mm/dd/yyyy format, click cell **C13**, and then type Relocated data to the left, deleted some blank rows.

g. Click the **Sheet1 worksheet tab**.

h. Press $\boxed{\text{Ctrl}}+\boxed{\text{Home}}$, and then click **Save** $\boxed{\blacksquare}$.

Merge & Center vs. Center Across

The titles in the golf cart analysis worksheet are entered in cells A1:A3. Although they contain the correct information to communicate the purpose of the golf cart analysis worksheet, they might better present that information with some formatting improvements. Titles that identify the general purpose of a worksheet are often at the top and centered above worksheet content. Additionally, they are often displayed in a different, larger font and may be bolded or italicized. Merge & Center ⊞ combines selected cells into a single cell and centers the content in the left and/or top cell in the resulting single cell—all other data is lost. Merge & Center can be applied both horizontally and vertically. Center Across Selection erases the borders between cells such that a selected range looks like a single cell, but the original cells remain, the borders between them are removed and the content is centered. Center Across Selection can only be applied horizontally. Additionally, Center Across Selection will never cause a loss of data.

To Merge, Center, and Format Headings

a. Select cell range **A1:G1**, and then click **Merge & Center** in the Alignment group.

b. Select cell range **A2:G3**, and then click **Merge & Center** in the Alignment group. Notice the warning message.

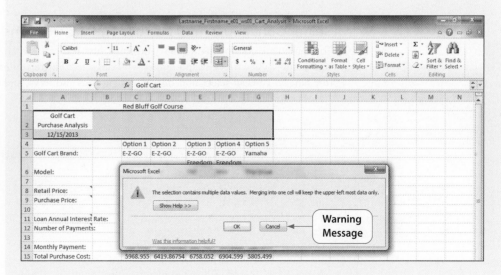

Figure 15 Merge and center a range containing multiple values and data

c. Click **Cancel**, you do not want to lose the data in cell A3.

d. Click the **Alignment dialog box launcher** ⬜. This launches the Alignment tab of the Format Cells dialog box. Click **Center Across Selection** in the Horizontal list box.

e. Click **OK**. Cell A2 content is centered across cell range A2:G2, and cell A3 content is centered across cell range A3:G3.

f. Click the **Sheet3 worksheet tab**.

g. Click cell **A14**, type today's date in mm/dd/yyyy format, click cell **C14**, type Centered titles, and then press ⌷Enter⌷.

h. Click the **Sheet1 worksheet tab**.

i. Press ⌷Ctrl⌷+⌷Home⌷, and then click **Save** ⬜.

CONSIDER THIS │ **When Would You Choose Merge & Center?**

Try this. In the Sheet1 worksheet of the Lastname_Firstname_e01_ws01_Cart_Analysis worksheet, select cell range A1:D16. Try to select cell range A1:B9.

Now try to select cell range A2:D16. Try to select cell range A2:B9.

Merge & Center ⬜ creates a single cell that can cause problems if you want to select a range of cells that includes only part of the merged cell range.

There are Excel experts who feel Merge & Center should never be used—should not even be part of Excel. Do you agree?

Manipulate Columns and Rows

By default any worksheet you create has set column widths and row heights. As you build, refine, and modify a worksheet, it is often necessary to add and/or delete columns and rows for formatting and content purposes. Fortunately, Excel makes these activities extremely easy to accomplish.

Select Contiguous and Noncontiguous Columns and Rows

To manipulate columns and rows, you must first indicate which of each you wish to affect by your actions. As with cells and ranges, you can select entire columns, rows, column ranges, and row ranges. You can select noncontiguous columns and rows, and even select ranges of columns and rows at the same time.

Quick Reference   Selecting Columns and Rows

To select an individual column or row click the heading (letter or number respectively) in the header.

To select a range of contiguous columns or rows, click and hold the heading at the start of the range you want to select. Then drag the mouse to select additional columns or rows, or click the heading of the column or row at one end of the range you want to select then press and hold [Shift] and click the heading of the column or row at the other end of the range you want to select.

To select noncontiguous columns or rows, click the heading of the first column or row you want to select. Press and hold [Ctrl], and then click the headings of any additional columns and/or rows you want to select. Contiguous ranges of columns or rows can be part of a noncontiguous range. To use the methods listed above for selecting a range of contiguous columns or rows, simply hold down [Ctrl] during the first step.

Use [Ctrl], not [Shift], when moving between selecting columns and rows in the same noncontiguous range.

To select all cells in a worksheet, place the pointer over the Select All ▨ button and the pointer will change to ✛, then click the left mouse button. Alternatively press [Ctrl]+[A].

Inserting Columns and Rows

A selected range is defined as a contiguous set of cells, columns, or rows that are all part of a single contiguous selection. However, how you select columns and rows determines whether they are a single, contiguous range or are considered separate, individual selections.

If you click column C, press and hold [Shift], and click column E, you have created a contiguous selection of columns C:E. All three columns are highlighted as a group. But, if you click column C, press and hold [Ctrl], click column D, and then click column E, you have just selected three individual columns—three individual selections. In this situation, columns C, D, and E are treated by Excel as noncontiguous columns—there is a slight border highlighted between the columns. Whether columns (or rows) are a selected range or are noncontiguous has an effect on how actions such as Insert are applied to a worksheet.

There is still a need to add some white space to the cart analysis worksheet—the columns of information for the different carts are too close together. One way to add white space is to insert a blank column between each column of cart information. Additionally, there is enough definitional difference between the Monthly Payment and the Purchase and Interest totals that some white space to separate them may be advisable. This can be accomplished by inserting a row in the appropriate locations.

To Insert a Column Between Each Column of Cart Data

a. Click the heading for column **D** to select column D, press and hold [Shift], and then select column **G**.

b. Click **Insert** in the Cells group. Four contiguous columns were inserted to the right of column C.

c. Press [Ctrl]+[Z] to undo the last change. This is not what you wanted.

d. Click on the heading for column **D**, press and hold [Ctrl], and then select column **E**, column **F**, and column **G** by clicking on each column heading individually. Notice the white line between each column selection—this is not a selected range of columns, it is four individually selected columns.

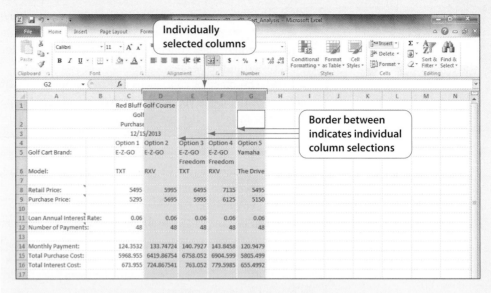

Figure 16 Use Ctrl to select individual columns, rows, cells, or ranges

e. Click **Insert** in the Cells group.

   A column has been inserted to the left of each selected column because columns D, E, F, and G were selected as noncontiguous individual columns.

f. Click the heading for row **15**. Press and hold Ctrl, select row **4**, click **Insert** in the Cells group, and then press Ctrl+Home.

g. Click the **Sheet3 worksheet tab**.

h. Click cell **A15**, type today's date in mm/dd/yyyy format, click cell **C15**, and then type Added more white space.

i. Click the **Sheet1 worksheet tab**.

j. Click **Save** .

SIDE NOTE

A Faster Way to Insert

When columns or rows are selected for the purpose of inserting them into the worksheet, you can click the right mouse button and select Insert from the shortcut menu.

Column Width and Row Height

You've inserted columns and rows to add additional white space, but there is still a need to refine the amount of white space in the worksheet. At this point there is too much—the information is spread too far apart.

Column width and row height often need to be adjusted for a couple of reasons. One reason is to reduce the amount of white space a blank column or row represents in a worksheet, the other is to allow the content of cells in a row or column to be displayed properly.

Column width is defined in characters. The default width is 8.43 characters. The maximum width of a column is 255 characters.

Row height is defined in points. A point is approximately 1/72 of an inch (0.035 cm). The default row height in Excel is 15 points, or approximately 1/6 of an inch (0.4 cm). A row can be up to 409 points in height (about 5.4 inches).

To Manually Adjust Column Width and Row Height

a. Select column **D**, press and hold Ctrl, and then select columns **F**, **H**, and **J**.

b. Click **Format** in the Cells group, click **Column Width** from the Cell Size menu, and then type **2** in the Column Width dialog box.

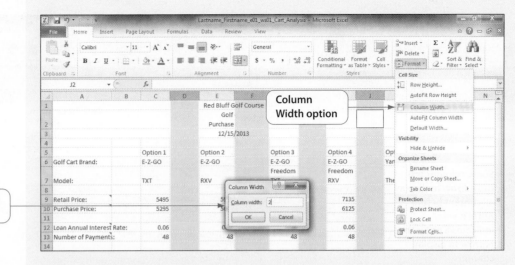

Figure 17 Column Width dialog box

c. Click **OK**, click row **4**, press and hold Ctrl, and then select rows **8**, **11**, **14**, and **16**.

d. Click **Format** in the Cells group, and then click **Row Height** in the Cell Size menu.

e. Type **7** in the Row Height dialog box.

f. Click **OK**, and then press Ctrl + Home.

g. Click the **Sheet3 worksheet tab**.

h. Click cell **A16**, type today's date in mm/dd/yyyy format, click cell **C16**, and then type Resized some rows and columns.

i. Click the **Sheet1 worksheet tab**.

j. Click **Save**.

Changing Column Widths Using AutoFit

Column width and row height can also be adjusted automatically—or AutoFit—based on the width and height of selected content. The width of columns will be adjusted to allow selected content to fit into the column. Care is required in that data in cells not selected may be truncated or not displayed properly.

To AutoFit Column Width

a. Click cell **A7**, press and hold Ctrl, and then select cells **C7**, **E7**, **G7**, **I7**, and **K7**.

b. Click **Format** in the Cells group, and then click **AutoFit Column Width**.

Since AutoFit sizes columns (also notice there is an AutoFit Row Height command, which works in exactly the same manner) to the selected content, columns C and E are too narrow to display most of the numeric data, which is then displayed as a series of number signs (#). Notice also that columns A and B together are too narrow to display the content of cells A12 and A13, so they are truncated on the right.

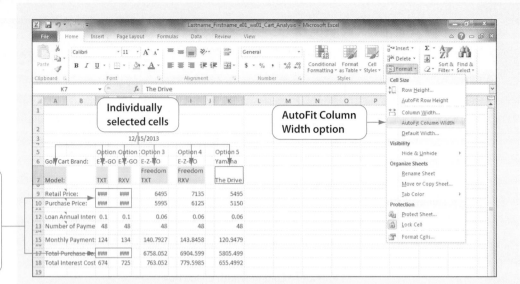

Some columns are too narrow to display all content before AutoFit—### indicates a cell is too narrow to display contents

Figure 18 AutoFit Column Width results for selected cells

c. Select column **A**, press and hold Ctrl, select columns **C**, **E**, **G**, **I**, and **K**, and then click **Format** in the Cells group.

d. Click **AutoFit Column Width** from the Cell Size menu.

Since columns were selected instead of individual cells the columns are AutoFit to the widest content in the column, resulting in no number signs. AutoFit Column Width made the columns wide enough to display seven (7) digits to the right of the decimal place in the Monthly Payment row. That's more than is necessary for what is obviously a dollar amount.

e. Select cell range **C15:K18,** and then click **Decrease Decimal** in the Number group repeatedly until only two decimal places are visible.

f. Select column **C**, press and hold **Ctrl**, and then select columns **E, G, I**, and **K**. Click **Format** in the Cells group, and then click **AutoFit Column Width** on the Cell Size menu.

Column width can also be set manually. Column A could be a little wider than set by AutoFit Column Width.

g. Place the mouse pointer over the **border** between column A and column B. The pointer should change to ✛. Click and hold the left mouse button, and then drag the mouse to the right until column A is about ¼ inch wider. **Press** Ctrl + Home.

SIDE NOTE
There Is an Increase Decimal Too

What do you do if you click Decrease Decimal too many times? Click Increase Decimal as many times as is necessary to display the correct number of decimal places.

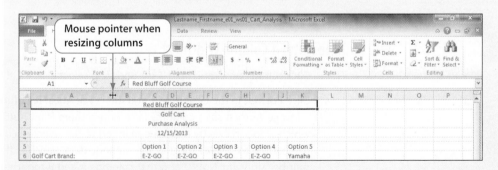

Mouse pointer when resizing columns

Figure 19 Manually Adjust Column Width

h. Click the **Sheet3 worksheet tab**.

i. Click cell **A17**, type today's date in mm/dd/yyyy format, click cell **C17**, and then type Resized columns using AutoFit.

j. Click the **Sheet1 worksheet tab**.

k. Click **Save** 🔲.

Real World Advice — Fast Ways to Adjust Column Width and Row Height

For small worksheets in particular, you will often want to simply adjust a column width or row height using the content you can see on the screen.

1. Hover the mouse pointer over the column header between two columns. The mouse pointer will change to ➕.

2. Click and hold the left mouse button and move the mouse left or right to adjust the width of the column to the left of the cursor, or double-click to AutoFit. The same procedure can be used to adjust row height.

1. Hover the mouse pointer between two row headers; it should change to ➕.

2. Click and hold the left mouse button and move the mouse up or down to adjust the height of the row above the cursor, or double-click to AutoFit.

If multiple columns or rows are selected, adjusting width or height for one selected column or row adjusts the width or height for all.

Delete vs. Clear

When removing data from a cell or cells in a worksheet, data can be cleared or deleted (there is a difference between the two). Clearing contents from a cell does not change the location of other cells in the worksheet. Deleting a cell shifts surrounding cells in a direction determined from a prompt.

Delete works exactly as you would expect when editing a string of characters or a formula in a cell in edit mode. However, when you are not in edit mode, pressing Delete actually clears content, it does not delete a cell, column, or row. This distinction is important because clearing content doesn't shift the location of other cells in the worksheet. Deleting cells, columns, or rows requires the use of either the Delete option in the Cells group of the Home tab, or the use of the Delete option in the shortcut menu displayed via a right-click of the mouse button on the selected cells—and it does shift other cells in the worksheet.

Earlier in this workshop you deleted columns and rows by selecting cells and cell ranges, selecting Delete in the Cells group and then choosing a shift direction from the Delete dialog box. Once you have selected a row or column by clicking on the header, follow the same process to delete the column or row, but there is no Delete dialog box. Since an entire column or row is selected, there is no need to prompt for the direction to move adjacent cells.

The golf cart analysis worksheet is formatted well, but after adjusting the width of column A, column B is no longer necessary to avoid truncation of the text in cells A12 and A13. Further, Barry has decided that the E-Z-GO Freedom TXT and the E-Z-GO Freedom RXV are not options to be further considered so they are to be removed from the analysis. The date in row 3 isn't necessary so you've been asked to delete that content as well.

To Delete Columns and Rows

a. Click and hold the heading for column **F**, and then drag the mouse pointer to the right until columns **F** through **I** are selected. Press and hold Ctrl, and then select Column **B**.

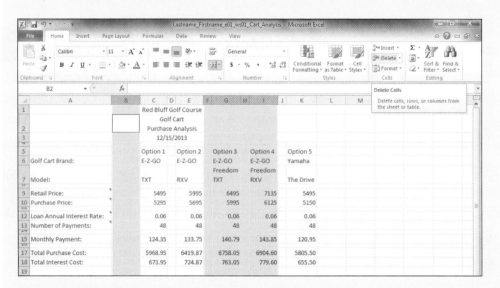

Figure 20 Multiple columns selected for deletion

b. Click **Delete** in the Cells group.

c. Select cell **A3**, and then press Delete.

You have just cleared the contents of cell A3. Recall that for the cell range that includes the centered date, you used Center Across Selection. Clearing the contents of cell A3 doesn't affect the cell that contains the centered date.

d. Select row **3** by clicking on the row heading.

e. Click **Delete** in the Cells group—now you've cleared the date. Also, notice the borders between all cells in row 3 are again visible.

f. Select cell **F4**, and then type Option 3.

g. Click on **Sheet3**, click cell **A18**, type today's date in mm/dd/yyyy format, click cell **C18**, and then type Removed carts no longer under consideration.

h. Click the **Sheet1 worksheet tab**.

i. Press Ctrl + Home, and then click **Save** 💾.

Inserting Columns That Contain Data

Barry has asked that the analysis include multiple payment schedules for 24, 36, and 48 months of interest for each of the three remaining golf carts in the analysis. The interest rate for 24-month financing is 5.0%, for 36-month financing is 5.5%, and for 48-month financing is 6.0%. Expanding the analysis to include additional payment schedules is easily accomplished by inserting new columns that have been copied to the clipboard and then editing the newly inserted columns.

To Expand the Analysis by Reusing and Editing Column Data

a. Select column **B**, and then click **Copy** in the Clipboard group. Right-click the heading for column **B**.

b. Click **Insert Copied Cells** in the shortcut menu. Press ⏎Enter.

c. Repeat Steps a–b one more time.

d. Select column **F**, right-click the heading for column **F**, and then click **Copy** in the shortcut menu.

e. Right-click the heading for column **F**, and then click **Insert Copied Cells** in the shortcut menu. Press ⏎Enter.

f. Repeat Steps d–e one more time.

g. Select column **J**. Right-click the heading for column **J**, and then click **Copy** in the shortcut menu.

h. Right-click the heading for column **J**, and then click **Insert Copied Cells** in the shortcut menu. Press ⏎Enter.

i. Repeat Steps g–h one more time. Press Esc.

j. Click cell **B11**, type 0.05, and then press Ctrl+⏎Enter to apply the change and to keep cell **B11** selected. Press Ctrl+C to copy cell B11 to the clipboard. Select cell **F11**, press and hold Ctrl, and then select **J11**. Press Ctrl+V to paste cell B11 into cells F11 and J11. Press Esc.

k. Click cell **C11**, type 0.055, and then press Ctrl+⏎Enter. Press Ctrl+C. Click cell **G11**, press Ctrl, select cell **K11**, and then press Ctrl+V. Press Esc.

l. Click cell **B12**, type 24, and then press Tab. Type 36, and then press ⏎Enter. Select cell range **B12:C12**, and then press Ctrl+C. Select cell **F12**, press and hold Ctrl, select cell **J12**, press Ctrl+V, and then press Esc.

m. Select column **C**, press and hold Ctrl, and then select columns **D**, **G**, **H**, **K**, and **L** (be sure to click each column heading rather than drag across). Click **Insert** in the Cells group.

n. Select column **C**, press and hold Ctrl, and then select columns **E**, **I**, **K**, **O**, and **Q**—you may have to scroll right to access all the columns while still pressing Ctrl while scrolling. Click **Format** in the Cells group, and then select **Column Width** from the Cell Size menu. Type 1 in the Column Width dialog box, and then click **OK**.

o. Select cell range **B4:F4**, and then click **Merge & Center** in the Alignment group. Click **OK** when the warning message appears.

p. Repeat Step o for cell ranges **H4:L4** and **N4:R4**. Press `Ctrl`+`Home`.

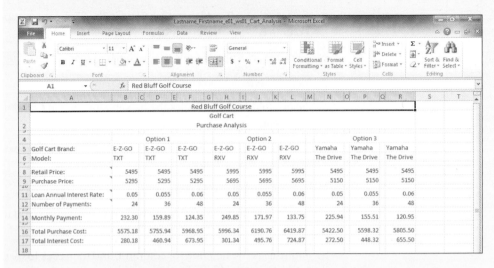

Figure 21 Golf cart analysis with option headings centered and new white space

q. Click the **Sheet3 worksheet tab**.

r. Click cell **A19**, type today's date in mm/dd/yyyy format, click cell **C19**, and then type Added analysis for 24 and 36 month loans.

s. Click the **Sheet1 worksheet tab**.

t. Press `Ctrl`+`Home`, and then click **Save**.

Printing Worksheets and Manipulating Workbooks

Worksheets must often be printed for discussion at meetings or for distribution in venues where paper is the most effective media. Excel has a lot of built-in functionality that makes printed worksheets easy to read and understand. Further, as workbooks grow to include multiple worksheets and evolve to require maintenance, it is necessary to be able to create new worksheets, copy worksheets, delete worksheets, and reorder worksheets.

In this section you will learn to utilize Excel's print functionality to ensure that your worksheets are usable when presented on paper and will learn to create, copy, delete, and reorder worksheets in a workbook.

Preview and Print Worksheets

The golf cart analysis is now ready to distribute as part of a package that will be given to management at the next board meeting. This will require that the analysis be printed on paper with appropriate headings and so forth.

Excel has a great deal of flexibility built into its printing functionality. To appropriately present your work in printed form, it is important that you understand how to take advantage of Excel's print features.

Worksheet Views

In the bottom-right corner of the application window are three icons that control the worksheet view. Normal view ⊞ is what you use most of the time when building and editing a worksheet. Only the cells in the worksheet are visible; print specific features such as margins and page breaks are not shown.

Page Layout view ▣ shows page margins, print headers, and page breaks. It presents you with a reasonable preview of how a worksheet will print on paper.

Page Break Preview ▦ does not show page margins, but allows you to manually adjust the location of page breaks. This is particularly helpful when you would like to force a page break after a set of summary values and/or between data categories, and force the next part of a worksheet to print on a new page.

Quick Reference   Switching Among Worksheet Views

On the right side of the status bar do the following:
1. Click ▦ for Normal view.
2. Click ▣ for Page Layout view.
3. Click ▤ for Page Break Preview view.

To Switch Among Worksheet Views and Manipulate Page Breaks

a. Click **Page Layout** ▣ on the status bar.

b. Use the **Zoom Slider** ⊖───○───⊕ on the status bar to adjust the view until two pages are completely visible.

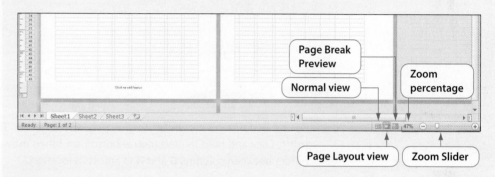

Figure 22 Page Layout view

c. Click **Page Break Preview** ▤ on the status bar.
Only the part of the worksheet that will print is displayed. A dashed blue border indicates where printing will break from one page to another.

d. Use the **Zoom Slider** 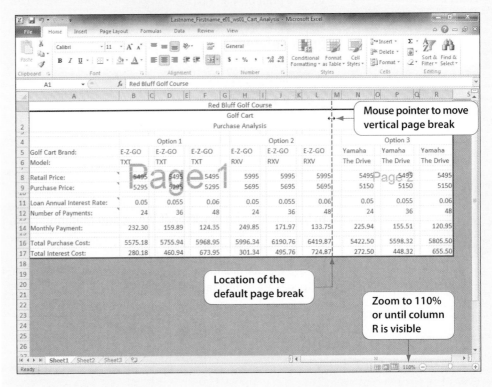 to adjust zoom level to make the pages as large as possible without hiding any data off the visible application window.

Figure 23 Page Break Preview

e. Point the mouse pointer over the blue page break border. The mouse pointer changes to ↔. Click and hold the left mouse button, and then move the page break to the cell border between columns **G** and **H** to adjust its location.

f. Click the **Page Layout tab** on the Ribbon—not Page Layout on the status bar. Now you need to insert another page break so each of the three golf carts still under consideration will print on a separate page.

g. Select cell **N4**, and then click **Breaks** in the Page Setup group.

h. Click **Insert Page Break**.

Two page breaks are inserted, a horizontal page break above the active cell, and a vertical page break to the left of the active cell. You only want the vertical page break between columns M and N.

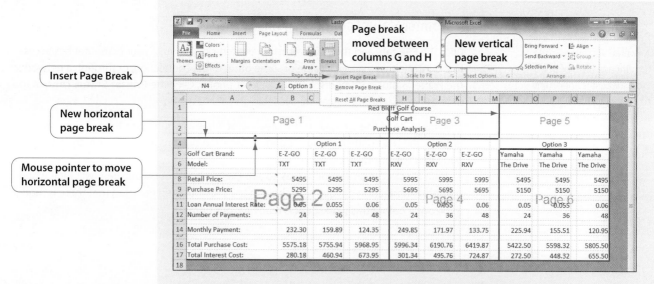

Figure 24 Insert Horizontal and Vertical Page Breaks in Page Break Preview view

i. Point to the horizontal page break, and the mouse pointer will change to ⬍. Drag the horizontal page break off the bottom (or top) of the print area to remove it. There should now be page breaks after column G and after column M.

j. Click **Normal** ⊞ on the status bar. The dotted lines between columns G and H and columns M and N are the page breaks you just created.

   Notice that the titles in rows 1 and 2 will be split between two pages and won't print at all on the third page. Remove them from the print area.

k. Click **Page Break Preview** ⊞ on the status bar. Point to the top border, and the mouse pointer will change to ⬍. Click and hold the left mouse button, and then move the top border down until it is between rows 3 and 4.

l. Click **Normal** ⊞ on the status bar. The dotted lines show the print area and the location of page breaks.

m. Click the **Sheet3 worksheet tab**.

n. Click cell **A20**, type today's date in mm/dd/yyyy format, click cell **C20**, and then type Adjusted page breaks.

o. Click the **Sheet1 worksheet tab**.

p. Press Ctrl + Home , and then click **Save** 🖫.

Print Preview, Printer Selection, and Print

Enter Backstage view by clicking the File tab and selecting Print in the left menu. The right side of the screen is Print Preview. **Print Preview** presents a facsimile of your document printed. You can use the scroll bar on the right or the paging control on the bottom to view additional pages if your worksheet requires more than one page to print.

Often a computer is connected to a local area network, or LAN. More than one print device can be made available to a computer via LAN. You must be sure to select the printer/device you want to use from the Printer Status control. The default printer is selected automatically and is usually acceptable. When a different printer is required, click the Printer Status arrow on the right side of the printer status control to see a list of available devices.

Printing a worksheet is as simple as clicking the Print button. If more than one copy is desired, change the number in the Copies box to the right of the Print button. The copy count can be increased or decreased by clicking the arrows or by clicking in the Copies box and entering the number of copies from the keyboard.

SIDE NOTE
Print Preview
Any time you are going
to print any or all of a
worksheet, it is important
to preview what will print
to avoid wasting time
and paper.

To Use Printer Status Control and Print Preview

a. Click the **File tab**, and then click **Print** on the left side menu. If your computer has access to a printer, either via a USB cable or some other direct connection, or through a network, the Printer Status control displays the default printer. Click the **Printer Status control** to determine what print devices are available on your network.

b. The right side of the window is the preview of what will print. Use the scroll bar on the right, or the Next page or Previous page navigation buttons at the bottom to view each page that will print.

Print Preview is an excellent way to see exactly how your worksheet will look when printed. Examination of your worksheet in the previous step revealed that there is more to be done before this worksheet is ready for printing.

Print Titles

When a worksheet is too large to print on a single page, it is often difficult to keep track of data from one page to another. Identifying headers, such as those in column A of the golf cart analysis, are only printed on the first page.

Print titles can be specified to print on each page. Every column and/or row is labeled and easily identified from one page to another depending on the structure of the worksheet.

To Specify Print Titles

a. Click the **Page Layout tab**, and then click **Print Titles** in the Page Setup group. The Page Setup dialog box will appear.

b. On the Sheet tab of the Page Setup dialog box, under Print titles, type A:A in the Columns to repeat at left text box.

Since the golf cart analysis worksheet contains too many columns to print on a single page, you should print at least one column on each page that identifies cell contents in each row—it may seem odd, but the Print Titles feature requires the specification of a range, even when only a single column will be printed, thus the need to enter column A as A:A.

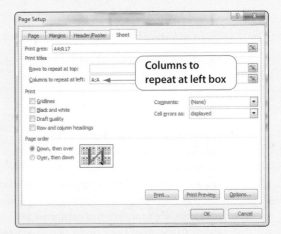

Figure 25 The Sheet Tab in the Page Setup dialog box for creating print titles

c. Click **OK**, click the **File tab**, and then click **Print** on the left side menu.

d. In the Print Preview pane, use the scroll bar on the right, or the Next page or Previous page navigation buttons at the bottom, to view each page that will print.

e. Click the **Home tab**. Click the **Sheet3 worksheet tab**.

f. Click cell **A21**, type today's date in mm/dd/yyyy format, click cell **C21**, and then type Specified print titles.

g. Click the **Sheet1 worksheet tab**, and then press [Ctrl]+[Home].

h. Click **Save** 🔲.

Print Headers/Footers

There are often items of information that should be included on a printed document that are not necessary in a worksheet. These items might include the following:

- Print date
- Print time
- Company name

- Page number
- Total number of pages
- File name and location

The print header and footer are divided into three sections: left, center, and right—information can be placed in any section or all sections. Print headers place information at the top of each printed page. Print footers place information at the bottom of each printed page. You may include information in either or both the print header and print footer as deemed necessary.

To Add a Print Header and Print Footer

a. Click **Page Layout** 🔲 on the status bar. If necessary, use the **Zoom Slider** [⊖———▽———⊕] to adjust zoom to 100%.

b. Select **Click to add header** in the top margin of Page Layout view. The Design tab for Header & Footer Tools will appear in the Ribbon.

c. Select the **left section** of the print header, and then click **Current Date** in the Header & Footer Elements group.

d. Select the **center section** of the print header, type Red Bluff Golf Club, press [Enter], and then type Cart Purchase Analysis.

e. Select the **right section** of the print header, click **Page Number** in the Header & Footer Elements group, press [Spacebar] to add a space, and then type of. Press [Spacebar] to add a space again, and then click **Number of Pages** in the Header & Footer Elements group.

f. Click **Go to Footer** in the Navigation group, or alternatively click **Click to add footer** at the bottom margin of Page Layout view—you may have to scroll down to find it.

g. Select the **left section** of the print footer, and then click **File Name** in the Header & Footer Elements group.

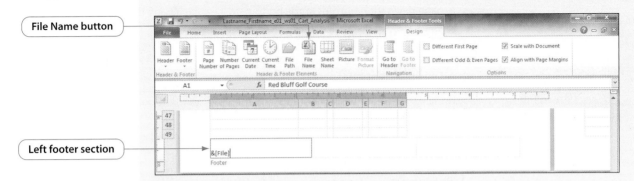

File Name button

Left footer section

Figure 26 Page Layout View—Add information to the page footer

h. Select any cell in the worksheet, press Ctrl+Home, and then click **Normal** ⊞ on the status bar.

i. Repeat Steps b–h for the **Sheet2** and **Sheet3** worksheets.

j. Click the **Sheet1 worksheet tab**. Click the **File tab**, and then click **Print** on the left side menu.

k. Use the scroll bar on the right or the page navigation buttons to view each page that will print. Notice the header and footers are added.

    Once again, there is still more to be done to the worksheet before printing.

l. Click the **Home tab**. Click the **Sheet3 worksheet tab**.

m. Click cell **A22**, type today's date in mm/dd/yyyy format, click cell **C22**, and then type Added print header and footer.

n. Click the **Sheet1 worksheet tab**.

o. Click **Save** 🖫.

Page Margins

Page margins are the white space left at the edges of the printed page. Normal margins for Excel are 0.7 inches on the left and right sides of the page, 0.75 inches on the top and bottom of the page, and 0.3 inches for header and footer, if included.

Margins can be changed to suit conventions or standards for an organization, to better locate information on the page, or to avoid a page break at the last column or line of a worksheet. For the golf cart analysis, there is no need to change page margins.

Quick Reference — Setting Page Margins

Page margins can be changed as follows:

1. Click the File tab.
2. Click Print on the left side menu.
3. Under Settings, the margins control is the second from the bottom.
4. Margins can be set to several preset values: **Normal**, **Wide**, or **Narrow**.
5. Click Custom Margins to reveal the Margins tab in the Page Setup dialog box.

Page margins can also be changed as follows:

1. Click the Page Layout tab.
2. In the Page Setup group, select Margins to reveal the same Margins control as displayed in the File tab, Print menu.

Page Orientation

Worksheets are printed on paper that are seldom, if ever, in the form of an exact square. Consequently, worksheets can be oriented to print on paper in one of two ways, **portrait**—the vertical dimension of the paper is longer, or **landscape**—the horizontal dimension of the paper is longer. Landscape is generally used when a worksheet has too many columns to fit into a single page in portrait orientation. Scaling the worksheet to fit all columns on a single page can work in portrait orientation, but if scaling makes the data too small to be readable, landscape orientation is an option to resolve the problem.

To Change Page Orientation

a. Click the **File tab**, and then click **Print** on the left side menu.

b. Click **Landscape Orientation** in the Orientation control—fourth from the bottom under Settings.

c. The right side of the window is the preview of what will print. Use the scroll bar on the right or the page navigation buttons at the bottom to view each page that will print.

d. Use the scroll bar on the right or the page navigation buttons to view each page that will print. Notice there is now quite a lot of white space on the right side of every page.

e. Click the **Home tab**. Click the **Sheet3 worksheet tab**.

f. Click cell **A23**, type today's date in mm/dd/yyyy format, click cell **C23**, and then type Set page orientation to landscape.

g. Click the **Sheet1 worksheet tab**.

h. Click **Save** 🔲.

Scaling

It is not uncommon for worksheets to be just a little too large to print on a single page, or to be so small that they appear dwarfed in the top-left hand corner of the page. Scaling changes the size of the print font to allow more of a worksheet to print on a page or for a worksheet to print larger and use more page space. A printed worksheet that has been scaled to fit a sheet of paper generally looks more professional and is easier to read and understand than a worksheet that prints on two pages that uses only a small part of the second page.

To Change Page Scaling

a. Click the **File tab**, and then click **Print** on the left side menu.

b. Click **Fit All Columns on One Page** in the Scaling control—the bottom control under Settings.

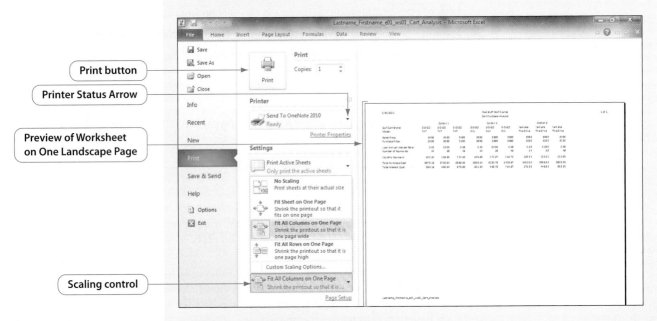

Print button

Printer Status Arrow

Preview of Worksheet on One Landscape Page

Scaling control

Figure 27 Print—Scaling control in Backstage view

c. If your computer is attached to a printer, the Printer Status control displays the default printer. If you want to print to a different printer (if your computer has access to more than one printer), click the **Printer Status arrow** next to the printer name, and then select the desired printer from the list. Click **Print** or submit your workbook file as directed by your instructor.

d. If necessary, click the **Home tab**. Click the **Sheet3 worksheet tab**.

e. Click cell **A24**, type today's date in mm/dd/yyyy format, click cell **C24**, and then type Scaled worksheet to print all columns on one page.

f. Click the **Sheet1 worksheet tab**.

g. Click **Save** 🖫.

SIDE NOTE
Navigate Between Worksheets in a Workbook

1. Click the worksheet tab of an inactive worksheet to make it the active worksheet.

or

2. Press [Ctrl]+[PgUp] to go to the prior worksheet or [Ctrl]+[PgDn] to go to the next worksheet.

Manipulate Worksheets and Workbooks

When there are two (or more) worksheets in a workbook, there is a need to navigate between (or among) the worksheets. Worksheets can be added to a workbook, deleted from a workbook, moved within a workbook or moved to other workbooks. Sheet names are displayed on each sheet's tab at the bottom of the application window, just above the status bar. See Figure 28. The white worksheet tab identifies the active worksheet. Gray worksheet tabs identify hidden worksheets.

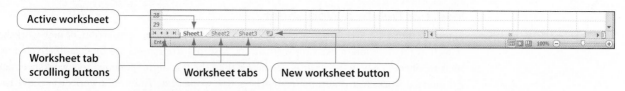

Figure 28 Worksheet tabs and navigation controls

When a workbook contains a large number of worksheets or when worksheets have very long names, some worksheet tabs may not be visible in the application window. To bring tabs that are not visible into view, use the worksheet tab scrolling buttons to the left of the worksheet tabs.

Name a Worksheet

When worksheets are created, whether among the default three in a new workbook, or the dozens that can be added to a workbook, the default name is "Sheet*n*" where *n* is a sequential integer: if you add a fourth worksheet to a workbook, its default name will be "Sheet4."

The default worksheet names are not particularly descriptive and do nothing to help document the contents or purpose of a worksheet in a workbook. Worksheets can be renamed by double-clicking the worksheet tab or by right-clicking the worksheet tab and clicking Rename in the shortcut menu. Worksheet names can be up to 31 characters long.

SIDE NOTE
Navigate Between Workbooks

In Windows 7, pressing Windows + Tab reveals a 3D display to rotate through open applications. Hold Windows and press Tab repeatedly to rotate through open applications—release Windows when the desired application is at the front of the rotation.

To Navigate Among and Rename Worksheets in a Workbook

a. Double-click **Sheet1 worksheet tab**. Sheet1 is the active worksheet, and the Sheet1 name in the worksheet tab is highlighted as selected text.

b. Type RBGC_Golf_Cart_Purch_Analysis, and then press Enter.

c. Double-click **Sheet2 worksheet tab**. Sheet2 is the active worksheet, and the Sheet2 name in the worksheet tab is highlighted as selected text.

d. Type RBGC_Golf_Cart_Usage_Analysis, and then press Enter.

e. Double-click the **Sheet3 worksheet tab**. Sheet3 is the active worksheet, and the Sheet3 name in the worksheet tab is highlighted as selected text.

f. Type Documentation, and then press Enter.

g. Click the **RBGC_Golf_Cart_Purch_Analysis worksheet tab**.

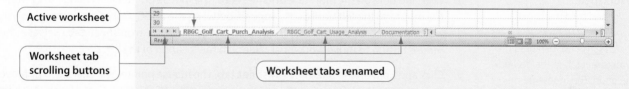

Figure 29 Worksheet tabs after renaming

h. Click the **Documentation worksheet tab**, click cell **A25**, and then type today's date in mm/dd/yyyy format. Click cell **C25**, type Renamed worksheets. Click cell **B32**. Type RBGC_Golf_Cart_Purch_Analysis. Click cell **B38**. Type RBGC_Golf_Cart_Usage_Analysis. Click cell **B44**. Type Documentation and then press Ctrl + Home.

i. Click the **RBGC_Golf_Cart_Purch_Analysis worksheet tab**. Press Ctrl + Home.

j. Click **Save**.

Insert or Delete a Worksheet

Manipulating a workbook will occasionally require the creation, or insertion, of new worksheets as well as the deletion of existing worksheets. Inserted worksheets are by default given a name such as "Sheet4" where the digit is one larger than the last digit appended to a worksheet name. An inserted worksheet is automatically the active worksheet. To insert a worksheet move to the right of the list of worksheet tabs and click Insert Worksheet.

To delete a worksheet, right-click the tab of the worksheet you want to delete and click Delete in the shortcut menu.

To Insert a Worksheet

a. Click the **Insert Worksheet tab** to the right of the worksheet tabs. You may have to use the worksheet tab scrolling buttons to access the Insert Worksheet tab.

b. Click the **Insert Worksheet tab** a second time.

c. Click **Save**.

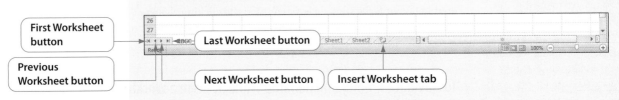

First Worksheet button

Previous Worksheet button

Last Worksheet button

Next Worksheet button

Insert Worksheet tab

Figure 30 Renamed worksheet tabs and two inserted worksheets

Move a Worksheet

The order of worksheets in a workbook can be changed by reordering the worksheet tabs. To move a worksheet, make the target worksheet the active worksheet by clicking on its tab. Click and hold on the worksheet tab, drag the worksheet tab to its new location, and drop it by releasing the mouse button. As a worksheet is dragged, a ▼ will appear between worksheet tabs. This indicates where the worksheet location will be inserted if the left mouse button is released.

To Move a Worksheet

a. Click and hold on the **Sheet2 worksheet tab**. The mouse pointer will change to ▲. Move the mouse to the left until a ▼ appears between the RBGC_Golf_Cart_Purch_Analysis worksheet tab and the RBGC_Golf_Cart_Usage_Analysis worksheet tab. Release the mouse button to move worksheet Sheet2 to the location of the ▼.

b. Click and hold on the **Sheet1 worksheet tab**. The mouse pointer will change to ▲. Move the mouse to the left until a ▼ appears between the RBGC_Golf_Cart_Usage_Analysis worksheet tab and the Documentation worksheet tab. Release the mouse button to move Sheet1 to the location.

c. Click **Save**.

SIDE NOTE

A Fast Way to Copy a Worksheet

Click and hold the target worksheet tab. Press and hold Ctrl, and then drag the worksheet tab to the desired location. The mouse pointer changes to ▲ to show that you are copying. Release the mouse button.

SIDE NOTE

Move Quickly Between Workbooks

To move quickly between workbooks, press Ctrl + Tab.

Figure 31 Worksheet tabs—Sheet 1 and Sheet2 moved

Deleting a Worksheet

Deleting a worksheet is most commonly done to remove blank worksheets that will not be used from a workbook—recall that a new workbook contains three worksheets by default and many workbooks do not require three worksheets. Unused worksheets are a form of clutter in a workbook and add unnecessary size to the stored workbook file. The deletion process is the same whether or not the worksheet that is to be deleted is blank.

To Delete a Worksheet

a. Click the **Sheet2 tab** to make it the active worksheet tab. Right-click, and then click **Delete** from the shortcut menu.

b. Use the worksheet navigation buttons to locate and click the **Sheet1** worksheet to make it the active tab. Right-click and click **Delete** from the shortcut menu. Click the **RBGC_ Golf_Cart_Purch_Analysis tab** to make the first worksheet the active sheet.

c. Click **Save** . Print or submit your documents as directed by your instructor. Close Excel.

1. The instructor in one of your classes distributed a syllabus that includes the following statement: "Late assignments are not accepted unless university policy specifically addresses your situation, such as family tragedy or personal medical malady—both of which require written validation. Computer and network problems are not an excuse, so *back up your work!*"

   What strategy will you implement to ensure you will not miss a due date owing to a computer or network problem, or because of the loss of a USB drive or other portable storage medium?

2. Often, acceptance into a college requires a specific grade point average (GPA) in a student's first two years of coursework. Acceptance into graduate school or a professional school such as law or medical school requires a minimum undergraduate GPA. Many students could make use of a worksheet into which they can enter courses they have taken and the grades they earned, as well as courses they *will* take. The worksheet could then calculate both the current GPA and the GPA that would result from expected grades in future courses.

   Plan such a worksheet. What data will you need? What calculations will you need to make? How will you structure the worksheet?

3. Although Merge & Center and Center Across result in exactly the same look in your worksheet, they function differently. How are they different? When would you recommend to use one over the other and why?

4. Print titles, page headers, and page footers, if used properly, can make your printed worksheets easier to read and appear more professional. Explain what each does, why, and when you would use them.

5. Page orientation and scaling can be used together when printing your worksheet. What does each do, and how can they be used in tandem to allow you to efficiently print a professional-looking worksheet?

Active cell   43
Active worksheet   45
AutoFill   55
Cell   40
Cell reference   43
Column   43
Field   40

Formula   40
Function   40
Landscape   75
Portrait   75
Print Preview   71
Range   52
Record   40

Row   43
Spreadsheet   40
What-if analysis   40
White space   57
Workbook   41
Worksheet   40
Worksheet navigation   43

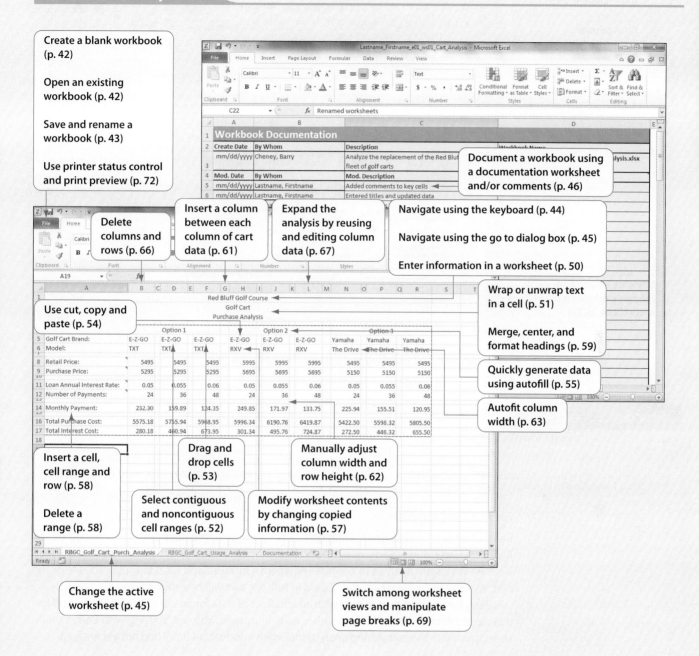

Create a blank workbook (p. 42)

Open an existing workbook (p. 42)

Save and rename a workbook (p. 43)

Use printer status control and print preview (p. 72)

Document a workbook using a documentation worksheet and/or comments (p. 46)

Delete columns and rows (p. 66)

Insert a column between each column of cart data (p. 61)

Expand the analysis by reusing and editing column data (p. 67)

Navigate using the keyboard (p. 44)

Navigate using the go to dialog box (p. 45)

Enter information in a worksheet (p. 50)

Use cut, copy and paste (p. 54)

Wrap or unwrap text in a cell (p. 51)

Merge, center, and format headings (p. 59)

Quickly generate data using autofill (p. 55)

Autofit column width (p. 63)

Insert a cell, cell range and row (p. 58)

Delete a range (p. 58)

Drag and drop cells (p. 53)

Manually adjust column width and row height (p. 62)

Select contiguous and noncontiguous cell ranges (p. 52)

Modify worksheet contents by changing copied information (p. 57)

Change the active worksheet (p. 45)

Switch among worksheet views and manipulate page breaks (p. 69)

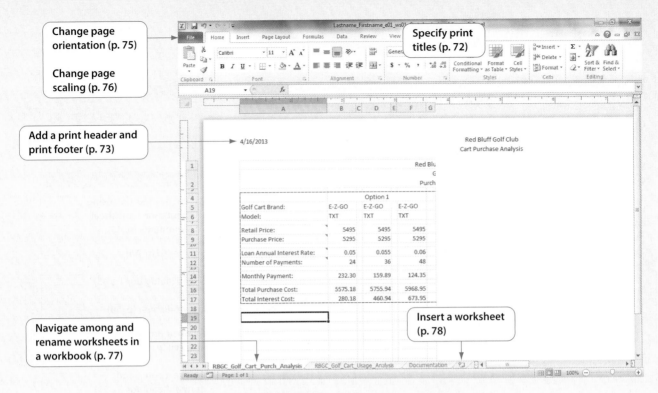

Change page orientation (p. 75)

Change page scaling (p. 76)

Specify print titles (p. 72)

Add a print header and print footer (p. 73)

Navigate among and rename worksheets in a workbook (p. 77)

Insert a worksheet (p. 78)

Figure 32 Red Bluff Golf Club Golf Cart Purchase Analysis Final

---

Practice 1

Student data file needed:

e01_ws01_Lease_Analysis

You will save your file as:

Lastname_Firstname_e01_ws01_Lease_Analysis

Golf Cart Lease

Barry Cheney is considering leasing golf carts to augment the fleet of 10 carts owned by the Red Bluff Golf Course. Barry wants a detailed financial analysis of the lease versus buy decision. He wants the analysis to consider payments, interest, and total cost over the life of the cart. Assume once a lease or loan is paid in full, the cart will be replaced.

Barry has created a worksheet with an initial set of data for an E-Z-GO TXT golf cart and has a table of information for a couple other carts of interest. You will, starting with Barry's worksheet, complete the cart leasing analysis including information Barry had not yet entered.

a. Start **Excel**. Click the **File tab**, and then click **Open**. Click the disk drive in the left pane where your student data files are located, navigate through the folder structure, and then click **e01_ws01_Lease_Analysis**. Click the **File tab**, and then click **Save As**. In the Save As dialog box, navigate to the location where you are saving your files. In the File name box, type Lastname_Firstname_e01_ws01_Lease_Analysis replacing Lastname_Firstname with your name.

b. Double-click the **Sheet1 worksheet tab**, type Golf_Cart_Lease_Analysis as the new name for the worksheet, and then press [Enter].

c. Double-click the **Sheet2 worksheet tab**, type Documentation as the new name for the worksheet, and then press [Enter]. Click cell **B16**, type Golf_Cart_Lease_Analysis and then press [Enter].

d. Click the **Golf_Cart_Lease_Analysis worksheet tab**.

e. Enter the following information into the worksheet for the appropriate row heading:

Column A Row Heading	Column F	Column G	Column I	Column J
Golf Cart Brand	E-Z-GO	E-Z-GO	Yamaha	Yamaha
Model	RXV	RXV	The Drive	The Drive
Retail Price	5995	5995	5495	5495
Negotiated Price	5695	5695	5150	5150
Residual Value	1200	1000	1100	900
Number of Payments	36	48	36	48
Annual Interest Rate	0.05	0.055	0.0525	0.06

f. Click cell **E3**, press and hold [Ctrl], and then click cell **H3**. Click **Format** in the Cells group, click **Column Width**, and then set Column Width to 3. Click **OK**.

g. Select column **A** by clicking the column header. In the Cells group click **Format**, and then click **AutoFit Column Width**.

h. Select cell range **C11:D13**, and then in the Clipboard group, click **Copy**.

i. Click cell **F11**, and then in the Clipboard group, click **Paste**.

j. If necessary, use the mouse pointer to select cell range **F11:G13**. Hover the mouse pointer over the border of the selected range. Press and hold [Ctrl], and when the mouse pointer changes to include a plus sign, drag and drop the selected range to range **I11:J13**.

k. Select cell range **C11:J13**. Click the **Decrease Decimal** in the Number group until exactly 2 decimal places are shown in the selected range.

l. Select the cell range **A2:A3**, click the **Insert arrow** in the Cells group, and then click **Insert Sheet Rows**.

m. Click cell **C3**, type Option A, click cell **F3**, and then type Option B. Click cell **I3**, and then type Option C.

n. Select cell range **C3:D3**. Press and hold [Ctrl], and then select ranges **F3:G3** and **I3:J3**. Click **Merge & Center** in the Alignment group.

o. Select cell **A1**, type Golf Cart Lease Analysis, and then press [Ctrl]+[Enter]. Select the cell range A1:J1, and then click **Merge & Center** in the Alignment group.

p. Click the **header** for row 10 to select the entire row. Click **Delete**, in the Cells group, and then press [Ctrl]+[Home].

q. Click the **Page Layout tab**, and then click **Print Titles** in the Page Setup group. Click the **Header/Footer tab** in the Page Setup dialog box, and then click the **Custom Footer button**.

r. Click in the **Left section** of the Footer dialog box.

s. Click **Insert File Name**, click **OK** in the Footer dialog box, and then click **OK** in the Page Setup dialog box. Press [Ctrl]+[Home].

t. Click the **Documentation worksheet tab**, click cell **A5**, and then enter today's date in mm/dd/yyyy format. Click cell **B5**, and then type your name in Lastname, Firstname format. Click cell **C5**, type Completed Mr. Cheney's initial work, and then press [Ctrl]+[Home]. Click the **Golf_Cart_Lease_Analysis worksheet tab**.

u. Click **Save**. Print and/or turn in workbook files as directed by your instructor. Close Excel.

Student data file needed:

e01_ws01_Wedding_Worksheet

You will save your file as:

Lastname_Firstname_e01_ws01_Wedding_Worksheet

Red Bluff Resort Wedding Planning Worksheet

Weddings are becoming an important part of the resort's business. Thus, Patti Rochelle started a worksheet to improve the wedding planning process for her staff. Last year, on average, the resort hosted three weddings per week and has done as many as six in a weekend. The worksheet Patti wants you to finish will allow for changes in pricing to be immediately reflected in the planning process.

You've been given a workbook that includes product/service categories, prices, and an initial worksheet structure in order to help standardize the process and pricing of weddings. You will build a worksheet that calculates the price of a wedding and doubles as a checklist to use as weddings are set up to ensure subcontractors, such as DJs, are reserved in a timely fashion and that all contracted services are delivered.

a. Start **Excel**, click the **File tab**, and then click **Open**. Click the disk drive in the left pane where your student data files are located, navigate through the folder structure, and click **e01_ws01_Wedding_Worksheet**. Click the **File tab**, and then click **Save As**. In the Save As dialog box, navigate to the location where you are saving your files. In the File name box, type Lastname_Firstname_e01_ws01_Wedding_Worksheet replacing Lastname_Firstname with your name.

b. Double-click the **Sheet1 worksheet tab**, type Wedding_Planner, and then press Enter.

c. Double-click the **Sheet2 worksheet tab**, and then type Documentation as the new name for the worksheet. Press Enter, click cell **B16**, and then type Wedding_Planner. Press Ctrl+Home.

d. Click the **Wedding_Planner worksheet tab**.

e. Type the Value information into the cell indicated as follows:

Data Item	Value	Cell
Wedding Date	6/18/2014	B2
Start Time	4:00 PM	D2
End Time	5:00 PM	G2
Reception Start Time	6:00 PM	D3
Reception End Time	12:00 AM	G3
Total Hours	8	B5
Reception Hours	6	D5
Estimated guests	125	B7
Ceremony	650	H11
Reception	750	H12
Catering	17	H13
Flowers	1250	H18
Decorations	1500	H19
Photography Package	1500	H24
Webcast	250	H25
Entertainment Hours Played		
Piano Player (Hours)	1	C28
String Quartet (Hours)	2	C29

Data Item	Value	Cell
DJ (Hours)	4	C32
Discount	-0.05	H33

f. Select cell range **F3:G3**, click the **Home tab**, click **Cut** in the Clipboard group, click cell **H8** to make it the active cell, and then click **Paste** in the Clipboard group.

g. Select cell range **C3:D3**, click **Cut** in the Clipboard group, click cell **H7**, and then click **Paste** in the Clipboard group.

h. Click cell **B3**. Hover over the border of the active cell, when the mouse pointer changes, click and hold the left mouse button, drag cell **B3** to cell **G7**, and then release the mouse button to drop.

i. Select cell range **F2:G2**, press Ctrl+X, click cell **H5**, and then press Ctrl+V.

j. Select cell range **C2:D2**, press Ctrl+X. Click cell **H4**, and then press Ctrl+V.

k. Select cell range **A2:B2**, press Ctrl+X, and then click cell **G3** to make it the active cell. Press Ctrl+V, select the column range **G:H**, click the **Format arrow** in the Cells group, and then click **AutoFit Column Width**.

l. Press Ctrl+Home. Hover over the border of the active cell, when the mouse pointer changes to the move pointer click and hold the left mouse button, and then drag cell **A1** to cell **G1**.

m. Select cell range **B9:C9**, press Ctrl, and then select cell range **B34:C34**. Click **Merge & Center** in the Alignment group.

n. Select columns **B:C**, click **Format** in the Cells group, and then click **Column Width**. Type 17 in the Column Width box, and then click **OK**.

o. Click cell **A27**, click the **Insert arrow** in the Cells group, and then click **Insert Sheet Rows**.

p. Click the header for column **E**. Right-click and select **Delete** from the shortcut menu. In the Cells group, click the **Format arrow**, and then click **Column Width**. Type 2 in the Column Width text box, and then click **OK**.

q. Select cell range **A5:A35**. Press Ctrl and select cell ranges **B10:D10, B17:C17, B23:C23, B28:D28, F1:F35, G4:G8, G10:H10** and cells **C5, B35, G14, G21, G26** and **H35**. Press Ctrl+B.

r. Click **Page Layout** on the Status bar. Scroll to the bottom of the worksheet and click **Click to add footer**.

s. Click in the **Left section** of the Footer.

t. If necessary, click the **Design tab** under Header & Footer tools. Click **File Name** in the Header & Footer Elements group, click a cell in the worksheet. Press Ctrl+Home. Click **Normal** on the Status bar.

u. Click the **Documentation worksheet tab**, and then click cell **A5**. Enter today's date in mm/dd/yyyy format. Click cell **B5**, and then type Lastname, Firstname replacing Lastname, Firstname with your actual name. Click cell **C5**, type Completed Ms. Rochelle's initial work - reorganized worksheet to function better as a checklist, and then press Ctrl+Home.

v. Right-click the **Sheet3 worksheet tab**, and then click **Delete**. Click the **Wedding_ Planner worksheet tab**, select cell range **F1:H35**, click the **File tab**, and then click **Print** from the menu on the left. Under Settings, click the **Print Active Sheets arrow**, and then click **Print Selection**. Click **Print** and/or submit your workbook file as directed by your instructor. On the Wedding_Planner worksheet tab, press Ctrl+Home.

w. Save and close the workbook.

Objectives

1. Format cells, cell ranges, and worksheets.   p. 88

2. Create information with functions and formulas.   p. 103

3. Use conditional formatting to assist decision making.   p. 115

Formatting, Formulas, and Functions

PREPARE CASE
Red Bluff Golf Club Pro Shop Sales Analysis

The Red Bluff Golf Course Pro Shop sells products to members that range from golf clubs and accessories to clothing displaying the club logo. In addition, the Pro Shop collects fees for rounds of golf and services such as lessons from golf pro John Schilling.

Manager Aleeta Herriott needs to track Pro Shop sales by category on a day-by-day basis. Sales, at least to some extent, are a reflection of traffic in the Pro Shop and can be used to help determine staffing requirements on different days of the week. In addition, summary sales data can be compared to inventory investments to determine if product mix is optimal, given the demands of clientele.

Each item or service at the time of sale, is recorded in the Pro Shop point-of-sale (POS) system. At the end of each day, the POS system produces a cash register report with categorized sales for the day. This is the data source of each day's sales for the worksheet. Aleeta has created an initial layout for a sales analysis workbook, but she needs you to finish it.

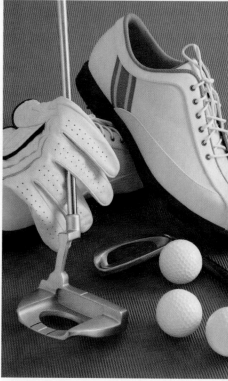
Courtesy of www.Shutterstock.com

Student data files needed for this workshop:

 e01_ws02_Weekly_Sales

 e01_ws02_Documentation_Template

You will save your file as:

 Lastname_Firstname_e01_ws02_Weekly_Sales

Worksheet Formatting

In Excel you can easily manipulate cells, cell ranges, and worksheets in a workbook as well as print worksheet information. However, manipulating information is not enough. To be of value, information must be effectively communicated. Effective communication of information generally requires that the information is formatted in a manner that aids in proper interpretation and understanding.

Some of the most revolutionary ideas in history have been initially recorded on a handy scrap of paper, a yellow legal pad, a tape recorder, and even paper napkin. Communication of those ideas generally required they be presented in a different medium and that they be formatted in a manner that aided others' understanding. The content may not have changed at all, but the format of the presentation is important. People are more receptive to well-formatted information which is easier to understand and absorb. While accuracy of the information is of utmost importance, what use is misunderstood accurate data? In this section, you will manipulate a worksheet by formatting numbers, aligning and rotating text, changing cell fill color and borders, using built-in cell and table styles, and applying workbook themes.

Format Cells, Cell Ranges, and Worksheets

There are several ways to present information. If different technologies, mediums, and audiences are considered, a list of more than 50 ways to present information would be easy to produce—the list could include such varied communication methods as books, speeches, websites, tweets, RSS feeds, and bumper stickers. An analysis of such a list however, would reveal a short list of generic communication methodologies:

- Oral
- Written narrative
- Tabular
- Graphical

Excel is an application specifically designed to present information in tabular and graphical formats. **Tabular format** is the presentation of information (text and numbers) in tables—essentially organized in labeled rows and columns. **Graphical format** is the presentation of information in charts, graphs, and pictures. Excel facilitates the graphical presentation of information via charts and graphs based on the tabular information in worksheets. This workshop is focused on formatting information for tabular presentation.

To Get Started

a. Click the **Start** button 🎯. From the Start Menu, locate and then start **Microsoft Excel 2010**.

b. Click the **File tab**, and then click **Open** in the menu on the left.

c. In the Open dialog box, click the disk drive in the left pane where your student data files are located, navigate through the folder structure, click **e01_ws02_Weekly_Sales**, and then click **Open**.

d. Click the **File tab**, click **Save As**, and then in the Save As dialog box, navigate to the location where you are saving your files. In the File name box type Lastname_Firstname_ e01_ws02_Weekly_Sales replacing Lastname_Firstname with your own name, and then click **Save**.

e. Double-click the **Sheet1 worksheet tab**. Type Weekly_Sales as the new name for the sheet, and then press [Enter].

f. Press [Ctrl]+[Home]. Click **Save** 💾.

Copying a Document from One Workbook to Another

One way to easily document workbooks is to have a standard documentation template that you can reuse in any workbook. To reuse a documentation template, you will need to be able to copy and insert the documentation template into your workbooks with little effort. Copying a worksheet from one workbook into another can be accomplished in just a few steps.

To Copy a Documentation Template From Another Workbook

a. Click the **File tab**, and then click **Open**. In the Open dialog box, click the disk drive in the left pane where your student data files are located, navigate through the folder structure, click **e01_ws02_Documentation_Template**, and then click **Open**.

b. Click **Select All** in the top-left corner of the Documentation worksheet.

c. Press Ctrl+C.

d. Press Ctrl+Tab to switch to e01_ws02_Weekly_Sales.

e. Click **Insert Worksheet** to the right of the worksheet tabs.

f. Press Ctrl+V.

g. Double-click the **Sheet1 worksheet tab**. You will now update the new documentation worksheet.

h. Type Documentation as the new name for the Sheet3 worksheet, and then press Enter.

i. Click cell **A3**, type 8/25/2013, click cell **B3**, and then type Herriott, Aleeta.

j. Click cell **C3**, and then type Pro Shop weekly sales analysis.

k. Click cell **A5**, and then press Ctrl+; to enter today's date.

l. Click cell **B5**, and then type your name in Lastname, Firstname format.

m. Click cell **B16**, and then type Weekly_Sales to replace and update the sheet name text.

n. Click cell **B17**, type Herriott, Aleeta, click cell **B23**, and then type Herriott, Aleeta.

o. Click cell **B18**, type 8/25/2013, click cell **B24**, and then type 8/25/2013.

p. Click cell **B19**, and then type Analyze weekly Pro Shop sales by item category and subcategory.

q. Click cell **B25**, and then type Analyze a day's sales by subcategory and time.

r. Click the **Weekly_Sales worksheet tab**.

s. Click **Save**. Press Ctrl+Tab to make e01_ws02_Documentation_Template the active workbook. Click to close e01_ws02_Documentation_Template without saving if prompted.

Numbers

Number formatting is probably more important than text formatting in an application such as Excel. Through number formatting, context can be given to numbers that make text labeling unnecessary, such as with a date value or a time value. Most of the world's currencies can be represented in Excel through number formatting. Financial numbers, scientific numbers, percentages, dates, times, and so on all have special formatting requirements and can be properly displayed in a worksheet. The ability to manipulate and properly display many different types of numeric information is the feature that makes Excel an incredibly powerful and ubiquitously popular application in almost all walks of life.

Formats

Numbers can be formatted in many ways in Excel as shown in Figure 1.

Ribbon Button	Menu Button	Format Name	Example
General ▾	ABC 123	General	1234
General ▾	12	Number	1,234.00
General ▾		Currency	$1,234.00
$ ▾		Accounting	$ 1,234.00
General ▾		Short Date	6/15/2010
General ▾	⏱	Time	6:00:00 PM
%	%	Percentage	7.50%

Figure 1   Common number formats

To Format Numbers

a. Select cell **B6**, and then click the **Number Format arrow** General ▾ in the Number group. A list of formats will appear. Click **Currency**.

b. Select cell range **B20:H25**, and then click **Accounting Number Format** $ ▾ in the Number group. If any of the cells in B20:H25 display number signs (#), click **Format** in the Cells group, and then click **AutoFit Column Width**.

c. Press Ctrl + Home , and then click **Save** .

Real World Advice   Accounting Number Format vs. Currency Number Format

The Accounting and Currency formats are both intended for the identification and display of monetary values. Characteristics of the accounting format are as follows:

• The accounting format always displays negative numbers in parentheses, thus a consistent right margin space is maintained to accommodate parentheses when needed.

• The currency symbol is aligned with the left side of the cell.

• Zero values are displayed as a long dash (—) aligned at the decimal position.

• The decimal place is aligned.
  Currency is a more complex format than the accounting format as shown in Figure 2. The currency format has several formatting options:

• Negative numbers can be identified with a dash (—), parentheses, or displayed in a red font color. The red font color option can be combined with parentheses as well.

• The currency symbol is placed directly left of the value and inside the parentheses if they are used to denote negative numbers.

• Zero values are displayed as 0 with zeroes in each decimal place.

Continued

Continued

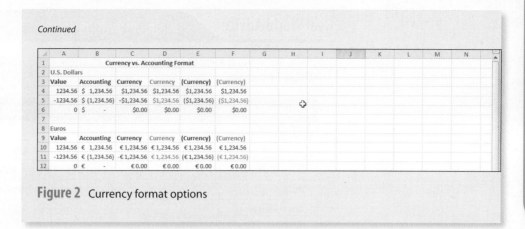

	A	B	C	D	E	F	G	H	I	J	K	L	M	N
1			Currency vs. Accounting Format											
2	U.S. Dollars													
3	Value	Accounting	Currency	Currency	(Currency)	(Currency)								
4	1234.56	$ 1,234.56	$1,234.56	$1,234.56	$1,234.56	$1,234.56								
5	-1234.56	$ (1,234.56)	-$1,234.56	$1,234.56	($1,234.56)	($1,234.56)								
6	0	$ -	$0.00	$0.00	$0.00	$0.00								
7														
8	Euros													
9	Value	Accounting	Currency	Currency	(Currency)	(Currency)								
10	1234.56	€ 1,234.56	€ 1,234.56	€ 1,234.56	€ 1,234.56	€ 1,234.56								
11	-1234.56	€ (1,234.56)	-€ 1,234.56	€ 1,234.56	(€ 1,234.56)	(€ 1,234.56)								
12	0	€ -	€ 0.00	€ 0.00	€ 0.00	€ 0.00								

Figure 2 Currency format options

Negative Values and Color

Negative numbers often warrant more than parentheses or a hyphen to call attention to the fact that a particular value is below zero. The phrase "in the red" is often used to describe financial values that have fallen below zero so, not surprisingly, Excel makes it very easy to display negative numbers in a red font color.

To Display Negative Numbers in Red

a. Select cell range **B20:H25**, click the **Number Format arrow** | General ▾ | in the Number group, and then click **More Number Formats**.

b. Under Category, click **Number**. If necessary, enter 2 in the Decimal places box. Make sure **Use 1000 Separator (,)** is checked.

c. Under Negative numbers, select the red negative number format **(1,234.10)**, and then click **OK**.

    To apply the red formatting to the negative number, be sure to select the red version of the negative number format (1,234.10). If any of the cells in B20:H25 display number signs, click Format in the Cells group, and click AutoFit Column Width in the Cell Size menu.

d. Press [Ctrl]+[Home], and then click **Save** 🖫.

CONSIDER THIS | **Usability and Color-Blindness**

Approximately 8–12% of people of European descent are color-blind. This doesn't mean they can't see any color, but for about 99% of the them, it means they have trouble distinguishing between reds and greens. How should this information affect the way you format your worksheets?

There are several keyboard shortcuts that allow rapid application of specific number formats:

Keyboard Shortcut	Number Format
Ctrl + Shift + ~	General
Ctrl + Shift + 1	Number -1,234.10
Ctrl + Shift + 2	Time hh:mm AM/PM
Ctrl + Shift + 3	Date dd-mmm-yy
Ctrl + Shift + 4 or Ctrl + Shift + $	Currency ($1,234.10)
Ctrl + Shift + 5 or Ctrl + Shift + %	Percentage
Ctrl + Shift + 6 or Ctrl + Shift + ^	Scientific (Exponential)

Figure 3   Number format keyboard shortcuts

Dates and Times

Excel stores a date and time as a real number where the number to the left of the decimal place, or the absolute value, is the number of complete days since January 1, 1900, inclusive. The right side of the decimal place is the decimal portion of the day. This kind of date system allows Excel to use dates in calculations. For example, if you add 1 to today's date, you will get tomorrow's date.

While useful for computer systems and applications like Excel, people have not been taught to interpret time in this manner, so unformatted date and time values (those displayed in General format) mean little or nothing. Date and time formatting allows Excel date and time values to be displayed in a fashion that allows proper reader interpretation. A heading that identifies a column as date values gives context to the information, but in the case of date information, without proper formatting, it is for the most part not interpretable by the reader.

To Format a Cell or Cell Range as a Date or as Time

a. Select cell **B4**, type 12/1/2013, and then press Ctrl + Enter to accept the data and to keep cell B4 selected.

b. Click the **Number Format arrow** [General ▾] in the Number group, and then click **General**.

   Cell B4 is no longer formatted to display the date you entered in month/day/year format. The number in cell B4 (*41609* in this example) is what Excel actually stores for the date you entered.

c. Click the **fill handle** by holding down the left mouse button. Drag the fill handle right until the border around the active cell expands to include cells **B4:H4**, and then release the left mouse button. The General formatted number has been copied to each of the cells in C4:H4.

d. Click **AutoFill Options** ▦, which appears as it is attached to the fill handle.

Click **Fill Series** in the AutoFill Options menu. The numbers in B4:H4 are now incremented by 1 in each cell from left to right.

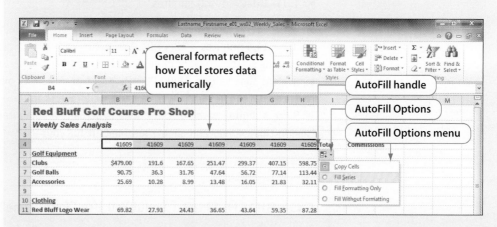

Figure 4 AutoFill and AutoFill options

e. Click the **Number Format arrow** [General ▾] in the Number group, and then click **Short Date**. If any of the cells in B4:H4 display number signs, click **Format** in the Cells group, and then click **AutoFit Column Width** in the Cell Size menu.

f. Click cell **A1**, and then click **Save** 🖫.

g. Double-click the **Sheet2 worksheet tab** to make Sheet2 the active sheet and to enter edit mode. Type Hourly_Sales_Sunday as the new name for Sheet2, and then press [Enter].

h. Select cell range **A6:A7**. Position the mouse over the bottom-right corner fill handle, drag the fill handle down to include cells **A6:A28**.

The series in cell range A6:A7 has been expanded through cell A28. The number series is formatted as General numbers.

i. Click the **Number Format arrow** [General ▾] in the Number group, and then click **Time**.

If any of the cells in A6:A28 display number signs, click Format in the Cells group, and click AutoFit Column Width in the Cell Size menu.

The default time format includes a value for seconds. This isn't necessary and adds clutter in the form of an additional ":00" to every time value.

j. With cells A6:A28 still selected, click the **Number Format arrow** [General ▾] in the Number group, and then click **More Number Formats**.

k. Under Category box, click **Time** if necessary. Under Type box, select **1:30 PM**.

l. Click **OK**.

m. Click the **Documentation worksheet tab**, click cell **B22**, and then type Hourly_Sales_Sunday to document the name change for this worksheet.

n. Press [Ctrl]+[Home], and then click **Save** 🖫.

Excel stores time values as decimal portions of one day as follows:

- 1.0 = 1 day = 1,440 minutes

- 0.1 = 144 minutes = 2:24 AM

- .01 = 14.4 minutes = 12:14:24 AM

For this system to work in conjunction with date values, 0 and 1 display as equivalent time values: 12:00:00 AM. However, in reality once a time value increases to 1, the date increments by 1 day and time reverts to 0.

Since a digital watch or cell phone is actually a computer, do you think it handles time in this manner and simply reformats it for your use?

CONSIDER THIS | Could You Use "Excel Time"?

Would you be able to adapt if your digital watch or cell phone showed time the way Excel stores it? Would there be any advantages if time were actually displayed and handled in this format? What about date values?

Cell Alignment

Cell alignment allows for cell content to be left-aligned, centered, and right-aligned on the horizontal axis; top-aligned, middle-aligned, and bottom-aligned on the vertical axis. Certain cell formats align left or right by default. Most number formats align right. Date and time formats align right as well. Most text formatting aligns left by default and for the most part, horizontal alignment changes will be made to alphabetic content such as titles, headings, and labels.

To Right-Align Text, Increase Indent, and Bottom Align

a. Click the **Weekly_Sales worksheet tab**. Select cell range **A5:A25**, and then click **Align Text Right** in the Alignment group.

b. Click cell **A5**, press Ctrl, and then select cells **A10**, **A15**, and **A19**. Click **Increase Indent** in the Alignment Group.

c. Select cell range **I4:J4**, and then click **Align Text Right** in the Alignment group.

d. If necessary, click **Bottom Align** in the Alignment group.

e. Click cell **J4**, click **Format** in the Cells group, and then select **AutoFit Column Width** in the Cell Size menu.

f. Press Ctrl+Home, and then click **Save**.

Content Orientation

Sometimes, it is helpful to display information at an angle or even vertically rather than the standard horizontal left to right. This is particularly true for tabular information. When formatting charts and graphs, rotating textual content can be very helpful in presenting information in a space-efficient yet readable manner.

To Rotate Text

a. Select cell range **B4:H4**, and then click **Orientation** in the Alignment group. A menu will appear.

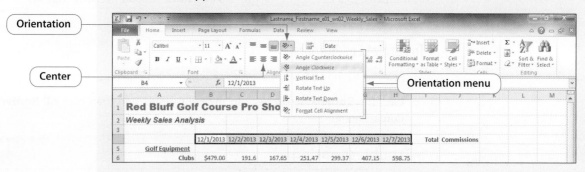

Figure 5 Orientation menu

b. Click **Angle Clockwise** in the Orientation menu, and then click **Center** in the Alignment group.

c. Press Ctrl+B to bold the dates in B4:H4.

d. Select cell range **B4:H25**, click **Format** in the Cells group, and then select **AutoFit Column Width** in the Cell Size menu in the Cells group.

e. Press Ctrl+Home, and then click **Save**.

Fill Color

Fill color refers to the background color of a cell. It can be used to categorize information, to band rows or columns as a means to assist the reader to follow information across or down a worksheet, or to highlight extreme values.

Unless you are using fill color to highlight information that is potentially erroneous, it is generally a best practice to use muted or pastel fill colors. Bright colors are difficult to look at for long periods of time and often make reading information in the cell(s) very difficult.

To Change Cell Background Color

a. Select cell range **B4:H4**, press Ctrl, and then select cell range **A5:A25**. Click the **Fill Color arrow** in the Font group to display the color palette.

b. Under Theme Colors, point to any color in the left column and a ScreenTip will appear identifying the color name. Select **White, Background 1, Darker 15%** (first column, third row).

c. Click cell **A4**, press Ctrl, and then select cells **I4** and **J4**. Click the **Fill Color arrow** in the Font group. Under Theme Colors, click **White, Background 1, Darker 50%**.

d. Click cell **A9**, press Ctrl, and then select cells **A14** and **A18**. Click the **Fill Color arrow** in the Font group, and then click **No Fill**.

e. Press Ctrl+Home, and then click **Save**.

SIDE NOTE
To Remove Cell Fill Color
To remove cell fill color simply select the cell(s) you want to apply the change to, click the Fill Color arrow, and then select No Fill.

Cell Borders

In the last exercise you changed the background color in a range of cells. When the background color is changed for a range of contiguous cells, the cell borders may no longer be visible. If, for readability or other reasons, it would be preferable to have cell borders visible, cell borders can be formatted in a number of ways to make them visible and to clarify content.

To Format Cell Borders

a. Select cell range **B4:J4**, press Ctrl, and then select cell range **A5:A25**.

b. Click the **Borders arrow** ⊞ ▾ in the Font group, and then click **All Borders** in the Borders menu.

Troubleshooting

The Borders button may look different in your Excel application window than it does when referenced in this text. The reason for that is the Borders button in the Font group of the Home tab always displays the last border setting applied.

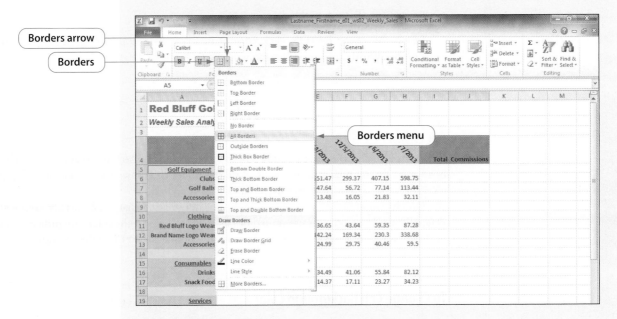

Figure 6 Border menu

c. Click cell **A5**, press Ctrl, and then select cells **A10**, **A15**, and **A19**. Click the **Borders arrow** ⊞ ▾ in the Font group, and then click **Thick Bottom Border** in the Borders menu.

d. Select cell range **B9:I9**, click the **Borders arrow** ⊞ ▾ in the Font group, and then click **Top and Bottom Border** in the Borders menu.

e. Select cell range **B14:I14**, press Ctrl, and then select cell ranges **B18:I18** and **B26:I26**. Click **Top and Bottom Border** ⊞ ▾ in the Font group.

f. Select cell range **B27:I27**, click the **Borders arrow** ⊞ ▾ in the Font group, and then click **Bottom Double Border** in the Borders menu.

g. Press Ctrl + Home, and then click **Save** 🖫.

SIDE NOTE
Want to See More of Your Worksheet? Hide the Ribbon

Double-click the Home tab to hide the Ribbon if you would like to see more rows of the Weekly_Sales worksheet. You can double-click the Home tab again to unhide it.

Real World Advice — Formatting—less is more

Excel, between text and numbers, offers many formatting options. Be careful to avoid overusing formatting in your worksheets. Too much variety in formatting creates a worksheet that is hard on the eyes, difficult to read, seems haphazard in its design, and conveys a sense that the designer did not have a plan. The following are some suggested guidelines for general formatting:

- Formatting should be done for a reason, not simply for appearances.
- Use no more than three fonts in a worksheet. Use each font for a purpose such as text, numbers, headings, and titles.
- Use color sparingly. Only use color to assist in readability, categorization, or identification purposes. For example, use organization colors for titles, bright colors to call attention to small details and background colors to separate categories. In particular, where coloration of text and numbers is concerned, treat color as though it is expensive to include.
- When color is used as a background, use calm and soothing pale or pastel colors. Large amounts of bright colors are tiring for the reader and can actually become painful to look at after long periods of time.
- Special characters such as the $ should be applied only as necessary. The first value in a column of numbers is sufficient to tell the user that column values are monetary. Then values such as subtotals and totals can be formatted with a $ to identify them as a value of importance.

Copying Formats

Developing a worksheet with clarity requires more than just setting a font and font size. Formatting a cell can consist of several steps involving fonts, colors, sizes, borders, and alignment. You gain a significant efficiency advantage by reusing your work. Once a cell is formatted properly, you can apply the formatting properties to a different cell. The ability to copy formats from one cell to another saves a great deal of time and often frustration.

Format Painter is a tool that facilitates rapid application of formats from one cell to another cell or to a range of cells. To use the Format Painter, simply select the cell that is the source of the format you want to copy, click the Format Painter in the Clipboard group of the Home tab, and then select the cell or range of cells you want to "paint" with the source cell's formatting.

To Use the Format Painter to Copy Formats

a. Select cell **B20**, and then click the **Format Painter** in the Clipboard group. The mouse pointer will change to. Select cell range **B16:H17**.

b. Click **Save**.

Paste Options/Paste Special

When a cell is copied to the Clipboard, there can be much more than a simple value ready to be pasted to another location. Formats, formulas, and values are all copied and can be selectively pasted to other locations in a workbook.

Different paste options are shown in Figure 7. Although there are a large number of paste options, most worksheet activities require only a few of these options. Paste, 📋 Paste Formats %, and Paste Values 123 will accomplish most of what you will need to do. The various paste options are also additive, in that you can first paste a link to a copied cell and then paste the format from the copied cell, after which you could paste the formula from the copied cell.

Button	Function	Description
📋	Paste	Pastes all content from the Clipboard to a cell
%	Formatting	Pastes only the formatting from the Clipboard to a cell
123	Values	Pastes only the value from the Clipboard to a cell
fx	Formulas	Pastes only the formula from the Clipboard to a cell
📋	Paste Link	Pastes a link (e.g., =A25) to the source cell from the Clipboard to a cell
📋	Transpose	Pastes a range of cells to a new range of cells with columns and rows switched

Figure 7 Paste options

To Use Paste Options and Paste Special to Copy Formats

a. Select cell **B20**, press [Ctrl]+[C] to copy cell B20 to the Clipboard, and then select cell range **B11:H13**.

b. Right-click the **selected range**. The shortcut menu will appear, which includes options that are determined by the context of the object that is the focus of the action.

c. Move the mouse pointer over each button in the Paste Options menu and notice what happens in the selected cell range. Click **Formatting** % in the Paste Options menu. Press [Esc] to cancel further paste options when finished.

d. Select cell **B11**, press [Ctrl]+[C] to copy cell B11 to the Clipboard, and then select cell range **B6:H8**.

e. Right-click the **selected range**. The shortcut menu will appear. Point to each button in the Paste Options menu, and notice what happens in the selected cell range.

f. Point to **Paste Special**. The Paste Special shortcut menu in will appear. Select **Formatting** % under Other Paste Options.

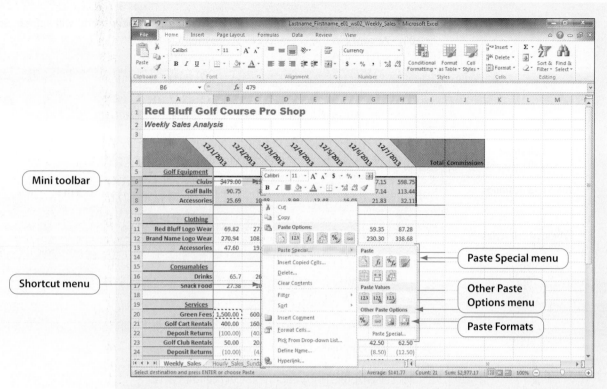

Figure 8 Paste Special

g. Press Ctrl + Home, and then click **Save** 📇.

Built-in Cell Styles

Built-in cell styles are predefined and named combinations of cell and content formatting properties that can be applied to a cell or range of cells to define several formatting properties of a cell at once. A built-in cell style can set font, font size and color, number format, background color, borders, and alignment with a couple clicks of the mouse. Built-in cell styles allow for rapid and accurate changes to the appearance of a workbook with very little effort.

To Apply Built-in Cell Styles

a. Click the **Hourly_Sales_Sunday worksheet tab**. Select cell range **B4:D4**, press Ctrl, and then select cell ranges **E4:G4**, **H4:I4**, and **J4:O4**. Each range is a distinct selection. Click **Merge & Center** in the Alignment group.

b. Click cell **B4**, press Ctrl, and then select cell **H4**.

c. Click **Cell Styles** in the Styles group. The Cell Styles gallery menu will appear. Select **20% - Accent2** in the Themed Cell Styles menu.

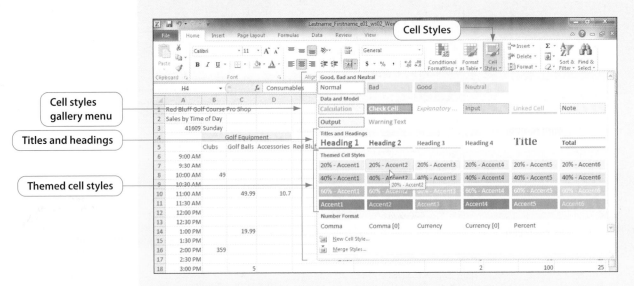

Figure 9 Cell styles gallery menu

d. Click cell **E4**, press Ctrl, and then select cell **J4**.

e. Click **Cell Styles** in the Styles group, and then select **40% - Accent2** in the Themed Cell Styles menu.

f. Select cell range **A3:B3**, press Ctrl, and then select cell ranges **B4:O5** and **A6:A29**.

g. Click **Cell Styles** in the Styles group. Select **Heading 4** under the Titles and Headings menu. Notice that in cell range B4:O4, the Accent2 cell background colors have not changed.

h. Select cell range **B29:O29**, click **Cell Styles** in the Styles group, and then select **Total** in the Titles and Headings menu.

i. Press Ctrl+Home.

j. Click the **Weekly_Sales worksheet tab**, select cell range **A1:A2**, and then press Ctrl+C.

k. Click the **Hourly_Sales_Sunday worksheet tab**, select cell range **A1:A2**, right-click the selected range, and then click **Formatting** in the Paste Options menu.

l. Click cell **A3**, click the **Number Format arrow** General, and then select **Short Date**.

m. Select cell range **B6:O29**, click the **Number Format arrow** General, and then click **More Number Formats** to reveal the Format Cells dialog box.

n. Click **Number** under the Category box. If necessary, enter 2 in the Decimal places box. Make sure **Use 1000 Separator (,)** is checked. Select red negative number format **(1,234.10)** in the Negative numbers box. Click **OK**.

o. Press Ctrl+Home. Click **Save**.

SIDE NOTE

Multiple Built-In Styles Can Be Applied to One Cell

Cells are not limited to a single built-in style. Different styles affect different cell elements. The end result of applying multiple styles to a single cell is determined by the order in which the styles are applied.

Table Styles

A **table** is a powerful tabular data-formatting tool that facilitates data sorting, filtering, and calculations. Once a collection of data has been defined as a table by the application of a table style, it has special table properties not available to data simply entered into rows and columns of cells.

A **table style** is a predefined set of formatting properties that determine the appearance of a table. One of the useful features of a table style is the ability to "band" rows and columns. **Banding** is alternating the background color of rows and/or columns to assist in tracking information. Banding can be accomplished manually by changing the background color of a range of cells (a row for example) and then pasting the formatting into every other row. Manually banding a table is a tedious process at best. By applying a table style to a selected range of rows and columns, banding is accomplished in a couple of clicks. Most importantly, table banding is dynamic. If a row or column is inserted into—or deleted from—the worksheet, the banding is automatically updated. If banding is done manually, insertions and deletions require manual updating as well.

Tables also allow for calculations in a total row such as summations, averages, or counts for each column in the table. These calculations are possible without table formatting. However, a table makes the calculation simple and dynamic. Thus, if a new column or row is added to the table, the new information is automatically calculated in the totals row.

To Apply a Table Style to a Cell Range

a. Right-click the **Hourly_Sales_Sunday worksheet tab**, and then in the shortcut menu, click **Move or Copy**. In the Move or Copy dialog box, under Before sheet, click **Documentation** so the new sheet copy will be positioned before this sheet. Click **Create a copy check box** at the bottom of the dialog box, and then click **OK**.

b. Double-click the **new worksheet tab**, type Hourly_Sales_Sunday_2, and then press Enter to accept the new tab name adjustments.

c. With the Hourly_Sales_Sunday_2 worksheet as the active tab, select cell range **A5:O28**, and then click **Format as Table** in the Styles group. The gallery menu will appear.

d. Select **Table Style Medium 3** in Medium table styles. The Format As Table dialog box appears. Be sure **My table has headers** is checked, and then click **OK**. The Ribbon switches to the Table Tools Design tab.

e. Double-click cell **A5** to edit the cell contents. Double-click cell **A5** again to highlight the Column1 text, and then type Time. Press Ctrl + Enter.

   Cell A5 was titled Column1 since no column heading existed. Time is a more appropriate heading.

f. Click the **Home tab**, click **Cell Styles** in the Styles group, and then select **Heading 4**. Click **Align Text Right** ☰ in the Alignment group, and then click **Increase Indent** 🔠 in the Alignment group two times.

g. Click the **Filter arrow** ▾ in the Time column, and then click **Sort Largest to Smallest** in the Filter menu.

   The order of the rows in the table is reversed. The filter next to each column heading in the table in row 5 allows you to sort the entire table by the information in each column.

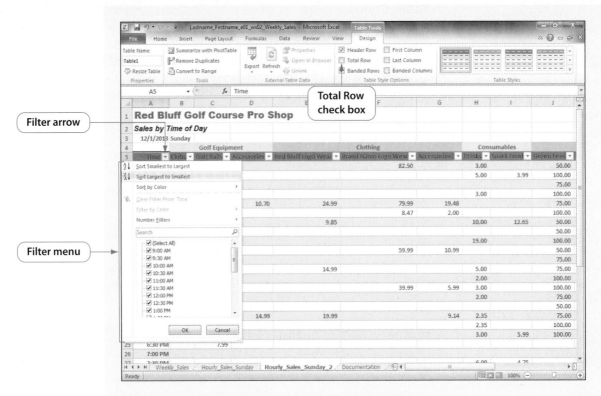

Figure 10 Table Tools Ribbon and Table filter menu

h. Click the **Filter arrow** in the Time column, and then select **Sort Smallest to Largest** to revert to the original order.

i. Click **Sort & Filter** in the Editing group, and then click **Filter** to toggle off data filtering. Since sorting by time or any of the other columns in the table is not really necessary, the Filter arrows can be removed.

j. The table format did not override the font style applied to the header row when you copied formats from the Hourly_Sales_Sunday worksheet. The blue font color is difficult to read on the red background. Select cell **A5**, press Shift + End + → to select cell range A5:O5. In the Styles group, click **Cell Styles**, and then select **Accent2**.

k. Click the **Table Tools Design tab**, and then check **Total Row** in the Table Style Options group. This adds a special total row that works with the table style to total each column as appropriate.

l. Select row 30 by clicking on the **row 30 header** when the cursor appears as → . Right-click the selected row, and then click **Delete** on the shortcut menu to delete the unnecessary total row copied from the Hourly_Sales_Sunday worksheet.

m. Click cell **C7**, and then scroll down until row 5 disappears at the top of the application window.

Notice what happens to the column headers. As long as the active cell is inside the table, if you scroll down the table column headings of the visible application window, table column headings replace worksheet column headings.

n. Click the **Documentation worksheet tab**, click cell **B28**, and then type Hourly_Sales_Sunday_2. Click cell **B29**, enter your Lastname, Firstname, click cell **B30**, and then type today's date in mm/dd/yyyy format.

SIDE NOTE
Column Names in a Table Must Be Unique

Each column in a table must have a unique label. Excel forces column labels to be unique by appending a number to duplicates. In the Hourly_Sales_Sunday_2 worksheet, notice the "Accessories2" and the "Deposit Returns3" column labels.

o. Click the **Hourly_Sales_Sunday_2 worksheet tab**.

p. Press Ctrl+Home, and then click **Save** 🖫.

Troubleshooting

Is the Table Tools Design tab not available when you want to select it? Check to make sure the active cell is somewhere in the table you formatted. A worksheet can contain many tables. Excel only makes the Table Tools Design tab available when the active cell is part of a formatted table.

Workbook Themes

A **workbook theme** is a collection of built-in cell styles all associated with a theme name. The **default** workbook theme, the theme that is automatically applied unless you specify otherwise, in Excel is the Office theme. Changing the assigned theme is a way to very quickly change the appearance of your worksheet(s). When a different workbook theme is applied, the built-in cell styles in the Styles group on the Home tab change to reflect the new workbook theme. Workbook themes are a way to rapidly change the look of the worksheets in a workbook and are particularly helpful for those who suffer from color blindness or who do not have a good eye for design. Applying a workbook theme assures a consistent, well-designed look throughout your workbook.

To Change the Workbook Theme

a. Click the **Hourly_Sales_Sunday worksheet tab**, click the **Page Layout tab**, and then click **Themes** in the Themes group. The gallery menu appears.

b. Point to the **Black Tie** built-in workbook theme. Note that any cell that was assigned a Cell Style now reflects the corresponding cell style in the Black Tie workbook theme.

c. If necessary, scroll down using the scroll bar on the right side of the Themes menu, and then click the **Horizon** theme. Some cells, such as cell A1 where color and font were explicitly set, are not affected by a change to the Horizon workbook theme.

d. Click the **Weekly_Sales worksheet tab**. Notice that the background colors that were set using cell formatting are not affected by the new workbook theme.

e. Click the **Hourly_Sales_Sunday_2 worksheet tab**. The table style applied to this worksheet reveals the extent to which a change in workbook theme can change the appearance of a worksheet.

f. Press Ctrl+Home, and then click **Save** 🖫.

Creating Information for Decision Making

New information is most often produced in Excel through the use of functions and/or formulas to make calculations against information in the workbook.

Often, the objective is to improve decision making by providing more informative information. Decision making can be improved by presenting information in a manner that calls attention to important trends and thresholds. In this section, you will manipulate data using functions and formulas and will assist in decision-making using conditional formatting to highlight or categorize information based on problem-specific parameters.

What Is a Function?

Functions are one of Excel's most powerful features. A **function** is a small program that performs operations on data. Function syntax takes the form of functionname (*argument* 1,..., *argument* n) where "functionname" is the name of the function and **arguments** inside the parentheses are the variables or values the function requires. In Excel, a **variable** is simply a value in a cell that is referenced in a formula or function. Different functions require different arguments. Some functions do not require any arguments at all—they are commonly referred to as null functions. There are more than 400 functions built-in to Excel that can be categorized as financial, statistical, mathematical, date and time, text, and several others—collectively these are referred to, not surprisingly, as **built-in functions**.

Arguments can be entered as letters, numbers, cell references, cell ranges, or other functions depending on the function's requirements. A few of the most common mathematical functions are grouped into AutoSum functions available in both the Editing group on the Home tab and the Function Library group on the Formulas tab. AutoSum functions include SUM( ), COUNT( ), AVERAGE( ), MIN( ), and MAX( ).

The power of functions is two-fold:

1. Functions allow you to take advantage of code that has been thoroughly tested to make complex calculations, to access operating system variables, to manipulate strings of text characters, and to make logical decisions.

2. Functions are easily copied and pasted to new locations in your worksheet to facilitate the reuse of code.

Part of what makes functions so useful in a worksheet is the use of cell references as arguments. Cell references enable you to specify that information from a particular cell or cell range be used in a function. Recall, that a **cell reference** is the combination of a cell's column and row addresses. When a function that includes a cell reference as an argument is copied, the cell reference is changed to reflect the copied location in reference to the original location. For example, say a function in cell B26 calculates the sum of cells B1:B25; if you copy the function from cell B26 to cell C26, the function in cell C26 will automatically be changed to summate C1:C25. You copied the function one column to the right, relative to the original location. All cell references will be relatively adjusted one column to the right.

AutoSum Functions

Of the more than 400 functions built into Excel, the most commonly used are the **AutoSum functions**. Since SUM( ), COUNT( ), AVERAGE( ), MIN( ), and MAX( ) are used so often, Excel makes them more readily available than any other function via AutoSum $\boxed{\Sigma}$, which is available in the Function Library group on the Formulas tab or in the Editing group on the Home tab. Further, when these functions are invoked using the AutoSum button, Excel inspects your worksheet and automatically includes a range adjacent to the active cell. In general, adjacent cells above are used by default. If there are no adjacent cells above, then adjacent cells to the left are used for the range. Excel does not inspect cell ranges to the right or below the active cell for AutoSum functions.

SUM( )

The SUM( ) function produces a sum of all numeric information in a specified range, list of numbers, list of cells, or any combination. Figure 11 contains examples of the different ways in which data can be included in a SUM( ) function.

Type of Data	Function
Numbers	=SUM(1,3,5,7,11,13)
Cell range	=SUM(B3:B25)
List of noncontiguous cells	=SUM(B3,B9,C5,D14)
Combination	=SUM(B3,B9:B15,C12/100)

Figure 11 SUM( ) function variations

To Use the AutoSum Sum( ) Function

a. Click the **Weekly_Sales worksheet tab**, click the **Formulas tab**, and then select cell **H9**.

b. Click the **AutoSum** button in the Function Library group. Excel will try to predict the cell range to sum by examining the cells directly above H9. Since there is numeric information in the three rows above H9, H6:H8 is automatically inserted into the function. This is correct. Press Enter .

AutoSum button

Formula bar shows formula or value in selected cell

Range selected by AutoSum

Formula built by AutoSum

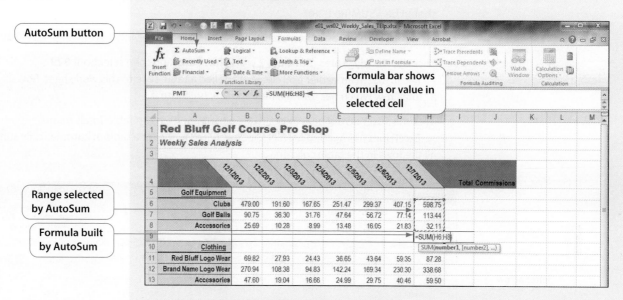

Figure 12 AutoSum SUM( ) function

c. Repeat Step c. for cells **H14**, **H18**, and **H26**.

d. Select cell **H9**. Use the fill handle to copy cell H9 directly to the left in cell range **B9:H9**. Click on the fill handle again and fill to the right through cell **I9**. Click cell **E9**.

Look at the formula displayed in the formula bar. The relative cell references in the formula were changed when you copied the original formula from cell H9. If any of the cells in B9:I9 display number signs, click Format in the Cells group of the Home tab, and then click AutoFit Column Width in the Cell Size menu.

e. Repeat Step d to copy cell **H14** to cell range **B14:I14**.

f. Repeat Step d to copy cell **H18** to cell range **B18:I18**.

g. Repeat Step d to copy cell **H26** to cell range **B26:I26**.

h. Click the Formulas tab, select cell **I6**, and then click **AutoSum** in the Function Library group. Excel tries to predict the cell range to sum and in this case chooses the seven columns to the left of I6, which is correct. Press Enter .

i. Select cell **I6**. Use the fill handle to copy cell I6 to cell range **I7:I8**. Notice the automatic recalculation of the sum in cell I9.

j. Select cell **I8**. Press Ctrl + C to place the formula in I8 on the Clipboard. Select cell range **I11:I13**, and then press Ctrl + V to paste the formula from the Clipboard into the selected cell range.

k. Select cell range **I16:I17**, press Ctrl + V , and then select cell range **I20:I25**. Press Ctrl + V to paste the formula from the Clipboard into the selected cell ranges, and then press Esc when finished pasting.

l. Click the heading for **column I**. Click the **Home tab**, click **Format** in the Cells group, and then select **AutoFit Column Width** in the Cell Size menu.

m. Click the **Hourly_Sales_Sunday worksheet tab**, and then click the **Formulas tab**.

n. Select cell **B29**, and then click **AutoSum** Σ in the Function Library group.

In this case Excel does not predict the summated range properly. The predicted range is outlined with a moving dotted line. Excel predicts range B20:B28. You want to sum the cells that represent all the day's time slots. Point to the top corner of the dotted outline so the mouse pointer changes to $\nwarrow$ or $\nearrow$. Drag the top of the summated range upward to encompass B6:B28. The formula displayed in the formula bar should be =SUM(B6:B28).

o. Press $\boxed{\text{Ctrl}}$+$\boxed{\text{Enter}}$, and then use the fill handle to copy cell B29 to cell range **C29:O29**.

p. Click the **Hourly_Sales_Sunday_2 worksheet tab**, and then select cell **B29**.

Recall that in an earlier exercise you applied a table style to this worksheet. Row 29 is a "Total" row which has formula functionality built into it.

q. Click the **Filter arrow** next to cell B29. Select **Sum** from the Table Totals menu.

Excel does not need to predict the summated range for a table. It automatically sums all the rows in the table column.

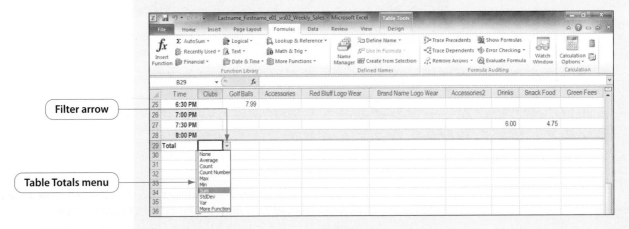

Figure 13 Calculating sum in a table total row

r. Use the fill handle to copy cell B29 to cell range **C29:O29**.

s. Press $\boxed{\text{Ctrl}}$+$\boxed{\text{Home}}$, and then click **Save** $\boxed{\blacksquare}$.

SIDE NOTE
Double-Click AutoSum
Rather than click AutoSum and press $\boxed{\text{Enter}}$, double-click AutoSum—the result is the same, but you get there more quickly. Double-check the resulting formula to make sure the correct range was selected.

COUNT( )

The **COUNT( ) function** returns the number of cells in a range of cells that contain numbers. It can be used to generate information such as the number of sales in a period by counting invoice numbers, the number of people in a group by counting Social Security numbers, and so on.

To Use the AutoSum COUNT( ) Function

a. Click the **Home tab**. Click the **Hourly_Sales_Sunday worksheet tab**, select cell **A30**, type # of Sales, and then press $\boxed{\text{Enter}}$. Select cell range **A29:A30**, click **Align Text Right** $\boxed{\equiv}$ in the Alignment group, click cell **A30**, and then click **Bold** $\boxed{\text{B}}$ in the Font group.

b. Click the **Formulas tab**, select cell **B30**, and then click the **AutoSum arrow** Σ in the Function Library group. The AutoSum menu will appear. Select **Count Numbers**.

c. Select cell range **B6:B28**. The cell range should be outlined in a moving dotted line and cell B30 should display =COUNT(B6:B28). Press $\boxed{\text{Ctrl}}$+$\boxed{\text{Enter}}$.

d. Use the fill handle to copy cell B30 to cell range **C30:O30**.

e. Click the heading for **row 30** to select the entire row, and then press $\boxed{\text{Ctrl}}$+$\boxed{\text{C}}$ to copy row 30 to the Clipboard.

f. Click the **Hourly_Sales_Sunday_2 worksheet tab**, click the heading for row **30**, and then press $\boxed{\text{Ctrl}}$+$\boxed{\text{V}}$ to paste row 30 from the Clipboard.

g. Press $\boxed{\text{Ctrl}}$+$\boxed{\text{Home}}$, and then click **Save** 💾. Rows 29 and 30 in the Hourly_Sales_Sunday and Hourly_Sales_Sunday_2 worksheets should contain matching data results.

AVERAGE( )

The **AVERAGE( ) function** returns a weighted average from a specified range of cells. The sum of all numeric values in the range is calculated and then divided by the count of numbers in the range. Essentially the AVERAGE( ) function is SUM( )/COUNT( ).

To Use the AVERAGE( ) AutoSum Function

a. Click the **Hourly_Sales_Sunday** worksheet, and then click the **Home tab**.

b. Select cell **A31**, type Average Sale, and then press $\boxed{\text{Ctrl}}$+$\boxed{\text{Enter}}$ to accept the changes and keep cell A31 selected. Click **Align Text Right** 📰 in the Alignment group, and then click **Bold** 𝐁 in the Font group.

c. Select cell **B31**, click the **Formulas tab**, click the **AutoSum arrow** $\boxed{\Sigma}$ in the Function Library group, and then select **Average**.

d. Select cell range **B6:B28**. The cell range should be outlined in a moving dotted line and cell B31 should display =AVERAGE(B6:B28). Press $\boxed{\text{Enter}}$.

e. Select cell **B31**, and then use the fill handle to copy cell B31 to cell range **C31:O31**.

f. Click the heading for **row 31** to select the row. Press $\boxed{\text{Ctrl}}$+$\boxed{\text{C}}$ to copy row 31 to the Clipboard.

g. Click the **Hourly_Sales_Sunday_2 worksheet tab**, click the heading for **row 31**, and then press $\boxed{\text{Ctrl}}$+$\boxed{\text{V}}$ to paste row 31 from the Clipboard.

h. Press $\boxed{\text{Ctrl}}$+$\boxed{\text{Home}}$, and then click **Save** 💾.

Min( ) and Max( )

An average gives you an incomplete picture. If your instructor stated that the average on the exam is 75%, you do not have any information about the actual score distribution. Everyone in the class may have gotten a C with the low of 71% and high of 79%. Conversely, no one may have gotten a C with half the class getting an A and half getting an F. Both situations could have a 75% average but are very different distributions. The average should never be relied on without looking at additional statistics that help complete the picture of actual scores. While many statistics exist to do this, the minimum and the maximum value provide at least a little more insight into the distribution of the data by defining the extremes. The **MIN( ) and MAX( ) functions** examine all numeric values in a specified range and return the minimum value and the maximum value respectively.

To Use the AutoSum MIN( ) and MAX( ) Functions

a. Click the **Hourly_Sales_Sunday worksheet tab**.

b. Click the **Home tab**, select cell **A32**, and then type Max. Sale Select cell **A33**, type Min. Sale and then select cell **A31**. Click **Format Painter** ✄ in the Clipboard group, and then select cell range **A32:A33**.

c. Click cell **B32**, click the **Formulas tab**, click the **AutoSum arrow** Σ in the Function Library group, and then click **Max**.

d. Select cell range **B6:B28**. The cell range should be outlined in a moving dotted line, and cell B32 should display =MAX(B6:B28). Press Enter. Cell B33 should be the active cell.

e. Click the **AutoSum arrow** Σ in the Function Library group, and then click **Min**.

f. Select cell range **B6:B28**. The cell range should be outlined in a moving dotted line, and cell B33 should display =MIN(B6:B28). Press Enter.

g. Select cell range **B32:B33**, and then use the fill handle to copy cell range B32:B33 to cell range **C32:O33**.

h. Select the headings for **rows 32** and **33**, and then press Ctrl + C to copy rows 32:33 to the Clipboard.

i. Click the **Hourly_Sales_Sunday_2 worksheet tab**, click the heading for **row 32**, and then press Ctrl + V to paste rows 32:33 from the Clipboard. Press Ctrl + Home.

j. Click the **Hourly_Sales_Sunday worksheet tab**. Press Esc.

k. Press Ctrl + Home, and then click **Save** 💾.

29	TOTAL	479.00	90.95	25.69	69.82	270.94	47.60	65.70	27.38	1,500.00	400.00
30	# of Sales	3	5	2	4	5	5	13	4	19	12
31	Average Sale	159.67	18.19	12.85	17.46	54.19	9.52	5.05	6.85	78.95	33.33
32	Max. Sale	359.00	49.99	14.99	24.99	82.50	19.48	19.00	12.65	100.00	50.00
33	Min. Sale	49.00	5.00	10.70	9.85	8.47	2.00	2.00	3.99	50.00	25.00
34											
35											

Figure 14 AutoSum AVERAGE( ), MAX( ), and MIN( )

What Is a Formula?

A **formula** allows you to perform basic mathematical calculations using information in the active worksheet (and others) to calculate new values and can contain cell references, constants, functions, and mathematical operators. Formulas in Excel have a very specific syntax. In Excel, formulas always begin with an equal sign (=). Formulas can contain references to specific cells that contain information; a **constant**, which is a number that never changes, such as the value for π; and **mathematical operators** such as +, -, *, /, ^, and functions. Cells that contain formulas can be treated like any other worksheet cell. They can be edited, formatted, copied, and pasted.

If the formula contains a cell reference, when copied and then pasted into a new location, the cell reference in the formula changes. The new cell reference reflects a new location relative to the old location. This is called a **relative cell reference**. For example, as shown in Figure 15, when the formula in the left column is copied one column to the right and two rows down, the cell references in the formula change to reflect the destination cell relative to the original cell. Consequently, columns A and J are changed to B and K respectively—one column right, and rows 3 and 12 are changed to 5 and 14, two rows down. Note that the column and row numbers of the cells that contain the formulas are not shown in Figure 15. The active cell address doesn't matter in relative addressing. All that matters is the relative shift in columns and rows from source to destination, and the cell references in the formula—source and target addresses are irrelevant.

Figure 15 Relative referencing when copying from a source cell to a destination cell

Relative cell references create a powerful opportunity for the reuse of formulas in a well-designed worksheet. You can enter a formula once and use the formula many times without having to reenter it in each location. Simply copy and paste it to new locations.

Further, relative references are a powerful means by which worksheets adjust formulas to ensure correctness when the structure of the worksheet changes. If a column is inserted to the left of a cell referenced in a formula, or a row is inserted above a cell referenced in a formula, the cells referenced by the formula will be adjusted to ensure the formula still references the same relative locations.

Operators

Excel formulas are constructed using basic mathematical operators very similar to those used in a mathematics class and exactly the same as used in most programming languages. Figure 16 contains the mathematical operators recognized in Excel.

Operation	Operator	Example	Formula Entered in Current Cell
Addition	+	=B4+B5	Assign the sum of B4 and B5 to the current cell
Subtraction	-	=B5-B4	Assign the difference of B4 and B5 to the current cell
Multiplication	*	=B5*3.14	Assign B5 multiplied by 3.14 to the current cell
Division	/	=B5/B4	Assign the quotient of B5 divided by B4 to the current cell
Exponentiation	^	=B4^2	Assign the square of B4 to the current cell

Figure 16 Mathematical operators in Excel

To Use a Formula to Sum Totals

a. Click the **Weekly_Sales worksheet tab**, click the **Home tab**, select cell **B27**, and then type =B9+B14+B18+B26. Press Ctrl+Enter.

b. Press Ctrl+C to copy cell B27 to the Clipboard.

c. Select cell range **C27:I27**, and then press Ctrl+V to paste cell B27 from the Clipboard. If any of the cells in B27:I27 display number signs, click **Format** in the Cells group, and then click **AutoFit Column Width** in the Cell Size menu.

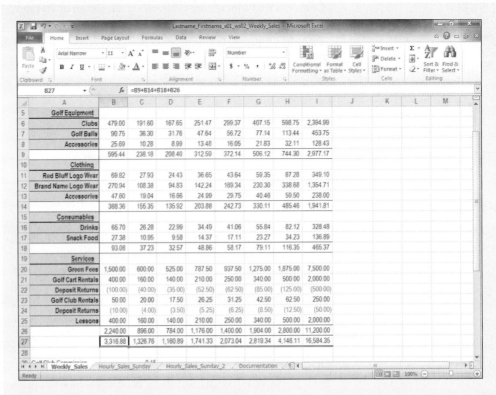

Figure 17 Use of a formula to sum subtotals

d. Press Ctrl+Home, and then click **Save** 💾.

Troubleshooting

Excel allows you to copy formulas from one location to another and adjusts cell references to ensure calculation accuracy. This is not necessarily true when a formula is moved from one location to another, however. If you move a formula by dragging it from one location to another, cell references *do not* change. Be sure you double check a formula after you move it to ensure it is still producing a correct result.

SIDE NOTE

How to Copy a Formula and Not Change Relative References

To copy a formula from one cell to another and not have relative cell references adjusted, highlight the formula in the formula bar, press Ctrl+C, press Esc, select the destination cell, and press Ctrl+V.

Real World Advice An Alternative to Typing Cell References

An alternative and more accurate method to typing cell references into a formula is to type only the operators and then select the cells from the worksheet. The steps to enter the daily sales total in the Weekly_Sales worksheet would be as follows:

a. Select cell B27

b. Type =

c. Click cell B9, and then type +

d. Click cell B14, and then type +

e. Click cell B18, and then type +

f. Click cell B26, and then press Enter

Order of Operations

Another consideration to take into account when applying formulas to ensure the desired results when using more than one operator is to understand and control the **order of operations**. Order of operations is the order in which Excel processes calculations in a formula that contains more than one operator. Mathematical operations execute in a specific order:

1. Parentheses
2. Exponentiation
3. Multiplication and division
4. Addition and subtraction

Excel scans a formula from left to right while performing the calculations using the above order of operation rules. Thus you can control which part of a calculation is performed first by enclosing parts of a formula in parentheses. Portions of a formula enclosed in parentheses are evaluated first, following the previously listed order. Figure 18 contains some examples of the effect of order of operations on formula results.

Formula	Result	Formula	Result
=4-2*5^2	-46	=(5+5)*4/2-3*6	2
=(4-2)*5^2	50	=(5+5)*4/(2-3)*6	-240
=5+5*4/2-3*6	-3	=(5+5)*4/(2-3*6)	-2.5

Figure 18 Order of operations

SIDE NOTE

How to Remember Order of Operations

An old acronym that is often used to remember order of operations is PEDMAS.

- **P**arentheses
- **E**xponentiation
- **D**ivision and/or **M**ultiplication
- **A**ddition and/or **S**ubtraction

Golf pro John Schilling is paid on a commission of sales. He receives 70% of all lesson fees received by the Pro Shop. Additionally, he must report all tips on a weekly basis for tax purposes. Pro Shop manager Aleeta Herriott is in charge of all golf club sales. She receives a 15% commission on all sales of clubs and a 10% commission on golf balls and accessories.

To Enter Formulas to Calculate Commissions

a. Select cell **J25**, and then type =I25*C33.

b. Select cell **J6**, and then type =I6*C29.

c. Select cell **J7**, and then type =(I7+I8)*C30.

d. Select cell **I6**, and then double-click **Format Painter** in the Clipboard group.

e. Select cell range **J6:J7**, click cell **J9**, and then click cell **J25**.
Although cell J9 does not contain data, the Format Painter can still be used to change its format. Data, or a formula, entered later will be displayed with the "painted" format.

f. Click **Format Painter** in the Clipboard group to toggle off the Format Painter.

g. Select cell range **J7:J8**. On the Home tab, click the **Merge & Center arrow** in the Alignment group, and then click **Merge Cells** from the menu.
The merged cell J7 will contain the formatting applied in Step f.

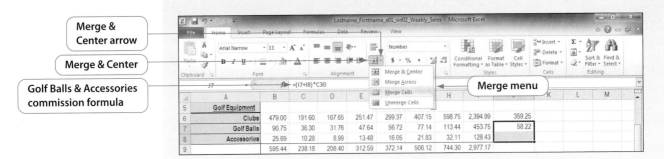

Figure 19 Merge & Center the Golf Balls & Accessories Commission

h. Press Ctrl + Home, and then click **Save** 🖫.

Real World Advice **Use Parameters, Don't Hard-Code Numbers in Formulas**

Hard-coding means the inclusion of an explicit value in a formula, an actual number—in the formula =H12/60, the number 60 is hard-coded. Excel formulas and functions can include what are called constants. A constant is a number that never changes, such as the number of hours in a day, or the number of minutes in an hour. Hard-coding constants is acceptable. For example, to calculate the area of a circle, if the radius was stored in cell C2, the area could be calculated as =C2*3.14 since the value of π never changes.

However, for the majority of values, there is a probability of change. Most numbers, such as tax rates, commission percentages, age limits, and interest rates will potentially change over time. Such values should be treated as parameters. A **parameter** is a special form of variable included in a worksheet for the sole purpose of inclusion in formulas and functions. A value is treated as a parameter by placing it in a cell, giving it a label (which is important for documentation), and referencing the value in formulas and/or functions via its cell address, rather than explicitly typing it into formulas and/or functions.

In Figure 20, the values in rows 29 through 34 are parameters. To use them in a formula you would reference them by cell address. For example, to calculate the commission on the sale of a $1,600 set of golf clubs, if the value of the sale were stored in cell B5, the formula would be =B5*C29, not =B5*0.15 or =1600*0.15. Cell C29 is a parameter—it stores the commission percentage for pro shop golf club sales for use in worksheet calculations.

The elegance of parameters is that the value of a parameter can be changed in its cell, and any of potentially hundreds of formulas that reference that parameter will instantly reflect the change in value. If the value were entered explicitly into each of hundreds of formulas, each formula would have to be changed, one at a time, by hand. Use parameters.

Hiding Information in a Worksheet

A worksheet can contain information that may not be necessary, or even desirable, to have displayed most of the time. This is often true of a list of parameters. It can also be the case that detailed information used to calculate totals can be hidden until such time that the person using the worksheet would like to see more detail.

Hiding information in a worksheet is relatively simple. Entire worksheet rows and columns can be hidden. Simply select the rows and/or columns to be hidden by clicking on the row or column heading. Right-click with the mouse pointer over the heading or in the selected row(s) or column(s), and click Hide in the menu that appears.

To Hide and Unhide Rows in a Worksheet

a. Select **row 29** by clicking on the row heading, press [Shift], and then click the heading for **row 34**.

b. Point to the **selected rows**, and then right-click. Click **Hide** in the shortcut menu.

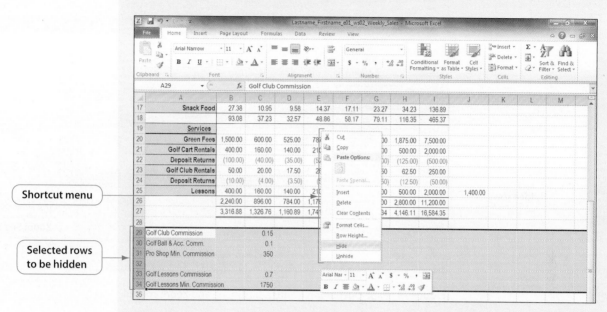

Shortcut menu

Selected rows to be hidden

Figure 20 Hide rows using the shortcut menu

c. Select row 28 by clicking on the row heading, press [Shift], and then click the heading for **row 35**.

d. Point to the **selected rows**, and then right-click to display the shortcut menu. Click **Unhide**.

e. Press [Ctrl]+[Z] to undo and leave rows 29:34 hidden.

f. Press [Ctrl]+[Home]. Click **Save** [💾].

Show Functions and Formulas

What is displayed in a cell that contains a function or a formula is the calculated result. The function or formula that generated the displayed value is only visible one cell at a time by selecting a cell and then looking at the formula bar. The keystroke combination [Ctrl]+[`] toggles Show Formulas on and off. When Show Formulas is on, the calculated results are hidden, and functions and formulas are shown in the cells instead whenever applicable.

Show Formulas is very helpful in understanding how a worksheet is structured. It is an essential debugging aid when something in a worksheet is in error. A worksheet that has Show Formulas toggled on can be printed for documentation purposes.

To View and Print All Formulas in a Worksheet

SIDE NOTE

A Faster Way to Show Formulas

Don't want to use the Ribbon to Show Formulas? Press [Ctrl]+[`] to toggle Show Formulas.

a. Click the **Formulas tab**, and then click **Show Formulas** in the Formula Auditing group. Cells will display formulas rather than values.

b. Use the **Zoom Slider** [⊖———◻———⊕] on the status bar to move the zoom level so you can view the entire worksheet on the monitor. If necessary, scroll the worksheet to the right to view formulas through column J.

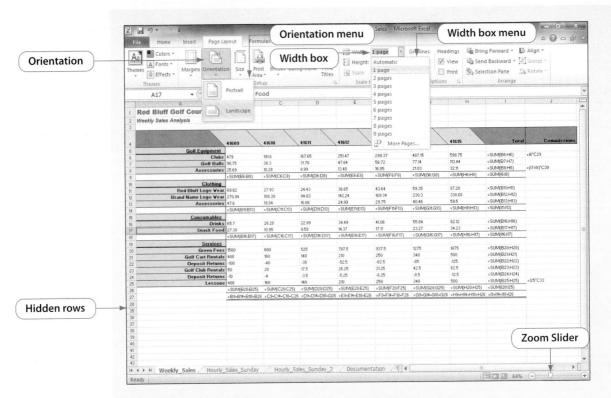

Figure 21 Page Orientation, Width adjustment, and Zoom control

c. Click the **Page Layout tab**, click **Orientation** in the Page Setup group, and then select **Landscape** in the menu.

d. Click the **Width Box arrow** in the Scale to Fit group, and then click **1 page**. This will scale your worksheet to print in the width of a single page.

e. Click the **Height Box arrow** in the Scale to Fit group, and then click **1 page**. This will scale your document to print in the height of a single page.

f. Click **Print Titles** in the Page Setup group, click the **Header/Footer tab** in the Page Setup dialog box, and then click **Custom Footer**.

g. Click in the **Left section** of the Footer dialog box, click **Insert File Name** , click **OK** in the Footer dialog box, and then click **OK** in the Page Setup dialog box.

h. Click the **File tab** to enter Backstage View, click **Print** in the left menu, and then look over the Print Preview of the worksheet displayed on the left side (notice the file name footer).

i. Make sure the top button under **Settings** is set to **Print Active Sheets** to ensure you only print the Weekly_Sales worksheet.

j. Make sure you have selected the proper printer under Printer, and then click **Print**.

k. Press Ctrl+` to toggle **Show Formulas** off, and return to the default Normal view.

l. Use the **Zoom Slider** on the status bar to set the zoom to **100%**.

m. Click **Save** .

Real World Advice — Print Function View for Documentation

You need to document your workbooks. As the worksheets you develop become more complex—use more functions and formulas—the need for documentation increases. Once your worksheet is complete, one vital documentation step is to print a Formula view of your worksheet. If anything ever goes wrong with your worksheet in the future, a Formula view printout may be the fastest way to fix it. Remember, an environmentally friendly documentation option can be to print to PDF. **Portable Document Format (PDF)** was developed by Adobe Systems in 1993 and is a file format that has become a standard for storing files. PDF preserves exactly the original "look and feel" of a document but allows its viewing in many different applications.

Decision Making

As discussed previously, one of the primary purposes of the analysis of information in Excel worksheets is to assist in decision making. People are often influenced by the format by which information is presented. Worksheets can be huge—thousands of rows and dozens of columns of information. The number of calculated items can be daunting to analyze, digest, and interpret. To the extent Excel can be used to assist the decision maker in understanding the information, decision making speed and quality should improve.

Conditional formatting is one way Excel can aid the decision maker by changing the way information is displayed based on rules specific to the problem the worksheet is designed to address.

Conditional Formatting

Conditional formatting allows the specification of rules that apply formatting to a cell as determined by the rule outcome. It is a way to dynamically change the visual presentation of information in a manner that actually adds information to the worksheet.

Conditional formatting can be used to highlight information by changing cell fill color, font color, font style, font size, border, and/or number format.

To Highlight Above and Below Average Daily Sales

a. Click the **Home tab**, select cell range **B6:H6**, and then click **Conditional Formatting** in the Styles group. Point to **Top/Bottom Rules**, and then select **Above Average** from the menu.

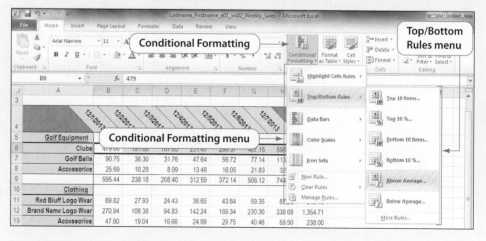

Figure 22 Conditional Formatting menus

b. In the Above Average dialog box, click the **for the selected range with arrow**, select **Green Fill with Dark Green Text**, and then click **OK**.

c. Click **Conditional Formatting** in the Styles group, point to **Top/Bottom Rules**, and then select **Below Average**. In the Below Average dialog box, click the **for the selected range with arrow**, select **Light Red Fill with Dark Red Text**, and then click **OK**.

d. Press Ctrl+C to copy the cell range to the Clipboard.

e. Select cell **B7** and right-click. In the shortcut menu that appears, click **Formatting** 📋 in the Paste Options menu. This will create a new set of rules for cell range B7:H7.

f. Repeat Step **e** for cells **B8**, **B11**, **B12**, **B13**, **B16**, **B17**, **B20**, **B21**, **B22**, **B23**, **B24**, and **B25**.

Troubleshooting

Conditional formatting is very sensitive to relative references. Copy and paste very carefully. Be sure to double check the results of any copy-and-paste activity when conditional formatting is involved. In the Hands-on Project, the row of cells that contain conditional formatting is copied to the Clipboard. The row must be pasted from the Clipboard, Paste Formatting 📋, one row at a time or the conditional formatting rules will be broken.

g. Click the heading for **row 28**, press Shift, and then click the heading for row **35**. Right-click and select **Unhide** in the shortcut menu. You need access to the parameters hidden in rows 29:34.

h. Click cell **J9**, click the **Borders arrow** in the Font group, and then select **Top Border** in the Borders menu.

i. Click **AutoSum** in the Editing group, and then press Ctrl+Enter.

j. Click **Conditional Formatting** in the Styles group, point to **Icon Sets**, and then click **More Rules**.

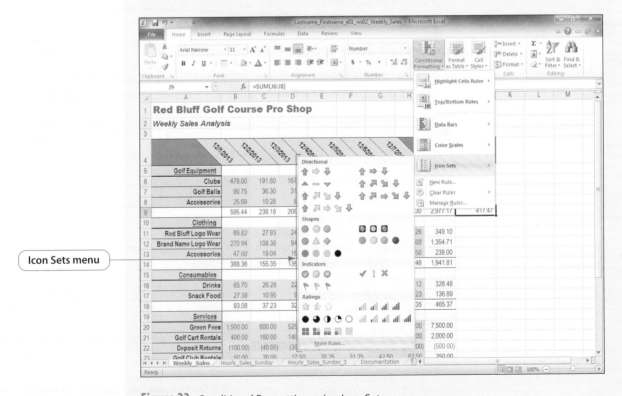

Icon Sets menu

Figure 23 Conditional Formatting using Icon Sets

k. In the New Formatting Rule dialog box, select **Format all cells based on their values** under Select a Rule Type. Click **3 Arrows (Colored)** in the Icon Style box—you may have to scroll up.

l. Under **Icon**, select the **Red Down Arrow** for the middle Icon box—the Icon Style box will change to Custom. Select **No Cell Icon** in the bottom Icon box, and then select **Number** in both Type boxes.

m. Double-click the top **Value** box. Select cell **C31**—the minimum commission for the Pro Shop manager, and then click **OK**.

n. Select cell **J25**, click **Conditional Formatting** in the Styles group, point to **Icon Sets**, and then select **More Rules**.

o. In the New Formatting Rule dialog box, select **Format all cells based on their values** under Select a Rule Type. Click **3 Flags** in the Icon Style box.

p. Under **Icon**, select the **Red Flag** in the middle Icon box—the Icon Style box will change to Custom. Select **No Cell Icon** in the bottom Icon box, and then select **Number** in both Type boxes.

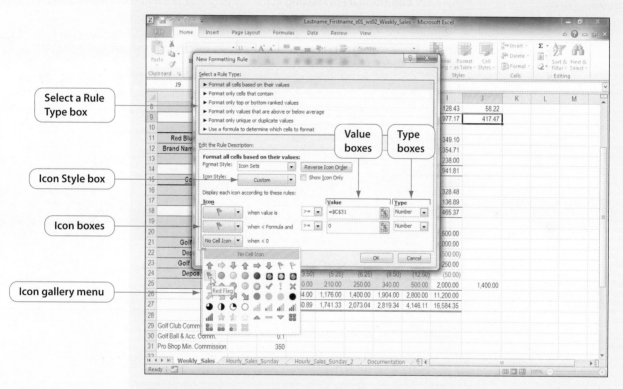

Select a Rule Type box

Icon Style box

Icon boxes

Icon gallery menu

Value boxes

Type boxes

Figure 24 New Formatting Rule dialog box

q. Click **Collapse Dialog Box** in the top Value box. The New Formatting Rule dialog box collapses in size, and the Collapse Dialog button toggles to the Expand Dialog button.

r. Click cell **C34**—the minimum commission for the RBGC golf pro. Click **Expand Dialog box**. Click **OK**.

s. Select **rows 29:34** using the row headings. Point to the selected rows, right-click, and then click **Hide** in the shortcut menu.

t. Press Ctrl+Home, and then click **Save**.

Removing Conditional Formatting

Once conditional formatting has been applied to a cell or range of cells, it may be necessary to remove the conditional formatting without affecting other cell formatting or cell contents. Conditional formatting can be removed from a selected cell or cell range, and can be removed from the entire sheet, depending upon which option is chosen.

CONSIDER THIS | **How Might You Use Conditional Formatting?**

Can you think of ways you could use conditional formatting in worksheets to aid personal decisions? Could you use conditional formatting as an aid in tracking your stock portfolio? Monthly budget and expenses? Checking account?

To Remove Conditional Formatting from a Range of Cells

a. Select cell range **B22:H22**, press Ctrl, and then select cell range **B24:H24**.

b. Click **Conditional Formatting** in the Styles group, point to **Clear Rules**, and then select **Clear Rules from Selected Cells**.

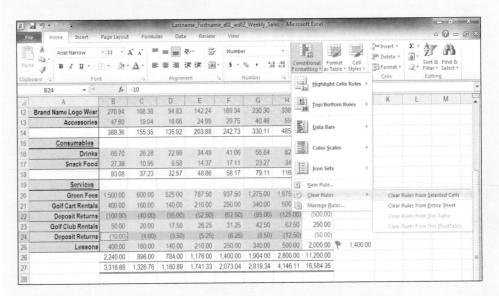

Figure 25 How to clear conditional formatting

Troubleshooting

Did all the conditional formatting in your worksheet disappear? You probably selected Clear Rules from Entire Sheet by mistake. Press Ctrl+Z to undo, and carefully select Clear Rules from Selected Cells.

c. Press Ctrl+Home, and then click **Save** 💾.

d. To see more of the worksheet, click the **View tab**. Uncheck **Formula Bar** in the Show group, and then double-click the **View tab**.

e. Double-click the **View tab**, and then check **Formula Bar** in the Show group.

f. Click the **Documentation worksheet tab**, click cell **C5**, and then type Formatted for appearance and clarity.

g. Select cell **C6**, and then type Added column and row totals where appropriate. Include punctuation.

h. Select cell **C7**, and then type Applied cell themes and workbook theme (Horizon). Include punctuation.

i. Select cell **C8**, and then type Applied conditional formatting to show above and below average daily sales. Applied conditional formatting to indicate commission status. Include punctuation.

j. Press Ctrl+Home, and then click **Save** 💾. Submit your work as directed by your instructor. **Close** ✕ Excel.

Real World Advice ▸ The Power and Risk of "Machine Decision Making"

Never forget that tools like Excel are decision-making aids, *not* decision makers. Certainly there are highly structured decisions that can be programmed into a worksheet in Excel such that the result is the decision, for example a product mix problem. Excel is more often used for the analysis of information in less highly structured problems. In addition, generally not all factors in a decision can be quantified and programmed into a worksheet. Never forget that Excel and other tools are decision-making *aids*, not decision makers. Computers make calculations; people make decisions.

1. Jon, who works with you in accounting, is creating a new workbook. This workbook will be used to present information to clients outside the department and will form the standard of appearance for all worksheets in the accounting department. Jon's supervisor has asked that the workbook be flexible enough to allow for easy changes to formatting that would affect all worksheets in the workbook with minimal effort. Jon admits he is not very good with formatting. His primary concern at the moment is column headings. What advice would you give Jon to enhance the appearance and readability of column headings while satisfying his supervisor's desire for flexibility and workbook-wide changeability?

2. Your supervisor, Shannon, has asked you to update a financial worksheet because some of the upper-level managers who read it are having difficulty finding information they need—mostly totals and other aggregate data. The worksheet currently contains no special formatting other than the numbers that all display with two decimal places. List five things you could do to make the worksheet more readable for upper-level managers.

3. You have been asked to add a new section of data to a worksheet. The additional data will require the same formatting that is used by other data in the worksheet. There are several ways to set the formatting for the new cells to reflect what is already in place. The most difficult way is to set the formatting manually (changing each cell or cell range). What are two easier ways to set the formatting for the new data?

4. Approximately 99% of color-blind individuals have trouble distinguishing between the colors red and green. For financial worksheets, where green may be used as conditional formatting for positive numbers and red may be used for negative numbers, color blindness would make such an informational aid difficult. What other things could you do with conditional formatting to ensure color-blind readers have the similar differential formatting as non-color-blind readers?

5. Documentation is a vital part of ensuring that a workbook is usable over time and that the information presented in a workbook will be correct. One of the most powerful capabilities of a worksheet is the creation of new information by aggregating data and by applying various functions to data and ranges of data. The formulas and functions that are used to create new information are not generally of interest to workbook readers, but at times they are very important to people responsible for maintaining and enhancing a workbook. Rebuilding an accidentally deleted or modified formula can be frustrating and time consuming. How would you document the formulas and functions to assist future users in maintaining and enhancing a workbook?

Key Terms

Argument 104
AutoSum function 104
AVERAGE() function 107
Banding 101
Built-in cell style 99
Built-in function 104
Cell alignment 94
Cell reference 104

Conditional formatting 115
Constant 108
COUNT() function 106
Default 103
Fill color 95
Format Painter 97
Formula 108

Function 104
Graphical format 88
Hard-coding 112
Mathematical operator 108
MAX() function 107
MIN() function 107
Order of operations 111
Parameter 112

Portable Document Format (PDF) 115
Relative cell reference 108
Table 101
Table style 101
Tabular format 88
Variable 104
Workbook theme 103

View and print all formulas in a worksheet (p. 113)

Format a cell or cell range as a date or as time (p. 92)

Rotate text (p. 95)

Change cell background color (p. 95)

Format cell borders (p. 96)

Use the AutoSum Sum() function (p. 105)

Display negative numbers in red (p. 91)

Get started, open the weekly_sales workbook in Excel and rename sheet1 (p. 88)

Format numbers (p. 90)

Highlight above and below average daily sales (p. 115)

Right-align text, increase indent, and bottom align (p. 94)

Use paste options and paste special to copy formats (p. 98)

Use the format painter to copy formats (p. 97)

Copy a documentation template from another workbook (p. 89)

Remove conditional formatting from a range of cells (p. 118)

Use a formula to summate totals (p. 109)

Hide and unhide rows in a worksheet (p. 113)

Enter formulas to calculate commissions (p. 111)

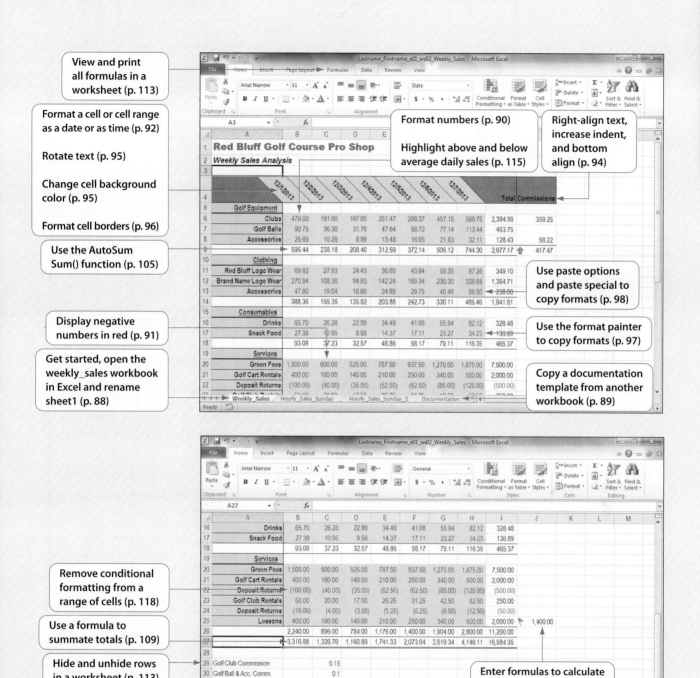

Apply built-in cell styles (p. 99)

Change the workbook theme (p. 103)

Use the Average() AutoSum function (p. 107)

Use the AutoSum Min() and Max() functions (p. 108)

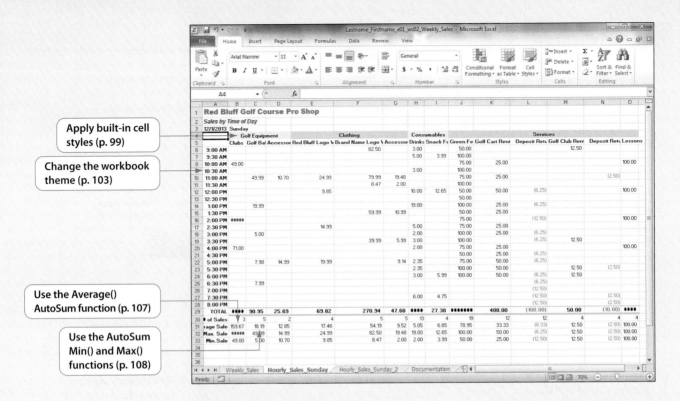

Apply a table style to a cell range (p. 101)

Use the AutoSum Count() function (p. 106)

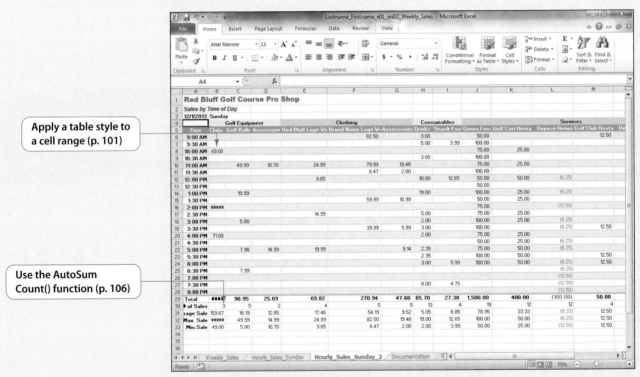

Figure 26 Red Bluff Golf Club Pro Shop Sales Analysis Final

Student data file needed:

e01_ws02_ProShop_Budget

You will save your file as:

Lastname_Firstname_e01_ws02_ProShop_Budget

Pro Shop Budget

After you completed the Pro Shop sales analysis, Aleeta realized the value of the worksheet would be enhanced if sales budget analysis could be added to it. She added the budget figures to the WS2_Practice1 worksheet. You are to use number formatting and conditional formatting to add information to the worksheet that indicates whether or not WS2_Practice1 meets budget goals.

a. Start **Excel** and then open **e01_ws02_ProShop_Budget**. Click the **File tab**, and click **Save As**. In the Save As dialog box, navigate to the location where you are saving your files, and then in the File name box, type Lastname_Firstname_e01_ws02_ProShop_Budget.

b. Click cell **B41**, click the **Formulas tab**, and then click **AutoSum** in the Function Library group. Press Enter.

c. Click cell **B41**, click the fill handle in the bottom-right corner of cell B41, and then drag to select the cell range **B41:I41**.

d. Click cell **I37**, click **AutoSum** in the Function Library group, and then press Enter.

e. Click cell **I37**, click on the fill handle in the bottom-right corner of cell I37, and then drag to select the cell range **I37:I40**.

f. Click cell **B36**, and then click the fill handle and drag the mouse to the right until cell range **B36:H36** is selected. Next you want to add conditional formatting to cell B9 to identify whether the category sales for each day met budgeted amounts.

g. Click cell **B9**, click the **Home tab**, and then click **Conditional Formatting** in the Styles group. Point to **Highlight Cells Rules**, and then select **More Rules**. In the New Formatting Rule dialog box, under Select a Rule Type, click **Use a formula to determine which cells to format**.

h. Under Edit the Rule Description, in the Format values where this formula is true box, type =B9>=B37. Click **Format**, and then click **Bold** under Font style. In the Color box, click **More Colors**. If necessary, click the **Custom tab** in the Colors dialog box. Set Color model to **RGB**. Red to **0**, Green to **100**, and Blue to **0**. Click **OK**, click **OK** in the Format Cells dialog box, and then click **OK** in the New Formatting Rule dialog box.

i. In the Styles group, click **Conditional Formatting**, point to **Highlight Cells Rules**, and then select **More Rules**. In the New Formatting Rule dialog box, under Select a Rule Type, click **Use a formula to determine which cells to format**.

j. Under Edit the Rule Description, in the Format values where this formula is true box, type =B9<B37. Click **Format**, and then under Colors, click **Red**, second from the left in Standard Colors. Click **OK**, and then click **OK** in the New Formatting Rule dialog box.

k. Click the **fill handle**, and then drag the mouse right until cells **B9:I9** are selected. Click **AutoFill Options**, and then select **Fill Formatting Only**.

l. Repeat Steps g–k for cells **B14**, **B18**, **B26**, and **B27** and cell ranges **B14:I14**, **B18:I18**, **B26:I26**, and **B27:I27**. Modify the formulas in the Conditional Formatting Rule dialog box to compare each cell to the proper budget figure; for example, for cell B14 the formula for Step i is =B14>=B38.

m. Add Data Bar conditional formatting to the daily totals in row 27 by selecting cell range **B27:I27**. Click **Conditional Formatting** in the Styles group, point to **Data Bars**, and then under Gradient Fill, click **Green Data Bar**.

n. Select cell range **I37:I41**, press Ctrl, and then select cell range **B41:H41**. Press Ctrl+B.

o. Format the budget amounts with two decimal places and a comma separator. If necessary, click the **Home tab**. Select cell range **B37:I41**. In the Number group, click the **Number Format arrow**, and then click **More Number Formats**. Under Category, click **Number**. If necessary, in the Decimal places box, enter 2. Make sure **Use 1000 Separator (,)** is checked. Click **OK**. If any of the cells in B:I display number signs, select column headings **B:I**, click **Format** in the Cells group, and then select **AutoFit Column Width** in the Cell Size menu.

p. Select cell range **A36:A41**, press [Ctrl], and then select cell range **B36:I36**. Press [Ctrl]+[B]. In the Alignment group, click **Align Text Right**.

q. To add cell borders to better differentiate individual budget figures from budget totals, select cell range **A41:I41**. Click the **Borders arrow** in the Font group, and then click **Top Border** in the Borders menu. Select cell range **I36:I41**, click the **Borders arrow** in the Font group, select **Left Border** from the Borders menu, and then press [Ctrl]+[Home].

r. Click the **Documentation worksheet tab**, click cell **A5**, and then press [Ctrl]+[;] to replace the date format with current date.

s. Click cell **A9**, and then type today's date in mm/dd/yyyy format.

t. Click cell **B9**, and then type your Lastname, Firstname replacing Lastname and Firstname with your own name.

u. Click cell **C9**, and then type Added budget analysis using daily budgets by category and conditional formatting. Press [Ctrl]+[Home].

v. Click the **Page Layout tab**, click **Print Titles** in the Page Setup group, click the **Header/Footer tab** in the Page Setup dialog box, and then click **Custom Footer**. Click in the **Left section** box, click **Insert File Name**, click **OK** in the Footer dialog box, and then click **OK** in the Page Setup dialog box.

w. Click the **WS2_Practice1 worksheet tab**. Repeat step v.

x. Click **Save**, and then submit your project as directed by your instructor. Close Excel.

Practice 2

Student data file needed:	You will save your file as:
e01_ws02_Gift_Shop	Lastname_Firstname_e01_ws02_Gift_Shop

Gift Shop Sales Analysis

The Painted Treasures Gift Shop offers a variety of products in the following areas: Toiletries, Clothing, Spa, Golf, Toys, and Local. While clothing is the most popular product in the Gift Shop, spa products are another popular offering. Gift Shop sales are tracked on several dimensions, including time of day, day of the week, and product category. The resort also tracks the average sales by hour for each product category. Some gift shop sales data has been included for a few categories. The Gift Shop recently opened for a full day on Sunday, so hourly information for Sunday sales is of particular interest to determine if Sunday opening is fiscally responsible.

a. Start **Excel** and then open **e01_ws02_Gift_Shop**.

b. Click the **File tab**, and then click **Save As**. In the Save As dialog box, navigate to the location where you are saving your files. In the File name box, type Lastname_Firstname_ e01_ws02_Gift_Shop replacing Lastname and Firstname with your own name.

c. Click the **Home tab**, select columns **B:I** using the column headings, click **Format** in the Cells group, and then click **Column Width** in the Cell Size menu. Enter 12 in the Column Width: box, and then click **OK**.

d. Select cell range **B5:I22**, click the **Number Format arrow** in the Number group, and then select **Number**.

e. Click cell **I5**, click **AutoSum** in the Editing group, and then press [Enter].

f. Click cell **I5**, click on the fill handle, and then drag the mouse down until cells **I5:I8** are selected.

g. Click cell **I8**, press [Ctrl]+[C] to copy cell I8 to the Clipboard, and then select cell range **I11:I13**. Press [Ctrl]+[V], and then select cell range **I16:I21**. Press [Ctrl]+[V] to copy the contents of the Clipboard to the selected ranges. Press [Esc].

h. Click cell **B9**, click **AutoSum** in the Editing group, and then press [Enter].

i. Click cell **B9**, click the fill handle, and then drag the mouse across until cells **B9:I9** are selected.

j. Repeat Steps h–i for cell **B14** and cell range **B14:I14**, cell **B22**, and cell range **B22:I22**.

k. Click cell **H25**, click the **AutoSum arrow** in the Editing group, and then select **Average**. Point to the top-left corner of the dotted cell range outline so the mouse pointer changes. Click the **diagonal arrow** in the corner, and then drag the mouse to the left to expand the selected cells to **B25:G25**. Press [Enter].

   Notice next to the left of cell H25 is an Error Message and a green error triangle in the top-left corner. Click Error Message to reveal the Error tag menu. "Formula Omits Adjacent Cells" indicates that column A contains a number and is adjacent to the range B25:G25. The error is a warning that you may have missed a cell when specifying the range—you did not—you do not want to add the Excel value for 6:00:00 AM to the row total.

   You can ignore this error or alternatively click on Ignore Error in the Error tag menu to remove the green triangle. Further, you can select Error Checking Options and uncheck Formulas which omit cells in a region in the Error Checking Rules menu to stop this form of error checking in the future. This type of error checking can be turned back on in the File tab, Options dialog box, Formulas menu.

l. Select cell **H25**, click the fill handle, and then drag the mouse down until cells **H25:H41** are selected.

m. Click **Increase Decimal** in the Number group once.

n. Select cell range **B9:H9**, and then click **Accounting Number Format** in the Number group. Select cell range **I5:I9**, and then click **Accounting Number Format**.

o. Double-click **Format Painter**. The mouse pointer will change. Select cell range **B14:H14**, cell range **I11:I14**, cell range **B22:H22**, and cell range **I16:I22**. Click **I22**. Toggle off **Format Painter** when done.

p. Select cell range **B9:I9**, press [Ctrl], and then select the cell ranges **B14:I14** and **B22:I22**. Click the **Borders arrow**, and then click **Top Border**.

q. Select cell range **A3:I22**, click **Format as Table** in the Styles group, and then select **Table Style Medium 9**. Check the **My table has headers** check box in the Format As Table dialog box, and then click **OK**.

r. Click the **Home tab**, click **Sort & Filter** in the Editing group, and then click **Filter** to turn off column filters in the table headings.

s. Select cell range **B24:H24**, click **Wrap Text** in the Alignment Group, and then select **row 24** by clicking on its heading. Click **Format** in the Cells group, and then click **AutoFit Row Height**.

t. Double-click cell **A24**. Use the arrow keys or the mouse pointer to position the cursor immediately following **Analysis**. Press [Delete] to remove the space, and then press [Alt]+[Enter] to insert a hard return. Press [Enter], click cell **A24**, and then click **Center** in the Alignment group.

u. Select **column A** by clicking on its heading. Click **Format** in the Cells group, and then click **AutoFit Column Width** in the Cell Size menu.

v. Select cell range **A2:I3**. Hold down Ctrl, and then select cell range **A4:A41** and cell range **B24:H24**. Click **Bold** in the Font group, click cell **A1**, and then change the font to **Arial Black** and font color to **Dark Red** (first color on the left under Standard Colors).

w. Click the **Documentation worksheet tab**.

- Click cell **A3**, and then type today's date in mm/dd/yyyy format.
- Click cell **B3**, and then type your Lastname, Firstname.
- Click cell **C3**, and then type Gift Shop Sales Analysis by Day, Category and Product. Includes hourly analysis for Sunday. Include punctuation. Press Enter.
- Click cell **B16**, and then type WS2_Practice2.
- Click cell **B17**, and then type your Lastname, Firstname.
- Click cell **B18**, and then type today's date in mm/dd/yyyy format, or press Ctrl+ ; .
- Click cell **C3**, and then press Ctrl+ +C . Click cell **B19**, press Ctrl+ V , and then press Esc . Press Ctrl+ Home .

x. Click the **Page Layout tab**, and then click **Print Titles** in the Page Setup group. Click the **Header/Footer tab** in the Page Setup dialog box, and then click **Custom Footer**. Click in the **Left section** box, click **Insert File Name**, and then click **OK** in the Footer dialog box. Click **OK** in the Page Setup dialog box.

y. Click the **WS2_Practice2 worksheet tab**. Repeat step x. Click **Orientation** in the Page Setup group, click **Landscape**, and then select **1 page** for Width and Height in the Scale to Fit group.

z. Click **Save**, and then turn in your files as directed by your instructor. Close the workbook, and then close Excel.

Student data file needed:

e01_mp_Beverage_Sales

You will save your file as:

Lastname_Firstname_e01_mp_Beverage_Sales

Beverage Sales/Inventory Analysis

The Painted Paradise Resort and Spa offers a wide assortment of beverages through the Indigo 5 restaurant and bar. The resort must track the inventory levels of these beverages as well as the sales and costs associated with each item. Analyze the inventory and sales data found in the worksheet. There are four categories of beverages: Beer, Wine, Soda, and Water. You also have three inventory figures: Starting, Delivered, and Ending. Resort management wants you to generate an analysis of beverage sales in which you identify units sold of each beverage, cost of goods sold, revenue, profit, profit margin, and appropriate totals and averages.

a. Start **Excel**, and then open **e01_mp_Beverage_Sales**. Save the file in with the name Lastname_Firstname_e01_mp_Beverage_Sales replacing Lastname_Firstname with your own name.

b. Click the **Documentation worksheet tab**, click cell **A3**, and then press Ctrl+; to enter today's date. Click cell **B3**, and then type your Lastname, Firstname. Click cell **C3**, type Formatting More_Practice worksheet, and then press Ctrl+Home.

c. Type More_Practice in cell **B16**. Type your Lastname, Firstname in cell **B17**. Enter today's date into cell **B18**. Enter a descriptive sentence or two that accurately reflect the activities in this exercise. Press Ctrl+Home. Click the **More_Practice worksheet tab**.

d. Select cell range **A1:K1**, and then click **Merge & Center** for the selected range. Apply the **Title** cell style to the selected range. If necessary, on the Home tab, in the Cells group, click **Format**, and then click **AutoFit Row Height**.

e. Select cell range **A2:K2**, and then click **Merge & Center** for the selected range. Apply the **Heading 4** cell style to the selected range.

f. Insert a hard return at the specified locations in the following cells—be sure to remove any spaces between the words, and then press Alt+Enter:
   - Between **Starting** and **Inventory** in **C6**
   - Between **Inventory** and **Delivered** in **D6**
   - Between **Ending** and **Inventory** in **E6**
   - Between **Units** and **Sold** in **F6**
   - Between **Cost** and **Per Unit** in **G6**
   - Between **Cost of** and **Goods Sold** in **H6**
   - Between **Sale Price** and **Per Unit** in **I6**
   - Between **Profit** and **Margin** in **K6**

g. Format the height of row 6 to 30, select cell range **A6:K29**, and apply **AutoFit Column Width**. Select cell range **C6:K6** along with cells **B13**, **B19**, **B26**, **B30**, and **B31**. Apply **Align Text Right**.

h. Select cell ranges **C13:K13**, **C19:K19**, **C26:K26**, and **C30:K30**. Add a **Top and Bottom Border** to the selected cell ranges. Select cell range **C31:K31**, and then add a **Bottom Double Border** to the selected range.

i. Select cell range **C7:F31**. Format the selected range as **Number** with a comma separator and zero decimal places. Select cell range **G7:J31**, and then format the selected range as **Number** with a comma separator and two decimal places. If any cells contain a string of pound signs (#), select the columns, and then apply **AutoFit Column Width**.

j. Select cell **F7**. Calculate Units Sold by adding Starting Inventory to Inventory Delivered and subtract Ending Inventory. Type =C7+D7-E7, and then copy cell **F7** to cell ranges **F8:F12**, **F15:F18**, **F21:F25**, and **F28:F29**. Press Esc when done to cancel the target copy cell. If any cells contain a string of pound signs (#), select the column, and then apply **AutoFit Column Width**.

k. Select cell **H7**. Calculate Cost of Goods Sold as Units Sold multiplied by Cost Per Unit. Type =F7*G7, copy cell H7 to cell ranges **H8:H12**, **H15:H18**, **H21:H25**, and **H28:H29**. If any cells contain a string of pound signs (#), select the column, and then apply **AutoFit Column Width**.

l. Select cell **J7**. Calculate Revenue as Units Sold multiplied by Sale Price Per Unit. Type =F7*I7 and then copy cell **J7** to cell ranges **J8:J12**, **J15:J18**, **J21:J25**, and **J28:J29**. If any cells contain a string of pound signs (#), select the column, and then apply **AutoFit Column Width**.

m. Select cell **K7**. Calculate Profit Margin as (Revenue – Cost of Goods Sold)/Revenue. Type =(J7-H7)/J7 and then copy cell **K7** to cell ranges **K8:K12**, **K15:K18**, **K21:K25**, and **K28:K29**.

n. Select cell range **C13:F13**, press Ctrl, and then select cells **H13** and **J13**. Click **AutoSum**. If any cells contain a string of number signs (#), select the cells, and then apply **AutoFit Column Width**.

o. Select cell range **C19:F19**. Press Ctrl, and then select cells **H19** and **J19**. Click **AutoSum**. If any cells contain a string of number signs (#), select the cells, and then apply **AutoFit Column Width**.

p. Select cell range **C26:F26**. Press Ctrl, and then select cells **H26** and **J26**. Click **AutoSum**. If any cells contain a string of number signs (#), select the cells, and then apply **AutoFit Column Width**.

q. Select cell range **C30:F30**, press Ctrl, and then select cells **H30** and **J30**. Click **AutoSum**. If any cells contain a string of number signs (#), select the cells, and then apply **AutoFit Column Width**.

r. Select cell **C31**. Calculate the total number of items in Starting Inventory for all categories combined by using the SUM() formula. Type =SUM(C13,C19,C26,C30) and copy cell **C31** to cell range **D31:F31** as well as cells **H31** and **J31**. If any cells contain a string of number signs (#), select the cells, and then apply **AutoFit Column Width**.

s. Copy cell **K12**, and then from **Paste Options**, paste **Formulas** into cells **K13**, **K19**, **K26**, **K30**, and **K31**. Select cell range **K7:K31**. Format the selected range as **%** with one decimal place. If any cells contain a string of pound signs (#), select the cells, and then apply **AutoFit Column Width**.

t. Select cells **H13**, **J13**, **H19**, **J19**, **H26**, **J26**, **H30**, **J30**, **H31**, and **J31**. Format the selected cells as **Currency**. If any cells contain a string of pound signs (#), select the cells, and then apply **AutoFit Column Width**.

u. Select cell range **F7:F12**. Use **Conditional Formatting** to highlight the beer with the highest number of units sold for the week as **Green Fill with Dark Green Text**—use **Top 10 Items** in **Top/Bottom Rules** and change the number of ranked items to **1**.

v. Repeat Step u with cell ranges **J7:J12**, **F15:F18**, **J15:J18**, **F21:F25**, **J21:J25**, **F28:F29**, and **J28:J29**. Do not use Ctrl to select all the above ranges at the same time, repeat Step u seven times, once for each range.

w. Select cell range **A6:K6**, press Ctrl, and then click cells **A14**, **A20**, and **A27**. Apply **20% - Accent1** in the Themed Cell Styles to the selected cells. Select cell range **A4:B4**, press Ctrl, and then select cell ranges **A6:K6**, **B13:K13**, **B19:K19**, **B26:K26**, **B30:K31**, as well as cells **A14**, **A20**, and **A27**. Click **Bold**.

x. Click the **Page Layout tab**, and in the Themes group click **Themes**, and then click **Adjacency** to change the workbook theme to Adjacency.

y. Click **Print Titles**, click the **Header/Footer tab** in the Page Setup dialog box, and then click the **Custom Footer** button. Click in the **Left section** of the Footer dialog box, click **Insert File Name**, click **OK**, and then click **OK** again to close the Page Setup dialog box.

z. Press Ctrl+Home, click **Save**, and then close **Excel**.

Problem Solve 1

Student data file needed:	You will save your file as:
e01_ps1_Hotel_ Discounts	Lastname_Firstname_e01_ps1_Hotel_ Discounts

Analysis of Hotel Sales Discounts

The Painted Paradise Resort and Spa has 700 rooms. The Paradise Resort and Spa gives discounts to guests who meet certain conditions. First, the Paradise Club discount, a 9% discount applicable to all products and services at the resort, is offered to guests who opt into the resort's rewards program. Another 10% discount, good on hotel rooms and services, is offered to groups who book a large block of rooms. Finally, at the discretion of the resort management, rooms may be charged at a complimentary rate. The resort's management would like to get an idea of how much revenue is lost to discounts on Friday and Saturday nights, the busiest nights of the week.

a. Start **Excel**, and then open **e01_ps1_Hotel_Discounts**. Save the file with the name Lastname_Firstname_e01_ps1_Hotel_Discounts replacing Lastname and Firstname with your own name.

b. Click the **Documentation worksheet tab**, click cell **A3**, and then press Ctrl+; to enter today's date. Click cell B3, type your Lastname, Firstname, click cell **C3**, and then type Formatting Problem_Solve_1 worksheet.

c. Type Problem_Solve_1 in cell **B16**, and then type your Lastname, Firstname into cell **B17**. Enter today's date into cell **B18**. Enter a descriptive sentence or two that accurately reflect the activities in this exercise.

d. Press Ctrl+HOME, and then click the **Problem_Solve_1 worksheet tab**.

e. Apply the **Title** cell style to cell **A1**. Apply the **Heading 4** cell style to cells **A2**, **A12**, **A24**, and **A41**.

f. Apply the **Heading 3** cell style to cells **A3:G3** and **A7**.

g. Change the font in cells **A4:A5** and **A8:A10** to **Dark Blue, Text 2** and **Bold**.

h. Format the range **B8:G10** as **%** with one decimal place.

i. Format cells **A13:G17** as **Table Style Light 9** with the option **My table has headers** checked. On the **Table Tools Design tab**, check **First Column** in the Table Style Options group. In the Tools group, click **Convert to Range**, and then click **Yes** in response to "Do you want to convert the table to a normal range?"

Convert to Range enables you to apply table formatting for appearance purposes without some of the overhead and restrictions of a table in manipulating data in the range. Of course, you also lose the power of tables for sorting, totals, and so on. Convert to Range should only be used when you are quite certain rows will not be inserted into, or deleted from, the range since the banding of a normal range would be affected.

j. Format cells **A18:G22** as **Table Style Light 9** with **My table has headers** checked. Check **First Column**, and then convert the table to a normal range.

k. Format cells **A25:H31** as **Table Style Medium 2** with **My table has headers**. Check **First Column** and **Last Column**, and then convert the table to a normal range.

l. Format cells **A33:H39** as **Table Style Medium 2** with **My table has headers**. Check **First Column** and **Last Column**, and then convert the table to a normal range.

m. Format cells **A42:H46** as **Table Style Medium 2** with **My table has headers.** Check **First Column** and **Last Column**, and then convert the table to a normal range.

n. Format cells **B26:G29**, **B34:G37**, and **B43:G45** as **Number** as follows: **(1,234.00)**. Negative numbers should **not** be displayed in red. **2 decimal places** and **Use 1000 Separator (,)** should be checked.

o. Format cells **B30:H31**, **H26:H29**, **B38:H39**, **H34:H37**, **B46:H46**, and **H43:H45** as Accounting.

p. In cell **B26** enter a formula to multiply the total number of One Double rooms rented on Friday by the Standard Rate for a One Double room. Click **AutoSum**, and then select the cell range **B14:B17**. Edit the formula to multiply the SUM() function by the Standard Rate for a One Double room. Copy the formula to cell range **C26:G26**.

q. Calculate the discount total for the Paradise Club for each room type for Friday night in cell **B27**. Enter a formula to multiply the number of Paradise Club One Double rooms rented on Friday by the Standard Rate for a One Double room by the Paradise Club discount. The result will be a negative number to reflect the discount total. Copy the formula to cell range **C27:G27**.

r. Calculate the following:
   - Group discount total for each room type for Friday night in cell range **B28:G28**
   - Comp discount total for each room type for Friday night in cell range **B29:G29**
   - Gross Sales for One Double rooms for Saturday night in cell range **B34:G34**
   - Paradise Club discount total for all room types for Saturday night in cell range **B35:G35**
   - Group discount total for all rooms for Saturday night in cell range **B36:G36**
   - Comp discount total for all rooms for Saturday night in cell range **B37:G37**

s. Calculate the Paradise Club discounts for Friday and Saturday night for One Double rooms in cell **B43**, and then copy the formula to cell range **B43:G45**—be sure not to copy over any formatting.

t. In cell **H26**, calculate the Total Gross Sales using **AutoSum**. Copy the formula in cell **H26** to cell ranges **H27:H29**, **H34:H37**, and **H43:H45**—be sure to copy and paste **Formulas** only so the table formatting is not disturbed.

u. In cell **B30**, use **AutoSum** to calculate Net Sales, the sum of Gross Sales, and all discounts for One Double rooms on Friday. Copy the formula to cell range **C30:H30**—be sure not to copy over any formatting.

v. In cell **B31**, calculate Total Discounts for Friday for One Double rooms by subtracting Gross Sales from Net Sales. Copy the formula to cell range **C31:H31**—be sure not to copy over any formatting.

w. Copy the formulas in cell range **B30:H31** to cell range **B38:H39**.

x. Calculate the total discounts for One Double rooms for the weekend by using **AutoSum** in cell **B46**. Copy the formula to cell range **C46:H46**—be sure not to copy over any formatting.

y. Bold cell ranges **B31:G31**, **B39:G39**, and **B46:G46**. Apply **AutoFit Column Width** for columns **A:H**, and then insert **File Name** into the **Left section** of the **Custom Footer**.

z. Press ⌐Ctrl¬+⌐Home¬, click **Save**, and then close **Excel**.

Problem Solve 2

Student data file needed: **You will save your file as:**

e01_ps2_Room_Service_Analysis   Lastname_Firstname_e01_ps2_Room_Service_Analysis

Room Service Charges Analysis

The Painted Paradise Resort and Spa offers an extensive array of food and drink available for delivery to guests' rooms. For the convenience of in-room delivery, guests pay a premium price for the service. Recently, the resort has asked representatives from both the hotel and the restaurants to start tracking the charges by room type and day of the week. From this information, management hopes to determine what menu items are being ordered and which types of guests are ordering.

a. Start **Excel,** and then open **e01_ps2_Room_Service**. Save the file with the name Lastname_Firstname_e01_ps2_Room_Service replacing Lastname_Firstname with your own name.

b. Click the **Documentation worksheet tab**, click cell **A3**, and then press ⌐Ctrl¬+⌐:¬ to enter today's date. Click cell **B3**, type your Lastname, Firstname, click cell **C3**, and then type Formatting Problem_Solve_2 worksheet.

c. Type Problem_Solve_2 in cell **B16**, type your Lastname, Firstname into cell **B17**, and then enter today's date into cell **B18**. Enter a descriptive sentence or two that accurately reflect the activities in this exercise.

d. Press ⌐Ctrl¬+⌐Home¬, and then click the **Problem_Solve_2 worksheet tab**.

e. Merge across, but do not center, cell range **B4:C4**, and then apply the **Comma Style (,)** number style to cell range **B7:H20**.

f. Format cell ranges **A4:A23** and **B6:H6** as **Bold** and **Align Text Right**. Select cell ranges **A7:A23** and **B6:H6**, and then set the Fill Color to **White, Background 1, Darker 15%**. Click cell **A6**, and then set the Fill Color to **White, Background 1, Darker 25%**.

g. Place a **hard return** between **Grand** and **Villa** in cell **G6** (remember to remove the space between the two words).

h. Set the width of **column A** using **AutoFit Column Width**. Set the column width to 12 for columns **B:H**.

i. Calculate the total room service charges for One Double rooms for the week in cell **B14**. Copy the function to cells **C14:G14**.

j. Calculate the average room service charges for One Double rooms for the week in cell **B15**. Copy the function to cells **C15:G15**. Be careful not to include the total room service charges in the average calculation.

k. Calculate the minimum room service charges for One Double rooms for the week in cell **B16**. Copy the function to cell range **C16:G16**.

l. Calculate the maximum room service charges for One Double rooms for the week in cell **B17**. Copy the function to cell range **C17:G17**.

m. Calculate the total room service charges for Sunday in cell **H7**, copy the function to cell range **H8:H22**, and then delete the function from cells **H18** and **H21**. Change the number of decimal places in cell **H22** to 0.

n. Click cell **I19**, type <-Total press Ctrl+Enter, apply **Bold**, and then copy it into cell **I20**.

o. Change the Fill Color in cell range **H19:I19** to **White, Background 1, Darker 15%**. Change the Fill Color in cell range **H20:I20** to **White, Background 1, Darker 25%**.

p. Calculate the average individual sale in cell **B23**, and then select cell **B23**. Divide the total sales for the week by the number of rooms and the number of days in a week. Copy the formula to cell range **C23:H23**.

q. Select cell range **B7:B15**. Use **Conditional Formatting** to apply Bold if a cell value is greater than or equal to the daily target for One Double rooms—use **Highlight Cells Rules**, **More Rules**, and then click **Format only cells that contain**.

r. Repeat step q for cell ranges **C7:C15**, **D7:D15**, **E7:E15**, **F7:F15**, **G7:G15**, and **H7:H15**. Make sure the cell values in each column are compared to the daily target for that column (row 19).

s. Clear conditional formatting from cell range **B14:H14**. Apply the **Total** built-in cell style to cell range **A14:H14**, and then apply **Accounting Number Format** to cell ranges **B14:H17**, **H7:H13**, and **B23:H23**.

t. Apply **Solid Fill Green Data Bars** to cell range **B14:H14**, and then apply **Solid Fill Green Data Bars** to cell range **H7:H14**.

u. Use **Conditional Formatting** to put a gold star in cell **H14** if the total room service charges for the week meet or exceed the total Weekly Target. If any cells contain a string of number signs (#), select the column, and then **AutoFit Column Width**.

v. Change the font in cell **A1** to **Arial Black**, and then make the text color **Dark Red**.

w. **Insert File Name** into the left section of the **Custom Footer** in the **Print Titles**.

x. Click **Save**, and then close **Excel**.

Problem Solve 3

Student data file needed:

e01_ps3_Housekeeping_Analysis

You will save your file as:

Lastname_Firstname_e01_ps3_Housekeeping_Analysis

Housekeeping Staff Performance

The Painted Paradise Resort and Spa takes great pride in the efficiency of its housekeeping staff. The housekeeping staff at the Painted Paradise Resort and Spa is expected to properly clean a hotel room in an average of 25 minutes and never more than 30 minutes. Management is interested in how long it takes to actually begin cleaning rooms after guests check out. This is referred to as lag time—time when a room cannot be rented. The Painted Paradise Resort and Spa wants guests to be able to check in early at no charge as long as there is a room available. By keeping lag time to a minimum, room availability is maximized.

a. Start **Excel**, and then open **e01_ps3_Housekeeping_Analysis**.

b. Save the file as Lastname_Firstname_e01_ps3_Housekeeping_Analysis replacing Lastname_Firstname with your own name.

c. Click the **Documentation worksheet tab**, click cell **A3**, and then press Ctrl+; to enter today's date. Click cell **B3**, type your Lastname, Firstname, click cell **C3**, and then type Formatting Problem_Solve_3 worksheet.

d. Type Problem_Solve_3 in cell **B16**, and then type your Lastname, Firstname into cell **B17**. Enter today's date into cell **B18**. Enter a descriptive sentence or two that accurately reflect the activities in this exercise.

e. Press Ctrl + HOME , and then click the **Problem_Solve_3 worksheet tab**.

f. Apply **Merge & Center** to cell ranges **A24:B24**, **A25:B25**, **A26:B26**, **A27:B27**, **A29:B29**, **C22:D22**, and **E22:F22**.

g. In cell range **C8:F8**, replace the hyphen and any surrounding spaces with a hard return. In cell **B8**, replace the space between **Checkout** and **Time** with a hard return.

h. Apply **AutoFit Column Width** in columns **A:H**.

i. Apply **Merge & Center** in cell range **B7:D7**, and then apply **AutoFit Column Width** to column **B**.

j. Apply **Align Text Right** to cell ranges **A3:A5**, **E3:E4**, **A24:A29**, **C23:F23** and cells **A8**, **C3**, and **H8**.

k. Center-align cell ranges **B8:F8**.

l. Apply the **20% Accent1** cell style to cells **A2**, **B7**, and **C22**. Apply the **40% Accent1** cell style to cell **E22**.

m. Apply the **Heading 2** cell style to cell **A2**. Apply the **Heading 3** cell style to cell range **A8:H8** and cells **B7**, **C22**, and **E22**. Apply the **Heading 4** cell style to cell ranges **A3:A5**, **E3:E4**, **A24:A29**, and cell **C3**.

n. Adjust the **Column Width** for the following columns:
   - Column **A** to **18**
   - Columns **B:F** to **12**
   - Column **H** to **10**

o. Calculate the following:
   - Room Clean Lag Time in cell **E9** by subtracting the Checkout Time from the Room Clean Start Time. Copy the formula you just created to cell range **E10:E20**.
     Notice that the cells that contain formulas that subtract one time value from another time value are automatically formatted as time values.
   - Room Clean Duration in cell **F9** by subtracting the Room Clean Start Time from the Room Clean End Time. Copy the formula you just created to cell range **F10:F20**.
   - Total Room Cleaning Time—Lag in cell **D24** by summing all individual Room Clean Lag Time.
   - Total Room Cleaning Time—Duration in cell **F24** by summing all individual Room Clean Duration.

p. Calculate the following:
   - Average Room Cleaning Time—Lag and Duration in cells **D25** and **F25**, respectively
   - Minimum Room Cleaning Time—Lag and Duration in cells **D26** and **F26**, respectively
   - Maximum Room Cleaning Time—Lag and Duration in cells **D27** and **F27**, respectively

q. Calculate the number of Maintenance Issues Reported in cell **C29**. Format cell **C29** as **Number** with zero decimal places.

r. Apply **Conditional Formatting** to the cell range **E9:E20** so Room Clean Lag Times that are greater than the Allowed Average Room Clean Time Lag displays cell values in **Red Text**.

s. Apply **Conditional Formatting** to the cell range **F9:F20** so Room Clean Durations that are greater than the Allowed Average Room Clean Time Duration displays cell values in **Red Text**.

t. Apply **Conditional Formatting** to change the font color in the following:
- Cell **D24** to **Red Text** if the value in D24 > the value in cell C24
- Cell **D25** to **Red Text** if the value in D25 > the value in cell C25
- Cell **D26** to **Red Text** if the value in D26 > the value in cell C26
- Cell **D27** to **Red Text** if the value in D27 > the value in cell C27
- Cell **F24** to **Red Text** if the value in F24 > the value in cell E24
- Cell **F25** to **Red Text** if the value in F25 > the value in cell E25
- Cell **F26** to **Red Text** if the value in F26 > the value in cell E26
- Cell **F27** to **Red Text** if the value in F27 > the value in cell E27

u. Format the cell ranges **E9:F20**, **D24:D27**, **F9:F20** and **F24:F27** with a Green font color.

In earlier exercises you have also applied Conditional Formatting to display the opposite in green, meaning if D24 < C24 then display D24 in red text; the opposite is that if D24 >= C24 then display D24 with a green font. By formatting all the cells in the conditionally formatted ranges with a green font, you accomplish the same result, but you only have to apply Conditional Formatting once, rather than twice.

v. Apply the **Foundry** workbook theme.

w. **Insert File Name** in the left section of the Custom Footer.

x. Press Ctrl + Home, click **Save**, and then close **Excel**.

Perform 1: Perform in Your Life

Student data file needed:	You will save your file as:
Blank Excel document	Lastname_Firstname_e01_pf1_Grade_Analysis

Grade Analysis

Most students are concerned about grades and want to have some means of easily tracking grades, analyzing performance, and calculating the current grade (as much as is possible) in every class.

a. Start **Excel**, and then open a blank document. Save the file as Lastname_Firstname_e01_pf1_Grade_Analysis replacing Lastname_Firstname with your own name.

b. Look in your syllabus or ask your instructor for the grading scale in this course. Your grading scale may also be given by points rather than percentage. Enter the grading scale into Excel under a title for each course.

c. Look in your syllabus for a list of assignments, exams, and other point-earning activities. Enter the assignments into Excel. For completed assignments, enter the points possible and your score. Be sure to label all data items.

d. Calculate the percentage score for each point-earning activity, and then use conditional formatting to indicate whether you received an A, B, C, or below a C on each assignment.

e. Calculate the possible points earned to date and total points earned to date in the class.

f. Calculate the current overall percentage earned in the class.

g. Calculate the percentage you need to earn on the final examination to achieve an A, B, and C given the points possible to date and points earned to date.

h. Conditionally format the percentage required to achieve an A in the course to visually indicate how hard you may have to study for the final examination.

For example, if you will have to score at least an 80% on the final examination to achieve an A in this course, color the cell that contains the points required to achieve an *A* red to show that you have to study pretty hard for the final examination. Use other colors to indicate whether or not you must score less than 80% or less than 70% on the final examination to achieve an A in the course. Use parameters to identify the cutoff values for A, B and C.

i. Repeat Step h for the percentage required to achieve a *B* in the course.

j. Repeat Step h for the percentage required to achieve a *C* in the course.

k. Also add conditional formatting to visually indicate if an *A* is not possible because the percentage required on the final examination to achieve an *A* exceeds 100%.

l. Repeat Step k for the percentage required on the final examination to achieve a *B* in the course.

m. Repeat Step k for the percentage required on the final examination to achieve a *C* in the course.

n. Ask your instructor whether to include any other courses you are currently taking.

o. Insert the filename in the left Custom Footer section of the Print Titles on all worksheets in the workbook.

p. Press Ctrl + HOME , save and close your file, and exit Excel.

Perform 2: Perform in Your Career

Student data file needed:	You will save your file as:
Blank Excel document	Lastname_Firstname_e01_pf2_Time_Tracking

Personal Time Tracking

You have started working as a computer programmer with BetaWerks Software Corporation. The company requires you to track the time that you spend doing different things during the day each week. This helps the company determine how many of your hours are billable to customers. You have several different projects to work on as well as a few training sessions throughout the week. The company pays for one 15-minute coffee break and one 30-minute lunch each day. Any additional time is considered personal time.

a. Start **Excel**, and then open a blank Excel document. Save the file as Lastname_Firstname_ e01_pf2_Time_Tracking replacing Lastname_Firstname with your own name.

b. Create a spreadsheet to track your time for the company this week. The following requirements must be met:

- Your time must be broken down by project/client and weekdays.
- Time not billable to a project should be classified as Unbillable.
- Unbillable time should be broken into at least two categories: Breaks and Work.

c. Set up your worksheet so you can easily calculate the amount of time you spent working on each account, in meetings, in training, and on breaks according to the information below:

- Monday, you spent two hours in a meeting with your development team. This is billable to the BetaWerks Software company as unbillable hours. Following the meeting, you took a 20 minute coffee break. After your break, you spent two hours and 15 minutes working on your project for the Garske Advising. After an one-hour lunch, you attended a two-hour training and development meeting. Before heading home for the day, you spent two hours working on the United National Distributors (UND) project.

- Tuesday morning you spent four hours on the Klemisch Kompany project. To help break up the morning, you took a 20-minute coffee break at 10:00. You only had time for a 30-minute lunch because you had to get back to the office for a team-building activity. The activity lasted 40 minutes. To finish the day, you spent a solid four hours working on the Garske Advising assignment.

- Wednesday morning, you spent two hours each on the Garske Advising and Klemisch Kompany projects. Lunch was a quick 30 minutes because you had a conference call with Mr. Atkinson from UND at 1 p.m. The conference call took one hour, and then you spent an additional three hours working on the project.

- Thursday, the day started with a 30-minute update with your supervisor. Following the meeting, you were able to spend two hours on the UND project. After a 15-minute coffee break, you started on a new project for K&M Worldwide for 90 minutes. You took a 45-minute lunch break, and then spent two and a half hours on the Klemisch Kompany project and two hours on your work for L&H United.

- Friday started with a two-hour training and development session about a new software package that BetaWerks is starting to implement, followed by a 15-minute coffee break. After your coffee break, you were able to squeeze in two more hours for L&H United before taking a one-hour lunch. After lunch, you put in four hours on the Klemisch Kompany project before finally going home for the week.

d. BetaWerks bills your time spent on each account according to the following rates:

Klemisch Kompany	$250
Garske Advising	$250
United National Distributors	$175
K&M Worldwide	$150
L&H United	$200

e. Your salary is $100,000/year with benefits. Given two weeks of vacation, you cost BetaWorks $2,000 in salary and benefits/week.

f. Include in your worksheet a calculation of your profit/loss to BetaWorks for the week.

g. Be sure to document your worksheet using a documentation worksheet, comments, and instructions.

h. Insert the filename in the left custom footer section of the print titles footer.

i. Press Ctrl+Home, save your file, and then exit Excel.

Perform 3: Perform in Your Career

Student data file needed:

Blank Excel document

You will save your file as:

Lastname_Firstname_e01_pf3_Check_Register

Check Register

You volunteer your time with a local nonprofit, the Mayville Community Theatre. Because of your business background, the board of directors has asked you to serve as the new treasurer and to track all of the monetary transactions for the group.

a. Start **Excel**, and then open a blank document. Save the file as Lastname_Firstname_e01_ pf3_Check_Register replacing Lastname and Firstname with your own name.

b. Create a spreadsheet to track receipts and expenditures that should be assigned to one of the following categories: Costumes, Marketing, Operating and Maintenance, Scripts and Royalties, and Set Construction. Also track the following for each receipt or expenditure: the date, amount of payment, check/reference number, recipient, and item description.

c. Enter the following receipts and expenditures under the appropriate category.

d. Periodically, money is deposited into the checking account. Include a way to track deposits.

e. Finally, include a running balance. This should be updated any time money is deposited or withdrawn from the account.

Date	Item	Paid To	Check or Ref. #	Amount
11/1/2013	Starting Balance	N/A		$1793.08
11/2/2013	Royalties for "The Cubicle"	Office Publishing Company	9520	-$300.00
11/2/2013	Scripts for "The Cubicle"	Office Publishing Company	9521	-$200.00
11/5/2013	Building Maintenance—Ticket Office	Fix It Palace	9522	-$187.92
11/8/2013	Patron Donation	N/A	53339	$1,000.00
11/12/2013	Costumes for "The Cubicle"	Jane's Fabrics	9523	-$300.00
11/22/2013	Building Materials for set construction of "The Cubicle"	Fix It Palace	9524	-$430.00
11/30/2013	TV and Radio ads for "The Cubicle"	AdSpace	9525	-$229.18
11/30/2013	General Theater Operating Expenses—November	The Electric Co-op, City Water Works	9526	-$149.98
12/15/2013	Ticket Revenue from "The Cubicle"	N/A	59431	$1,115.50
12/30/2013	General Theater Operating Expenses—December	The Electric Co-op, City Water Works	9527	-$195.13

f. If the running account balance drops below $1,000 there should be a conditional formatting alert for any balance figure below the threshold.

g. Document the check register using a documentation worksheet, explicit instructions, and comments where helpful.

h. Insert the filename in the left custom footer section of the print titles footer on all worksheets in the workbook.

i. Press Ctrl+Home, save your file, and then exit Excel.

Student data file needed:

e01_pf4_Project_Billing

You will save your file as:

Lastname_Firstname_e01_pf4_Project_Billing

Project Management Billing

John Smith works with you at The Excellent Consulting Company. Each week, consultants are required to track how much time they spend on each project. A spreadsheet is used to track the date, start time, end time, project code, a description of work performed, and the number of billable hours completed. At the bottom of the spreadsheet, the hours spent on each project are summarized so clients can be billed. In your role as an internal auditor, you have been asked to double-check a tracking sheet each week. By random selection, Mr. Smith's tracking worksheet needs to be checked this week. Make sure his numbers are accurate, and ensure that his spreadsheet is set up to minimize errors. His worksheet is also badly in need of some formatting for appearance and clarity, and it is completely lacking in documentation.

a. Start **Excel**, and then open **e01_pf4_Project_Billing**. Save the file as Lastname_Firstname_e01_pf4_Project_Billing replacing Lastname_Firstname with your own name.

b. Make sure all calculated figures are correct—if you subtract Start Time from End Time and multiply the difference by 24, the result is the number of hours between the two times. Do the Client Totals look correct to you? What about the total hours for the week?

c. What formatting changes would make the worksheet more attractive?

d. Are there formatting changes that would make the worksheet easier to understand and to use?

e. Add documentation.

f. Insert the filename in the left custom footer section of the print titles footer on all worksheets in the workbook.

g. Press Ctrl + Home , save your file, and exit Excel.

WORKSHOP 3

Objectives

1. Reference cells within formulas or functions.   p. 142

2. Create, modify, and use named ranges within formulas or functions.   p. 149

3. Understand the syntax of a function.   p. 154

4. Introduce common function categories.   p. 157

Conducting Excel Analysis Through Functions and Charts

PREPARE CASE
Massage Table Analysis

The Turquoise Oasis Spa currently has a set of two massage tables. Irene, the spa manager, is considering purchasing more tables. Before any decision can be made, an analysis of existing data is needed pertaining to maintenance costs, including the replacement of the thermostats that control the heating unit on the massage tables. Irene has given you the task of completing a spreadsheet started by another staff member. This spreadsheet will be used to order replacement parts and track maintenance of the massage tables as well as evaluate purchase decisions.

Courtesy of www.Shutterstock.com

Student data file needed for this workshop:

 e02_ws03_Spa_Equipment

You will save your file as:

 Lastname_Firstname_e02_ws03_Spa_Equipment

Cell References and Formula Basics

The value of Excel expands as you move from using the spreadsheet for displaying data to analyzing data in order to make informed decisions. As the complexity of a spreadsheet increases, techniques that promote effective and efficient development of the spreadsheet become of utmost importance. Integrating cell references within formulas and working with functions are common methods used in developing effective spreadsheets. These skills will become the foundation for more advanced skills.

A **cell reference** is used when you refer to a particular cell or range of cells within a formula or function instead of a value. When a formula is created, you can simply use values, like =5*5. However, Excel formulas typically refer to a cell or range of cells, like =B4*C4, where cells B4 and C4 contain values to be used in the calculation. The formula now references a cell rather than a value, which is preferable as it improves efficiency should cell data change over time.

Importantly, anyone who uses the spreadsheet can easily view and change the value in the referenced cell. Every time you change the value within a referenced cell, the formula computes a new result. Changing the value in a cell is easier than editing the formula every time a value needs to be changed. Additionally, you can reference the same cell in multiple formulas or functions. Thus, changing the value once in a cell is superior to changing the value multiple times in every formula that uses that value. Cell referencing increases a spreadsheet's flexibility.

There is also another level of cell referencing which Excel uses to offer built-in intelligence for moving or copying formulas to other cell locations within a spreadsheet or workbook. By default, cells are referenced in formulas in a relative manner, where directions for locating the cell are *relative* to where the formula is placed. For instance, the cell referenced is viewed as being two cells to the right and three cells below the cell containing the formula. When you copy the formula to many cells, that reference will remain relative to where the formula resides.

Conversely, there may be circumstances in which you want a cell reference to remain stationary when a formula is copied to other cells. You do not want the reference to be copied or moved *relative* to the original formula location but rather in an *absolute* manner. In this situation, an absolute location is indicated in the formula so the cell reference does not change as the formula is copied to other cells. It does not matter where the formula is placed, it will continually reference the same absolute referenced cell location.

Real World Advice — Hard-Coding Data within a Spreadsheet

Some users always use numbers in their formulas. Including actual data in a formula, like =5*25, is known as **hard-coding** the values. Hard-coding decreases the ability to easily update data in the spreadsheet and adapt to change. When developing a spreadsheet, build in flexibility and include cells with data and then reference those cells.

To calculate a monthly payment, the loan amount, loan period, and interest rate are required. If the loan amount needs to be changed, it is intuitive to change it in cell B2. For example, the user may want to change from 10,000 to 20,000 and would simply change it in cell B2. However, because the 10,000 was hard-coded within the formula, you would also need to change it within the formula before the answer would be correct. The model shows a loan amount for 20,000, but the answer is still calculated for a loan of 10,000 as shown in Figure 1. Hard-coding means you must understand the formula and be able to modify it.

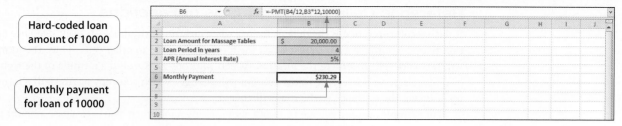

Figure 1 Hard-coding a formula

As you change the loan amount, the number of years, or interest rate in cells B2, B3, and B4 respectively, the formula automatically recalculates the solution. When the loan is changed in B2 from 10,000 to 20,000 the monthly payment is automatically calculated in B6 as shown in Figure 2. That is, you do not have to change the formula. This approach makes it easier to change the values and thus is more flexible.

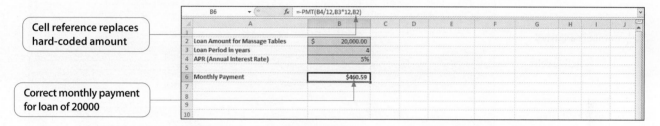

Figure 2 Cell referencing in formula

Not only is it easier to distinguish between data and formulas for editing data, using *relative* versus *absolute* cell referencing allows you to quickly replicate formulas. There is no need to create each formula individually. For example, if a spreadsheet needs to list the prices, you can calculate the total price by multiplying quantity and price. Rather than creating a formula multiple times, with relative cell referencing you can create just one formula, then use AutoFill to copy the formula. Excel automatically adjusts the cell references to use the correct cells for the calculation of each product. Figure 3 shows how the formula is automatically adjusted to reference the two cells to the left of the formula after the formula in E5 has been AutoFilled down through E16.

	A	B	C	D	E	F	G
				Order Date		Estimated Arrival	
2							
3	PURCHASE ORDER						
4	Item	Unit #	Quantity	Unit Price	Price	Shipping	Tax
5	Thermostat	HD504	3	145.95	=C5*D5		
6	Thermostat	HD704	1	185	=C6*D6		
7	Heating Unit	CR3300	2	43.25	=C7*D7		
8	Heating Unit	XR3500	3	34	=C8*D8		
9					=C9*D9		
10					=C10*D10		
11					=C11*D11		
12					=C12*D12		
13					=C13*D13		
14					=C14*D14		
15					=C15*D15		
16					=C16*D16		
17	TOTALS						
18							

Figure 3 AutoFill to copy

There are three ways in which a cell can be referenced. Mastering cell reference techniques allows you to increase the speed of development of your worksheet. The three ways cells can be referenced in formulas or functions are relative, absolute, and mixed.

Reference Cells within Formulas or Functions

Relative cell reference is the default format when creating formulas with a cell reference position that will automatically adjust when the formula is copied to other cells. Thus, the formula will reference cells *relative* to the location. When you copy or AutoFill a formula to the right or left, the relative cell reference to the column will change. When you copy or AutoFill a formula up or down, the reference to the row will change.

For example, assume you are thinking about taking a job where you earn a base amount plus commission on sales. When you start, you earn 10% of sales in addition to your base pay. You have the potential of increasing your commission rate to 15%, 20%, and 25% as you get more experience. Additionally, you have been told that $1,000 in sales is a conservative estimate, an average is $2,000, and $3,000 is really good. You want to see the potential for how much you can make in a week given these numbers. Figure 4 shows the percentages you can earn and three estimates of projected sales. The formula entered in cell B5 was AutoFilled down and to the right to show what happens to the cells referenced when they are all relative.

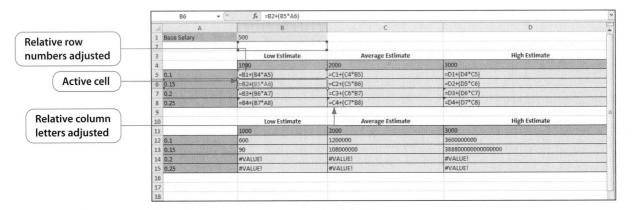

Figure 4 AutoFill with incorrect cell reference

Notice the cell reference, B1, in the formula changed to B2, B3, and so forth as the formula was AutoFilled downward. Because the formula was only moving down rows, row numbers were adjusted in a relative manner. When it was copied to the right, the B1 changed to a C1 and D1. The formula was being moved across columns and remaining in the same row, so only column letters were adjusted in a relative manner. As the formula was copied to other cells, the relative cell addresses also adjusted, relative to the new location of the formula. In this example, the B1 cell in the formula should stay as B1 regardless of where the formula is copied.

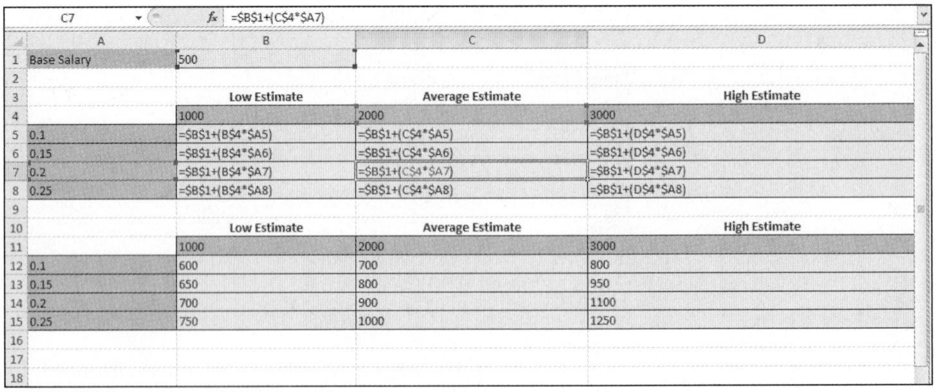

Figure 5 AutoFill with correct cell reference

In Figure 5, starting with the formula in cell B5, the cells referenced have dollar signs ($) entered in the formula in B5. A dollar symbol in front of both column and row creates an absolute cell reference to ensure the cell reference location will not change. Placing a dollar symbol in front of only a row number or only the column letter creates a mixed reference to ensure the respective row reference or column reference will not change. The formula in cell B5 was then AutoFilled down, and the column of formulas—column B—were AutoFilled to the right. Now, you should be able to see that cell B1, which is referenced as an absolute value using $B$1, continues to reference B1. It doesn't move relative to the formula but stays absolutely where it is referenced. Additionally, the $A5 reference in the formula in cell B5 is relative so the 5 changes to a 6, 7, and 8 as the formula is AutoFilled down. The B4 reference in the formula, shown as B$4 in cell B5, is relative so it changes to C and D as the formula is AutoFilled to the right.

The results of the relative references are shown in the second table of Figure 4 so you can see the formulas in B5:D8 and the corresponding formula results in B12:D15. The formulas currently used in B5:D8 result in monthly payments that grow exponentially with some value errors because the formula in B5 was copied to the rest of the range with relative cell references. Some of the cells in the formulas refer to an empty cell reference or a cell with formulas, which result in the #VALUE! math error as shown in Figure 4. The same table has been altered to make some of the references absolute and some relative so the formula correctly references cells after the formula has been copied from B5 to the cell range of B5:D8 as shown in Figure 5.

To Work with Relative Cell Referencing

a. Click the **Start** button ⊙. From the Start Menu, locate and then start **Microsoft Excel 2010**.

b. Click the **File tab**, and then click **Open**.

c. In the Open dialog box, click the disk drive in the left pane where your student data files are located, navigate through the folder structure, click **e02_ws03_Spa_Equipment**, and then click **Open**.

d. Click the **Documentation worksheet tab**, click cell **A6**, and then enter the current date in mm/dd/yyyy format. Press Tab.

e. In cell **B6**, type your first name and last name, and then press Tab.

f. In cell **C6**, type Continuing to develop file, and then press Tab.

g. In cell **D6**, type e02_ws03_Spa_Equipment, and then press Enter.

h. Click the **File tab**, and then click **Save As** 🖫. The Save As dialog box will appear.

i. In the Save As dialog box, navigate to the location where you are saving your files. In the File name box, type Lastname_Firstname_e02_ws03_Spa_Equipment, replacing Lastname and Firstname with your own name, and then click **Save**.

j. Click the **Insert tab**, and then click **Header & Footer** in the Text group to insert a footer with the filename. Click the **Design tab**, and then click **Go to Footer** in the Navigation group. If necessary, click on the left section of the footer, and then click **File Name** in the Header & Footer Elements group.

k. Click any cell in the spreadsheet to move out of the footer. Click the **View tab**, and then click **Normal** in the Workbook Views group. Press Ctrl + Home.

l. Click the **Thermostats worksheet tab**.

Notice the worksheet is in Page Layout view so you can see what the layout will be on the printed order form. As you work on the report you will want to ensure everything fits on one page.

m. Click cell **E5**, type =C5*D5, and then press Enter.

The active cell moves to E6 and Excel displays a price value for the HD504 thermostat in cell E5. A similar formula needs to be created for all of the remaining thermostats. While this could be done individually, just like you did in cell E5, Excel allows you to extend the formula to the necessary cells since relative cell referencing will work in addressing the Price column.

n. Click cell **E5**, click the **AutoFill handle** in the lower-right corner of the cell, and then drag down to copy the formula down to cell **E16**.

Troubleshooting

The AutoFill handle is in the lower-right corner of the active cell or range of cells. To select it, hover the mouse pointer over the corner and the pointer will turn to a black plus sign as shown in Figure 6.

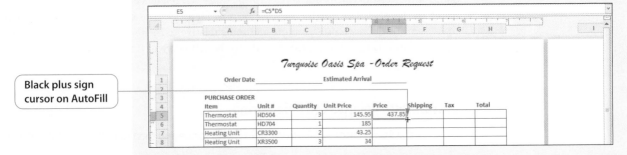

Black plus sign cursor on AutoFill

Figure 6 AutoFill handle

o. Click cell **E16** and notice that the formula has changed to =C16*D16. It is relative to the formula location—multiplying the two cells that are to the immediate left of the formula.

p. Press Ctrl + □ to toggle the Show Formulas feature on. Alternatively, click the Formulas tab, and click Show Formulas in the Formula Auditing group.

You should see the formulas displayed on the spreadsheet instead of the results from the formulas. You may need to scroll to the right or left to see all of the columns as they expand in size to accommodate showing the full formulas. **Show Formulas view** is when the cells display the formulas instead of the output, or values.

q. Press Ctrl + □ again to toggle back to Normal view.

r. Click **Save** 🖫.

SIDE NOTE
Super Quick AutoFill
To AutoFill a large data range, you can hover over the bottom-right corner, where the AutoFill handle is located, and double-click. Excel will attempt to offer the desired result and copy the formula to the bottom of the data set.

Real World Advice   The Cost Benefit of Documentation

Irene already started the spreadsheet and has asked you to continue development. There is basic information in the workbook including the project details on the documentation sheet. This is an internal file that few people will see or use, so a lot of detail may not be required.

There are many factors that determine the information required for the documentation on each file, such as your boss, the situation, the number of people working on the project, and who will see the project. In the business world, it is a matter of balance. It would be great to have lots of detail about the spreadsheet, but from a practical viewpoint, the documentation will vary from file to file.

Absolute Cell Reference

Absolute cell references are used when a formula needs to be copied and the reference to one or more cells within the formula should not change as the formula is copied. **Absolute cell reference** refers to the address of a cell, when both the column and row needs to remain constant regardless of the position of the cell when the formula is copied to other cells.

To make a cell reference absolute means to *freeze* the reference so Excel doesn't change the reference when the formula is copied to other cells. Dollar signs within the cell reference are used to let Excel know to keep that reference. For example, a formula, =A1*B4 located in C4 has relative cell referencing. If you need to copy that formula to C5:C10, and you need the formula to continue to refer to cell A1, you would change it to =$A$1*B4. The dollar sign before the A freezes column A and the dollar sign before the 1 freezes row 1. When the formula is copied to cells in any direction, either left, right, up, or down, the formula reference to cell $A$1 will absolutely stay referenced to the exact cell address of $A$1. The relative reference to cell B4 will move in a relative manner as the formula is copied in the direction of left, right, up, or down. To make a reference absolute, the dollar signs need to be before both the column letter and the row number.

To Work with Absolute Cell References

a. Select cell **G5**.

b. Type =E5*$D$29 and then press [Enter].

This will calculate the tax, based on the current tax rate listed in D29. Since the tax rate is the same for all products, the formula needs to be copied to the other items purchased in the list. The reference to the tax rate cell should not change, but the reference to the price of the item in column E should change.

c. Click cell **G5**. Click the **AutoFill handle**, and then extend the formula in G5 down through **G16**.

Notice the formulas in cells G5 through G16 are now identical except the E5 has changed to E6, E7, and so forth. Also, note the numeric results contain more than 2 decimal points in some cells, and less than 2 decimal places in other cells. Since this is currency, the cells need to be formatted to eliminate the extra decimals. This will be adjusted and fixed later in this workshop.

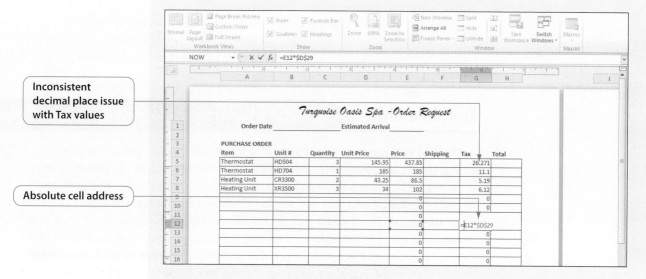

Inconsistent decimal place issue with Tax values

Absolute cell address

Figure 7 Absolute cell reference

Mixed Cell Reference

Mixed cell references within formulas are less common but can be useful in the development of spreadsheets. **Mixed cell reference** refers to referencing a cell within the formula where part of the cell address is preceded by a dollar sign to lock—either the column letter or the row value—as absolute and leaving the other part of the cell as relatively referenced.

Recall that a cell reference is composed of two components, the column and the row reference. Cell B10 is referencing column *B* and row *10*. When you want to make a cell reference totally absolute, you insert a dollar sign in front of the column letter so it will not change when the formula is copied into cells to the left or right. Additionally, you would insert a second dollar sign in front of the row number to make it absolute so it will not change when the formula is copied up or down. When you add one dollar sign, but not the other, you have a mixed reference. If you only want to make the column absolute, you only put a dollar sign in front of the column reference. For example, as you copy $B10 to other cells, the B column would remain unchanged in the formula. The row reference, however, would change relative to where the formula was placed. Likewise, if you referenced a cell as B$10 then column B would change when copied to other cells and row 10 would never change.

If you are creating a spreadsheet and developing a formula that will not be copied elsewhere, relative and absolute cell referencing is not an issue. However, you may have data in a table and need to add a column of formulas beside the data that does calculations on each row, or record. In this case you need to incorporate cell referencing. Thus, when you are developing a spreadsheet, you should consider whether you will need to copy a formula or not. Having established the need to copy a formula, you should also establish where the formula will be copied. Remember, the issue revolves around which cell references need to move as you copy the formula and which should remain constant when copied. This thought process, in considering when to use absolute, relative, or mixed can be broken into four cases.

First, if the formula is not to be copied, using the default of relative cell addressing is the quickest and simplest solution. It really does not matter if you make any of the cell references relative or absolute.

Second, if a formula will be copied only over rows, up or down, the only part of the cell reference that would change is the row number. In this case, it is only necessary to consider whether the row number needs to be relative or absolute. The column would not change. Consequently, it doesn't matter if you make the column letter relative or absolute.

Third, if a formula is only going to be copied sideways, left or right, the only part of the cell reference that would change is the column letter. The row will not change. Thus, it doesn't matter if you make the row relative or absolute.

Finally, if a formula is going to be copied both across rows and columns, you must consider both parts of the cell reference. You must consider whether each cell referenced in the formula needs the row and the column reference to remain constant or move relative to the formula.

Real World Advice — Layout of a Spreadsheet Model

Think of a spreadsheet as a report. In a report you have an executive summary first that is supported with your details. On a spreadsheet, it can be useful to have a section along the top that has the summary data and any text that will guide the user. Along with the summary data you can include the inputs you need for the model. These would include any values, like a tax rate or credit limit that would be used in calculations. Then, put the data set below the summary or, if necessary, on another sheet. This makes it easy for any user to see the summary data first, at the top of a spreadsheet, then, look for supporting data, analysis, and details as needed.

If you need to verify the formula has the correct relative and absolute referencing after it has been copied or moved into other cells within the spreadsheet, a quick and easy verification is to examine one of the cells in edit mode. Best practice dictates following these steps:

1. Double-click a cell containing the formula to enter edit mode.

2. In edit mode, notice the color-coded borders around cells match the cell address references in the formula. Using the color-coding as a guide, verify that the cell(s) are referenced correctly.

3. If the referencing is incorrect, notice which cells are not referenced correctly.

4. Exit out of edit mode by pressing Esc and returning to the original formula.

5. Edit the cell references, and then copy or AutoFill the corrected formula again.

6. Always recheck the formula again to see if your correction worked when copied into other cells or cell ranges.

Repeat this process as needed. Instead of typing the dollar signs within your cell references, F4 is a handy toggle to use. If the insertion point is placed within a cell reference in your formula, press F4 one time and Excel will insert dollar signs in front of both the row reference and column reference. If you press F4 again, Excel places a dollar sign in front of the row number only. Press F4 as needed to toggle through the remaining variations.

Quick Reference · Using the F4 Key Toggle

1. Press F4 one time to place a $ in front of both the column and row value.
2. Press F4 a second time to place a $ in front of the row value only.
3. Press F4 a third time to place a $ in front of the column value only.
4. Press F4 a fourth time to remove all $ characters.
5. Press F4 a fifth time to start the sequence again.

For the comfort of the spa's customers, the massage tables have heating components with thermostats to adjust the temperature. The usage and energy costs need to be tracked. This allows the company to determine the true costs for running the business and ensure the business is generating revenue. Irene has requested the model be set to show 30 days so the model can easily be verified. Later it can be scaled to handle the normal life of a thermostat. Because of this, she wants you to use cell referencing as you create formulas in the model.

Real World Advice · Building for Scalability

When you develop a spreadsheet you should consider scalability and accuracy. A good spreadsheet model allows the user to add more data as needed. If you are making a spreadsheet to track your sales staff, you need to consider how many sales staff you may have in the future.

Instead of assuming current conditions will never change, your spreadsheet should be built to accommodate growth. You need to consider a reasonable growth of sales people so you do not have to change the spreadsheet layout and formulas every time the number of sales staff changes. It may make sense, given the size of the company and growth potential, to build in the ability to have up to 10 staff.

While developing the model, use hypothetical data so you can see how the model will look when it has real data. Work on a small scale so you can work out the kinks. It is much easier to see, check, and modify a model that uses 30 records than one that uses 1,000 records.

To Work with Mixed Cell Referencing

a. Click the **Table_Life worksheet tab**, and then click cell **C18**.

b. Type =B18*B9, which is the Usage (minutes) times Energy cost per minute. Press Enter.

   Notice that cell B18 does not need any dollar signs. You will need to AutoFill the formula down. The row will change, thus, you need to evaluate the row references in the formula. The B18 cell reference has a row reference of 18, and as you copy the formula down, the row value 18 will change to a 19, 20, and so on. Thus, that reference is relative, and you will leave it as B18 so it remains as relative.

c. Notice that the reference to cell B9 needs one dollar sign. Select just the **B9** in the formula in cell C18. Press F4 until the B9 changes to B$9. Once it appears as B$9 in the formula, press Enter.

   Since you need to extend the formula down, the row will change. Thus, you need to evaluate the row references in the formula. Cell B9 has a row reference of 9. As you copy the formula down, you need the 9 to stay at a constant value as row 9—that's where the Energy cost per minute resides. Thus, the 9 needs to be frozen. You need to put the $ sign immediately on the left of the 9.

d. Click cell **C18** again. Click the **AutoFill handle**, and then extend the formula in C18 down through **C31**.

e. Double-click cell **C31** to enter edit mode. Following the best practice, verify that the color borders are around B9 and B31.

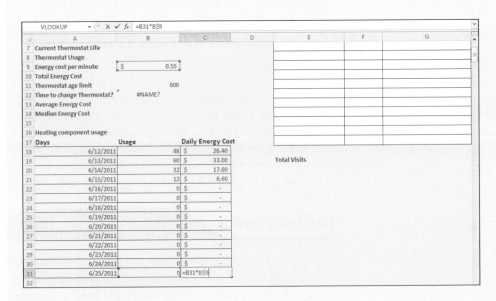

Figure 8 Verify AutoFill

f. Press ESC to exit edit mode.

CONSIDER THIS | **Relative Addresses**

In the exercise, you placed a $ before the 9, but not the B. Would it have been incorrect to place the $ before the B in this particular situation, as in $B$9? Describe a situation where a dollar sign would be optional. Describe a situation where you must use mixed referencing.

Working with Named Ranges

Once you are comfortable working with formulas and cells there is a natural progression to using named ranges and functions. Named ranges are an extension of cell references and provide a quick alternative for commonly used cell references or cell ranges.

Spreadsheet formulas that use cell references such as =C5*C6 may be easy to interpret when simple. However, as the size and complexity of the workbook increases, so does the difficulty and time needed to incorporate cell references in formulas. This is especially the case with workbooks that use multiple worksheets. The use of named ranges enables a developer to quickly develop formulas that make sense.

A **named range** is a set of cells that have been given a name that can then be used within a formula or function. For example, you may not understand =SUM(C4:C20)*B2 until you determine what is in those cells. You can quickly understand the formula if it is written with assigned names you designate. For instance, if you named the range C4:C20 as *Sales* and B2 as *Bonus*, you can write the formula as =SUM(Sales)*Bonus, which is easier to understand.

Creating Named Ranges in the Name Box

Named ranges are easy to create as you develop a spreadsheet. A named range can be either a single cell or a set of cells. Most named ranges are sets of cells used within multiple formulas. The simplest way to name a range is to select the range and use the Name Box to create the name.

You must follow a few rules when naming ranges.

- Names for ranges must start with a letter, an underscore (_), or a backslash (\).

- You should use words that provide meaning. If you have a set of numbers representing sales, then name the range *Sales*.

- Do not use spaces when using multiple words. Either put a hyphen or underscore in lieu of a space, or capitalize the first letter of each word in the phrase to avoid using a space. Thus, *Sales_2012* or *NetSales* are both acceptable and convey meaning.

- Do not use names that are Excel words, like function names or conjunctions. Excel will allow you to name a range SUM. However, a formula such as =SUM(SUM) does not convey meaning. Thus, stay away from AND, COUNT, ROW, and other Excel words. They may confuse you, other users, or possibly Excel.

- Whenever using a combination of letters and numbers, do not use a combination that creates a reference to a cell. In other words, *Sales2012* is acceptable but *S2012* is not. A cell in column S and row 2012 already exists.

To Create a Named Range Using the Name Box

a. Click the **Thermostats worksheet tab**, and then click cell **D29**.

b. Click in the **Name Box**, which is to the left of the formula bar and should currently display **D29**. The text will be highlighted when you click in the Name Box.

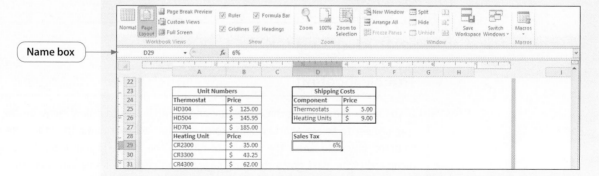

Figure 9 Name box

c. Type **TaxRate** replacing the existing cell name.

d. Press Enter.

The Name Box displays TaxRate instead of the cell address D29. Now that D29 is named TaxRate, you could use the named range instead of using absolute cell referencing in the formulas in cells G5:G16. Excel does not automatically update cell references already existing in formulas.

Name box with named range

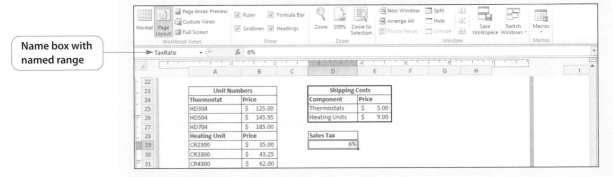

Figure 10 Name Box with named range

e. Click cell **G5**. Notice the formula did not change the $D$29 to TaxRate.

f. Click the **Formulas tab**, click the **Define Name arrow** in the Defined Names group, and then click **Apply Names**. The Apply Names dialog box appears with TaxRate highlighted.

g. Click **OK**. Notice the range of cells G5:G16 now show the TaxRate named range.

With named ranges, you can see the listing of current names by clicking on the Name Box arrow. When there are multiple named ranges, you can select one, and Excel will take you to that range with the range cells selected. This is useful when you want to determine the location of the named range.

h. Click the **Name Box arrow** to see the listing of current named ranges, and then click **Thermostat**.

Notice that the active cell is A24, which is named Thermostat. You will use this named range later as a part of determining the shipping cost in column F.

Figure 11 Name box drop down

Troubleshooting

If you enter the name in the Name Box and then click onto a new range on the spreadsheet to select another range to name, that will not name the range. Be sure to press Enter to finish the process of naming the range. If you name the range incorrectly, you must go to the Formulas tab and click the Name Manager. There, you can delete named ranges or edit and modify them as needed.

Creating Named Ranges from Selections

Using the Name Box is the most convenient method for creating named ranges. This allows for naming ranges as you develop a spreadsheet. At times your worksheet's data will be organized in such a way that the names for your ranges exist in a cell in the form of a heading, either for each row or each column in the data set. Rather than selecting each row or column separately in a time-consuming process, you can use the Create from Selection method.

The Create from Selection method is a process that produces multiple named ranges from the headings in rows, columns, or both, from the data set. The key element is to realize that the names for the ranges need to exist in a cell either above the data range for naming columns, or to the left for naming rows. Most commonly, these names are column headers that make for very convenient names for each column of data.

To Create a Set of Named Ranges from Selection

a. Select the range **E4:G16**. This includes the column headers that will be used for the names of each range.

b. Click the **Formulas tab**, and then click **Create from Selection** in the Defined Names group.

   The dialog box that appears will have options for top, left, bottom, and right column or rows. Excel will try to guess what you want to use for the names of the ranges. Be sure to include the heading cells in the target selection, and verify that Excel offered the correct checked option in the Create Names from Selection dialog box—and if necessary, correct the appropriate option or accordingly.

c. In the Create Names from Selection dialog box, click the **Top row** check box, make sure all other check boxes are unchecked, and then click **OK**.

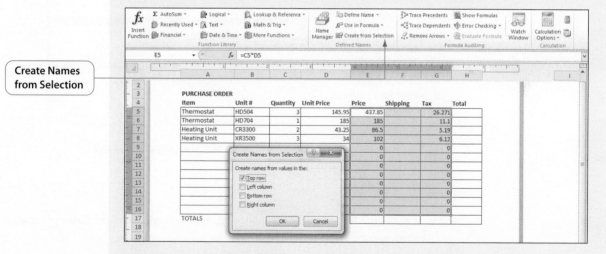

Create Names from Selection

Figure 12 Create from selection

d. To check the named ranges, click the **Name Box arrow** and you should see the new names—Price, Shipping, and Tax—in addition to previously existing named ranges.

SIDE NOTE

Labels for Named Ranges

Since named ranges cannot have spaces, if you have names with spaces, the Create from Selection method will insert an underscore (_) to replace the spaces.

Modifying Named Ranges

As you create named ranges, you may need to make a change to an existing named range. You may also have names that are no longer required and need to be deleted. These kinds of changes need to be made with the Name Manager—which is also found on the Formulas tab—in the Defined Names group.

To Modify a Named Range

a. Click the **Table_Life worksheet tab** to make it the active sheet.

The Table_Life worksheet had some initial named ranges created. It is always wise to check named ranges to determine if they are correct for the current model. Notice, the template will record the number of minutes the massage table heating thermostat is on each day in the Usage column. An employee will enter the data daily. Currently the model will handle two weeks' worth of data. Thus, the named range needs to be modified to include this full column range.

b. If necessary, click the **Formulas tab**, and click **Name Manager** in the Defined Names group.

c. In the Name Manager dialog box, click the Name **Usage**. Notice, under the Refers To column, the range is indicated as =Table_Life!$B$18:$B$20. If needed, you can resize the Refers To column to see the details better by double-clicking the border in the column heading between Refers To and Scope.

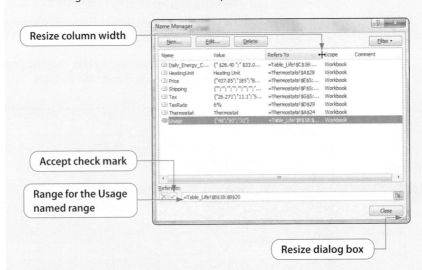

Figure 13 Name Manager dialog box

d. Click in the **Refers to** box, highlight **20**, and then type **31**. Click **Enter** ✔ to accept the changes and set the new range.

e. In the Name Manager dialog box, click the Name range **Daily_Energy_Cost**, as it also needs modification. In the Refers to box, highlight **20**, and type **31**. Click **Enter** ✔ to set the new range.

f. Click **Close**, and then click **Save** 🖫 to save changes to the workbook.

Using Named Ranges

As you begin creating your own formulas, the usage of named ranges is a simple element within the process. You can use them in formulas like the tax calculation you already applied to column G on the Thermostats worksheet. However, when you want to indicate the range of cells, you simply type in the named range instead of having to select the cells. There are two methods for using named ranges in formulas or functions. First, you can start typing the named range and a drop-down list will appear to show not only function names, but also named ranges. You can select the named range from the drop-down list by using ↓ and pressing Tab to select the name (or alternatively double-clicking on the name when it appears in the list). Conversely, if you forget the name of the range, you can press F3. Pressing F3 opens a dialog box listing all the available named ranges.

Creating Formulas Using a Named Range

On the Table_Life worksheet, you need to calculate the total minutes for Thermostat Usage.

To Create a Formula Using a Named Range

a. Click cell **B8**. You need to calculate the total minutes used in this cell.

b. Type =sum. As you start typing, when you see SUM appear in the drop-down list, double-click on it to complete the typing.

c. Press F3. From the Paste name list of named ranges, click **Usage**.

d. Click **OK**.

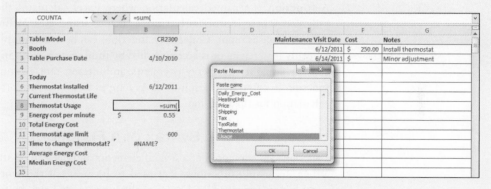

Figure 14   Paste name

e. Press Enter to have Excel add the closing parenthesis and accept the formula. Notice, this function now totals the range named Usage.

f. Click cell **B10**, and then type =sum(da.
    Notice, a drop-down list including the Daily_Energy_Cost named range appears. The named ranges appear with the ⊟ next to the name of the range in the drop-down list while the functions have fx to the left of the function name.

g. If Daily_Energy_Cost is not highlighted, press ↑ or ↓ until **Daily_Energy_Cost** is highlighted. Press Tab to select that named range and have it inserted into the SUM function.

Symbol representing a named range

Symbol representing a function

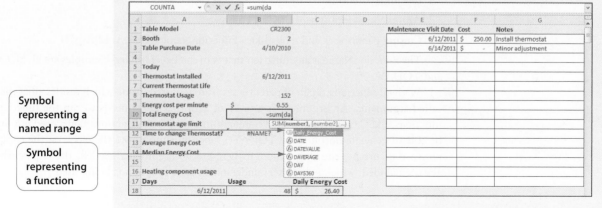

Figure 15   Formula drop-down list

h. Press Enter to finish the formula, and then click **Save** 💾.

Named ranges are useful. However, they can also be overused. Named ranges make it easy to understand formulas, such as =Sales*Bonus and can also be used to select a range of cells quickly. However, you must invest time and effort to create and use the named ranges. If others won't be using the spreadsheet, your time may be better spent. Named ranges have the most value when sets of data are used in multiple formulas or when other users need to understand the construction of the spreadsheet. You should do a mental cost-benefit analysis to ensure it is worth the time and effort. Your decision on when to use named ranges will become easier with practice and experience.

Functions

A **function** is a named calculation where Excel calculates the output based on the input provided. These can be fairly simple such as using a SUM function that will add any cell address range as input. Conversely, functions can be more complex. For example, calculating a monthly loan payment is accomplished by indicating various inputs, known as **arguments**—the loan amount, number of payments, and interest rate. Arguments are any inputs used by a function to compute the solution. As long as you have the correct inputs, Excel will run the calculation for the function.

Understand the Syntax of a Function

Functions are composed of a several elements and need to be structured in a particular order. When discussing functions, you need to be aware of the syntax of an Excel function. The **syntax** is the structure and order of the function and the arguments needed for Excel to run the function. If you understand the syntax of a function you can easily learn how to use new functions quickly. There are a couple of techniques for creating functions once you learn the structure of a function.

Function Structure

Functions have a particular structure and rules for construction. Once learned, you will be able to quickly learn and use any function within the Excel library. The structure, or syntax, for a function consists of the following:

1. =
2. Function name
3. Opening parenthesis
4. Arguments—inputs separated by commas
5. Closing parenthesis and looks like:=FunctionName (Arg1,Arg2,ArgN)

The FunctionName is any function that is in the Excel library. Examples are SUM, COUNT, and TODAY.

With all functions, a pair of parentheses () are required inside which resides all of the inputs, called arguments. An argument is a piece of data that Excel needs to run the function. Some functions, like TODAY() don't have any arguments. These functions don't need any inputs to be able to generate output. The TODAY() function simply uses the clock on the computer to return the current date. Even though there are no arguments needed, the () parentheses are always included, which helps Excel understand that a function is being used.

CONSIDER THIS | **Exploring Functions**

Use the Insert Function button in the formula bar to peruse the listing of functions. Find a function you have never heard of before. Read the description for the Function in the Insert Function dialog box. Use Microsoft Help or the Internet to determine what the function does, what arguments are needed, and share it with another person.

Arguments can either be required or optional. The required arguments always come first, before the optional arguments. All arguments are separated with commas. Optional arguments are identified in the ScreenTip or help file with square brackets [ ] around the argument name. You never type the square brackets into the actual construction of the function. They are only used to inform you that the argument is optional.

For example, the PMT function is a handy financial function that calculates a periodic payment, like a monthly car payment, given some standard inputs. When you insert a function by hand, Excel provides a ScreenTip as shown in Figure 16 that offers guidance for the expected arguments needed for any function. The ScreenTip for a PMT function shows PMT(rate, nper, pv, [fv], [type]). The (rate, nper, and pv) arguments are required, but the [fv] and [type] arguments are optional. Commas are used between the arguments you list.

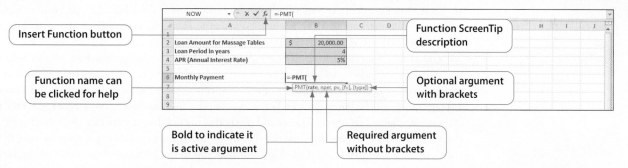

Figure 16 Function ScreenTip

Arguments, like variables in a math equation, need to be appropriate values that are suitable for the function. With Excel, the acceptable values can take six common forms, including other functions, as shown in Figure 17:

Form of Input	Example	Explanation
Numeric Value	5	Type the value
Cell Reference	C5	Type the cell or range of cells
Named Range	SALES	Type the name of the range
Text String	"Bonus"	Type the text with quotes " " so Excel will recognize it as a text string rather than a named range
Function	SUM(C5:C19)	Type a function following the correct syntax of the function name, pair of parentheses, and any arguments
Formula	(C5+D5)/100	Type the formula following correct mathematical formula structure

Figure 17 Function Argument Formats

Functions are typically categorized for easy access. The primary categories are shown in Figure 18. Over time, you will develop knowledge of functions that are specific to your needs. For this reason, you must learn where to find functions and the basic syntax. If you learn this, you can quickly learn how to use new functions as the need arises.

Category	Description
Financial	Working with common financial formulas
Logical	Evaluating expressions or conditions as being either True or False
Text	Working with text strings
Date & Time	Working with dates and times
Lookup & Reference	Working with indexing and retrieving information from data sets
Math & Trig	Working with mathematics
Statistical	Working with common statistical calculations
Engineering	Working with engineering formulas and calculations
Cube	Working with data and filtering, similar to pivot tables
Information	Providing data about cell content within a worksheet
Compatibility	A set of functions that are compatible with older versions of Excel

Figure 18 Function Categories

Function Construction with the Function Arguments Dialog Box

There are two common methods for creating functions: through the Function Arguments dialog box and by typing in the function. When you are first developing the skills for using functions in Excel, the Function Arguments dialog box can be very valuable. As you become familiar with specific functions, it will become easier to type in the functions. Even then, the Function Arguments dialog box is also helpful for trouble-shooting.

Creating a function through the Function Arguments dialog box first entails selecting the cell location where you want the results to be displayed. There are two ways to access the Function Arguments dialog box. First, you can use the category buttons in the Function Library group on the Formulas tab. When you select a function from the category, the Function Arguments dialog box opens. The second method is to click Insert Function fx, which is located between the Name box and formula bar. When the Insert Function dialog box opens, type or find the desired function and click OK. This will take you to the Function Arguments dialog box for the chosen function.

The Function Arguments dialog box will list the arguments. The arguments in bold are required and listed first. Then, the optional arguments are listed next but are not bold. To the right of the argument name is the box where you will input the information needed for the argument. On the far right, the result is displayed for that argument once you input information. Below the listing of arguments, you will find a description of the argument currently selected. Finally, at the bottom you will find the formula result and a link that will take you to the Excel Help for the function as shown in Figure 19.

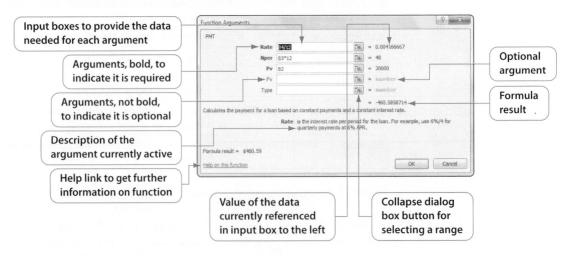

Figure 19 Function Arguments dialog box

Function Construction with the Formula Bar

Functions can also be constructed without using the Function Arguments dialog box. This is accomplished by typing the equal sign and typing the function name directly into the cell. Excel will still provide guidance using this method. Additionally, as needed, you can always jump into the Function Arguments dialog box to get more assistance.

When you initially type in the beginning of a function name, an AutoComplete listing of functions will be shown from which you can select the appropriate function as shown in Figure 20. The list will automatically reflect changes as you type in more letters. Excel will even display a short description of the function when the function name is highlighted. As the function names appear you can use ⬇, ⬆, ➡, ⬅, or your mouse to move through the listing. To select a function, press Tab or double-click the selected function.

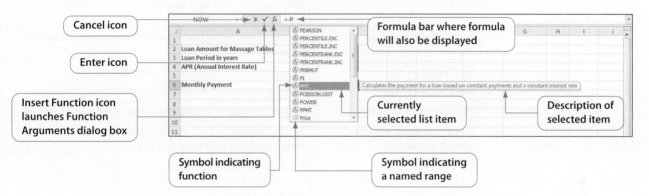

Figure 20 Function drop-down list

Once the function is selected, the arguments will be listed in a movable tag to provide a guide. The argument you are currently working on will be displayed in bold. The optional arguments, as stated previously will be listed but with square brackets [ ] as shown in Figure 21. If you have entered some of the arguments, you can click on the argument in the movable tag, and Excel will relocate the insertion point to that argument. Finally, you can click the Insert Function button *fx* any time to switch to the Function Arguments dialog box.

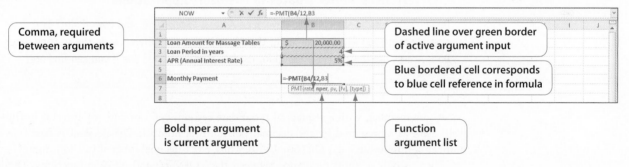

Figure 21 Function ScreenTip

Common Functions

Remember, there are hundreds of functions available, although most users will primarily use a small set of very common functions. The following is an explanation of common functions that will provide a strong foundation for building powerful spreadsheets. Learning these functions will also provide the skill set needed for learning additional functions on your own.

Date and Time Functions

Date and Time functions are useful for putting in the current day and time as well as calculating time intervals. This category of functions is based on a serial date system where each day is represented sequentially from a starting point. In Microsoft, that standard is 1/1/1900 which has a serial number of 1. Thus, dates prior to that will not be recognized by the system. Interestingly, when Apple initially made its starting point, it began in 1904. Excel settings can be changed to use the Apple starting point, but it is generally accepted practice to keep the default setting of 1/1/1900 as the starting point. You can only imagine the potential issues when the two different starting points are used in Excel spreadsheets. Common date and time functions are shown in Figure 22.

Date & Time Functions	Usage
NOW()	Will use computer system to give date and time
TODAY()	Will use computer system to give date
DATEDIF(Date1,Date2,Interval)	Will return the time unit specified between two dates, including the two dates (inclusive)
DATE(Year,Month,Day)	Returns the number that represents the date in Microsoft Excel date-time code
DAY(Serial_number)	Returns the day of the month, a number from 1 to 31
MONTH(Serial_number)	Returns the month, a number from 1 to 12
YEAR(Serial_number)	Returns the year of a date, an integer in the range 1900–9999
WEEKDAY(Serial_number, [return_number], [Return_type])	Returns a number from 1 to 7 representing the day of the week. Can be set to return 0–6 or 1–7
WEEKNUM(Serial_number, [Return_type])	Returns the week number in the year, which week of the year the date occurs
NETWORKDAYS(Start_date, End_date,[Holidays])	Returns the number of whole workdays between two dates, inclusive; doesn't count weekends and can skip holidays that are listed

Figure 22 Date and Time Functions

CONSIDER THIS | **Dates in Microsoft Applications**

Do you suppose the same people developed Access, Excel, Word, and PowerPoint? Is it possible that even within a company, there may have been differences in the starting date? Does Access use the same 1/1/1900 for its date starting point? See if you can find out.

Also remember, with a sequential serial date system, you can find any interval in time as well. Time is represented by the decimal portion of a number. The decimal is based on the number of minutes in a day (24*60=1440). Thus, a 0.1 decimal is equal to 144 minutes.

There is only a slight difference between the TODAY() and NOW() functions. The key difference is that the TODAY() function simply puts in the date while the NOW() function puts in the date and time. If you think about it, the TODAY() function only works with integer representation of days while the NOW() function uses decimals to include the time in addition to the day. Both functions can be formatted to show just the date, and you can work with time calculations that mix the two functions.

Real World Advice   Using NOW and TODAY functions

Be careful using NOW() versus TODAY(), especially when doing date calculations. Both functions use a serial number, counting from 1/1/1900. But, the NOW() function also includes decimals for the time of day while TODAY() works with integer serial numbers. At noon, on 5/1/2013 the NOW() function has the value of 41395.5 while the TODAY() function has a value of 41395.0. If you are using these date functions inside an IF statement this could change the result if you are comparing a date the user input. It is suggested to use the TODAY() function if a user will be inserting the date into Excel by hand so the hand-typed value will be compared or used in a calculation with the function, eliminating the decimal issue.

To Work with the TODAY Function

a. If necessary, click the **Table_Life worksheet tab** to make it the active worksheet, and then click cell **B5**.

b. Click **Insert Function** f_x beside the formula bar to open the Insert Function dialog box. Click the **Or select a category arrow**, and then click **Date & Time**.

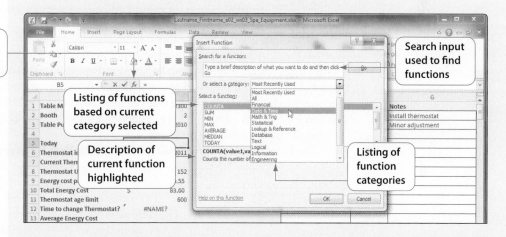

Insert Function to launch Insert Function dialog box

Listing of functions based on current category selected

Description of current function highlighted

Search input used to find functions

Listing of function categories

Figure 23   Insert Function dialog box

SIDE NOTE
Typing Functions and Cell References

Although functions and cell references are typically shown in uppercase, they can be typed in lowercase. Excel converts cell references and function names to uppercase in formulas.

c. In the **Select a function** box, scroll and click **TODAY**. Click **OK**, read the information in the Function Arguments dialog box, and then click **OK** when done.

d. Click the **Thermostats worksheet tab**, and then click cell **B1**. Type **=NOW**. Notice that as you type each letter, the list of functions decreases the options until only the one you need is listed.

e. Press [Tab], and the NOW function is selected.

f. Press [Enter], and Excel adds the closing parenthesis and you see the current date and time.

g. Right-click cell **B1**, and then click **Format Cells** from the shortcut menu.

h. If necessary, click the **Number tab**, and then click **Date**. In the Type box list, click the **14-Mar-01** format, click **OK**, and then click **Save** 🔲.

Troubleshooting

Do you get a #NAME? error when you start putting in your function? When creating a function and choosing a function name from the drop-down list, be sure to press ⌜Tab⌟ instead of ⌜Enter⌟. ⌜Enter⌟ simply enters what you have currently typed and moves to the next cell below. ⌜Tab⌟ moves to the function and inserts it into the cell.

CONSIDER THIS | **Where Did DATEDIF Originate?**

Search the Internet for Excel DATEDIF. Can you find speculation as to why it does not have the same coverage as other Excel functions? If you cannot find any speculation, can you imagine any reasons why?

DATEDIF is a useful date function because it enables you to find the time between two dates. The function can return the time unit as days, months, or years. However, while all the other functions are listed and can be found in Excel help, you will not find any information on the DATEDIF function unless you search the Microsoft site. Since no information exists on it within Excel, this is one function that you must hand type and do the research to understand the syntax (or function arguments). The Function Library will not help. Nonetheless, DATEDIF is one of the more useful date functions.

The syntax of the function is DATEDIF(Date1, Date2, Interval).

The first argument is the starting date in time—the older date—while the second argument is the ending date in time—the newer, more recent date. It may be helpful to remember that time lines are usually depicted as moving left to right, just like you read. So, the earlier date comes first, or to the left. The third argument is the interval that should be used, like the number of months, weeks, or days between the two dates. The unit is expressed as a text value and therefore must be surrounded by quotes for correct syntax. The viable unit value options are shown in Figure 24.

Unit Value	Description
"D"	Returns the number of complete days between the dates
"M"	Returns the number of complete months between the dates
"Y"	Returns the number of complete years between the dates
"YM"	Returns the months remaining, after subtracting completed full years
"YD"	Returns the days remaining, after subtracting the completed full years
"MD"	Returns the days remaining, after subtracting the completed full months and full years

Figure 24 Unit value options

> **CONSIDER THIS | Calculating Time**
>
> Since Excel uses the 1900 date system, do you really need to use the DATEDIF function to calculate the difference between days—the "D" unit? What other way could you calculate the difference? What would that formula look like?

To Work with the DATEDIF Function

a. Click the **Table_Life worksheet tab**, and then click cell **B7**.

b. Type =datedif(B6,B5,"D") and then press Enter.

Notice, you want to determine the age of the current thermostat. The date the thermostat was installed is entered one time. It would not be a function, like TODAY or NOW since these functions would be updated each time the spreadsheet is opened. Thus, the user would type the date into cell B6. Then, you need to find the current age, so the current date is needed in cell B5 also. Rather than type it in each time the spreadsheet is opened, the TODAY function is used to get the current date. The DATEDIF function uses three arguments. The first argument is the date the thermostat was installed, which would be the older date, or the date closest to 1/1/1900. The second argument is the current date, the date furthest from 1/1/1900. The third argument is the units of time to use. In this case, the number of days between the two dates was used, thus the "D" argument.

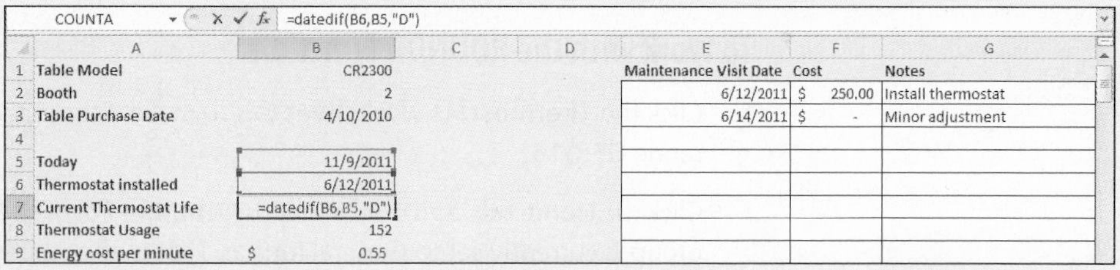

Figure 25 DATEDIF function

Troubleshooting

> Do you get a #NUM! error when you construct a DATEDIF function? The most common error is mixing up the order of the two dates within the function. The first date should be the date that is closest to 1/1/1900. The other common error is actually typing in a date as the argument. Typing 12/3/2000 will be interpreted as division instead of a date. The value must be in serial date format. Thus, it is highly recommended you put the dates in cells and reference the cells in the function. One more possible common error is to neglect putting quotation marks around the last argument for the interval unit.

Math and Trig Functions

The Math and Trig functions are useful for various numerical manipulations. Commonly used math functions are shown in Figure 26. Of the common math functions, the work horse would have to be the SUM function. You can specify values, ranges, and named ranges to be summed. You can indicate multiple ranges and values, separated by commas.

Math and Trig Functions	Usage
SUM(Number1,[Number2],...)	Adds all the numbers in a range of cells
INT(Number)	Rounds a number down to the nearest integer
ABS(Number)	Returns the absolute value of a number, a number without its (negative) sign
RAND()	Returns a random number greater than or equal to 0 and less than 1
RANDBETWEEN(Bottom,Top)	Returns a random integer between the numbers you specify
ROUND(Number,Num_digits)	Rounds a number to a specified number of digits (decimal places)
ROUNDDOWN(Number, Num_digits)	Rounds a number down, toward zero (to a specified number of decimal places)
ROUNDUP(Number, Num_digits")	Rounds a number up, away from zero (to a specified number of decimal places)

Figure 26 Math and Trig functions

The ROUND function is important when you have calculations that result in answers with more decimals than you need in the result. One common occurrence is with calculating money. For the spa, when the order form was being developed, recall that the calculations of the Tax column can and did result in values with three or more decimal places and in some instances, one decimal place. For currency results, the ROUND function can come to the rescue. It is important to understand that formatting numbers can mask or hide the true values underneath.

To Work with the ROUND() Function

a. Click the **Thermostats worksheet tab** to make it the active tab, and then select the cell range **G5:G16**.

b. Click the **Home tab**, and notice that the **Number Format** [General ▾] in the Number group is currently set to General format. That is, the values currently have a General format with no specific format.

c. On the Home tab, click the **Number Format arrow** [General ▾] in the Number group, and then click **Accounting**. Notice the values now show two decimal places. The values have not changed, just how they are displayed has changed.

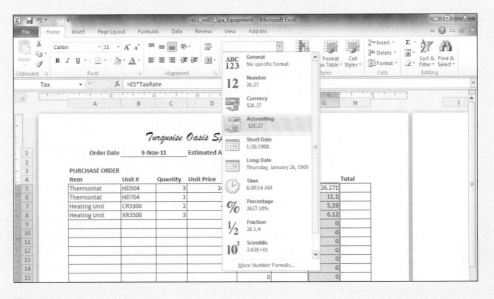

Figure 27 Cell formatting

d. On the Home tab, click the **Number Format arrow** General ▾ in the Number group, and then click **General**. Notice the values now show two of the variable decimal places. Now it is time to edit the formula to ROUND the result so the value will have values to the second decimal place and no more.

e. Click cell **G5** to select this cell only.

f. Press F2 to enter into edit mode for the formula, and then place the insertion point between the = and **E5** within the formula.

g. Type ROUND(.

   Notice that as you type, the drop-down list of functions appears and changes as you type the word. It will show the arguments needed and the first argument, number, is bold. This indicates that you are currently working in that section of the ROUND function.

h. Position the insertion point at the end of the formula after TaxRate so you can type the last argument of the ROUND function.

   Notice that the E5*TaxRate is still a part of the number argument (which is still bold) and is the part of the formula that provides the raw answer. That result is what needs to be rounded.

i. Type a , and notice that the bold shifts from the number argument to the num_digits argument indicating you are ready to put in the number of decimals you want with the result.

j. Type 2 Finish the formula and type).

   As you type in the) notice that the pair of () will turn bold for a moment. This is Excel indicating what it considers to be a pair of () and is a visual cue that you are inserting the function correctly.

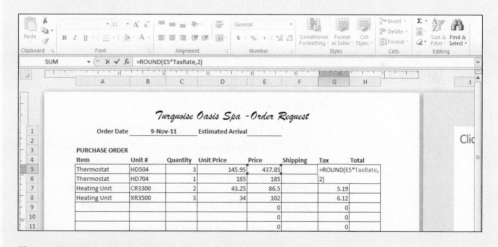

Figure 28 Round function

k. Press Enter, click cell **G5**, hover over the bottom-right corner of the cell, and then double-click to AutoFill the formula for the range **G5:G16**.

l. Select **D5:H16** since the entire range should be formatted the same. Click the **Accounting Number Format** $ ▾ button in the Number group, and then click **Save** 🖫.

Statistical Functions

Similar to mathematical functions, statistical functions, as shown in Figure 29, handle common statistical calculations such as averages, minimums, and maximums. Statistical functions are extremely useful for business analysis as they aggregate and compare data. Common descriptive statistics are used to describe the data. The average, median, and mode are common descriptive statistics that help describe the nature of a data set. They help understand and predict future data.

Statistical Functions	Usage
AVERAGE(Number1,[Number2],...)	Returns the mean from a set of numbers
COUNT(Value1,[Value2],...)	Counts the number of cells in a range that contain numbers
COUNTA(Value1,[Value2],...)	Counts the number of cells in a range that are not empty
COUNTBLANK(Range)	Counts the number of empty cells in a range
MEDIAN(Number1,[Number2],...)	Returns the number in the middle of a set of numbers
MAX(Number1,[Number2],...)	Returns the largest number from a set of numbers
MIN(Number1,[Number2],...)	Returns the smallest number from a set of numbers
MODE(Number1,[Number2],...)	Returns the value that occurs most often within a set

Figure 29

The AVERAGE function is commonly used in business analysis. It requires only one argument, a set of values. While many use AVERAGE by itself to help understand data, it is important to be careful when using this by itself. For example, if you were looking at the average starting salaries of graduates among universities in order to determine which school to attend, the University of North Carolina would stand out as having enormous average starting salaries for their graduates in 1984. However, further exploration might reveal this was due to Michael Jordan's huge NBA salary. Thus, it is wise to consider multiple statistics in analyzing data.

The thermostat life is being tracked on the Table_Life worksheet. To have a better idea of the usage on a daily basis, the model needs to show the average and the median of the usage.

To Work with Statistical Functions

a. Click the **Table_Life worksheet tab** to make it the active worksheet, and then click cell **B13**. Click **Insert Function** f_x next to the formula bar. Under Or select a category, click **Statistical**, and then click **Average** from the function list. Click **OK**.

b. In the Function Arguments dialog box, place the insertion point in the Number1 box, press F3, and then click **Daily_Energy_Cost**. Click **OK**, and then click **OK** again.

c. Click cell **B14**. Click **Insert Function** f_x. Under Or select a category, click **Statistical**, and then click **MEDIAN** from the function list. Click **OK**.

d. In the Function Arguments dialog box, the Number1 input box will be active, press F3, click **Daily_Energy_Cost**, and then click **OK**. Click **OK** to finish the function. Click **Save** .

Note the current solution for the median and average energy cost. The median is 0 and the average is 5.97. These formulas are using all the cells in the Daily_Energy_Cost range because the cells actually have numbers in every cell. Thus, while the median and average are calculated correctly, the range has 0 values for cells that have no daily energy cost. The functions are using the 0 values in their calculation resulting in incorrect results. The Daily Energy cost formulas need to be changed so they show numbers when there is usage and don't show numbers when there has not been usage. This issue will be addressed later in this workshop.

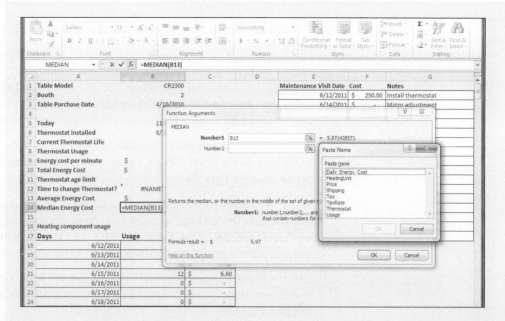

Figure 30 Paste name in function argument

e. Click the **Table_Usage worksheet tab** to make it the active worksheet, and then click cell **B8**. Click **Insert Function** ƒₓ next to the formula bar. Under Or select a category, click **Statistical**, and then click **AVERAGE** from the function list. Click **OK**.

   In addition to the Table_Life calculations, the spa has two portable massage tables that the therapists share. Irene wants to track the usage and has started two worksheets that the receptionist will use to check the tables in and out. These two worksheets, Table_Port1 and Table_Port2, are included, but they do not provide any consolidated information. The Table_Usage worksheet will be used to develop statistical information about the table usage based on information logged into the two Table_Port worksheets. Irene wants you to develop the formulas in the simple grid provided for the needed statistics on the Table_Usage worksheet.

f. In the Function Arguments dialog box, place the insertion point in the Number1 box, click ▦ to collapse the dialog box, and then click the **Table_Port1** worksheet tab. Select the range **E4:E23**.

g. Click **Expand Dialog Box** ▦ to expand the dialog box and return to the Function Arguments dialog box. Click **OK**.

   Notice the formula will include the worksheet name, Table_Port1, with an exclamation mark (!) between the worksheet and the range. Since there is a range E4:E23 on every worksheet, this formula is specifying which worksheet has the range that is to be averaged. So, anytime you are working with a formula that has cells referenced that are on other worksheets, you need to include the worksheet name with an exclamation mark.

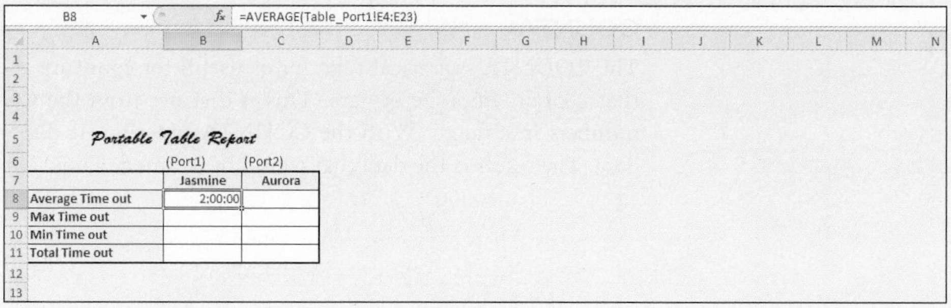

Figure 31 Formula referencing another worksheet

SIDE NOTE

Watch that Function List

Keep an eye on the function list to learn how functions are listed. You might be used to using AVG, but in Excel the function name is AVERAGE.

h. Click cell **B9**. Click **Insert Function** f_x next to the formula bar. Under Or select a category, click **Statistical**, and then click **MAX**. Click **OK**.

i. In the Function Arguments dialog box, place the insertion point in the Number1 box, click to collapse the dialog box, and then click the **Table_Port1 worksheet tab**. Select the range **E4:E23**. Click **Expand Dialog Box** to expand the dialog box, and then return to the Function Arguments dialog box and click **OK**.

j. Click the **Table_Usage worksheet tab**, and click cell **B10**. Click **Insert Function** f_x next to the formula bar. Under Or select a category, click **Statistical**, and then click **MIN** from the function list. Click **OK**.

k. In the Function Arguments dialog box, place the insertion point in the Number1 box, click **Collapse Dialog Box** to collapse the dialog box, and then click the **Table_Port1 worksheet tab**. Select the range **E4:E23**. Click **Expand Dialog Box** to expand the dialog box and return to the Function Arguments dialog box. Click **OK**.

l. Click the **Table_Usage worksheet tab**, and click cell **B11**. Click **Insert Function** f_x next to the formula bar. Under Or select a category, click **All**, click **SUM** from the function list, and then click **OK**.

m. Click **Collapse Dialog Box** to collapse the dialog box, click the **Table_Port1 worksheet tab**, and then select the range **E4:E23**. Click **Expand Dialog Box** to expand the dialog box and return to the Function Arguments dialog box. Click **OK**.

n. Click the **Insert tab**, click the **Header & Footer** button to insert a footer with the filename. Click the **Design tab**, and then click the **Go to Footer** button. If necessary click on the left section of the footer, and then click **File Name** in the Header & Footer Elements group.

o. Click any cell on the spreadsheet to move out of the footer, and then press Ctrl + Home. Click the **View tab**, and then click the **Normal** button in the Workbook Views group.

p. Click the **Table_Port1 worksheet tab**, click the **Insert tab**, and then click the **Header & Footer** button. On the **Design tab**, click the **Go to Footer** button. Click in the left footer section, and then click the **File Name** button in the Header & Footer Elements group.

q. Click any cell on the spreadsheet to move out of the footer, and then press Ctrl + Home. Click the **View tab**, and then click the **Normal** button in the Workbook Views group.

r. Click the **Table_Port2** worksheet tab, click the **Insert tab**, and then click the **Header & Footer** button. Click the **Design tab**, and then click the **Go to Footer** button. Click in the left footer section, and then click **File Name** in the Header & Footer Elements group.

s. Click any cell on the spreadsheet to move out of the footer, and then press Ctrl + Home. Click the **View tab**, and then click **Normal** in the Workbook Views group.

COUNTA

The COUNTA statistical function is useful for counting the number of cells within a range that contain any type of data. This is distinct from the COUNT function that only counts numbers in a range. With the COUNTA function, it does not consider a function as being data. The result is the data that would be counted. Thus, On the Table_Life worksheet, if you were to use the COUNTA function on the Daily Energy cost it would have a result of 4. It would not count all the cells that have formulas, only the values returned. This is different from the Average that did use the formulas in the entire range in determining the average daily energy cost.

Using COUNTA is a great way to count the number of records in a data set. With the maintenance for the massage tables, it may be that a technician would visit but not incur any charges. In this case, it would not be correct to simply count the cost column as there may not be a cost. However, the table would have a date for each visit and that could be counted using the COUNTA function.

To Work with the COUNTA() Function

a. Click the **Table_Life worksheet tab**, and then click cell **F19**.

b. Click **Insert Function** f_x next to the formula bar. Under Or select a category, click **Statistical**, and then click **COUNTA** from the function list. Click **OK**.

c. Click **Collapse Dialog Box** 🔳 to collapse the dialog box, and then select the range **E2:E17**.

d. Click **Expand Dialog Box** 🔲 to expand the dialog box and return to the Function Arguments dialog box, click **OK**, and then click **Save** 🔲.

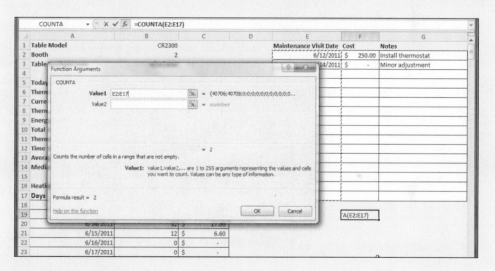

Figure 32 COUNTA function

Financial Functions

Excel has many financial functions available to help businesses make decisions. A foundation for a successful business is generating revenue—any income brought into the business, prior to paying any expenses out—and hopefully yielding net profits. This also applies to personal finances where individuals generate income with the main goal of covering their expenses as they go through life with a net profit to spare. Having a foundational knowledge of financial terms is thus an important element of succeeding in both your personal and professional life. Some common financial terms that you will see and hear or possibly make use of in an Excel spreadsheet are shown in Figure 33.

Financial Term	Definition
APR	The annual percentage rate, an interest rate expressed in an annual equivalent
Compounding interest	A process of charging interest on both the principal and the interest that accumulates on a loan
Interest payment	The amount of a payment that goes toward paying the interest accrued
NPV	The net present value of future investments
Period	The time period of payments, such as making payments monthly
Principal payment	The amount of a payment that goes toward reducing the principal amount
Principal value	The original amount borrowed or loaned
PV	Present value—the total amount that a series of future payments is worth now
Rate (and APR)	The interest rate per period of a loan or an investment
Simple interest	The interest charged on the principal amount of a loan only
Term	The total time of a loan, typically expressed in years or months
Time value of money	Recognizing that earning one dollar today is worth more than earning one dollar in the future

Figure 33 Financial Terminology

One of the most common and useful financial functions in Excel is the PMT function for determining the periodic payment for a loan. The PMT function by default returns a negative value. The function is really calculating an outflow of cash, a payment to be made. Within the financial and accounting industry, an outflow of cash is considered a negative value. In other words, this function assumes you are actually making a payment—taking money out of your pocket to give to someone else, or a negative value. Since some people may be confused seeing the value as negative, the value can be made positive by simply inserting a negative sign prior to the function or placing the absolute value function—ABS()—around the payment function.

The PMT function uses three required arguments. The first is the **rate**, which is the periodic interest rate. Importantly, the interest rate must be for each period. Most loans are discussed in terms of annual percentage rate (APR), while the period would be a shorter time period such as quarterly or monthly. The APR would need to be divided by 12 to get an equivalent monthly interest rate.

The second argument is **nper**, which is the number of periods or total number of payments that will be made for the loan. Again, many loans are discussed in years while the payments would be monthly. Thus, you will need to determine the total number of periodic payments.

The third, and final, required argument is **PV** which is the present value of an investment or loan—the amount borrowed that needs to be paid back.

There are other common financial functions that are useful for both personal and business analysis. These are listed below in Figure 34.

Financial Functions	Usage
PMT	Calculates periodic payment for a loan based on a constant interest rate and constant payment amounts
IPMT	Calculates periodic interest payment for a loan based on a constant interest rate and constant payment amounts
PPMT	Calculates periodic principal payment for a loan based on a constant interest rate and constant payment amounts
NPV	Calculates the net present value based on a discount interest rate, a series of future payments, and future income

Figure 34 Financial Functions

Within the spa, the managers would like your help analyzing the costs and benefits of purchasing and using equipment. This involves looking at the total cost of purchasing equipment including any interest that may be charged for borrowed money. You then need to look at the revenues generated to determine if they cover the payments and, over time, offer more revenue in than expenses out. Not only does the equipment purchased need to generate enough revenue to cover the total cost, it also needs to generate enough revenue in the short term to make the monthly payments on time. It may not be feasible to try to pay back a loan in six months if the equipment can't generate enough revenue quickly. Other factors may influence the decision. For example, a longer loan may have lower monthly payments. But, the interest is typically higher for longer term loans. Thus, you need to develop a model that will allow you and the managers to examine various interest rates, principal amounts, and time periods to determine a monthly payment that would work for your business needs.

To Work with the PMT() Function

a. Click the **Table_Purchase worksheet tab** to make it the active worksheet, and then click cell **B6**.

b. Click **Insert Function** f_x next to the formula bar. Under Or select a category, click **Financial**, and then click **PMT** from the function list. Click **OK**.

c. Click in the **Rate** box, and type B4/12 so you will have the correct interest rate per number of annual payments.

   The division by 12 is to convert an annual year rate, which is typically how the loan would be discussed, in months, which is the payment period length. Again, when discussing a loan, it is typical to speak in terms of an APR—the annual percentage rate rather than the period interest rate. Thus a conversion is needed to get the equivalent monthly interest rate.

d. Click in the **Nper** box, and then type B3*12 so the total number of payments for the loan can be calculated, in this case the number of years times the number of months since the payments are on a monthly rate.

e. Click in the **Pv** box, and then type B2.

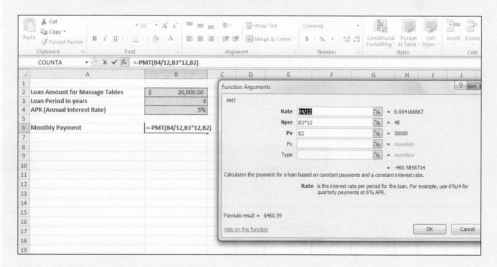

Figure 35 PMT function

f. Click **OK**. Notice the result will be in red with parentheses, which is due to the result being a negative number.

g. Press F2 to enter edit mode. Move the cursor to the right of the = sign and type – (a negative sign), and press Enter. The result is now displayed as a positive number.

h. Click the **Insert tab**, and then click the **Header & Footer button**. Click the **Design tab**, click the **Go to Footer** button, click in the left footer section, and then click the **File Name** button in the Header & Footer Elements group.

i. Click any cell in the spreadsheet to move out of the footer, and then press Ctrl + Home. Click the **View tab**, and then click the **Normal** button in the Workbook Views group. Click **Save** 🔲.

Logical Functions

Logical functions are statements, or declarations, that can be evaluated as being either true or false. For example, the statement "the sky is blue" is a declaration that can be evaluated as true. If the statement was "Is the sky blue?" the response would be a yes/no instead of true/false. So, all logical functions are structured around the concept of declaring a position or statement that Excel will evaluate and return as True or False.

The best way to think of a declaration is to think of using comparison symbols like the =, <, >, or >= symbols as shown in Figure 36. When you set up a statement of X>Y, Excel can evaluate that comparison as true or false.

Comparison Operator Symbol	Example	Declarative Clause
<	A < B	A is less than B
>	A > B	A is greater than B
=	A = B	A is equal to B
<=	A <= B	A is less than or equal to B
>=	A >= B	A is greater than or equal to B
<>	A <> B	A does not equal B

Figure 36 Comparison operator symbols

It is possible to create intricate logical statements using the AND and the OR functions which allow you to evaluate multiple logical statements. The IFERROR function can be useful to eliminate an error message that might otherwise confuse the user. The common logical functions and their usage are listed in Figure 37. It is very common to have the AND and OR functions as arguments within an IF statement. The components can incorporate values, cells, named ranges, and even other functions.

Logical Functions	Usage
IF	Returns one of two values, depending upon whether the logical statement is evaluated as being true or false
IFERROR	Returns a specified value if a function or formula is showing an error, otherwise it returns the value of the function or formula
AND	Allows multiple logical statements to be evaluated; returns a true result if all of the logical statements are true
OR	Allows multiple logical statements to be evaluated; returns a true result if one or more of the logical statements are true

Figure 37 Logical functions

The most common logical function to learn is the IF function:
IF(Logical_test,[Value_if_true],[Value_if_false])

With this function, you will put in the Logical_test, the declarative equation, as the first argument. Excel will then evaluate it as either true or false. The second argument is the result you want returned in the cell if the expression is evaluated as true. The third argument is the result you want in the cell if the expression is evaluated as false.

Notice that only the expression is required. The last two arguments are optional. If you leave them out, Excel will automatically return the word TRUE or FALSE. However, it is much more common and expected that you will put in something for all three arguments. If you consider the context, logical statement, and results of the IF function, the structure begins to fall into place. Figure 38 has some examples of evaluating a context and constructing the components into a logical IF statement.

CONSIDER THIS | **Variations in Constructing Formulas**

In Excel, there can be many ways that a formula can be written. Some are more efficient than others. At a minimum, every IF statement can be written two ways. Why? Provide an example with both ways.

Context: Display the word Good if the exam score in J10 is better than or equal to the target goal of 80, which is in cell B2. If it is worse than 80, display the word Bad.

Example: =IF(J10>=$B$2,"Good","Bad")

Interpretation: If the value of cell J10 is greater than or equal to the value in B2, the text Good is displayed. Otherwise, the text Bad is displayed.

Context: Display the status of an employee meeting their goal of getting a number of transactions, where transactions are listed in the range of A2:A30 and the target number of transactions are in cell C3.

Example: =IF(COUNT(A2:A30)<C3,"Below Goal","Met Goal")

Interpretation: If the count of transactions that are listed in range A2:A30 is below the value in C3 (the target goal for our employee), then the employee did not make their goal and the text Below Goal should be displayed. Otherwise, the goal must have been met and the text Met Goal should be displayed.

Context: For tracking any projects that have not been completed, check the text in H20 and if it does not say Complete, assume the project is not complete and calculate how many months are left when A3 has today's date and A4 has the targeted completion date.

Example: =IF(H20<>"Complete",DATEDIF(A3,A4,"M"),0)

Interpretation: If H20 doesn't say Complete to represent a completed project, calculate the number of months left, based on dates in cells A3 and A4. Otherwise, show a zero.

Context: Determine salary by checking if the employee generated less revenue than their goal, listed in B2. If so, they simply get their base pay. If they do meet their goal or generate more revenue than their goal, they get a bonus, which is a percent of sales added to their base pay. Since this may result in a value that has more than two decimals, the result needs to be rounded to two decimals.

Example: =ROUND(IF(SUM(Sales)<B2,Base,Base+BonusPercent*(Sum(Sales))),2)

Interpretation: The ROUND() function will round the result to two decimals. Inside the ROUND function, the SUM(Sales) functions will sum the range named Sales to give the total sales. The IF statement then indicates that IF the total Sales is less than the value in B2 (the sales goal), provide the value that is in the range called Base (Base pay). Otherwise, the total Sales must be greater than B2 and the pay would be calculated as the Base (Base pay) plus the value in the named range, BonusPercent times the total Sales.

Figure 38 Evaluating IF statements

Real World Advice   Function Construction Production

As you develop a spreadsheet, there are guidelines to help when developing formulas and functions. Some of the common guidelines include the following:

1. Use parentheses for grouping operations in calculations in order to get the correct order. However, do not overuse parentheses as it quickly adds to the complexity of the formula. For example, use =SUM(Sales) instead of =(SUM(Sales)).

2. Insert numbers without formatting such as 10000. Do not enter 10,000 using a comma. The comma is a formatting element and in Excel is used to separate arguments.

3. Insert currency as 4.34 instead of $4.34 as this will get confusing with relative and absolute cell referencing. Then, format the cell that will contain the result as Accounting or Currency. Recall that an even better practice for functions and formulas is to enter the 4.34 value in a cell and the cell address in the formula.

4. Enter percentages as decimals, such as .04. Then, format the number as a percentage.

5. Logical conditions have three parts—two components to compare and the comparison sign. Do not type >5 when there is no value to evaluate as being greater than 5.

6. Use the negative sign, such as -333 to indicate negative numbers in formulas as opposed to (333).

7. Always put quotes around text unless it is a named range. Also, numeric values do not require quotes unless the number will be used in a textual context and not for a mathematical equation, such as displaying a zip code or telephone number.

Pseudocode is the rough draft of a formula or code. It is intended to help you understand the logic and determine the structure of a problem before you develop the actual formula. When you get a logical statement, especially when it is complex, it is helpful to write it in a manner to focus on the logical aspect of what needs to be accomplished without worrying about the formula syntax or formatting. The proper placement of commas or parentheses won't matter if you don't have a clear plan of the logical intent needed.

The shipping cost varies depending on whether the component is a thermostat or heating unit. So, without worrying about getting the syntax exactly correct when you write the logic of the IF statement in pseudocode, the logical statement is as follows:

IF the component is a thermostat, the shipping cost will be $5.00. Since there are only two items and the item is not a thermostat, the item must be a heating unit. Thus by process of elimination, the shipping will be $9.00.

This could be written again in the following format:

IF(x = Thermostat, Thermostat shipping cost, Heating Unit shipping cost)

This form is closer to the actual syntax but conveys the logic of making your logical test, putting in what will happen if the logical test is true and what will happen if it is false. You can then break it down to the three parts, focusing on the syntax of each argument separately.

The logical test could be stated as either x="Thermostat" or x="Heating Unit." Both could be evaluated as true or false so it doesn't matter which logical test is used as long as the true and false correspond properly.

To Use the IF() Function

a. Click the **Thermostats worksheet tab**, and then click cell **F5**, the cell in which the shipping cost will be calculated.

b. Click **Insert Function** f_x next to the formula bar. Under Or select a category, click **Logical**, and then click **IF** from the function list. Click **OK**.

c. Click the **Logical_test** argument input box, and then type A5="Thermostat" with quotes so Excel will know that Thermostat is a text string and not a named range.

d. Click in the **Value_if_true** argument input box, and then type $E$25*C5.

e. Click in the **Value_if_false** argument input box, type $E$26*C5, and then click **OK**.

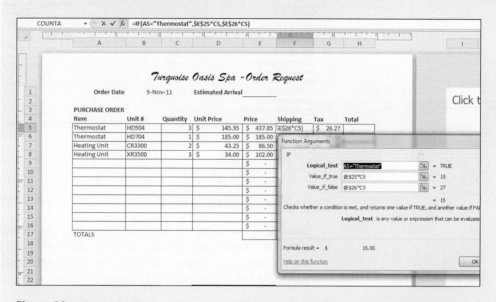

Figure 39 IF function

f. Click the **AutoFill handle** on cell F5, and then drag down to copy the formula to cell **F16**.

g. Click the **Insert tab**, and then click the **Header & Footer** button. Click the **Design tab**, and then click the **Go to Footer** button. Click in the left footer section, and then click the **File Name button** in the Header & Footer Elements group.

h. Click in any cell on the spreadsheet to move out of the footer, and then press Ctrl + Home. Click the **View tab**, and then click the **Normal button** in the Workbook Views group.

i. Click **Save** .

Adding an IF Function to an Existing Formula

The IF statement can return either text or numbers. It can even mix the data in the same IF statement, returning a value for the true argument and text for the false argument. This can be useful when you are doing other statistics on the results as you saw on the Table_Life worksheet.

The formula in the Daily Energy Cost range on the Table_Life worksheet, C18:C31, is causing a value to be seen for every cell with the average and median calculations. Since these functions will only use numbers, if we change the value to a text string when there is no energy cost, the functions will then be calculated correctly. So, the existing formula needs to be modified to check if there is usage. If there is, then the daily energy cost will be calculated. If there is not any usage, an empty text string will be put in, which will be ignored by the average and median functions in B13 and B14.

To Add an IF Function to an Existing Formula

a. Click the **Table_Life worksheet tab**, and then click cell **C18**.

b. Click the formula bar, put your cursor between the = and **B**, type IF(B18>0, move the cursor to the end of the formula and type ,""), and then press [Enter].

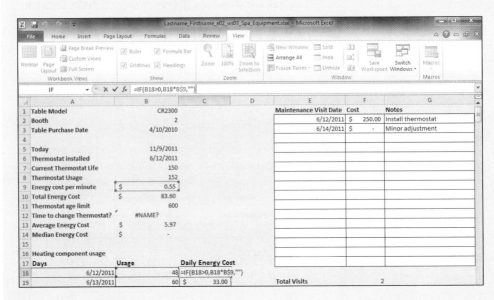

Figure 40 Incorporate an IF function

c. Select **C18** and using the AutoFill handle, copy the formula down through C19:C31. Notice the median and average are being calculated using the four data points rather than including the empty cells. As Usage data is added, the daily energy cost will be calculated with the average and median being updated.

Editing and Troubleshooting Functions

Logical functions dramatically increase the value of a spreadsheet. However, on the path to learning how to use functions, and even as an experienced spreadsheet user, you will still make typing errors during the development of functions. Excel does an excellent job of incorporating cues to help you determine where you have gone astray with a function.

When you make a mistake with a function that prevents Excel from returning a viable result, Excel will provide an error message. While these may seem cryptic initially, they actually can be interpreted. Typically an error message will be prefaced with a number symbol (#). Examples would be #VALUE!, #N/A, #NAME?, or #REF!. Over time you will learn to recognize common issues that would cause these error messages.

Quick Reference — Common Error Messages

1. **#NAME?**—Excel does not recognize text in a formula and believes there is a named range being listed that does not exist. Commonly, this is due to using a text string and forgetting the quotes or, mistyping the function or named range.

2. **#REF!**—Excel is showing a reference to a cell range location that it cannot find. This happens often in development when big changes occur like deleting a worksheet. A formula on Sheet2 may have worked originally but when Sheet1 is deleted, the formula on Sheet2 can no longer find the cell on Sheet1 and will replace it with a #REF! error.

3. **#N/A**—This error indicates that a value is not available in one or more cells specified. Common causes occur in functions that try to find a value in a list but the value doesn't exist. Rather than returning an empty set—no value—Excel returns this error instead.

4. **#VALUE!**—This error occurs when the wrong type of argument or operand is being used, such as entering a text value when the formula requires a number. Common causes can be the wrong cell reference that contains a text value rather than a numeric value.

5. **#DIV/0!**—This is a division by 0 error and occurs when a number is divided by zero or by a cell that contains no value. While it can occur due to an actual error in the design of a formula, it also may occur simply due to the current conditions within the spreadsheet data. In other words, this is common when a spreadsheet model is still in the creation process and data has not yet been entered into the necessary cells. Once proper numeric data does exist, the error will disappear.

When you encounter errors, you should click the Insert Function button f_x and examine the arguments and corresponding values in the Function Arguments dialog box. When something is contained in the argument input box that cannot be evaluated by Excel, it displays an error message to the right of the offending argument input box. Most helpfully, it will also be in red. If Excel can interpret the input information for the argument, it displays the current value(s) to the right. Using the visual clues and values in the dialog box can at the very least aid in guiding you as to where Excel is struggling with the function construction.

On the Table_Life worksheet, there is a function applied by one of the managers, and the function results are displaying an error message. The manager looked at the function and believes the logic is correct. So, your debugging skills are needed.

To Edit a Function with the Insert Function Button

a.	Click the **Table_Life worksheet tab** to make it active, and then click cell **B12** and notice that it currently displays the **#NAME?** error.

b.	Click the **Insert Function** f_x to the left of the formula bar.

This will bring up the Function Arguments dialog box. Notice, the Value_if_true and the Value_if_false inputs have error messages to the right. They both are bold and red indicating that there is a name issue. Recall, the #NAME? error is common when you input a text string without using quotes to surround the text. A text string should always have quotes around it unless it is a reference to a function name or named range. Without the quotes, Excel will believe the text is a named range. Excel cannot find a range that has been named Thermostat, Age, Limit, Reached, and so on for all of the individual words typed in the input box; therefore, Excel is confused and letting you know that it has not found a name in the list of named ranges.

c. Click once inside the **Value_if_true** box to enter edit mode.

d. Click in the **Value_if_false** box and Excel will automatically adjust to add quotes for the text in the Value_if_true box. You should also see the red, bold #NAME? error disappear and be replaced with the appropriate text string for that argument value.

e. With the insertion point now in the Value_if_false argument input box, click in the **Logical_test** input box and Excel will adjust the Value_if_false box so that quotes appear around the text again. The red #NAME? error is replaced with appropriate text string value. Click **OK**.

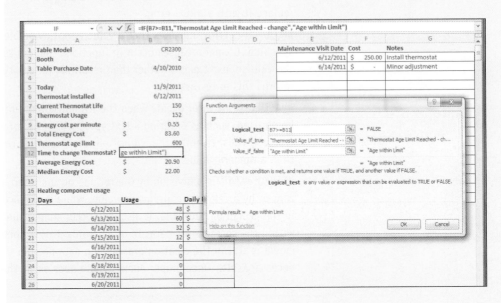

Figure 41 Function corrected

f. Click the **Insert tab**, and then click the **Header & Footer** button. Click the **Design tab**, and then click the **Go to Footer** button. Click in the left footer section of the footer, and then click the **File Name** button in the Header & Footer Elements group.

g. Click any cell in the spreadsheet to move out of the footer, press [Ctrl] + [Home], click the **View tab**, and then click **Normal** in the Workbook Views group.

h. Click **Save**. Submit or print your project as directed by your instructor. **Close** Excel.

Concept Check

1. You are the manager of the production department and need to create a spreadsheet to track projections. What differences would exist if this spreadsheet were to be used only by you versus being accessed by other staff employees?

2. You have a spreadsheet that contains performance data for the staff. How would you organize this data considering that it would be data used for annual performance reviews for each staff member? What are some of the ethical considerations to keep in mind when using this data?

3. You are reviewing a spreadsheet for your employee and notice the formula that calculates production costs as =B25*10000, where B25 is the unit cost and 10000 is the estimated production. What is wrong with how this formula has been structured and what suggestions would you offer to correct the formula to make it more efficient?

4. You have a range C4:C8 that are the number of transactions for each division of your company. The sum of the transactions is in C9. You want a formula in D4:D8 that will figure the percent of transactions for each division. The formula in D4 is =C4/C9, which works for the first division, but when that formula is copied down through D8, errors occur for the other divisions. Why? How would you fix the formula so it could be copied to other cells and work correctly?

5. You are creating a PMT function and you see PMT(rate,nper,pv,[fv],[type]) just below where you are typing. Why is the nper bold? Why are there [ ] brackets around the fv and type arguments?

Key Terms

Absolute cell reference 145
Argument 154
Cell reference 140
Function 154
Hard-coding 140

Mixed cell reference 146
Named range 149
Nper 168
Pseudocode 172
PV 168

Rate 168
Relative cell reference 142
Show Formulas view 144
Syntax 154

Create a set of named ranges from selection (p. 151)

Work with relative cell referencing (p. 143)

Create a named range using the Name Box (p. 149)

Use the IF() function (p. 173)

Work with absolute cell references (p. 145)

Work with the ROUND() function (p. 162)

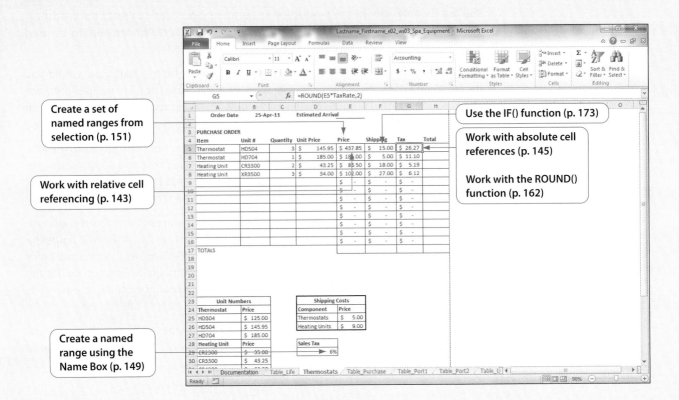

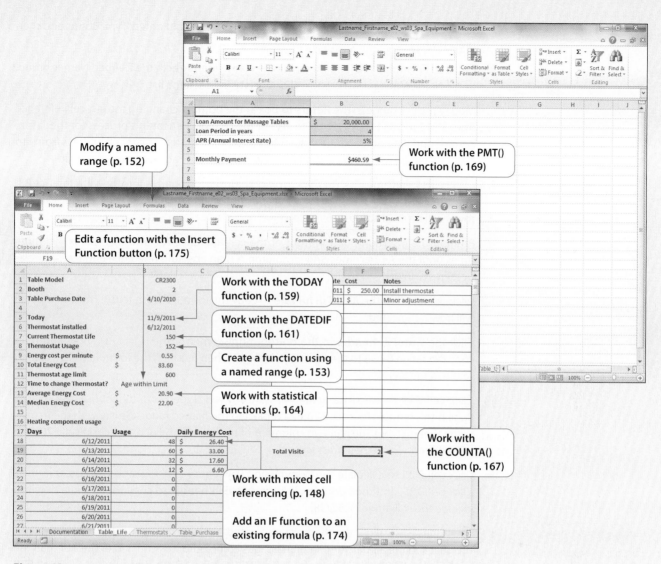

Figure 42 Massage Table Analysis Final Spreadsheet

Student data file needed:

e02_ws03_Bonus

You will save your file as:

Lastname_Firstname_e02_ws03_Bonus

Massage Therapists Bonus Report

Two managers, Irene and Meda, have been discussing a worksheet that would enable them to coordinate the goals for the massage therapists and calculate their pay. The massage therapists have a base pay plus they earn commission for massages along with a bonus. Meda is heading to a conference so they have asked you to make some modifications and complete the worksheet.

a. Start **Excel**, and then open **e02_ws03_Bonus**. A spreadsheet with a partially completed model for bonuses will be displayed. Click the **File tab**, and then click **Save As**. In the Save As dialog box, navigate to where you are saving your files, and type Lastname_Firstname_e02_ws03_Bonus, replacing Lastname and Firstname with your own name.

b. On the **Bonus worksheet tab**, click cell **J17**.

c. Click in the **Name Box**. The cell address J17 should be highlighted. Type Bonus and then press Enter .

d. Click the **Formulas tab**, and then click the **Name Manager** in the Defined Names group. In the Name Manager dialog box, click **Christy** in the Name list.

e. Modify the cell range in the **Refers to** box at the bottom, changing the last cell reference from $I$12 to $K$12. Click Enter to accept the change. Repeat this process for the Jason, Kendra, and Pat named ranges, changing the column letter for last cell address from I to K so the named ranges include all the massage data for each massage therapist.

f. Click cell **B4**, and type =B3*A4. Click to place the insertion point before the cell reference **B3**, and then press F4 twice until the B3 becomes B$3 so column B will be relative and row 3 will be an absolute reference.

g. Position the insertion point in front of the cell reference **A4**, and then press F4 three times until the A4 becomes $A4 so column A is an absolute reference and row 4 is relative. Press Enter .

h. Click cell **B4**. Click the **AutoFill handle** to copy the formula down to **B8**. The range B4:B8 will now be selected.

i. Click the **AutoFill handle** in the bottom-right corner of the selected range, and then copy the range B4:B8 to the right to column K. When finished, the formula will be copied to the range B4:K8.

j. Click cell **F19** to calculate actual Massages given. Type =SUM(Christy). Press Enter . Repeat this formula for cells **F20:F22** replacing the named range Christy with the named range that matches the name in column A of the same row. For example, in cell F20 type =SUM(Kendra) and then press Enter .

k. Click cell **D25** to calculate the Commission Pay. Type =C19*C25 and then press Enter . Click cell **D25**, and then double-click the **AutoFill handle** to copy the formula down to include the cell range D25:D28.

l. The bonus is earned if the therapist generated actual revenue equal to or greater than the goal and the actual number of massages completed was equal to or greater than the goal. Click cell **E25**, and then type =IF(D19*G19=1,"Yes","No"). Press Enter . Click cell **E25** and then double-click the **AutoFill handle** to copy the formula down to include the cell range E25:E28. This formula takes the met revenue goal value and multiplies it by the met massages goal value. The formulas in both these columns yield a numeric value of zero for no and a value of 1 for yes, thus multiplying these two numbers together will only yield a value of 1 if both goals are met (represented by 1). Any met goal represented by a zero will yield a zero since multiplying any number times zero results in zero.

m. Click cell **F25**, and then type =IF(E25="Yes",Bonus,0). Press Enter . Click cell **F25**, and then double-click the **AutoFill handle** to copy the formula down to include the cell range F25:F28.

n. Click cell **G25**, and then type =B25+D25+F25. Press Enter , click cell **G25**, and then double-click the **AutoFill handle** to copy the formula down to include the cell range G25:G28.

o. Click the **Insert tab**, and then click the **Header & Footer** button. Click the **Design tab**, and then click the **Go to Footer** button. Click in the left footer section, and then click the **File Name** button in the Header & Footer Elements group.

p. Click in any cell on the spreadsheet to move out of the footer, press Ctrl + Home , click the **View tab**, and then click the **Normal** button in the Workbook Views group.

q. Click **Save**.

Student data file needed:
e02_ws03_Giftshop_Schedule

You will save your file as:
Lastname_Firstname_e02_ws03_Giftshop_Schedule

Gift Shop Work Schedule

The managers of the gift shop want to be able to track the schedule for the staff working at the shop. With the schedule, it is possible that people will swap hours or stay over and get overtime. Management would like to limit the amount of overtime given since overtime is paid at time and a half. So, the worksheet should track overtime pay, and help the managers control overtime.

Because of privacy issues, the spreadsheet is being developed with no actual names and with hypothetical data. Once developed, the actual data will be incorporated. The spreadsheet has been started and your skills are being requested to continue work on the worksheet. There are no actual employee hours scheduled. Once formulas are created, some hours will be put in to test the formulas.

a. Start **Excel**, and then open **e02_ws03_Giftshop_Schedule**. A spreadsheet with a par- tially completed model for employees will be displayed. Click the **File tab**, and then click **Save As**. In the Save As dialog box, navigate to where you are saving your files, and then type Lastname_Firstname_e02_ws03_Giftshop_Schedule, replacing Lastname and Firstname with your own name.

b. On the **Schedule worksheet tab**, click **B1**, and then type =WEEKNUM(TODAY()), which will show the week of the current date. Since the report will be kept weekly through the year, the managers want to know which week the schedule is showing rather than simply knowing a date. Press Enter .

c. If necessary, click cell **B2** and insert your name, showing that you prepared the report.

d. Click cell **I7**, and then click the **Insert Function** button. Under Or select a category, click **Math & Trig**, and then click **SUM** from the function list. Click **OK**.

e. In the Function Arguments dialog box, place the insertion point in the Number1 box, and then click **Collapse Dialog Box**. Select the range **B7:H7**, click **Expand Dialog Box** to restore the Function Arguments dialog box, and then click **OK**. Click cell **I7**, and then use the **AutoFill handle** to copy the formula to the cell range **I7:I14**.

f. Click cell **K7**, type =IF(I7<J7,"No","Yes"), and press Enter . Using the **AutoFill handle**, copy the formula in cell K7 down through K14. This column will allow the managers to know if they have scheduled enough hours for each employee.

g. Click cell **B17**, and then type =IF(B15<B16,B16-B15,"OK"). Press Enter . Using the **AutoFill handle**, copy the formula in cell **B17** across through **H17**.

   This formula will test if enough hours have been scheduled for the day. If there are not enough hours scheduled, the hours needed will be displayed, otherwise, the word OK is displayed.

h. Click cell **B18**, and then type =COUNT(B7:B14). Press Enter . Using the **AutoFill handle**, copy the formula in cell B18 across through H18.

i. Click cell **J22**.

   Notice the error message #DIV/0! occurring in range J22:J29. Recall when division is in a formula, a zero in a cell or a blank cell reference can cause a division by zero error. The formula should be checked. There is a green triangle on the top-left corner with an error message for cell J22. Hover on the cell error message to see that the error is noting a formula that is divid- ing by 0. The source of the problem is the fact that no employees have any hours scheduled. The error message is acceptable and will disappear once employees are scheduled for work in range B7:H14 so their total hours are greater than 0. If there are only five employees, that would mean there would be no data for employee six, seven, or eight, and the error would show up for those three rows. The error can be fixed to display "NA" (to suggest Not Available) when division by zero occurs by adding an IFERROR function.

j. Click in the formula bar to place the insertion point after the = (equals sign). Type to adjust the formula as follows =IFERROR(I22/I7,"NA") and then press Enter. Click cell **J22**, and then double-click the AutoFill handle to copy the formula down to include the cell range J22:J29. All cells in this range should now display the text NA instead of an error message.

As you have developed some of the formulas, it would be helpful to insert some data so you can confirm that functions and formulas are working correctly. You should vary the data so you can test various scenarios, such as people getting close to 40 hours.

k. Click in **D7** and type 8, click in **G8** and type 6, and then click **D22** and type 7.
   - For EMP 3, type 8 for each cell in B9:F9 so the total hours will be 40.
   - For EMP 3 in range B24:F24, also type 8 for each day indicating actual hours worked.
   - For EMP 4 in range B25:F25, type in a 9 for each of those days indicating the actual hours worked. Note this person will get overtime. Confirm that totals are working correctly. Note the total hours for each employee, their total actual hours worked, as well as their % of schedule.

l. Click cell **M22** to calculate an OT Hours formula. Type =IF(I22<E1,"No OT",I22-E1) and then press Enter. Click cell **M22**, and then double-click the **AutoFill handle** to copy the formula down to include the cell range **M22:M29**.

m. Double-click cell **M29** to evaluate the formula to ensure it is correct.

Notice the green cell referenced is E8, which is not correct. That cell reference adjusted when the original formula was copied down. Thus it is currently relative when the row reference should be absolute.

n. Press Esc, and then double-click cell **M22**. Place the insertion point in the formula to the left of the row number 1 for the first E1 reference. Type a $ sign to the left of the row number, E$1. Repeat the same correction for the last E1 cell reference to reflect E$1, then press Enter. Click cell **M22** again, and double-click the **AutoFill handle** to copy the formula in M22 down through M29. Double-click cell **M29** to ensure the cell references are correctly referencing the appropriate cells. Press Esc to leave edit mode.

o. Click cell **N22**, type =MIN(E$1,I22)*L22, and then press Enter. Click cell **N22**, and then double-click the **AutoFill handle** to copy the formula in N22 down through N29. Double-click cell **N29** to check that the cell references are correct, press Esc to get out of edit mode when done.

The MIN function was used to compare the actual hours accrued by the employee with 40, which is the maximum hours an employee could be paid at the regular pay rate. If the employee has less than 40 hours, it would take the actual hours, which would be the minimum value. If the employee has more than 40 actual hours they would get 40 hours paid at the regular pay and the extra—overtime hours—would be at the overtime rate. So, the MIN function will always pick the lower of the two values.

p. Click cell **O22**, type =MAX(I22-E$1,0)*(L22*E$2), and press Enter. Click cell **O22**, and then double-click the **AutoFill handle** to copy the formula in O22 down through O29.

q. Click the **Insert tab**, and then click the **Header & Footer button**. Click the **Design tab**, and then click the **Go to Footer button**. Click in the left footer section, and then click the **File Name button** in the Header & Footer Elements group.

r. Click any cell on the spreadsheet to move out of the footer, and then press Ctrl + Home. Click the **View** tab, and then click **Normal** in the Workbook Views group.

s. Click **Save**.

Objectives

1. Explore chart types, layouts, and styles in the design process. p. 184

2. Explore positioning of charts. p. 187

3. Use labels, objects, axes, and gridlines to develop a cohesive layout. p. 197

4. Learn to edit and format a chart using objects, text, and 3-D effects. p. 204

5. Develop a statement by emphasizing data, using sparklines, data bars, color scales, and icon sets. p. 208

6. Correct confusing charts. p. 213

7. Prepare a chart for printing and copying. p. 216

Using Charts

PREPARE CASE
Turquoise Oasis Spa Sales Reports

The Turquoise Oasis Spa managers, Irene and Meda, are pleased with your work and would like to see you continue to improve the spa spreadsheets. They want to use graphs to learn more about the spa. To do this Meda has given you a spreadsheet with some data, and she would like you to develop some charts. These charts will provide knowledge about the spa for decision-making purposes.

Courtesy of www.Shutterstock.com

Student data files needed for this workshop:

 e02_ws04_Spa_Sales

 e02_ws04_Couple

You will save your file as:

 Lastname_Firstname_e02_ws04_Spa_Sales

Designing a Chart

With Excel you can organize data so it has context and meaning, converting data into information. Now, you want to use the documented information and develop charts that convey the information in a visual manner to help interpret and analyze the data more clearly. Charts enlighten you as you compare, contrast, and examine how information changes over time. Learning how to work with charts means not only knowing how to create them but also realizing that different knowledge can be discovered or emphasized by each type of chart.

While it may seem simple to create a pie chart or bar chart, there are many considerations in creating your charts. Charts, as with pictures, are worth a thousand words. However, people interpret charts differently if the chart is not well developed. A well-developed chart should provide context for the information, without overshadowing key points to focus the message. Finally, it is pretty easy to confuse people with the choice and layout of a chart. You should create charts that convey true, real information, and your objective should be to provide a focused, accurate message.

In today's world of technology, it is probable that there will be a great deal of data available while working with charts, and many interpretations or messages can be extracted from the data. With a chart you will be trying to accomplish a couple of objectives with regard to the vast number of messages that are hidden within the data.

First, you may simply explore the data, and try to evaluate and prioritize all the messages. There may be a need to create multiple charts, using a variety of source data ranges, layouts, and designs as you interpret the data. In this case, examine the data, and let the charts tell a story.

Secondly, you may have some ideas or hypotheses about the data. Maybe a belief that a certain salesperson has a better performance or that certain types of massages are more popular with certain types of customers. Charts can visually support or refute a hypothesis.

Finally, you may have goals for which you want to use data to visually support your position. In this case you will need to select a specific and appropriate chart layout, use the necessary data, and design a chart that conveys your message clearly and unambiguously.

Regardless of the objective, just a small set of data allows you to create a variety of charts, each offering a different understanding of the data. In this workshop, you will start with understanding concepts for creating a chart in Excel, and understand which type of chart will depict the information in the best and most efficient manner.

Exploring Chart Characteristics—Types, Layouts, and Styles

When you decide to represent data visually, you need to make some initial decisions about the basic design of the chart. These initial decisions include the location of the chart, the type of chart, the general layout and style, and what data you will be using. These elements can be set initially and modified later. Best practice dictates that you first consider and develop the basic design of the chart.

Regardless of the location or type of chart, the process of creating a chart starts with the organization of the data on the spreadsheet. The typical structure is to have labels across the top of the data, along the left side of the data, or both. For example, you could have labels for each massage type in one column and the revenue for each in the column beside the labels. Or, you could have revenue columns, one for each of the past five years with labels across the top for each year. You do not have to have the labels and data sitting beside each other, although it helps when selecting data and making your chart.

Not all data, however, is organized to facilitate the creation of charts. For example, salesperson data on individual worksheets could be organized nicely on each worksheet, but this is not appropriate for creating a chart that would compare the various sales people. Ultimately, there may be a need to reorganize data prior to creating a chart.

When ready to create a chart, select the cells that contain both the label headings and the data. Rarely do people create a perfect chart the first time. Initially, you may start a chart, work with it for a while, and then realize a different chart would better convey the information. Fortunately, there is flexibility when designing. Thus, if you change your mind, you can modify the chart or simply start over.

Navigating a Chart

When you select the outer edge of a chart, you activate the largest component of the chart—the chart area. It will be highlighted on the border while the middle of the sides and the corners will have light, small dots used to signal resizing handles for the chart. The border edge can also be used to move the entire chart to a new location within the spreadsheet.

When a chart is selected, the data used in creating the chart will be highlighted in the data-sheet offering a visual clue of the associated data. This is the data that is being used within the chart. The purple border surrounds the data that represents the legend labels. The range with a blue border is the data that represents the data series for the pie slices. A **data series** is a set of data to be charted. A **data point** is an individual piece of data in a data series. There can be multiple data series.

Subcomponents of the chart can also be selected, such as the background, various text elements, and even the individual chart elements themselves. Click components to make them active, and adjust specific items through either the Ribbon options or by right-clicking to display the shortcut menu to see available options. In the pie chart constructed on the TableUse worksheet, the various components, like the chart background and the plot area, are easy to see because they use textured backgrounds. Obviously, this may not be the best color scheme as it is difficult to read the legend along the right side and the title.

While navigating through a chart, the Ribbon will display the Chart Tools contextual tabs, which include the Design, Layout, and Format tabs. These are specific tabs associated with formatting and adjusting chart elements. Click anywhere outside the chart border area, and this group of tabs will disappear. Click anywhere within the chart, and this group of contextual tabs will reappear.

Documentation in a worksheet is an internal document that details changes made to that workbook. This helps others to understand what and who made changes in the past and is an internal document that only a few people will see or use. You will want to practice safe file development procedures by saving the file and creating backups as needed.

To Update Documentation and Navigate a Chart

a. Click the **Start** button ⊕. From the Start Menu, locate and then start **Microsoft Excel 2010**.

b. Click the **File tab**, and then click **Open**. In the Open dialog box, click the **disk drive** in the left pane where your student data files are located, navigate through the folder structure, and then click **e02_ws04_Spa_Sales**.

c. Click the **Documentation worksheet tab** to make it the active worksheet, click cell **A6**, and then press ⌷Ctrl⌷+⌷;⌷ to input the current date. Click cell **B6**, and then type your first name and last name.

d. Click the **File tab**, click **Save As**, and then in the Save As dialog box, navigate to the location where you are saving your files. In the File name box, type Lastname_Firstname_e02_ws04_Spa_Sales, replacing Lastname with and Firstname with your own name, and then click **Save**.

e. Click the **Insert tab**, and then click the **Header & Footer** button in the Text group. Click the **Design tab**, and then click the **Go to Footer** button. Click in the **left footer section**, and then click **File Name** in the Header & Footer Elements group.

f. Click any cell on the spreadsheet to move out of the footer, press ⌷Ctrl⌷+⌷Home⌷, click the **View tab**, and then click **Normal** in the Workbook Views group.

g. Click the **TableUse worksheet tab** to view the pie chart on this worksheet, and then click **Save** ⊟.

 Notice that while the pie chart shows the data in a positive way, the design is overwhelming the data and message.

h. Click the **outer border edge** of the chart to select the chart and display the Chart Tools contextual tabs.

i. Click the **Layout tab**. If necessary, click the **Chart Elements arrow** in the Current Selection group, and then choose **Chart Area**. The Chart Elements box indicates that the Chart Area is the current selection.

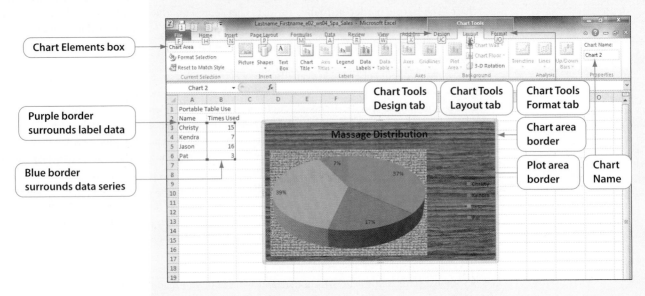

Figure 1 Navigating through a chart

j. With the border currently selected, click the **chart title** area. Notice the border appears around the chart title indicating it is the active component. The Chart Elements box in the Current Selection group will change to display Chart Title.

k. Click the **pie chart**. Notice the pie becomes the active component. You can then select individual pie slices by clicking the desired pie slice. The Chart Elements box will reflect the current selection.

l. Click the **green pie slice**. With the green slice as the active component, right-click the green slice to display the shortcut menu that contains options available for that component.

Troubleshooting

If you clicked on a pie slice and the percentage label displays a border with corner handles around it, then you have clicked on that element accidentally. You should click one more time on the pie slice, but not on any of the text labels.

m. Click the **Chart Elements arrow** in the Current Selection group, and then click **Plot Area**. It now becomes the active component with circle handles displayed on the four corners. These can be used to resize the plot area or change the background.

n. Click **Save** 💾. Click cell **A1**. Notice that the Chart Tools tabs have disappeared.

Real World Advice | First Impressions

First impressions are important with charts. You want the audience to receive the correct message during the initial moments. If the audience is distracted by the look and feel of the chart, they may stop looking for the message in the chart or extend the chaotic personality of the chart to the presenter. Thus, the chart can become a reflection upon you and your company.

CONSIDER THIS | Misleading Charts

Charts are supposed to frame information. But, have you ever seen a chart in a newspaper, online article, or magazine that would lead the viewer to an incorrect assumption or conclusion? Look for a chart that is misleading, discuss the context and possible incorrect conclusions that could be made, and consider the ethical aspect of the creator for that chart.

Quick Reference | Working with Chart Objects

It is possible to navigate through a chart using some of the guidelines below:
1. Click the chart edge to activate the Chart Tools group of tabs.
2. Click chart objects to select individual chart components.
3. Click again to select subobjects of any larger chart object.
4. Click another chart outside of an object or press Esc to deselect an object.
5. Use the Chart Elements list to select object components.
6. Use border corner handles to resize selected objects.
7. Click the border edge and drag to move a chart object.

Chart Locations

When developing a chart, consider the chart location as this might affect the flexibility of moving and resizing your chart components. There are two general locations for a chart—either within an existing worksheet or on a separate worksheet referred to as a chart sheet.

Creating Charts in an Existing Worksheet

Placing a chart within a worksheet can be very helpful, allowing you to display the chart beside the associated data source. When comparing charts side by side, placing the charts on the same worksheet can be handy. Additionally, placing a chart within the worksheet may offer easy access to chart components when copying and pasting components into other applications.

Your manager, Irene, would like you to work on some compiled data. Irene would like the data presented and organized in an effective graphical manner to aid in the analysis of the data so it is more informative.

To Create a Chart in an Existing Worksheet

a. Click the **Product_Data worksheet tab**, and then select the range **A3:I13** to use the data for creating a chart. Do not include the Totals in column J.

b. Click the **Insert tab**, and then click **Column** in the Charts group to display a gallery menu for column chart options.

c. Click **Clustered Column** under 2-D column. Notice the chart appears on the currently active spreadsheet and shows colored borders surrounding the associated data linked to the chart.

d. Click the **chart border** when the cursor appears as a four-way arrow [icon]. Be careful not to click the corners or middle areas of the border that are designated by small handles and used for resizing the chart. Drag the border to move the chart to the right of the data so the top-left chart corner is approximately in cell L3. Click **Save** [icon].

SIDE NOTE
Hover to See Icon Information

Remember, when presented with a set of icons such as the chart types, hover the mouse over an icon and a ScreenTip appears to offer descriptive information.

Modifying a Chart's Position

Charts created within the worksheet will appear as objects that "float" on top of the worksheet. It should be noted that the default property settings resize the chart shape if any of the underlying rows or columns are changed or adjusted. However, it is possible to change the setting to lock the size and position of the chart so it cannot be resized or moved.

To Modify the Chart Position on a Worksheet

a. Click the **TableUse worksheet tab**, and then click the **border edge** of the chart to select it. Right-click the **border edge** of the chart, and then click **Format Chart Area**.

b. In the Format Chart Area dialog box, click **Properties** to display the Properties settings.

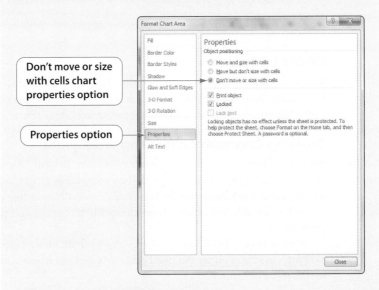

Figure 2 Format chart area

c. Click **Don't move or size with cells**, and then click **Close**. Click **Save** [icon].

The chart size will not change or be resized if the width or height of the columns or rows underneath are changed or adjusted. From here, you can easily move the chart by dragging the border, or you can resize the chart by clicking and dragging the corners.

Placing Charts on a Chart Sheet

A chart can also be created on a separate sheet. Having the chart on a separate chart sheet can make it easier to isolate and print on a page. A **chart sheet** is a worksheet with a tab at the bottom similar to other worksheets. However, the sheet replaces the cell grid with the actual chart. This is useful when you want to create a set of charts and easily navigate between them by sheet tab names rather than hunting for them on various worksheets.

SIDE NOTE

Color Code Your Chart Sheet Tabs

For easy management of your chart sheets, color the tabs of all the chart sheets the same so you can easily distinguish charts from worksheets.

SIDE NOTE

Moving a Chart Between a Chart Sheet and a Worksheet

The Move Chart button is the only simple method for transferring a chart from a worksheet to a chart sheet. This action cannot be undone once the chart is moved between the two locations.

To Create a Chart in a Chart Sheet

a. Click the **Product_Data worksheet tab**, select the range **A4:A13**, hold down CTRL, and then select **J4:J13** to create a pie chart showing the distribution of massage totals over the eight-week period.

b. Click the **Insert tab**, click the **Pie** button in the Charts group, and then under the 3-D Pie category, click **Pie in 3-D**. The chart will be inserted on the worksheet so you will need to move it to a chart sheet.

c. If necessary, click the **Design tab** on the Chart Tools contextual tab, and then click **Move Chart** in the Location group. The Move Chart dialog box is displayed.

d. Click the **New sheet** option. In the New sheet box, clear the existing name and type **MassageComparison**. Click **OK**. Notice, that you now have a new chart sheet tab in your workbook file. This chart sheet is exclusively for the chart and will not have the normal spreadsheet look and feel. Click **Save** .

Chart Types

The next thing you will need to do is decide what chart type to use. Each chart type conveys information differently. The chart type sets the tone for the basic format of the data and what kind of data is included. Thus, it helps to become familiar with the types of charts that are commonly used for business decision making and for presentations. Always consider which type is appropriate for the message you are trying to convey.

Pie Charts

Pie charts are commonly used for depicting parts of the whole such as comparing staff performance within a department or comparing the number of transactions of each product category within a time period.

For a pie chart you need two sets of data, the labels, and a set of corresponding values that make up the pie similar to the data selection made in the TableUse sheet to indicate the percentage of times each person used the portable massage table. Note that the data can be described as a percentage of the whole as in the chart.

The questions you have will influence what textual data you will include in any chart. If you are exploring a use fee then having the percentage would indicate which therapist would be contributing the most fees, and the actual numbers may not be a crucial element. When you create a chart, examine it to see if it answers your questions.

Line Charts

Line charts help convey change over a period of time. These are great for exploring how data in a business, such as sales or production, changes over time. Line charts help people to interpret why the data is changing and to make decisions about how to proceed. For example, when a doctor examines a heart rate on an electrocardiogram, he or she is looking at data over time to see what has been happening. The doctor wants to determine if there are issues, and then make decisions whether the patient should go home, be given medications, or have surgery.

To create a line chart you need to have at least one set of labels and at least one set of corresponding data. It is possible to have multiple sets of numbers, each set representing a line on the chart. For example, you may want to examine the number of massages given on a weekly basis. Each week would be a point on the line that is created. Each massage type would be a separate line on the chart.

To Create a Line Chart

a. Click the **Product_Data worksheet tab**, and then select the range **A3:I13** to include both the data and the labels.

b. Click the **Insert tab**, click the **Line** button in the Charts group, and then under 2-D Lines click **Line with Markers**.

c. With the chart still selected, click the **border edge** of the chart (not the corner), and then drag to move the graph below the data set so the top-left corner is in cell A15.

d. Position the mouse pointer over the bottom-right corner of the chart until the pointer changes to 🔲, and then drag to resize the chart so the bottom-right corner is over cell I30. Notice this chart is pretty chaotic, so it will need some editing later. Click **Save** 🖫.

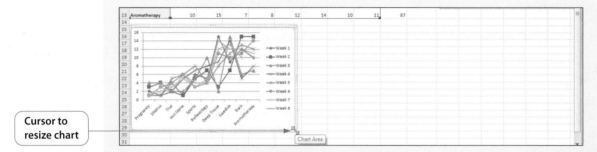

Cursor to resize chart

Figure 3 Resize chart

Troubleshooting

If you end up with a chart that looks dramatically different than what you would expect, check the colored borders around the linked data set. It is very common to select all the data in a table when the intention was to grab just some of the data. If too much data was selected, you can delete the selected chart by pressing Delete. Alternatively, you could select the corner of a colored link data border and drag the border to adjust the set of data. The blue-border data is displayed in the chart. When that border is adjusted, the associated label data is automatically adjusted accordingly. The chart is also automatically adjusted so changes can be immediately seen.

Column Charts

Column charts are useful for comparing data sets that are categorized, like departments, product categories, or survey results. Column charts are also useful for showing categories over time where each column represents a unit of time. Column charts are good for comparisons both individually, in groups, or stacked. Column chart data can easily allow for grouping of data so comparisons of the groups can occur.

To Create a Column Chart

a. Select the range **A3:I7** to include both the data and labels for the first four types of massages.

b. Click the **Insert tab**, click **Column** in the Charts group, and then click **Stacked Column in 3-D**. Notice the chart shows the massages grouped by weeks on the x-axis.

c. With the chart still selected, click the **Design tab**, and then click **Switch Row/Column** in the Data group. The chart changes to group by massage type along the x-axis for weekly stacked totals.

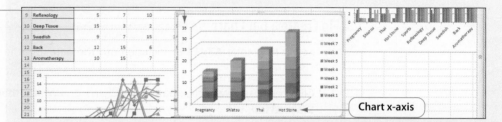

Figure 4 Chart Design tab

d. Click the **border edge** of the chart (not the corner), and then drag to move it to the right of the first column chart you created until the top-left corner is in cell W3.

e. If necessary, click the **bottom-right corner**, and then resize the chart so the bottom-right corner is over cell AD12. Click **Save** 🖫.

Notice the colors are the same for the weeks between massage types creating a visual comparison for all four massage types. For example, the first bottom blue strip for each column represents Week 1 for each type of massage. Thus, the column chart provides multiple perspectives and more information through the arrangement.

Even though the data could have been prepared with all ten types of massages over an eight-week period, you do not have to use all the data. Maybe the goal is to examine the data and extract a portion of the information, like the fact that several massage types are given a lot more than others. The types given most often are the Deep Tissue, Swedish, Back, and Aromatherapy.

In determining how to proceed once the data has been initially examined, start developing hypotheses and questions. For example, it may be that Shiatsu and Thai massages are very new and need to be marketed more. Develop questions and then use the data to determine the validity of the questions and make strategic decisions.

Real World Advice   Stacked or Grouped Columns

Should you stack or group a set of data? The column chart just created groups eight weeks of data for each of the four massage types. This allows for a visual comparison of the weeks for each massage type to easily see that the Hot Stone massage is chosen more than the other three types. This was not obvious before the row and column data were switched.

When the weeks are on the x-axis it may be better to group the massage types rather than stacking them. By grouping, the chart can visually compare the size of each column by week. Stacking the massage types would make the comparison within each week difficult. Ultimately it depends on what message you are trying to convey in the chart.

Bar Charts

Bar charts are useful for comparing data in groups and are similar to column charts. The bars are horizontal representations of the data rather than vertical. Like column charts, bar charts can depict a single piece of data, can be grouped sets of data, and even stacked.

Typically, bar charts would not be used with time components since time is traditionally shown on the x-axis. Stacked charts are useful when you want to see how the individual parts add up to create the entire length of each bar. For example, with the product data, you may want to compare each type of massage and see how the individual week's data is accumulating over time. While it is the same data as used for the line chart, it conveys information about an output without the emphasis on time that is inherent with the line chart.

To Create a Bar Chart

a. Select the range **A3:I13** to include both the data and the labels without the totals column.

b. Click the **Insert tab**, click **Bar** in the Charts group, and then under 2-D Bar click the **Stacked Bar**.

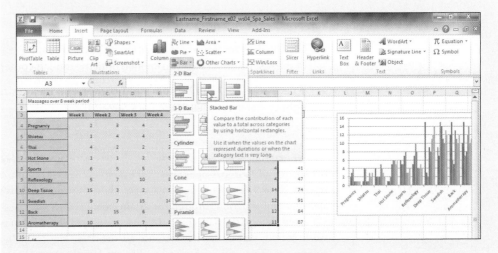

Figure 5 Bar chart options

c. With the chart still selected, click the **border edge** of the graph (not the corner) chart, and then drag so the top-left corner is over cell A33.

d. Click the **bottom-right corner**, and resize the chart until the bottom-right corner is over cell I47. Click **Save** 🖫.

The resulting chart depicts each type of massage. For each bar, each week is a different color, and the length is relative to the value for that week. The overall length of each bar is the cumulative total for that type of massage. From this we can see that for the eight-week period, three types of massages—Aromatherapy, Back, and Swedish—have the most overall number of massages, while Pregnancy has the least.

Scatter Charts

Scatter charts are a particular type of chart that conveys the relationship between two numeric variables. This type of chart is very common as a statistical tool depicting the correlation between the two variables. The standard format is to have the x-axis data on the leftmost column and the y-axis data in a column on the right side.

The data for a scatter plot could be categorical, such as gender and age, but this would produce two lines of data, one for male and one for female with the data points being the age. This can provide some knowledge for analysis but it can also be confusing when you first see the resultant chart.

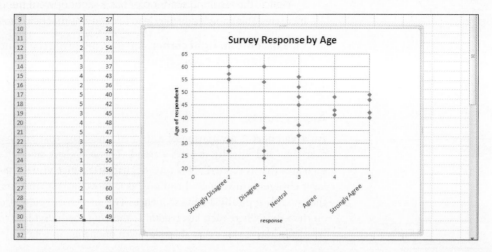

Figure 6 Categorical scatter plot

More typical is having the two sets of data being on the line of a continuum, such as age and the time the person has been on Facebook, as shown in Figure 7. With this chart, the data is on a continuum along the x-axis and y-axis rather than in categories. For the spa, the managers have data from a survey showing the requested temperature of the room used for massages and the age of the customer. With this data, you would have a wider range of temperatures and of ages, producing a more traditional scatter plot. This data may reveal important information as to what temperature is typically requested by different age groups.

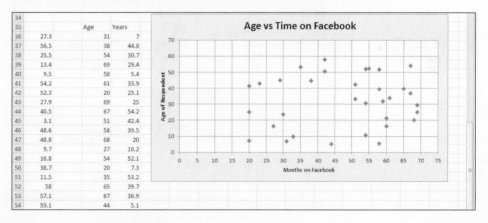

Figure 7 Scatter plot with continuous data

To Create a Scatter Chart

a. Click the **Survey worksheet tab** to make it active, select the range **A4:B34** to include the data and labels for Age and Temp Request.

b. Click the **Insert tab**, click **Scatter** in the Chart group, and then click **Scatter with only Markers**.

c. With the chart still selected, click the **border edge** of the graph (not the corner) chart, and then drag to move it below the chart to the right of the data, so the top-left corner is over cell E4.

   Notice, the resulting scatter plot has a slight upward trend as the age of the customer increases. This knowledge may lead to decisions that help provide better customer service.

d. Click the **bottom-right corner**, and then resize the chart until the bottom-right corner is over cell L20. Click **Save** 📄.

Area Charts

An **area chart** is a variation of a stacked line chart that emphasizes the magnitude of change over time and visually depicts a trend. The area chart stacks a set of data series and colorizes each area that is created. This type of chart has a nice visual characteristic because each colored layer changes, growing or shrinking, as it moves across time periods. Thus, with an area chart, the x-axis is typically a time sequence. The area chart could also use categories instead of time on the x-axis where each layer again is showing the individual contribution to the area; thus, it is a quantitative chart that shows growth or change in totals.

To Create an Area Chart

a. Click the **Product_Data worksheet tab**, and then select the range **A3:I13** to include the data and labels.

b. Click the **Insert tab**, click **Area** in the Chart group, and then under 2D Area click **Stacked Area**.

Figure 8 Stacked area chart

c. Click the **Design tab**, and then click **Switch Row/Column** in the Data group so the data will have the weeks as the x-axis scale.

d. With the chart still selected, click along the border edge of the chart (not the corner), and then drag to move the chart below the column chart so the top-left corner is over cell L14.

e. Click the **bottom-right corner**, and then resize the chart so the bottom-right corner is over cell S30.

f. Click **Save** 📄.

Quick Reference / Chart Selection Guide

The common types of charts and their usage are listed below:
1. Pie—Great for comparing parts of a whole
2. Line—Shows changes within a data series; used a lot with time as the x-axis
3. Column—Compares data vertically; can incorporate a time element and groups
4. Bar—Compares data horizontally; stacked bar can show progress, growth
5. Scatter—Used for correlations, exploring the relationship between two variables
6. Area—Used to highlight areas showing growth over time or for categories; a variation of a line chart

Chart Layouts, Styles, and Data

While the default chart settings are pleasant visually, you can still improve the look and feel of the chart. The chart layouts are clustered on the Design tab within the Chart Tools, in the Chart Layouts group. Excel provides a great deal of variety in arranging the components on a chart. This includes placement of the titles and legends as well as the display of information such as the data point values.

Chart styles are a variation of chart layouts. Where chart layouts focus on location of components, styles focus more on the color coordination and effects of the components. The chart styles are located on the Design tab within the Chart Tools group of tabs, in the Chart Styles group. The choices mix color options with shadows and 3-D effects to create a variety of templates. You can also start with a template then adapt it for individual tastes.

Chart data is the underlying data for the chart and labels. There can be many reasons for modifying data, and it can be accomplished through various methods. For example, if the data needs to be swapped between the data points and the axis data, you can use the Ribbon.

One helpful component of creating charts in Excel is that you may create the chart and then realize a need to correct some data errors. Because the chart is tied to data on the spreadsheet, changes are automatically reflected in the linked chart. This is extremely useful if you have a model that is using some calculations that are then used in a chart. You can do what-if analysis by changing the inputs and see the corresponding changes on the chart.

A second problem, as seen with some of the charts created, is when the chart has too much information making it difficult to get a clear picture. The initial charts may guide you to look at a smaller subset of data rather than all the data at once. The line chart on the Product_Data worksheet is one that is pretty chaotic, and it should be broken down a bit so it uses less data.

A third problem can occur when creating a chart and then discovering a need to add additional data to the chart. If the new data is adjacent to the existing data, it is a simple process to expand the existing data series. This is achieved by resizing the borders around the data series after activating the chart. If the data is on another sheet or location, it is advisable to relocate the new data so it is adjacent to the current data to simplify resizing the current data series borders.

To Work with Layouts, Styles, and Data

a. If necessary, click the **Product_Data worksheet tab**, and then click the **border edge** of the line chart (inside the chart border). Notice the purple, blue, and green borders around the source data. It may be that only the first four weeks of data needs to be examined since the current eight weeks of data is overwhelming.

b. Click the **bottom-right corner** of the blue border in cell I13, and then drag it to the left so the blue border only surrounds the cell range B3:E13. You should notice that the data on the chart changes and the legend only displays four weeks. Click **Save** 💾.

   Notice, the chart currently shows the different types of massages, each being depicted as a week. This doesn't really make sense. A clearer data presentation would have each line represent a type of massage and have each data point be one week. The current chart has a line made up of all the massage types, and thus it is difficult to interpret. If you have the weeks along the x-axis instead of the massage types, interpretation would be easier.

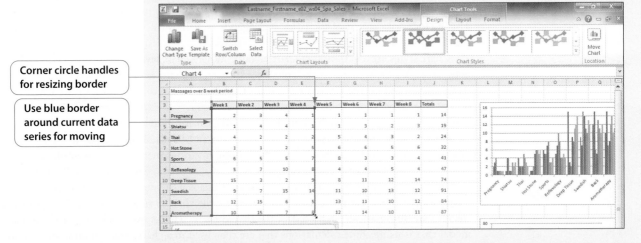

Corner circle handles for resizing border

Use blue border around current data series for moving

Figure 9 Adjust data in chart

Troubleshooting

If you click on the chart to see the source data associated with the chart and only see some of the data selected with a blue border, a chart component might have been clicked by mistake instead of the full chart area. To get the entire data set associated for the entire chart, click the border edge of the chart. When clicking a chart component, such as the bars, columns, pie slices, or a line, the selected chart component will determine which bordered linked data will display only blue.

c. With the chart still selected, click the **Design tab**, and then click **Switch Row/Column** in the Data group. Notice the data will be updated to show the weeks along the x-axis.

   If you want to split up the data set so only a few of the massage types are showing, but the set you want isn't together, you can still alter the data without having to start over. In Excel, you can reselect subsets of the source data.

d. Click the Design tab, click **Select Data**. The Select Data Source dialog box appears.

e. In the Chart data range input box, select the **13** at the end of the range reference, and then type **4**.

f. Type **,** (a comma) at the end of the range to signal adding a second range of data.

g. Click the **Collapse Dialog Box** , and then select the cell range **A8:E9**.

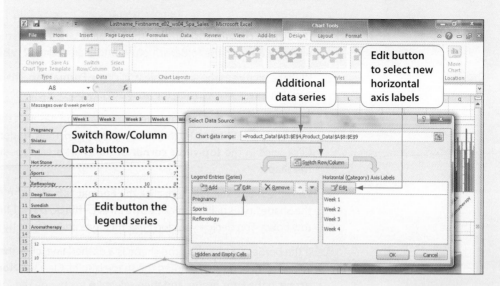

Figure 10 Select data source

h. Click the **Expand Dialog Box** to return to the dialog box, and then click **OK**. Notice that the chart should now have Pregnancy, Sports, and Reflexology as the three types of massages, over four weeks. The data source has been changed to be two separate sets of data without starting from scratch. Click **Save** .

Laying out a Chart

As you have seen, a chart can help answer questions or may even generate more questions. This helps move toward the understanding of information, which can also lead to better decision-making. Creating these initial charts to explore data is quick, efficient, and informs the user.

When presenting a chart to others, the context of the chart is of utmost importance. Without context, your audience will try to guess the context. You need to provide meaning.

Providing context means providing textual guidance to the audience. The audience will see the pie chart, but you need to inform them more about the data. This includes putting in titles, labels, and any miscellaneous objects that provide textual guidance. These components are found on the Layout tab within the Chart Tools.

Inserting Objects

If you work for a company, it would be useful to insert the company logo into any chart that is used outside the company. After all, marketing occurs everywhere. It may also be useful to use images to help convey the tone of the presentation. This can be accomplished with an image inserted into the chart.

To Insert Objects into a Chart

a. Click the **MassageComparison worksheet tab** containing the pie chart.

b. Click the **Layout tab**, and then click **Picture** in the Insert group. In the Insert Picture dialog box, click the disk drive in the left pane where your student data files are located, navigate through the folder structure, and then click **e02_ws04_Couple**. Click **Insert**.

c. With the picture as the active object, click the **Format tab**, change the **Shape Height** to 1", and then press Enter. Drag the image to position it in the bottom-left corner of the chart.

d. Click the **edge** of the chart to select the chart and deselect the picture. Click the **Layout tab**, click the **Shapes** in the Insert group, and then under Basic Shapes click **Oval**. Click once in the **top-right corner** of the chart area. Type Massage Distribution into the shape.

e. With the shape still selected, click the **Format tab**, click the **More** ⬇ button to display the Shape Styles gallery. Click **Subtle Effect – Black, Dark 1** from the first column, fourth row down. You decide you don't like this style and undo it by pressing Ctrl+Z.

f. If the border surrounding the shape is a dashed line, click the surrounding border once so the border line surrounding the shape is solid. Click the **Home tab**, click the **Font Size arrow** in the Font group, and then select **16** to change the font size.

g. Click the **Format tab**, and then change the **Shape Height** in the Size group to 1" and the **Shape Width** to 2". Press Enter.

h. Click the **border** of the shape, and then drag the shape to the top-right corner of the graph area. Click the **edge** of the chart sheet to deselect the shape. Click **Save** 💾.

Working with Labels

Labels are another crucial element needed to provide context in charts. The labels include the chart title and axes titles, the legend, and the labels for the data. All these elements should work cohesively to convey a complete picture of what the chart is trying to convey to the audience.

Titles for the Chart and Axes

Chart and axes titles are input easily through the Layout tab within the Chart Tools set of tabs. The Labels group has all the elements for inserting and positioning the labels.

To Work with Titles

a. Click the **Product_Data worksheet tab**, and then click the **line chart** directly under the data to display the set of Chart Tools tabs. Click the **Layout tab**, click **Chart Title** in the Labels group, and then click **Above Chart**.

b. Select the **Chart Title text**, if necessary, and type Massage Monthly Highlights. Press Enter to apply the changes to the title above the chart.

c. On the Layout tab, click the **Axis Titles** button in the Labels group, point to **Primary Horizontal Axis Title**, and then click **Title Below Axis**.

d. With the x-axis title selected, type Week and then click the edge of the chart to apply the title change and deselect the component.

e. On the **Layout tab**, click the **Axis Titles** button in the Labels group, point to **Primary Vertical Axis Title**, and then click **Vertical Title**.

f. With the y-axis title selected, type **No. of massages**. Notice the typed text appears in the formula bar, but the component still displays the text Axis Title. Press Enter or alternatively click the edge of the chart to apply the title changes.

g. Click the **border edge** of the bar chart below the line charts to make it the active chart.

h. On the **Layout tab**, click **Chart Title** in the Labels group, and then click **Above Chart**. Notice the title is the active component.

i. Click in the **formula bar** and type =, click cell **A1**, and then press Enter. The bar chart now reflects the text contained in cell A1 on the Product_Data worksheet. Click **Save** 💾.

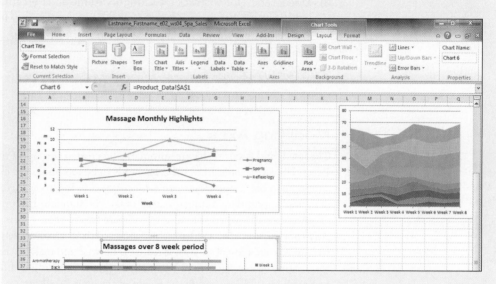

Figure 11 Formula bar with chart title

CONSIDER THIS | **The Unit of Analysis**

You are presented with a chart titled "2012 Sales Report" and the x-axis is showing 20, 30, 40, and so on for the scale. What is this report depicting? Is it the number of sales transactions—number sold—or the revenue for 2012? Are the 20, 30, and 40 the actual numbers or in hundreds or thousands? What context should there be to make certain the audience knows? Should the term "Sales" ever be used without qualifying whether it is sales revenue or sales volume?

Working with the Legend and Labeling the Data

The legend is an index within a chart that provides information about the data. With some charts the legend is automatic and adds context. With other charts, such as pie charts, it is possible to incorporate the legend information beside each pie slice. When the parts are labeled on the chart, the legend is not needed and can be removed. This is accomplished by clicking on the Legend button on the Layout tab and choosing None. If the legend is missing, go to the same location and simply add the legend to the chart using any of the various options listed.

Labels can also be added alongside of the data on the chart. This is quite informative as it moves the information from a legend to the data. This can be a visually useful addition. The data labels can be added, moved, or removed through the Data Labels button on the Layout tab.

To Work with Legends and Labeling

a. Click the **MassageComparison worksheet tab** and, if necessary, click the **border edge** of the chart to display the Chart Tools contextual tabs.

b. Click the **Layout tab**, click **Legend** in the Labels group, and then click **None**. Notice that the legend disappears from the chart and the chart enlarges to fit the space.

c. Click the Layout tab, click **Data Labels**, and then click **More Data Label Options**. The Format Data Labels dialog box is displayed.

d. Under Label Options, click the **Category Name** and **Percentage** check boxes. Leave the other options Value and Show Leader Lines selected, and then click **Close**. Notice the data labels are now showing the massage type, the value, and the percentage represented by each pie slice.

e. Click **Save** 🖫.

Modifying Axes

The x-axis and y-axis scales are automatically created through a mathematical algorithm within Excel. However, sometimes the scale needs to be modified. For example, when the numbers are spread out a bit, a significant gap can exist near 0. In this case, you can modify the scale to start at a more appropriate number instead of 0—the standard minimum value for Excel.

Additionally, when you need to compare two or more charts, the scales must be consistent. Any time you put charts side by side, you need to also make sure your x-axis and y-axis scales are the same. Your audience may not realize otherwise and make incorrect assumptions or decisions.

Lastly, the axis data could be jammed together, making it difficult to read. In this situation, you would be able to modify the layout of the scale by adjusting the alignment of the data. The data on the axis can be vertical, horizontal, or even placed at an angle.

For these elements and more, you work through the Layout tab in the Axes group. Choose the Axes button and at the bottom of all the gallery menus for Labels and Axes buttons, there is always a choice for more options. These additional options will provide a dialog box that offers more choices beyond the most common options offered on the gallery menu, options such as formatting the background fill, border color, styles, and number formats, as well as many others.

SIDE NOTE
The Quick Right-Click
Remember, if you select a component, such as the y-axis, right-click over the selected area and choose a format option from the menu to quickly get the dialog box that pertains to the selected component.

To Work with Axes

a. Click the **Product_Data worksheet tab**, and then click the **border edge** of the clustered column chart—the chart positioned just to the right of the data starting at cell L3.

b. Click the y-axis vertical numbers, so that component is selected. Looking at the y-axis scale, the scale goes up to 16, but the highest bar column is at 15, which is also the highest value in the weekly data. That scale maximum can be changed.

c. Click the **Layout tab**, click **Axes** in the Axes group, and then point to **Primary Vertical Axis** to view the submenu. Notice some standard options for the axis, including numbers in thousands or millions. Click **More Primary Vertical Axis Options**.

d. In the Format Axis dialog box, click **Axis Options**, if necessary, and then under Maximum click **Fixed**. In the Maximum input box, select 16, type 17, and then click **Close**.

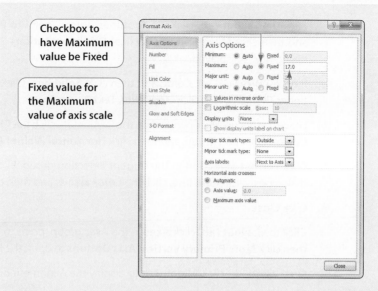

Checkbox to have Maximum value be Fixed

Fixed value for the Maximum value of axis scale

Figure 12 Format Axis options

e. Click the **border edge** of the line chart that starts in cell A15 so it becomes the active chart.

f. On the Layout tab, click **Axes**, point to **Primary Horizontal Axis**, and then click **More Primary Horizontal Axis Options**. The Format Axis dialog box appears.

g. On the left side, click **Alignment** to display the alignment options.

h. Under Text layout, click the **Custom angle arrow** until **25** is displayed.

i. Click **Close**. The horizontal axis weekly labels should now be displayed at an angle.

j. Click **Save** .

Changing Gridlines

Gridlines are the lines that go across charts to help gauge the size of the bars, columns, or data lines. In Excel, the default is to display the major gridlines (the gridlines at the designated label values) and not to display the minor gridlines (the gridlines between the label values). If the chart is a line or column chart it will put in the horizontal major gridlines while the bar chart will put in vertical major gridlines. The default is a good starting point, but personal preferences can dictate which lines to display.

The Format Axis dialog box is handy for manually setting the axis options for consistency between a set of charts. Under the Axis Options, the default Excel setting is Auto. This is also where to find the Excel settings for the major and minor gridline units. To change and adjust these units, change the Auto option to Fixed, then adjust the corresponding fixed value. If the source data for the chart is changed, the scale will remain fixed (and will not automatically be updated); therefore, any fixed values may also need to be reevaluated as source data changes.

To Work with Gridlines

a. Click the **border edge** of the stacked bar chart found starting in cell A33.

b. Click the **Layout tab**, and then click **Gridlines** in the Axes group. Point to **Primary Vertical Gridlines**, and then click **Minor Gridlines**. This will increase the number of vertical gridlines on the chart.

If you cannot find the minor gridline option on the Chart Elements list in the Current Selection group of the Layout tab, that is because the Minor gridlines must first be added to the chart.

c. Click the **Layout tab**, click the **Gridlines** button, point to **Primary Vertical Gridlines**, and then click **More Primary Vertical Gridlines Options**. The Format Major Gridlines dialog box is displayed.

d. If necessary, click **Line Color**, and then click **Solid line**. Click the **Color arrow**, and then under Theme Colors, click **Dark Blue, Text 2**.

e. Leave the dialog box open and on the Layout tab, click the **Chart Elements arrow** in the Current Selection group, and then click **Horizontal (Value) Axis Minor Gridlines**.

f. Click **Format Selection** in the Current Selection group. In the Format Minor Gridlines dialog box, click **Solid line**, click the **Color arrow**, and then click **Dark Red**.

g. Click **Close**.

h. Click the **Layout tab**, click **Axes** in the Axes group, point to **Primary Vertical Axis**, and then click **More Primary Vertical Axis Options** to open the Format Axis dialog box.

i. On the left side, click **Alignment** to display the Alignment options.

j. Under the Text layout section, click in the **Custom angle** box, and then type **-45** degrees.

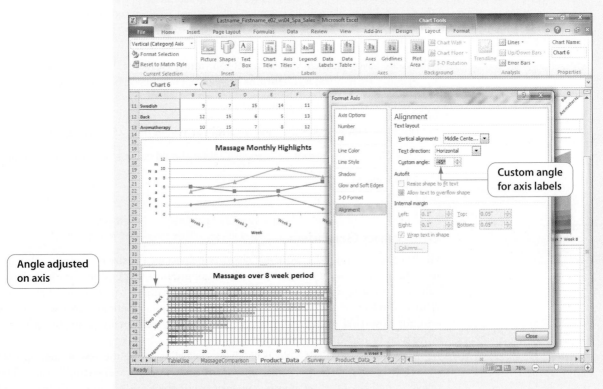

Figure 13 Horizontal vertical alignment

k. Click **Close**.

l. Click the border of the stacked bar chart. Click **Format tab**, click in the **Shape Height** box in the Size group, type **4.5"**, and then press [Enter] to expand the display of the massage types along the y-axis. Click **Save** 🔲.

Analysis with Trendlines

Excel has a few tools that can help analyze data within a chart. The Analysis group is on the Layout tab within the Chart Tools contextual tabs. One of the most common analysis tools is the trendline. A **trendline** is a line that uses current data to show a trend or general direction of the data. Data, however, can have a variety of patterns. For scatter plots that explore how two variables interact, a linear trend may be seen. For example, as the price for Oreo cookies drop, we would expect sales of milk to increase because everyone knows a glass of milk is the perfect companion for dunking cookies.

If the data fluctuates or varies a great deal, it may be more desirable to use a moving average trendline. Instead of creating a straight line based on all the current data, the moving average trendline uses the average of small subsets of data to set short trend segments over time. The moving average trendline will curve and adjust as the data moves up or down.

The trend or pattern of the data may suggest or predict what will happen in the future. For linear trends, the predicted data can be charted using the Linear Forecast Analysis feature and the current trend of the data.

The trendline for the Survey worksheet data indicates older customers may desire a warmer room than younger customers. This may lead the staff to adjust the room temperature prior to a customer arriving. The staff could predict the desired temperature based on the age of the customer. The data suggests a correlation between age and room temperature. This could help improve customer satisfaction. Again, you may want to consider other demographics—characteristics—of the customers that allow for providing a customized and personalized service that will build customer loyalty and repeat business. It is easier to retain customers than find customers.

To Insert a Trendline

a. Click the **Survey worksheet tab**, and then click the **border edge** of the chart to select it.

b. Click the **Layout tab**, click **Trendline** in the Analysis group, and then click **Linear Trendline**. Click **Save**.

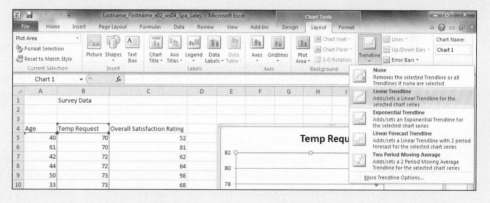

Figure 14 Insert linear trendline

Editing and Formatting Charts

When formatting a chart it is important to have a plan in mind as to the overall layout and look and feel. With a thought-out plan, it will be easy to apply the desired adjustments to the components with regard to position, color, and emphasis. Typically, you can either create a unique layout or modify one of Excel's many layouts. Either way, being able to make formatting changes is easy and a very useful and powerful way to convey information. In this section, you will explore various ways to format a chart.

Colorizing Objects

Working some color into charts can be helpful from a marketing perspective. To change the colors of objects within the chart, simply select the item and use the Format tab within the Chart Tools contextual tabs. Excel offers options that allow changing the interior color as well as the border color. When examining the properties of any component within a properties dialog box for that component, you will typically see options on the left side indicating Fill, Line Color, Line Style, and so on. These are formatting and color options. Keep in mind, while it is possible to spruce up charts with color, it is also possible to overdo it.

To Work with Formatting and Color

a. Click the **Product_Data worksheet tab**, and then click the **border edge** to select the line chart beginning in cell A15.

b. Click the **Format tab**, and then change the **Shape Height** in the Size group to 4" and the **Shape Width** to 8". Press [Enter].

c. Click the **Format tab**, and verify that the Chart Elements box in the Current Selection group is displaying **Chart Area**. If necessary, click the **Chart Elements arrow**, and then click **Chart Area**.

d. Click the **Format tab**, click the **Shape Fill** button in the Shape Styles group, and then select **Olive Green, Accent 3, Lighter 80%**.

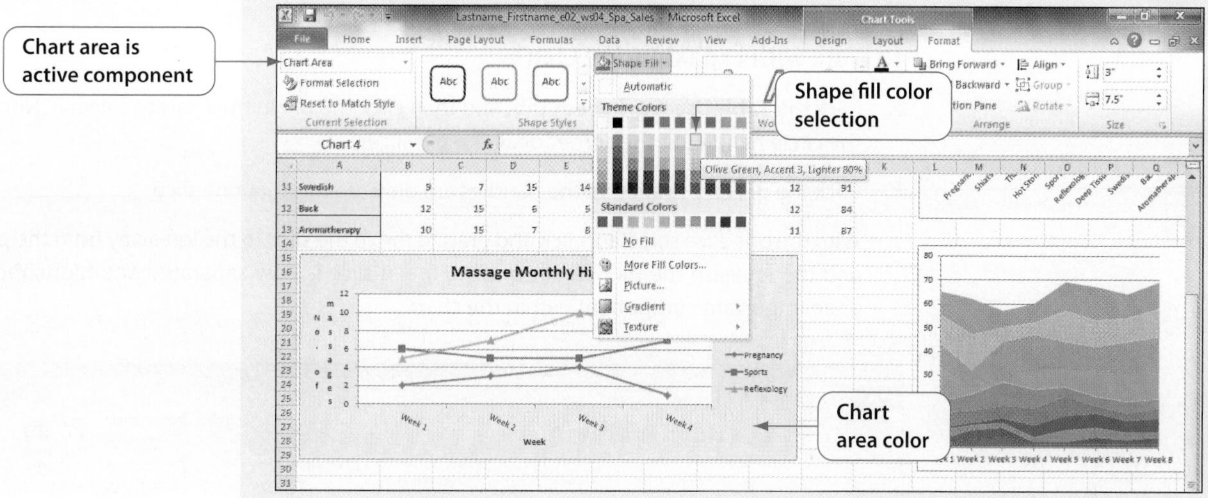

Chart area is active component

Shape fill color selection

Chart area color

Figure 15 Shape fill with color

e. Click the **Layout tab**, click the **Chart Elements arrow** in the Current Selection group, and then click **Legend**.

f. Click the **Format tab**, click the **Shape Outline** button in the Shape Styles group, and then click the **Black, Text 1** to apply a black border to the legend.

g. On the Format tab, click the **Shape Outline** button again, point to **Weight**, and then click the **1½ pt** weight line. If necessary, click the **border edge** of the bar chart below the line chart, and then drag it down and position it in a row so it does not overlap the line chart. Click **Save** .

Working with Text

Whether the text is in a text box, title, legend, or axis scale you can format the text in one of two methods. For some stylish formatting of text, use the Format tab and select the buttons from the Ribbon. This is where you would select WordArt Styles or Shape Styles. However, to change font characteristics such as font type or size, you can do this from the Home tab or by right-clicking the selected text and using the Mini toolbar options.

To Format Text Within a Chart

a. Click the **Survey worksheet tab**, and then click the **chart title** once to make it active. Verify the border surrounding the title component is a solid line and not a dashed line. If necessary, click the **title border edge** again to make the surrounding border solid.

b. Type Temperature Survey and then press Enter to apply the change.

c. With the title still selected, click the **Format tab**, click the **Text Fill** button in the WordArt Styles group, and then click **Dark Red**.

d. Click the **Home tab**, click the **Font arrow**, and then scroll as necessary to locate and click **Brush Script MT**. Click **Save** .

Exploding Pie Charts

The traditional pie chart is a pie with all the slices together. Preset options offer a pie chart with a slice pulled slightly away from the main pie or you can manually move a slice outward creating an exploded pie chart. This technique allows for highlighting a particular part of the pie. To explode a pie slice, simply click to select the correct pie slice and then drag it away from the rest of the pie.

To Work with Exploding Pie Charts

a. Click the **TableUse worksheet tab**, and then click the **pie** in the chart to select it. Notice the circle handles at the corner of all the pie slices.

b. Click the **green pie slice** so the handles are only around that one slice.

c. With the one slice selected, click and drag to move the slice to the left away from the pie, and then release the mouse button. The green slice is now separated and highlighted as an important component within the chart.

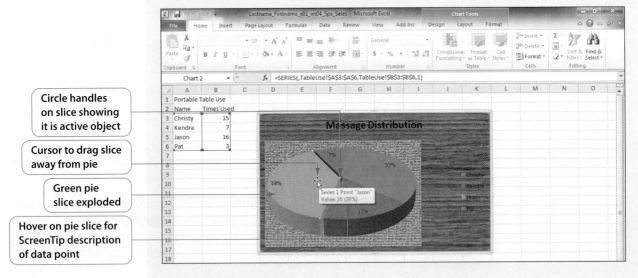

Circle handles on slice showing it is active object

Cursor to drag slice away from pie

Green pie slice exploded

Hover on pie slice for ScreenTip description of data point

Figure 16 Explode pie slice

d. Click the **blue textured border edge** to select the **Plot Area**. Click the **Format tab**, click the **Shape Fill** button, and then select **White, Background 1**. Click the **chart border edge** to select the entire chart area, click the **Shape Fill** button again, and then click **White, Background 1** to fill the chart area and plot area with the same color. Press [Esc] to deselect the chart.

e. Click the **Insert tab**, and then click the **Header & Footer** button in the Text group. Click the **Design tab**, and then click the **Go to Footer** button. Click in the left footer section, and then click the **File Name** button in the Header & Footer Elements group.

f. Click any cell on the spreadsheet to move out of the footer, and then press [Ctrl]+[Home]. Click the **View tab**, and then click the **Normal** button in the Workbook Views group. Click **Save** 🖫.

3-D Charts and Rotation of Charts

The 3-D effect and rotation of charts is something that should be used conservatively. The effect can be done well, or it can be abused, resulting in a chart that goes overboard and distracts from the information. You can choose the 3-D effect when starting to develop a chart. Additionally, options are available to rotate the 3-D effect, giving the chart a crisp distinctive look. The 3-D

Format and rotation options are found in the Format dialog box. The 3-D format can be applied to a variety of objects. The 3-D Rotation setting is intended for the chart area only.

The column chart is still too busy with all the weeks and massage types. You may explore a subset of data and realize that showing a smaller set will allow you to make a point about certain massage types or weeks. Then, you will apply formatting to add a little pop to the chart.

To Work with 3-D and Rotating Charts

a. Click the **Product_Data worksheet tab**, click the **border** of the stacked column chart that is found in cell L3 so the chart displays the borders around the source data series.

b. Using the corner handles of the blue data border, resize the border so it surrounds the cell range **F10:I13** to display the four massage types for weeks five through eight.

c. Click the **Design tab**, click **Change Chart Type** in the Type group, and then click **3-D Clustered Column**. Click **OK**.

d. Click the **Layout tab**, and then click **3-D Rotation** in the Background group to display the Format Chart Area dialog box.

e. Under Rotation, select the **20** in the X: box, and then type **30**. Select the **15** in the Y: box, and then type **10**. Click **Close**.

Figure 17 3-D rotation

The 3-D option can be reset as needed by clicking the Reset button in the Format Chart Area dialog box. The 3-D effect becomes more dramatic if you include some color changes to the chart area, particularly to the walls and floor.

f. Click the **Layout tab**, click the **Chart Elements** arrow in the Current Selection group, and then click **Walls**.

g. Click **Format Selection** in the Current Selection group to display the Format Walls dialog box. Under Fill, click **Solid fill**, click the **Color arrow**, and then click **Tan, Background 2, Darker 10%**. Keep the dialog box open.

h. Click the **Layout tab**, click the **Chart Elements arrow**, and then click **Floor**.

i. In the Format Floor dialog box, under Fill, click **Solid fill**, click the **Color arrow**, and then click **Tan, Background 2, Darker 50%**.

j. Click **Close**, and then press Esc to deselect the chart.

k. Click any cell outside the chart. Click the **Insert tab**, and then click the **Header & Footer** button. On the Design tab, click the **Go to Footer** button. Click in the left footer section, and then click the **File Name** button in the Header & Footer Elements group.

l. Click any cell on the spreadsheet to move out of the footer, press Ctrl+Home, click the **View tab**, and then click the **Normal** button in the Workbook Views group.

m. Click **Save** .

Quick Reference / Formatting Options for Chart Objects

Below are format options for charts and their descriptions:
1. Number—Format data as currency, date, time, etc.
2. Fill—Fill the background of a component with a color, picture, or pattern
3. Border Color—Set the color of the border for a component
4. Border Styles—Set the thickness and type of border for a component
5. Shadow—Add shadowing effect to a component
6. Glow and Soft Edges—Add glow and edge effects to a component
7. 3-D Format—Add 3-D effects to component
8. Alignment—Align text direction for a component, left, top, vertical, horizontal, etc.

Effectively Using Charts

The effectiveness of a chart is dependent on the chart type, the layout, and formatting of the data. Charts should provide clarity and expand the understanding of the data. Charts used in a presentation should support the ideas you want to convey. The charts should highlight key components about an issue or topic being addressed in the presentation. Providing too much information on a chart can confuse or hide the issue being discussed. It can be difficult to get a point across if the chart is confusing, cluttered, or packed with too much information.

Strategic Statements with Charts

The same data can be viewed through various perspectives, emphasizing different parts of information. Charts typically do three things:

- Support or refute assertions
- Clarify information
- Help the audience understand trends

Emphasizing Data

As with any set of data, you can reasonably expect to find multiple ideas that could be emphasized. Typically within a business, one to three key issues might be chosen for discussion. The idea is to eliminate any extraneous data from the chart that does not pertain to the issues being emphasized. Common methods can be employed to emphasize the idea in the chart. When using a single chart, highlight a particular data set within the chart to help focus attention to a key point. Depending on the chart type, the emphasis may be depicted differently as shown in Figure 18.

Single Chart Types	Common Emphasis Methods
Pie chart	Explode a pie slice
Bar/Column	Use an emphasizing color on the bar/column
Line	Line color, weight, and marker size
Scatter	Adding a trendline

Figure 18 Single chart types

Another way of emphasizing information on a chart is to create a chart that uses two types of charts. This is useful when you have a clustered column chart, where data has been grouped in columns but you also want to show the average of each group. Rather than have the average of the group shown as yet another column in the cluster, it is possible to have the averages of each cluster depicted as a line chart that overlays the clustered columns. This is an effective method for comparing clusters of data. The technique requires combining all the data together into one chart, then taking a specific subset of data and converting it to a second chart type.

To Combine Two Chart Types

a. Click the **Product_Data worksheet tab**, click cell **K3**, and then type Average. Click cell J3, click the **Home tab**, in the Clipboard group click **Format Painter**, and then click cell **K3** to apply the same cell border formatting to the new cell heading.

b. Click cell **K4**, and then type =AVERAGE(B4:I4). Press Enter.

c. Click cell **K4**, and then double-click the **Auto Fill handle** to extend the formula in K4 down through K13.

d. Select the range **A3:I13**, then hold down Ctrl, and select range **K3:K13** so both ranges are selected, excluding the totals column.

e. Click the **Insert tab**, click **Column** in the Charts group, and then click the **Clustered Column**.

f. Click the **Format tab**, select the **Shape Height** box, and then type 5". Select the **Shape Width** box, and then type 8". Press Enter. Notice on the chart that the last series in the legend is **Average**. Click the **border edge** of the chart, and then drag to reposition the chart so the top-left corner is over cell L33.

g. Click the **Format tab**, click the **Chart Elements arrow** in the Current Selection group, and then click **Series "Average"** to select that series as the active component within the chart.

h. Click the **Design tab**, click the **Change Chart Type** button in the Type group, click **Line**, and then click the **Line with Markers**. Click **OK**.

i.   Click the **Format tab**, click the **Chart Elements arrow** in the Current Selection group, and then click **Series** "**Average.**" Click **Format Selection** in the Current Selection group to display the Format Data Series dialog box.

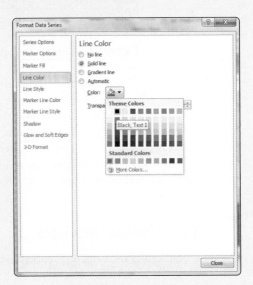

Figure 19   Series chart elements

j.   In the Format Data Series dialog box, click **Line Color**, click **Solid line**, click the **Color arrow**, and then click **Black, Text 1**.

k.   In the Format Data Series dialog box, click **Line Style**, and then in the **Width** box, select **2.25 pt** and type 3.5. Click **Close**.

Notice the Average data for the clusters is clearly shown with a thick black line. The line representing the average for each cluster helps clarify the information trend.

l.   Click **Save** .

Sparklines

Sparklines are small charts that are embedded into a spreadsheet, usually beside the data to facilitate quick analysis of trends. A sparkline can be used within a spreadsheet to give an immediate visual trend analysis, and it adjusts as the source data changes.

The sparkline can graphically depict the data over time through either a line chart or a bar chart that accumulates the data. For example, for the spa, during a week of massage specials, the daily number of massages could be added to a spreadsheet and the totals would appear in a sparkline to show the progress for each therapist.

To Work with Sparklines

a. On the Product_Data worksheet, right-click **column A**, and then click **Insert**. Right-click the new **column A**, and then click **Column Width**. In the **Column width** box type **25** to expand the width setting. Click **OK**.

b. Select the cell range **A4:A13**. This is the target cell range to create a set of sparklines showing the trend over time for each of the massage types.

c. Click the **Insert tab**, and then click the **Line** button in the Sparklines group to display a Create Sparklines dialog box.

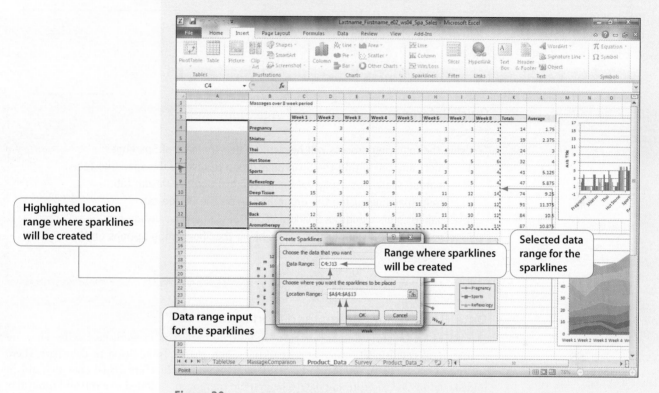

Highlighted location range where sparklines will be created

Range where sparklines will be created

Selected data range for the sparklines

Data range input for the sparklines

Figure 20 Creating a sparkline

d. In the Create Sparklines dialog box, in the Data Range input box, click **Collapse Dialog Box** , and then select the range C4:J13.

e. To the right of the input box, click **Expand Dialog Box** , and then click **OK**.

   The Sparklines appear in column A and display the trend over the eight-week period for each massage. The sparklines are grouped together by default so if any one cell in the group is selected, an outline is displayed surrounding the entire set—in this case the cell range A4:A13. When changes are applied, they will be applied for all the sparklines in that group. Sparklines can be edited to change colors or to display markers on the highest or lowest points.

f. If necessary, select the range **A4:A13**.

g. Click the **Design tab**, click the **Sparkline Color** button in the Style group, and click **Dark Red** to change the line color.

h. Click the **Design tab**, and then click to select **Markers** in the Show group to display the data markers on the sparklines. Click **Save** 💾 .

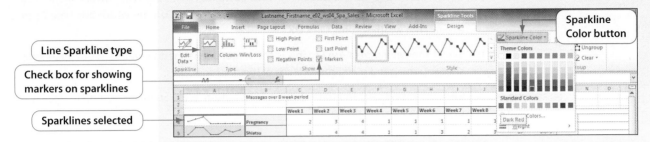

Figure 21 Sparkline Design tab

Quick Reference Working with Sparklines

Using the following process will help in the development of Sparklines:
1. Select any cell within the Sparklines group to display the Sparkline Tools.
2. Ungroup sparklines using the Ungroup button on the Design tab.
3. Group sparklines using the Group button on the Design tab.
4. Change colors using the Sparkline Color button on the Design tab.
5. Choose to show high or low points using the Show group options on the Design tab.

Data Bars, Color Scales, and Icon Sets

Data bars are graphic components that are overlaid onto data in worksheet cells. They are a mixture of conditional formatting, sparklines, and charts. In addition to data bars, there are color scales and icon sets that work the same way. All three are visual cues that aid in understanding and interpreting data. The graphic component is added to a cell and interprets a set of data in a range giving color codes or images that help a spreadsheet user gain a quick understanding of the data.

These Excel components are found on the Home tab in the Styles group as gallery menu options on the Conditional Formatting button. The data bars can be applied as a one-color solid fill or a gradient fill from left to right as the numerical value gets bigger. With the Color Scales, the color shifts as the numerical values change. A low score could be red, while a high score could be green. The icon sets provide images to indicate the good/bad or positive/negative rating to the value. This technique can be employed with scores, ratings, or other data where the user would want to do a visual inspection to see a relative scale on the data. With the spa, the survey data includes an overall satisfaction rating. Using these visual cues would enable a manager to glance through the data and quickly distinguish the lowest or highest scores.

To Work with Data Bars

a. Click the **Survey worksheet tab**, select the cell range **C5:C34** to select the Overall Satisfaction Rating data. Since the data represents a collection of scores, where low scores are bad and high scores are good, it would be useful to have a color scale.

b. Click the **Home tab**, click **Conditional Formatting** in the Styles group, point to **Color Scales**, and then click **Green – Yellow – Red Color Scale**.

   Notice the lower numbers are red while the high numbers are green. Using this technique it is possible to scan through the data to get a sense that there are not many low satisfaction scores and there is a higher incidence of high scores.

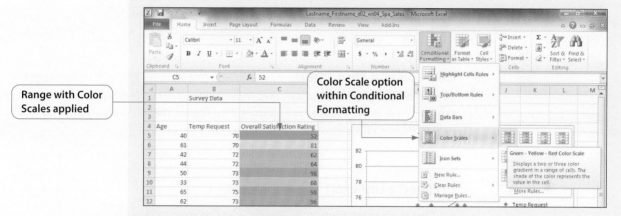

Figure 22 Color scales on data

c. Click the **Insert tab**, and then click the **Header & Footer** button. Click the **Design tab**, click the **Go to Footer** button, click in the left footer section, and then click the **File Name** button in the Header & Footer Elements group.

d. Click any cell on the spreadsheet to move out of the footer, and then press [Ctrl]+[Home]. Click the **View tab**, and then click the **Normal** button in the Workbook Views group.

e. Click **Save** 📙.

Recognizing and Correcting Confusing Charts

The process of working with and creating visually appealing charts with clear messages involves recognizing when you have a confusing chart. It is possible to have too much information, ambiguous information, or even inappropriate chart types for the data. Irene has included a worksheet that contains questions the managers want to explore with charts. Irene has requested that you take a look at the charts a previous staff member started.

The Massage Sales column chart was to address the question of highlighting massage data over the eight-week period. However, there is so much information that it is difficult to get a clear picture of any particular highlights. Additionally, it appears the scaling is off. Examining the data shows the chart includes the totals—making the y-axis scale ineffective. Changing this and focusing on only a few weeks and few massage types can accentuate some details about the data.

To Correct an Overloaded Chart

a. Click the **Product_Data_2 worksheet tab**, and then click the **border edge** of the Massage Sales – 8 Week Report column chart to select the chart. This chart shows so much information that there is no clear message.

b. In the source data for the chart, drag the **bottom-right corner** of the blue border in the data area toward the left until it is over cell D13.

c. In the source data for the chart, drag the **top-right corner** down until the blue border is over row 10 and includes the range B10:D13. The chart now has less information, which emphasizes the data for four massage types compared for three weeks.

d. Click **Save** 🖫.

Correcting a Line Chart

The second question explores sales over the time period. The Weekly Sales chart shows that the time period is not being depicted on the x-axis. Rather, the weeks are in the legend. The chart did not include all the labels.

To Correct a Line Chart

a. Click the **border edge** of the Weekly Sales line chart to select it.

b. Click the **Design tab**, and then click **Select Data** in the Data group.

c. In the Select Data Source dialog box, under the Horizontal (Category) Axis Labels, click the **Edit** button. The number labels need to be changed to reference the names of the massage types.

d. In the Axis label range box, click **Collapse Dialog Box** 🔲, and then select the cell range **A4:A13**. Click the **Expand Dialog Box** button 🔲, and then click **OK**. This will place the massage type names along the x-axis; however, the desired result would be to switch the legend week labels with the massage types.

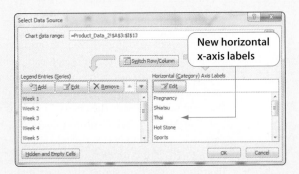

Figure 23 Axis labels—corrected

e. In the Select Data Source dialog box, click the **Switch Row/Column** button to make the legend list the massage types and the x-axis labeled by weeks. Click **OK**.

f. Click the **Format tab**, change the **Shape Height** in the Size group to **4.5"** and the **Shape Width** to **7.5"**. Press Enter. Looking carefully, you notice that the Hot Stone massages have been increasing. But it is lost in all the data.

g. With the Weekly Sales chart still selected, drag the **bottom-right corner** of the blue bor-
    der up to adjust the range of data from B4:I13 to B4:I7 to display the four massage types.

h. Click once on the **Hot Stone data series** in the Weekly Sales line chart to select this
    component.

i. Click the **Format tab**, verify that the **Chart Elements** box in the Current Selection group
    displays **Series** "**Hot Stone**", and then click **Format Selection** to display the Format Data
    Series dialog box.

j. On the left side of the dialog box, click **Line Style**, and then in the **Width** box change the
    width from 2.25 to **6 pt**. Click **Close**. The Hot Stone line will be emphasized in the chart.
    Now, with less data the growth of the Hot Stone massages is accentuated.

k. Click **Save** 🖫.

Changing the Chart Type and Legend

Finally, the Sales Comparison chart was an attempt to compare totals by week. The line chart
does have totals, but the x-axis is showing the totals for each massage type labeling them
numerically since no labels have been set up. Secondly, the chart does not really allow comparison of the massages for the entire time period. A pie chart would be more appropriate.

To Change Chart Type and Legend

a. Click the **border edge** of the Sales Comparison chart.

b. Click the **Design tab**, click **Change Chart Type** in the Type group, and then under the
    Pie category click **Pie**. Click **OK**.

c. Click the **Design tab**, and click **Select Data** in the Data group to display the Select Data
    Source dialog box. Under Horizontal (Category) Axis Labels, click the **Edit** button so the
    legend can be changed.

d. With the insertion point in the Axis label range input box, select the range **A4:A13**, and
    then click **OK**. This will put the massage types as the legend. Click **OK** to close the Select
    Data Source dialog box.

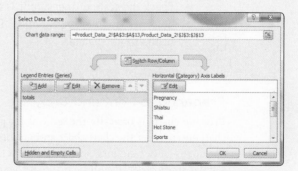

Figure 24 Edit Horizontal Axis Label

e. Click the **Layout tab**, click the **Data Labels** button, and then click **More Data Label
    Options**.

f. In the Format Data Labels dialog box, under Label Options, click to select **Percentage** so both Value and Percentage are shown (as well as Show Leader Lines). Click **Close**. Press Esc to deselect the chart.

The pie chart now allows a comparison of the massage types over the entire time period. By including both the percentage and the value, it provides more complete information for the decision makers.

g. Click the **Insert tab**, and then click the **Header & Footer** button. Click the **Design tab**, and then click the **Go to Footer** button. Click in the left footer section, and then click the **File Name** button in the Header & Footer Elements group.

h. Click any cell on the spreadsheet to move out of the footer, and then press Ctrl + Home. Click the **View tab**, and then click the **Normal** button in the Workbook Views group. Click **Save** .

Quick Reference / Common Charting Issues

These are common issues you should try to avoid in the development of charts.
1. Not enough context; users don't understand the chart
   - Add titles to x-axis and y-axis.
   - Add a chart title that conveys context of time and scope.
   - Add data labels to show percentages or values of chart elements.
2. Too much information on the chart
   - Use a subset of the data, rather than all the data.
   - Summarize the data so it is consolidated.
3. Incorrect chart type
   - Choose a type more appropriate, such as a line chart for trends.
4. Chart readability issues
   - Check the color scheme to ensure text is readable.
   - Check font characteristics such as font type or font size.
   - Move data labels, and remove excess information.
   - Resize the overall chart to provide more area to work.
   - Check the color scheme and formatting so it is professional and doesn't hide chart information or text.
5. Misleading information or labeling
   - Check the scaling to ensure it is appropriate and labeled for the correct units.
   - Consider the following wording: Does "Sales" mean the number of transactions or the total revenue?

Preparing to Print and Copy

Printing charts is basically the same as for printing any portion of a spreadsheet. If printing a chart sheet, select the chart sheet and go through the normal printing process and adjust print options as you would for a spreadsheet. The chart will be a full-page display. If the chart is on a regular spreadsheet, it will be printed if you choose to print everything on the spreadsheet. In this case, the chart will be the size you developed on the spreadsheet. This is convenient when you want to print some tables or other data along with the chart. Finally, if you want to print just the chart on the spreadsheet, select the chart first, then choose the print option to Print Selected Chart to print only the current chart.

Another useful technique when exploring data through charts is the ability to create static copies of the chart that can be used to compare with later versions. You can, in essence, take a picture of a chart that will not retain the underlying data. Maybe after exploring changes to the chart, a second or third static picture is taken to use for chart comparisons. The process of creating a picture of the chart is to select the chart, copy it, then use the Paste Special option and paste it as a picture. When pasting as a picture, there are multiple picture format options such as a PNG, JPEG, or GIF file.

To Create a Chart Picture

a. Click the **Product_Data worksheet tab**, and then click the **border edge** of the chart starting in cell M14.

b. Click the **Home tab**, click **Copy** in the Clipboard group, and then press [Esc] or click outside the chart (on the worksheet) to deselect the chart.

c. On the **Home tab**, click the **Paste arrow**, and then click **Paste Special** to display the Paste Special dialog box.

d. Click **Picture (GIF)**, and then click **OK**.

   The picture will be inserted and can be resized or moved as needed. The picture can even be used in another application like Word or PowerPoint.

e. Using the border of the picture, move the picture so the top-left corner is over cell B58.

f. Press [Esc] or click outside the chart to deselect the chart element.

g. Click the **Massage Comparison worksheet tab**, click the **Insert tab**, and then click the **Header & Footer** button to display the Page Setup dialog box.

h. Click the **Custom Footer** button to display the Footer dialog box, and then click to place the insertion point in the **Left section** box. Click **Insert File Name** 🗎 to insert the file name in a left footer section when the chart sheet is printed.

i. Click **OK**, and then click **OK** again.

j. Click **Save** 🖫, and then close Excel.

1. Describe a scenario where you would want to use a line chart.

2. You want to compare the revenue that each of your departments has generated as a portion of total revenue. What type of chart would you choose and why?

3. You have transaction data pertaining to three types of gasoline sold at the gas station. Think of questions that you might explore and the type of chart that would help answer those questions.

4. List the ways in which context for a chart is provided.

5. What ethical issues arise when creating charts?

Key Terms

Area chart 194
Bar chart 192
Chart sheet 189
Column chart 190

Data bars 212
Data point 185
Data series 185
Line chart 189

Pie chart 189
Scatter chart 192
Sparkline 210
Trendline 203

Visual Summary

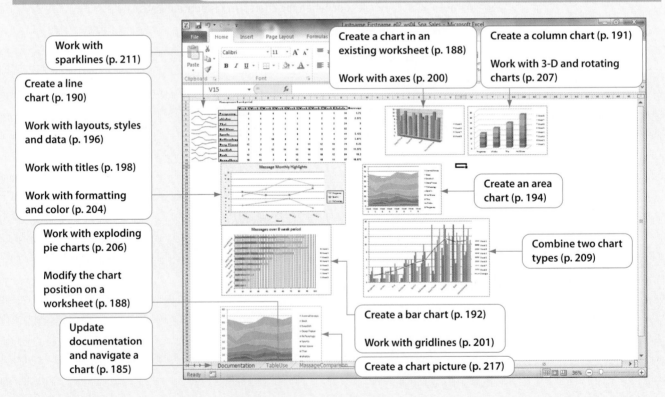

Work with sparklines (p. 211)

Create a line chart (p. 190)

Work with layouts, styles and data (p. 196)

Work with titles (p. 198)

Work with formatting and color (p. 204)

Work with exploding pie charts (p. 206)

Modify the chart position on a worksheet (p. 188)

Update documentation and navigate a chart (p. 185)

Create a chart in an existing worksheet (p. 188)

Work with axes (p. 200)

Create a column chart (p. 191)

Work with 3-D and rotating charts (p. 207)

Create an area chart (p. 194)

Combine two chart types (p. 209)

Create a bar chart (p. 192)

Work with gridlines (p. 201)

Create a chart picture (p. 217)

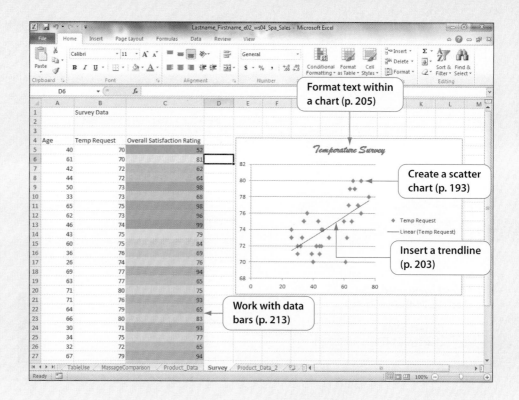

Format text within a chart (p. 205)

Create a scatter chart (p. 193)

Insert a trendline (p. 203)

Work with data bars (p. 213)

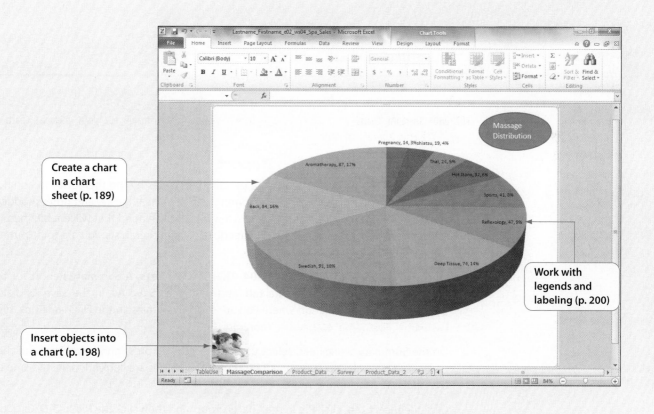

Create a chart in a chart sheet (p. 189)

Work with legends and labeling (p. 200)

Insert objects into a chart (p. 198)

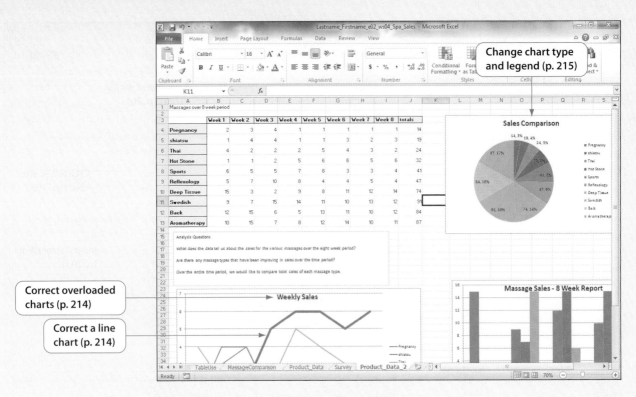

Figure 25 Turquoise Oasis Spa Sales Final Reports

Practice 1

Student data file needed:
e02_ws04_Therapist_Charts

You will save your file as:
Lastname_Firstname_e02_ws04_Therapist_Charts

Therapist Product Sales Report

The managers have pulled together data pertaining to sales by the therapists. In addition to massages, the therapists should also promote skin care, health care, and other products. With the monthly data, the managers want a few charts developed that will enable them to look at trends, compare sales, and provide feedback to the therapists. You are to help them create the charts.

a. Start **Excel**, and then open **e02_ws04_Therapist_Charts**. A Summary Report for the month is displayed. Click the **File tab**, and then click **Save As**. In the Save As dialog box, navigate to the location where you are saving your files. In the File name box, type Lastname_Firstname_e02_ws04_Therapist_Charts.

b. On the Summary worksheet, select the range **B12:J12**, press and hold Ctrl, and then make a second selection of range **B17:J17** so two ranges are currently selected, one for the labels and one for the Totals.

c. Click the **Insert tab**, click **Pie** in the Charts group, and then click the **Pie in 3-D**. Click the **border edge** of the chart, and then drag to the right to reposition the chart until the top-left corner of the chart is in cell M1. Click the **Format tab**, and then change the **Shape Height** to 4" and the **Shape Width** to 6". Press Enter.

d. Click the **Layout tab**, click the **Chart Title** button, and then click **Above Chart**. Type Therapist Transactions for the Month and then press Esc.

e. On the **Layout tab**, click the **Chart Elements arrow** in the Current Selection group, and then click **Series 1**. Click **Data Labels**, and then click **More Data Label Options** to display the Format Data Labels dialog box. Under Label Options, click to select **Percentage** so percent is included along with **Value** and **Show Leader Lines**. Click **Close**.

f. Click the **Pie** (be careful not to click the label text). Click once again on the **red pie slice** to select the one slice. Click and drag the slice to the right so it is exploded from the rest of the pie.

g. Select the range **A20:J24**, click the **Insert tab**, click the **Bar** button, and then under 2-D Bar click **Stacked Bar**. Click the **border edge** of the chart, and drag down to reposition the chart until the top-left corner of the chart is in cell A27.

h. Click the **Layout tab**, click the **Chart Elements arrow** in the Current Selection group, and then click **Plot Area**. Click **Format Selection**, and then under Fill, click **Solid fill**. Click the **Color arrow**, and then click **Tan, Background 2**. Leave the dialog box open.

i. Click the Layout tab, click the **Chart Elements arrow**, and then click **Horizontal (Value) Axis** to select the x-axis in the chart. The dialog box changes to the Format Axis dialog box. Under Axis Options, click **Fixed** for the Minimum value and type 200 for the minimum fixed value. On the left side of the dialog box, click **Alignment**, and adjust the **Custom angle** to 40 degrees. Click **Close**.

j. Select the range **B25:J25** for creating a set of sparklines for the revenue data.

k. Click the **Insert tab**, and then click the **Line** button in the Sparklines group to display the Create Sparklines dialog box.

l. To the right of the **Data Range** box, click the **Collapse Dialog Box**, and then select the range **B21:J24**. Click the **Expand Dialog Box**, and then click **OK**. Click on any cell outside of the sparklines to deselect the sparklines.

m. Click the **Insert tab**, and then click the **Header & Footer** button. Click the **Design tab**, and then click the **Go to Footer** button. Click in the **left footer section**, and then click the **File Name** button in the Header & Footer Elements group.

n. Click any cell on the spreadsheet to move out of the footer, and then press Ctrl + Home. Click the **View tab**, and then click the **Normal** button in the Workbook Views group.

o. Click **Save**.

Practice 2

Student data file needed:	You will save your file as:
e02_ws04_Giftshop_Charts	Lastname_Firstname_e02_ws04_Giftshop_Charts

Gift Shop Sales Analysis

The managers of the gift shop have pulled together sales data for the store. The data was collected over a three-month period and summarizes the average daily sales revenues. The managers are interested in examining the trends to see if there are differences in revenues based on time of day and day of the week. They wonder how revenue compares with different time periods. Using the data provided, create a set of charts that may reveal information they can use with regard to staffing needs and projecting future sales.

a. Start **Excel**, and then open **e02_ws04_Giftshop_Charts**. A sales spreadsheet will be displayed. Click the **File tab**, and then click **Save As**. In the Save As dialog box, navigate to the location where you are saving your files. In the File name box, type Lastname_ Firstname_e02_ws04_Giftshop_Charts.

b. On the SalesData worksheet, select the range **A4:A16**. Hold down the Ctrl key, and then select the cell range **F3:H16**. Click the **Insert tab**, click **Column** in the Chart group, and then under 3-D Column, click **Stacked Column in 3-D**.

c. Click the **border edge** of the chart, and then drag it down to reposition the chart until the top-left corner is over cell A18. Click the **Format tab**, change the **Shape Height** to 4" and the **Shape Width** to 7". Press Enter.

d. Click the **Layout tab**, click the **Chart Title** button, and then click **Centered Overlay Title**. With the title selected, in the formula bar type Daily Revenue by Hour and then press Esc. On the Layout tab, click **Format Selection** in the Current Selection group to continue to format the title.

e. In the Format Chart Title dialog box, under Fill, click **Solid fill**, click the **Color arrow**, and then click **Blue, Accent 1** if necessary. On the left side of the dialog box, click **Border Color**. Under the Border Color options, click **Solid line**, click the **Color arrow**, and then if necessary, click **Blue, Accent 1**.

f. With the dialog box open, click the **Layout tab**, if necessary click the **Chart Elements arrow** in the Current Selection group, and then click **Walls**. In the Format Walls dialog box, under Fill, click **Solid fill**, click the **Color arrow**, and then click **Tan, Background 2**.

g. With the dialog box still open, click the **Chart Elements arrow**, and then click **Horizontal (Category) Axis** to select the x-axis scale to change the alignment for the scale. In the Format Axis dialog box, on the left side of the dialog box, click **Alignment**, and change the **Custom angle** to 30 degrees. Click **Close**.

h. Click the **border edge** of the chart to deselect the components. Click the **Design tab**, and then click **Select Data** in the Data group. In the Select Data Source dialog box, under Horizontal (Category) Axis Labels, click the **Edit** button. With the insertion point in the Axis label range box, select the cell range **A4:A16**, click **OK**, and then click **OK** again.

i. On the SalesData worksheet, select the range **A3:F16**. Click the **Insert tab**, click the **Line** button, and then click **Stacked line with Markers**.

j. Click the **border edge** of the chart, and then drag to the right to reposition the chart until the top-left corner is over cell K3.

k. Click the **Layout tab**, click the **Chart Title** button, and then click **Above Chart**. Notice the formula bar as you type Revenue Generated Hourly and then press Enter.

l. On the **Layout tab**, click the **Axis Titles** button, point to **Primary Horizontal Axis Title**, and then click **Title BelowAxis**. Notice the formula bar as you type Time of Day and then press Enter.

m. On the **Layout tab**, click the **Axis Titles** button, point to **Primary Vertical Axis Title**, and then click **Rotated Title**. Notice the formula bar as you type Revenue and then press Enter.

n. On the SalesData worksheet, select the range **A3:H16**. Click the **Insert tab**, click the **Area** button, and then under 2-D Area click **Stacked Area**.

o. Click the **Design tab**, click the **Switch Row/Column** button in the Data group so the day of the week is the x-axis labels and the hours of the day are listed in the legend labels.

p. Click the **border edge** of the chart and drag down and to the right to reposition the chart until the top-left corner is over cell K20.

q. Click the **Layout tab**, click the **Chart Title** button, and then select **Above Chart**. Notice the formula bar as you type Revenue Generated Daily and then press Enter.

r. Click the **Axis Titles** button, point to **Primary Horizontal Axis Title**, and then click **Title Below Axis**. Notice the formula bar as you type Day and then press Enter.

s. On the Layout tab, click the **Axis Titles** button, point to **Primary Vertical Axis Title**, and then click **Rotated Title**. Notice the formula bar as you type Revenue and then press Enter. Press Esc to deselect the chart.

t. Click the **Insert tab**, and then click the **Header & Footer** button. Click the **Design tab**, and then click the **Go to Footer** button. Click in the **left footer section**, and then click the **File Name** button in the Header & Footer Elements group.

u. Click any cell on the spreadsheet to move out of the footer, and then press Ctrl+Home. Click the **View tab**, and then click the **Normal** button in the Workbook Views group.

v. Click **Save** .

MODULE CAPSTONE

More Practice 1

Student data file needed:
e02_mp_Restaurant_Sales

You will save your file as:
Lastname_Firstname_e02_mp_Restaurant_Sales

Restaurant Marketing Analysis

The restaurant receives data on a daily basis that can be used for analysis to gauge its performance and determine needed changes. The restaurant is considering entering into a long-term agreement with a poultry company and getting a new refrigeration unit to store the chicken. The restaurant also ran a marketing campaign for its Chicken Caliente because a chef recently modified the dish. Management would like you to analyze some trends with the restaurant's chicken dishes, see if the marketing is working for the new dish, and explore an amortization table for the refrigerator loan.

a. Start **Excel**, and then open **e02_mp_Restaurant_Sales**. Click the **Documentation worksheet tab**. Click in cell **A6**, and then press Ctrl+; to input the current date. Click cell **B6**, and then type in your first name and last name.

b. Save the file as Lastname_Firstname_e02_mp_Restaurant_Sales.

c. Click the **Summary worksheet tab**, and then click cell **C2**. Type =TODAY() and then press Enter.

d. You need to consolidate the weekly quantity sold on the Summary sheet.
    - Click cell **C28**, type =, and then select the **Week1 worksheet tab**. Click cell **C5**, and then press Enter.
    - Click cell **D28**, type =, and then select the **Week2 worksheet tab**. Click cell **C5**, and then press Enter.
    - Click cell **E28**, type =, and then select the **Week3 worksheet tab**. Click cell **C5**, and then press Enter.
    - Click cell **F28**, type =, and then select the **Week4 worksheet tab**. Click cell **C5**, and then press Enter.
    - Select range **C28:F28**, click the **AutoFill handle**, and then drag down through row 35 to copy those four formulas for the remaining cell range C29:F35.

e. You also need to summarize the data to calculate the totals and average for each item.
    - Click cell **F5**, type =SUM(C28:J28), and then press Enter.
    - Click cell **G5**, type =SUM(C17:J17), and then press Enter.
    - Click cell **H5**, type =AVERAGE(C28:J28), and then press Enter.
    - Select range **F5:H5**, click the **AutoFill handle**, and then drag down through row 12 to copy those three formulas for the remaining cell range F6:H12.

f. Click cell **D5**, type =E5*F5, and then press Enter. Click cell **D5**, click the **AutoFill handle**, and then drag to copy the formula down through cell D12.

g. Click cell **L17**, type =IF((C28-C17)/C17>=$N$14,1,0), and press Enter. Click cell **L17**, click the **AutoFill handle**, and then drag down to copy the formula through L24. Use the AutoFill feature across to column O so the formula is copied into the range L17:O24.

h. Click cell **T17**, type =SUM(L17:S17), and then press ⎵Enter⎴. Click cell **T17**, click the **AutoFill handle**, and then drag down to copy the formula through cell T24.

i. Click cell **A17**, type =IF(T17=MAX($T$17:$T$24),"Top Performer",""), and then press ⎵Enter⎴. Click cell **A17**, click the **AutoFill handle**, and then drag down to copy the formula through cell A24.

j. Select the range **A28:A35**. Click the **Insert tab**, and then click **Line** in the Sparklines group. To the right of the Data Range box, click the **Collapse Dialog Box**, select the range **C28:J35**, click **Expand Dialog Box**, and then click **OK**. Click the **Design tab**, and then click the **Markers** check box in the Show group to toggle this feature on.

k. Select range **B27:F35** so you can create a growth chart for chicken sales by type of dish.

- Click the **Insert tab**, click **Bar** in the Charts group, and then click **Stacked Bar** (first row, second column).

- Click the **Layout tab**, click the **Chart Title** button in the Labels group, click the **Above Chart** option, type Chicken Sales — Accumulative, and then press ⎵Enter⎴.

- Click the edge of the border chart area, and then drag to reposition the chart so the top-left corner falls in cell A37. Click near the right border chart edge, and then when the resize cursor appears click and drag to the right to resize until the right chart edge fills column E.

- Click the **Layout tab**, and then click the **Format Selection** button in the Current Selection group.

- Under Fill, click the **Solid fill** option button, click the **Color** button, click **Orange, Accent 6, Lighter 40%** (fourth row, last column), and then click **Close**. Press ⎵Esc⎴ to deselect the chart.

l. Select range **B27:F35** so you can create a line chart showing the Caliente dish sales.

- Click the **Insert tab**, click **Line** in the Charts group, and then click **Line** (first row, first column).

- Click the border edge, and then drag to move the chart so the top-left corner is over **G37** (across from the previous chart). Click near the right border chart edge when the resize cursor appears, and then click and drag to the right to resize until the right chart edge fills column N.

- Click the **Design tab**, and then click **Switch Row/Column** in the Data group.

- Click and drag the top-left corner of the blue border that surrounds the linked data range C28:F35 until the border only surrounds the range **C33:F35**.

- Click the **Layout tab**, and then click **Format Selection** to change the chart area background.

- Under Fill, click the **Solid fill** option button, click the **Color** button, and then click **Orange, Accent 6, Lighter 40%**. Leave the dialog box open.

- Click the **Layout tab**, click the **Chart Elements arrow** in the Current Selection group, and then click **Series "Chicken Caliente"**.

- On the left side of the Format Data Series dialog box, click **Line Color**. Under Line Color, click **Solid line**, click **Color**, and then click **Red**.

- On the left side of the Format Data Series dialog box, click **Line Style**, and then change the **Width** to 4.25 pt. Leave the dialog box open.

- Click the **Layout tab**, click the **Chart Elements arrow** in the Current Selection group, and then click **Vertical (Value) Axis**. Under the Axis Options, click the **Fixed Minimum** option, and then adjust the minimum value by typing 20.0. Click **Close**.

- Click the **Layout tab**, click **Chart Title** in the Labels group, click **Above Chart**, and then type Caliente - New Recipe Promotional Sales. Press ⎵Enter⎴. If necessary, widen the title so the text is on one line. Press ⎵Esc⎴, and then press ⎵Ctrl⎴+⎵Home⎴.

m. Click the **Loan worksheet tab**. Click cell **C7**, type =-PMT(C6/12,C5*12,C4), and then press Enter. Note: Be sure to type a negative character between the equal sign and the PMT function name.

n. On the Loan worksheet tab, add the following formulas for the amortization table.

- Click cell **B12**, and then type =C4 since the beginning balance in the first month is the loan amount. Press Enter.

- Click cell **B13**, type =F12, and then press Enter since the beginning balance for the remainder of this column is the ending balance from the previous month. Click to select **B13** again, and then double-click the **AutoFill handle** to copy the formula down through the range B13:B131.

- Click cell **C12**, type =$C$6/12*B12, and then press Enter.

- Click cell **D12**, type =IF(B12<$C$7,B12+C12,$C$7), and then press Enter. This will check the balance, and if it is less than the normal monthly payment, the payment will be the balance plus the interest for that month. If the balance is greater than the payment, the normal payment will be made.

- Click cell **E12**, type =D12-C12, and then press Enter. This is the amount of the payment that goes towards reducing the principal loan amount.

- Click cell **F12**, type =B12-E12, and then press Enter. This will give the ending balance for the month.

- Select the range **C12:F12**, and then double-click the **AutoFill handle** to copy the formulas down through the range C12:F131.

o. Select the range **C12:C131**, click in the **Name Box**, type Interest, and then press Enter.

p. Click cell **C9**, type =SUM(Interest), and then press Enter so the total interest is calculated. Notice the total interest paid on $15,000 for 10 years is $4,091.79. If you change the number of years from 10 to 5 in cell C5, the total interest paid would be $1,984.11—a lot less interest to pay.

q. Insert the file name Lastname_Firstname_e02_mp_Restaurant_Sales into the left section of the footer.

r. Press Ctrl+Home. Click **Save**, and then close Excel.

Problem Solve 1

Student data file needed:	You will save your file as:
e02_ps1_Hotel_Survey	Lastname_Firstname_e02_ps1_Hotel_Survey

Hotel Marketing Survey

The hotel periodically surveys guest satisfaction prior to the guest leaving. You need to chart this data. The hotel is also considering hiring a company to complete a comprehensive customer satisfaction and marketing research analysis. This project would require a loan of $50,000 to be paid in quarterly payments over one year. The manager would like a simple amortization schedule for this loan.

The Survey_Q10 worksheet contains a set of recent customer survey data in A23:J98. The respondents marked their rating for the question asking for the likelihood they would return. A response of 1 indicates no intention of returning, and a response of 10 indicates a high likelihood of returning. Above the data, you need to create summary information and a chart of all the scores.

a. Start **Excel**, and then open **e02_ps1_Hotel_Survey**. Click the **Documentation worksheet tab**. In A6, press Ctrl+; to input the current date. Click cell **B6**, and then type your first name and last name. Save the file as Lastname_Firstname_e02_ps1_Hotel_Survey.

b. Click the **Survey_Q10 worksheet tab**. Click cell **B8**, and then enter a COUNTA that ignores blank cells while counting the number of x's for the choice 1, in range A24:A98. Calculate a similar COUNTA formula in cells B9:B17 using the appropriate range corresponding to the Score number.

c. With the scores tallied, create a **Clustered Cylinder** column chart showing the count by score. In creating the chart, develop the following:

   - Position the top-left corner of the chart over cell G2.
   - Resize the chart to have a height of 3.5" and width of 6".
   - Change the Chart background to **Orange, Accent 6, Lighter 80%**.
   - Insert a chart title above the chart that displays Plans to Return, Move the chart title to the top-left corner of the graph area. Remove the chart legend.
   - Add a text box that states 10 - Definitely will on the first line and 1- Definitely will not on the second line. Make the text box .5" high and 1.5" wide, and then position it in the top-right corner of the graph area.
   - Change the columns for 7, 8, 9, and 10 to **Olive Green, Accent 3, Darker 25%**.
   - Change the columns for 4, 5, and 6 to **Yellow**.
   - Change the columns for 2 and 3 to **Red**.
   - Change the Chart Area **3-D Rotation** to a 15 degree Perspective. Hint: Click the Format Selection button and appropriate option from the resulting dialog box, and then uncheck the **Right Angle Axes** to adjust perspective value.
   - Change the Vertical (Value) Axis to a Fixed Major unit of 5.0.

d. Click the **Satisfaction worksheet tab**, select cell ranges **A4:A9** and **E4:F9**, and then create a **3-D Clustered Column** chart for the Quality of Service. Develop the chart with the following elements:

   - The chart should cluster the age groups by Restaurant and Hotel only providing a group of Restaurant data and a second group of Hotel data. If necessary, apply the Switch Row/Column button.
   - Position the top-left corner of the chart over cell H2.
   - Make the chart 7" wide and 3" high.
   - Create a chart title above the chart that says Quality of Service by Age Group.
   - Change the properties of the chart to **Don't move or size with cells**.

e. Select the ranges **A15:A49** and **C15:C49**, and then create a **Scatter with only Markers** scatter chart for the Overall Satisfaction. Develop the chart with the following elements.

   - Position the top-left corner of the chart over cell E20.
   - Make the graph 4" high and 8" wide.
   - If necessary, create a chart title above the chart that states Overall Satisfaction.
   - Modify the Vertical scale so it starts at minimum of 3 and only goes up to 10 maximum.
   - Modify the Horizontal scale so it starts at minimum of 20.
   - Add primary vertical gridlines and major gridlines.
   - Change the properties of the chart to include the **Don't move or size with cells** option.

f. Select the cell range **B16:B49**, click in the **Name Box** to name the cell range, type TotalBill, and then press Enter.

g. Click cell **B11**, and then create a formula that will provide the average bill amount for cell range TotalBill.

h. Click cell **B12**, and then create a formula that will provide the minimum bill amount for cell range TotalBill.

i. Click cell **B13**, and then create a formula that will provide the maximum bill amount for cell range TotalBill.

j. Click the **Name Box arrow**, click **TotalBill** to select the TotalBill cell range, hold down the Ctrl, add the cell range **B11:B13** to the selection, and then apply the Accounting format with two decimal places.

k. Click the **AdLoan worksheet tab**, click cell **C4**, and then create a formula that will use the loan amount (or present value) in C1, number of payments in C2, and the annual interest rate in C3 to calculate the quarterly payment amount for the loan.

l. Click cell **B9**, and then add a cell reference to the beginning Loan Amount. Then, for cells B10:B12 add a cell reference of a beginning balance that should reference the ending balance cell for the previous quarter's Ending Balance.

m. Click cell **C9**, and then add a cell reference with an absolute reference to the Quarterly Payments. Use the AutoFill feature to copy the formula cell reference in the cell range **C10:C12**.

n. Click cell **D9**, and calculate the interest charged, which is the quarterly Annual Interest Rate times the Beginning Balance. Use the AutoFill feature to copy this formula down to D10:D12.

o. Click cell **E9**, and calculate the principal amount of the quarterly payment. This would be the total payment minus the interest charged for that quarter. Use the AutoFill feature to copy this formula down to E10:E12.

p. Click cell **F9**, and calculate the ending balance, which is the Beginning Balance minus the Principal. Use the AutoFill feature to copy this formula down to F10:F12.

q. Click the **Documentation worksheet tab**. Hold Shift, and then click on the **AdLoan worksheet tab**. This will select all the tabs as a group, and you will see [Group] appear in the title bar at the top of the window. Click the **Insert tab**, and then insert the file name Lastname_Firstname_e02_ps1_Hotel_Survey into the left footer section. Click out of the footer, and then return to Normal view. Press Ctrl+Home, right-click one of the worksheet tabs, and then click **Ungroup Sheets**.

r. Click **Save**. Close Excel.

Problem Solve 2

Student data file needed:
e02_ps2_Advertising

You will save your file as:
Lastname_Firstname_e02_ps2_Advertising

Resort Advertising Review

The resort has been investing in advertising using different advertising media. When customers book travel to the resort, they reference how they learned about the resort which could include magazine ads, radio ads, the Internet or from referrals of past customers. Data that shows this advertising has been gathered on the Advertising worksheet. You will develop charts for an upcoming presentation that will discuss a marketing strategy.

The Magazines worksheet contains cost and inquiry data for four magazine ads. The ads were placed into one monthly issue of each magazine. Each customer contact is an enquiry. If the customer actually booked business, it is a sale. You will create charts to compare performance of the magazines.

a. Start **Excel**, and then open **e02_ps2_Advertising**. Click the **Documentation worksheet tab**. In A6, press ⌈Ctrl⌉+⌈;⌉ to input the current date. Click cell **B6**, and then type your first name and last name. Save the file as Lastname_Firstname_e02_ps2_Advertising.

b. Click the **Advertising worksheet tab**.

   The data in the cell range A4:D8 shows transactions that came from advertising for specific travel packages to the resort. Some totals need to be developed using this data.

   - In cell **B9** create a formula that will sum the Romance transactions in B5:B8, then use the AutoFill feature to insert the formula to C9:D9, for Golf and Relax travel packages.
   - In cell **E5**, create a formula that will sum all the transactions generated from the Magazine ads, in range B5:D5.
   - In cell **F5**, create a formula that will determine the cost per transaction using the Cost table that shows the total Magazine costs in C12 and the total number of packages generated by the magazine ad, found in cell E5.
   - Select the range **E5:F5**, and then use the AutoFill feature to copy these formulas down to E6:F8 for the other advertising types.

c. Using the range A4:D8, create a 2-D Bar, Stacked Bar chart grouping the packages by Advertising Type. As you develop this chart include the following:

   - Position the chart so the top-left corner is over H3.
   - Change the width of the chart to be 5" and the height to be 3".
   - Create a chart title above the chart that says Resort Package Advertising Results.
   - Create an axis title below the horizontal axis, and then type # of Packages Sold.
   - Create an axis title for the vertical axis, rotate the title, and then type Advertising Type.
   - Adjust the scaling for the horizontal axis so the maximum is 25.

d. Using all the monthly data in A20:D44, create a 2-D, Line chart that will show the three magazine types, Travel, Business, and Health, over time.

   - Position the top-left corner of the chart over cell F20. Make the width of the chart 8" and the height 3".
   - Create a chart title using the **Centered Overlay Title** style, and then type Advertising Results by Magazine Type 2010-2011.
   - Change the Shape Fill color of the Chart Title text box to **Orange**.
   - Create an axis title for the vertical axis, rotate the title, and then type # of Transactions.

e. Click the **Magazines worksheet tab**, and then in cell C17 create a sum formula that will total all the transactions for Spaaaah for Month 1 through Month 6. Use the AutoFill feature to insert the formula down from C17 to C18:C20.

f. In cell F17, use the DATEDIF function to calculate the number of days between the Start Date of Advertising using an absolute reference to cell C14 and the Date of Last Inquiry for Spaaaah, in cell E17. Use the AutoFill feature to insert the formula in F17 down through F18:F20.

g. In cell G17 create a formula that will find the cost per inquiry, given the cost of advertising in B17 and the total number of Spaaaah inquiries in C17. Round the formula to two decimal places. Use the AutoFill feature to insert the formula down from G17 to G18:G20.

h. In cell H17 create a formula that will find the cost per number of sales, given the cost of advertising in B17 and the total number of Spaaaah sales in D17. Round the formula to two decimal places. Use the AutoFill feature to insert the formula down from H17 to H18:H20.

i. In cell I17 create a formula that will find the number of inquiries per day using the number of inquiries in C17 over the number of total days the inquiries were being received in F17. Round the formula to two decimal places. Use the AutoFill feature to insert the formula down from I17 to I18:I20.

j. In cell B7 create a formula that will determine the percentage of inquiries for Spaaaah that occurred in Month 1, given the month 1 data in B2 and the number of Spaaaah inquiries in C17. Use the AutoFill feature to insert the formula in B7 down to B8:B10, and then copy the formulas in B7:B10 over C7:G10. Be sure to check your formula in G10 to ensure you have it correct. (Hint: Assess if cell references need to be absolute or relative.)

k. Select **B7:G10**, and then add a conditional formatting **Gradient Fill Blue Data Bar**. This will indicate the effectiveness over time of the advertising.

l. Select **A16:A20** and **C16:D20**, and then create a **2-D Column, Clustered Column** chart on the worksheet. As you develop the chart include the following:
    - Position the top-left corner over cell A22.
    - Change the width to 6.5" and the height to 3.5".
    - Create a chart title above the chart, and then type Inquiry vs Transactions by Magazine.
    - For the Travel Zone data point that represents the highest # of Sales from Inquiries, change the column color from red to green.

m. Select **A16:A20** and **H16:H20**, and then create a **Clustered Bar in 3-D** chart on the worksheet. As you develop the chart include the following:
    - Position the top-left corner over cell **G22**.
    - Change the width to 6.5" and the height to 3.5".
    - Create a chart title using the **Centered Overlay Title** style, and then type Average Cost per Transaction.
    - Change the alignment for the vertical axis to have a custom angle of −45 degrees.
    - Show the data labels for the bars. Format the data labels to be bold and font size of 14.
    - For the data point that represents the best—lowest—Cost/Sale, change the column color from blue to green.
    - Delete the legend.
    - Change the chart area background fill color to **Aqua, Accent 5, Lighter** 80%.

n. Insert the file name Lastname_Firstname_e02_ps2_Advertising into the left footer section for all worksheets.

o. Press Ctrl + Home . Click **Save**. Close Excel.

Problem Solve 3

Student data file needed:
e02_ps3_Hotel_Occupancy

You will save your file as:
Lastname_Firstname_e02_ps3_Hotel_Occupancy

Hotel Occupancy Analysis

Painted Paradise Resort and Spa would like to review the occupancy and profitability of the various rooms in the hotel with the data on the Occupancy worksheet. Further, Painted Paradise is developing a VIP club that will provide rewards based on points earned. The points are earned based on the guest's usage of the different areas within the resort. The hotel manager has asked you to analyze the potential points program using the data on the Villa worksheet. After your analysis, management may want to change some of the point levels and values. Thus, all of your formulas must be updated appropriately if those values changed.

a. Start **Excel**, and then open **e02_ps3_Hotel_Occupancy**. Click the **Documentation worksheet tab**. In A6, press Ctrl + ; to input the current date. Click cell **B6**, and then type in your first name and last name. Save the file as Lastname_Firstname_e02_ps3_Hotel_Occupancy.

b. Click the **Villa worksheet tab**, click cell **I14**, and then calculate the Resort Points for the customer.

    If the customer has a combined total of five or more Golf and Spa activities, found in columns F and G, then, they earn Resort points. If the customer does not have a total of five activities, they will earn zero Resort points. Resort points are earned by taking the Spa Activities times the Spa Resort Points plus the Golf activities times the Golf Resort Points. Pay attention to construct the formula so cell references can be automatically filled down the column for all the customers. (Note: If a green error triangle appears in the top-left corner of the cell after a formula is applied, it often occurs if reference cells aren't adjacent. Click the arrow next to the Error Checking options icon that appears next to the selected cells, and then click Ignore Error.)

c. In cell J14 calculate the Hotel Points by multiplying the Villa Points per Night for the customer with the Number of Nights the customer stayed. The formula should be constructed so it can be automatically filled down the column for all the customers.

d. In cell K14, use functions to create a formula that will determine the Gift Shop Points earned.

    The formula should check to determine if the customer has purchased more than the Gift Shop Minimum, in which case they will earn points based on the Gift Shop Point Percentage of their total Gift Shop purchases. If a customer's purchases are less than the minimum, the customer would earn zero points. Since the calculation may give a result with decimal points, add a round function to round the results to 0 decimals. The formula should be constructed so it can be automatically filled down the column for all the customers

e. Click **L14**, and then calculate the Total Points by adding the Resort Points, Hotel Points, and Gift Shop Points for the first customer.

f. Make sure all formulas created in I14:L14 are automatically copied to I15:L32 so points are calculated for all customers.

g. For the total points range, L14:L32, use Conditional Formatting to add a **Gradient Fill Green Data Bar**.

h. Click the **Occupancy worksheet tab**, and then calculate the following:
    *   In cell B19 create a Total formula that will add up all the rooms used for the One Double week days found in range B12:B18.
    *   In cell B20 calculate the average daily occupancy for the One Double room type in range B12:B18.
    *   Copy the formulas in the range B19:B20 to the range C19:G20, so the total and average for each room type is calculated.
    *   Select the cell range **B11:G18**. Click the **Create from Selection** option to create named ranges for each room type and usage data.

    Be sure to click the Top row option when defining the named ranges—an example of the result will be the range B12:B18 will be a named range of One_Double defined by the heading in cell B11.

i. In B6 calculate the Revenue for the One Double room type in B19, times the Average Room Rate in B5.

j. In B7 calculate the Gross Profit, which is the Revenue in B6 times the profit Margin in B4.

k. Use the AutoFill feature to copy the formulas in the range B6:B7 right across the table to fill the range C6:G7.

l. Using the range **A2:G2** and **A7:G7**, create a 2-D Pie chart showing a comparison of Gross Profit by room type. For the chart, make the following changes:
    *   Add data labels with the percentages showing but not the values.

- Select the red piece of pie that has 23%, and then pull it away from the rest of the pie so it is emphasized.
- Add or adjust a chart title above the chart that says Comparison of Gross Profit by Room Type.
- Resize the chart to have a height of 3" and width of 6".
- Position the top-left corner of the chart over cell I2.

m. Select the range **A2:G3** and **A20:G20**, and then create a Clustered Bar, 2-D Bar chart showing the Average Occupancy clustered with the Number of Rooms for each room type.

n. For this second chart, make the following changes.
- Change the Chart Layout to **Layout 3**.
- Add data labels—using the **Outside End** option.
- Move the chart to a chart sheet that is named Room Utilization and if necessary, move the Room Utilization chart sheet to position it after the Occupancy sheet.
- Add or adjust a chart title above the chart so it states Average Room Utilization by Room Type.
- Change the chart background to **Tan, Background 2, Darker 10%**.
- Change the plot background to **Tan, Background 2**.
- Add a custom footer to insert a file name footer in the left footer section.

o. Insert the file name Lastname_Firstname_e02_ps3_Hotel_Occupancy into the left footer section for all remaining worksheets—Documentation, Villa, and Occupancy.

p. **Save** your file. Close Excel.

Perform 1: Perform in Your Life

Student data file needed:
Blank Excel workbook

You will save your file as:
Lastname_Firstname_e02_pf1_Investment_Portfolio

Personal Investment Portfolio

You have started working and realize the importance of paying off current debt, managing expenses, and preparing for your retirement. You need to start paying down school loans and thinking about investing for the future. You want to start a spreadsheet that you can use to track some stock investments.

Either use the data provided for the stock below, or choose current stock data from the Internet per your instructor's preference. If using the Internet, use one of several known stock sites that provide historical data such as finance.yahoo.com.

Company	Nobel Energy, Inc
Ticker	NBL
Date	Closing Share Price
1/2/2008	72.58
4/1/2008	87.00
7/1/2008	73.87
10/1/2008	58.82
1/2/2009	48.93
4/1/2009	56.75
7/1/2009	61.12

Company	Nobel Energy, Inc
Ticker	NBL
Date	Closing Share Price
10/1/2009	65.63
1/4/2010	73.94
4/1/2010	76.40
7/1/2010	67.06
10/1/2010	81.48
1/3/2011	91.10

a. Open a new, blank Excel workbook. Save it as Lastname_Firstname_e02_pf1_ Investment_Portfolio.

b. Start with a worksheet named Investment and with one stock. Create labels showing the name of the stock and the tracking information such as the account name and ticker symbol.

c. Create a table that will track investments into the stock. You would track the following data:
   - Date of investment
   - The investment amount
   - The share price on date of purchase
   - The number of shares purchased, which is the investment divided by the share price.
   - Add a column that will show the accumulated total number of shares purchased.

d. Next, the stock activity needs to be tracked on a quarterly basis. Create a table that will record quarterly activity including the following:
   - A Quarter column labeling the first date of each quarter
   - A Value column showing the current overall value of your investment at the start of the quarter (this would be the share price times the number of shares you possess)
   - A Quarterly Investment column showing total amount invested in that quarter (this would be the quarterly investment, the money you invested each quarter based on your investments table)
   - A Total Investment column that records the total amount invested to date—accumulated
   - A Total Growth column of the investment to date (this would be the total value minus the total investment)
   - A Total Growth % column that records the percentage growth for that quarter (this is the current total growth divided by the total investment)
   - A Qtrly Growth column that calculates the growth of the investment minus the total investment from the previous quarter
   - A Qtrly Growth % column that calculates the percentage growth for the quarter (this is the current total quarterly growth divided by the total investment)

e. To test the worksheet, put in either the data provided or use the quarterly data from the Internet for a chosen stock.

f. Create an appropriate chart that will track the total amount invested and total value of the investment over time.

g. Insert the file name Lastname_Firstname_e02_pf1_Investment_Portfolio into the left footer section for the worksheets.

h. Save your work, and then close Excel.

Student data file needed:
Blank Excel workbook

You will save your file as:
Firstname_Lastname_e02_pf2_Loan_Amortization

Loan Amortization

You are doing some consulting for the owners of a small business who want spreadsheets created so they can track loans. They would like to track the payment of the loans by splitting up the monthly payment into the amount going to interest and the amount going to principal. They would like to incorporate extra payments and then determine the total interest paid over the life of the loan. Finally, they would like to track their progress on the repayment.

a. Open a new, blank Excel workbook. Save it as Lastname_Firstname_e02_pf2_Loan_Amortization. Create a spreadsheet that calculates the monthly payment for a standard loan based on the time period, loan amount, and interest rate. Your calculations should be set up so the time period, loan amount, and interest rate can easily be changed. Then, the spreadsheet should track the monthly payment for the loan in a table format. You can assume the loan is for three years. At a minimum, this amortization table should include the following:
    - The beginning balance for each time period
    - The interest charged for the month
    - The payment that month
    - The amount of the payment that would go toward the principal
    - The ending loan balance after the principal has been paid
    - In addition to the standard monthly payment, also calculate the total amount of interest paid if the owner pays off the loan with no extra payments.

b. In conjunction with the loan payment, create a table that can then be used to create a chart that demonstrates that the total amount of interest charged for a loan that goes up as the number of years to repay the loan goes up. Have the table tie into the interest rate and loan amount used for the above calculations.

c. Create a second amortization table that would allow the owner to make an additional payment that would go towards the principal during any month. Allow flexibility so the owner could change the amount of the extra payment any month. At a minimum, this amortization table should include the following:
    - The beginning balance for each time period
    - The interest charged for the month
    - The payment that month
    - The amount of the payment that would go toward the principal
    - The extra payment made that month
    - The ending loan balance after the principal has been paid

d. Create summaries of the two amortization tables to show the total interest for the first payment schedule and the second payment schedule if the owner pays an amount greater than the standard monthly payment.

e. Create a chart showing the total interest paid with the two plans: paying the minimum payment and when paying more than the minimum payment.

f. Insert the file name Lastname_Firstname_e02_pf2_Loan_Amortization into the left footer section for all worksheets.

g. Save and close your file.

Student data file needed:
e02_pf3_Tolerance_Charts

You will save your file as:
Lastname_Firstname_e02_pf3_Tolerance_Charts

Manufacturing Tolerance Analysis

You have started a job with a manufacturer for components used in medical instrumentation. One of your duties is to get data about the components coming off the manufacturing floor so you can determine the quality of the components. Your task is to analyze measurements of a small silicon tube that is used to give medicines intravenously. When the machines get out of alignment over time they need to be adjusted.

The width of the tubing is within tolerance if the width is within .025 centimeters of the target diameter of .3 centimeters. Thus if the tubing is between .275 and .325 in diameter, it is good quality. Otherwise it is out of tolerance and the machinery needs adjusting. The spreadsheet will compare the sample to the target diameter of the tube, determine how much it is off from the specification, then graph the sample data over time to see if the machine is still aligned or needs to be adjusted up, down, or totally recalibrated.

a. Start **Excel**, and then open **e02_pf3_Tolerance_Charts**. Save the file as Lastname_Firstname_e02_pf3_Tolerance_Charts.

b. On the Tolerance_Data worksheet you will find 30 samples taken from the line over the past 30 days. Each sample is taken from the manufacturing line daily. So Sample 1 is the part that was pulled on day 1. Sample 10 was pulled on day 10. The width in centimeters is taken of the tube diameter. Add formulas to the new columns to calculate the data to determine the error—the difference between the actual diameter and the required, or specified, diameter of the tubing—and then determine if the diameter is wider than the specification or narrower than the specification.

c. You should determine some base statistics of the diameter of the samples. Determine the minimum, maximum, and average diameter of the samples in the provided cells.

d. A table has been started that will tally the results of the error analysis so you can determine how many samples were out of tolerance. Add formulas to complete the table as follows:
   • Add a function for the total number of samples that had widths that were wider than the allowable tolerance
   • Add a function for the total number of samples that had widths that were narrower than the allowable tolerance
   • Add a function for total number of samples that were within the tolerance.

e. As a part of the table, targets have been set to determine when the machine needs to be adjusted. It is the goal that 25 or more of the samples overall will be within the tolerance. Add a function to the Note column cells to test if the Totals are greater than the Target, and place a note to Check Machine if totals exceed target, otherwise the Note cell can remain blank.

f. To help visualize the samples, chart the error measurement over time. Consider the following as you create the chart:
   • Review and adjust the axis scales if needed.
   • Create textual guidance with titles and text so the chart is self-explanatory.
   • Keep the chart professional as it may be printed with a report that is given to the manufacturing team.

g. A second chart should be created that compares the counts of OK, High, and Low relative to the total counts. This chart should also be professional.

h. Insert the file name Lastname_Firstname_e02_pf3_Tolerance_Charts into the left footer section for the worksheets.

i. Save your work, and then close Excel.

Perform 4: How Others Perform

Student data file needed:
e02_pf4_BMI_Analysis

You will save your file as:
Lastname_Firstname_e02_pf4_BMI_Analysis

BMI Health Analysis

A state health agency wants to examine health data on college students starting with the body mass index (BMI). The agency has provided a file with a dataset of average BMI numbers for males and females from 1952 through 2011. In addition to looking at that data, the agency has some current data and wants to be able to work with current clients to analyze their health condition using the BMI. You've been hired to look at the data, correct some issues, and create some new components on the spreadsheet.

The BMI is calculated using the height (in inches) and the weight (in pounds). The formula for BMI is as follows:

$Weight/Height^2*703$

For example, if a client weighs 120 pounds and is 5 foot 6 inches tall, their BMI would be $120/66^2*703=19.37$

The BMI has categories as follows:

- Underweight   less than 18.5
- Normal   18.5 or greater and less than 25
- Overweight   25 or greater and less than 30
- Obese   30 or greater

a. Start **Excel**, and then open **e02_pf4_BMI_Analysis**. Save the as Lastname_Firstname_e02_pf4_BMI_Analysis.

b. Click the **Historical worksheet tab**. The historical data, showing average BMI numbers for males and females, has been collected. The agency wants to see the trend of average BMI index numbers for males and females over the entire time period. However, the chart that has been created does not depict the trend over time. Add an additional graph to offer a trend analysis. The new updated chart should consider the following:

- The chart should be a more appropriate chart type that would show the trend over time for males and females.
- The chart should have clear titles, including for the x-axis and y-axis.
- The chart should have a professional, business look so it can be used by the state agency in a presentation.
- Adjust the scales and create gridlines that help convey the context as appropriate.

c. Click the **Donor worksheet tab**. The agency has included a copy of current raw survey data. The data includes the ID, Height, Weight, and Gender of the respondent. The agency would like to use this data to create a few graphs. It would like to compare the numbers of males in each BMI category to the total number of females surveyed to determine the percentage of males in each category compared to female. You should sort and regroup the data as needed so the agency can easily tally the number of males and the number or females in separate tables that also include a column to calculate BMI. This summary data should be organized so you can create the two graphs.

- The two charts should have similar look and feel and be arranged side by side for comparison.

- The charts should be an appropriate type that allows comparison of the pieces as a part of the whole.
- The charts should be formatted to look professional in preparation for being in a brochure.

d. The agency would also like a simple input table to act as a calculator to determine the BMI for any client along with a table that uses formulas to calculate BMI index values that could be printed and used as a reference in the office when a computer is not handy. These two elements should be on the Donor worksheet.

- The BMI calculator should use cells where the client's Height and Weight information is input and the BMI is calculated.
- The BMI table should show a range of heights in inches down the side and a range of weights along the top. The ranges should be reasonable for typical adults. The ranges would not have to handle extremes heights or weights.
- The BMI table should also include color scaling so the higher BMI values are white and the low values are green.
- The table should provide guidance, but it does not have to be to the exact pound. The table should be a reasonable size that could fit on a normal sheet of paper and be readable.

e. Insert the file name Lastname_Firstname_e02_pf4_BMI_Analysis into the left footer section for all worksheets.

f. Save your work, and then close Excel.

WORKSHOP 5

Objectives

1. Build nested IF functions.   p. 241

2. Integrate conjunction functions into IF statements.   p. 248

3. Learn conditional statistical functions. p. 253

4. Develop math conditional functions.   p. 256

5. Explore LOOKUP functions.   p. 260

6. Work with data retrieval using MATCH and INDEX.   p. 264

7. Learn how to handle error messages.   p. 269

Integrating Complex Functions into Excel Analysis

PREPARE CASE
Red Bluff Pro Shop Sales Analysis

The Red Bluff Pro Shop has a golf shop that sells golf equipment and supplies. Barry Cheney receives revenue data on a monthly basis. He would like to have some reports developed that will help track sales. He has a spreadsheet started with some sample data and wants you to continue developing some reports.

Courtesy of www.Shutterstock.com

Student data file needed for this workshop:

 e03_ws05_Golf_Sales

You will save your file as:

 Lastname_Firstname_e03_ws05_Golf_Sales

Integrating Logical Functions

Making decisions involves evaluation and choices. Golfers use logic as they play, evaluating the situation as it changes with every shot. If they are 300 yards away from the green and have a clear shot, they choose one club. If they are in a sand trap, they choose a different club. Likewise, a business succeeds based upon the ability to choose whether to buy or lease, build or buy from a supplier, or advertise in a magazine or on the radio. Being able to evaluate conditions and apply logic in choosing the best option is the foundation of logical functions. **Logical functions** are functions that return a result, or output, based upon evaluating whether a logical test is true or false. Logical functions enable evaluation and choices to be integrated into a spreadsheet. The most common logical functions include IF, AND, OR, and NOT. Another logical function, IFERROR, is a special function that is included at the end of the workshop.

The foundation of logical functions is a logical expression or logical test. A **logical test** is an equation that involves logical operators that can be evaluated as being either true or false. The evaluation of the logical test determines the outcome or result. For example, "the distance left to the green is more than 300 yards" compares the actual distance to 300 yards. The test, comparing whether the ball is lying more than or less than 300 yards away determines the result: which club will be chosen. Logical operators, as listed in Figure 1, are used to create logical tests.

Operator	Description	TRUE	FALSE
<	Less than	5 < 7	10 < 3
>	Greater than	10 > 3	3 > 10
<=	Less than or equal to	5 <= 5	5 <= 4
>=	Greater than or equal to	5 >= 4	3 >= 10
<>	Not equal to	2 <> 4	2 <> 2

Figure 1   Logical Operators

Barry has asked you to develop a spreadsheet to help with decision making. Another staff member had started the spreadsheet and populated it with some sample data. When Barry realized the person was simply entering values for the calculated fields rather than using formulas, he decided to turn the project over to you. He put some data in to demonstrate what he wants it to look like; however, the manually inserted calculations need to be replaced with formulas.

The Inputs worksheet has been set up to handle all the data within the spreadsheet that might need to be updated occasionally but that should not be on the actual revenue report. Keeping the supporting data on a separate sheet makes it easier to streamline the printed report.

Additionally, the worksheet needs to be set up to analyze different amounts of data. There could be 113 transactions in one time period and 154 in another. Barry believes having enough room for 200 transactions will be sufficient.

Within the spreadsheet, named ranges have already been created for most, but not all, of the data. Using these named ranges makes creating formulas easier. You should open and update the documentation in preparation to make changes.

To Open a Spreadsheet

a. Start **Excel**.

b. Click the **File tab**, and then click **Open**. In the Open dialog box, navigate to where your student data files are located, click **e03_ws05_Golf_Sales**, and then click **Open**.

c. Click the **Documentation worksheet tab** to make it the active worksheet, click cell **A6**, and then press Ctrl+; to input the current date. Click cell **B6**, type Firstname Lastname using your own first name and last name, and then press Ctrl+Home.

d. Click the **File tab**, click **Save As**, and then in the Save As dialog box, navigate to the location where you are saving your files. In the File name box, type Lastname_Firstname_e03_ws05_Golf_Sales replacing Lastname and Firstname with your own name. Click **Save**.

e. Click the **Insert tab**, and then click **Header & Footer** in the Text group. Click **Go to Footer** in the Navigation group. Click in the **left footer section**, and then click **File Name** in the Header & Footer Elements group. Repeat this process with all worksheets in the file.

f. Click any cell on the spreadsheet to move out of the footer, press Ctrl+Home, click the **View tab**, and then click **Normal** in the Workbook Views group.

g. Click the **Inputs worksheet tab**, click cell I48, press F3, and then click **Paste List** so the current ranges with the names are listed.

Figure 2 Paste list of named ranges

Barry would like you to analyze the monthly Red Bluff Pro Shop sales data to transform the data into information that he can use to make sound business decisions. Being able to address the following questions may provide insight into ways to increase sales, decrease expenses, or provide better customer service.

- What types of products sell well in the store?
- What percent of the transactions come from credit card sales?
- What is the average transaction amount?
- Who buys more, hotel guests or local customers?
- Which sales team members sell the most? Which sell the least?

Based on the analysis, he might decide to create a marketing strategy to increase the average sales to local customers or ask the human resource department to provide sales training.

Exploring the data, finding the answers to questions, and developing knowledge from the information will help the pro shop gain and maintain a competitive advantage. Thus, Barry is hopeful that developing the spreadsheets properly will help with decision making. In this section you will build nested IF statements and integrate other functions to create complex functions for decision-making purposes.

Using Nested IF Functions

The IF function is the most common logical function and evaluates a logical test. The logical test can involve either values or other functions. It can also employ other logical functions nested within as arguments. The IF function has three arguments—where two are optional:

=IF(logical_test, [value_if_true], [value_if_false])

Remember, the logical test is evaluating a logical condition, or statement, as being either true or false. Suppose you want a list of all golf club members who have a handicap at or below 0. A golfer who has a handicap of 0 or below is known as a scratch golfer. A function could be created that would check the handicap and return the words "Scratch Golfer" if the handicap is less than or equal to 0. You could then establish an initial IF statement that starts as:

=IF(C5<=0)

If cell C5 contains a value that is less than or equal to 0, Excel will return a value of TRUE to the cell that has the function. Otherwise, Excel returns a value of FALSE. However, simply returning a value of TRUE or FALSE is of minimum value and is not usually the best practice or desired result. Instead, you normally provide two values for Excel to return. So, it is more acceptable to use:

=IF(C5<0,"Scratch Golfer","Handicapped Golfer")

This way, instead of a generic TRUE or FALSE response, the user would see "Scratch Golfer" if the value in C5 is less than or equal to 0. Otherwise, "Handicapped Golfer" would be returned. The IF function is exclusive in that it only has two outcomes, one when the logical test is true and a second when the logical test is false.

The data on the Transactions worksheet is set up with two sections. The first section is data that Barry will receive on a monthly basis from the IT staff. It contains the transaction data listed in Figure 3.

Data Field	Description
Trans_ID	Transaction number
Trans_Time	Time of the transaction
SKU	Product ID number
Pay_Type	Method of payment
Trans_Qty	Purchase quantity
Coupon_Num	Coupon number, if used
Emp_ID	Employee that completed the transaction
Cust_Cat	Customer category

Figure 3 Sales data descriptions

The other section of the data has fields that need to be calculated. Currently the data has been manually calculated and typed into the spreadsheet, a very inefficient practice. You need to replace the data in this section with calculations. The fields' descriptions are briefly detailed in Figure 4.

Data Field	Description for Calculated Fields
SKU_Cat	Product category
Emp_Position	Employee position
Shift	Time period when the transaction occurred
Coupon_Target	Type of customer targeted for the coupon
Coupon_hit	Whether the coupon was submitted by the correct customer type
Coupon_Amt	Percentage off for the coupon
Retail	Retail price of the product
Line_Item_Total	Total revenue (price x qty – coupon)
Card_Charge	Whether the transaction used a credit card
Trans_Group	Category of transaction based on the amount of the transaction
Big_Ticket_Item	Category of nonaccessory items
Sales_Point1	Incentive points calculation for sales team
Sales_Point2	Incentive points calculation for sales team

Figure 4 Calculated fields descriptions

The credit card company charges for every transaction. Barry would like to track credit card usage versus other types of transactions. In the worksheet, he needs a column to indicate whether a transaction used a credit card. If it did, he wants Excel to return "Charge." Otherwise, he does not want anything to appear in the cell.

To Create an IF Function

a. Click the **Transactions worksheet tab**, click cell **Q21**, type =IF(D21="Ccard","Charge",""), and then press Ctrl+Enter.

This checks if the Pay_Type value in D21 is equal to "Ccard." If that is true, the word "Charge" will be returned. Otherwise, an empty set, indicated with the double quotes with nothing between, will be returned.

b. With cell Q21 selected, click the **AutoFill** handle in the bottom-right corner of the cell, and then drag it down to copy the formula down to cell **Q220**.

Rows where there are no records will be evaluated as FALSE and return the empty set.

c. Click cell **M21**. The coupon is a Coupon Match when the Cust_Cat is the same as the Coupon_Target. When they are different, it is a No Match. Type =IF(H21<>L21,"No Match", "Coupon Match"), and then press Ctrl+Enter.

The logical test is stating that H21 is not equal to L21. Thus, when they are equal, the test returns a value of FALSE and it is a Coupon Match.

d. With cell **M21** selected, click the **AutoFill** handle in the bottom-right corner of the cell, and then drag down to copy the formula down to cell **M220**. While the formula is not giving an error message, the result is not correct. This is a modeling issue that we will address later in this chapter. Click **Save** 💾.

As previously mentioned the [value_if_true] and [value_if_false] arguments are both optional and could be omitted from the function. In this case, the values TRUE and FALSE are returned from the evaluation of the function. While this may be intuitive, it is not user friendly. You can use a variety of elements, including numerical values, text strings, cell references, named ranges, and other functions for the arguments in an IF function. Figure 5 provides an example.

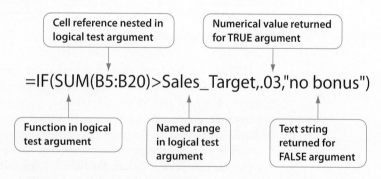

Figure 5 Function argument example

In this example, the .03 is a numerical value. With numerical values, you do not need to include formatting, such as a dollar sign. The "No Bonus" is a text string and should have quotes around the string. Quotes, shown as double primes—not the curly quotation marks you use in writing papers—let Excel know that the element is a text string and not a numeric value, cell reference, or named range. Sales_Target is a named range. This may look like a text string, but because it does not have quotes, Excel will look for a range that is named Sales_Target. If a Sales_Target named range does not exist, Excel will return the error #Name?. Finally, SUM(B5:B20) is a function that is part of the logical test. Excel will automatically recognize function names.

To Use Different Elements in an IF Statement

a. Click the **Rev_Rpt worksheet tab**, and then click cell **E21**.

   Barry wants to evaluate the number of items being sold. If the total number of items sold is more than 50, then the current goal is met. If that is true, he wants to have "Goal Met" displayed; otherwise, he wants "Under Goal" displayed.

b. Type =IF(SUM(, press [F3], scroll down as needed, in the Paste Name dialog box, click to select **Trans_Qty** , and then click **OK**. Type)>50,"Goal Met","Under Goal"), and then press [Ctrl]+[Enter].

   This will evaluate whether the sum of the quantity sold is greater than 50. However, it uses a value for 50 in the logical test. If the goal changes, the function will no longer be valid.

c. With cell **E21** selected, press [F2] to go into edit mode. Select the **50** within the formula, and then type E20. Press [Ctrl]+[Enter], and then click **Save** [💾].

   Notice that as E20 was typed in the formula, Excel recognized it as a valid cell reference and changed it to blue with a blue border surrounding it. By using a cell reference rather than a numeric value, when the goal value in cell E20 changes, the Sold Status formula will still make the evaluation of the quantity sold correctly.

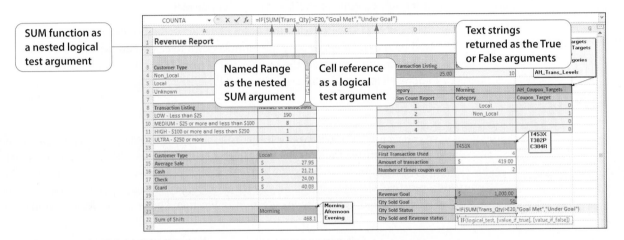

Figure 6 IF function

The function developed thus far is a **complex function**, a function that combines multiple functions into a formula. In the Sales Rating example, the logical test involved evaluating a function. A special type of complex function is a nested IF. A single IF statement provides two outcomes to a single logical test. But what happens if you have three or four options or outcomes? A **nested IF** function uses IF functions as arguments within another IF function. A nested IF increases the logical outcomes that can be expressed.

The purchase price is included in the sales data and Barry would like to categorize the transactions as Low, Medium, High, or Ultra, depending on this amount. The business requirements for each category are provided in Figure 7.

	Greater than or equal	Less than
Low	0	25
Medium	25	100
High	100	250
Ultra	250	

Figure 7 Transaction ratings

Creating a number line of the business requirements similar to the one shown in Figure 8 can be helpful in visualizing the logic. When looking at the number line and breaking it up based on the $25, $100, and $250 amounts, it is possible to see there are four possible categories or alternatives. One IF function cannot handle four outcomes, so nested IF functions are needed.

Figure 8 Nested IF number line

Working from left to right across a number line, an initial logical statement will check for the left-most range. The initial logical statement starts with

=IF(P21<25,"Low", "everything else")

It is checking whether the value is less than $25, and thus a Low transaction. If this is true, the value of "Low" will be returned as the outcome. If false, Excel will return the "everything else" value. This is similar to assuming there are only two options, Low if the test is true; otherwise, the result is "everything else" as shown in Figure 9, Part 1.

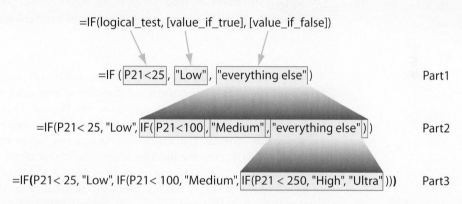

Figure 9 Nested IF logic

To Start a Nested IF Function

a. Click the **Transactions worksheet tab**, click cell **R21**, type =IF(P21<Inputs!$K$20,Inputs! $I$20,"everything else"), and then press Ctrl + Enter.

b. With cell **R21** selected, click the **AutoFill** handle, drag down to copy the formula down to cell **R220**, and then click **Save** 💾.

   Notice "Low" shows up for Purchase Prices less than $25 and "everything else" is displayed for all other values. Also, note that when there is no price in the column P cell reference—no value—the IF statement is returning a result of Low. This will be explored in a later exercise.

Real World Advice   Working with IF Function Ranges

In the real world, it helps to work with real numbers, like 25, 100, and 250, when developing the logic of the formula. However, it is hazardous to use the numbers in the formula when they may change. It is much better to build for flexibility. It is easier to change a spreadsheet cell value than it is to search formulas to find the number you need to update. Whenever possible, use a cell reference in a formula instead of a number.

The initial function works well when there are two outcomes, in this case "Low" and "everything else." However, when the value is greater than $25, you have established that it is *not* a low transaction. You still do not know if it is Medium, High, or Ultra. Thus, you need a second logical statement for the [value_if_false] argument replacing the "everything else" as depicted in Figure 9, Part 2. The values below $25 have been eliminated by the first IF statement and do not need to be checked again. Thus, the next IF statement should check for values below $100. Development of the function would continue as:

=IF(P21<25,"Low",IF(P21<100,"Medium","everything else"))

To Nest a Second IF Function

a. On the Transactions worksheet tab, click cell **R21**, and press [F2] to go into edit mode. Select **"everything else"**including quotes, replace it by typing IF(P21<Inputs!$K$21,Inputs!$I$21,"everything else"), and then press [Ctrl]+[Enter] so the same cell remains active.

b. Double-click the **AutoFill** handle for cell R21 to copy the formula down the column, and then click **Save** [disk icon].

   Notice Low shows up for Line_Item_Total prices less than $25, and now the Medium value is also being returned for values less than $100 but greater than or equal to $25. All other values return "everything else," unless the price column cell is empty.

If it is *not* a Low purchase price, the second nested IF statement will check whether it is less than $100. If it is, then the text "Medium" will be returned. The possibility of the price being less than $25 was eliminated with the first [logical_test]. This is why best practice dictates working left to right with the number line. It allows you to take advantage of the process of elimination. The function checks for the left-most range first, and if the first logical test evaluates to TRUE, then the function knows it is in that range, the outcome is known, and the other nested IF functions will not run or be evaluated. However if both the first and the second IF logical tests evaluate to FALSE, indicating that the price is $100 or greater, you need yet another IF function to determine the outcome to be High (if third test returns TRUE) or Ultra (if third test returns FALSE).

This means adding one more IF function in the [value_if_false] at the end of the second IF function, as shown in Figure 9 in the transition to Part 3. The nested function would be expanded to be:

=IF(P21<25,"Low",IF(P21<100,"Medium",IF(P21 <250,"High","Ultra")))

To Nest a Third IF Function

a. On the **Transactions worksheet tab**, click cell **R21**, and then press [F2] to go into edit mode. Select **"everything else"**including quotes, replace it by typing IF(P21<Inputs!$K$22,Inputs!$I$22,Inputs!$I$23), and then press [Ctrl]+[Enter] so the same cell remains active.

b. Double-click the **AutoFill** handle to copy the formula down the column, and then click **Save** [disk icon].

   Recall that Low is still displayed for empty price cells and will be addressed in a later section. Notice the price cells that contain data have one of four outcomes returned appropriately for each Line_Item_Total price. There are three parentheses at the far right of the formula, one for each IF function. The options are exhaustive in that any number that is provided for the Line_Item_Total price will fall into one of the four groups.

This process of nesting the IF statements allows you to generate multiple outcomes to the logical statement. As a guide, count the number of options or outcomes there are in the situation. Then, subtract 1 to determine how many IF statements are needed. For example, to use IF statements to convert exam scores to a letter grade, A, B, C, D, or F, there are five outcomes, so $5 - 1 = 4$. Four IF statements are needed to develop the nested function to convert the numerical grade to a letter grade.

This logic is demonstrated by looking at the logical diagram in Figure 10. In the exercise, three results come through three [value_if_true] arguments. Then, by process of elimination, since the logic worked from left to right across the range, the only remaining option could utilize the last, [value_if_false].

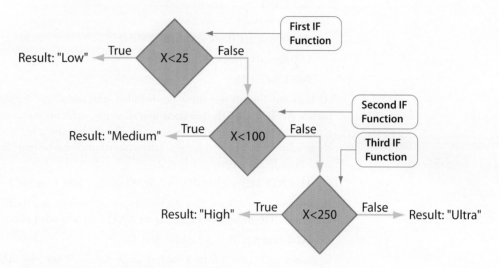

Figure 10 Logic of the nested IF function

CONSIDER THIS | **Left or Right When Working with Nested IFs**

Consider the process of working with the ranges on a number line in a left to right fashion. Would it be possible to start on the right side and work to the left? Do you suppose it would be possible to start with any range and construct the logic of the options in any order?

Real World Advice Working with IF Function Ranges

You will want to consider whether your ranges go to the left or right of infinity or if you have actual lower and upper bounds. If a value should never be negative, then it may be necessary to incorporate a starting point for the left-most range. The same would apply for the right side. For some values, such as the credit limit, you may want to check that the value is not above $50,000. While data validation can be used to limit the values, if you actually have a lower or upper limit, you will need to consider whether to test for this in the IF statements.

Using Conjunction Functions in IF Functions

While nesting IF functions allows handling more than two outcomes, **conjunction functions** allow evaluation of multiple logical tests and enable linking or joining of functions or formulas. The conjunction functions within Excel are AND, OR, and NOT. The AND function is used when the logical tests must all be true, whereas the OR function is used when any combination of logical tests has at least one TRUE outcome. The NOT function is appropriate when there are many options that do fit the desired criteria and only one option that does not fit the criteria. It is important to realize the syntax for these functions is similar to any other function: the arguments are parenthetical following the function name. A user might think the syntax would be something like:

X AND Y

The syntax is really:

AND(logical1,[logical2],...)

OR(logical1, [logical2],...)

NOT(logical1)

At least one logical test must be included, and additional logical test arguments are optional for the AND or the OR functions. For example, students wanting to be eligible for a university scholarship must have an ACT score of 30 or more *and* a high school GPA of 3.5 or better. If these values are in named ranges, both conditions must be met, thus an AND function could be used in an IF statement as follows:

IF(AND(ACT>=30,GPA>=3.5),"Eligible","Not Eligible")

In this case, the ACT>=30 is the first logical argument and the GPA>=3.5 is the second logical argument. The logic for evaluating an AND function with two logical tests:

AND(Logical Test *A*,Logical Test *B*)

is shown in Figure 11 in a logical truth table. When the AND function is nested in the logical_test argument of an IF function, both logical tests need to be evaluated as TRUE for the [value_if_true] argument to be returned. If either evaluates to FALSE, then the AND function will return a FALSE for the logical test. Of the four outcomes, only one would return a value of TRUE.

Logical Test 'A'	Logical Test 'B'	AND Function Result
TRUE	TRUE	TRUE
TRUE	FALSE	FALSE
FALSE	TRUE	FALSE
FALSE	FALSE	FALSE

Figure 11　AND logical truth table

Barry wants to evaluate the status of employees. If an employee is an assistant manager and the Percent of Goal is greater than 25%, then he wants to have the status be "On Target". Otherwise, it should return a result of "Increase Sales". Because there are two conditions that lead to the results and they both must be true, an AND function can be used within the logical test for the IF function.

To Use the AND Function Within an IF Function

a.　Click the **Emp_Rpt worksheet tab**, and then click cell **B19**.

b.　Type =IF(AND(B6="Asst Manager",B11>0.25),"On Target","Increase Sales"), press Enter, and then click **Save** 🔲.

　　Both logical tests in the AND function must be evaluated to TRUE for the AND to return a TRUE to the IF Function.

The OR function works in the same way as an AND function, except the logical evaluation of the arguments is different. Whereas the AND function requires all arguments to be TRUE, the OR function requires at least one of the arguments to be evaluated as TRUE. So, the OR function, with two logical tests—OR(Logical Test 'A',Logical Test 'B')—depicted in the logical truth table in Figure 12, shows that three of the four combinations would return a result of TRUE.

Logical Test 'A'	Logical Test 'B'	OR Function Result
TRUE	TRUE	TRUE
TRUE	FALSE	TRUE
FALSE	TRUE	TRUE
FALSE	FALSE	FALSE

Figure 12   OR logical truth table

Because there are two Non_Local coupons listed in the Coupons table on the Inputs worksheet tab, the Coupon_Num value on the Transactions worksheet can be either; thus, an OR function can be used in conjunction with an IF statement to convert the data. Once the target for the coupon is known, it is possible to determine whether a Non_Local customer used a Non_Local coupon, which is the desired use. Management would like to know whether Local customers are using Local coupons.

To Use the OR Function in an IF Function

a. Click the **Transactions worksheet tab**, and then click cell **L21**.

b. Type =IF(OR(F21=, click on the **Inputs worksheet tab**, click cell **I5**, press F4, then type ,F21=, click cell **I7**, press F4, type), then click **L5**, press F4, type ,, click cell **L6**, press F4, type), and then press Ctrl+Enter. If either one of the logical tests in the OR evaluates to TRUE, then the logical test for the IF function will be TRUE and "Non_Local" will be the result.

c. Click cell **L21**, click the **AutoFill** handle, and then drag down to copy the formula down to cell **L220**. Click **Save**.

   Notice that this provides a "Local" result for rows where there is no data. This will be explored and changed in a later section.

The NOT function allows creation of logical statements in which it creates the opposite or reverse result. This is particularly useful when there are many values that would result in a TRUE and only one that would return a FALSE. For example, if you wanted to charge state tax to all states except Texas, you could use NOT(State = "Texas") so if the value were Texas, that is TRUE and the result of the NOT function would be FALSE. If it were Ohio, then Ohio = Texas is FALSE, and NOT FALSE is TRUE. So, all other states would return the same result.

Barry recognizes that the accessories items do not cost a lot or take up much space. All of the other categories of products found in the SKU_Cat column are big-ticket items where there is a larger margin. The shop makes a larger profit from selling the big-ticket items, so Barry may want some analyses on just those items. He would like a column that distinguishes the big-ticket items, regardless of the category. You can accomplish this task in one logical test using the NOT function.

To Use the NOT Function in an IF Function

a. On the Transactions worksheet tab, click cell **S21**.

b. Type =IF(NOT(I21="Accessories"),"Big Ticket Item",""), and then press ⌐Ctrl⌐+⌐Enter⌐.

If the category is Accessories, the logical expression in the NOT function will evaluate to TRUE but the NOT function will reverse it to be NOT TRUE, or FALSE. When FALSE, the result will be nothing, indicated by double quotes. The double quotes indicate an empty text string.

c. With cell **S21** selected, click the **AutoFill** handle, and then drag down to copy the formula down to cell **S220**. Click **Save** 🖫.

Notice that this provides a "Big Ticket Item" result for rows where there is no data. The formula should check whether there is a transaction. This will be evaluated and changed later.

There are more complex situations where it is necessary to combine the OR with the AND function. This can be tricky because you need to determine whether to put the AND inside the OR, or vice versa. A lot depends upon the situation. Just as in math, you need to be careful with the grouping.

Barry wants to give motivational points to the sales team for certain transactions. Sales_Point1 will look for Trans_Group results of High or Ultra transactions that occur in the morning or afternoon shift and will award one point. Otherwise it will return zero points. The logic for this is illustrated in Figure 13. The formula requires both an OR function and AND function within the IF statement. The initial step is to think through the situation and organize the conditions using some pseudo-code. **Pseudocode** is using the structure of the functions but with wording that is for logical understanding. Here, there are four conditions to evaluate. The first two are the shift is Morning or the shift is Afternoon. They cannot be joined with an AND, since they are exclusive. So, they need an OR. The same applies to the Trans_Group because a transaction cannot be both High and Ultra. The requirement mentions the High transactions have to occur in one of the two shifts, so an AND needs to be used to combine the high transaction with either of the shifts. Thus, the AND is the outer function with two OR functions inside.

Logic:

A) Right Shift   **OR**   Shift is Morning
                                     Shift is Afternoon

         AND

B) Right Trans_Group   **OR**   Trans_Group is High
                                       Trans_Group is Ultra

Pseudo code:

IF(**AND**(Right Shift, Right Trans_Group), earn a point, no points)

IF(**AND**(**OR**(Morning, Afternoon), **OR**(High, Ultra)), 1, 0)

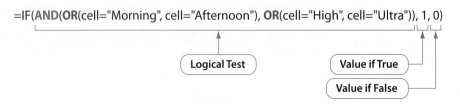

=IF(**AND**(**OR**(cell="Morning", cell="Afternoon"), **OR**(cell="High", cell="Ultra")), 1, 0)

Logical Test   Value if True

Value if False

Figure 13 Logic of nesting OR in AND functions

To Use an OR Function Nested in an AND Function

a. On the Transactions worksheet tab, click cell **T21**, type =IF(AND(OR(K21="Morning", K21="Afternoon"),OR(R21="High",R21="Ultra")),1,0) and then press Ctrl + Enter .

b. With cell **T21** selected, click the **AutoFill** handle, drag down to copy the formula down to cell **T220**, and then click **Save** 💾.

   This shows a point will be awarded when the shift is Morning or Afternoon, and has the added condition that the Trans_Group results display either High or Ultra. The second OR needs to be added and the two OR functions will be combined with an AND, requiring each to return a TRUE result.

Real World Advice   Working Complex AND, OR Conditions

In the real world, you will want to confirm complex conditions. For example, the statement, "All employees in division X or division Y with more than three years of experience get training" can be interpreted as follows: All employees from the two divisions that have more than three years of experience get training. Or, it could mean that all employees from division X get training and all employees from division Y with more than three years experience get training. If you are unsure of the conditions being requested, get clarification before proceeding.

For the second set of motivational points, Barry wants to give points to encourage the sales team to increase the purchasing of both the local and out-of-town—nonlocal—customers. He believes nonlocal customers tend to buy more than the local customers, so the transaction amount for them is set higher than for the local customers. Ultimately, he would like to see the average transactions increase for all customers. He may change the transaction amounts that determine the points, so these have been included on the spreadsheet. For a point to be earned, the transaction needs to be either a local customer with more than $50 spent or a nonlocal customer that spent more than $100. The structure of this logical statement is shown in Figure 14 with pseudocode. It shows there are two ways to earn the points, and either will work, thus an OR function is the outer function. The two ways of earning points both require an AND function. The AND functions combine the Line_Item_Total condition with the Cust_Cat condition, requiring both to be evaluated as TRUE.

Logic:

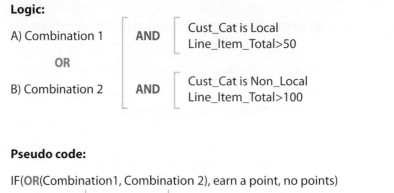

A) Combination 1   **AND**   Cust_Cat is Local
                                   Line_Item_Total>50

           OR

B) Combination 2   **AND**   Cust_Cat is Non_Local
                                     Line_Item_Total>100

Pseudo code:

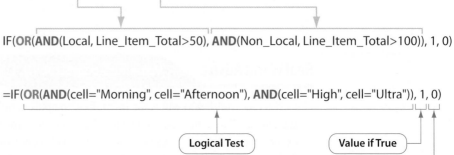

IF(**OR**(Combination1, Combination 2), earn a point, no points)

IF(**OR**(**AND**(Local, Line_Item_Total>50), **AND**(Non_Local, Line_Item_Total>100)), 1, 0)

=IF(**OR**(**AND**(cell="Morning", cell="Afternoon"), **AND**(cell="High", cell="Ultra")), 1, 0)

Logical Test   Value if True

Value if False

Figure 14   Logic of nesting AND in OR functions

To Use the AND Function Nested in an OR Function

a. One part of the function will be addressed to see how it works. On the Transactions worksheet tab, click cell **U21**, type =IF(AND(H21=, click the **Inputs worksheet tab**, click **I14** and press ⎋F4, then type ,P21>, click on **J14**, press ⎋F4, type),1,0), and then press ⎈Ctrl+⏎Enter.

b. Click the **AutoFill** handle, and drag to copy the formula down to cell **U220**.

    This will show that transactions from local customers spending more than $50 will get 1 point, but no others will get a point. The second inside logical AND condition to test for nonlocal customers spending more than $100 needs to be added with the OR as the outside joining function.

c. Click cell **U21**, press ⎋F2, and then position the cursor to the right of the **IF(**. Type OR(AND(H21=Inputs!$I$13,P21>Inputs!$J$13),. Place the cursor to the right of the **$J$14**), and then type) so there is a closing parenthesis to the OR that was just added. Press ⎈Ctrl+⏎Enter.

d. Double-click the **AutoFill** handle and copy the formula down to cell **U220**. Now, if either of the AND logical statements evaluate to TRUE, there will be a point given. Click **Save** 🔲.

SIDE NOTE
Setting up Reference
The values have been set up on the Inputs worksheet. This allows the managers to change and adapt their criteria without having to go find the values within formulas.

Using Conditional Aggregate Functions

It is quite common to run a calculation, like adding or averaging sales, and then evaluating whether the average or total met a goal or benchmark. This incorporates calculation and a logical decision. This is possible to handle by nesting the SUM or AVERAGE function within the IF function. However, these functions will calculate the entire range selected. With a spreadsheet that uses more sophisticated decision-making models, it is often desirable to do calculations on some of the data in the range, based upon some criteria. For example, in a data set of sales transactions, it may be useful to sum all of the credit card sales, ignoring the cash or check sales.

While this was a complex task to accomplish in previous versions of Excel, the addition of conditional aggregate functions in Excel 2010 makes this task manageable. **Conditional aggregate functions** are functions that consolidate or summarize a subset of data that has been filtered based upon one or more criteria. This is different from the traditional functions that calculate using all cells that are in a specified range. If SUM(A1:C10) is used, it adds all the values in all the cells in that range. With an aggregate function, a range would still be provided, but the aggregation would only use cells that meet a given criteria. The criteria can be on the data that is being aggregated or on associated data.

The criteria for determining which subset of data can be constructed in a variety of ways, as defined in Figure 15. Quotes are needed with the logical operators. The ampersand is used for adding the logical operator with another component. Elements like named ranges and cell references cannot go inside quotes because Excel would interpret them as text strings rather than named ranges or cell references. For example, "> B4" would check for values greater than the string >B4 instead of a value that is in the cell B4. This applies to all the functions discussed here.

In this section, conditional functions and database functions will be developed using this foundation. The functions will provide analysis of a data set for the purpose of gaining knowledge from the information.

Criteria	Action
B4	Selects if the value equals the value in B4
">10"	Selects if the value is greater than 10
">="&Goal	Selects if the value is greater than or equal to the value in the named range 'Goal'
"<>"&B5	Selects if the value is not equal to the value in B5

Figure 15 Criteria options

Using Conditional Statistical Functions

Excel 2010 recognizes the need for having statistical functions that would calculate on a subset of data that meets the specified criteria. There is set of common functions that have been merged with the logical functions, including the COUNT and AVERAGE functions. They have been set to handle both a single criterion and multiple criteria for filtering.

The COUNTIF and COUNTIFS Functions

The COUNTIF and COUNTIFS functions count the number of cells that meet the specified criteria. This differs from the SUMIF and SUMIFS functions, which sum the data in the cells that meet the given criteria. Both variations of the COUNT function will *count* the number of cells in a range that meet certain criteria. For example, a COUNTIF function that uses a range with 12 cells would return a value between 1 and 12 because the cells are counted. If the same range was used with a SUMIF, the result is determined by the sum of the values within the cells, not the number of cells.

The COUNTIF function only has two arguments, a range and one criterion. The syntax for the COUNTIF is

COUNTIF(range, criteria)

The range is the cells that will be counted, and the criteria is the logical statement that will determine which cells to count within the formula cell range. For example if there were a range of data in which the cells contained the data "Handicapped Golfer" or "Scratch Golfer" and the criteria was "Scratch Golfer", the function would count every occurrence in the cell range where the cell data content (criteria) equals "Scratch Golfer".

Barry wants to count the transactions based upon the transaction amount. You can accomplish this using the Trans_Group data range that has been classified as Low, Medium, High, and Ultra. Counting each of those will give the number by group.

To Create a COUNTIF Function

a. Click the **Rev_Rpt worksheet tab**, click cell **B9**, type =COUNTIF(Trans_Group,Inputs!I20), and then press Ctrl + Enter.

b. With cell **B9** selected, double-click the **AutoFill** handle to copy the formula down to cell **B12**.

   Notice the 190 value seems unusually high compared to the remaining values. This is due to the fact that the formula returns a value of Low in any remaining cells on the Transactions sheet where reference cells in the formula are blank. This is an example of why a formula needs to account for all possibilities when validating the information.

c. Barry would like to count the number of times a specific coupon is used. Click cell **E16**, type =COUNTIF(Coupon_Num,E13), and then press Enter. This will count the times the coupon listed in E13 was used in the Coupon_Num range found on the Transactions worksheet.

d. Finally, Barry wants to count the number of transactions greater than or equal to a specific value. This value can change, so it definitely needs to be referenced. Click cell **E4**.

e. Type =COUNTIF(Line_Item_Total,">="&D4), and then press Enter. This is different in that the criteria is set up so the value in D4 is used instead of looking for the string "D4". Click **Save**.

SIDE NOTE
Criteria for COUNTIF

Logical symbols, like > or <, are alphanumeric and are within quotes. However, D4 is a cell reference and does not use quotes. The ampersand (&) is a plus sign adding the text in the quotes with the value in the cell reference.

Real World Advice — Working Complex AND, OR Conditions

In the real world, you would error check as you develop a spreadsheet, looking for odd numbers. Try testing data to ensure formulas work. It may be that an issue is caused by cells being referenced in a formula rather than the formula itself. Develop techniques, such as using formula auditing and testing a range of data possibilities to ensure correct calculations.

The COUNTIFS function allows for multiple criteria in multiple ranges to be evaluated and counted. The syntax for the COUNTIFS is:

COUNTIFS(criteria_range1, criteria1, [criteria_range2, criteria2],…)

There is no distinction between a criteria_range argument found in the COUNTIFS and a range argument used in the COUNTIF. When counting, it simply counts the cells that meet the criteria, so the range of cells to count and the criteria_range are the same range.

However, when using multiple criteria, all criteria ranges must have exactly the same shape, with the same number of rows and same number of columns. Then, the cells within the multiple ranges are compared and all criteria have to evaluate to TRUE to be counted. In Figure 16, the first set of cells will be TRUE if the value is 392. Cells A1 and B3 would be TRUE. In the second range, the cells would be evaluated as TRUE if they have a value of 28. Cells F1, F2, and G3 meet that second criteria. However, cells in the same relative position within the two ranges must both be TRUE to be counted. Thus the pairs A1 & F1 and B3 & G3 both are TRUE so the COUNTIF would return a value of 2 for this COUNTIFS example. The criterion is met for the cell in F2, the first column, second row, for the second range, but it is not met for cell A2 in row 2, column 1, for the first criteria range, so that set is not counted. Thus, the number of cells in one range determines the maximum count that can be obtained.

COUNTIFS(A1:B3, "=392", F1:G3, "=28")

	A	B			F	G
1	**392**	439		**1**	**28**	83
2	439	375		**2**	**28**	37
3	827	**392**		**3**	48	**28**

Figure 16 COUNTIFS calculation

Barry wants to count the number of transactions, grouped by the coupon target and the shift. The table on the Transactions worksheet has been set up to show the coupon targets and the current shift desired. The shift may change so it needs to be referenced. Two criteria must be matched for a count to occur. The two ranges checked will be the Shift and the Coupon_Target. Both are the same shape, so the first cell in both ranges will be evaluated. *If* both are true for their criteria, that pair will be counted, and so on for the remaining cells in the two ranges.

To Create a COUNTIFS Function

a. On the **Rev_Rpt worksheet tab**, click cell **F8**, type =COUNTIFS(Shift,$E$6,Coupon_Target,E8), and then press [Ctrl]+[Enter].

   This checks for the Shift category of "Morning" and for "Local" coupon targets. When both occur, the set is counted.

b. With cell **F8** selected, double-click its **AutoFill** handle to copy the formula down to cell **F11**, and then click **Save** 🖫.

The AVERAGEIF and AVERAGEIFS Functions

The AVERAGEIF and AVERAGEIFS functions are similar in that they average a range of data selecting data to average based on the criteria specified. The AVERAGEIF has three arguments, two required and one optional. The syntax for the AVERAGEIF is as follows:

=AVERAGEIF(range, criteria, [average_range])

If the option argument is left out, Excel assumes the same range specified in the first range argument will be used for filtering the data and for averaging. For example, if Barry wanted to find the average for only the scratch golfers, he would average the handicaps for people that have a handicap greater than 0. This would filter based on the handicap and would average the same range.

With the AVERAGEIF, the third argument is only required if one range of data is being averaged based on criteria of a second range. Similar to the COUNTIFS function, the two ranges must be the same shape, having the same number of rows and columns. With the AVERAGEIFS function all ranges must be the same size, although they do not have to be adjacent nor even on the same page.

For the revenue report, the average sales will be calculated for the local customers. Next an average will be calculated for the type of transaction used for the local customers. Thus, it will pull the local customers that used cash and average the line item total for those records. The same thing needs to be done for the checks and credit card transactions for the local customer transactions.

To Use the AVERAGEIF Function

a. On the **Rev_Rpt worksheet tab**, click cell **B15**, type =AVERAGEIF(Cust_Cat,B14,Line_Item_Total), and then press [Enter]. Click **Save** 🖫.

The AVERAGEIFS function expands on the AVERAGEIF function, allowing multiple criteria to determine the subset of data. However, it is important to note that the order of the arguments changes. The syntax for the AVERAGIFS is:

=AVERAGEIFS(average_range, criteria_range1, criteria1, [criteria_range2, criteria2], …)

The average range is moved to become the first argument on the assumption that different ranges would be used for determining the filtered subset of data. After the average range, there are pairs of criteria ranges and criteria. In this fashion multiple criteria can be used to filter the data to be averaged.

Barry wants to find the average Line_Item_Total based on the Cust_Cat and the Pay_Type. He would like flexibility so the criteria will be set in cells and need to be referenced in the formula.

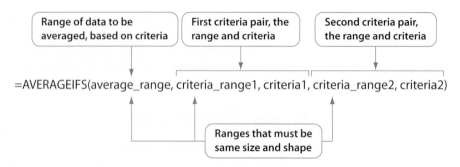

Figure 17 AVERAGEIFS function

To Use the AVERAGEIFS Function

a. On the Rev_Rpt worksheet tab, click cell **B16**, if necessary, and then type =AVERAGEIFS(Li, and then double-click **Line_Item_Total** when it appears in the AutoComplete list.

b. Type ,Cu, and then double-click **Cust_Cat** when it appears in the AutoComplete list.

c. Type ,$B$14,P, and then double-click **Pay _Type** when it appears in the AutoComplete list.

d. Type ,A16), and then press [Ctrl]+[Enter].
   Now the Customer Type can be changed in B14, and the Average will automatically adjust.

e. Click cell **B16**, double-click the **AutoFill** handle to copy the formula down through **B18**, and then click **Save** 🔲.

Using Conditional Math Functions

Conditional math functions work in a similar fashion as the statistical functions just covered. The conditional math functions include the SUMIF and SUMIFS functions.

The SUMIF Function

The SUMIF and SUMIFS functions exist to select values from a range of data based on criteria and then add those values together. The SUMIF function sums data based on one criterion. The SUMIFS function does the same thing but allows for more than one filtering criteria. The syntax for the two functions, while using similar arguments, has a different order for the arguments:

SUMIF(range, criteria, [sum_range])

SUMIFS(sum_range, criteria_range1, criteria1, [criteria_range2, criteria2],…)

For the SUMIF function, because there is only one criterion allowed, the first argument is the range associated with the criterion. The second argument is the criterion itself, which will determine which values are summed. The third argument is an optional [sum_range]. This is optional because you can set the criterion on the actual sum range. If the sum_range argument is omitted, the default is to assume the range and the sum_range are the same. However, a great feature with this function is that the criteria can be set on one range, like the payment type, while summing a second range, like the payment amount.

To Use a SUMIF Function

a. On the **Rev_Rpt worksheet tab**, click cell **B22**, type =SUMIF(Shift,B21,Line_Item_Total), and then press Enter .

   This will select those transactions that occurred during the morning shift and sum the Line_Item_Total values.

b. The Revenue needs to be summed for each customer type in the same manner. Click cell **B4**, type =SUMIF(Cust_Cat,A4,Line_Item_Total), and then press Ctrl + Enter .

c. In cell **B4**, double-click the **AutoFill** handle and copy the formula down through cell **B6**, and then click **Save** .

   Now each subset of line item totals has been summed, grouped by the customer type.

The SUMIFS Function

With the SUMIFS function, it is assumed that multiple criteria would be set, thus having a sum_range different from at least one criteria_range. Thus, the order is changed to have the sum_range first, then add a criteria_range and criteria for each constraint or filter. For example, you could indicate the sales range to sum and have a criterion of only summing transactions that were made online and were set up as gifts. Recall the syntax for the SUMIFS is

   SUMIFS(sum_range, criteria_range1, criteria1, [criteria_range2, criteria2],…)

The structure for the arguments is the same as with the AVERAGEIFS. The criteria ranges have to match the sum_range in shape. If there are multiple criteria, the cells are evaluated for each criterion with a result of TRUE to be used in the subset of data, as shown in Figure 18.

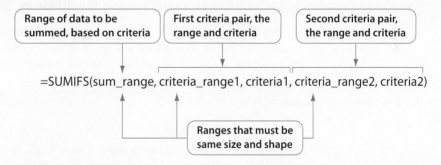

Figure 18 SUMIFS calculation

The report has been set up to sum the Line_Item_Total range filtered by the SKU_Cat and the Cust_Cat. This way, the report will show a grid indicating revenue from Local, Non_Local, and Unknown, grouped by the Product Categories of Clothing, Clubs, Accessories, and Shoes.

To Use a SUMIFS function

a. On the **Rev_Rpt worksheet tab**, click cell **B25**, type =SUMIFS(Line_Item_Total,SKU_Cat,$A25,Cust_Cat,B$24), and then press Ctrl + Enter .

   The mixed cell referencing the formula can be copied to the other cells within the grid.

b. In cell **B25**, double-click the **AutoFill** handle to copy the formula down to cell **B28**.

c. With the range **B25:B28** still selected, click the **AutoFill** handle on the lower-right corner of the range, and then drag to the right to cell **D28** to copy the formula over to cell range **B25:D28**. Press Ctrl+Home.

d. Click the **Emp_Rpt worksheet tab**, and then click cell **B8**.

   The Employee Sales Report also needs some conditional sums. The Total Sales Revenue for a sales staff needs to be calculated. The current Sales Staff is an Asst Manager named Hample who has a Staff ID Number of 15, which will be used as the conditional filter.

e. Type =SUMIF(Emp_ID,A8,Line_Item_Total), and then press Enter.

f. Click cell **B15**. The staff has a goal for each product category.

   Currently clothing is listed in B13 and the associated goal for Hample is also provided. The percentage of that goal is Hample's sales for clothing divided by the goal.

g. Type =SUMIFS(Line_Item_Total,SKU_Cat,B13,Emp_ID,A8)/B14, and then press Enter.

   This will sum the records if both the SKU category is clothing and the employee ID is 15. Referencing the cells allow the category and sales staff to be changed, incorporating flexibility.

h. Click cell **B17**. The incentive points need to be added up for the staff person listed. Type =SUMIF(Emp_ID,A8,Sales_Point1)+SUMIF(Emp_ID,A8,Sales_Point2), press Enter, and then click **Save** 🖫.

   This has to be done by adding two SUMIF functions. It cannot be done in one SUMIFS as that sums on multiple criteria and the only criteria in this case is the Emp_ID. The sale point columns cannot be combined into one sum range as the Sales_Point1 and Sales_Point2 data would not match up in the same cells for the same range shape, thus they need to be tallied separately and then combined.

CONSIDER THIS | **Using the SUMIF vs. SUMIFS Function**

The two functions are very similar in what they accomplish. Could you simply use the SUMIFS function all the time and get used to its format? Could any situation that would use the SUMIF be written using the SUMIFS?

The DSUM Function

The SUMIFS function has a competitor within Excel. The DSUM function is a database function that is great for setting up a criteria range and then calculating the sum based on the filters within that criteria range. An advantage is that you can see the criteria on the spreadsheet and understand the calculation. Secondly, the criteria can be modified on the sheet and the result will automatically be updated. So instead of editing a SUMIFS function, in DSUM the criteria are changed in cells and there is no need to alter the function. The structure of the DSUM is

   =DSUM(database, field, criteria)

The database argument is a range of cells that make up the set of records, like the transaction data, with records and fields. The field is the field label of the column to be summed. The criteria are a range of cells that contains the conditions you specify. The criteria range includes a column field label or list of field labels on the top row and one or more cell rows below the field label(s) for the criteria condition. Criteria can be put onto multiple fields at the same time. When this is done, all the criteria must be evaluated to TRUE for the record to be included in the summation of the fields. Common database functions are described in Figure 19.

Database Function	Description
DAVERAGE	Averages the values in the column field of records in a list or database that match conditions you specify
DCOUNT	Counts the cells that contain numbers in a field (column) of records in the database that match the conditions you specify
DCOUNTA	Counts nonblank cells in the field (column) of records in the database that match the conditions you specify
DGET	Extracts a single value from a column of a database that matches the conditions you specify
DMAX	Returns the largest number in the field (column) of records in the database that match the conditions you specify
DMIN	Returns the smallest number in the field (column) of records in the database that match the conditions you specify
DPRODUCT	Multiplies the values in the field (column) of records in the database that match the conditions you specify
DSTDEV	Estimates the standard deviation based on a sample by using numbers in a field of records in a database that match conditions that you specify
DSTDEVP	Calculates the standard deviation based on the entire population by using numbers in a field of records in a database that match conditions that you specify
DSUM	Adds the numbers in a field (column) of records in the database that match conditions you specify
DVAR	Estimates the variance based on a sample by using the numbers in a field of records in a database that match conditions that you specify
DVARP	Calculates the variance based on the entire population by using the numbers in a field of records in a database that match conditions that you specify

Figure 19 Database functions

To Use a DSUM Function

a. Click the **DB_Sums worksheet**, select **G2**, type Non_Local, and then press Enter.
This value is the constraint for filtering the records. Only records that are nonlocal customers will be used with the DSUM function.

b. Click the **DB_Sums worksheet**, click cell **B10**, type =DSUM(DataSet,B9,A1:K2), and then press Enter.
The DataSet is the transaction database data found on the Transactions worksheet. B9 is the field that will be summed. A1:K2 is the two rows of information that is the criteria. Press Ctrl+Home, and then click **Save**.

c. Select **A2**, type Check, and then press Enter. This changes the value reflected in B10 immediately.

Once again, flexibility has been integrated into the formula. B9 is the field to be summed. If Barry wants to sum the line item total or the transaction quantity, he simply puts the field name into B9. The formula will automatically be updated. The field chosen for B9 should be a numerical field like the Line_Item_Total or the Trans_Qty.

Retrieving Data Using LOOKUP and Reference Functions

With sets of data, it is also useful to be able to look for and retrieve specific data. For example, you may have exam scores and you need to convert the numerical score into a letter grade. Within a business, you may need to convert a coupon number into a percentage number so the amount of the discount can be computed. In both cases, you want to search for, or look up a value, and then retrieve some corresponding information. You need to refer to or retrieve specific information. A variety of functions exist for this type of data analysis. In this section you will create functions that will look up information based on the initial data set. Then you will work to evaluate and eliminate errors within the spreadsheet model.

Using LOOKUP Functions

There are two LOOKUP functions you can use to look up a value and then, using that value as a reference, return data that is associated with that value. LOOKUP functions are extremely valuable when working with tables where the data is in rows or columns.

The VLOOKUP function is the more commonly used LOOKUP function. It has four arguments, three of which are required; the other is optional. The syntax for the VLOOKUP is:

VLOOKUP(lookup_value, table_array, col_index_number, [range_lookup])

The V in VLOOKUP stands for vertical and is used when your comparison values are located in a column to the left of the data that you want to find. For example, a teacher could use a VLOOKUP to look up an exam score and retrieve the corresponding letter grade. The setup for a VLOOKUP shown in Figure 20 uses a TRUE value for the optional range_lookup argument. It should be noted that if this optional argument is omitted, Excel defaults to the TRUE argument, which will find the next lower value for a specified value. Because a TRUE argument will not search for an exact match and will return the next lower match that it finds, it should also be noted that the left-most lookup_value column must be sorted in ascending order to ensure the appropriate value is returned. In Figure 20, the lookup_value is 72, and when Excel encounters the value of 80, Excel will assume the closest value in this example will be approximate to the lower 70 score value. A score of 79 will also drop down to the closest match less than that value, so 79 would also return the 70 value result. Recall, the default for the VLOOKUP, when leaving off the optional argument is to assume TRUE for an approximate match result. If the fourth argument is assigned a FALSE, or 0 value, the VLOOKUP will return an exact match, and it will not be necessary to sort the lookup_value column in ascending order.

VLOOKUP(B1, table, 2, TRUE)

Cell A1	Cell B1		
C	72	**SCORE**	**GRADE**
		0	F
		60	D
		70	C
		80	B
		90	A

Figure 20 VLOOKUP function

For the employee report, Barry wants to give incentives to staff that do well in selling products. He is awarding points for certain transactions and a set of rewards has been set up for redeeming points earned during the time period. The more points earned, the better the rewards. He will adjust the awards and point levels needed to attain the various choices. On the employee report, the incentive points have been added. The point value needs to be converted to show their reward level. There are four reward levels, and no reward is an additional possibility. As Figure 20 shows, a VLOOKUP can be used to find the approximate match and return the appropriate result to the points attained.

To Find an Approximate Match in VLOOKUP

a. Click the **Emp_Rpt worksheet tab**, and then click cell **B18**. The table has been set up as IncentivePts and resides on the Inputs worksheet. Type **=VLOOKUP(B17,Incentive Pts,2,TRUE)**, and then press Enter. With only a few incentive points, Hample needs to improve sales to the targets customers. Click **Save** 📄.

The other optional argument for a VLOOKUP hunts for an exact match. You search for an exact match daily in a contact list when looking for a phone number associated with a name. You search for a name and from the name obtain the phone number or other data that has been stored in the little table such as the one shown in Figure 21 that demonstrates the process and components of a phone contact list within the structure of a VLOOKUP. Each row contains the information for a person. The value you look up is the name. The information returned is in the adjacent columns to the right of the name. The lookup_value is the value Excel will look for in the left-most column of the table array. For a phone number, an exact match is needed. This is achieved with the optional [range-lookup] argument set to FALSE or a 1. If the VLOOKUP does not find an exact match in the left column of the table_array, it will return a #N/A error—not available. The order of the first column does not need to be sorted for an exact match argument.

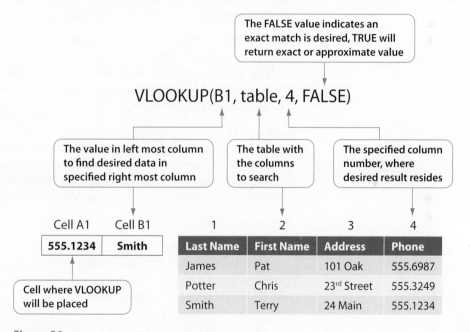

Figure 21 Exact match VLOOKUP for phone number

The SKU_Cat will be included with the data brought into the Transactions worksheet but the retail purchase price will not be included. This data, however, can be found by referencing a SKU List table that is maintained on the Inputs worksheet. The Item ID will need to be found in the SKU List table and the corresponding Retail_Price can then be included. This means the first column of the range where the search will occur must contain the Item ID. Because an exact match must be found, the table does not have to be sorted.

To Find an Exact Match in VLOOKUP

a. Click the **Transactions worksheet tab**, click cell **O21**, type =VLOOKUP(C21,SKU_List,6,FALSE), and press Ctrl+Enter. The SKU_List on the Inputs worksheet has the list and is a named range. The Item ID in cell reference C21 is also located in the first column of the table. The corresponding Retail Price is pulled from the sixth column, counting from left to right within the SKU List table.

b. With cell **O21** selected, click the **AutoFill** handle, and then drag down to copy the formula down to cell **O220**.

The formula will display a #N/A error for any cells referencing a blank cell in column C, but this will be corrected in a later exercise when the worksheet is checked and updated for errors.

c. On the Transactions worksheet tab, click cell **N21**.

The coupon percentage needs to be determined from the coupon number provided in column F. The Coupons table is setup on the Inputs worksheet and is a range named Coupons.

d. Type =VLOOKUP(F21,Coupons,2,FALSE), and then press Ctrl+Enter.

Note the #N/A appears. This is because there was no coupon used in the transaction column F cell reference, thus it cannot find an exact match and returns an error message that means it is *not applicable* or *not available*.

e. With cell **N21** selected, click the **AutoFill** handle, and then drag down to copy the formula down to cell **N220**.

Note the error messages occur for all the transactions that do not have a Coupon_Num entry listed in the F column cell. This can be corrected when the worksheet is checked and updated for errors.

f. Click cell **I21**.

The SKU_Cat needs to be determined by looking at the SKU in column C. The SKU_List on the Inputs worksheet has the Item ID on the left side so it can be searched. Looking at the SKU List table, the Category is listed in the third column. The search needs to find an exact match, not approximate. From that, the VLOOKUP can be created.

g. Type =VLOOKUP(C21,SKU_List,3,FALSE), and press Ctrl+Enter.

h. In cell **I21**, click the **AutoFill** handle, and then drag down to copy the formula down to cell **I220**. The formula will display a #N/A error for any cells referencing a blank cell in column C, but this will be corrected in a later exercise when the worksheet is checked and updated for errors. Click **Save** 🖫.

The HLOOKUP works in the same manner as the VLOOKUP function except the lookup_value is checked horizontally in the top row of the table_array. As seen in Figure 22, the HLOOKUP wants a row_index_number indicating which row below the lookup row the target value can be found. By comparison, the VLOOKUP used a col_index_num. All the remaining arguments are the same and operate in a similar manner. The HLOOKUP also uses the optional [range_lookup] argument with the same approximate or exact match options.

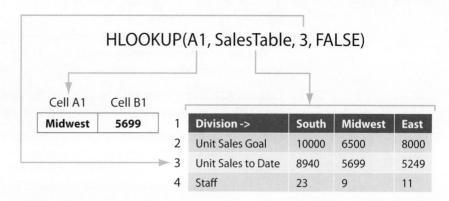

Figure 22 HLOOKUP function

For the report, a section is set up to analyze individual staff. With an individual listed, formulas will be created to pull information pertaining to that person. In particular, their goal for revenue will be pulled.

Barry would also like to be able to pull data about the Transaction Groups, the Shifts data, or the Coupons data that has been established on the Inputs sheet. Because it needs to be flexible, he wants to be able to choose one of those options and have the categories appear for that option and calculate the sum when it can be applied to appropriate categories on the Transactions worksheet. But first, an adjustment to the Rev_Rpt worksheet will be developed. The Coupon_Target cells in F8:F11 have already been taken care of, and now we will focus on the Category E8:E11 cells. Using the numbering in column D, the formula can be set up to use those numbers to go to the correct row_index_num value to return the correct value from the AH_ReportTable. The range for the table has not been set up, so first we need to do that to make it easier to set up the formula.

To Create an HLOOKUP Function

a. Click the **Inputs worksheet tab**, and then select **B12:G17**. This is the data including the headings for the HLOOKUP function to search in the first row for the different reporting groups as needed.

b. Click the **Formulas tab**, click **Define Name**, and then in the New Name dialog box, in the Name input box type AH_ReportTable, replacing the **AH_Shifts** that is in the Name input box. Click **OK**. Now the table can be referenced easily in formulas.

c. On the Formulas tab, click **Create from Selection**, make sure only the **Top row** check box is checked, and then click **OK**. Now, each report group has also been named so they can easily be referenced.

d. Click the **Rev_Rpt worksheet tab**, click cell **E8**, type =HLOOKUP($F$6,AH_Report Table,D8+1,FALSE) replacing the text that is in that cell, and then press Ctrl + Enter .

This will look for the Ad Hoc Report Name listed in F6 within the ReportTable on the Inputs worksheet. Once that data is found, Excel will drop down and retrieve the category item. Because the function has FALSE as the last argument, Excel will look for an exact match to the value in F6.

e. Click cell **E8**, click the **AutoFill** handle and copy the formula down through **E11**.

Using the numbers in column D, allow the formula to be copied. If it had been hardcoded into the formula, it could not have been copied to the other cells without editing.

f. Click the **Transactions worksheet tab**, and then click cell **K21**.

The Shift needs to be determined from the time of the transaction. The Shifts named range has been set up on the Inputs worksheet for A20:D21. The times fall within ranges so hunting for an exact match would rarely succeed. Instead, an approximate match is needed.

g. Type =HLOOKUP(B21,Shifts,2,TRUE), and then press Ctrl+Enter.

This will find an approximate match, then pull the corresponding result from the second row in the table.

h. Click cell **K21**, click the **AutoFill** handle, and then drag down to copy the formula to cell **K220**. Again, ignore the #N/A errors, which will be corrected later.

i. Click the **Emp_Rpt worksheet tab**, and then click cell **B10**.

The Overall Goal for the staff, currently Hample, needs to be retrieved. The staffs' goals are listed on the Inputs worksheet. The data can be pulled from the table and can be flexible so it will be updated when the staff member in A6 changes.

j. Type =HLOOKUP(A6,Inputs!B4:F9,6,FALSE), and then press Enter.

k. Click cell **B11**, type =B8/B10, and then press Enter so the percent of goal is now determined. Click **Save** 🖫.

CONSIDER THIS | Using VLOOKUP or Nested IF

Take the situation of converting an exam score to a letter grade. Could you create an IF function statement that would accomplish the same task? What logical issues would lead you to use a VLOOKUP versus a nested IF?

Retrieving Data with MATCH, INDEX, and INDIRECT

VLOOKUP and HLOOKUP look in the first column of data and "look" to the right or down to retrieve a value. Returning to the phone book metaphor, what if I asked you for the name of the person with the phone number (555) 555-1234? Would that be easy to do? Unfortunately, the task becomes more difficult because a traditional phone book is organized by name, not by phone number.

To overcome this limitation in the VLOOKUP and HLOOKUP, the MATCH and INDEX functions work to accomplish the same type of process. The primary difference is that these two functions together overcome the limitation of data arrangement. With the MATCH and INDEX functions you have the added flexibility of multiple data ranges that can be located throughout the spreadsheet. The ability to use MATCH and INDEX together is a powerful skill.

The MATCH Function

The MATCH function looks for a value within a range and returns the position of that value within the range. The position is a relative location starting from the top row of the table array. The syntax for the MATCH function is:

MATCH(lookup_value, lookup_array, [match_type])

The optional match_type argument uses a value of -1, 0, or 1. The default value of 1 is assumed (if omitted). A match_type value of 0 is used for an exact match, a 1 returns a match for the largest value that is less than or equal to the lookup_value, and a -1 finds the smallest value that is greater than or equal to the lookup_value. The exact match will return the row where the first occurrence of the match resides. This means that if there are multiple occurrences of a value, it will return the first one it finds, from the top. It will not find subsequent values. The 1 will find the location of the value that is closest to the value but not greater than the value. The -1 value will return the position of the value that is closest to the lookup_value but not less than the lookup_value. Thus, by being able to return either the next lowest or next higher value, the match has a little more flexibility than the VLOOKUP function. In either the 1, or the -1, options, the data has to be sorted in ascending order or descending order, respectively, or the match process will not work correctly.

The MATCH function returns a number that indicates the position, or row, in which the match was found. This value will be relative to the top row of the range. While the function indicates the lookup_array is one range, the range must be one continuous range that is only in one column. If you try to use a range that includes more than one column, the MATCH function will not work.

For the revenue report, Barry wants to be able to check the transactions and see when the first transaction that used a coupon occurred. Using the MATCH function will enable him to determine the transaction number of the first occurrence.

To Use the MATCH Function

a. Click the **Rev_Rpt worksheet tab**, click cell **E14**, type =MATCH(E13,Coupon_Num,0), and then press Enter. Click **Save** 🔲. The coupon listed in E13 will be searched in the CouponNum field as the lookup_array within the Transactions worksheet. The third argument in the function is 0 indicating the search should be for an exact match.

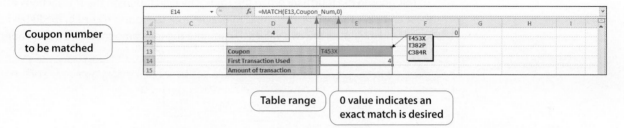

Figure 23 MATCH function

If the discount coupon listed in E13 is not used in any of the transactions, it will return a #N/A error, which indicates it could not find the coupon listed. If the coupon listed was typed incorrectly, this would also return a #N/A error. It would not be easy to determine whether a #N/A error indicates if the discount coupon typed in was simply not used or if it was not a valid coupon.

Real World Advice   Typing Errors

With a short list of options, like coupon number, using a comment to list the coupon codes is a reasonable solution. But, it is still possible to make typing errors. To minimize typing errors, designers typically create a drop-down list of the options. This eliminates typing errors and is a more efficient method. Learning to incorporate drop-down lists in a cell is handled in another workshop. It is a valuable tool to use in validating data.

The Index Function

The INDEX function works in conjunction with the MATCH function. The INDEX function returns the value of an element in a table or array selected by the row and column number indexes. INDEX has two argument lists to choose. The first list of arguments uses an array and returns a value from a specified cell or range. The second list of arguments uses a reference and returns a reference to specified cells. The more common set of arguments, which will be discussed here, is with the array that returns a value. The value gets returned from a range based on the row and column indicated. The indexing starts from the top-left corner of the table. Thus, the left column, first row, of the table would be row 1 and column 1. The index is relative based on the top-left corner of the array. The syntax for the INDEX function is:

INDEX(array, row_number, [column_number])

The array is the range of data, the row_number is the row in which the value will be found, and if the column_number is provided, it will be the column number, starting from the left of the range from which the result will be pulled. INDEX works with the MATCH function well because MATCH indicates the row where a match was found, and then the INDEX can go to that row and another column to retrieve associated data.

To Use the INDEX Function

a. On the Rev_Rpt worksheet tab, click cell **E15**, if necessary.

   Knowing when the first transaction occurred, the amount of the transaction prior to the discount could be pulled from the transaction data using the INDEX function. The transaction total would be the price times the quantity for that transaction, which is on row 4 of the data.

b. Type =INDEX(Trans_Qty,E14)*INDEX(Retail,E14), and then press Enter.

   This goes to the fourth record in the Trans_Qty field found on the Transactions worksheet and pulls that value, then pulls the value from the fourth record in the Retail field range, and multiplies the two values to compute the total amount of the transaction.

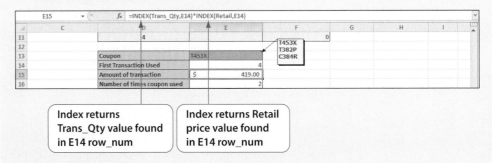

Figure 24 INDEX function

c. Click the **Emp_Rpt worksheet tab**, and then click cell **B22**.

   Barry wants to be able to list the rewards for the different levels so it is available as he talks with his staff. Currently, it shows Level_1 in B21. He wants the three Level_1 rewards to be listed below. He can use the INDEX function, and the numbers in column A to retrieve the information.

d. Type =INDEX(Level_1,A22), and press Ctrl+Enter.

e. In cell **B22**, use the **AutoFill** handle to copy the formula down to **B24**.

   Now the items available for Level_1 are listed. However, the formulas would need to be changed if a different level was desired. In a later section, this will be modified to automatically update when B21 is change.

f. Click cell **B6**.

   The position for the staff, Hample currently, needs to be retrieved. However, in the table, Hample is not the first column. It could still be searched, but using a VLOOKUP would not work because the position field is to the *left* of the Last Name field in the table on the Inputs worksheet. The MATCH can locate the row where Hample exists, then go to the same row for the positions and pull his position.

g. Type =MATCH(A6,Inputs!L27:L31), and then press Ctrl+Enter. This will show the row where Hample is located.

h. Press F2 to edit cell **B6**. Click in the **formula bar** to position the insertion point to the right of the = sign, type INDEX(Inputs!I27:I31,. Position the cursor at the end of the formula and type), and then press Enter. Now it will retrieve Hample's position value using the nested MATCH function to determine the row_num argument.

i. Click the **Transactions worksheet tab**, and then click cell **J21**.

    The employee position for all the transactions needs to be retrieved and accomplished in a similar manner as retrieving Hample's position.

j. Type =INDEX(Inputs!$I$27:$I$31,MATCH(G21,Inputs!$J$27:$J$31,0)), and then press Ctrl+Enter.

    The dollar signs ($), which make the references absolute, are necessary because the ranges need to stay in place as the formula is copied down the column.

k. Click cell **J21**, click the **AutoFill** handle, and then copy the formula down to cell **J220**. The errors will be fixed later when the sheet is error checked.

l. Click the **Emp_Rpt worksheet tab**, and then click cell **B14**.

    Currently the value is 200 for the clothing goal for Hample. But, for flexibility, Barry wants this number to be updated if the staff member changes and if the product category changes. Fortunately, the Sales Goals table found on the Inputs table has all the goal values listed for each category for each staff member, and has been named Goals.

m. Click the **Name** box, and then choose **Goals** from the list of named ranges.

    You will see it selects the data associated with the staff and the goals for each category. If the row and column within the table is known, the INDEX function can be used to pull the value for the appropriate goal value. Using the MATCH functions within the INDEX function, the goal can be retrieved. Building it a piece at a time will help with the development by testing the subcomponents.

n. On the Emp_Rpt worksheet tab, click cell **D10**, type =MATCH(B13,Inputs!A5:A9,0), and then press Ctrl+Enter.

    This is the first piece and shows the row where the lookup_value from B13 (in this case, Clothing) is found in the Goals range. The last argument, with 0, indicates an exact match should be found.

o. Click cell **D11**, type =MATCH(A6, Inputs!B4:F4,0), and then press Ctrl+Enter.

    The formula returns the column where the staff member is located in the Goals named range on the Inputs worksheet.

p. Click cell **B14**.

    Knowing the MATCH functions work, the complex function can be constructed.

q. Type =INDEX(Goals,MATCH(B13,Inputs!A5:A9,0),MATCH(A6,Inputs!B4:F4,0)) and press Enter.

    The Goals range on the Inputs worksheet array is used. The first MATCH is the row within the table while the second MATCH is the column within the range. Using those coordinates the INDEX function returns the correct goal value.

Named range where result is located

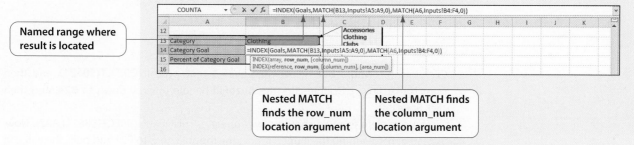

Nested MATCH finds the row_num location argument

Nested MATCH finds the column_num location argument

Figure 25 The INDEX function with a nested MATCH function

r. Select cells **D10:D11**, press Delete to remove the test functions, and then click **Save**.

The INDIRECT Function

The INDIRECT function is another reference function that can be used to add flexibility to a spreadsheet. The INDIRECT function is valuable because it can change a text string within a cell to a cell reference. The syntax for the INDIRECT is:

=INDIRECT(ref_text, [a1])

The argument typically is a cell reference or a text string. Within the cell you can put in a cell, range, or named range. The function tells Excel to interpret the cell's value as a reference rather than a text string. In other words, the cell referenced in the INDIRECT function, reroutes to a new reference. In Figure 26 the formula in cell A1 does not use a specific named range. The AVERAGE function does not go directly to the named range. It goes indirectly, to B1, which redirects the function to use the range listed in B1. The INDIRECT function pulls the value in B1, the range named "Pat" as a range to be averaged. Instead of changing the named range in the formula, the name can be changed in cell B1 from Pat to Chris and it would give the average for Chris. This adds flexibility to choose which named range to average.

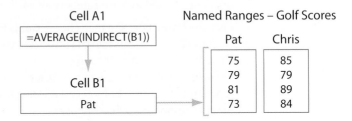

Figure 26 INDIRECT function logic

The optional INDIRECT argument will not be a concern for the average user. The function defaults to the A1 reference method if the A1 argument is omitted, which merely refers to the method for cell references. Typically Excel is set to interpret references by the A1 method of column letter and row number. The alternative method is referred to as a R1C1 reference style, which means to refer to the row and column number. For example, if a value is in the third row and fourth column, the cell reference would be R3C4. Excel allows you to set the R1C1 reference style check box as a default option under Formulas within the Excel Options dialog box.

On the employee report (Emp_Rpt worksheet), if Barry wants to look at the different rewards in the different levels, the formulas would need to be changed again. Preferably, the cell in B21 could show the level that is to be displayed. And, since it is the name of the range that holds the list of rewards, it could be used in the three formulas. Using the INDIRECT function would allow the value in cell B21 to change, and the reward list would automatically be updated.

To Use the INDIRECT Function

a. On the Emp_Rpt worksheet tab, click cell **B22**.

b. Click in the **formula bar**, select the **Level_1 text**, type INDIRECT($B$21), and then press Ctrl + Enter. Double-click the **AutoFill** handle to copy down to **B24**, and then click **Save**.

The complete formula should now appear as =INDEX(INDIRECT($B$21),A22). Now, instead of hard-coding the named range, the formula goes to B21 and pulls the value in B21 to use as the range, indirectly, by going first to B21, and B21 is directing the formula to use the Level_1 value contained in the cell as the named cell range.

Handling Errors with the IFERROR Function

Because logical functions are used in decision-making scenarios where flexibility and scalability is desirable, there are times in the development of the formulas when the functions may return error messages. Because there could be multiple users of varying skills, it is important to minimize the occurrence of error messages within the spreadsheet. Error messages tend to make users uncomfortable. Additionally, if the error message is legitimate, and other calculations reference those cells, the errors will carry forward into the next formula, compounding the problem.

The solution is to be aware of when errors may occur, such as a division by 0 due to no data being in a template, and create functions in a way that eliminates the error message from being viewed. During development, it is possible to anticipate and handle errors within the formula if you consider the values being used and the possible answers. The IFERROR function is a useful tool for detecting an error and displaying something more user friendly than the error message.

Real World Advice — Using a Blank or a Zero to Hide an Error

Does it matter what you put in for a result or outcome for an IF statement? What are the implications when you use "" versus a 0? This is not an easy decision if the cell will be used in another formula. When a calculation refers to a cell where you have used a blank, created with the double quotes, the result will be a #VALUE! error or #Div/0! error. The calculation will not be able to compute the blank as a numerical value. Conversely, if you put in a 0 for a value so it is numerical, then, that number would be used in aggregate functions. This would potentially drive an average down artificially. So you have to be careful when you decide to put in either the blank or a 0. Consider how the result will be used. If it is not going to be used in later calculations, then using the blank is a viable solution. Otherwise you may need to use a 0. A workaround to consider when cells in a range contain a 0 is to use a calculation formula that allows you to filter based on certain criteria. For example, if you need to average your results that contain cells with a 0, you can use the AVERAGEIF and only average the numbers that are greater than 0.

With the IFERROR function it is possible to evaluate if an error occurs and replace an error message with another value that you specify; otherwise, the formula result will be returned. The syntax for the IFERROR function is:

IFERROR(value, value_if_error)

The first argument, value, is the formula that is going to be checked for existing errors. IF the value works and a valid output exists, that formula value will be returned from the IFERROR function. However, if the value returns any error message, such as #N/A or #DIV/0!, then the value_if_error value will be returned.

When examining the Transactions worksheet, you will see there are error messages showing up within the range in two different contexts. First, when there are not any transaction records, error messages exist throughout. Secondly, in a few fields error messages occur even when there are transactions. The #N/A is not only distracting, it is confusing to users. They may believe there are errors in the calculations when in actuality these errors are valid errors.

In the process of checking the values and eliminating errors, it is best to start with formulas that are simple and do not reference other cells that have formulas. For example, if an error exists in a formula in cell A1, that error will create an error in any other formula that references A1. For the Transactions data, it also makes sense to first correct fields where the error message occurs only where there are no records. Checking the formulas, it appears that fields such as SKU_Cat, Emp_Position, and Shift have errors only when there is no record. A simple way to eliminate this kind of error is to check for a field that must exist for every record. If it does not, then put nothing in for the calculation.

To Eliminate Errors

a. Click the **Transactions worksheet tab**, click cell **I21**, click in the **formula bar** to place the insertion point to the right of the equal sign, and then type IFERROR(.

b. Reposition the cursor at the end of the formula, type ,""), and then press Ctrl+Enter.

c. In cell **I21**, double-click the **AutoFill** handle to automatically update the entire column of formulas.

d. Click cell **J21**, click in the **formula bar** to place the insertion point to the right of the equal sign, and then type IFERROR(. Click to place the insertion point at the end of the formula, type ,""), and then press Ctrl+Enter.

e. Click cell **K21**, click in the **formula bar** to place the insertion point to the right of the equal sign, and then type IFERROR(. Click to place the insertion point at the end of the formula, type ,""), and then press Ctrl+Enter.

f. Select **J21: K21**, double-click the **AutoFill** handle in the bottom-right corner of the range to copy the formula down to **J220:K220**. This will update any error cells with a blank cell whenever there is no record for the formula cell references in those fields.

g. Click cell **L21**.

With this column, there are no error messages. But, it is showing "Local" whenever there is not a value in the Coupon_Num field. Evaluating any calculations on the formula results, such as a COUNT formula, would be erroneous because of the incorrect "Local" values. The formula needs to show nothing when there is no coupon. An IF function that checks if the Coupon_Num field is empty will eliminate the issue.

h. Click in the **formula bar** to place the insertion point to the right of the equal sign, type IF(F21<>"",, and then click to reposition the insertion point at the end of the formula. Type ,""), and press Ctrl+Enter.

This will check F21 using the <> "" to see if it contains any values. IF it does, it will check for the coupon. If it does not have a value, it will return a blank cell value.

i. Click cell **L21**, double-click the **AutoFill** handle to automatically update the entire column of formulas.

j. Click cell **M21**. This column has the same issue as the Coupon_Target field. Click in the **formula bar** to place the insertion point to the right of the equal sign, type IF(H21<>"",, and then click to reposition the insertion point at the end of the formula. Type ,""), and then press Ctrl+Enter. This will check H21 using the <>"" (not blank) to see if it contains any values. If it does, it will check for the coupon. If it does not, it will return a blank cell value.

k. Click cell **M21**, double-click the **AutoFill** handle to automatically update the entire column of formulas.

l. Click cell **N21**.

This cell has the #N/A error because the formula cannot locate an exact VLOOKUP value to match a blank cell found in the Coupon_Num field. Correcting with an IFERROR will correct for this issue.

m. In cell **N21**, click in the **formula bar** to place the insertion point to the right of the equal sign, and then type IFERROR(. Click to reposition the insertion point at the end of the formula, type ,0), and press Ctrl+Enter. Click cell **N21**, and then double-click the **AutoFill** handle to automatically update the entire column of formulas.

n. Click cell **O21**, click in the **formula bar** to place the insertion point to the right of the equal sign, and then type IFERROR(. Click to reposition the insertion point at the end of the formula, type ,0), and then press Ctrl+Enter. Click cell **O21**, and then double-click the **AutoFill** handle to automatically update the entire column of formulas. Checking columns N and O, the formulas look correct and are not giving values that would cause issues.

o. Click cell **P21**. This is still just values so this should have a formula to show a correct calculation for the Line_Item_Total. Type =ROUND(O21*E21-(O21*E21*N21),2), which rounds the calculation to take Retail price times Trans_Qty and subtracts the discount calculations. Press Ctrl+Enter. Drag the **AutoFill** handle to copy the formula down through **P220**.

Earlier we used IFERROR to correct column N (Coupon_Amt) by placing a zero for any error references, but what if we had used a blank cell correction instead? When a 0 or blank is put into a formula, the spreadsheet should be checked that the 0 or blank does not interfere with formulas that reference those values. For example, a 0 would affect any AVERAGE function. If there is a 0 where there is no record, this would cause the average to be incorrect.

To Evaluate and Eliminate Errors

a. Click cell **N21**, click in the **formula bar**, select the **0** at the end (before the last closing parenthesis), and then type "" to replace the zero with an empty text string. Press Ctrl+Enter. Notice the #VALUE! error displays in cells P21, R21, T21, and U21. Click cell **N21**, and then double-click the **AutoFill** handle to automatically update the entire column of formulas. Notice the #VALUE! errors that appear in numerous cells for the affected columns. Press Ctrl+Z to undo the AutoFill. Press Ctrl+Z again to undo the formula change to cell N21, and the worksheet should return to normal without the errors.

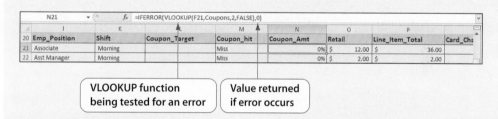

Figure 27 IFERROR calculation with zero

b. Click cell **R21**.
   The formula in column R returns a Low value for records that have no transactions.

c. Click the **Rev_Rpt worksheet tab**, and then click cell **B9**.
   Recall that B9 counts the number of Low values on the Transaction worksheet for the Trans_Group column; thus, the 190 is correct for the current amount of Low values, but the count is not valid or accurate. This supports the need to carefully evaluate the formulas throughout the entire spreadsheet.

d. Click the **Transactions worksheet tab**, and then if necessary, click cell **R21**. Click in the **formula bar** to place the insertion point to the right of the equal sign, type IF(A21<>"",, and then click to reposition the cursor at the end of the formula. Type ,""), and then press Ctrl+Enter. This checks if there is a transaction ID in Trans_ID. If there is a transaction ID, the formula does the calculation; otherwise, it leaves the cell blank. Using the "" is appropriate as the field is a text-oriented field. In cell **R21**, double-click the **AutoFill** handle to automatically update the entire column of formulas.

e. Click cell **S21**. This column has the same issue of values for the nonexistent transactions. Setting it up like column R will correct this issue. Click in the **formula bar** to place the insertion point to the right of the equal sign, type IF(A21<>"",, and then click to reposition the cursor at the end of the formula. Type ,""), and then press Ctrl + Enter. If there is a transaction, the formula calculation continues; otherwise, a blank value is returned to the cell. Using the "" is appropriate as the field is a text-oriented field. Click cell **S21**, and then double-click the **AutoFill** handle to automatically update the entire column of formulas.

f. Since you may need to print the Rev_Rpt, it is useful to check Print Preview. Click the **File tab**, and then select **Print**. The worksheet currently breaks in a way that makes it difficult to use.

g. Click **Portrait Orientation**, and then change it to **Landscape**. Click **No Scaling**, and then click **Fit All Columns to One Page**.

h. Click the **Home tab**, and then click the **Emp_Rpt worksheet**. Click **File**, and then click **Print**. Confirm that the worksheet will print on one sheet. Click the **Home tab**.

i. Select the **DB_Sums** worksheet, click **File**, and then click **Print**. Confirm the worksheet has been set so it will print on one page, and then click the **Home tab**.

j. Click **Save**. Print or submit your file as directed by your instructor. Exit **Excel**.

Concept Check

1. Describe at least three types of inputs that can be used for arguments within a function.

2. Construct pseudocode for the situation where the result "Loan" is given for an applicant that has either salary greater than $100,000 and a credit score of at least 700 or a salary greater than $50,000 and a credit score of at least 750. Otherwise, the result is "No Loan".

3. Provide examples of when you would use the options for the fourth argument in a VLOOKUP.

4. What is the primary advantage of using the MATCH/INDEX combination versus a VLOOKUP function?

5. What benefit is there to use the IFERROR when it increases the complexity of the formulas?

Key Terms

Complex function 244
Conditional aggregate functions 253
Conjunction function 248

Logical function 240
Logical test 240
Nested IF 244

Pseudocode 250

Visual Summary

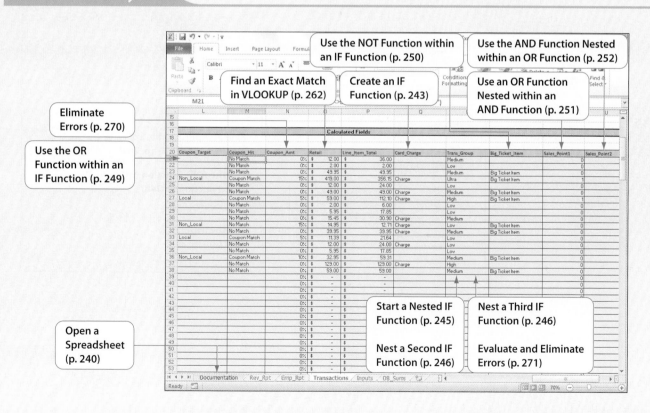

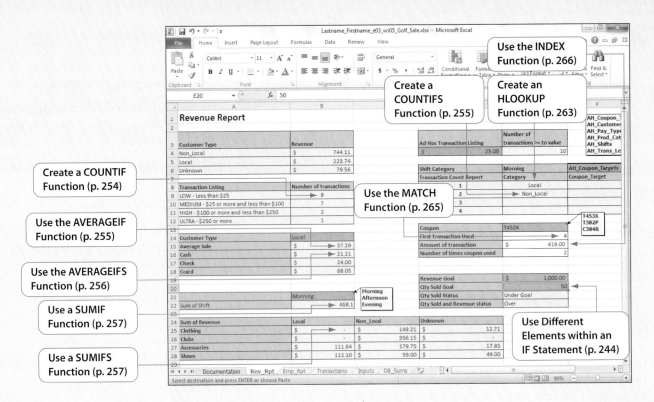

Create a COUNTIF Function (p. 254)

Use the AVERAGEIF Function (p. 255)

Use the AVERAGEIFS Function (p. 256)

Use a SUMIF Function (p. 257)

Use a SUMIFS Function (p. 257)

Create a COUNTIFS Function (p. 255)

Create an HLOOKUP Function (p. 263)

Use the INDEX Function (p. 266)

Use the MATCH Function (p. 265)

Use Different Elements within an IF Statement (p. 244)

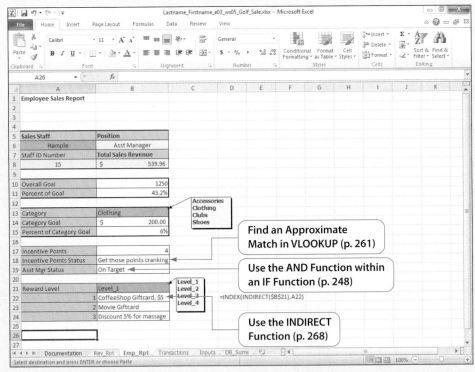

Find an Approximate Match in VLOOKUP (p. 261)

Use the AND Function within an IF Function (p. 248)

=INDEX(INDIRECT($B$21),A22)

Use the INDIRECT Function (p. 268)

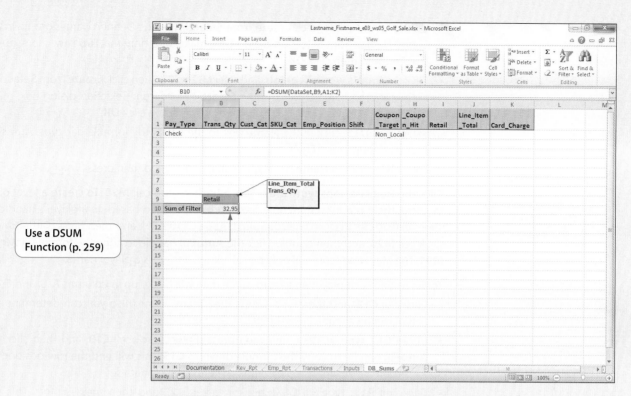

Use a DSUM
Function (p. 259)

Figure 28 Red Bluff Pro Shop Sales Analysis final spreadsheets

---

Practice 1

Student data file needed:	You will save your file as:
e03_ws05_Golf_Scramble	Lastname_Firstname_e03_ws05_Golf_Scramble

Golf Scramble Registration

The golf course is getting set up for another golf tournament for charity. Because they do this periodically, they would like a spreadsheet developed that could track information about the registrations. The spreadsheet would track the teams for the golf scramble including tracking the registration, T-shirts, and fees. Your task is to take the beginning file and continue the development of reports to support decision making for the tournament.

a. You will need to open the file and update the Documentation worksheet.

- Start **Excel**, click the **File tab**, click **Open**, navigate to the student data files, and then open the **e03_ws05_Golf_Scramble** workbook.

- Click the **Documentation worksheet tab** to make it the active worksheet, click cell **A6**, and then press Ctrl+; to input the current date.

- Click cell **B6**, and type Firstname Lastname using your first name and last name, and then press Ctrl+Home.

- Click the **File tab**, and then click **Save As**. In the Save As dialog box, navigate to where you are saving your student files, and in the File name box type Lastname_Firstname_ e03_ws05_Golf_Scramble replacing Lastname and Firstname with your own name.

b. Some named ranges will help with the development of the formulas.

- Click the **Registrations worksheet**, click cell **B20**, and then press Ctrl+A to select the range of data.

- Click the **Formulas tab**, click **Define Name**, type ScrambleData in the Name input box, and then press Enter.

- On the Formulas tab, click **Create from Selection** in the Defined Names group. In the Create Names from Selection dialog box, make sure only the **Top row** check box is checked, and then click **OK**.
- Click the **Inputs worksheet tab**, and select **B24:E27**, then click **Create from Selection** in the Defined Names group. In the Create Names from Selection dialog box, make sure only the **Top row** check box is checked, and then click **OK**.
- Select **B13:D15**, click in the **Name** box to the left of the formula bar, type Sponsor_ Fees, and then press Enter.
- Select **B2**, click the **Name** box, type Mulligan_Fee, and then press Enter.

c. Click the **Registrations worksheet tab**, and then click cell **M20**. To create a level playing field, there is a maximum hole score to be calculated based on a player's handicap. Type =IF(E20<>"",VLOOKUP(H20,Inputs!$A$6:$C$10,3),""), and then press Ctrl+Enter. Click cell **M20**, and then double-click the **AutoFill** handle to copy the formula down to **M91**. The Max Hole score will only be calculated if there is a player name.

d. To determine each player on a team, some data will be set up in Columns A, B, and C.
- Click cell **C12**, and then type =MATCH(e2,Team_Name,0) so you can determine the first player on a team. Press Enter.
- In cell C13, type =C12+1, and then press Enter. Click cell **C13**, and then click the **AutoFill** handle to copy the formula down to **C15**. This will find the row position for the other players on the team within the Registration data set.
- Click cell **B12**, type =INDEX(Sponsor_Level,C12), and then press Enter. This will determine their sponsor level, if it exists.
- Click cell **A12**, type =INDEX(Early_Bird,C12), and then press Enter. This will pull the Early bird information for each of the players on the team.
- Select cells **A12:B12**, and then use the **AutoFill** handle to copy the formula down through **B15**.

e. Click **E2**, type Hole in One, and then press Enter. Click **F4**, type Mulligans, and then press Enter. In cell F5 type =DSUM(ScrambleData,F4,E1:M2), and then press Enter. This will create a DSUM section that will use the filtering in E1:M2 for the criteria and the field listed in F4 for the summation field.

f. Click the **Report worksheet tab**. Tee it Up is a team listed in E2 currently. Data about this team should be compiled below. Click cell **E3**, type =AVERAGEIF(Team_Name,E2,Handicap), and then press Enter.

g. Click cell **E4**, type =IF(I12="Yes",B12,IF(I13="Yes", B13,IF(I14="Yes",B14,B15))), and press Enter.

h. In **E5**, type =IF(I12="Yes",A12,IF(I13="Yes",A13,IF(I14="Yes",A14,A15))), and then press Enter.

i. In cell **E6** type =IF(E3<Inputs!A19,Inputs!B19,IF(E3<Inputs!A20,Inputs!B20,Inputs!B21)), and then press Enter.

j. In cell **E7**, type =SUM(H12:H15), and then press Enter. In cell **E8** type =IF(OR(SUM(H12 :H15)>=8,AND(E5="yes",SUM(H12:H15)>=6)),2,0)+VLOOKUP(E4,Inputs!F2:G4,2,FALSE), and then press Enter.

k. Click cell **E18**. The listing of team names need to be pulled from the registration table. Type =IFERROR(INDEX(Team_name,MATCH(d18,Registration_Number,0)),""), and then press Enter. Click cell **E18**, and then click the **AutoFill** handle to copy the formula down through **E35**.

l. Click cell **F18**, type =SUMIF(Team_Name,E18,Mulligans), and then press Ctrl+Enter. Double-click the **AutoFill** handle to copy the formula down to cell **F35**.

m. Click cell **H3**, type =HLOOKUP(E4,Sponsor_Fees,IF(Report!E5="yes",2,3),FALSE), and then press Enter .

n. In cell **H4**, type =SUMIF(Team_Name,E2,Mulligans)*Mulligan_Fee, and then press Enter .

o. In cell **H5**, type =SUM(H3:H4), and then press Enter .

p. Click cell **K4**, type =COUNTIF(Shirt_Size,J3), and then press Enter . In cell K5, type =INDEX (INDIRECT(J3),MATCH(K4,Inputs!A25:A27,1)), and then press Enter .

q. Select columns **A:C**, right-click, and select **Hide** from the list of options so these columns will be hidden from the user.

r. To complete the information for each player, their data can be pulled from the Registration data based on the row where their data exists. The row was determined in column C. Each person was listed for their team, but they still need to register with their shirt size and other informatiom. If the player has not registered, they will need to be reminded to register.

- Click cell **E12**, type =IF(INDEX(Shirt_Size,C12)= "","No","Yes"), and then press Tab . This will look if a shirt size has been input, indicating they have registered.

- Type =INDEX(Registrations!$D$20:$D$91,C12), and then press Tab . This will pull the first name of the person.

- Type =INDEX(Registrations!$E$20:$E$91,C12), and then press Tab . This will pull the last name of the person.

- Type =IF(INDEX(Registrations!$I$20:$I$91,C12)="","Missing", INDEX(Registrations!I 20:$I$91,C12)), and then press Tab . This will return "Missing" if the person did not sign up for any Mulligans. If they did, it will return how many they purchased.

- Type =IF(INDEX(Captain,C12)= "y", "Yes",""), and press Tab . This will check the record to see if the person was designated in column C on the Registration as the captain. If they are, it will return a Yes. Otherwise it will return nothing.

- Type IF(OR(COUNTIF($H$12:$H$15,"Missing")>0,SUM($H$12:$H$15)<5),"Contact Captain-Mulligans",""), and then press Enter . This provides a note to indicating the captain should be notified encouraging them to purchase some Mulligans. The note will be given if any registrations are missing or if the total number of Mulligans is less than five for the team.

- Select **E12:J12**, and then use the **AutoFill** handle to copy the formula down through **J15**.

s. Click the **Documentation worksheet tab**. Click the **Insert tab**, and then click **Header & Footer** in the Text group. Click **Go to Footer** in the Navigation group. Click in the **left footer** section, and then click **File Name** in the Header & Footer Elements group. Click any cell on the spreadsheet to move out of the footer, press Home , and then click the **Normal** button at the bottom right of the Excel window status bar (near the navigation slider). Repeat this process for every worksheet within the file.

t. Click the **Report worksheet**. Click **File**, and then click **Print** so the layout can be adjusted. Click **Portrait Orientation**, and then change to **Landscape Orientation**. Click **No Scaling**, and then click **Fit All Columns on One Page**.

u. Click **Save**. Print or submit your file as directed by your instructor. Close Excel.

Practice 2

Student data file needed:

e03_ws05_GiftShop_Inventory

You will save your file as:

Lastname_FirstName_e03_ws05_GiftShop_Inventory

Gift Shop Inventory

The gift shop staff wants to track inventory so they can audit their system, reduce the times they run out of inventory, and be more effective with reordering. They need a template designed that will hold all the product information and then analyze daily transactions that are brought in at the end of every month. They do not have data currently, so the spreadsheet will be designed using fake data so the formulas can be created and checked. Your job is to work on developing the reporting components of the spreadsheet.

a. You will need to open the file and update the Documentation worksheet.

- Start **Excel**, click the **File tab**, click **Open**, navigate to your student data files, and then open the **e03_ws05_GiftShop_Inventory** workbook. A spreadsheet with a partially completed model for the gift shop will be displayed. The initial inputs have been created along with named ranges.
- Click the **Documentation worksheet** tab to make it the active worksheet, click cell **A6**, and then press `Ctrl`+`;` to input the current date.
- Click cell **B6**, and then type Firstname Lastname using your first name and last name. Press `Ctrl`+`Home`.
- Click the **File tab**, and then click **Save As**. In the Save As dialog box, navigate to where you are saving your student files, and then in the File name box type Lastname_Firstname_ e03_ws05_GiftShop_Inventory replacing Lastname and Firstname with your own name.

b. Click the **Inventory worksheet tab**, click cell **L19**, type =IF(AND(K19="N",H19<=J19),"Rush",IF(AND(K19="N",H19<I19),"ReOrder","OK")), and then press `Ctrl`+`Enter`. In cell L19, double-click the **AutoFill** handle to copy the formula down through cell **L38**.

c. Click the **DailyTransactions worksheet tab**, click cell **D2**, and then type Food. Click cell **E2**, type Fri, and then press `Enter`.

d. Click cell **F11**. The Trans_Sold is the number of items sold. If the Trans_Qty is negative, that is inventory that was sold. If it is positive, it means that inventory was received from the supplier. Type =IF(C11<0,-C11,""), and then press `Tab`. Use the **AutoFill** handle to copy the formula down the column.

e. In **G11**, type =IF(C11>0,C11,""), and then press `Enter`. This takes the positive Trans_Qty, which are deliveries, and puts in the value if it was positive. If it was negative, nothing is put into the result. Use the **AutoFill** handle to copy the formula down the column.

f. Click cell **C6**, type =DSUM(A10:G40,C5,Criteria), and then press `Enter`. In cell **C7**, type =DAVERAGE(A10:G40,C5,Criteria), and then press `Enter`.

g. The table in A2:D17 on the Inventory Audit needs to be filled out based upon the category that is listed in B1. Currently that is the Massage category. The table will have the information about each item for that listed category.

- Click the **Inventory_Audit worksheet tab**, and then click cell **B3**.
- Type =IFERROR(INDEX(INDIRECT($B$1),A3,1),""), and then press `Tab`. This will pull the Item information for the category. If the category does not exist, the IF statement will return nothing.
- In cell C3, type =IFERROR(INDEX(INDIRECT($B$1),A3,2),""), and then press `Tab`. This will find the projected sales for the category.
- In cell D3, type =SUMIF(Trans_Item,B3,Trans_Sold), and then press `Ctrl`+`Enter`. This will add up the total qty sold for the category.
- Select **B3:D3**, and then double-click the **AutoFill** handle to copy the three formulas down through cell range **B4:D17**.

h. The total qty sold for each category on each day needs to be calculated in B20:I26. Using the field labels on row 20 and column B, the totals can be determined.

- Click cell **C21**, type =IFERROR(SUMIFS(Trans_Sold,WeekDay,Inventory_Audit!C$20, Trans_Category,$B21),0), and then press `Ctrl`+`Enter`.
- Click cell **C21**, and then double-click the **AutoFill** handle to copy the formula down through **C26**.
- Use the **AutoFill** handle again to copy the formulas to the right through cell range **C21:I26**.

i. The total qty sold for each category needs to be calculated in D32:D51 based on the item in column A. Then, the total quantity that was delivered can be calculated. Finally, the Ending inventory is the beginning inventory minus the quantity sold plus the quantity that was delivered.

- Click cell **D32**, type =SUMIF(Trans_Item,B32,Trans_Sold), and then press Tab.
- In cell E32, type =SUMIF(Trans_Item,B32,Trans_Delivered), and then press Tab.
- In cell F32, type =C32-D32+E32, and then press Tab.
- In cell G32, type =VLOOKUP(B32,Inventory!$A$19:$L$38,7,FALSE), and then press Tab. This will look up the actual inventory.
- Select **D32:G32**, and then double-click the **AutoFill** handle to copy the formula down through **G51**.

j. Inventory goes down as product is sold and goes up as deliveries are made. Inventory can also go down due to theft or damage. Thus, it is useful to analyze the difference between what should be in inventory and what is really in inventory. If actual is less than it should be, the missing amount should be returned. If there is more, then the overage amount should be returned. Otherwise, it is on target.

- Click cell **I32**, type =IF(G32<F32,"missing "&F32-G32,IF(G32>F32,"over by "&G32-F32,"On Target")), and then press Tab. The & adds the text string to the value as the result.
- In cell **J32**, type =D32/H32, and then press Tab.
- In cell K32, type =VLOOKUP(B32,Inventory!$A$19:$M$38,2,FALSE), and then press Ctrl+Enter. This will list the description of the item for the report.
- Select **I32:K32**, and then use the **AutoFill** handle to copy the formula down through **K51**. Because this is a starting spreadsheet, not all of the product data has been included, but it will be later. The formulas should be for all the items.

k. Click the **Documentation worksheet tab**. Click the **Insert tab**, and then click **Header & Footer** in the Text group. Click **Go to Footer** in the Navigation group. Click in the **left footer** section, and then click **File Name** in the Header & Footer Elements group. Click any cell on the spreadsheet to move out of the footer, press Home, and then click the **Normal** button at the bottom right of the Excel window status bar (near the navigation slider). Repeat this process for every worksheet within the file.

l. Click the **Inventory_Audit worksheet**. Click **File**, and then click **Print** so the layout can be adjusted. Click **Portrait Orientation**, and then click **Landscape Orientation**. Click **No Scaling**, and then click **Fit All Columns on One Page**.

m. Click **Save**. Print or submit your file as directed by your instructor. Close Excel.

Objectives

1. Work with data tables. p. 282

2. Use the SUBTOTAL function with tables. p. 290

3. Develop PivotTables. p. 293

4. Create PivotCharts. p. 305

Analyzing Data Using Tables

PREPARE CASE
Golf Course Marketing Strategies

The Red Bluff Pro Shop would like to develop marketing strategies for increasing golf course patronage. Aleeta Herriott—the manager—has asked for data about the golf activity over the past years. Aleeta needs to be able to work with the data to understand the current patronage. Exploring the data is key in determining the marketing strategy and presenting her ideas to the board of directors.

Courtesy of www.Shutterstock.com

Student data file needed for this workshop:

 e03_ws06_Golf_Marketing

You will save your file as:

 Firstname_Lastname_e03_ws06_Golf_Marketing

Organizing Data with Tables

While Excel can analyze large amounts of data, users can sometimes be overwhelmed with the volume of data that needs to be explored. With many rows and columns, information overload can quickly set in as it becomes difficult to track the data across each row. However, using tools within Excel can help you understand the data. For example, viewing data in tables allows you to examine the data an organized manner. In this section, you will learn how to establish a table with data.

The Golf Pro Shop manager, Aleeta, wants to analyze some course data. Daily transactions from the past 10 years exist, but that would be a lot of records to bring into Excel. Rather, she has requested a random sample of data for initial analysis. The database administrator was able to run a query on the database and provide a set of data to explore. In this section, you will develop an understanding of the data and organize it so it can be analyzed.

To Open an Excel File

a. Start **Excel**, click the **File tab**, and then click **Open**. In the Open dialog box, navigate to where your student data files are located, click **e03_ws06_Golf_Marketing**, and then click **Open**.

b. Click the **Documentation worksheet tab** if it is not the active worksheet, click cell **A6**, and then press Ctrl+; to input the current date. Click cell **B6**, and type Firstname Lastname using your own first name and last name.

c. Click the **File tab**, click **Save As**, and then in the Save As dialog box, navigate to the location where you are saving your student files. In the File name box, type Lastname_ Firstname_e03_ws06_Golf_Marketing replacing Lastname and Firstname with your own name. Click **Save**.

d. Click the **Insert tab**, and then click **Header & Footer** in the Text group. Click the **Design tab**, and then click **Go to Footer**. Click in the **left footer section**, and then click **File Name** in the Header & Footer Elements group.

e. Click any cell in the spreadsheet to move out of the footer, press Ctrl+Home, click the **View tab**, and then click **Normal** in the Workbook Views group. Repeat this process on all worksheets within the file. Click **Save** 🖫.

Working with Tables of Data

Regardless of the career you choose, the need to work with data is common. **Raw data** is considered to be elements or raw facts—numeric or text—that may or may not have meaning or relevance. For example, data such as "blue" or "brown" is raw data without context, and thus is of minimal value to anyone. **Information**, however, is data that has context, meaning, and relevance and therefore is valuable to a user. The value is determined by the user and may vary between users. Thus information is created by users when they organize, interpret, and present data in a meaningful context.

Data sets are a named collection of related sets of information that are composed of separate elements—the data. If a set of data is not organized, it is difficult to determine the context and transform the data into information. The user is informed by understanding context in which the data has been gathered and organized. For example, the raw data, "blue" and "brown", by itself may not have any significance. Putting this raw data into the context of studying the eye color of men and women and knowing the data was collected from a set of subjects—this allows information to be created. A user can determine whether one eye color is more prevalent in males. Excel is a great tool to manipulate data so the user can transform the data into information leading to good decision making. Organizing the data using an Excel table is a good first step toward creating and evaluating information effectively.

Organizing Data Sets

With data, care should be taken to protect its integrity. This includes keeping a backup of the original data so if errors occur it is possible to return to the original data and start over. Whenever possible, check your data for completeness and accuracy. Also, strive to organize data within the workbook in a meaningful and efficient manner that allows for new data to be added as needed. Finally, it is best to keep sets of data separated. Avoid using cells immediately surrounding the sets of data. This will minimize the possibility of mistakenly assuming the content in the adjacent cells is part of the main data set. When possible, keep related data on one worksheet while reporting and analyzing another worksheet.

To Prepare a Backup Copy of Data

a. Right-click the **Golf_Data worksheet tab**, and click **Move or Copy** to display the Move or Copy dialog box.

b. In the Before sheet box, click the **(move to end)** option, click to check the **Create a copy** check box, and then click **OK**. A new worksheet is displayed with the name Golf_Data (2).

c. Right-click the **Golf_Data (2) worksheet tab**, and then click **Rename**. Select the **2** in the name, type backup, and then press Enter to create a backup of the data.

d. Click the **Golf_Data worksheet tab** to return to the worksheet that will be modified.

e. On the Golf_Data worksheet, select **rows 1 through 19**. Right-click a selected row, and then click **Insert** from the menu. This will insert 19 rows and push the data set down to row 20 starting with the field headings. Click **Save** .

CONSIDER THIS | **Placement of Calculations and Analysis**

You could place the data and subsequent analysis anywhere within a spreadsheet. Why place the analysis at the top of the data set? Why not place it at the bottom of the data set? What are the advantages and disadvantages of either? How about placing the analysis on another worksheet?

Real World Advice   Back Up Your Work

Hopefully, you will never need to use your backup, but in reality, someday you may mess up, lose, or destroy your data. Make a habit of creating backups of your work. This can include quick backups, such as backup worksheets as done with the files in this chapter. But, you should also backup the entire file on a regular basis, such as every day or after major revisions. Keep backup files in a different physical location than the originals, such as with a backup service or company site.

Organizing a Data Set Within a Table

While the data may be set up in a spreadsheet, an Excel table establishes the data as more than a simple collection or range of raw facts presented in rows and columns. An Excel table can help provide context to the user by organizing the data in a meaningful way. Data can be converted to an Excel table that offers additional capability allowing the user to manipulate the data and to generate information and value for a variety of needs. The table has both flexibility and scalability. New columns and rows can be added, and the table will extend to include them automatically. Formatting and formula references automatically adjust as well.

To Create a Table in Excel

a. On the Golf_Data worksheet, select cell **D25**.

b. Click the **Insert tab**, and then click **Table** in the Tables group.

c. In the Create Table dialog box, be sure the **My table has headers** check box is checked and that the range is $A$20:$H$220.

Troubleshooting

If Excel fails to guess the correct range selection, you can either adjust the range by typing in the correct range or drag to select the correct range.

d. Click **OK**.

An Excel table will be created with banded coloring. Additionally, the Table Tools Design tab will appear containing all the options available for a table.

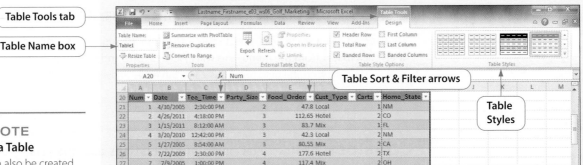

Figure 1 Excel table

e. Click the Design tab, click the **Table Name** box. Type Golf_Data, and then press Enter. This will name the table Golf_Data and create a named range for the entire data set, excluding the field headings.

f. Click the **Formulas tab**, then click **Name Manager** in the Defined Names group.

g. In the list found in the Name Manager dialog box, click the **Golf_Data** named range if it is not selected, and notice at the bottom of the dialog box that the Refers to range is displayed as Golf_Data!$A$21:$H$220. The tag beside the Golf_Data range is a small table, indicating it is associated with the table. The option to delete this range is not available since it is associated with the Excel table. Click **Close**.

h. Click cell **I20**, type Tax, then press Enter. Notice Excel automatically applied the formatting color to the newly added table cells to match the rest of the table.

i. In cell I21, type =Golf_Report!$B$3*, click **E21**, and then press Enter.

Notice [@[Food_Order]] is inserted at the end of the formula. Excel uses a structured reference rather than a regular cell reference. It inserted [@[Food_Order]] instead of E21 because it automatically sets ranges within the table that will adjust as columns or rows are added or deleted. The table also automatically copies the formula down the entire column similar to applying Auto Fill.

j. Scroll down until cell A221 is visible. Notice the field heading in row 20 replaces the column lettering when you scroll. Click cell **A221** to add a new record to the data.

SIDE NOTE
Reference the Tax Rates
Tax rates change. Keep these
input values on a work-
sheet so they can be easily
updated as needed and
referenced in formulas.

Notice the field headings in Row 20 replace the column lettering when you scroll down. The field headings again disappear and are replaced with column letters when you click in cell A221 because this cell is outside the table range. However, the field headings reappear after you type the data for the first cell in the new row. Using the data below, add a new record in Row 221, pressing Tab after each entry. Notice that the banded color formatting appears as soon as data are initially entered and that the Tax field is copied down automatically because it is a calculation.

Field	Data
Num	201
Date	4/8/2010
Tee_Time	8:30:00 AM
Party_Size	4
Food_Order	104.8
Cust_Type	Hotel
Carts	2
Home_State	LA

Figure 2 New record

Table field headings replace column headings

New record with banding automatically added

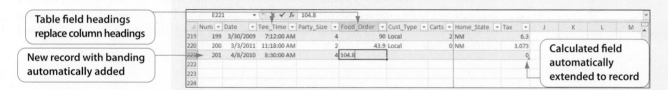

Calculated field automatically extended to record

Figure 3 Excel table adding a new record

k. If necessary, click the **Formulas tab**, then click **Name Manager** in the Defined Names group. In the list on the Name Manager dialog box, click the **Golf_Data** named range and notice the range is now $A$21:$I$221. Click **Close**. The range has changed to include the newly created column and row. Click **Save** 🔲.

A table defaults to a table style that has banded rows, making it easier to read data across rows. There are options to change the applied style for banded rows (and/or columns) with alternating colors. As new rows of data are added, the range expands with formatting. Similar to rows, new columns are also automatically formatted and added to the table. The new column added in the above exercise is included in the Golf_Data named range.

When a formula is created in a cell of a new column, it will automatically copy it to the rest of that column in the table. In the above exercise, a cell reference was added by clicking cell E21. Excel substituted the table field heading reference for the cell name. However, E21 could have been typed into the formula and the results would have been the same.

It is also possible to remove the Excel table structure as well as the extra functionality. When the table is converted back to a range of data using Convert to Range in the Tools group on the Design tab, the formatting remains behind, but the functionality of tables, such as adding new columns or rows, will no longer automatically be added or updated to the ranges and formulas and would need to be manually copied down a column.

Filtering Data Sets

The data sets used in business may be large and contain numerous fields. It is useful to gain an understanding of the data by looking at subsets of data rather than the entire set at one time. Filtering data sets is useful and makes it possible to view specific data. Filtering is also useful for selecting and copying a subset of data to move to a new worksheet. **Filtering** is a process of hiding records that do not meet specified criteria in a data set. It enables a user to examine and analyze, if desired, a subset of records.

Filters can be established on either a range of data or on an Excel table. For a range of data, a filter can be set by clicking the Filter button in the Sort & Filter group on the Data tab. When applying a filter to a data range, be sure the active cell is within the range to help ensure the correct data range is selected. However, if an Excel table has been created; the range will be established based upon the initial creation process, decreasing the chance for error. Additionally, the filter is a standard part of the Excel table, eliminating the need to apply a filter feature to the data set.

The filter feature adds arrow buttons for each field heading, which offer drop-down lists of filtering options to select the criteria for each field. By selecting criteria for a certain field heading, any records that do not meet the criteria will be hidden until the filter criterion is removed. The filters can be added, modified, and cleared as needed. Additionally, multiple filtering criteria using multiple fields can be applied. So, it would be possible to filter for a specific Party_Size number and on the number of golf carts used within the Golf_Data table.

Filtering allows the exploration of the data. For example, the golf manager, Aleeta may want to determine how many instances of two-person golf parties spend more than $75 on food. For this example, Aleeta would filter for parties containing two people, which would exclude any parties that contained a number other than two people. Then, the data would further be explored by filtering the records based on the total spent on food for everyone in the two-person parties. The golfing parties that had two people and spent more than $75 are then displayed and available for easy analysis.

To Filter Data

a. On the Golf_Data worksheet, click the **Party_Size filter arrow** ▼, and then click to uncheck the **(Select All)**. Click to check the **2** check box, and then click **OK**. All the other options will be hidden or filtered, showing only the records that meet the checked criteria.

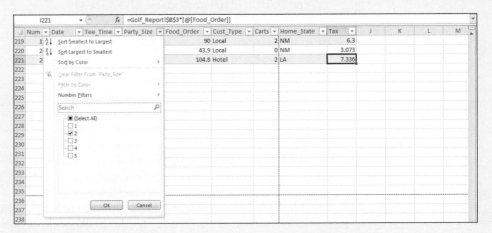

Figure 4 Filter list

SIDE NOTE

One Filter per Worksheet

The filtering function can be applied to only one data set on a worksheet. Thus, if there are multiple data sets that need to be filtered, the data sets should be placed on separate worksheets.

b. Click the **Food_Order filter arrow** ▼, and then select **Number Filters**. Click **Greater Than**. Notice the Filter icon is displayed on the filter button as a visual cue that the field heading has a filter applied.

c. In the Custom AutoFilter, click in the **text box** at the top and to the right side of the is greater than box. Type **75**, and then press ⌐Enter⌐. Examine the row numbers and notice the visible row numbers start at 20 and jump to 51, 53, 55, 147, and 158. The other rows of data are still there but are hidden. The data still exists, and it can be redisplayed. Click **Save** 🖫.

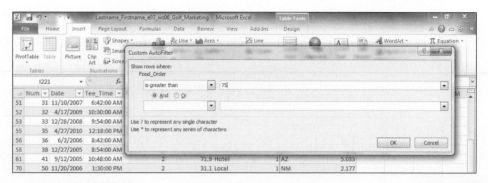

Figure 5 Filtered table

Filtering hides the rows of data that do not fit the criteria. In this case, both criteria must be true for the rows to be displayed. It is easy to remove, or clear, filters and apply other filters. The standard filter displays the values in the field that can be toggled on and off through the check boxes. If those do not handle the desired criteria, there are options above the check boxes that are specific for the type of data contained in the field. For example, the options available for fields with numeric values will differ from the options available if the field data were date or text values.

Real World Advice   Developing Questions for Data Analysis

It is vital to have an understanding of the company data so relevant questions can be explored using the data. The managers could find the average size of the golf parties, but this does not provide much value. However, it may be useful to know whether larger groups tend to order more food per person than smaller groups. Based on the answer, a marketing strategy could be developed. Always consider the value of the question.

To Clear and Change Filters

a. On the Golf_Data worksheet tab, click the **Party_Size filter arrow** ▾ in cell D20, and then click **Clear Filter from "Party_Size"**.

b. Click the **Date filter arrow** ▾ in cell B20. Notice it has a listing of years with plus signs. Click the **plus sign** beside 2009. It will expand to months, and if needed, individual days could be shown and selected.

c. Select **Date Filters** and notice the list of options are specific for dates. Click **Between** to display the Custom AutoFilter dialog box.

d. Click in the text box at the top and to the right of the box displaying **is after or equal to**, type 1/1/2009, and then in the text box below and to the right of the box displaying **is before or equal to**, type 12/31/2009. Click **OK**. The results will display food orders over $75 that occurred in 2009.

e. Point to the **Date filter arrow** ☑ for cell B20 to display a ScreenTip indicating the details of the filter. The filter arrow button will also have a smaller triangle next to a filter icon, which indicates that the field has a filter applied.

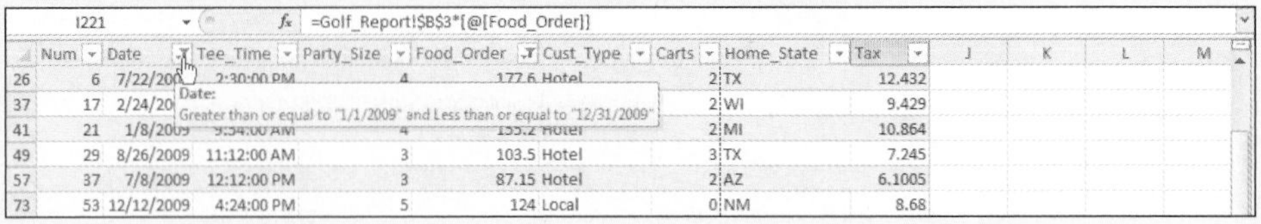

	Num	Date	Tee_Time	Party_Size	Food_Order	Cust_Type	Carts	Home_State	Tax	J	K	L	M
26	6	7/22/20	2:30:00 PM	4	177.6	Hotel	2	TX	12.432				
37	17	2/24/20					2	WI	9.429				
41	21	1/8/2009	9:54:00 AM	4	155.2	Hotel	2	MI	10.864				
49	29	8/26/2009	11:12:00 AM	3	103.5	Hotel	3	TX	7.245				
57	37	7/8/2009	12:12:00 PM	3	87.15	Hotel	2	AZ	6.1005				
73	53	12/12/2009	4:24:00 PM	5	124	Local	0	NM	8.68				

Formula bar: I221 =Golf_Report!$B$3*[@[Food_Order]]

Date: Greater than or equal to "1/1/2009" and Less than or equal to "12/31/2009"

Figure 6 Display filter information

f. Select the filtered range **A20:I219**, and then press Ctrl + C.

g. Click the **Insert Worksheet button** 🗋. This will create a new worksheet with cell A1 being the active cell. Press CTRL + V. The subset of data will be pasted into the new worksheet.

Having data filtered can be useful, especially when there is a complete data set and someone else needs to examine some , but not all of the data. The filtered data can be copied and pasted to a new worksheet so it can be analyzed separately.

h. Right-click the **worksheet name**, and then click **Rename**. Type 2009_Data, and then press Enter. Ensure that columns **A:I** are selected. Click the **Home tab**, click **Format** in the Cells group, and then click **AutoFit Column Width** so the data fits within the columns. Press Ctrl + Home.

i. Click the **Insert tab**, and then click **Header & Footer** in the Text group. Click the **Design tab**, and then click **Go to Footer**. Click in the **left footer section**, and then click **File Name** in the Header & Footer Elements group.

j. Click any cell on the spreadsheet to move out of the footer, press Ctrl + Home, click the **View tab**, and then click **Normal** in the Workbook Views group. Click **Save** 🖫.

Using the Advanced Filter Feature

While the filtering feature is great for ad hoc and spur-of-the-moment exploration of the data, the filtering mechanism makes it difficult to easily see what filters exist. A user would need to hover over or click the displayed filter arrows to evaluate what filters are applied. With the Advanced Filter feature, the filtering criteria are on the spreadsheet. The filtering criteria must be set up in a specific format. A top row with the field headings that are identical to the data set must be established. Then, criteria can be set up in one or more cells below the field names. Once the criteria area has been set up, the Advanced Filter can be applied. It will hide records in the same manner as the filters on the data set. Only records matching the criteria will be shown.

To Create an Advanced Filter

a. Click the **Golf_Data worksheet tab**, select **B20:I20**, press Ctrl+C, select **B12**, and then press Ctrl+V. Press Esc.

b. Click cell **A20**. If necessary, click the **Data tab**, and then click **Clear** in the Sort & Filter group to clear all current filters that have been applied to the data set.

c. Click cell **F13**, and then type Hotel. Press Enter.

The range B12:I13 will be the data criteria area. The first row is the field names that could potentially be used for setting constraints or criteria. The second row and below could be used for the criteria for particular fields. In this case, there is only one criterion set, the customer type being Hotel. With this arrangement, the advanced filter is ready to be set up to find the records that meet those criteria.

d. Click the **Data tab**, and then click **Advanced** in the Sort & Filter group to display the Advance Filter dialog box.

e. Click in the **List range** text box, and then remove any range references currently listed.

f. Select the cell range **A20:I221**. The List range will change to display Golf_Data[#All], recognizing the data range of the table.

g. Click in the **Criteria range** input box, and then select **B12:I13**. Make sure the **Filter the list, in-place** check box is checked, and then click **OK**.

The data in the table will be filtered to show only the Hotel Cust_Type transactions. It is possible to add additional criteria. All criteria have to be met for the record to be shown. If only Hotel customers from Texas with food orders over $100 were shown, all three of those constraints must be true for the record to be displayed. The three constraints are thus joined with an AND clause. If Cust_Type equals Hotel AND Home_State equals TX AND the Food_Order is greater than $100, the record will be displayed. By listing all three constraints on one row, Excel will know to have all three arguments set to true for the record to be included in the results.

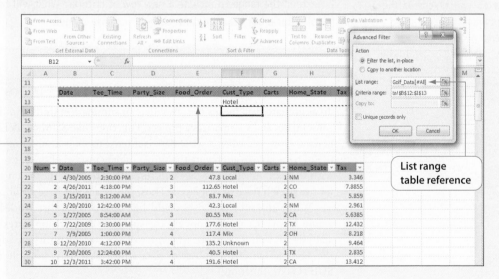

Figure 7 Advanced Filter

h. Click cell **E13**, type >100, and then press Enter. Click **H13**, type TX, and then press Enter.

i. Click **Advanced** in the Sort & Filter group, and since the ranges should still be the same, click **OK**.

The settings in the Advanced Filter will remain from the previous time so the List range and Criteria range will still be the same. The data set should adjust to show Hotel customers from Texas, with food orders greater than 100. To add additional criteria, add it to the criteria range. For example, to also include all records that have a Party_Size of 1 with customer type of Local, a second row would be used. Criteria on an individual row must all be true as mentioned. Each row of criteria acts like an OR, joining the two sets of filtering criteria. Records meeting either the first row of criteria or the second row of criteria will be displayed.

j. Click cell **D14**, type 1, and then press Enter . Click cell **F14**, type Local, and then press Enter .

k. Click the **Data tab**, click **Advanced** in the Sort & Filter group. Click to place your insertion point at the end of the **Criteria range** text box, press Backspace to remove the **3**, and then type 4 so the Criteria range displays **$B$12:$I$14**. Click **OK**.

When adding a second row of criteria, the criteria in the Advanced Filter must also be adjusted. The same would apply if the additional row of criteria were removed from the Advanced Filter.

l. Click **Save** 💾 .

The results will show records for food orders greater than $100 from Texas Hotel customers and all parties with 1 for Local customers. The constraints on one row will not impact the constraints on another row. Thus there are parties of 1 that did not spend more than $100.

CONSIDER THIS | Rows of Criteria

Be careful when creating criteria for the filters. What would happen if you forget to adjust the criteria range as you work with criteria? What will happen if you do not extend the range to include a new row of criteria? What will happen if you delete a row of criteria but leave that row in your criteria range?

Using the SUBTOTAL Function and Filters with Tables

To **aggregate** data means to consolidate or summarize; similar to the way an executive summary consolidates and summarizes a project. Functions like SUM or AVERAGE aggregate an entire set of data. However, when a set of data is filtered to show a subset of the entire data set, it would be useful to be able to aggregate the subset of data instead of the entire set of data. This is impossible with standard functions as they will run calculations on the data regardless of whether the records (or rows) are hidden or displayed. Thus, the data filters have no impact on standard functions.

While the subset of data could be copied to another worksheet and then aggregated, it would be inefficient. By copying the subset of data, it duplicates the data and complicates the analysis. It would be more efficient to have the flexibility of adjusting the filter and having the aggregation of the subset of data adjust also. It is possible to accomplish this using the SUBTOTAL function.

The SUBTOTAL function is specific to the filtering mechanism and will only run calculations on the data that is in the subset when a filter is applied. Any records that are on hidden rows will not be used in the calculation of the SUBTOTAL function. The SUBTOTAL function has two arguments. The first argument requires a function number to indicate which aggregate function to apply, such as SUM, AVERAGE, or COUNT. The second argument is one or more ranges to be aggregated:

SUBTOTAL(function_num, ref1, [ref2],…)

The function_num argument informs Excel which function to use on the subset of records. When typing this function, a list will appear to help if you are not familiar with which argument number to use. There are two sets of function numbers, 1–11 and 101–111, as shown in Figure 8. The first set, 1–11, will return result values for rows that are visible and rows that have been hidden using the Hide Rows command. The second set, 101–111 will ignore rows that have been formatted to be hidden, again using the Hide Rows command, thus returning a value of visible rows only. Keep in mind, that the SUBTOTAL function ignores any rows not included when a filter is applied, no matter which function_num value you use. Thus, the difference between these two sets of argument values only comes into importance when using the Hide Rows command and is of no importance when applied to filtered data.

Function_Num (includes hidden values)	Function_Num (ignores hidden values)	Function
1	101	AVERAGE
2	102	COUNT
3	103	COUNTA
4	104	MAX
5	105	MIN
6	106	PRODUCT
7	107	STDEV.S
8	108	STDEV.P
9	109	SUM
10	110	VAR.S
11	111	VAR.P

Figure 8 Subtotal Function List

Real World Advice Hiding Rows and Filtering

It is unusual to use the Hide Rows feature when filtering, and is not a recommended practice. Any time filters are removed, any hidden rows will become unhidden. It becomes complicated to try and work with both filtering data and hiding rows. It is recommended that all records be visible when filtering. Any records that should not be used in the SUBTOTAL calculations should be excluded using the filtering process.

To Summarize a Data Set

a. Click the **Golf_Data worksheet tab**, click **B6**, type Averages, and then press Enter. In cell B7 type Overall, and then press Enter. In cell B8, type Filter, and then press Enter. In cell B9 type By State, and then press Enter. In cell B10 type Customer Type, and then press Enter.

b. Click cell **D9**, type NM, and then press Enter. In cell D10 type Local. Click cell **E9**, type Number of Records, and then press Enter. In cell E10, type Sum of Food Order, and then press Enter. Select columns **B:E**, and then double-click the **border margin** between column B and column C to make columns B through E automatically fit the text.

c. Select range **B6:B10**, press and hold Ctrl, and then select range **E9:E10**. Press Ctrl+B to bold these cells.

SIDE NOTE
Named Ranges

To edit or view existing named ranges, click on the Name Manager button on the Formulas tab. When creating named ranges on a table using Create from Selection, the named range will expand as additional rows of data are added.

d. Select cells **A20:I221**. Click the **Create from Selection** button in the Defined Names group on the Formulas tab. Click the check box next to **Right Column** to deselect it, and click **OK**.

e. Click cell **C7**, type =AVERAGE(Food_Order), and then press ⏎Enter.
The Overall average uses the named range and will calculate using every record. The AVERAGE function uses all data even if it is hidden.

f. In cell C8, type =SUBTOTAL(. Notice that a listing for the function number will appear with the available choices for the function that will be used on the filtered records.

g. Double-click **1-AVERAGE** from the list.

Number for functions in SUBTOTAL

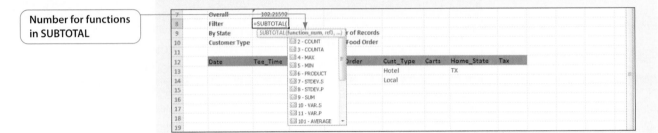

Figure 9 Subtotal function

h. Type ,Food_Order), and then press ⏎Enter. The SUBTOTAL function ignores any data that is hidden due to the filtering.

i. In cell C9, type =AVERAGEIF(Home_State,D9,Food_Order), and then press ⏎Enter. The AVERAGEIF function will include hidden records, just like the AVERAGE function.

j. In cell C10, type =AVERAGEIF(Cust_Type,D10,Food_Order), and then press ⏎Enter.

k. Click cell **F9**, type =SUBTOTAL(2,Num), and then press ⏎Enter. This will count the number of records that are visible and would be included in any subtotal calculation.

l. In cell F10 type =SUBTOTAL(9,Food_Order), and then press ⏎Enter. This will sum up the values in any records or rows that are visible within the data set.

m. Click **Save** 🖫.

With these options it is possible to see the differences in the different averages that have been computed. Notice, only the SUBTOTAL function ignores hidden records and calculates only visible filtered records. The other functions provide results based upon all the records, without regard to visible and hidden records.

Organizing and Analyzing with PivotTables and PivotCharts

It is possible to accomplish quite a lot through the use of tables and filters, the SUBTOTAL function, and other aggregate functions like SUMIF or AVERAGEIF. But, what if there is a need to really dig deep and explore a data set asking all kinds of questions? What if there is a need to let the initial questions drive subsequent questions?

PivotTables provide a more expanded solution for exploring data; they are especially useful when you are looking at a huge table of data that can become overwhelming. **PivotTables** are interactive tables that extract, organize, and summarize data. They are used for data analysis and looking for trends and patterns for decision-making purposes. Examples of questions PivotTables can help to answer are:

- How often are clubs rented for a round of golf?
- How many customers came from each state last year?
- Has the mix between hotel and local customers changed over time?

These questions can be answered with a PivotTable report. PivotTables can easily group the time period to years, quarters, months, or all three. The flexibility comes from using an interface that allows the table to be built without having to create formulas and functions to do the grouping, summary, or calculations. And, because PivotTables are interactive, they can be adjusted with a few clicks and rearranged or cleared to start the process over if the layout becomes too messy. In this section you will develop skills working with PivotTables and PivotCharts.

Developing PivotTables

An understanding of the general process is helpful when working with PivotTables. First, it is important to make sure the data set is well organized. A PivotTable can be created on an existing worksheet or new worksheet. When it is created, a link is established to a source range of data. After determining the data source and location to insert a blank PivotTable, the interactive part begins. The PivotTable initially is blank or clear, but it can be developed by considering what to group and what to summarize. The final step is to explore and work with the options within the PivotTable to fine-tune the layout to fit your specific needs. If needed, it is possible to create PivotCharts, covered later, which chart data based on PivotTable adjustments, thus offering charted data based on extracted subsets of data analysis.

Creating PivotTables

The creation of a PivotTable is a two-step process: selecting the data set and location where the PivotTable will be created and working with the data fields to group and summarize the selected data. A few guidelines will help with these two steps.

There are a couple of concepts to consider before creating a PivotTable. First, be sure the source data are arranged in an area with column headings representing each field and the rows representing each record, preferably with no other information or content in cells that are adjacent to the data set. In addition, there should be clear, concise field headings in the top column cell for each column of data. Excel will use these as the labels within the PivotTable. Finally, if there are automatic subtotals or other summary functions at the bottom of the data, be sure to remove these. They will cause confusion if they are incorporated into a PivotTable.

Real World Advice   Consider the Fields Needed for the PivotTable

You should consider if you are going to add data and want to name the data set range so you can add data to the named range. Add any calculated fields to the data initially. For example, with quantity and price, there may be a need to add a new column that is the price times the quantity. Or, if there is a field that has both the city and state, you might want to separate those into two columns so it is possible to group by city or by state. If there are potential changes, working with a table is optimal as it makes adding fields easy and those new fields can be incorporated into PivotTables simply by refreshing the data.

There are only a couple of options with regard to the location of a PivotTable. A PivotTable can be created on a new worksheet or an existing worksheet. PivotTables automatically expand and contract on a worksheet as variables are added, removed, and rearranged. Creating a PivotTable on a new worksheet will set it apart and reduce the chance of the PivotTable interfering or disturbing other data. If a PivotTable is placed on an existing worksheet with other data, it is best to choose a location where it is below or to the right of any existing data. This allows the PivotTable room to expand to the right or down as needed, without interfering with existing data. While it is possible to create multiple PivotTables from the same data set, only one PivotTable is allowed per worksheet.

Real World Advice   PivotTables Add to File Size

PivotTables, while valuable, quickly add to the size of an Excel file. It is better to use PivotTables for multiple purposes than to create a set of separate PivotTables. As the file size increases, there is added risk of corruption. Thus it becomes important to remember to backup and maintain your backup files.

SIDE NOTE
Pivot Tables and Hidden Data
A filter applied to the data set will not affect the PivotTable creation process. The PivotTable will ignore the filter and use all the data—including the hidden data.

Similar to creating an Excel Table, when creating a PivotTable from a data set, one cell within the data set should be the active cell. Excel will automatically detect the range in the process of setting up the initial PivotTable area. It is possible to adjust the data range used if Excel mistakenly includes other information that is not needed in the PivotTable data range. If the data has been established as a Table, the creation of a PivotTable is based upon the current range for the Table.

To Create a PivotTable from an Excel Table

a. On the Golf_Data worksheet tab, click cell **H20**.

b. Click the **Design tab**, and then click **Summarize with PivotTable** in the Tools group to display the Create PivotTable dialog box.

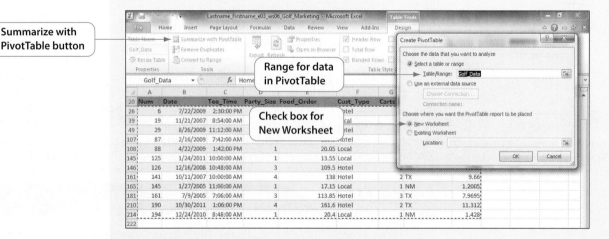

Figure 10 Create a PivotTable

Troubleshooting

If the data are not a table, go to the Insert tab and click the Insert PivotTable button in the Tables group.

Also, if you have a few cells selected in a data set when you start the process of creating a PivotTable, you may end up creating a PivotTable that only has the subset selection as the range. It is best to only have one cell selected in your data set when you create the PivotTable.

c. Confirm that the **New Worksheet** option is selected, and then click **OK**.

d. Double-click the newly created **worksheet tab**, type Pivot_Analysis, replacing the default worksheet name, and then press Enter.

e. Click cell **A1**. Notice that context-sensitive PivotTable Tools tabs on the Ribbon disappear and only a blank PivotTable area is showing below cell A1.

f. Click any one cell within the PivotTable area in the range A3:C20. Now, the PivotTable Field List will reappear on the right side of the screen. The PivotTable Tools Options tab and Design tab are available, and the Field List is docked on the right side.

g. Click **Save** 💾.

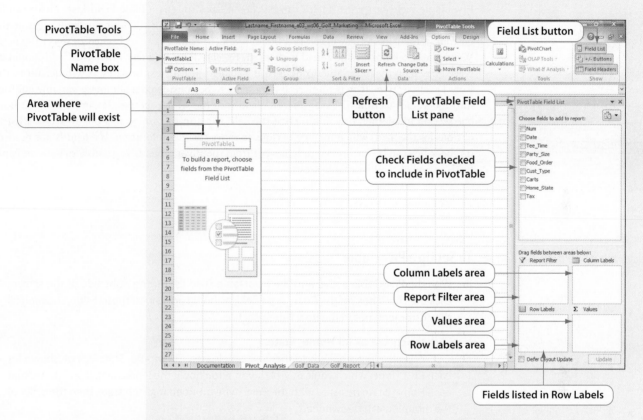

Figure 11 PivotTable

Troubleshooting

If you close the PivotTable Field List pane and need to display it again, be sure a cell in the PivotTable is selected, and then on the PivotTable Tools Option tab, click Field List in the Show group.

Once the area is set up for the PivotTable, the interactive part of the process begins. The focus is to construct a table that will group and summarize subsets of the data in a useful and meaningful manner. There are a few guidelines for choosing how to arrange the fields.

It helps to distinguish fields as either grouping variables or summary variables, because these two types get placed in different areas within the PivotTable. **Grouping variables** can be thought of as any fields within the data set that could be used to categorize or group for comparison. For example, gender is a common variable used to group and analyze data. It may be necessary to compare the salaries between females and males. Dates are also great for grouping into months, quarters, and years to explore trends over time. Conversely, **summary variables** are data that are not categorical in nature and would likely be used for summarization. Summary variables are data that can be aggregated by summing, counting, or averaging.

Exam scores, quantity, or price are examples of data variables that would be aggregated by summing, averaging, or counting. Grouping variables go along the top or the left side. The aggregation of data occurs when records in the data are grouped by selected variables. The results would be placed in the bottom-right side of the aggregate summary. This layout is shown in Figure 11, when looking at the layout of the table along the bottom-right corner, when developing a PivotTable.

The grouping variables are put into the Column Labels or Row Labels areas at the bottom of the PivotTable Field List. The summary variables are put into the Values section below the PivotTable Field List pane. Fields can be chosen from the PivotTable Field List. Fields can be dragged and dropped from the PivotTable Field List to any of the four quadrant areas at the bottom of the pane, or the check box beside the field names can be checked to select the field. When the check box beside a field is checked, Excel will try to guess where that field should be placed based on the data values contained in the field. If it is text or dates, it will default to the Row Labels section. If it is numerical data, it may be considered a summary variable and put into the Values section. If Excel puts the field into the wrong section, it can be dragged from one section to another, or you can click the field name in the target area box to access a list of options for the field, which include options to move the field's location. If a field is not needed, its check box can be unchecked to remove it from the PivotTable. It is possible to have multiple fields in any of the PivotTable areas.

To Set Up a PivotTable

a. With the PivotTable active and the PivotTable Field list on the right side of the screen, click the check box for the **Cust_Type** field. It should appear on the left side, showing all the customer types in the Row Labels section.

b. Click the check box for **Home_State**.

   Excel will add both fields to the Row Labels area. The Home_State will be shown for each Cust_Type, which you can view if you scroll down the worksheet. If you prefer that each Home_State be listed with the Cust_Type grouped for each state, then the order of the grouping can be switched.

c. Click the **Home_State** field in the Row Labels area, and then click the **Move Up** option. This will change the order of the groups for the two fields within the Row Labels area.

Figure 12 Row Labels field order

d. In the PivotTable Field List, click the check box for **Food_Order**, and then click cell **B5**.

   Excel, detecting numerical data, puts this into the Values area and defaults to summing the values. Notice the label in B3 indicates the field being aggregated and what calculation is being applied, in this case, Sum. The cell B5 is showing the sum of the golf parties that stayed at the hotel with a home state of Arkansas. The value is calculated, but there is no formula within the cell.

e. Click the **Golf_Data worksheet tab**, click cell **H13**, type **AR**, and then press Enter. Click cell **E13**, and then press Delete. Select **D14:F14**, and then press Delete.

f. Click the **Data tab**, and then click **Advanced** in the Sort & Filter group. Confirm that the List range data is set to $A$20:$I$221, click in the **Criteria range** text box, select the cell range **B12:I13**, and then click **OK**.

Notice the Sum of Food Order in cell F10 is now 545.2. This is the same as in the PivotTable in cell B5. So, while it is possible to use formulas and filtering to get an answer, the PivotTable generates the answers for all the groups with less effort involved. Thus, PivotTables facilitate comparing summary data more efficiently.

g. Click the **Pivot_Analysis tab**, and then click in the PivotTable if it is not active. Drag the **Cust_Type** field in the Row Labels area over to the Column Labels area.

Previously, the table had consisted of many rows that stretched down the worksheet. Now, the number of rows and columns are more evenly distributed, thus making the PivotTable more readable.

The columns in the PivotTable should now show the different types of customers. Now, in cell B5, it is showing the sum of the food purchased by the hotel golf parties that are from Arkansas. Also note that in cell A33 the value indicates blanks. That is because there are records where there is no home state indicated. Finally notice how the PivotTable expands both in rows and columns as the fields are added and removed in determining how they will be grouped. This is the interactive attribute of a PivotTable and also why it is best to have a PivotTable on a worksheet by itself.

h. Click the check box for **Home_State** to remove it from the PivotTable, and then click the check box for **Date**. Date will now be on the left column in the Row Labels area. Most of the time it will group within each unique date, so it would be helpful if the dates could be aggregated some more.

i. Right-click **A9**, and then click **Group** from the menu options to display the Grouping dialog box. Currently the Months are highlighted in the By list.

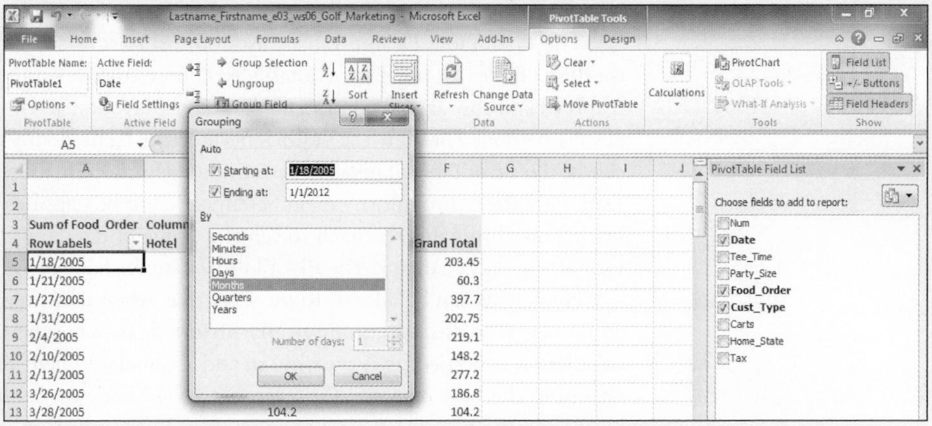

SIDE NOTE
Grouping When Data Are Missing

When grouping dates, the PivotTable will not know how to group blank data. So, a date must exist for every record before a grouping can be applied.

Figure 13 Grouping dates

j. Click one time on **Months** to remove the blue highlighting, click one time on **Quarters** and click once on **Years**, and then click **OK**. Click **Save**.

The dates will now be grouped by year, and within each year four quarters will be listed. Over in the PivotTable Field List it will now also show a Years field. Looking down in the Row Labels area you can see the first grouping is with Years. Within each Year the subgroup is Date, which is the Quarters. If the grouping needs to be changed, right-click one of the cells in column A and select Group again to change the grouping options. Or, select Ungroup and the individual dates will reappear.

CONSIDER THIS | **Group on Rows or Columns**

Obviously the fields for grouping could be all in the Row Labels area, all in the Column Labels area, or a mixture. What issues may arise if you have all the grouping fields as Row Labels or all as Column Labels? What would you use as a rule of thumb for the number of groups within each area?

Real World Advice   Which Fields Are Better for Row Labels?

While it is possible to choose any grouping field on either the Row Labels or Column Labels, there are some guidelines. Typically you want your PivotTable to go down more than across. People are more accustomed to scrolling up or down in a document rather than left or right. So, if you have a lot of groups within a field, it is better to put those fields along the row side of the PivotTable instead of across the top in columns. It is better to have the user scroll up or down instead of across.

PivotTable Options

With PivotTables there are two context-sensitive tabs available to aid in the control of PivotTable elements: one is the Options tab and the other is the Design tab. The Options tab has all the options for fine-tuning the PivotTable. Many of these options can also be accessed by right-clicking any cell within the PivotTable. Some are very useful in structuring the PivotTable.

The PivotTable Design tab focuses on formatting and the appearance aspect of designing the PivotTable. Options are available to choose from a variety of styles, and whether or not to display band row and/or column colors, report layouts, and so on. Additionally, formatting can always be done through the traditional Format Cells dialog box found by right-clicking any cell in the PivotTable. This is not recommended though, as it will only format the selected cell. Data formatted through the Field Settings dialog box applies to all other cells within the same field. This eliminates the need to select a range of data and for being concerned with how the formatting will change as the PivotTable changes shape or is restructured.

New fields can be added. Remember that when data are in an Excel table, it is possible to add a new field that is automatically included. If, while working with the PivotTable, a new calculation is needed, it is possible to add a calculated field directly to the PivotTable without changing the base data set. Or, even better, go back to the underlying data and use an Excel table, add the new fields, and then use the Refresh button on the Options tab to update the PivotTable data for any changes made to the source data.

Finally, it is possible to change the layout, adding totals, grand totals, and labels within the PivotTable to enhance the look and feel of the PivotTable. This is useful in creating a structure that will be used in a presentation.

To Work with PivotTable Options

a. Click cell **B6**, which displays the data for the Sum of Food_Order in the first quarter of 2005 for parties staying at the hotel.

b. Click the **Options tab** in the PivotTables Tools, and then click **Field Settings** in the Active Field group to display the Value Field Settings dialog box.

c. Click **Number Format**, and then click **Currency** from the Category list. Click **OK**, and then click **OK** again. Notice that all values within the Values section have now changed to Currency.

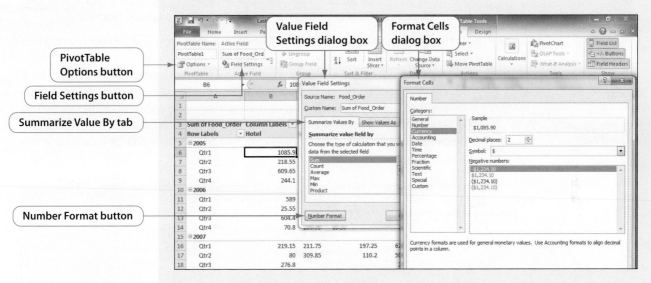

Figure 14 Number format in field settings

SIDE NOTE

PivotTable Formatting

It is not recommended to use the standard formatting techniques found on the Home tab with PivotTables. The PivotTable is dynamic, and the regular formatting techniques will not make use of the dynamic attributes.

d. Click the Options tab, click **Summarize Values By** in the Calculations group. If necessary, click the Calculations button. Summarize Values By offers a list of options for summarizing the data values. Currently the PivotTable is summing the values.

e. Select **Average**. It may be useful to compare the values. For example, it may be good to know how the hotel average compares to the overall average within each time period.

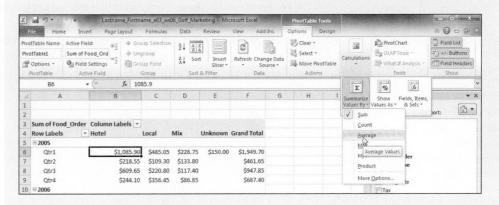

Figure 15 Summarize by average

f. Click the Options tab, click **Summarize Values By** again and change back to Sum. Click **Show Values As** in the Calculations group, and then select the **% of Row Total**.

Because the values are sums, the Grand Total row average is 100%. So, in Qtr 1 of 2006, the three percentages will add up to the 100%.

Keep in mind that this average is based on the average Food_Order purchases for each Cust_Type golfing party. However, golfing parties have anywhere from one to five people, so if the average purchases per person was desired, the PivotTable would need to be adjusted to calculate an average by dividing the Food_Order by Party_Size.

g. In the PivotTable Field List, uncheck the **Food_Order** field.

h. Click the Options tab, click **Fields, Items, & Sets** in the Calculations group, and then select **Calculated Field** to display the Insert Calculated Field dialog box.

i. In the Name text box type Food_Per_Person, and then press [Tab]. In the Formula text box type =Food_Order/Party_Size, click **Add**, and then click **OK**.

The average food cost per person will now be seen. For example, B6 is the total food order for all hotel parties during Qtr1 of 2005 divided by the sum of all the party sizes during that same time period. Notice there are some #DIV/0! errors in the table. This is because those are cells where there was no activity, so Excel is trying to divide by 0. Because this error message is a valid error that could reasonably be expected, it can also be hidden.

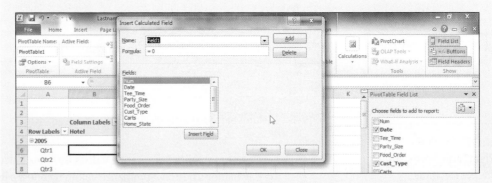

Figure 16 Calculated field

j. If necessary, click cell **B6**. Click the Options tab, click **Options** in the PivotTable group to display the PivotTable Options dialog box. Click the **Layout & Format tab**, and then click the **For error values show** check box under the Format section. Because nothing should show, click **OK**.

Notice the error messages are now replaced with a blank cell. Now the data from 2005 through 2011 should be showing, by quarter. However, if the analysis were to focus on just a couple of years, the data could be filtered even more.

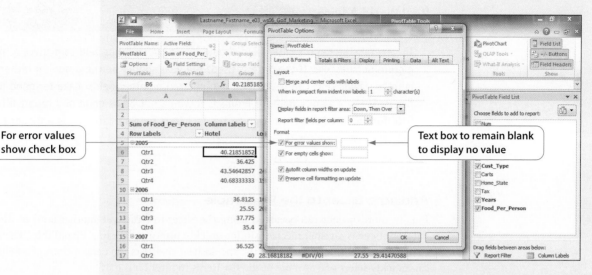

Figure 17 PivotTable Options

For error values show check box

Text box to remain blank to display no value

SIDE NOTE
Retaining Labels

When you change the Column Labels or Row Labels name within the PivotTable, the new label name will be retained. If the PivotTable is restructured, removing that field then adding it again, the new label will be retained.

k. Click cell **A4**, and then click the **Row Labels arrow** and Filter menu options will be available. Click the **(Select All)** check box to toggle all the options off. Click the **2006**, **2007**, and **2008** check boxes, and then click **OK**. This allows quick filtering of the records. The updated results are displayed.

l. Click cell **B3**, type **Customer Types**, and then press Enter.

This will replace the Column Labels text name and make the name more informative to the users. Only those three filter years will be showing for the Row Labels. Notice within the PivotTable Field List, there is now a filter icon to the right of the Years field to indicate a filter has been applied. If another level of grouping is required, but not on the table, the Report Filter can be used. It allows an overarching level of grouping to be added. Fields, such as Year, Party_Size, or Carts, where there are minimal options with lots of records make good selections for the Report Filter.

m. In the PivotTable Field List, click the **Home_State** check box. Drag the **Home_State** field listed in the Row Labels area to the Report Filter area (above the Row Labels area). Home_State will now appear in cells A1:B1.

n. Click cell **B1**, click the **Filter arrow**, and then click the **Select Multiple Items** check box. Click the **(All)** check box to clear all the check boxes, and then click the **AR** and **AZ** check boxes to select the Arizona and Arkansas data to be used in the PivotTable. Click **OK**, and then click **Save**.

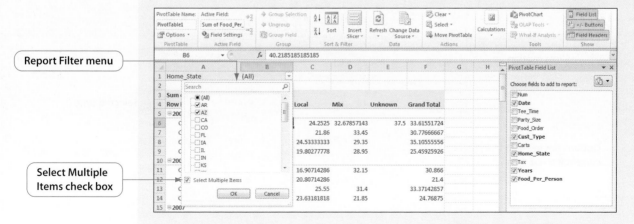

Report Filter menu

Select Multiple Items check box

Figure 18 Report filter

Organizing and Analyzing with PivotTables and PivotCharts   301

Workshop 6

In general, the Report Filter field should be an overarching field that gives a big picture perspective. If the date is used, the year should be the grouping rather than months. Fields that can be further manipulated by other fields make for good report filters. If there were a field for Product, it would not be as good of a report filter as a field for Product Category owing to the fact that product category is a bigger picture field that can be filtered for fewer items as needed.

Adding a Slicer to the PivotTable

Finally, more options can be added using the Slicer to create yet another layer of slicing to the data. A **slicer** is a visual mechanism for quickly filtering data in a PivotTable. The slicer is an object that sits or floats on top of the spreadsheet that lists the data options of a field. The user can quickly select one or more of the list items to filter on the fly.

To Add a Slicer

a. Click the **Options tab**, and then click **Insert Slicer** in the Sort & Filter group. Click the **Tee_Time** check box from the list of Insert Slicers field options, and then click **OK**.

Troubleshooting

Click the Insert Slicer arrow and the gallery menu will appear, click the Insert Slicer button to go directly to the Insert Slicers dialog box.

b. Click the **9:18:00 AM** time slot in the Tee_Time slicer. Press and hold Ctrl, and then click the **3:24:00 PM** time slot. The data for those time slots will be incorporated into the PivotTable. Click **Save**.

The slicer floats on the spreadsheet with all available Tee_Times. The PivotTable will reflect the filters applied to the slicer. Shift can be used to select a range of options, or you can use Ctrl to pick and choose options to include in the PivotTable. With the Tee_Time slicer, there are three times listed at the top that are displayed as bolder text compared to the rest of the times, which are listed as gray text. This is because within the Arizona and Arkansas data there are only records that have those tee times. There are no records in the subset of data that have other tee times.

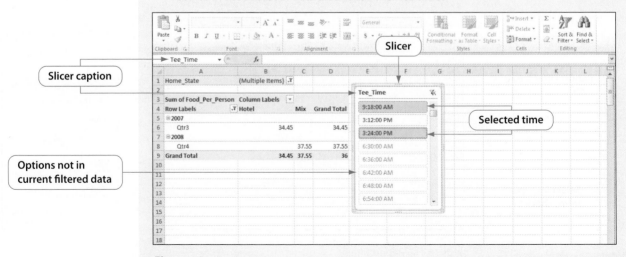

Figure 19 Slicer

Design Options within PivotTables

Design options on the Design tab focus on the look and feel of the PivotTables. The options available include layout and styles. To get a perspective of the design options, it will be useful to clear out the current PivotTable and work with a basic structure.

To Clear a PivotTable and Work with Totals

a. Right-click the **Tee_Time** slicer border, and then click **Remove "Tee Time"** from the menu.

b. In the PivotTable Field List, uncheck all of the fields that are currently checked.

   This returns the PivotTable back to the starting point. Notice there will be filter icons to the right of field names in the PivotTable Field List. These indicate the filter is still available with the previous settings and can be brought back into the PivotTable by checking the check box.

c. Click the field check boxes to select **Date**, **Cust_Type**, **Food_Order**, and **Years**. The years are grouped within each quarter, so in the Row Labels area, click the **Years field arrow**, and then select **Move to Beginning** so the quarters are subgroups within each year. Notice the filter is still only showing 2006 through 2008.

d. In the Row Labels area, drag the **Cust_Type** field over to the Column Labels area.

e. Click the **Design tab**, and then click the **Subtotals arrow** in the Layout group to see the options. Click **Show all Subtotals at Bottom of Group**.

<hr>
SIDE NOTE
Grand Totals

The default is for the PivotTable to show a grand total for both columns and rows. On the Design tab, the Grand Totals button enables you to turn row and column totals off or to pick only row or column totals.

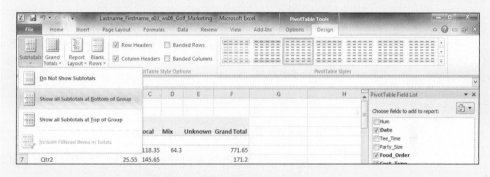

Figure 20 PivotTable subtotals

f. On the Design tab, click the **Banded Rows** check box.

   This will put alternating colors on the rows. A PivotTable style, which are templates, can also be selected if desired.

g. Click the Design tab, and then click **PivotTable Styles More**. In the PivotTable Styles gallery menu, under Medium, click **Pivot Style Medium 2** in the first row, second column. Click **Save**.

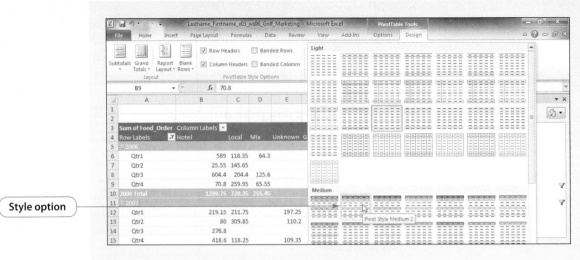

Figure 21 PivotTable styles

Style option

Updating and Sharing Data in PivotTables

There are a lot of options for organizing and summarizing data. What happens if the data changes? And what are the options for giving a subset of data to another person? These capabilities are available in PivotTables. If adding data to a PivotTable is necessary, the data source and range of data can be changed. After making changes to the source data set, the PivotTable data should be refreshed so the changes are updated in the PivotTable as well.

It is also possible to give a subset of data to people without having to provide data they do not need or should not have in the first place with a technique called drilling down. **Drilling down** is a method for accessing the detailed records that were used in a PivotTable to get to the aggregated data. It allows a user to select an individual piece of the data in the PivotTable and then create a copy of individual records that were used to get that summary data on another worksheet.

To Update, Refresh, and Drill Down

a. Click the **Golf_Data worksheet tab**, click the **Data tab**, and then click **Clear** in the Sort & Filter group to clear all the filters.

b. Click cell **J20**, type Region, and then press Enter. Click cell **J21**, type =IF(OR(H21= "NM",H21="TX",H21="AZ"),"Tri_State",""), and then press Enter. Notice the formula will fill in for the new column.

c. Click the **Pivot_Analysis worksheet tab**, click cell **A6**, click the **Options tab**, and then click the **Refresh button**. Notice the new field for Region now appears in the PivotTable Field List and could be integrated into the PivotTable as needed.

d. Click cell **C6**.

   This is the food order revenue from local customers during the first quarter of 2006. The underlying records that were used in generating the 118.35 total need to be retrieved.

e. Double-click cell **C6**. The action of double-clicking any cell within the PivotTable initiates the drill-down process where Excel will copy and paste the records that are associated with that value to another worksheet.

f. Double-click the newly created **worksheet tab**, type 2006_Local, and then press Enter.

g. On the 2006_Local Worksheet tab, click cell **E4**, type =SUM(E2:E3), and then press Ctrl+Enter. Notice the sum is 118.35, which corresponds to the data in the PivotTable. Click **Save** 💾.

SIDE NOTE
Cells References Compared to Table References

When adding the new field Region, you typed the cell references. If you click on H21, Excel will insert [@[Home_State]] into the formula instead of H21. Either method will yield the same result.

Real World Advice — Dates on the Row Labels

In general, if dates are going to be a grouping variable, it is customary to put them on the Row Labels. Typically grouping by quarter or month with the date on the Row Labels follows a financial or accounting format. If only grouping by year, it may be suitable to put the date field in the Column Labels area.

Creating PivotCharts

The visual representation of data through charts can be powerful. **PivotCharts** are charts that are tied to the data within a PivotTable. When the PivotTable data are rearranged, it is automatically updated in the PivotChart. Conversely, when making changes to the PivotChart the corresponding changes are seen in the PivotTable.

PivotCharts have an added component of filtering. The chart has drop-down elements with filtering options. Multiple PivotCharts can be associated with one PivotTable; however, because they are all tied together, best practice dictates having only one PivotChart associated with a PivotTable. Additionally, be careful when making use of a PivotChart in a presentation so that no changes occur accidentally within the PivotTable that could yield unwanted changes to the chart. Once a PivotChart is created, all formatting elements from a regular chart are available.

To Add a PivotChart

a. Click the **Pivot_Analysis worksheet tab**. With the PivotTable active, click the **Options tab** in the PivotTable Tools.

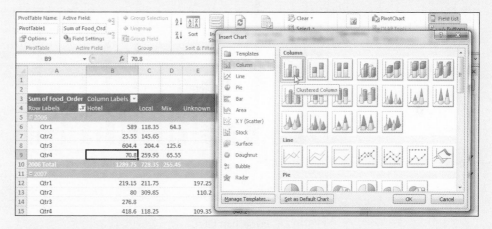

Figure 22 Create a PivotChart

b. Click **PivotChart** in the Tools group to display the Insert Chart dialog box. Click the **Clustered Column** chart in the first row, first column, and then click **OK**.

c. With the chart selected, click the **Design tab**, and then click **Move Chart** to display the Move Chart dialog box. Click **New sheet**, and then in the New sheet text box, replace the existing name and type Pivot_Chart. Click **OK**. There will be filtering options on the chart that allow the user to change the filters within the chart.

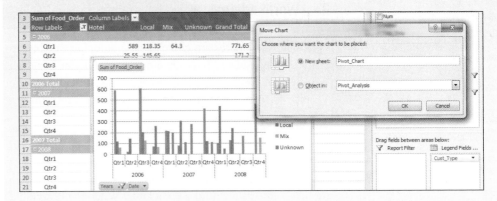

Figure 23 Move PivotChart

d. On the Pivot_Chart worksheet tab, click the **Cust_Type** Filter button to display the filter option menu. Click to uncheck the **Mix** and the **Unknown** check boxes, and then click **OK**.

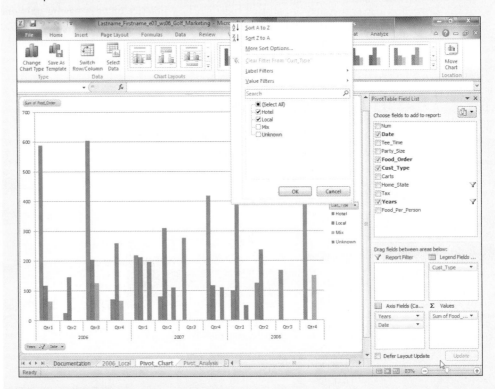

Figure 24 PivotChart filter

e. Click the **Layout tab**, click the **Chart Title**, and then click **Centered Overlay Title**. Type Food Purchases by Hotel and Local Customers, 2006-2008, and press [Enter].

f. If printing, click the **File tab**, and then change the orientation to **Landscape** to improve the layout of pages that are wide. Click **Save** 🖫. Submit your project as directed by your instructor. **Close** [X] Excel.

Concept Check

1. You have a batch of data in a spreadsheet that you are going to analyze. What are some tips for working with the data set to help prevent and correct errors?

2. Describe at least two benefits of using an Excel table over an Excel range of data.

3. You are chatting with a colleague who mentions that the SUBTOTAL function performs sum, average, count, or other functions, and questions why a person would use that function when there already is a SUM, AVERAGE, and COUNT function. What is the difference when using the SUBTOTAL to sum versus the SUM function?

4. What type of data would work well for the row and column labels within a PivotTable? What are some examples?

5. An Excel spreadsheet has a huge set of data pertaining to all members of the sales team. You would like to share the data with your team but only that data that pertains to each person. How would you go about slicing the data and getting a copy of the records to each person without giving them records they should not receive?

Key Terms

Aggregate 290
Data set 282
Drilling down 304
Filtering 286

Grouping variable 295
Information 282
PivotChart 305
PivotTable 292

Raw data 282
Slicer 302
Summary variable 296

Visual Summary

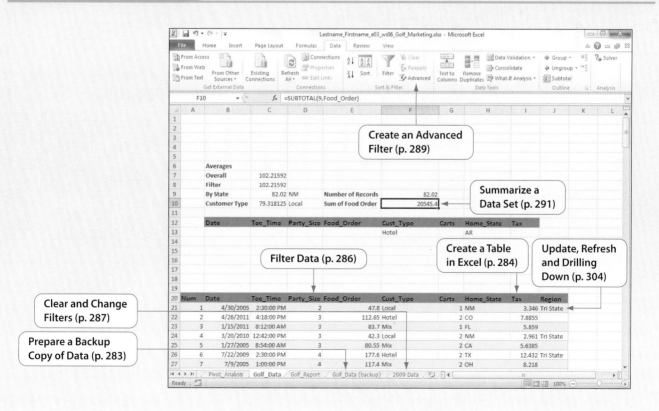

Create an Advanced Filter (p. 289)

Summarize a Data Set (p. 291)

Create a Table in Excel (p. 284)

Update, Refresh and Drilling Down (p. 304)

Filter Data (p. 286)

Clear and Change Filters (p. 287)

Prepare a Backup Copy of Data (p. 283)

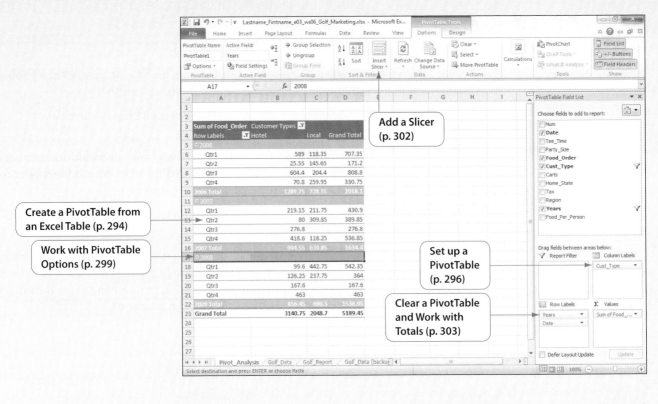

- Create a PivotTable from an Excel Table (p. 294)
- Work with PivotTable Options (p. 299)
- Add a Slicer (p. 302)
- Set up a PivotTable (p. 296)
- Clear a PivotTable and Work with Totals (p. 303)

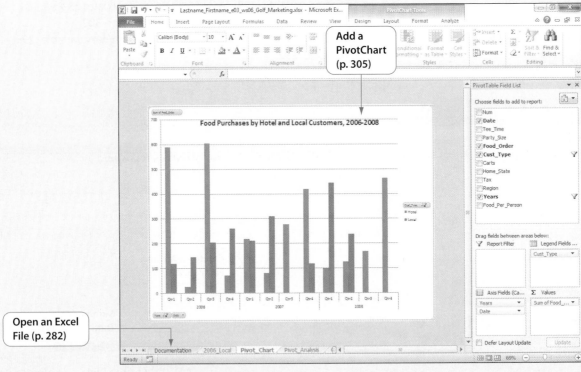

- Add a PivotChart (p. 305)
- Open an Excel File (p. 282)

Figure 25 Golf Course Market Strategies final workbook

Student data file needed:

e03_ws06_Employee_Sales

You will save your file as:

Lastname_Firstname_e03_ws06_Employee_Sales

Golf New Employee Sales Analysis

The management team has requested data from the information systems team on the new employees in the golf shop. The data are from the database on sales and only includes the sales for three employees over a week. With that data they would like you to set up some analysis for them to review. In addition, they have some questions they would like answered. These questions are representative of the type of analysis they will use with the data. You must set up PivotTables that will help them understand the data.

a. Start **Excel**, and then open **e03_ws06_Employee_Sales**. A spreadsheet with a range of data will be displayed. Click the **File tab**, and then click **Save As**. In the Save As dialog box, navigate to the location where you are saving your student files. In the File name box, type Lastname_Firstname_e03_ws06_Employee_Sales, replacing Lastname_Firstname with your own name, and then click **Save**.

b. Click the Documentation worksheet tab if it is not the active worksheet. Click cell **A6**, and then press Ctrl+; to input the current date. Click cell **B6**, and type Firstname Lastname using your own first name and last name.

c. Click the **Insert tab**, and then click **Header & Footer** in the Text group. Click the **Design tab**, and then click **Go to Footer**. Click in the **left footer section**, and then click **File Name** in the Header & Footer Elements group.

d. Click any cell on the spreadsheet to move out of the footer, press Ctrl+Home, click the **View tab**, and then click **Normal** in the Workbook Views group.

e. Right-click the **Golf_ShopData worksheet tab**, and then click **Move or Copy** to display the Move or Copy dialog box. Click to select the **(move to end)** option, click to check the **Create a copy** check box, and then click **OK**. A new worksheet will appear that is named Golf_ShopData (2). Right-click the **Golf_ShopData(2)** worksheet tab, and then click **Rename**. Highlight the **2** in the name, and then type backup. Press Enter to create a backup copy of the data.

f. Click the **Golf_ShopData worksheet tab**, click cell **C20**, click the **Insert tab**, and then click **Table**. Verify the table range text box displays $A$20:$K$90 and the **My table has headers** check box is checked, and then click **OK**. With the data still selected, click the **Formulas tab**, and then click **Create from Selection**. Verify that only the Top row check box is checked, and then click **OK**.

g. Select **A20:K20**, press Ctrl+C to copy the range, click cell **A1**, and then press Ctrl+V to paste the field labels in row 1. Click cell **C2**, type Accessories, click cell **K2**, type Friday, and then press Enter.

h. Click cell **G20**, and then press Ctrl+A to select the data. Click the **Data tab**, and then click **Advanced**. If a message asking to include the column labels in the selection to allow the Filter command to work properly displays, click **Yes**. In the Advanced Filter dialog box, click in the **Criteria range** text box, and then select **A1:K2**. Ensure that Excel automatically made the Criteria range an absolute reference. Verify the Filter the list, in-place check box is selected, and then click **OK**.

i. Select **A20:K72**, press Ctrl+C to copy the filtered data, and then click **Insert Worksheet** 🗐 to insert a new worksheet. Select **A1**, press Ctrl+V to paste the subset of data, and then press Esc.

j. Click the **Golf_ShopData worksheet tab**, click cell **C20**, click the **Insert tab**, and then click **PivotTable** in the Tables group. Click the **Existing Worksheet** check box, and then click in the **Location** text box and, if necessary, clear any existing text. Click the **Golf_Report worksheet tab**, and then click cell **A20**. In the Create PivotTable dialog box click **OK**.

k. In the PivotTable Field List, click check boxes for **Category**, **QTY**, and **Emp_ID** fields in the PivotTable Field list.

   - In the Values area, click **Sum of Emp_ID**, and then click **Move to Column Labels**.

l. The Employee IDs are not informative, so they should be changed to the employee's first names.

   - Select **B21**, and then type Pat.
   - Select **C21**, and then type Chris.
   - Select **D21**, and then type Tori.
   - Double-click to use the AutoFit feature on the column width for columns C and D so the employee names can be seen.
   - Select **A3**, and then type 26.
   - Select **A5**, and then type Tori.
   - Select **B5**, and then type 10.

m. Click any cell in the PivotTable, and then click to uncheck the **Category**, **QTY**, and **Emp_ID** fields.

n. Click cell **A20**, click the **Options tab**, and then in the Calculations group, click **Fields, Items, & Sets**. Click **Calculated Field**.

   - In the Name text box type SubTotal, and then press [Tab].
   - Click **Retail** in the Fields list.
   - Click **Insert Field**.
   - Type *.
   - Click the **QTY** field in the Fields list.
   - Click **Insert Field**.
   - Click **OK**.

o. Click the **Golf_ShopData worksheet tab**, and then select cell **L20**. Click the **Data tab**, and then click **Clear** in the Sort & Filter group. In L20, type SubTotal, press [Enter], and then type =. Click cell **F21**, type *, click cell **G21**, and then press [Enter] to calculate the subtotal for each line item.

p. Click the **Golf_Report worksheet tab**, and then click cell **A20**:

   - Click the **Options tab**, click **Fields, Items, & Sets** in the Calculations group, and then click **Calculated Field**.
   - With the Name text box selected, type Tax, and then press [Tab].
   - Click **SubTotal** from the Fields list, and then click **Insert Field**.
   - The insertion point will be at the end of the Formula text box. Type *.07, and then click **OK**.

q. In the PivotTable Field List, click **Product ID**, **Category**, and **Day**, in addition to the SubTotal and Tax field that was automatically added and checked when created:

   - Drag the **Day** field from the Row Labels to the Report Filter area.
   - Drag the **Product ID** in the Row Labels to be below the Category field in the Row Labels area.

- Click cell **B22**. Click the Options tab, click **Field Settings** in the Active Field group. Click the **Show Values As tab**, and then click **Number Format**. Click **Currency**, click **OK**, and then click **OK**.

- Click cell **C22**. Click the Options tab, click **Field Settings** in the Active Field group. Click the **Show Values As tab**, and then click **Number Format**. Click **Currency**, click **OK**, and then click **OK** again.

r. Click the Options tab, click **Insert Slicer**, click the **Emp_ID** check box, and then click **OK**. Click Emp_ID **Tori** in the Emp_ID slicer.

s. Click the **Filter arrow**, in cell **B18** to display the list. Click the **Select Multiple Items** check box. Click to uncheck the **(All)** check box, click to check the **Friday** and **Saturday** check boxes, and then click **OK**.

t. Click the **Design tab**, click the **Subtotals arrow**, and then click **Show all Subtotals at Bottom of Group**.

u. Click **Tori** in the Emp_ID slicer. Select **A8**, type 419, and then press Enter.

v. Click the **File tab**, change the orientation to **Landscape**, and then click **Save**.

w. Print or submit your project as directed by your instructor. Close Excel.

Practice 2

Student data file needed:

e03_ws06_GiftShop_Sales

You will save your file as:

Lastname_Firstname_e03_ws06_GiftShop_Sales

Gift Shop Sales Review

The sales team at the gift shop would like to review sales by the staff after some of the new staff has finished a training program. You have the data for May 2011 to use to set up this file, and more data will be added in the future. The sales team wants you to review the data, do some analysis, and answer some specific questions.

a. Start **Excel**, and then open **e03_ws06_GiftShop_Sales**. A spreadsheet with a range of data is displayed. Click the **File tab**, and then click **Save As**. In the Save As dialog box, navigate to the location where you are saving your student files. In the File name box, type Lastname_Firstname_e03_ws06_GiftShop_Sales, replacing Lastname_Firstname with your own name, and then click **Save**.

b. Click the **Documentation worksheet tab** if it is not the active worksheet, click cell **A6**, and then press Ctrl+: to input the current date. Click cell **B6**, and type Firstname Lastname using your own first name and last name.

c. Click the **Insert tab**, and then click **Header & Footer** in the Text group. Click the **Design tab**, and then click **Go to Footer**. Click in the **left footer section**, and then click **File Name** in the Header & Footer Elements group.

d. Click any cell on the spreadsheet to move out of the footer, press Ctrl+Home, click the **View tab**, and then click **Normal** in the Workbook Views group.

e. Right-click the **Sales worksheet tab**, and then click **Move or Copy** to display the Move or Copy dialog box. Click to select the **(move to end)** option, check the **Create a copy** check box, and then click **OK**. A new worksheet will appear that is named Sales (2). Right-click the **Sales (2) worksheet tab**, and then click **Rename**. Select to highlight the **2** in the name, type backup, and then press Enter to create a backup of the data.

f. Click the **Sales worksheet tab**, click cell **C18**, click the **Insert tab**, and then click **Table**. Verify that the range **$A$15:$I$212** is selected, verify the **My table has headers** check box is checked, and then click **OK**.

g. Select **A15:I15**, press [Ctrl]+[C] to copy the range, select cell **A1**, and then press [Ctrl]+[V] to paste the field labels in row 1. Click cell **G2**, type Receptionist, click cell **I2**, type Card, and then press [Enter].

h. Click cell **G17**, and then press [Ctrl]+[A] to select the data. Click the **Data tab**, and then click **Advanced**. When an Excel warning box appears asking if it should include the row with labels, click **Yes**. Click in the **Criteria range** input box, select **A1:I2**, and then in the Advanced Filter dialog box, verify the **Filter the list, in-place** check box is selected. Click **OK**.

i. Click cell **J15**, type Sub_Total, and then press [Enter]. In cell **J16**, type =, click cell **B16**, type *, click cell **E16**, and then press [Enter].

j. Select **C15**, and then press [Ctrl]+[A] to select all of the data including the column headings. Click the **Create from Selection** button in the Defined Names group on the Formulas tab. Click the check box next to **Right Column** to deselect and click **OK**.

k. Click cell **H7**, type =SUBTOTAL(3,Staff_Category), and then press [Enter]. In cell **H8**, type =SUBTOTAL(9,Units), and then press [Enter]. In cell **H9**, type =SUBTOTAL(9,Sub_Total), and then press [Enter]. In cell **H10** type =SUBTOTAL(1,Retail_Price), and then press [Enter].

l. Click the Data tab, click **Advanced** in the Sort & Filter group. The List range text box should be selected. Press [F3], and then click **Category** from the Paste name list of named ranges. Click **OK**. Select the range in the **Criteria range** text box, and then press [Delete]. Select the **Copy to another location** check box, click in the **Copy to** text box, and then type K2. Click to check the **Unique records only** check box, and then click **OK**. Click cell **K1**, press [Ctrl]+[B], and then type Category. Press [Enter]. Click the Home tab, click **Format** in the Cells group, and then click AutoFit Column Width for column K, so the data fits within the column. Alternatively, click **Column Width**, change the column width to **12**, and then press [Enter].

m. Click cell **C15**. Click the **Insert tab**, and then click **PivotTable** in the Tables group. Click **Existing Worksheet**. Click in the **Location** text box, click the **Sales_Analysis worksheet tab**, and then click cell **A15**. In the Create PivotTable dialog box, click **OK**.

n. In the PivotTable Field List, click to check the field check boxes for **Units**, **Staff**, and **Staff Category** since these are needed to determine the total units sold by nonmanagers:
   - In the Row Labels area, click **Staff_Category**, and then click **Move to Column Labels**.
   - On the PivotTable, click the **Column Labels arrow**, click to uncheck **Manager**, and then click **OK**.
   - Click cell **E17**. Click the **Options tab**, and then click **Sort Smallest to Largest** in the Sort & Filter group.
   - Click cell **A2**, type Kendra, press [Tab], and then in cell B2 type 73.
   - Click cell **A3**, type Christy, press [Tab], and then in cell B3 type 31.
   - Click cell **A5**, type Susan, press [Tab], and then in cell B5 type 24.
   - Click cell **A6**, type Jason, press [Tab], and then in cell B6 type 25.

o. Click to uncheck **Units** in the PivotTable Field List:
   - Click the check box for the **Category** field.
   - Drag the **Category** field from the Row Labels area to the Report Filter area.
   - Click the check box for the **Hotel Guest** field.
   - Click cell **A18**, replace No by typing Non Hotel Guest, and then press [Enter].
   - Widen column A so **Non Hotel Guest** can be seen in the cell.
   - In cell **A19** replace Yes by typing Hotel Guest, and then press [Ctrl]+[Enter].

p. Click cell **B18**. Click the **Options tab**, click the **Show Values As arrow** in the Calculations group, and then click **% of Grand Total**.

q. Click the **Design tab**, click the **Grand Totals arrow**, and then click **On for Columns Only**. Click the **Subtotals arrow**, and then click **Show all Subtotals at Bottom of Group**.

r. Select cell **A9** and type **71.39%**. Press Enter .

s. Click the **Options tab**, click **PivotChart** in the Tools group, and then click **Stacked Cylinder**, second row, second column. Click **OK**.

   • Click the **Design tab** of the PivotChart Tools, and then click **Move Chart**.

   • Click **New sheet**.

   • Click in the input box for the New sheet, type SalesChart, and then press Enter .

   • Click the **Layout tab** in the PivotChart Tools, click **Chart Title**, and then click **Centered Overlay Title**.

   • Type Percent Revenue Contribution, press Enter , and then click outside of the chart title to deselect it.

t. Click the **File tab**, and then click **Print**. Change the orientation to Landscape as needed to print, and then click **Save**.

u. Print or submit your project as directed by your instructor. Close Excel.

MODULE CAPSTONE

Student data file needed:	You will save your file as:
e03_mp_Restaurant_Dessert	Lastname_Firstname_e03_mp_Restaurant_Dessert

Restaurant Dessert Analysis

Robin Sanchez, the chef, was discussing dessert sales with the restaurant manager, Alberto Dimas. They want to examine the production levels and the sales of their signature desserts. As part of this, a spreadsheet with data has been provided so you can create some tools for analysis.

a. Start **Excel**.

- Click the **File tab**, and then click **Open**. In the Open dialog box, navigate to where your student data files are located, click **e03_mp_Restaurant_Dessert**, and then click **Open**.

- Click the **Documentation worksheet tab**, click cell **A6**, press Ctrl+; for the current date, and then press Tab.

- In cell B6 type your Firstname Lastname, and then press Ctrl+Enter. In the left footer section, insert the filename, and then return to **Normal** view.

- Click the **File tab**, click **Save As**, and then in the Save As dialog box, navigate to the location where you are saving your student files. In the File name box, type Lastname_Firstname_e03_mp_Restuarant_Dessert replacing Lastname and Firstname with your own name. Click **Save**.

b. Some named ranges need to be created. Click the **Lists worksheet tab**, and then select **A5:C10**.

- Click in the **Name** box, type Dessert_List, and then press Enter.

- Select **F5:G11**, click in the **Name** box, type Employee_List, and then press Enter.

- Select **B13:H14**, click in the **Name** box, type DailyGoal, and then press Enter.

- Select **A17:B19**, click in the **Name** box, type GoalGrade, and then press Enter. Press Ctrl+Home.

c. Click the **Dessert_Times worksheet tab**, and then click cell **B16**. Click the **Insert tab**, click **Table**, verify the entire table has been selected and that the check box is checked for **My table has headers**, and then click **OK**.

d. Click cell **E15** so some calculated fields can be created.

- Type Dessert, press Tab, type Day, and then press Tab. Type Category, press Tab, type Emp_Name, and then press Enter.

- In cell E16, type =VLOOKUP(B16,Dessert_List,2,FALSE), and then press Tab. The VLOOKUP will look up the Dessert_ID from the Dessert_List and return the name of the dessert. The FALSE indicates an exact match will be needed.

- In cell **F16**, type =INDEX(DailyGoal,1,WEEKDAY(C16,1)), and then press Tab. This will pull the value from the DailyGoal table, looking in Row 1. The WEEKDAY function will pull the day of the week, returning a number from 1 to 7, which will translate to the column field name within the DailyGoal Table.

- For the Category, Crème Brulee and Dutch Apple Pie are the two desserts that are made just prior to serving and are served hot. Thus, if the dessert is either of those, the category should be "Hot." Otherwise, it should be "Cool." In cell G16, type =IF(OR(E16="Crème Brulee",E16="Dutch Apple Pie"),"Hot","Cool"), and then press Tab.

- In cell H16, type =VLOOKUP(A16,Employee_List,2,FALSE), and then press Enter. The VLOOKUP will look up the Emp_ID from the Employee_List and pull the employee's name from the second column. The FALSE indicates an exact match will be needed.

e. A few named ranges need to be made on this worksheet also.

- Click cell **A15**, press Ctrl+A to select the entire table. Click in the **Name** box, type Dessert_All, and then press Enter.

- Click the **Formulas tab**, click **Create from Selection**, click as necessary to check the **Top row** check box only and click **OK**.

f. Select **A15:H15**, press Ctrl+C to copy the header information, click cell **A1**, and then press Ctrl+V to paste the headers. Click cell **A7**, and then press Ctrl+V to paste the headers.

g. Click cell **A2**, type 45, click cell **F2**, type Tuesday, press Tab, and then type Cool. Click cell **E8**, type Key Lime Pie, click cell **B5**, and then type Desserts Sold. Click cell **B10**, type Subtotal, and then press Tab.

h. Select cells **A15:H194**. Click the **Create from Selection** button in the Defined Names group on the Formulas tab. Click the check box next to **Right Column** to deselect it, and click **OK**.

i. To get the subtotal, in cell C10 type =SUBTOTAL(9,Qty), and then press Enter. The "9" indicates to SUM the filtered records on the Qty field for records currently showing in the table.

j. Click cell **C16**, click the **Data tab**, and then click **Advanced** in the Sort & Filter group. Confirm $A$15:H$215 is displayed in the List range input box, and if necessary, edit the range as specified to select the entire table. Click the **Criteria range** input box, select the range **A7:H8**, and then click **OK** to filter the data on Key Lime Pie desserts.

k. Click cell **C5**, type =DSUM(Dessert_All,D1,A1:H2), and then press Ctrl+Enter. This will create a database function to sum the Qty field from the table, using the criteria set up in A1:H2. It will sum all records, even records that are hidden by the filter that has been applied.

l. Click the **Report worksheet tab**, and then click cell **B3** so some functions can be created.

- Type =SUMIF(Dessert,A3,Qty), and then press Ctrl+Enter. Double-click the **AutoFill** handle to copy this formula down through B8.

- Click cell **B12**, type =SUMIFS(Qty,Dessert,$A12,Day,B$11), and then press Ctrl+Enter. Double-click the **AutoFill** handle to copy this formula down though **B17**, and then use the **AutoFill** handle to copy across to **H17** so the formula is copied to the range **B12:H17**. This sums the Qty field with both the dessert and day criteria is true.

- Click cell **B19**, type =SUM(B12:B17)/HLOOKUP(B11,DailyGoal,2,FALSE), and then press Enter. This sums the day's quantity sold and divides this value by the day's goal. The goal is found using the HLOOKUP in the DailyGoal table.

- In cell **B20**, type =VLOOKUP(B19,GoalGrade,2), and then press Enter.

- Select **B19:B20**, and then use the **AutoFill** handle to copy the formulas to fill the range **B19:H20**.

- Click cell **B24**, type =IF(B22="Employee","EMP_Name","Dessert"), and then press Enter. This determines which data named range is associated with the category that is in cell B22. It will then be used in other formulas to select that named range.

- In cell **B25**, type =SUMIF(INDIRECT(B24),B23,Qty), and then press ⎡Enter⎤. This uses the named range in B24 as the criteria range and sums the Qty field.

- In cell **B26**, type =AVERAGEIF(INDIRECT(B24),B23,Qty), and then press ⎡Ctrl⎤+⎡Enter⎤. This averages the Qty field, using the named range listed in B24 as the criteria field.

- Click cell **F3**. The End_Level is either Low or Okay. If the Bake Time is Day Bake and has an Ending_Qty lower than the Day Bake level listed in E17 on the Lists worksheet, the formula will return Low. The formula also returns Low if the Bake Time is Fresh Bake, and the Ending_Qty for the Fresh Bake item is less than the Fresh Bake value listed in cell E18 on the Lists worksheet. In cell F3, type =IF(OR(AND(E3="Day Bake",C3<Lists!$E$17), AND(E3="Fresh Bake",C3<Lists!$E$18)),"Low","Okay"), and then press ⎡Ctrl⎤+⎡Enter⎤.

- Double-click the **AutoFill** handle to copy the formula down to cell **F8**.

- The Adjust column checks if either of two situations are true. If either are true, it will indicate to "Produce More," otherwise it will show nothing with the "". If requests are more than 5, indicating items had sold out, more needs to be produced. Or, if the end level is low and the bake time is Day Bake, then more needs to be produced. Click cell **G3**, type =IF(OR(D3>5,AND(F3="Low",E3="Day Bake")),"Produce More", ""), and then press ⎡Ctrl⎤+⎡Enter⎤. Double-click the **AutoFill** handle to copy the formula down to cell **G8**. Press ⎡Ctrl⎤+⎡Home⎤.

m. Click the **Dessert_Times worksheet tab**, and then click cell **B16**. Click the **Insert tab**, click **PivotTable**, verify the proper table range is selected and that the New Worksheet option is selected, and then click **OK**. Double-click the **worksheet name**, type Pivot, and then press ⎡Enter⎤ to rename the worksheet.

n. In the PivotTable Field List Pane, click to check **Qty**, **Dessert**, **Day**, and **Category**.

- At the bottom of the PivotTable Field List area, drag as needed to make sure Day is in the Row Labels area, Dessert is in the Column Labels area, and Category is in the Report Filter area. The Sum of Qty should be in the Values area of the PivotTable Field List.

- Click cell **B4** and select **Column Labels filter button**, and then click **(Select All)** to deselect all the items. Click to check the **Crème Brulee** and **Personal Dutch Apple Pie** check boxes. Click **OK**.

o. Click the **Options tab**, click **PivotChart** in the Tools group, under Line, click the second style, the **Stacked Line**, and then click **OK**.

- Click the **Design tab**, and then click **Move Chart** in the Location group.

- In the Move Chart dialog box, select **New sheet**. Make sure the new sheet input box displays Chart1 as the sheet name, and then click **OK**.

p. Click **Save**. Click the **File tab**, click **Print**, and then select either **Portrait** Orientation or **Landscape** Orientation to ensure your worksheets print in a readable manner. Print or submit files as directed by your instructor. Click **Save**. Close Excel.

Problem Solve 1

Student data file needed:	You will save your file as:
e03_ps1_Hotel_Class	Lastname_Firstname_e03_ps1_Hotel_Class

Hotel Class Report

The hotel has started running exercise classes for guests. Guests can sign up for classes prior to their arrival or when they check into the hotel. There are several instructors to lead the classes, and each has multiple skills. The fitness center manager would like to have a spreadsheet developed that will track the class enrollment. The spreadsheet will provide an overview of enrollment with some decision-making tools. You have been asked to create that spreadsheet.

a. Start **Excel**, and then open **e03_ps1_Hotel_Class**.
- Click the **Report tab**, click cell **B1**, and then type your first name and last name.
- Click the **Documentation worksheet tab**, click **A6**, and then press Ctrl+; for the current date.
- Click cell **B6**, type your Firstname Lastname, and then press Enter.
- Click the **File tab**, click **Save As**, and then save your file as Lastname_Firstname_e03_ps1_Hotel_Class replacing Lastname and Firstname with your own name.

b. Click the **List worksheet tab**, and then select range **B11:H14**. Click the **Create from Selection** button as necessary to make sure **Top row** is the only check box checked to create a set of named ranges for each column in that range. Each range is the list of instructors that can teach individual classes.

c. Click the **Enrollment worksheet tab**, and then click cell **A14**. Click the **Insert tab**, and then click **Table** to create a table using the data on the worksheet. Verify that the table is selected and the check box for **My table has headers** is checked.

d. Click cell **D13**, and then create a new column header, Class Name. In cell **D14**, enter a HLOOKUP function that will look up the Class number in column B and use the ClassInfo table to return the Class Category name from the second row of that table with an exact match. Fill the formula for the column.

e. Select **A13:D106**, and then name the entire range Enrollment. Click the **Create from Selection** button to create named ranges for each **Top row** column in the selected range.

f. Select **A13:D13**, copy the selection, and then paste the headers to cell range **A1:D1** to set up a criteria header area.
- Click cell **C2**, and then type F.
- Click cell **D2**, and then type Yoga.
- Click cell **A5**, and then type Numbered Enrolled.

g. Click cell **B5**, and then create a DCOUNTA function to count the Student_ID field in the Enrollment table that meet the filter criteria specified in range A1:D2.

h. Click the **Report worksheet tab**, and then click cell **A4** to begin creating calculations. The user will put an x in E4:E10, indicating which class to report upon and an x in H4:H5 if they want a report on a specific gender.
- Click cell **A4**, use a MATCH nested in an INDEX function to retrieve the Class that was selected in E4:F10. The MATCH should find the row where the x is located and would be used within the INDEX to pull the associated Class value from the same row within F4:F10.
- Click cell **B4**, and then do the same for the gender, looking at the x in column H and returning the F or M for the Gender criteria. Using a MATCH nested in an INDEX function, retrieve the gender that was selected in H4:H5. Put this formula inside of an IFERROR, in case the user does not select a specific gender. The IFERROR should return a blank, using the "", if no gender is selected.
- Click cell **C4**, and then create a COUNTIF that counts the enrollment for the named range Class that has the class number listed in A4. The named range Class should reference the range Enrollment!$B$14:$B$106.
- Click cell **B7**, and then create a HLOOKUP formula that will look up the Class in A4 within the ClassInfo named range and return the max enrollment, which is in the third row of that table. The value should be looking for an exact match.
- Click cell **B8**, and then create another HLOOKUP that will use the Class in A4 and pull the Class Category type from the ClassInfo named range in row 2, also looking for an exact match.
- Click cell **B11**, and then create an IF function to indicate the Availability of spots. If the number enrolled in C4 is greater than or equal to the max enrollment in B7, then

FULL OR OVERBOOKED should be returned. Otherwise, Spots Available should be returned.

- The instructors for each class are listed on the List worksheet in B13:H15. The Instructors for the Swimmercize class needs to be counted. Click cell **B12**, and then create a complex function that will determine the number of instructors for the class that are listed in A4. (*Hint*: Use a MATCH nested in an INDEX to find the name of the range that has the instructors. Then, use that function nested inside of an INDIRECT to get the range that will be used in the COUNTA to count the nonblanks.)

- Click cell **B13**. Using an HLOOKUP nested in an AND function nested in an IF function, return either Split Class or Can't Split based on business options. Two conditions are needed to determine if a class can be split: Using the ClassInfo table, one row shows if a class can be split. That condition can be determined with a HLOOKUP. The second is if there is more than one instructor as shown in cell B12. If both conditions are met, the class can be split. Otherwise there can only be one class.

i. Click the **Enrollment worksheet tab**, and then click cell **A13**. Click the **Insert tab**, click **PivotTable** to create a PivotTable on a new worksheet. Rename the worksheet Pivot.

- In the PivotTable Field List, click to select **Student_ID**, **Gender**, and **Class Name** from the fields area.

- Make sure **Gender** is in the Column Labels area, **Class Name** is in the Row Labels area, and **Student_ID** is in the Values area and is being counted.

- Change the labels for gender from F to Female and from M to Male, and then resize the column width as needed.

j. Click the **Options tab** if necessary, click **PivotChart**, and then under the Bar category, click Clustered Bar, the first bar style. Reposition the PivotChart below the PivotTable.

k. Click the **Documentation worksheet tab**. Press [Shift], and then click the **Report worksheet tab**. This will select all worksheets as a group, and you will see [Group] appear in the title bar at the top of the window. Click the **Insert tab**, click **Header & Footer**, and insert the file name into the left footer section. Click out of the footer, and then return to **Normal** view. Press [Ctrl]+[Home], right-click one of the **worksheet tabs**, and then click **Ungroup Sheets**.

l. Click **Save**. Print or submit your files as directed by your instructor. Close Excel.

Problem Solve 2

Student data file needed:	You will save your file as:
e03_ps2_Hotel_Marketing	Lastname_Firstname_e03_ps2_Hotel_Marketing

Hotel Market Analysis

You have been assigned to do some market analysis development in Excel for the hotel. Data pertaining to guests has been compiled for a 30-day period. Using the initial data, tables, and information, your boss wants you to complete the workbook spreadsheets so it can be used for decision-making purposes.

a. Start **Excel**, and then open **e03_ps2_Hotel_Marketing**.

- Click the **Monthly Report worksheet tab**. Click cell **B1**, type your Firstname Lastname, and then press [Ctrl]+[Home].

- Click the **Documentation worksheet tab**, click cell **A6**, press [Ctrl]+[;] to get the current date, and then press [Tab].

- In cell B6, type your Firstname Lastname, and then press [Ctrl]+[Home].

- Save your file as Lastname_Firstname_e03_ps2_Hotel_Marketing replacing Lastname and Firstname with your own name.

b. Click the **List worksheet tab**, select range **F3:J4**, and then name that range MktRepList.

c. Click the **MonthlyStay worksheet tab**, and then click cell **A20** so a table can be created and some calculated fields can be added after a table has been established.

- Create an Excel table using the data set on the worksheet.
- Add a new field label named Coup_1 in cell K20.
- Add a new field label named Coup_2 in cell L20.
- Add a new field label named Rep_Name in cell M20.
- Click cell **K21**. Coup 1 is for determining which customers would get a promotional coupon. This coupon will be given to customers based on the pseudo-code information on the List worksheet in F8:I17. There are two ways for a coupon to be earned. First, if the customer stayed three or more days and had five or more in his party, then a coupon is given. Secondly, if the sum of their activities (enjoying the spa, playing golf, and dining) is greater than two (based on the data in columns F,G, and H of the MonthlyStay worksheet table) and there were two or more in the party, a coupon is given. Since these values may change, the cells should be referenced.
- Create an IF function in K21 using an AND nested inside an OR function that will return either Yes or No based on the conditions described to indicate if a coupon should be given.
- Click cell **L21**. Coup 2 is a second coupon to be given based on a second pseudo-code marketing strategy on the List worksheet in F20:I29.
- Create an IF function in L21 using an OR nested inside an AND function that will return either Yes or No based on the conditions described to indicate if a coupon should be given. On the List worksheet, the conditions are shown with the current values. If the Event_ID field of the MonthlyStay worksheet table is either an A or W and either the number of days is five or more or the sum of the spa, golf, and dining events (shown in columns F,G, and H) are greater than two, then the coupon will be given.
- Click cell **M21**. The Rep_Name is the name of the marketing rep. Create an HLOOKUP that looks up the Mkt_Rep field value from the MonthlyStay table within the MktRepList on the List worksheet and returns the name of the Representative in row 2 using an exact match.

d. Create an advanced filter to generate summary data for the Adhoc Report.

- Click the **MonthlyStay worksheet tab**, select **header labels** in A20:J20, copy the selection, and then paste into cell A1.
- Click cell **A1**, and then change that header label to be a second Date criteria field.
- Click cell **A2**, and then add the constraint <=6/15/2011.
- Click cell **B2**, and then add the constraint >6/7/2011.
- Click cell **J2**, and then add the constraint M33.
- Click the **Data tab**, and then use the Advanced filter to filter the data based on the criteria in A1:M2.
- Click cell **D6**, and then use the SUBTOTAL function to determine the average length of stay in Num_Days for the filtered data.
- Click cell **D7**, and then use the SUBTOTAL function to determine the maximum length of stay in Num_Days for the filtered data.
- Click cell **D8**, and then use the SUBTOTAL function to determine the number of customers in Cust_ID for the filtered data.

e. Create a PivotTable along with a PivotChart.

- Click cell **A20**. Using the MonthlyStay table data, create a PivotTable on a new worksheet named Pivot.
- In the PivotTable Field List, click and adjust to select the **Rep_Name** field in the Row Labels areas.

- Click the **Options tab**, and then click **Fields, Items, & Sets** to create a Calculated Field called Number_Activities that adds the Golf, Spa, and Dine fields. This calculated field should show in the Values area as Sum of Number_Activities.
- Create a Clustered Column PivotChart based on this PivotTable.
- Position the PivotChart under the PivotTable.

f. Click the **Monthly Report worksheet tab**, where some functions need to be created.

- Click cell **B4**. Create a function that will count the number of the activity listed in A4. Copy this formula down to B6.
- Click cell **B9**. Create a function that will sum the activities for the event range listed in A9. Copy this formula down to **B14**.
- Click cell **F4**. Create a function that will look up the rep ID and find the name of the rep based on the MktRepList named range. Copy this formula down to **F8**.
- Click cell **G4**. Create a function that will sum the range listed in G3 for the Rep listed in E4. Use appropriate cell referencing so you can copy the formula over the range G4:J8.
- Click cell **F14**. Create a function that will find the customer listed in the Monthly Stay data on the row that is listed in E13.
- Click cell **B18**. Create a database function that will use the criteria set up in A20:J21 that will find the sum of the category that is listed in B17.

g. Click the **Documentation worksheet tab**. Group the worksheets, and then insert the filename into the left footer section. Return to **Normal** view, and then ungroup the sheets.

h. Click **Save**. Print or submit your files as directed by your instructor. Close Excel.

<hr/>

Problem Solve 3

Student data file

e03_ps3_Hotel_CallCenter

You will save your file as:

Lastname_Firstname_e03_ps3_Hotel_CallCenter

Call Center Analysis

The Call Center wants a spreadsheet developed that will use call data. The spreadsheet will set up a variety of tools that will help assess the efficiency of the center and its staff. Your job is to develop the tools for the call center manager that will help with the assessment.

a. Start **Excel**, and then open **e03_ps3_Hotel_CallCenter**.

- Click the **Call_Report worksheet tab**. Click cell **B1**, and then type your Firstname Lastname.
- Click the **Documentation worksheet tab**, click cell **A6**, and then press Ctrl + ; to get the current date.
- Click cell **B6**, type your Firstname Lastname, and then press Ctrl + Home.
- Save your file as Lastname_Firstname_e03_ps3_Hotel_CallCenter, replacing Lastname and Firstname with your own name.

b. Create Named Ranges to use within formulas. Click the **Lists worksheet tab**.

- Name the range **A3:A8** as Department.
- Name the range **A16:B20** as GradeScale.
- Name the range **B11:H11** as DayofWeek.
- Select **E2:J6**, and create named ranges using the **Create from Selection** and **Top row** option.

c. Click the **Call_Data worksheet tab**, and then click cell **A11** to create a table and some calculated fields.

- Create an Excel table using the current data set.
- Click cell **H11**, and then add Issue as the field label.
- Click cell **I11**, and then add Grade as the field label.
- Click cell **J11**, and then add Weekday as the field label.
- Click cell **H12**, and then create an INDEX function that will use a nested INDIRECT reference to the Dept named range listed in column C, and also use the Reason field in column B as the row number to return for the department name in the referenced named range. Resize column width as needed.
- Click cell **I12**, and then create a function that will convert the Satisfaction_Score to a grade found in the second column of the GradeScale named range.
- Click cell **J12**, and then create an INDEX function that will convert the Call_Day to the actual weekday found in row 1 of the DayofWeek named range. Resize column width as needed.

d. Some ranges are needed on the Call_Data worksheet also.

- Click the **Call_Data worksheet**, name the entire data set, including the labels, as CallData_All.
- Also, use Create from Selection to name each Top row column of data labels as the range name.

e. On the Call_Data worksheet, create an advanced filter.

- Copy and paste all the A1:J1 labels from the data set to cell **A1**.
- Click cell **C2**, type Front_Desk, click cell **G2**, and then type Y.
- Run an advanced filter on the table data set using the criteria range A1:J2.
- Click cell **B5**, and then type Count of calls. Click cell **D5**, and then create a SUBTOTAL function that will count the number of Call_Hour cells returned for the subset of records that have been filtered.
- Click cell **B6**, and then type Average length of calls. Click cell **D6**, and then create a SUBTOTAL function that will determine the average Call_Length for the subset of records that have been filtered.

f. Click the **Call_Report worksheet**, as some functions need to be developed. Click cell **B3**, a department can be listed and the issues can be summarized for that department in B6:D9.

- Click cell **B6**. Create an INDEX function that will use an INDIRECT function to pull the department issue list that is listed in the B3 named range (use an absolute reference so AutoFill can be applied). Use a relative cell reference in A6 as the row_num argument. So, currently it would list the first issue for the Front_Desk department. Copy the formula down to cell **B9**.
- Click cell **C6**, and then create a COUNTIFS function that will count the number of Dept criteria_range1 for the department criteria listed in the absolute cell reference B3 and the Reason criteria_range2 using cell A6 as criteria 2. Copy **C6** down to cell **C9**.
- Click cell **D6**, and then create a COUNTIFS function that will count the number of calls coming from the department listed in B3, from issue 1 (cell A6) from the Reason criteria_range2 argument, and were listed as "Y" from the On_Hold as criteria_range3. Copy cell **D6** down to cell **D9**.
- Click cell **E6**, and then create an IF statement with a nested AND that will put in a status notice. If the # Calls on Issue in cell C6 is greater than 5 and the # On Hold in cell D6 is greater than 3, a message of Check Hold Issue should be returned. Otherwise, nothing should be returned. Copy cell **C6** down to cell **E9**.

g. Click cell **B12**, and then create the following formulas for this table report.

- Click cell **B12**, and then create an AVERAGEIF function that will find the average Call_Length for the Dept range and the criteria specified in cell A12.
- Click cell **C12**, and then create a COUNTIF function that will count the number of calls that were associated with the Dept range and the criteria specified in cell A12.
- Click cell **D12**, and then create a formula that sums two COUNTIFS formulas. The first COUNTIFS will count the number of calls associated with the Dept range and criteria specified in cell A12 that got a Grade "F", and the second COUNTIF will do the same for Grade "D".
- Click cell **E12**, and then create an IF statement using a nested OR function that will return either Explore Issues or a blank cell. One of two reasons will return an Explore Issues result: when there are more than 10 issues reported with a grade less than a C in cell D12, or when the number of scores less then C divided by the Total Calls in cell C12 is greater than 50%.
- Copy the formulas in **B12:E12** down through row **17**.

h. Because calls should be handled quickly, the longest call will be noted and checked.

- Click cell **H11** and create a MAX function that will show the maximum Call_Length minutes.
- Click cell **H12**, and then create an INDEX function that will pull the Dept range as the array associated with a MATCH function to determine the lookup_array for the longest call referenced in H11.
- Click cell **H13**, and then create an INDEX function that will pull the Satisfaction_Score associated with a MATCH function to determine the lookup_array for the longest call referenced in H11.

i. A final section is needed that will use database functions for some reports. The criteria can be easily changed and determine the satisfaction and call length for any subset of data.

- Click the **Call_Data worksheet tab**. Copy the header row **A11:J11**, click the **Call_Report worksheet tab** and then paste it into cell **A20**.
- Click cell **G21**, type Y, click cell **J21**, and then type Friday.
- Click cell **B25**, and then use a DCOUNT function for the CallData_All database to find the count of the Satisfaction_Score currently listed in cell B24 using the criteria set up in A20:J21. Use absolute values for cell references. Set up corresponding database functions in B26:B29 that find the DAVERAGE, DSUM, DMAX, and DMIN, respectively, for the Satisfaction_Score.
- Select cells **C25:C29**, and then use the same database functions and arguments used in B25:B29, with the exception that you want to find the statistics for the Call_Length currently listed in cell C24 (in lieu of the Satisfaction_Score listed in B24). Press Ctrl+Home.

j. Develop a PivotTable and PivotChart for further analysis.

- Click the **Call_Data worksheet tab**, and then click cell **A11** to use the Call_Data set to create a PivotTable on a new worksheet named Pivot.
- The PivotTable should have the **Call_Hour** field as the Report Filter, Dept as the Column Labels, Grade as the Row Labels, and Count of Reason in the Values area.
- Add a slicer for Weekday, and then choose Friday, Saturday, and Sunday. Position the slicer beside the PivotTable, on the right side.
- Create a Clustered Cone Column chart, and then position the chart below the PivotTable.

k. Click the **Documentation worksheet tab**. Group the worksheets and insert the file name into the left footer section. Click out of the footer, return to Normal view, and then ungroup the worksheets.

l. Click **Save**. Change the print orientation as necessary to provide a good fit for printing. Print or submit your files as directed by your instructor. Click **Save**, and then close Excel.

Student data file needed:

e03_pf1_Volunteer

You will save your file as:

Lastname_Firstname_e03_pf1_Volunteer

Student Club Volunteer Report

Your student club wants to set up a spreadsheet to track volunteer activities of the club members. This way, they can set goals, show they are helping the community, track how members are doing with their volunteer work, and feel good about life. Using the sample data provided in the file, set up a spreadsheet for tracking and monitoring volunteer activities.

a. Start **Excel** and open **e03_pf1_Volunteer**. Save your file as Lastname_Firstname_e03_pf1_Volunteer replacing Lastname and Firstname with your own name.

b. Click the **List worksheet tab**, and then name the data for the goals.
   - Select **A2:L12**, and then create named ranges from selection using Top row for each column, including the Goal list of jobs in column A.
   - Create a named range for the GoalStatus table in A18:B21.
   - Create a named range for the Goals for the range B3:L12.

c. Click the **VolunteerWork worksheet**, click cell **A10**, and then create a table with the VolunteerWork data set.
   - Create named ranges for each column in the data set.
   - Create a named range Vol_ALL for the entire data set, including the field labels.

d. Create an Advanced filter on the VolunteerWork worksheet.
   - Copy the range **A10:E10**, and then paste it into cell **A1** to set up the criteria field headings on Row 1.
   - Click cell **F1**, and then create an extra label heading for Date.
   - Click cell **B2**, type >1/1/2011, click cell **F2**, type <1/31/2011 to put in criteria to get records between 1/1/2011 and 1/31/2011, and then run the advanced filter.
   - Click cell **A4**, and then type Donations. Click cell **B4**, and then type Subtotal. Click cell **B5**, and then create a function to sum for the filtered data in the Donation field range.

e. Click the **Report worksheet tab**, and then create a tally for all the members.
   - Click cell **B1**, and then type your Firstname Lastname.
   - Click cell **B4**, and then create a function that will pull the goal for the member listed in B2 for the category listed in B3.
   - Click cell **B5**, and then create a function that will determine the actual time the member listed in B2 has actually logged for the category listed in B3.
   - Click cell **B6**, and then based on the Goal Status table in A18:B21 on the Lists worksheet, create a formula that provides status feedback for the member listed in B2.
   - Click cell **B7**, and then create a formula that will add up the overall goal of the member in B2 for all categories.
   - Click cell **B8**, and then create a formula that will calculate the total time logged for the member in B2 for all categories.
   - Click cell **B9**, and then create a formula that will determine how much has been raised by the member listed in B2.
   - For cells **B14:B24**, create a function for each cell that totals the entire Time of the Student range using criteria listed in column A.
   - For C14:C24, create a function for the Donation sum_range for each cell that will find the Student volunteering for the A column job and listed in the Work_Category range specified in cell C13. When that job changes, the totals should change for C14:C24 accordingly.
   - For D14:D24, create an INDEX function for the Goals array with two nested MATCH functions.

f. Click cell **E3**, and then create a function that will find the amount of the top donation. From that value find the other information associated with that donation.

- Click cell **E2**, and then create a function to find the first Student that received that donation (use a nested MATCH to find row number argument).
- Click cell **E4**, and then create a function to find the Work_Category activity that person did for the donation (use a nested MATCH to find row number argument).
- Click cell **E5**, and then use a function to count the number of people who received the Top Donation amount.

g. You need a graphical representation, similar to a thermometer, to show the progress toward the overall donation goal of $10,000.

- Click cell **H5**, and then create an IF function that will sum Donation and test if it is greater than G5. If true, it will return "XXXX"; otherwise, the function will return a blank cell. Use the AutoFill feature to fill in the formula down to **H24**.
- Select **H5:H24**, and then apply a conditional formatting with a custom format of an **Orange** background and **Orange** font color when the value equals "XXXX".

h. To set up some database filtering, perform the following.

- Click cell **D27**, and then type Lawn Mowing for the work category. Click cell **A27**, and then type Shoeless as the student member.
- Click cell **B31**, and then use a database function for the Vol_ALL database to determine the total Time field listed in cell B30 based on the criteria range A26:E27.
- Click cell **B32**, and then create a database function for the Vol_ALL database to determine the max donation field name listed in cell E26 based on the criteria A26:E27.

i. Click the **VolunteerWork worksheet tab**, click cell **A10**, and then create a PivotTable on a new worksheet named Pivot.

- The Student field should be on the Row Labels.
- The Donation field should be summed in the Values.
- The Date field should be in the Report Filter.
- Add a slicer for the Work_Category filtered for Paint. Move the slicer to the right of the PivotTable.

j. Insert the filename into the left footer section of all the worksheets in the file, and then return to Normal view. Save the file.

k. Change the print orientation to Landscape if necessary to determine a good fit for printing. Print or submit your files as directed by your instructor. Click Save, and then close Excel.

Perform 2: Perform in Your Career

Student data file needed:	You will save your file as:
e03_pf2_Student_Rental	Lastname_Firstname_e03_pf2_Student_Rental

Student Car Rental Service

A new business has started that keeps cars close to campus and rents them to students by the hour. They have GPS and can be reserved online. Students use their university ID as a means for reserving and renting the cars. This makes it easy for students without cars to run errands. A spreadsheet with old sample data has been provided for you, as a new hire, to work with in exploring the data. You have been asked to complete the model for the management team. Your success may lead to a quick promotion!

a. Start **Excel**, and then open **e03_pf2_Student_Rental**. Save your file as Lastname_Firstname_e03_pf2_Student_Rental replacing Lastname and Firstname with your own name.

b. Click the **Report worksheet tab**, click cell **B1**, and then type your Lastname Firstname.

c. Click the **Lists worksheet tab**, and then create named ranges.
   - Create a range name CheckupMiles for selected cells G5:J6.
   - Create named ranges from selection for the range L4:M7 using Top row.

d. On the **RentalData worksheet**, the data is compiled for analysis. It needs a couple of calculated fields after it is set up as a table.
   - Click cell **A11**, and then create an Excel Table with the data.
   - Add a new field label in K11 named Checkup.
   - Add a new field label in L11 named Model.
   - Click cell **K12**, and then create a logical function that will return a Y if the Note column equals either Damage or Repair; otherwise, the function will return N.
   - Click cell **L12**, and then create a function that will look up the Car_ID in the Lists worksheet table A5:C33 and return the Model of the car found in the third column.
   - Select the entire table range, including the labels in row 11, and then name the entire data set Rental_ALL.
   - Create named ranges from the selection for each column, using the Top row field labels as the range names.

e. Set up an Advanced filter by copying all the field labels (except for Cust_ID) in range B11:L11 and pasting the range to cell A1.
   - Click cell **J2**, type Y for Checkup, click cell **G2**, and then type M for the Gender fields as criteria.
   - Run the Advanced filter on the data using the criteria in A1:K2.
   - Click cell **B4**, and then type Miles. Click cell **A5**, and then type Average. Click cell **B5**, and then create a function that will find the average of range name listed in B4.

f. On the **Report worksheet**, some calculations need to be setup.
   - Click cell **B4**, and then create a formula that will sum the Car_ID range based on A4 criteria for the miles used by each car.
   - Click cell **C4**, and then create a formula that will count the times each Car_ID has made a trip based on A4 criteria.
   - Click cell **D4**, and then create a formula that will count the number of times each Car_ID based on A4 criteria needed to have a checkup indicated by a "Y" in the Checkup column range within the Rental Data.
   - Click cell **E4**, and then create a logical function that will return the result YES if the car needs to be pulled for a more thorough checkup; otherwise, a NO should be returned. Pseudo-code can be found on the Lists workshop in cells F14: I21. A car should be pulled in three different situations as outlined in the pseudo code on the Lists worksheet. First, a car should be pulled if it has more than 3000 miles. Secondly, a car should be pulled if it has more than 8 trips. Third, a car should be pulled if it has both more than 2000 miles and has had more than three trips. The logical test arguments within the formula should reference the pseudo-code cells on the Lists worksheet to allow for flexibility if the conditional values should be later adjusted.
   - Select **B4:E4**, and then double-click the **AutoFill** handle to copy down to row **32**.

g. Click cell **H4**, and then create a formula that will count the number of trips in the Miles range that have mileage greater than in H3.

h. The cell range G7:J11 will determine the number of rentals that had damage or a repair note. It is set up to input the Make in I7, currently listed as Honda, and all the associated Models will be listed in cell range H9:H11. Then, the number of Damage and Repair notices will be counted for each model.

- Click cell **H9**, and then create a function that will pull the first model from the range that is associated with the make that is listed in I7 (*Hint*: Use an INDIRECT function to reference the Make array, and G9 as the row number). Copy the formula down to **H11**.
- Click cell **I9**, and then create a formula that will count the number of records that have Damage (as defined in cell I8) for the Model that is listed in cell H9. This formula should be copied to **I9:I11**. Click cell **J9**, and then apply a similar formula, but replace the Damage criteria with the Repair criteria found in cell J8. Copy the formula down to **J11**.

i. Create a database function to find the most recent date a car was rented.

- Click the **RentalData worksheet tab**, and then copy the field labels **A11:L11**. Click the **Report worksheet tab**, and then paste the field headings to cell **A35**.
- Click cell **C36**, and then type H8. Click cell **A39**, and then type Car. Click cell **B38**, and then type Last Driven as the headings for the formula.
- Click cell **B39**, and then create a DMAX function using the Rental_ALL database to find the largest Date (B35) for the criteria range that has been set up (A35:L36). Using the MAX will find the largest number, which will equate to the latest or most recent date. Format cell B39 for Date.

j. Click the **RentalData worksheet tab**, click cell **A11**, and then create a PivotTable on a new worksheet named Pivot.

- The Note field should be the Report Filter.
- Date should be the Row Labels.
- Gender should be the Column Labels. Change the M, F to Male and Female.
- Price should be summed in the Values area as Sum of Price and formatted as Currency with two decimal places.
- Create a slicer for Standing and filter for Fresh. Position the slicer to the right of the PivotTable.
- Right-click any of the PivotTable date cells, and then click **Group**. In the Grouping dialog box, use 2/1/2011 as a starting date and 5/13/2011 as an ending date, and then click to group by Months.

k. Insert the filename into the left footer section of all the worksheets on the file. Return to **Normal** view.

l. As needed, change the print orientation to **Landscape** to determine a good fit for printing. Click **Save**. Print of submit your files as directed by your instructor. Close Excel.

Perform 3: Perform in Your Career

Student data file needed:

e03_pf3_Police_Training

You will save your file as:

Lastname_Firstname_e03_pf3_Police_Training

Police Training Tracker

One of the first jobs you have been assigned as a new hire with the local police department is to pull together a spreadsheet to track the various training activities offered on a regular basis to help keep all employees updated on preparedness. Some data has been placed into a spreadsheet that shows the training activities. For some training, there is a score and certification process. Other activities, such as exercise, do not require scoring or certification. Your task is to set up formulas to track the activities.

a. Start **Excel**, and then open **e03_pf3_Police_Training**. Save your file as Lastname_Firstname_ e03_pf3_Police_Training replacing Lastname and Firstname with your own name.

b. Click the **List worksheet tab**, select **A2:C19**, and then create ranges from selection with top row field name to be used as column range names.

c. Click the **Training worksheet tab**, and then click cell **A20** to set up a table as follows.
   - Create an Excel table with the Training data.
   - Click cell **G20**, and then add Class_Type as a field.
   - Click cell **H20**, and then add Reimbursement as a field.
   - Click cell **I20**, and then add Result as a field.
   - Click cell **J20**, and then add Points as a field.
   - Click cell **G21**, and then create a function with a nested OR function that will look at the Class_Name and, when equal to Combat or WeightLifting or Exercise, the Class_Type will return Physical; otherwise, the formula will return Class.
   - Click cell **H21**, and then create a function that will determine the level of reimbursement. The lookup value will be based on the Score field, but the reimbursement schedule is different for Physical training versus Class training. The table_array range will be based on whether the Class_Type is Physical or Class, to determine which reimbursement schedule will be provided from the List worksheet (*Hint*: Use an INDIRECT nested function). Format the Reimbursement column as Percentage with no decimal places.
   - Click cell **I21**, and then create a formula that will determine the outcome of the Score field. If the Score is greater than zero, a function can return the value from the second column in the Results array as Passed, Honors, or Retake. If the Score is not greater than zero, a blank cell formula result should be returned. The time for each activity is required to be in 30-minute increments.
   - Click cell **J21**, and then create a formula that divides the Time field value by 30 and multiples this value by an HLOOKUP value found in the third row of the ClassInfo array based on the Class_Name value. Format the Points column results with no decimal places.
   - Select the **entire table range**, including row 20 with field labels. Name the entire range Training_All. Create from the selection named ranges for each top row column field label.

d. Create an Advanced filter on the Training worksheet.
   - Copy the **A20:J20** data field labels, and then paste to cell **A1** for the criteria range. Click cell **C2**, and then type Weapons as the Class_Name criteria.
   - Run the Advanced filter, verify the correct table range is selected as the List range, and then use the A1:J2 criterion setup for the Criteria range.
   - Click cell **A5**, and then create a function that will sum the training Cost for the filtered records.
   - Click cell **A8**, and then create a function that will average the Score for the filtered records.

e. On the Report worksheet, calculations need to be created to track training further.
   - Click cell **B1**, and then type your Firstname Lastname.
   - Click cell **C4**, and then create a complex function to return the PID value for the Last Name in C3. Ensure no error messages will appear if no name exist in C3, having a No PID instead. (*Hint*: Work with INDEX and MATCH.)

f. For each officer, summary data should be calculated in the table that starts in cell **A7**.
   - Click cell **B8**, and then create a function that will count the number of PID_Entry training sessions for the officer that is listed in A8.
   - Click cell **C8**, and then create a function that will list the average Score obtained for the PID_Entry officer that is listed in A8.
   - Click cell **D8**, and then create a function that will count the number of times an "Honors" rating for the Result field was obtained for the PID_Entry officer that is listed in A8.

- Click cell **E8**, and then create a function that returns the value Gold if the B8 Courses result is greater than 4 courses, and the B8 Courses number equals the D8 Num Honors earned in all courses taken. Gold status should be returned if both conditions are met and a blank cell returned otherwise.

- Click cell **F8**, and then create a function that will add the Points earned by the PID_Entry officer listed in A8.

- Click cell **G8**, and then create a complex logical function that will evaluate the training and return an "Improvement Plan" or "Okay" Status. Two OR conditions need to be met to return an Okay Status. First, if the officer has Points greater than 7 *and* an Average Score better than 72. Secondly, if the Courses completed are greater than 3 *and* an Average Score greater than 78. If either combination is true, Okay should be returned; otherwise, Improvement Plan should be returned.

- Select **B8:G8**, and then double-click the **AutoFill handle** to copy the formulas down to row 24. Adjust the column widths as needed to display the contents.

g. A database criteria should be set up for looking at a subset of data.
- Click the **Training worksheet tab**, copy the field labels in **A20:J20** into cell **A27** on the Report worksheet.
- Click cell **C28**, and then type Weapons as a Class_Name criterion.
- Click cell **B32**, and then create a database function that will find the average B31 Score field in the Training_All database using the criteria in A27:J28.
- Click cell **E32**, and then create a database function that will find the total E31 Cost field in the Training_All database using the criteria in A27:J28.

h. Click the **Training worksheet tab**, click cell **A20**, and then create a PivotTable on a new worksheet named Pivot.
- The Cost should be summarized in the Values as Sum of Cost.
- Class_Type should be in the Column Labels.
- Class_Name should be in Row Labels under Date.
- Date should be in the Row Labels, grouped by quarter.
- Filter the Column Labels for Class.
- Group the Date by Quarters, and then if necessary click to deselect Months.
- Subtotals should be shown at the bottom of each quarter group.

i. Using the PivotTable, create a Clustered Bar PivotChart with chart style 2, on a new worksheet named Chart1.

j. Insert the filename into the left footer section of all the worksheets on the file. Return to **Normal** view.

k. Click **Save**. Change the print orientation to **Landscape**, if necessary, to determine a good fit for printing. Print or submit your files as directed by your instructor. Click **Save**, and then close Excel.

Perform 4: How Others Perform

Student data file needed:	You will save your file as:
e03_pf4_Shipping	Lastname_Firstname_e03_pf4_Shipping

ABC Distributor Shipping

ABC Distributor ships to its retail companies across the United States. Shipments are typically in quantities of 20 to 500 units. The company examines shipping data to evaluate and adjust the shipments of items and reduce shipping expenses. In the spreadsheet provided, they have data with some analysis started. They know there are issues and would like help getting things straightened out along with setting up and customizing additional information.

a. Start **Excel**, and then open **e03_pf4_Shipping**. Save your file as Lastname_Firstname_ e03_pf4_Shipping replacing Lastname and Firstname with your own name.

b. Click the **ShipData worksheet tab**, and then click cell **B6**. A table has been set up and a calculated field was added, but the formulas need to be developed and possibly corrected for the existing calculation.

- Click cell **H16**. The function that will retrieve the weight from the ProductWeights named range was set up, but it seems to be giving an error message. Check the formula and make sure it will retrieve the weight correctly.
- Click cell **I16**, and then create a function that will retrieve the Category in the second row of the Size_Category_List array, using the Weight field as the lookup value.
- Click cell **J16**, and then create a formula that will find the shipping Unit_Cost by dividing ShipCost by Qty shipped.

c. Create an Advanced filter on the ShipData worksheet.

- Copy **A15:J15**, and then paste it in cell **A1** to set up the criteria field headings on Row 1.
- Click cell **D2**, and then type Cleveland in as a criterion for City.
- Run the Advanced filter using the criteria range set up.

d. Set up some calculations on the filtered data based on one of three data fields specified in cell B5.

- Click cell **B6**, and then create a function that will find the average of the filtered data based upon the field name listed in B5.
- Click cell **B7**, and then create a function that will find the sum of the filtered data based upon the field name listed in B5.

e. Click the **Report worksheet tab**. Database stats need to be created or corrected.

- Click cell **B1** and type your Firstname Lastname.
- Set up a criteria range starting in cell A3.
- Click cell **E4**, and then type CA to add as criterion for the State.
- Click cell **B7**, and then create a function that will average the field listed in B6 for the ShipData_All database using the criteria range A3:J4.
- Click cell **B8**, and then create a function that will find the minimum of the field listed in B6 for the ShipData_All database using the criteria range A3:J4.
- Click cell **B9**, and then create a function that will find the maximum of the field listed in B6 for the ShipData_All database using the criteria range A3:J4.
- Click cell **B10**, and then create a function that will find the sum of the field listed in B6 for the ShipData_All database using the criteria range A3:J4.

f. The largest transactions need to be found.

- Click cell **G6**, and then find the largest ShipCost from the ShipData.
- Click cell **G7**, and then knowing the largest shipping cost value in G6, create a function to find the City location in conjunction with the row number for the largest shipping cost value in G6.
- Click cell **G9**, and then find the largest Qty shipped from the ShipData.
- Click cell **G10**, and then similar to the function developed in cell G7, find the City location for the row number that had the largest shipment quantity value in G9.

g. Summary data was started and needs to be completed for the cities where shipments have been sent.

- Click cell **B14**, and then use a function to find the average ShipCost of shipments to the City range listed in A14. Use the AutoFill feature to fill in the formula down to **B28**.

- Click cell **E14**, and then use a function to find the total number of shipments to the City listed in A14. Use the AutoFill feature to fill in the formula down to **E28**.

- Click cell **F14**. An IF function with a nested AND function has been created that should evaluate the shipments and return Evaluate if the record meets the criteria indicating that the shipment should be reviewed; otherwise, a blank cell is returned. The List worksheet offers pseudo-code for Evaluation 1 in cells D3:G7. The function will check if the number of Times_Rushed divided by Shipments to the city is greater than 0.25 (reflected in cell G5 on the List worksheet), and the average unit weight (Ave_Wt) is equal to LG in the Size_Category_List array, then the shipment will be evaluated. But, it appears that something may not have been set up correctly. Check the formula cell references to determine if it makes logical sense (*Hint*: Also name errors can sometimes indicate that text values are missing quotes). Correct the formula so it works correctly. Use the AutoFill feature to fill in the formula down to **F28**.

- Click cell **G14**, and then create an IF function that will evaluate the shipments a second time and return Evaluate if the shipment meets the criteria; otherwise, the formula should return a blank cell. For this second evaluation, two OR conditions should return an Evaluation result. First, if the Ave_Cost is greater than 300 or secondly, when the Ave_Cost is greater than 200 *and* the Times_Rushed have been three or more. The List worksheet offers pseudo-code for Evaluation 2 in cells D9:G14. Use the AutoFill feature to fill in the formula down to **G28**.

h. Click the **ShipData worksheet tab**, click cell **A15**, and then create a PivotTable that is on a new worksheet named Pivot.

- The City field should be in the Report Filter.

- The Size_Cat field should be in the Column Labels.

- The Date field should be in the Row Labels.

- The ShipCost field should be summed for Values as the Sum of ShipCost.

- The Date should be grouped by Months and Quarters.

- Subtotals should be included at the bottom of each quarter group.

i. Create a Line with Markers PivotChart for the PivotTable on a new worksheet that is named Pivot_Chart using the default chart style.

j. Insert the filename into the left footer section of all the worksheets on the file. Return to **Normal** view.

k. Save your file. Change the print orientation to **Landscape**, as needed, to determine a good fit for printing. Print or submit your files as directed by your instructor. Click **Save**, and then close Excel.

WORKSHOP 7

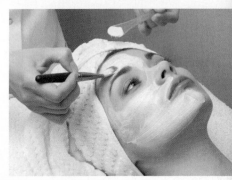
Courtesy of www.Shutterstock.com

Objectives

1. Group worksheets.
   p. 332

2. Fill contents and formats across worksheets.
   p. 340

3. Reference data between and among worksheets.
   p. 343

4. Work with multiple workbooks.   p. 352

5. Use and create templates.   p. 361

Working with Multiples and Templates

PREPARE CASE
Turquoise Oasis Spa Therapist Sales and Service Analysis

The Turquoise Oasis Spa serves resort guests with a full range of services ranging from traditional and alternative massage to aroma and detoxification therapy. The spa is open seven days a week. Meda Rodate, the spa manager, would like a workbook that allows her to summarize and compare the sales of each therapist and service for each day the spa is open.

A worksheet created from the salon and spa point-of-sales system each week can be used for the source of spa sales data. Each sale is listed by location, date, time, product, and therapist.

Student data files needed for this workshop:

 e04_ws07_Spa_Analysis   e04_ws07_SpaSales_Daily   e04_ws07_SpaSalon_Prices   e04_ws07_Invoice_w-tax.xltx

You will save your files as:

 Lastname_Firstname_e04_ws07_Amortization_Schedule   Lastname_Firstname_e04_ws07_Spa_Invoice

 Lastname_Firstname_e04_ws07_Spa_Analysis(linked)   Lastname_Firstname_e04_ws07_SpaSales_Daily

 Lastname_Firstname_e04_ws07_SpaInvoice_Template.xltx   Lastname_Firstname_e04_ws07_SpaSalon_Prices

 Lastname_Firstname_e04_ws07_SpaSalon_Prices(Kia)   Lastname_Firstname_e04_ws07_SpaSalon_Prices(Rodate)

 Lastname_Firstname_e04_ws07_Spa_Analysis   Lastname_Firstname_e04_ws07_TurquoiseSpa_Workspace.xlw

Working with Multiple Worksheets

An Excel workbook can contain many, potentially hundreds, of worksheets. A single work-sheet is a two-dimensional object: the rows are one dimension, and columns represent a second dimension. When a workbook contains more than one worksheet, the multiple worksheets can represent the third dimension as long as the worksheets share an identical layout. Data from multiple worksheets can be referenced to generate new data via formulas, functions, and consolidation. Data can be copied and pasted from one worksheet to another and can be filled from one worksheet to many worksheets. Multiple worksheets can be selected at the same time, called **grouping**, and actions such as data entry and formatting can affect all the worksheets in the group at once, greatly increasing efficiency.

Data can be accessed between worksheets using 3-D references, and even named ranges can include cells from multiple worksheets—these are called, not surprisingly, 3-D named ranges. In this section of the workshop, you will learn to work efficiently with multiple worksheets in a workbook.

To Get Started

a. Open **Excel**.

b. Click the **File tab**, and then click **Open**.

c. In the Open dialog box, navigate to where the student data files are located, and then double-click **e04_ws07_Spa_Analysis** to open the file.

   A workbook has already been started by Meda Rodate. She included data for product pricing in the Price_List worksheet and sales for December 16, 2013, in the Spa_Sales worksheet. She also created three worksheets, one for each of the spa therapists: Christy Istas, Kendra Mault, and Jason Niese.

d. Click the **File tab**, click **Save As**, and then in the Save As dialog box, navigate to the location where you are saving your files. In the File name box type Lastname_Firstname_e04_ws07_Spa_Analysis replacing Lastname_Firstname with your own name, and then click **Save**.

Grouping (and Ungrouping) Worksheets

Grouping worksheets allows you to perform certain tasks once and have those tasks affect the same cells for all worksheets in the group. There are a couple of ways to group worksheets. You can click the tab of a worksheet, hold down Ctrl, and then click the worksheet tab of additional worksheets you want to include in the group. The tabs of each worksheet included in the group will be highlighted with a white (or lighter) background color as a visual indicator. Alternatively, if all of the worksheets you would like to group are contiguous to one another, you can click the worksheet tab of a worksheet on one end, hold down Shift, and then click the worksheet tab on the other end of the contiguous worksheets.

Ungrouping worksheets is accomplished by either right-clicking a grouped worksheet tab and selecting Ungroup Sheets from the shortcut menu, or by clicking the tab of a worksheet that is not grouped.

There are many Excel features that are not available for grouped worksheets; for example, conditional formatting cannot be directly applied to grouped worksheets. But if your workbook contains several worksheets that share a similar structure, for actions like entering column and row headings, formatting text, entering formulas, and so on, grouping worksheets is a very efficient way to perform an action once and have it reflected in the content of several worksheets.

To Group and Ungroup Worksheets and to Identify Logical Worksheet Groups Using Tab Color

a. Click the **Istas_Christy worksheet tab**.

b. Press and hold Shift, and then click the **Niese_Jason worksheet tab**.

The Istas_Christy, Mault_Kendra and Niese_Jason worksheets are grouped. Shift can be used to click the first and the last of a group of worksheets—all worksheets between will be included in the group. Notice also the [Group] tag next to the filename in the title bar that indicates you are in grouped worksheet mode.

c. Right-click the **Istas_Christy worksheet tab**, click **Tab Color** from the shortcut menu, and then select **Dark Blue, Text 2, Lighter 60%** from the palette.

SIDE NOTE
An Alternative Way to Group

To select all the worksheets in a workbook, right-click on any worksheet tab and click Select All Sheets in the shortcut menu.

Figure 1 Color the tabs of grouped worksheets

d. Right-click the **Istas_Christy worksheet tab**, and then click **Ungroup Sheets** from the shortcut menu.

e. Click the **Price_List worksheet tab**, press and hold Ctrl, and then click the **Spa_Sales worksheet tab** to group the Price_List and Spa_Sales worksheets.

f. Right-click the **Price_List worksheet tab**, click **Tab Color** from the shortcut menu, and then select **Dark Blue, Text 2, Darker 25%** from the palette.

The Price_List and Spa_Sales worksheets contain source data, whereas the Istas_Christy, Mault_Kendra, and Niese_Jason worksheets will contain the analysis. By coloring their respective worksheet tabs differently, you are creating a visual differentiation between the two types of worksheets in the workbook.

g. Click the **Istas_Christy worksheet tab** to ungroup.

h. Click **Save**.

SIDE NOTE
An Alternative Way to Ungroup

You can also ungroup worksheets by clicking on the worksheet tab of a worksheet that is not in the group.

- Data can be copied from a single worksheet into grouped worksheets. Data can be copied from one set of grouped worksheets, then pasted into the same, or a different, set of grouped sheets. The criteria that determines whether or not clipboard data can be pasted into a new location are as follows:
  - The new location must have room available such that the pasted range has exactly the same shape as the copied range.
  - When multiple worksheets are grouped, the pasted range cannot overlap the copied range in any dimension; for example, copied cells from group Sheet1:Sheet2 cannot then be copied to a paste range in group Sheet2:Sheet3, but it could be pasted to Sheet1:Sheet2 as long as the rows and columns of the copied range and the paste range do not overlap.

- You can use worksheet grouping to reorder your worksheets, but remember that the group will move as one in the reordering process. If you want to reorder the placement of worksheets within a group, the worksheets need to be ungrouped and the reorder placement done manually.

- Be careful printing—if you print when worksheets are grouped, every worksheet in the group is available for print, not just the active worksheet. The Print Preview navigation information will display the available pages for printing from the group. If you only want one worksheet to print, either specify which pages to print in the print options, or ungroup and select the target worksheet.

- Many of Excel's functions are not available when worksheets are grouped, for example:
  - The entire Data tab
  - Table features and formatting
  - Conditional formatting
  - Shapes, charts, and sparklines

- *Remember to ungroup!* Everyone who works with grouped worksheets occasionally forgets to ungroup them and then makes changes to several worksheets when the objective was to make changes to the visible worksheet *only*. If you forget to ungroup worksheets, you can quickly create more work than you saved by grouping worksheets in the first place.

Data Entry

Grouping worksheets can save a lot of data entry time. Grouped worksheets make the entry of worksheet structural elements like titles, column headings, and row labels fast and efficient. Be careful though, errors made, such as misspellings or misplacement of a heading, are compounded across all grouped worksheets.

Of course you can enter structural data into a single worksheet and then copy and paste to additional worksheets one at a time, but that takes extra work and extra time, and if your workbook contains several dozen worksheets, it gets tedious. Plan ahead and group worksheets.

To Enter Data into Grouped Worksheets

a. Click the **Istas_Christy worksheet tab**, press and hold Shift, and then click the **Niese_Jason worksheet tab**.

b. Click cell **A1**, and then type Turquoise Oasis Spa.

c. Click cell **A2**, and then type A Passion for Helping People Relax.

d. Click cell **A4**, type 12/16/2013, and then press Ctrl+Enter to accept the changes and keep cell A4 selected. Click the Home tab, click **Format** in the Cells group, and then select **AutoFit Column Width**.

e. Click cell **A6**, type Time, and then press Tab. Type Service, and then press Tab. Type Charge/Hour, and then press Tab. Type Hours, and then press Tab. Type Total Charge, and then press Tab. Type Running Total.

f. Click cell **A7**, type 8:00 AM, and then press Enter. Type 8:30 AM in cell **A8**.

g. Click cell **A25**, and then type Total.

h. Select cell range **A7:A8**, grab the **AutoFill** handle, and then drag to cell **A24** to fill the selected range with time data. Cells A7:A24 should now contain a time entry for every half hour from 8:00 AM through 4:30 PM.

i. Click the **Mault_Kendra worksheet tab**. Notice that all the text entered into the Istas_Christy worksheet tab is also in the Mault_Kendra worksheet. Click the **Niese_Jason worksheet tab**—and find the same result.

j. Click the **Page Layout tab**, click **Print Titles** in the Page Setup group, click the **Header/Footer tab** in the Page Setup dialog box, and then click **Custom Footer**. Click in the **Left section** box, click **Insert File Name**, click **OK** in the Footer dialog box, and then click **OK** in the Page Setup dialog box. This inserts the file name into the footer of each grouped worksheet.

k. Press Ctrl+Home, right-click the **Istas_Christy worksheet tab**, and then select **Ungroup Sheets** from the shortcut menu.

l. Click **Save**.

Formula and Function Entry

Entering formulas and functions into grouped worksheets is a very efficient way to simultaneously create new data in multiple worksheets. Different worksheets may contain individually unique data, formulas, and cell references. To enter unique information, worksheets must not be grouped.

To Enter Formulas and Functions into Multiple Worksheets

a. Click the **Istas_Christy worksheet tab**, press and hold Shift, and then click the **Mault_Kendra worksheet tab** (the Niese_Jason worksheet is not included in this group).

b. Click cell **B7**, type =Spa_Sales!D2, and then press Ctrl+Enter to keep cell B7 active. Click the **AutoFill** handle, and then drag to cell **B24** to fill the range B8:B24.

c. Click the **Mault_Kendra worksheet tab**. Notice the formula entered and filled in the Istas_Christy worksheet was included here as well. Click the **Spa_Sales worksheet tab** to ungroup. Cell range D2:D19 includes the sales for Christy Istas, so inclusion of those formulas in the Kendra Mault worksheet is incorrect. The worksheets should not be grouped for the entry of this formula.

d. Click the **Istas_Christy worksheet tab**. Notice also the "0" in several of the cells in B7:B24. Those cells contain "0" because the source cell in the Spa_Sales worksheet is blank. The formula in each cell in the range B7:B24 is evaluated, and if it returns a blank, a zero is automatically inserted. By default, formulas that reference data from other worksheets cannot return blanks—blanks are replaced with "0". Click cell **B7**, and then type =IF(D7=0," ",Spa_Sales!D2).

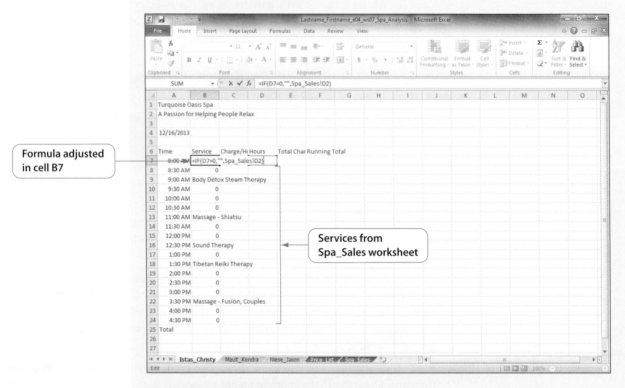

Formula adjusted in cell B7

Services from Spa_Sales worksheet

Figure 2 Spa services included from source data

e. Press Ctrl + Enter, click the **AutoFill** handle, and then drag down to cell **B24** to fill the cell range B8:B24—B7:B24 should show all blanks.

f. Click cell **D7**, type =, click the **Spa_Sales worksheet tab**, and then click cell **E2**. Press Ctrl + Enter, click the **AutoFill** handle, and then drag to cell **D4** to fill the cell range D8:D24.

g. Repeat steps d–f for the Mault_Kendra worksheet replacing the formula cell reference D2 with cell reference D20 in step d. In step f, click **E20** instead of E2.

h. Repeat steps d–f for the Niese_Jason worksheet replacing the formula cell reference D2 with cell reference D38 in step d. In step f, click **E38** instead of E2.

i. Click the **Istas_Christy worksheet tab**. Press and hold Shift, and then click the **Mault_Kendra worksheet tab**. The Niese_Jason worksheet is not selected as part of the group. You will use a different Excel feature to complete Mr. Niese's worksheet later in this exercise.

j. Click cell **C7**, type =VLOOKUP(B7,ProductTable[#Data],3,FALSE), and then press Ctrl + Enter. Use the **AutoFill** handle to copy the formula to the **C7:C24** cell range.
   ProductTable is the name of a table in the Price_List worksheet. ProductTable[#Data] is a "structured reference," a specific syntax by which tables references can be included in formulas.

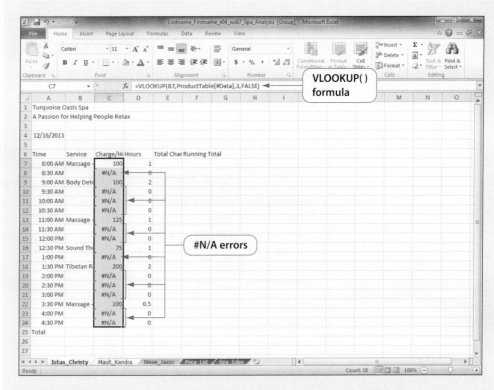

Figure 3 Charge/Hour included using the VLOOKUP function against a Price_List worksheet table

SIDE NOTE
#N/A?

When Excel displays "#/N/A" in a cell, this generally means that a value could not be found, such as a matching result in a VLOOKUP( ) function.

SIDE NOTE
A Shortcut to AutoSum

Rather than click the Home tab or the Formulas tab to gain access to the AutoSum function, you can press Alt+[=] to invoke the AutoSum function in the active cell at any time.

k. The #N/A values in many of the cells in cell range C7:C24 are unsightly. Click cell **C7**, type =IF(D7>0,VLOOKUP(B7,ProductTable[#Data],3,FALSE),0), and then press Ctrl+Enter. This formula only looks up the Charge/Hour if the value for the number of service hours is greater than 0.

l. Use the **AutoFill** handle to copy the formula to cell range **C8:C24**. click cell **E7**, type =D7*C7, press Ctrl+Enter. Use the **AutoFill** handle to copy the formula to cell range **E8:E24**.

m. Click cell **F7**, type =E7, and then press Enter. In cell **F8**, type =F7+E8, and then press Ctrl+Enter. Use the **AutoFill** handle to copy the F8 formula to cell range **F9:F24**.

n. Click cell **D25**, click the **Home tab**, and then click **AutoSum** Σ in the Editing group (alternately press Alt+[=]). Make sure the range D7:D24 is selected, and then press Ctrl+Enter.

o. Press Ctrl+C, click cell **E25**, and then press Ctrl+V.

p. Click cell **C25**, and then type =E25/8 to calculate the average charge per 8-hour work day. Press Ctrl+Enter.

q. Press Ctrl+Home, right-click the **Istas_Christy worksheet tab**, and then select **Ungroup Sheets** from the shortcut menu.

r. Click **Save** 🖫.

There is more than one way to identify table and range names that have been defined in a workbook:

- Click the Name Box arrow and a list of all table and range names will be displayed.

- To open the Name Manager dialog box:

  - Press Ctrl + F3 , or

  - Click the Formula tab, and then click the Name Manager button in the Defined Names group.

For ease of documentation, for range names only, you can select a location in your workbook that has room for two columns and several rows of data. Click Use in Formula in the Defined Names group of the Formulas tab. Select Paste Names from the menu, then click Paste List. This actually creates a list of range names and their definitions.

Cell Formatting

By grouping worksheets, you can apply cell formatting to multiple worksheets at once. For example, any of the formatting tools in the Font, Alignment, and Number groups can be applied to grouped worksheets. Any Ribbon tools that are not available when worksheets are grouped will be grayed out.

Formatting cannot be applied to grouped worksheets for any cells already formatted as part of a table. Table formatting cannot be applied to grouped worksheets, nor can any modifications to cell formats—or cell contents—inside a table be applied when worksheets are grouped. Entire tables can be filled across worksheets, the target worksheets will contain a new table, and parts of tables can be filled to other worksheets, but the results will not be formatted as a table.

To Format Cells in a Set of Grouped Worksheets

a. Click the **Page Layout tab**, click **Themes** in the Themes group, and then select **Flow** from the gallery.

b. Click the **Istas_Christy worksheet tab**, press and hold Shift , and then click the **Niese_ Jason worksheet tab**. Click the **Home tab**.

c. Click cell **A1**, click the **Font Size arrow** 11 ▾ , and then change the font size to **18**.

d. Click cell **A2**, click the **Font Size box** 11 ▾ , with font size text selected, type 13, and then press Enter .

e. Select cell range **A1:F2**, and then click the **Format Cells: Alignment dialog box launcher** ⊡ in the Alignment group. In the Format Cells dialog box, click the **Horizontal arrow**, select **Center Across Selection** on the Alignment tab, and then click **OK**.

f. Click the **Font Color arrow** A ▾ .

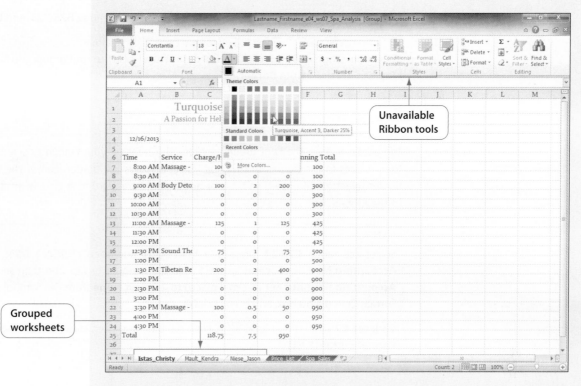

Figure 4 Formatting cells in a set of grouped worksheets

g. Select **Turquoise, Accent 3, Darker 25%** from the Theme Colors in the gallery, and then click **Bold** **B** in the Font group.

h. Select cell range **A2:F2**, click **Cell Styles** in the Styles group, and then select **Heading 2** under Titles and Headings in the gallery.

i. Click cell **A4**, and then click **Bold** **B** in the Font group.

j. Select columns **A:F**, click **Format** in the Cells group, and then click **AutoFit Column Width**.

k. Click the **Mault_Kendra worksheet tab**, and then click the **Niese_Jason worksheet tab**. Notice the formatting was applied to all three of the worksheets in the group.

l. Select cell range **A6:F25**. Notice that Format as Table in the Styles group is grayed out.
   It is not possible to format a cell range as a table when worksheets are grouped. The remainder of this exercise will be performed on the Istas_Christy worksheet only.

m. Right-click the **Istas_Christy worksheet tab**, and then select **Ungroup Sheets** from the shortcut menu.

n. With cell range A6:F25 still selected, click **Format as Table** in the Styles group. Click **Table Style Medium 18** from the gallery. Make sure the **My table has headers** check box is checked in the Format As Table dialog box, and then click **OK**.

o. If necessary, click the **Design tab**, click **Convert to Range** in the Tools group, and then click **Yes** in response to "Do you want to convert the table to a normal range?" Using the Fill option Across Worksheets will be much simpler in the coming exercises if you convert the table to a range.

p. Select cell range **A7:A25**, press and hold Ctrl, select cell range **B25:F25**, and then click **Bold** B in the Font group.

q. Select cell range **A25:F25**, click the **Borders arrow** in the Font group, and then select **Top and Thick Bottom Border**.

Troubleshooting

The border icon in the Font group may look different on your computer screen than it does in the figures in this text. Excel displays the border icon of the last border selection you used, so there is not a single standard icon that is displayed in the Ribbon.

r. Select cell range **C7:F24**, press and hold Ctrl, and then click cell **D25**. Click the **Accounting Number Format** arrow $ · in the Number group, and then select **More Accounting Formats**. Set Decimal places to **2**, select **None** from the Symbol list in the Format Cells dialog box, and then click **OK**.

s. Click cell **C25**, press and hold Ctrl, click cell **E25**, and then click **Accounting Number Format** button $ ·.

t. Press Ctrl + Home, and then click **Save** 💾.

Filling Contents and Formats Across Worksheets

Fill Across Worksheets can be used to copy cell contents, formats, or contents and formats (All) to worksheets in a group. The source and destination worksheets must all be included in the group. Unlike copy and paste, where cells can be copied from one location in a worksheet to a different location in the same worksheet or a different worksheet, Fill Across Worksheets will only fill to the same location in different worksheets; for example, cell A5 in Sheet1 can only be filled to cell A5 in other worksheets. The Istas_Christy worksheet is complete for both tabular content and format. To apply content and format to the other therapists' worksheets, care is required to avoid losing therapist-specific content in columns B and D.

Contents

When using Fill Across Worksheets, the decision of whether to fill All, Contents, or Formats is dependent on what exactly you need to copy. Choose Contents when the target worksheets are already formatted or will be formatted differently than the source worksheet.

In the next exercise, you will choose Contents and Fill to one worksheet that is already formatted and one that is not formatted to illustrate exactly what Fill Contents does.

To Fill Across Worksheets—Contents Only

a. Click the **Niese_Jason worksheet tab**. Notice that cell range C7:C24 does not contain any content. Click the **Istas_Christy worksheet tab**. Select cell range **C6:C24** in the Istas_Christy worksheet, press and hold Ctrl, and then click the **Niese_Jason worksheet tab**.

b. Click the Home tab, click **Fill** in the Editing group, select **Across Worksheets** in the menu, and then select **Contents** in the Fill Across Worksheets dialog box.

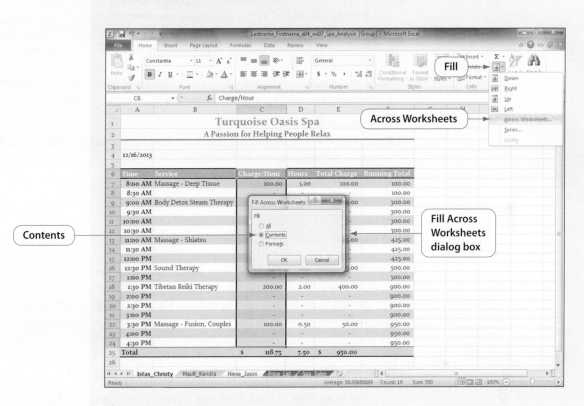

Figure 5 Istas_Christy:Niese_Jason worksheets grouped for Fill Across Worksheets

c. Click **OK**.

d. Click the **Niese_Jason worksheet tab**. Notice that the contents from cell range C6:C24 in the Istas_Christy worksheet have been filled to the Niese_Jason worksheet, but the formatting in the Niese_Jason worksheet was not changed.

e. Press Ctrl+Home, click the **Mault_Kendra worksheet tab** to ungroup the sheets, and then click **Save**.

SIDE NOTE

Fill Across Worksheets and Tables

Fill Across Worksheets will create new tables in target worksheets if an entire table is selected in the source worksheet.

Formats

Fill Across Worksheets—Formats should be used when the target worksheet(s) contain content that you do not want to overwrite. An example in this exercise is the formulas in cell range B7:B24. The content of each therapist's worksheet is unique and therefore copy formats will create identical formatting without affecting therapist-specific content.

To Fill Across Worksheets, Formats Only

a. Click the **Istas_Christy worksheet tab**, and then select cell range **A6:D24**.

b. Press and hold ⌈Shift⌉, and then click the **Niese_Jason worksheet tab**. Click the **Niese_Jason worksheet tab** and notice the lack of formatting. Click the **Mault_Kendra worksheet tab** and notice the lack of formatting. Click the **Istas_Christy worksheet tab**.

c. Click the **Home tab**, click **Fill** 🔽 in the Editing group, and then select **Across Worksheets** in the menu. Click the **Formats** option in the Fill Across Worksheets dialog box, and then click **OK**. Click the **Niese_Jason worksheet tab**. Notice that cell formats for range A6:D24 match the worksheet for Istas_Christy, but that cell content did not change. Click cell **B7**, and then notice that the content in cell B7 references Spa_Sales!D38, the sales data for Jason Niese. Click cell D7, and notice that the content still references Spa_Sales!D38. Since the Mault_Kendra worksheet is grouped as well, click the **Mault_Kendra worksheet tab**. Notice the filled formatting and that the content of the target range was not changed.

d. Press ⌈Ctrl⌉+⌈Home⌉. Right-click the **Istas_Christy worksheet tab**, select **Ungroup Sheets** from the shortcut menu, and then click **Save** 💾.

Contents and Formats

When you want the target worksheets to exactly duplicate the selected cell or cell range in the source worksheet, choose to fill both contents and formats.

In the example exercise, the content and formatting in row 25 in the Istas_Christy worksheet need to be duplicated in the other therapists' worksheets. The formulas in E7:F24 also need to be filled to the Niese_Jason worksheet. The next part of the exercise also illustrates how to apply AutoFit Column Width and Column Width to grouped worksheets.

To Fill Across Worksheets, All (Content and Formatting)

a. Click the **Istas_Christy worksheet tab**, and then select cell range **E6:F24**.

b. Press and hold ⌈Shift⌉, and then click the **Niese_Jason worksheet tab**. Click the **Mault_Kendra worksheet tab**. Notice the selected range contains formulas but not formatting.

c. Click the **Niese_Jason worksheet tab**. Notice the selected range contains neither formulas nor formatting. The selected range contains identical formulas in the Istas_Christy and Mault_Kendra worksheets, so filling All (both content and formulas) from Istas_Christy to Mault_Kendra will not damage the workbook and will allow you to "kill two birds with one stone"—fill the formatting in the Istas_Christy worksheet to the Mault_Kendra worksheet and to fill both the formatting and formulas to the Niese_Jason worksheet.

d. Click the **Istas_Christy worksheet tab**. Click the **Home tab**, click **Fill** 🔽 in the Editing group, select **Across Worksheets** in the menu, and then click **OK** in the Fill Across Worksheets dialog box.

e. Click the **Niese_Jason worksheet tab**, and then notice the results.

f. Click the **Mault_Kendra worksheet tab**, and then notice the results.

g. Click the **Istas_Christy worksheet tab**.

h. Select cell range **A25:F25**, click **Fill** 🔽 in the Editing group, select **Across Worksheets** in the menu, and then click **OK** in the Fill Across Worksheets dialog box.

i. Click the **Niese_Jason worksheet tab**, and then notice the results.

j. Click the **Mault_Kendra worksheet tab**, and then notice the results.

k. Click the **Istas_Christy worksheet tab**.

l. Select columns **A:F**, click **Format** in the Cells group, and then click **AutoFit Column Width**.

m. Click the header to select column **B**, click **Format** in the Cells group, and then select **Column Width**. Type **30** in the Column width box of the Column Width dialog box, and then click **OK**.

n. Press Ctrl+Home. Right-click the **Istas_Christy worksheet tab**, select **Ungroup Sheets** from the shortcut menu, and then click **Save** 📄.

Real World Advice Table Formatting and Fill Across Worksheets

When working with grouped worksheets, it may not be advisable to format cell ranges as a table. To apply table formatting to grouped worksheets, a workaround would be to format one worksheet as a table, then select the entire table including headings, and use Fill Across Worksheets to format any additional worksheets. However, when a range is formatted as a table, some of the functionality associated with grouped worksheets is lost. For example, data cannot be entered into tables in grouped worksheets. Table headings cannot be changed in group worksheets. Fill Across Worksheets will not fill data into tables in grouped worksheets. When you plan to work with grouped worksheets, Format as Table is an Excel feature that can be used to establish formatting quickly, but then Convert to Range may be your best plan.

Referencing Data Between and Among Worksheets

One of Excel's more powerful features is the ability to reference data between and among worksheets. If you think of a worksheet as a two-dimensional array, then multiple worksheets in a workbook can be thought of as a three-dimensional array. Multiple worksheets represent a third dimension; therefore, references that address data across multiple worksheets are called 3-D references and 3-D named ranges.

3-D References

Three-dimensional references, or **3-D references**, allow formulas and functions to utilized data from cells and cell ranges across worksheets. Cell and cell range references you have used thus far include components for columns and rows. 3-D references add a component, or dimension, for worksheets.

A 3-D reference has the following structure: Sheetname!ColumnRow. For example the 3-D reference to cell C25 in worksheet Sheet3 is Sheet3!C25. Individual cells in multiple worksheets can be referenced using a range of worksheets as well. For example, to reference cell C25 in Sheet1, Sheet2, and Sheet 3—assuming all three sheets are in that order and contiguous—the reference is specified as Sheet1:Sheet3!C25. Lastly, a range of cells can be referenced across several worksheets—the cell range C3:C25 in worksheets Sheet1 through Sheet3 is specified as Sheet1:Sheet3!C3:C25.

3-D Named Ranges

A **3-D named range** references the same cell, or range of cells, across multiple worksheets in a workbook. A 3-D named range cannot be defined in the name box; you must click Define Name in the Defined Names group of the Formulas tab.

To Create a 3-D Named Range Using a 3-D Reference

a. Click the **Istas_Christy worksheet tab**.

b. Click cell **E25**.

c. Click the **Formulas tab**, and then click **Name Manager** in the Defined Names group.

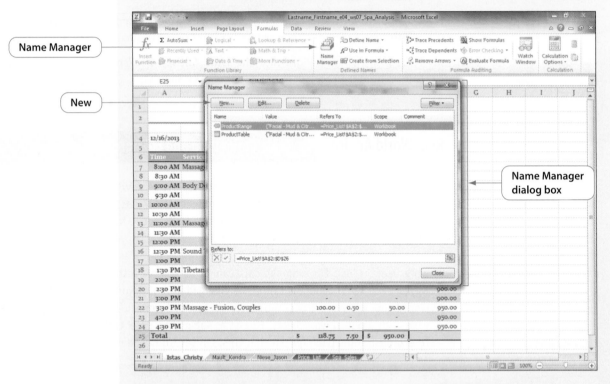

Figure 6 Name Manager dialog box

d. Click the **New button** in the Name Manager dialog box. The New Name dialog box will appear.

e. Type TotalCharge3D in the Name box.

f. To the right of the Refers to box, click the **Collapse Dialog Button** 📷. Press and hold Shift, click the **Niese_Jason worksheet tab**, and then click the **Expand Dialog Button** 📷. The Refers to box should now contain ='Istas_Christy:Niese_Jason'!$E$25.

Figure 7 New Name dialog box

g. **Click OK** in the New Name dialog box. Notice that TotalCharge3D is listed in the Name Manager. Click **Close** in the Name Manager dialog box.

h. Press Ctrl+Home. Click **Save** 💾.

Consolidating Data Across Worksheets

If your workbook contains multiple worksheets that contain either an identical structure, or data with identical row and/or column labels, you can create a summary worksheet using the Consolidate feature. Consolidated data can be generated with or without links to the original source data. Summary data created using the Consolidate feature that is not linked is not automatically updated when the source data are changed, but if you create a summary and link the consolidated data back to source data, then changes to source data are automatically reflected in the linked consolidation.

There are two ways data can be consolidated—by position and by category. **Consolidate by position** aggregates data in the same position in multiple worksheets. **Consolidate by category** aggregates data in cells with matching row and/or column labels; the labels do not need to be in the same row/column in each worksheet, there can be a different number of each label among the worksheets, and there can be a different mix of labels among the worksheets.

Consolidate Data by Position

Consolidate by position can be used to create a summary worksheet when the source worksheets all have an identical structure, such that the same location in each worksheet contains the same relative data—if cell A5 contains sales discounts for bulk sales in the January worksheet, cell A5 in worksheets February through December also contain sales discounts for bulk sales. The range selected in each worksheet must include the exact same number of rows and columns in each worksheet that is part of the consolidation.

In this exercise, you will consolidate data by position to summarize sales by appointment time.

To Consolidate Therapist Sales by Worksheet Position

a. Click the **Home tab**.

b. Click the **Insert Worksheet tab** 📝. Sheet1 will be inserted as the last worksheet in the workbook.

Troubleshooting

Can't see the Insert Worksheet tab 📝? This workbook currently contains six worksheets; you may need to scroll to the right using the tab scrolling buttons to see the Insert Worksheet tab. Alternatively, if you can see any of the Documentation worksheet tab, click on it, and the Insert Worksheet tab will be revealed to the right.

c. Drag the **Sheet1 worksheet tab** to between the Niese_Jason and Price_List worksheets.

d. Right-click on the **Sheet1 worksheet tab**, and then select **Rename** from the shortcut menu. Type Time_Summary as the new worksheet name, and then press ⏎Enter.

e. Click the **Niese_Jason worksheet tab**, select cell range **A1:F4**, press and hold ⌨Ctrl, and then click the **Time_Summary worksheet tab**. Click **Fill** in the Editing group, select **Across Worksheets**, and then click **OK**.

f. Select cell range **A6:A25**.

g. Click **Fill** in the Editing group, select **Across Worksheets,** and then click **OK**. Right-click the **Niese_Jason worksheet tab**, and then select **Ungroup Sheets** in the shortcut menu.

h. On the Niese_Jason worksheet tab, select cells **D6:F6**, and then press ⌨Ctrl+⌨C. Click the **Time_Summary worksheet tab**, click cell **B6**, and then press ⌨Ctrl+⌨V.

SIDE NOTE
Only One Per Worksheet!
A worksheet can store only one consolidation. If you want to create more than one consolidation, such as one that sums values and one that averages values, they should be placed into different worksheets.

i.   Click cell **B7**, click the **Data tab**, and then click **Consolidate** in the Data Tools group. The Consolidate dialog box will appear. In the Consolidate dialog box, make sure **Sum** is selected in the Function box. Click in the **Reference** box, click the **Istas_Christy worksheet tab**, and then select cell range **D7:F25**—you may need to scroll to the left in the worksheet tabs and move the Consolidate dialog box to make the selection.

j.   Click **Add** in the Consolidate dialog box.

k.   Click the **Mault_Kendra worksheet tab**, and then notice range D7:F25 is still selected.

l.   Click **Add** in the Consolidate dialog box.

m.   Click the **Niese_Jason worksheet tab**, and then click **Add** in the Consolidate dialog box.

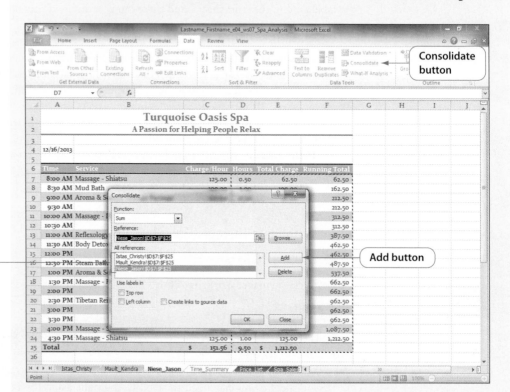

Figure 8 Consolidate dialog box

n.   Click **OK** in the Consolidate dialog box.

o.   On the Time_Summary worksheet tab, select columns **A:D**. Click the **Home tab**, click **Format** in the Cells group, and then select **AutoFit Column Width**.

p.   Click the **Niese_Jason worksheet tab**, select cell range **D6:F25**, and then press Ctrl+C. Click the **Time_Summary worksheet tab**, click cell **B6**, right-click cell **B6**, and then click **Formatting** in the Paste Options menu.

q.   Press Ctrl+Home, and then click **Save**.

Consolidate Data by Category

Consolidating by category is more flexible than consolidating by position. When consolidating by category, Excel examines row and/or column headings to determine which cells should contribute to a given calculation. Data do not need to be in the same relative position between and among worksheets; they simply need to share the same row and/or column labels. Labels can even be repeated multiple times in a single worksheet.

In this exercise you will consolidate therapists' sales by service, rather than by time. Because there is no way of knowing ahead of time where specific services will be located in the source worksheets, consolidation by category is the only realistic option.

To Consolidate Sales by Service Category

a. Right-click the **Price_List worksheet tab**, select **Insert** in the shortcut menu, and then click **OK** in the Insert dialog box. Sheet2 will be inserted to the left of the Price_List worksheet.

Troubleshooting

The sheet number of the new worksheet you created may not match the worksheet name specified in this exercise if you have saved and closed your workbook since starting this workshop exercise.

b. Double-click the **Sheet2 worksheet tab** to select the worksheet name. Type Service_ Summary as the new worksheet name, and then press ⎡Enter⎤.

c. Click the **Time_Summary worksheet tab**, select cell range **A1:F4**, press and hold ⎡Ctrl⎤, and then click the **Service_Summary worksheet tab**. Click the **Home tab,** click **Fill** in the Editing group, select **Across Worksheets**, and then click **OK**.

d. Click the **Niese_Jason worksheet tab** to ungroup the worksheets. Click the **Service_ Summary worksheet tab**.

e. Click cell **A6**, and then click the **Data tab**. Click **Consolidate** in the Data Tools group. In the Consolidate dialog box, make sure Sum is selected in the Function box, and then click in the **Reference** box.

f. Click the **Istas_Christy worksheet tab**, and then select cell range **B6:E24**. Note that you don't include the Running Total because a sum of Running Total by category would be a meaningless number.

g. Click **Add** in the Consolidate dialog box, and then click the **Mault_Kendra worksheet tab**. Click **Add** in the Consolidate dialog box, and then click the **Niese_Jason worksheet tab**. Click **Add** in the Consolidate dialog box, check the **Top row box** under the Use labels in section, and then check the **Left column box** under the Use labels in section.

Figure 9 Consolidate by category

h. Click **OK** in the Consolidate dialog box.

i. Click cell **A6**, and then type Service—it is a quirk of the consolidate functionality that it does not copy the title of the leftmost column. Press ⎡Ctrl⎤+⎡Enter⎤.

j.　Click the **Home tab**, select columns **A:D**, click **Format** in the Cells group, and then select **AutoFit Column Width**.

k.　Select cell range **A6:D20**, click **Format as Table** in the Styles group, and then select **Table Style Medium 18** in the gallery. If necessary, check **My table has headers**, and then click **OK** in the Format As Table dialog box.

l.　Click the **Filter arrow** ▼ next to Service in cell A6, and then select **Sort A to Z** in the menu.

m.　Click cell **A6**, or any cell in the consolidated table, click the **Data tab**, and then click **Filter** in the Sort & Filter group.

n.　Right-click **header for column B**, and then select **Hide**. There is no need to consolidate Charge/Hour, but since it is in the middle of the data, it is easiest to include the column in the consolidated worksheet and then hide it.

o.　Click cell **A20**, type Total, and then press ⌐Tab⌐. In cell **C20**, type =SUM(.

p.　Click the **Istas_Christy worksheet tab**, and then click cell **D25**. Press and hold ⌐Shift⌐, and then click the **Niese_Jason worksheet tab**. Press ⌐Ctrl⌐+⌐Enter⌐. Cell C20 in the Service_Summary worksheet should now contain =Sum(Istas_Christy:Niese_Jason!D25).

q.　Click cell **D20**, type =SUM(TotalCharge3D), and then press ⌐Enter⌐. This SUM( ) formula uses the 3-D named range created in an earlier exercise.

r.　Select cell range **A20:D20**, press ⌐Ctrl⌐+⌐B⌐, and then click cell **D20**. Click the **Home tab**, and then click **Accounting Number Format** $ ▼ in the Number group.

s.　Press ⌐Ctrl⌐+⌐Home⌐, and then click **Save** 🖫.

Creating Links to Source Data in Consolidation

A data consolidation that contains links to source data includes the cell references for cells from other worksheets that contributed to a consolidated data result. The source cell reference details are placed into hidden rows that can be electively viewed. When consolidating by category, the creation of links to source data requires careful consideration. Consolidations for data grouped by category are often unbalanced—an unequal number of cells contribute to consolidated data results; for example, five source values may be required to generate a sum for Category A and only three may be required to generate a sum for Category B. If source data are updated and change the number of values that are required to generate a result, the consolidation cannot change its structure to compensate. So, for example, if three values contribute to the calculation of the total charge for Massage – Deep Tissue, and you change one entry for Massage – Deep Tissue to Massage – Fusion, the consolidation cannot remove one entry from the detail for Massage – Deep Tissue and add one entry to Massage – Fusion. In such a case, the entire data consolidation must be deleted and then regenerated. Some would recommend you avoid linking to source data in situations where a consolidation by category will need to be occasionally updated unless consolidation by position could be used as well.

An additional caveat is that a consolidation that will include links to source data must be placed into a worksheet separate from all source data. The Consolidate feature cannot create links to the worksheet that contains the consolidation. In this exercise you will create a linked consolidation of sales by appointment time.

To Consolidate with Links to Source Data

a. Click the **Time_Summary worksheet tab**. Press and hold Ctrl, and then drag the **Time_Summary worksheet tab** to the right to create a new worksheet: Time_Summary (2) between the Time_Summary and Service_Summary worksheets.

b. Double-click the **Time_Summary (2) worksheet tab**, type Time_Summary_Linked as the new worksheet name, and then press Enter.

c. Select rows **6:25**, right-click in the selected rows, and then select **Delete** from the menu.

d. Click cell **A6**, click the **Data tab**, and then click **Consolidate** in the Data Tools group.

e. Click **Istas_Christy!$D$7:$F$25** in the All references box, and then click **Delete**.

f. Repeat step e for **Mault_Kendra!$D$7:$F$25** and **Niese_Jason!$D$7:$F$25**.

g. Make sure **Sum** is selected in the Function box, and then click in the **Reference** box in the Consolidate dialog box.

h. Click the **Niese_Jason worksheet tab**, select cell range **A6:F25**, and then click **Add** in the Consolidate dialog box.

i. Click the **Mault_Kendra worksheet tab**, and then click **Add** in the Consolidate dialog box.

j. Click the **Istas_Christy worksheet tab**, and then click **Add** in the Consolidate dialog box.

k. Check the **Top row box** under the Use labels in section, check the **Left column box** under the Use labels in section, and then check the **Create links to source data box**.

Create links to source data check box

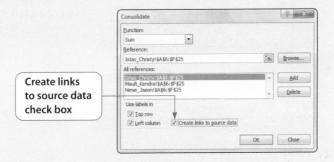

Figure 10 Consolidate data with links to source data

l. Click **OK** in the Consolidate dialog box.

m. Click the **Home tab**, click **Format** in the Cells group, and then select **AutoFit Column Width**. Click cell **A6**, and then type Time.

n. Select cell range **A10:A78**—notice that many rows are hidden, click the **Number Format arrow** General, and then select **More Number Formats** from the menu. Click **Time** in the Category box of the Format Cells dialog box, click **1:30 PM** in the Type box, and then click **OK**. Notice the Expand Outline buttons [+] to the left of rows 10:82. Click the **Expand Outline** button [+] next to row 14. Rows 11:13, which were previously hidden, are revealed. Notice the filename for your workbook is shown in column B. Consolidate can be used among multiple workbooks, and column B identifies the source workbook for each item of data. Because you are consolidating sheets in a single workbook, column B is not instructive. Click the **Collapse Outline** button [−] next to row 14 to hide rows 11:13 again.

Notice as well that column C is empty. Service names are text and cannot be summated, so column C does not contain any information. Further, Charge/Hour in column D is not particularly informative. A sum of Charge/Hour is not a meaningful number—its inclusion, while necessary for consolidation, is not meaningful.

o. Select columns **B:D**, right-click in the selected columns, and then select **Hide** from the menu.

p. Select cell range **A6:G82**, click **Format as Table** in the Styles group, and then select **Table Style Medium 18** from the gallery. Be sure **My table has headers is checked**, and then click **OK**. Click the **Home tab**, click **Sort & Filter** in the Editing group, and then click **Filter**.

q. Select cell range **A10:A78**, press and hold [Ctrl], and select cell range **A82:G82**. Press [Ctrl]+[B], and then click cell **A6**.

r. Click the **Level 2 outline** button [2] just to the left of the Select All button [ ]. The source data that contributes to each of the subtotals for a category (time in this case) is expanded.

s. Click cell **G8**. Notice the contents of the formula bar. The 50.00 in cell G8 came from source data in the Mault_Kendra worksheet, cell F7. Because a linked consolidation keeps track of the locations of source data, any changes to source data are automatically reflected in the consolidation.

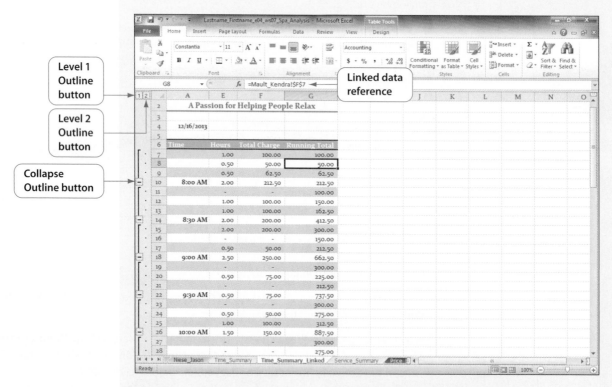

Figure 11 Level 2 Outline view of the consolidated and linked data

t. Click the **Level 1 outline** button [1], click the **Expand Outline** button [+] at row 30 to unhide the source data used to generate summated values for 10:30 AM, and then click the **Collapse Outline** button [-] to hide source data again.

u. Press [Ctrl]+[Home], and then click **Save** [ ].

Real World Advice — Consolidate Between Different Workbooks

Consolidation between workbooks can be done. The easiest way is to have all the source workbooks open, start defining the consolidation, and then navigate to each workbook, select the source range with the mouse, and add the reference to the consolidation.

Source data links work between workbooks, and data is updated if you recalculate the consolidation by pressing F9. However, just as with consolidation by category between worksheets, category labels cannot change. Changed labels will be treated as though the label had not changed for recalculation purposes.

To Document Your Work

a. Click the **Documentation worksheet tab**—you will probably have to scroll to the right by repeatedly clicking the next tab scrolling button ▶ or by clicking the last tab button ▶| once. Click cell **A5**, and then press Ctrl+;.

b. Click cell **B5**, and then type your Lastname, Firstname in that format.

c. Click cell **C5**, and then type Completed the analysis workbook for spa therapists.

d. Click cell **B5**, and then press Ctrl+C. Click cell **B17**, press and hold Ctrl, click cells **B23** and **B29**, and then press Ctrl+V.

e. Click cell **A5**, and press Ctrl+C. Click cell **B18**, press and hold Ctrl, click cells **B24** and **B30**, and then press Ctrl+V.

f. Click cell **B19**. Type Sales analysis for an individual therapist, and then press Ctrl+Enter. Press Ctrl+C. Click cell **B25**, press and hold Ctrl, and then click cell **B31**. Press Ctrl+V.

g. Select rows **27:32**, and then press Ctrl+C. Click cell **A33**, and then press Ctrl+V. Click cell **A39** (you may have to click just to the right of the Paste Options button 🗐), and then press Ctrl+V. Click cell **A45**, and then press Ctrl+V.

h. Click cell **B34**, and then type Time_Summary. Click cell **B37**, and then type Sales analysis by time of day.

i. Click cell **B40**, and then type Time_Summary_Linked. Click cell **B43**, and then type Sales analysis by time of day linked to source data.

j. Click cell **B46**, and then type Service_Summary. Click cell **B49**, type Sales analysis by spa service, and then press Enter.

k. Right-click the **Documentation worksheet tab**, and then click **Select All Sheets** in the shortcut menu. Press Ctrl+Home, right-click the **Istas_Christy worksheet tab**, and then select Ungroup Sheets in the shortcut menu.

l. Click **Save** 🖫. Leave your workbook open.

Accessing Data in Multiple Workbooks

Excel can access data in other workbooks using external references in formulas and functions. A primary advantage of the ability to reference data in multiple workbooks is that you can access data at its source—in its original location. You don't need to copy the data to your workbook and then be concerned about keeping the copied data up to date when the original data changes.

Working with Multiple Workbooks

You have already learned that when data in a workbook is changed, any data result from a formula that references that data changes. This concept holds true when the reference is to data located in another workbook as well. So you can access data in a different workbook that somebody else is responsible for maintaining. When that workbook's data values change, the values you reference in your workbook can be updated the next time you open it.

Create an Excel Workspace

Whether workbooks are linked through 3-D references or you simply need to be working on more than one workbook at a time, there is often a need to repeatedly open the same set of workbooks at the same time. The process of opening multiple workbooks can be simplified by creating an Excel Workspace. A **workspace** is a special file type that identifies multiple workbooks and remembers the manner in which you want them arranged.

A workspace is easy to create. Simply open the workbooks you want to include in the workspace, arrange them in a manner that you prefer, and save a workspace file by selecting Save Workspace in the Window group of the View tab. How you prefer to arrange your workbooks in a workspace is a function of your personal working style and possibly the resolution of your monitor. For low-resolution monitors, cascade works well, as does maximizing all workbooks and using Ctrl+Tab to move among them. For higher-resolution monitors you may want to arrange your workbooks vertically or horizontally, which ever works best for you. For this exercise you will create a workspace that includes three workbooks, place them in cascade view, and save them as a workspace.

SIDE NOTE
Try Cascade View in Your Workspaces
Cascade view overlaps all open Excel workbooks in such a way that all workbook title bars are visible and switching between workbooks can be accomplished by clicking a visible edge of the title bar for the workbook you want active. Cascade view works very well when creating a workspace if you are using a monitor with relatively low resolution, such as many netbook/notebook computers. It is easy to see at a glance all the workbooks in the workspace (as long as the number of workbooks in the workspace isn't too large).

To Create an Excel Workspace

a. Click the **File tab**, and then click **Open**.

b. In the Open dialog box, browse to navigate to where the student data files are located, click **e04_ws07_SpaSalon_Prices**, press and hold Ctrl, click **e04_ws07_SpaSales_Daily**, and then click **Open**.

c. If necessary, press and hold Ctrl and press Tab repeatedly until **Lastname_Firstname_ e04_ws07_Spa_Analysis** is the active workbook and you see the name of this file in the title bar.

d. Click the **View tab**, click **Arrange All** in the Window group, click the **Cascade** option in the Arrange Windows dialog box, and then click **OK**. Notice the active worksheet is placed on top when you put all open workbooks in the cascade arrangement.

Troubleshooting

Do you currently have more than three workbooks open? All open workbooks will be included in your workspace, so be sure to close any workbooks you do not want to include and repeat step d before saving your workspace.

e. Click **Save Workspace** in the Window group. If necessary navigate to the location where you are saving your Excel files, and then type Lastname_Firstname_e04_ws07_ TurquoiseSpa_Workspace in the File name box of the Save Workspace dialog box.

Workbooks in Cascade view

Workspace file type

Figure 12 Save an Excel workspace

SIDE NOTE

Workspaces Are Stored with a Different Extension

Recall that Excel workbooks are stored with an .xlsx extension. Workspaces are stored with an extension of .xlw.

f. Click **Save**. If prompted with a Microsoft Excel alert dialog that asks, "Do you want to save the changes...", click **Save**.

g. Click **Close** ☒ repeatedly until all open Excel workbooks are closed. If prompted with a Microsoft Excel alert dialog that asks, "Do you want to save the changes...", click **Don't Save**.

h. Click the **File tab**, and then click **Lastname_Firstname_e04_ws07_TurquoiseSpa_ Workspace** in the Recent Workbooks pane. Notice the workspace you just opened includes all three Excel workbooks.

Cell References between Workbooks—Linked Workbooks

As discussed earlier, when you need data from a different workbook, there is an advantage to referencing that data at its source rather than copying it into your workbook. Changes to data referenced in its source workbook can be reflected in your data when you open your workbook.

Excel recognizes when a workbook is linked to another workbook, or workbooks, through external reference and will prompt you when the workbook is opened, and ask whether or not you want to update links. The choice is then yours. If you want any updates to source data reflected in your workbook, select Update; otherwise, select Don't Update. Which option is the correct choice is dependent upon the workbook and the situation—whether you need the destination workbook to display the previously saved linked data or current linked data values.

Linking to other workbooks does create some potential problems, however. Links to workbooks are easily broken, especially if files are moved or deleted. Excel 2010 addresses linked workbooks by using relative addresses, where prior versions of Excel used absolute addresses. In a relative link, the address of a linked workbook is defined by its location in relation to the location of the destination workbook. If either workbook is moved when the destination workbook is closed, the links will be broken. If possible, it is considered good practice to store all workbooks in a linked relationship together in the same folder.

In this exercise you will link to two workbooks to reference data for the price of services and for therapist sales.

To Reference (Link to) Data in a Different Workbook

a. If necessary, use the [Ctrl]+[Tab] shortcut to make sure **Lastname_Firstname_e04_ ws07_Spa_Analysis** is the active workbook.

b. Click the **File tab**, and then click **Save As**. If necessary, navigate to where you are saving your student files, click in the File name box in the Save As dialog box, and then place the insertion point after **Analysis**. Type (linked).

   The file name box should contain Lastname_Firstname_e04_ws07_Spa_Analysis (linked).

c. Click **Save** in the Save As dialog box.

d. Click the **View tab**, click **Save Workspace** in the Window group, and then click **Save** in the Save Workspace dialog box. Click **Yes** if you are told the file already exists and are asked "Do you want to replace it?".

   Saving a worksheet with a new name from within a workspace does not change the file names associated with the workspace, so you had to save the workspace again to include the new file name.

e. Click the **Price_List worksheet tab**, press and hold [Ctrl], and then click the **Spa_Sales worksheet tab**. Right-click the **Spa_Sales worksheet tab**, and then select **Delete** from the shortcut menu. Click **Delete** in the Excel dialog box to confirm the deletion of the two selected worksheets, and then click the **Istas_Christy worksheet tab**.

   Notice all the formulas in columns B:F return a #REF!. When you deleted the Price_List and Spa_Sales worksheets in step e all the formulas in column B:F were broken since each formula references data in one or the other worksheet—or is dependent on a formula that does.

f. Click cell **B7** in the Istas_Christy worksheet. Click in the **formula bar**, and then highlight **#REF!D2** in the formula. Press [Ctrl]+[Tab] until the e04_ws07_SpaSales_Daily workbook is active. Click cell **D2**, and then press [Ctrl]+[Enter].

   Cell B7 in the Istas_Christy worksheet now contains a formula that references cell $D$2 in the 2013-12-16 worksheet in the e04_ws07_SpaSales_Daily workbook, but the absolute reference $D$2 is problematic in that you want this to be a relative reference when you copy this formula to the rest of the column.

g. Click in the **formula bar**, and then place the insertion point somewhere in the $D$2 absolute cell reference.

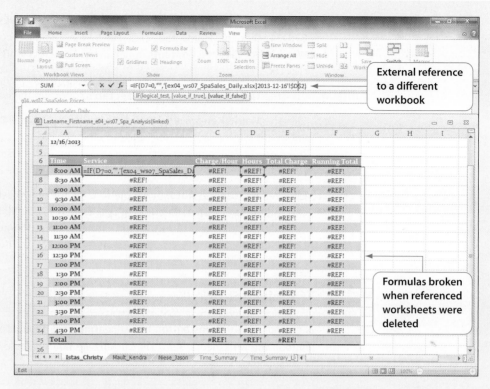

Figure 13 Edit formula to include reference to data in different workbook

h. Press F4 three times to change the absolute reference to a relative reference. Press Ctrl + Enter.

i. Click the **AutoFill** handle, and then drag down to copy to cell range **B8:B24**. A #REF! error will still be visible, but it will be fixed as remaining column data is adjusted.

j. Click the **Auto Fill Options** button ⊞, and then select **Fill Without Formatting**.

k. In the **Istas_Christy worksheet**, click cell **D7**, click in the **formula bar**, and then highlight **#REF!E2**. Press Ctrl + Tab to make the e04_ws07_SpaSales_Daily workbook active, and then click cell **E2**. Click in the **formula bar**, place the cursor somewhere in the absolute reference **$E$2**, and then press F4 three times to make the reference relative. Press Ctrl + Enter.

SIDE NOTE
A Shortcut for Moving between Open Workbooks
To move between open workbooks, press Ctrl + Tab. To move between open workbooks in the opposite order press Ctrl + Shift + Tab.

l. Use the **AutoFill** handle to copy to the cell range **D8:D24**. Click the **Auto Fill Options** button ⊞, and then select **Fill Without Formatting**.

m. In the **Christy_Istas worksheet**, click cell **C7**.

n. Click in the **formula bar**, and then highlight **#REF!**. Press Ctrl + Tab to make the e04_ws07_SpaSalon_Prices workbook active, and then select cell range **A2:D35**. This is a named range in the worksheet called **ProductRange**. Press Ctrl + Enter.

Troubleshooting

Remember that an error in Excel ends with an exclamation point! Be sure to highlight all of #REF! in the above step or the correction to the formula will not work.

o. Use the **AutoFill** handle to copy the active cell to the cell range **C8:C24**. Click the **Auto Fill Options** button ⊞, and select **Fill Without Formatting**.

p. Press and hold [Shift], and then click the **Niese_Jason worksheet tab**. Select cell range **B7:D24**, click the **Home tab**, click **Fill** in the Editing group, and then select **Across Worksheets**. Click the **Contents** option in the Fill Across Worksheets dialog box, and then click **OK**.

q. Click the **Time_Summary worksheet tab** to ungroup the worksheets.

r. Click the **Mault_Kendra worksheet tab**, and then click cell **B7**. Click in the **formula bar**, and then edit the last cell reference to change D2 to D20. The formulas in this worksheet need to reference Kendra Mault's sales, not Christy Istas'. Click cell **D7**, click in the **formula bar**, and then edit the last cell reference to change E2 to E20.

s. Click cell **B7**. Use the **AutoFill** handle to copy the active cell to the cell range **B8:B24**, click the **Auto Fill Options** button 🖳, and then select **Fill Without Formatting**. Click cell **D7**, and then use the **AutoFill** handle to copy the active cell to the cell range **D8:D24**. Click the **Auto Fill Options** button 🖳, select **Fill Without Formatting**, and then press [Ctrl]+[Home].

Troubleshooting

Is the Auto Fill Options button not appearing as it should? You probably did not ungroup the worksheets. Auto Fill Options are not available when worksheets are grouped.

t. Click the **Niese_Jason worksheet tab**, click cell **B7**, click in the **formula bar**, and then edit the last cell reference to change D2 to D38. The formulas in this worksheet need to reference Jason Niese's sales, not Christy Istas'. Click cell **D7**, click in the **formula bar**, and edit the last cell reference to change E2 to E38.

u. Click cell **B7**, and then use the **AutoFill** handle to copy the active cell to the cell range **B7:B24**. Click the **Auto Fill Options** button 🖳, and then select **Fill Without Formatting**. Click cell **D7**, and then use the **AutoFill** handle to copy the active cell to the cell range **D7:D24**. Click the **Auto Fill Options** button 🖳, select **Fill Without Formatting**, and then press [Ctrl]+[Home].

v. Click the **Istas_Christy worksheet tab**, click [Ctrl]+[Home], and then click **Save** 🖫.

Real World Advice — Don't Reference Tables in External Links

While VLOOKUP can reference linked table data in another workbook, it cannot do so unless the workbook that contains the table is open; any external table reference will return a #REF! error if the source workbook is not open. A workaround is to create a named range. Named ranges in external references are updated whether the source workbook is open or closed.

Collaborating Using Multiple Workbooks

Excel allows users to collaborate in the creation of a workbook; however, it is more common for users to collaborate in keeping data in a workbook up to date once the workbook has been developed. Excel enables collaboration by allowing you to share a workbook with other users. When a workbook is shared, you can save additional copies of your workbook for distribution. The shared copies can be changed by other users and the changes merged back into the master workbook.

The spa and salon have updated prices for a few of their services, and the price changes are not currently reflected in the e04_ws07_SpaSalon_Prices workbook. Rather than obtaining the updated prices from Meda Rodate and Irene Kia and entering them into the worksheet yourself—potentially a source of error because you would be acting as a transfer agent for the information—it is better to have Meda and Irene update copies of the workbook directly.

You need to share the e04_ws07_SpaSalon_Prices with Meda Rodate and Irene Kia and then merge their updated data into your master copy. Merging workbooks is not a functionality that is available by default in the Ribbon or Quick Access Toolbar, so you need to customize the Quick Access Toolbar to include the Compare and Merge Workbooks icon.

In the next exercise you will play three roles:

1. Yourself, as you create copies of a workbook for collaboration and later merge updated data from the copies back into the master workbook.
2. Meda Rodate, as you update prices for spa services in a collaboration copy of the e04_ws07_SpaSalon_Prices created for Meda.
3. Irene Kia, as you update prices for salon services in a collaboration copy of the e04_ws07_SpaSalon_Prices created for Irene.

To Share a Workbook for Collaborative Work

a. Press Ctrl+Tab to make e04_ws07_SpaSalon_Prices the active workbook. Click the **File tab**, click **Save As**, and then in the Save As dialog box, navigate to the folder where your student files are located. In the File name box of the Save As dialog box, type Lastname_Firstname_e04_ws07_SpaSalon_Prices, and then click **Save**.

Because Lastname_Firstname_e04_ws07_Spa_Analysis(linked) is open and it is linked to e04_ws07_SpaSalon_Prices, saving e04_ws07_SpaSalon_Prices with a new name will automatically update the links in Lastname_Firstname_e04_ws07_Spa_Analysis(linked).

b. Click the **Page Layout tab**, click **Print Titles** in the Page Setup group, click the **Header/Footer tab** in the Page Setup dialog box, and then click **Custom Footer**. Click in the **Left section** box, click **Insert File Name**, click **OK** in the Footer dialog box, and then click **OK** in the Page Setup dialog box.

c. Press Ctrl+Tab to make Lastname_Firstname_e04_ws07_Spa_Analysis(linked) the active workbook. Click **Save**, and then click **Close** to close the Lastname_Firstname_e04_ws07_Spa_Analysis(linked) workbook. If necessary, press Ctrl+Tab to make e04_ws07_SpaSales_Daily the active workbook. Click Close to close the e04_ws07_SpaSales_Daily workbook.

The Lastname_Firstname_e04_ws07_SpaSalon_Prices workbook should be the active workbook.

d. Right-click the **Quick Access Toolbar**, and then select **Customize Quick Access Toolbar** from the shortcut menu (or alternatively, click the **Customize Quick Access Toolbar** button and select **More Commands** from the menu)—you must do this before sharing the workbook because customizing the Quick Access Toolbar is not allowed in shared workbooks.

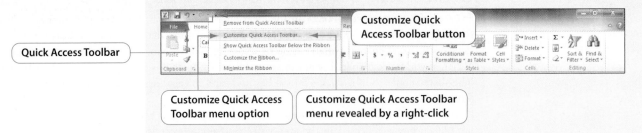

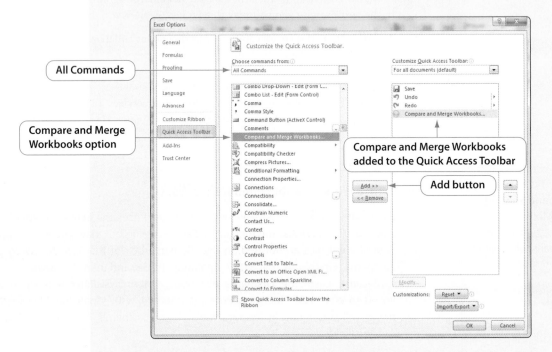

Figure 14 Customize Quick Access Toolbar shortcut menu

e. The Quick Access Toolbar pane, found in the Excel Options dialog box, will appear. Click the **Choose commands from arrow**, and then select **All Commands**. Scroll through the list of Commands, click to select **Compare and Merge Workbooks**, and then click the **Add button**.

Figure 15 Customize the Quick Access Toolbar using the Excel Options dialog box

f. Click **OK**. Compare and Merge Workbooks will now be in the Quick Access Toolbar.

g. Click the **Review tab**, and then click **Share Workbook** in the Changes group. The Share Workbook dialog box will appear. If necessary, click the **Editing tab** in the Share Workbook dialog box, check the **Allow changes by more than one user at the same time** box, and then click **OK**.

h. Click **OK** in the alert box that says This action will now save the workbook. Notice that once a workbook is shared, the Compare and Merge Workbooks icon changes to a green color .

Compare and Merge icon added to the Quick Access Toolbar

Be sure to check this box

User name you see will differ—this is the name of the user that is logged in

Share Workbook

Share Workbook dialog box

Figure 16 Share a workbook

i. Click the **File tab**, and then click **Save As**. If necessary, navigate to where you are saving your student files. In the File name box of the Save As dialog box, type Lastname_Firstname_e04_ws07_SpaSalon_Prices(Rodate), and then click **Save**.

j. Click the **File tab**, and then click **Save As**. If necessary, navigate to where you are saving your student files. In the File name box of the Save As dialog box, type Lastname_Firstname_e04_ws07_SpaSalon_Prices(Kia), and then click **Save**.

k. Irene Kia applied a few price changes for the salon a week ago. Make the following changes to the price column for the listed products in Irene's copy of the SpaSalon_Prices workbook:

Service	Price
Facial – Mud & Citrus	100
Makeup Consultation	100
Manicure & Pedicure Package	70
Manicure & Polish	45
Pedicure & Polish	45
Waxing – Body	75

Figure 17 Irene's price changes

l. Click **Save**, and then click the **Close** button ☒ in the top-right corner of the worksheet to close Lastname_Firstname_e04_ws07_SpaSalon_Prices(Kia).

m. Click the **File tab**, and then click **Firstname_Lastname_e04_ws07_SpaSalon_Prices(Rodate)** in the Recent Workbooks. If the worksheet is not maximized, click Maximize ▢ .

n. Meda Rodate put other price changes into effect for the spa a week ago. Make the following changes to the price column for the listed products in Meda's copy of the SpaSalon_Prices workbook:

Service	Price
Massage – Deep Tissue	125
Massage – Deep Tissue, Couples	112.50
Massage – Fusion	150
Massage – Fusion, Couples	137.50
Massage – Shiatsu	150
Steam Bath	75
Tibetan Reiki Therapy	225

Figure 18 Meda's price changes

o. Click **Save**. Click the **Close Window** button in the top-right corner of the worksheet pane to close Lastname_Firstname_e04_ws07_SpaSalon_Prices(Rodate).

p. Click the **File tab**, and then click **Lastname_Firstname_e04_ws07_SpaSalon_Prices** in the Recent Workbooks pane.

q. Click **Compare and Merge Workbooks** , and then click **OK** if prompted to save the workbook. Navigate to your student files and double-click **Lastname_Firstname_e04_ws07_SpaSalon_Prices(Kia)** in the Select Files to Merge Into Current Workbook dialog box. Any cell values that are changed as a result of the merge are highlighted.

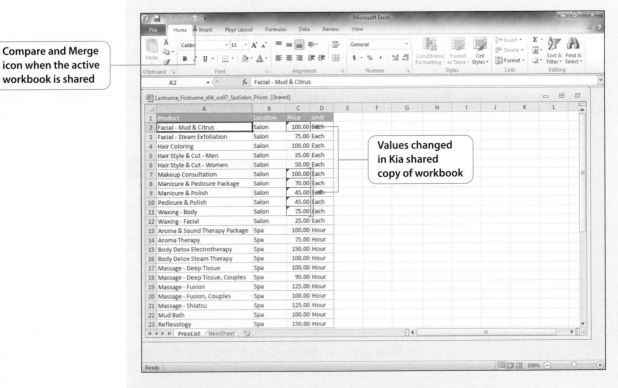

Figure 19 Values changed highlighted due to merging shared workbooks

r. Click **Compare and Merge Workbooks** ⊙, and then double-click **Lastname_ Firstname_e04_ws07_SpaSalon_Prices(Rodate)** in the Select Files to Merge Into Current Workbook dialog box.

s. Click the **Review tab**, and then click **Share Workbook** in the Changes group. In the Share Workbook dialog box, uncheck **Allow changes by more than one user at the same time**, click **OK**, and then click **Yes** in the alert that appears. The workbook is now not shared.

t. Click **Save**, and then click the **Close Window** button ☒ to close Lastname_Firstname_ e04_ws07_SpaSalon_Prices.

u. Click the **File tab**, and then click **Lastname_Firstname_e04_ws07_Spa_Analysis(linked)** in the Recent Workbooks pane.

v. Click **Update** in the This workbook contains links to other data sources alert. Alternatively, you may have to click **Enable Content** in the Security Warning bar below the ribbon.

w. Click the **Istas_Christy worksheet tab**.

Notice that, for example, the Charge/Hour for the 3:30 appointment for Massage – Fusion, Couples is now 137.50—cell C22.

x. Press ⌨Ctrl+⌨Home, click **Save** 💾, and then **Close** ☒ any remaining files.

Using Templates

Do a web search on "Excel templates" and you will find many different definitions—a model, a blueprint, just a workbook with a different extension, and so on. In reality, a template is all those things. In its simplest form, an Excel **template** is a workbook that provides a starting point for building other similar workbooks. In its intended form, a template is a worksheet framework, a worksheet that contains cell formats, structural data such as column headings and data labels, and formulas necessary to achieve the template's purpose, such as total invoice line items, calculate sales tax, or track and total the time spent on a project.

In reality, a template is just a workbook saved with a different extension—the .xltx extension. Templates, if stored in the default location, do have one special differentiator that may make their creation advantageous: they are readily available via the File tab when creating a new workbook by clicking the My templates button in the Available Templates menu. In addition, when opening templates from the default template location, the file will default to saving as a normal Excel workbook with the .xlsx extension, thereby leaving the original template file in its original form—ready to use again for future development needs.

Templates, by default, are saved to the system drive in the \Users\user name\AppData \Roaming\Microsoft\Templates folder. Any templates added to that folder are available in the My templates folder for easy access.

Any workbook can be used as a template for another workbook. Simply open a workbook and save it with the template extension and a new file name (optional).

Using Built-in Templates

Microsoft Excel has a number of built-in templates. **Built-in templates** are stored in the \Program Files\Microsoft Office\Templates\1033 folder. The number 1033 is the language ID number for English(US). This folder will change depending upon which language version of Office you have installed. Templates for all the Office applications are stored in this folder.

Built-in templates are accessed from the File tab by clicking the New tab, and then by clicking the Sample templates button in the Available Templates section. You can add your own templates to the built-in templates by saving, or moving, your templates to the built-in templates folder.

To Find, Open, and Use a Built-in Template

a. Click the **File tab**, and then click **New** in the left menu.

b. Click **Sample templates** under the Available Templates section.

c. Click the **Loan Amortization** built-in template in the gallery menu pane, and then click **Create** in the preview pane. If necessary, click **Maximize** ⬜.

d. Click the **File tab**, and then click **Save As**. Navigate to the folder where you are storing your assignment files, type Lastname_Firstname_e04_ws07_Amortization_Schedule into the File name box of the Save As dialog box, and then click **Save**.

e. Enter the following values into the amortization cells D5:D9:

	Enter values
Loan amount	250000
Annual interest rate	5
Loan period in years	30
Number of payments per year	12
Start date of loan	01/01/2014
Optional extra payments	

Figure 20 Amortization variable values

In cell range H5:J9 notice the Loan Summary. How much interest will you pay on this loan over its life? How does total cumulative interest compare to the loan amount?

f. Click the **Page Layout tab**, click **Print Titles** in the Page Setup group, click the **Header/Footer tab** in the Page Setup dialog box, and then click **Custom Footer**. Click in the **Left section** box, click **Insert File Name** 🗐, click **OK** in the Footer dialog box, and then click **OK** in the Page Setup dialog box.

g. Click **Save** 🖫, and then click **Close** ⊠ to close the workbook.

Built-in templates and templates in general are a great way to use work done by others. Remember the old saying, "Don't reinvent the wheel"? How long would it have taken you to build this loan amortization worksheet? Templates can be a big time saver.

CONSIDER THIS | **How Could Excel Facilitate Work as a Team?**

So far in this workshop, you have learned how to group worksheets, consolidate worksheets, to merge data from individual worksheets into a master worksheet, and to build and to use templates. Think about a couple of group or team projects you have been involved with in your educational career and consider how the Excel capabilities listed above might have aided your efforts with the following:

- Tracking team member contributions to a project
- Tracking project progress toward completion
- Bringing the work of team members together into one coherent final product
- Supporting a team member that is struggling with a part of the project by facilitating the involvement of other team members' assistance

How else might Excel facilitate team work in your education? How about in your career?

Using Templates on the Web (Office.com)

There are literally hundreds of Excel templates available on the World Wide Web. Microsoft, through its template site at Office.com, fosters a community of Office users who download templates posted by other users. Users can rate templates on a scale of 1 to 5 stars. User ratings are averaged, and the average is posted next to each template.

Some people are very good at generating data through formulas and functions; others are experts at presenting information graphically or at formatting tabular content attractively. People can post their templates to Office.com so others can benefit from their expertise.

In this exercise, you download a template from Office.com and use it to create a functional worksheet with a lot less effort than would be required to create it from scratch.

To Find, Open, and Use a Template at Office.com

a. Click the **File tab**, and then click **New** in the left menu.

b. Click **Invoices** in the Office.com Templates gallery, click **Service invoices** in the Invoices gallery, and then click **Invoice with tax calculation**.

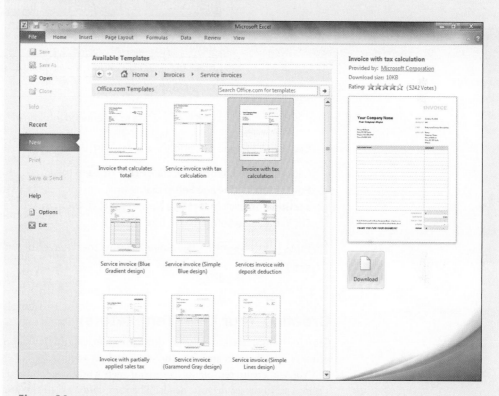

Figure 21 Office.com Templates Service invoices gallery menu

c. Click the **Download** button in the preview pane.

Troubleshooting

Office.com changes available templates occasionally. If this template is no longer available at Office.com, it is available in the student files for this workshop as e04_ws07_Invoice_w-tax.xlst.

d. Click the **File tab**, click **Save As**, and then navigate to the folder where you are storing your student files. In the File name box, type Lastname_Firstname_e04_ws07_Spa_Invoice in the Save As dialog box, and then click **Save**.

e. To personalize the company information in the template, click cell **B2**, and then type Turquoise Oasis Spa. Click cell **B3**, and then type A Passion for Helping People Relax. Click cell **B6**, and then type 3356 Hemmingway Circle. Click cell **B7**, and then type Santa Fe, NM 87549. Click cell **B8**, and then type Phone: 505.555.SPA1. Click cell **B9**, and then type Fax: 505.555.SPAx.

f. Select cell range **E7:E11**, and then press [Delete]. Click cell **D7**, and then type Room:. Click the **text box** at cell **B33**, edit the contents to change **Your Company Name** to Turquoise Oasis Spa. Be sure to keep the bold formatting.

g. Click cell **E7**, type 555, and then press [Ctrl]+[Enter]. Add the Description and Amount data starting in cell B14 using the following data:

Description	Amount
Body Detox Electrotherapy	150
Reflexology	150
Massage – Deep Tissue	125
Steam Bath	75

Figure 22   Data to be entered into the Invoice worksheet

h. Click cell **E31**, type 6.5, and then press [Ctrl]+[Enter].

i. Click the **Page Layout tab**, click **Print Titles** in the Page Setup group, click the **Header/Footer tab** in the Page Setup dialog box, and then click **Custom Footer**. Click in the **Left section** box, click **Insert File Name** 📄, click **OK** in the Footer dialog box, and then click **OK** in the Page Setup dialog box.

j. Press [Ctrl]+[Home]. Click **Save** 💾, and then leave the workbook open for the next exercise.

Creating Your Own Template(s)

Creating templates is really no different than creating workbooks—you simply remove any instance-specific data and save the workbook as a template.

You can create templates from your own workbooks, or you can create them by modifying a template to better fit your needs. The template used in the last exercise is not quite adequate for invoicing spa clients. It does not allow for the entry of the number of hours a service was delivered, and consequently it does not calculate the total for an individual service. Nor does it facilitate the lookup of service prices from an external workbook. In this exercise you will modify the invoice you created in the last exercise to create a template that is customized to the needs of the Turquoise Oasis Spa.

To Create a Template

a. Click the **File tab**, and then click **Save As** in the left menu pane. In the File name box, type Lastname_Firstname_e04_ws07_SpaInvoice_Template, and then in the Save As dialog box, select **Excel Template** in the Save as type box. The location for saving the file will change to the default templates folder—navigate to the folder where you save your student files.

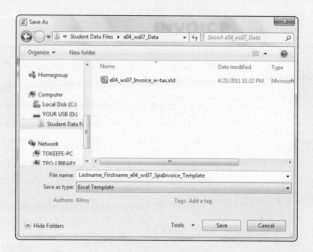

Figure 23 Save the Spa Invoice workbook as a template

b. Click **Save**.

c. Click the **Home tab**, select cell range **B13:B29**, and then press Delete. Click the **Merge & Center arrow** in the Alignment group, and then click **Unmerge Cells**.

d. Select cell range **E13:E29**, and then press Ctrl+C. Select cell range **C13:D29**, right-click the selected range, and then under Paste Options click **Formatting** in the shortcut menu.

e. Click cell **B13**, type SERVICE, and then press Tab. Type CHARGE/HOUR, press Tab, and then type HOURS.

f. Click cell **B15**, click **Format** in the Cells group, select **Column Width**, and then type 60 in the Column width box. Click **OK**.

g. Click cell **C15**, click **Format** in the Cells group, and then select **Column Width**. Type 17 in the Column width box, and then click **OK**.

h. Click cell **D15**, click **Format** in the Cells group, and then select **Column Width**. Type 10 in the Column width box, and then click **OK**.

i. Click cell **E15**, click **Format** in the Cells group, and then select **Column Width**. Type 15 in the Column width box, and then click **OK**. Select cell range **C13:E13**, and then click **Align Text Right** in the Alignment group.

j. Click cell **C14**. Type =IF(B14<>"",VLOOKUP(B14,Lastname_Firstname_e04_ws07_SpaSalon_Prices.xlsx!ProductRange,3,FALSE),0). Press Ctrl+Enter.

k. To test the formula in step e, click cell **B14**. Type Massage – Deep Tissue, and then press Ctrl+Enter. Cell C14 should show 125.00; if not, you probably mistyped something in either step j or step k.

l. Click cell **C14**, and then use the **AutoFill** handle to copy the active cell to cell range **C15:C29**. Click the **Auto Fill Options** button [⊞▾], and then select **Fill Without Formatting** from the shortcut menu.

m. Click cell **E14**, type =C14*D14, and then press ⌈Ctrl⌉+⌈Enter⌉. Use the **AutoFill** handle to copy the active cell to cell range **E15:E29**. Click the **Auto Fill Options** button [⊞▾], and then select **Fill Without Formatting** from the shortcut menu.

n. To test the formula in cell E14, click cell **D14**, type 1.5, and then press ⌈Ctrl⌉+⌈Enter⌉. Cell E14 should show 187.50, and cell E34 should show 199.69.

o. Click the **Page Layout tab**, click **Themes** in the Themes group, and then select **Flow** in the gallery. Click the **Home tab**, click cell **B2**, click **Cell Styles** in the Styles group, and then click **Title** in the Titles and Headings gallery.

p. Click **cell B3**, click **Cell Styles** in the Styles group, and then click **Heading4** in the Titles and Headings gallery. Select cell range **B13:E13**, click **Cell Styles** in the Styles group, and then click **60% - Accent1** in the Themed Cell Styles gallery.

q. Click cell **E30**, press and hold ⌈Ctrl⌉, and then click cells **E32** and **E34**. Click **Cell Styles** in the Styles group, and then click **20% - Accent1** in the Themed Cell Styles gallery menu.

r. Click cell **B14**, press and hold ⌈Ctrl⌉, click cell **D14**, and then press ⌈Delete⌉.

s. Click cell **E3**.

t. Click **Save** [🖫], and then click **Close** [✕] to close Excel.

CONSIDER THIS │ **Should Templates Contain External References?**

Templates generally are used to create worksheets or workbooks with consistent structure and format. While templates can, and often do, contain formulas, consider carefully before creating a template that incudes external references to other workbooks. For such a template to be used, the linked workbook must be available in the proper location. The probability of breaking external links in a template is quite high, even if the template is well documented. It would be very easy for a user to copy the template to a new folder, open it to create a new workbook and consequently break the external references (links).

   If you were creating a template and had to reference data in another workbook, what steps could you take to minimize the probability that the external links would get broken by someone using the template?

Concept Check

1. The ability to group worksheets creates an opportunity for you to greatly increase the efficiency of your work. List five ways in which grouping worksheets can increase the efficiency of developing a multiple worksheet workbook. Also list the major limitation, or requirement, in order for the use of worksheet grouping to be effective.

2. Consolidation is a means of rapidly making aggregate calculations across multiple worksheets. What are the different types of consolidation? If source data that was used to generate a consolidation changes, is the consolidation automatically updated? What is (are) the advantage(s) to a linked consolidation? Briefly explain the difference between consolidation by position and consolidation by category.

3. In this workshop, you were introduced to an Excel workspace. What is an Excel workspace? Does a workspace actually store the workbooks that have been included in the workspace as part of the workspace file?

4. A 3-D reference allows references to cells and ranges in other worksheets and even other workbooks. Referencing data in external workbooks has both advantages and disadvantages. List at least two advantages and two disadvantages associated with 3-D references to external workbooks.

5. In this workshop you learned that an Excel template is really just an Excel workbook stored with the .xltx file extension. What is the purpose of an Excel template, and if a template is just a worksheet with an .xltx file extension, why save a workbook as a template?

Key Terms

Visual Summary

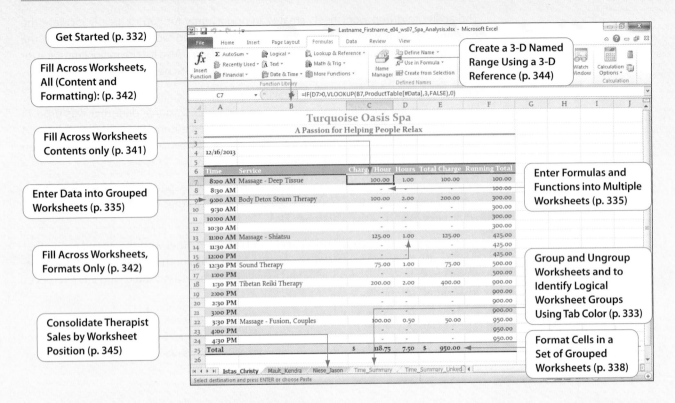

- Get Started (p. 332)
- Fill Across Worksheets, All (Content and Formatting): (p. 342)
- Fill Across Worksheets Contents only (p. 341)
- Enter Data into Grouped Worksheets (p. 335)
- Fill Across Worksheets, Formats Only (p. 342)
- Consolidate Therapist Sales by Worksheet Position (p. 345)
- Create a 3-D Named Range Using a 3-D Reference (p. 344)
- Enter Formulas and Functions into Multiple Worksheets (p. 335)
- Group and Ungroup Worksheets and to Identify Logical Worksheet Groups Using Tab Color (p. 333)
- Format Cells in a Set of Grouped Worksheets (p. 338)

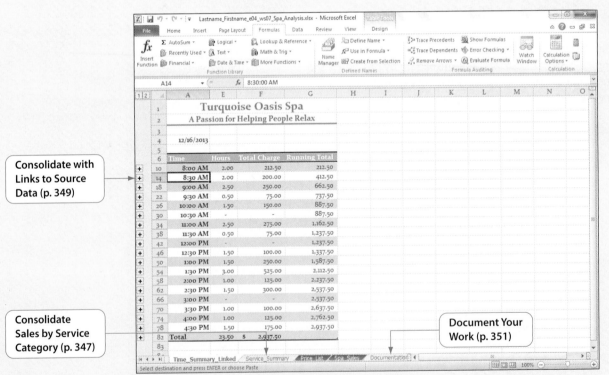

- Consolidate with Links to Source Data (p. 349)
- Consolidate Sales by Service Category (p. 347)
- Document Your Work (p. 351)

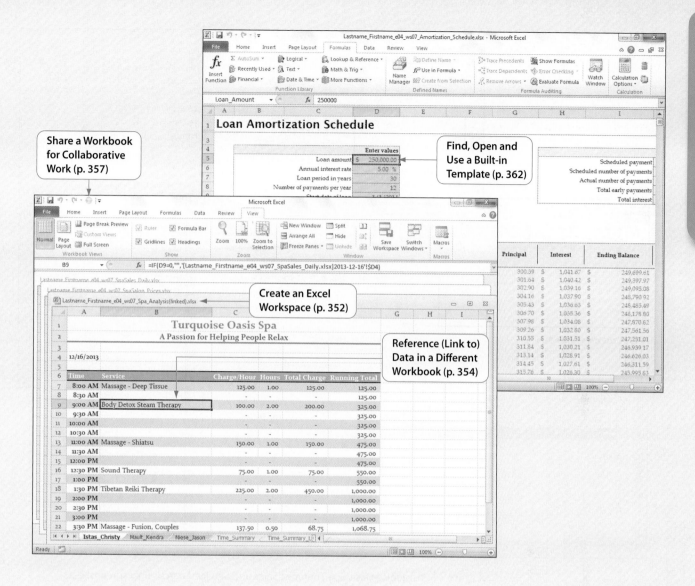

Share a Workbook for Collaborative Work (p. 357)

Find, Open and Use a Built-in Template (p. 362)

Create an Excel Workspace (p. 352)

Reference (Link to) Data in a Different Workbook (p. 354)

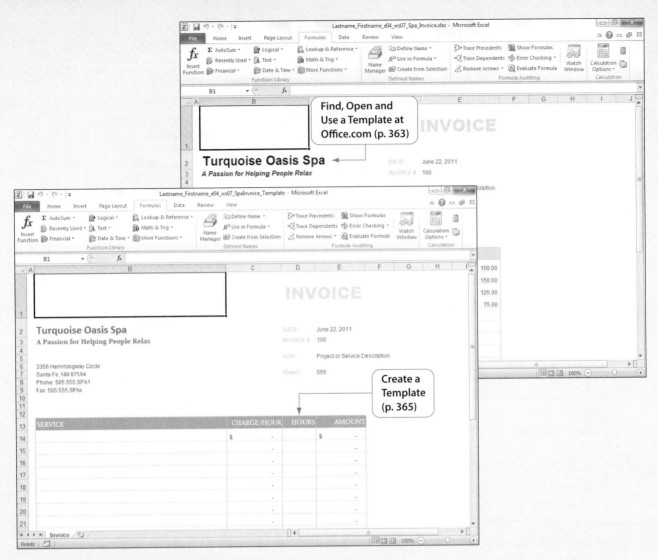

Figure 24 Turquoise Oasis Spa Therapist Sales and Service Analysis final spreadsheets

---

Practice 1

Student data file needed:

e04_ws07_Employee_Tips

You will save your file as:

Lastname_Firstname_e04_ws07_Employee_Tips

Therapist Tip Tracking

For Internal Revenue Service (IRS) purposes, employees in the spa and salon are required to track the tips they receive. The spa has decided on a policy that requires a 15% gratuity that is automatically added to a client's total tab for services. Meda Rodate wants a worksheet that will calculate the tips for each consultation for a week's sales.

Meda has created a workbook that includes a layout that she would like you to use for each employee in the spa. The workbook will be easily adapted to work for the salon, so you have been asked to first complete the workbook for the spa. The workbook includes the prices of the services in one worksheet and a worksheet for every day's sales for the week. You are to calculate every individual tip received during the week, total them by day, and calculate a total for the week in the proper place on each therapist's worksheet.

a. Start **Excel**, and then from the data files, open **e04_ws07_Employee_Tips**. Click the **File tab**, and then click **Save As**. In the Save As dialog box, navigate to the location where you are saving your student files, and then in the File name box, type Lastname_Firstname_e04_ws07_Employee_Tips, and click **Save**.

b. Click the **Istas_Christy worksheet tab**, press Shift, and then click the **Niese_Jason worksheet tab**. Select cell range **A1:I26**. If necessary, click the **Home tab**, click **Fill** in the Editing group, select **Across Worksheets**, and then click **OK** in the Fill Across Worksheets dialog box.

c. Apply the following formatting directives:

- Select column **A**, click **Format** in the Cells group, and then select **AutoFit Column Width**. Select columns **B:H**, click **Format** in the Cells group, and then select **Column Width** in the menu. Type 10 in the Column width box, and then click **OK**.

- Select cell range **B6:H23**, click the **Accounting Number Format arrow**, and then select **More Accounting Formats**. Select **None** in the Symbol box, set Decimal places to **2**, and then click **OK**.

- Select cell range **B24:I24**, press and hold Ctrl, and then select cell range **I6:I23**. Click the **Accounting Number Format** button, and then press Ctrl+B. Select cell range **B24:I24**. Click the **Border arrow**, and then select **Top and Double Bottom Border**.

d. Incrementally build the formula in cell B6 as follows:

- Click cell **B6**, type =IF(Spa_Sales_Sun!$D2<>0,Spa_Sales_Sun!$E2, ""), and then press Ctrl+Enter. This returns the duration of each appointment. The absolute references for the column values $D and $E allow you to copy this formula to columns D:H without Excel adjusting them relatively. Use the **AutoFill** handle to copy the active cell to cell range **B7:B23**.

- Click cell **B6**, click in the **formula bar**, and then place the insertion point between the first comma and the second Spa_Sales_Sun!. Type VLOOKUP(Spa_Sales_Sun!$D2,ProductTable[#Data],3,FALSE)*, and then press Ctrl+Enter to add this formula code to lookup the charge for the service in Spa_Sales_Sun!D2 and return the hourly charge, which is then multiplied by the duration of the appointment. The formula in cell B6 should match the following:

  =IF(Spa_Sales_Sun!$D2<>0,VLOOKUP(Spa_Sales_Sun!$D2,ProductTable[#Data],3,FALSE)*Spa_Sales_Sun!$E2,"")

- Use the **AutoFill** handle and copy the active cell to cell range **B7:B23**.

- Click cell **B6**, click in the **formula bar**, place the insertion point after *Spa_Sales_Sun!$E2 and then type *. Click cell **B26**, press F4 once to convert B26 to an absolute reference, and then press Ctrl+Enter. The formula in cell B6 should match the following:

  =IF(Spa_Sales_Sun!$D2<>0,VLOOKUP(Spa_Sales_Sun!$D2,ProductTable[#Data],3,FALSE)*Spa_Sales_Sun!$E2*$B$26,"")

- Use the **AutoFill** handle to copy the active cell to cell range **B7:B23**. Click cell **B6**, and then use the **AutoFill** handle to copy the active cell to cell range **C6:H6**.

e. Click cell **C6**, click in the **formula bar**, change all three references to worksheet Spa_Sales_Sun to Spa_Sales_Mon, and then press Tab.

- In cell **D6**, click in the **formula bar**, change all three references to worksheet Spa_Sales_Sun to Spa_Sales_Tue, and then press Tab.

- In cell **E6**, click in the **formula bar**, change all three references to worksheet Spa_Sales_Sun to Spa_Sales_Wed, and press Tab.

- In cell **F6**, click in the **formula bar**, change all three references to worksheet Spa_Sales_Sun to Spa_Sales_Thu, and then press Tab.

- In cell **G6**, click in the **formula bar**, change all three references to worksheet Spa_Sales_Sun to Spa_Sales_Fri, and then press Tab.

- In cell **H6**, click in the **formula bar**, change all three references to worksheet Spa_Sales_Sun to Spa_Sales_Sat, and then press Ctrl+Enter.

f. Select cell range **C6:H6**, and then use the **AutoFill** handle to copy the active cell to cell range **C7:H23**.

g. Click cell **B24**, and then click **AutoSum** in the Editing group. Adjust the predicted range to have the formula result sum cell range **B6:B23**, and then press Ctrl+Enter. Use the **AutoFill** handle to copy the active cell to cell range **C24:I24**.

h. Select cell range **B6:I23**, and then press Alt + = to AutoSum cells I6:I23, and then press Ctrl+Home.

i. Right-click the **Istas_Christy worksheet tab**, and then select **Ungroup Sheets**. Click the **Mault_Kendra worksheet tab**, and then click cell **B6**.

j. Click in the **formula bar**, and then change two cell references for cell D2 to D20 and one cell reference for cell E2 to E20. Press Tab.

k. Repeat step j for cells **C6**, **D6**, **E6**, **F6**, **G6**, and **H6**.

l. Select cell range **B6:H6**, and then use the **AutoFill** handle to copy the active cells to the cell range **B7:H23**. Press Ctrl+Home.

m. Click the **Niese_Jason worksheet tab**, and then click cell **B6**.

n. Click in the **formula bar**, and then change two cell references for cell D2 to D38 and one cell reference for cell E2 to E38. Press Tab.

o. Repeat step p for cells **C6**, **D6**, **E6**, **F6**, **G6**, and **H6**. Select cell range **B6:H6**, use the **AutoFill** handle to copy the active cells to the cell range **B7:H23**, and then press Ctrl+Home.

p. Right-click the **Price_List worksheet tab**, and then select **Insert** from the menu. Click **OK** to insert a new worksheet. Double-click the **Sheet1 worksheet tab**, type Totals, and then press Enter. Click the **Niese_Jason worksheet tab**, select cell range **A1:I5**, press and hold Shift, and then click the **Totals worksheet tab**. Click **Fill** in the Editing group, select **Across Worksheets**, and then click **OK**. Select cell range **A6:A24**, click **Fill** in the Editing group, select **Across Worksheets**, and then click **OK**. Press Ctrl+Home, right-click the **Totals worksheet tab**, and then select **Ungroup Sheets**.

q. In the Totals worksheet, click cell **B6**. Click the **Data tab**, click **Consolidate** in the Data Tools group, and then if necessary, select **Sum** in the Function box of the Consolidate dialog box. Click in the **Reference box**. Click the **Niese_Jason worksheet tab**, select cell range **B6:I24**, and then click **Add** in the Consolidate dialog box. Click the **Mault_Kendra worksheet tab**, and then click **Add** in the Consolidate dialog box. Click the **Istas_Christy worksheet tab**, click **Add** in the Consolidate dialog box, and then click **OK**.

r. Click the **Niese_Jason worksheet tab**, and then select cell range **B24:I24**. Click the **Home tab**, press and hold Ctrl, and then click the **Totals worksheet tab**. Click **Fill** in the Editing group, and then select **Across Worksheets** in the menu. Select **Formats** in the Fill Across Worksheets dialog box, and then click **OK**. Select cell range **I6:I23**, click **Fill** in the Editing group, and then select **Across Worksheets** in the menu. Select **Formats** in the Fill Across Worksheets dialog box, and then click **OK**. Right-click the **Totals worksheet tab**, and then select **Ungroup Sheets**. Select columns **A:I**, click **Format** in the Cells group, and then select **AutoFit Column Width**.

s. Right-click the **Totals worksheet tab**, and then select **Select All Sheets**. Click the **Page Layout tab**, click **Print Titles** in the Page Setup group, click the **Header/Footer tab** in the Page Setup dialog box, and then click **Custom Footer**. Click in the **Left section** box, click **Insert File Name**, click **OK** in the Footer dialog box, and then click **OK** in the Page Setup dialog box. Click the **Home tab**.

t. Press Ctrl+Home, right-click the **Istas_Christy worksheet tab**, and then select **Ungroup Sheets**.

u. Click the **Documentation worksheet tab**, click cell **A5**, and then press [Ctrl]+[;]. Click cell **B5**, and then type your Lastname, Firstname in that format. Click cell **C5**, and then type Completed the work begun by Meda. Select rows **27:32**, and then press [Ctrl]+[C]. Select row **33**, and then press [Ctrl]+[V]. Click cell **B34**, and then type Totals. Click cell **B35**, and then type your Lastname, Firstname in that format. Click cell **B36**, and then press [Ctrl]+[;]. Click cell **B37**, and then type Tip totals by day and time. Press [Ctrl]+[Home].

v. Click the **Istas_Christy worksheet tab**, click **Save**, and then close Excel.

Practice 2

Student data files needed:

e04_ws07_Corporate_Event
e04_ws07_EventFood_Pricing
e04_ws07_EventRoom_Pricing

You will save your files as:

Lastname_Firstname_e04_ws07_Corporate_Event
Lastname_Firstname_e04_ws07_Corporate_Event.xlw
Lastname_Firstname_e04_ws07_EventFood_Pricing
Lastname_Firstname_e04_ws07_EventRoom_Pricing
Lastname_Firstname_e04_ws07_Corporate_Event.xltx

Corporate Event Planning Template

The Painted Paradise Resort and Spa has several rooms that can be used to host events. Corporate events generally include small meetings, seminars, and conventions that require tables, seating, and often a meal. Room setup, tables, and seating are included in the room price, as are refreshments for guests during the event. A meal is an additional charge that is determined by the menu.

Patti Rochelle, the corporate event planner has requested that you design and build a template that she and her staff can use to list the services required for an event and to quickly price the event based on a standard cost workbook that Patti wishes to maintain separately.

Conference rooms are charged on a sliding scale that is determined by the number of rooms conference attendees will be renting in the hotel. The template must automatically adjust pricing according to the sliding scale.

Food prices will be pulled from an external worksheet maintained by Robert Sanchez, chef at the Indigo 5.

a. Start **Excel**, click the **File tab**, and click **Open**. Click **Close Window** to close the default Book1 workbook. If necessary navigate to the location of your student files. Press and hold [Ctrl], and then click **e04_ws07_Corporate_Event**, **e04_ws07_EventFood_Pricing**, and **e04_ws07_EventRoom_Pricing**. Click **Open**.

b. Press [Ctrl]+[Tab] once or twice to make e04_ws07_Corporate_Event the active worksheet. Click the **File tab**, and then click **Save As**. In the Save As dialog box, navigate to the location of your student files, and then in the File name box, type Lastname_Firstname_e04_ws07_Corporate_Event, and then click **Save**.

c. Press [Ctrl]+[Tab] to make e04_ws07_EventFood_Pricing the active workbook. Click the **File tab**, and then click **Save As**. In the Save As dialog box, navigate to the location of your student files, and then in the File name box, type Lastname_Firstname_e04_ws07_EventFood_Pricing, and then click **Save**.

d. Press [Ctrl]+[Tab] to make e04_ws07_EventRoom_Pricing the active workbook. Click the **File tab**, and then click **Save As**. In the Save As dialog box, navigate to the location of your student files, and then in the File name box, type Lastname_Firstname_e04_ws07_EventRoom_Pricing, and then click **Save**.

e. Press [Ctrl]+[Tab] until Lastname_Firstname_e04_ws07_Corporate_Event is the active worksheet. Click the **View tab**, click **Arrange All** in the Window group, select **Cascade** in the Arrange Windows dialog box, and then click **OK**.

f. Click **Save Workspace** in the Window group. Navigate to the location where you are saving your files, type Lastname_Firstname_e04_ws07_Corporate_Event in the File name box, and then click **Save** in the Save Workspace dialog box.

g. In the Lastname_Firstname_e04_ws07_Corporate_Event workbook, enter information as follows:

Cell	Value	Cell	Value
B9	12/31/2013	C17	Prime Rib – 10 oz.
B10	150	C18	Carrots – Baked
B11	50	C19	Potatoes – Baked
B12	Plate	C20	Shrimp Salad
C15	Muisca	C21	Waldorf

h. Add range names to aid in usability of the template.
   - Click cell **B10**, in the Name Box type GuestNumber, and then press Enter.
   - Click cell **B11**, in the Name Box type RoomBlockSize, and then press Enter.
   - Click cell **B12**, in the Name Box type DiningOption, and then press Enter.
   - Click cell **C15**, in the Name Box type RoomSelection, and then press Enter.
   - Click cell **C17**, in the Name Box type Meat, and then press Enter.
   - Click cell **C18**, in the Name Box type Side1, and then press Enter.
   - Click cell **C19**, in the Name Box type Side2, and then press Enter.
   - Click cell **C20**, in the Name Box type Side3, and then press Enter.
   - Click cell **C21**, in the Name Box type Salad, and then press Enter.

i. Press Ctrl+Tab to make Lastname_Firstname_e04_ws07_EventRoom_Pricing the active worksheet. Click the **Name Box arrow**, note the four range names in this worksheet, and then select the named range **Muisca**.

j. Press Ctrl+Tab once or twice to make Lastname_Firstname_e04_ws07_Corporate_Event the active worksheet. Click cell **B15**, type =VLOOKUP(RoomBlockSize,INDIRECT ("Lastname_Firstname_e04_ws07_EventRoom_Pricing.xlsx!"&RoomSelection),2), and press Enter. 5,000.00 will appear in cell B15 if you entered the formula correctly.

Troubleshooting

Important! Because this formula builds a dynamic reference using the INDIRECT( ) function, the worksheet reference will not be changed to an absolute reference that includes the folder path if the Lastname_Firstname_e04_ws07_EventRoom_Pricing worksheet is not open. Therefore, if linked data is to be updated properly, always open the workspace file to ensure all linked workbooks are open.

k. Click the **Review tab**, click cell **B15**, and then click **New Comment** in the Comments group. Select the user name and, in the comment box, type #REF! ERROR?, press Enter, and then then press Ctrl+B. Type If this cell displays a #REF! error, close this file and open the workspace file with the same name.

l. Click cell **B16**, type =IF(DiningOption="Plate",IF(GuestNumber>0,VLOOKUP(GuestNumber,Lastname_Firstname_e04_ws07_EventRoom_Pricing.xlsx!WaitStaff,2),""),""), and then press Enter.
   750.00 will appear in cell B16 if you entered the formula correctly.

m. Click cell B17, type =VLOOKUP(Meat,Lastname_Firstname_e04_ws07_EventFood_Pricing.xlsx!MeatPrices,IF(DiningOption="Plate",2,3),FALSE)*GuestNumber, and then press Enter.

 2,250.00 will appear in cell B17 if you entered the formula correctly.

n. Click cell **B18**, type =VLOOKUP(Side1,Lastname_Firstname_e04_ws07_EventFood_Pricing.xlsx!SideDishPrices,IF(DiningOption="Plate",2,3),FALSE)*GuestNumber, and then press Ctrl+Enter.

 600.00 should appear in cell B18 if you entered the formula correctly.

o. Press Ctrl+C, select cell range **B19:B21**, and then press Ctrl+V.

p. Click cell **B19**, click in the **formula bar**, and then change Side1 to Side2 in the formula. Press Enter.

 $675.00 will appear in cell B19 if you entered the formula correctly.

q. Click cell **B20**, click in the **formula bar**, and then change Side1 to Side3 in the formula. Press Enter.

 $1,050.00 will appear in cell B20 if you entered the formula correctly.

r. Click cell **B21**, click in the **formula bar**, and then change Side1 to Salad and SideDishPrices to SaladPrices in the formula. Press Enter.

 $1,200.00 will appear in cell B21 if you entered the formula correctly.

s. Right-click the **Event_Pricing worksheet tab**, and then click **Select All Sheets**. Click the **Page Layout tab**, click **Print Titles** in the Page Setup group, click the **Header/Footer tab** in the Page Setup dialog box, and then click **Custom Footer**. Click in the **Left section** box, click **Insert File Name**, click **OK** in the Footer dialog box, and then click **OK** in the Page Setup dialog box. Click the **Home tab**, right-click the **Event_Pricing worksheet tab**, and then click **Ungroup Sheets**.

t. Click the **Documentation worksheet tab**, and then do the following:

 • Click cell **A3**, and then type today's date in mm/dd/yyyy format.

 • Click cell **B3**, and then type your Lastname, Firstname in that format.

 • Click cell **C3**, and then type Corporate event pricing worksheet.

 • Click cell **A5**, and then type today's date in mm/dd/yyyy format.

 • Click cell **B5**, and then type your Lastname, Firstname in that format.

 • Click cell **C5**, and then type Created a template that can be used to price corporate events at the resort.

 • Click cell **B17**, and then type your Lastname, Firstname in that format.

 • Click cell **B18**, and then type today's date in mm/dd/yyyy format.

 • Click cell **B19**, and then type Calculate pricing for services required for a corporate event. Adjust pricing based on number of guests, the size of the hotel block reserved and the meal service type. Press Enter.

u. Press Ctrl+Home, and then click the **Event_Pricing worksheet tab**. Press Ctrl+Home, and then click **Save**.

v. Select cell range **B9:B12**, press and hold Ctrl, select cell range **C15:C21**, and then press Delete.

w. Click cell **B9**. Click the **File tab**, and then click **Save As**. Type Lastname_Firstname_e04_ws07_Corporate_Event in the File name box of the Save As dialog box. Select **Excel Template** in the Save As type box, navigate to where you are storing your student files, and then click **Save**. **Close** Excel.

WORKSHOP 8

1. Use data validation to control data entry.   p. 380
2. Audit formulas.   p. 391
3. Control navigation in a workbook.   p. 398
4. Automate activities with macros.   p. 403
5. Protect your worksheets and workbooks.   p. 412

Refining Your Excel Application

PREPARE CASE

Turquoise Oasis Spa Invoice Generation

Meda Rodate wants to improve the template she is using to produce invoices for the spa. She has built a template that has the layout she wants, but she does not know how to automate the invoice production process in a manner that will ensure data accuracy and consistency.

Courtesy of www.Shutterstock.com

Meda has asked you to use her invoice template as a start and to automate the invoice-generation process. Data entry should be minimized as much as possible. User actions should be guided as much as possible.

There are several workbooks available that you can use for source data, and Meda has made them available to you.

Student data files needed for this workshop:

 e04_ws08_Build_Invoice#.txt

 e04_ws08_Room#_Criteria.txt

 e04_ws08_Spa_Employees

 e04_ws08_SpaInvoice_Template.xltx

 e04_ws08_SpaSalon_Prices

You will save your files as:

 Lastname_Firstname_e04_ws08_Spa_Invoice

 Lastname_Firstname_e04_ws08_Spa_Invoice.xlsm

Controlling Data Entry

Probably the greatest single source of errors in a workbook, or in any application for that matter, is human error. People are notoriously fallible—they easily make mistakes for any number of reasons: fatigue, incorrect understanding of the worksheet purpose or function, misreading source material, using the wrong source material, and being bored, excited, too hot, too cold, too noisy, too quiet, and so on. Simply put, people make mistakes—particularly when keying in data.

It is impossible to eliminate human error in worksheet manipulation, but Excel makes data validation tools available that can help ensure data entry errors are kept to a minimum.

In this workshop you will develop an invoice application for the Turquoise Oasis Spa. Meda Rodate has started the application, but she is unable to finish it. The invoice application has several requirements she cannot satisfy:

- Data validation to minimize data entry errors
- Automatically generated invoice number
- Automated data cleanup using macros
- Protection of the application to stop users from mistakenly changing application content and structure.

You will use what Meda Rodate started and develop a polished invoice application for the Turquoise Oasis Spa. First, you must open Meda's initial template and save a copy as a workbook for further development.

To Get Started from a Template

a. Click the **Start** button ⊕ from the Start Menu, locate and then click to open **Microsoft Excel 2010**.

b. Click the **File tab**, and then click **Open**.

c. In the Open dialog box, navigate to where your student data files are located and double-click **e04_ws08_SpaInvoice_Template.xltx**. The template includes a formula to pull current service prices from an external workbook, so click **Don't Update** in the alert box.

   If the dialog box with Update and Don't Update buttons does not display, and instead you see a Security Warning below the Ribbon or a dialog box warning that links cannot be updated, see the Troubleshooting below to solve the problem.

Troubleshooting

If the message "Security Warning: Automatic update of links has been disabled" appears below the Ribbon, it is because you have not opened this file before and it contains links to an external document. Click Enable Content to enable external links. External links are considered active content that can contain malicious code. Active content can be Excel functionality such as a macro or an external link. You should only enable such content if you know and trust the source of the document. Once you enable active content in a workbook, Excel will not prompt you to do so again, unless you move the document to a different location.

Troubleshooting

If the message "This workbook contains one or more links that cannot be updated" appears in an Excel alert dialog box, Excel cannot find the file referenced in external links in the document. Close the file. Locate e04_ws08_SpaSalon_Prices, and then copy it into the same folder where e04_ws08_SpaInvoice_Template is located—the external links were defined with these two files in the same folder. Then open e04_ws08_SpaInvoice_Template again.

d. Click the **Invoice worksheet tab**, press and hold [Shift], and then click the **Documentation worksheet tab**. Click the **Page Layout tab**, click **Print Titles** in the Page Setup group, in the Page Setup dialog box click the **Header/Footer tab**, and then click **Custom Footer**. Click the **Left section** box, click **Insert File Name** [icon], in the Footer dialog box click **OK**, and then in the Page Setup dialog box click **OK**.

e. Click the **Documentation worksheet tab**. Then
- Click cell **A5**, and then press [Ctrl]+[;].
- Click cell **B5**, and then type your name in Lastname, Firstname format.
- Click cell **C5**, and then type Added data validation where appropriate. Press [Enter].
- In cell C6, type Corrected a problem with a summation formula, and then press [Enter].
- Type Created hyperlinks to ease navigation, and then press [Enter].
- Type Created macros to automate expanding and clearing the invoice, and then press [Enter].
- Type Cleaned up the interface by hiding unnecessary elements, and then press [Enter].
- Type Protected the worksheet and workbook, press [Enter], and then click the **Invoice worksheet tab**.

f. Click the **File tab**, click **Save As**, and then in the Save As dialog box, navigate to the location where you are saving your files. In the File name box type Lastname_Firstname_e04_ws08_Spa_Invoice, replacing Lastname_Firstname with your own name. If necessary, select **Excel Workbook** in the Save as type box, and then click **Save**.

g. If you saved Lastname_Firstname_e04_ws08_Spa_Invoice in a folder that does not contain the file e04_ws08_SpaSalon_Prices, then
    Click the **File tab**, and then click **Open**.
    In the Open dialog box, navigate to where your student data files are located, double-click **e04_ws08_SpaSalon_Prices**, click the **File tab**, and then click **Save As**.
    In the Save As dialog box, navigate to where you saved Lastname_Firstname_e04_ws08_Spa_Invoice, click **Save**, and then click **Close** [x].

Real World Advice — Speed Duplicate Data Entry with [Ctrl]+[Enter]

When you need to enter the same number or text into several cells, you do not need to enter the data into one cell and then copy and paste it into the rest. Instead, select all the cells, either as a contiguous range or as noncontiguous cells, enter the item of data into the active cell, and then press [Ctrl]+[Enter].

Controlling Data Entry with Data Validation

Data validation is any means of increasing the probability of correct data entry through programmatic tools and/or behavioral modifications. In this workshop, you will learn about programmatic data validation tools available in Excel.

Validation Criteria

Validation criteria are like constraints. A constraint can be defined as a limitation; validation criteria limit what worksheet users are allowed to enter into a particular cell. The types of validation criteria available in Excel are listed in the following Quick Reference:

Quick Reference / Types of Validation Criteria

1. Any value—Does not validate data, but does allow the use of the input message to give data entry instructions.
2. Whole number—Limits the data value in a cell to a specified range of integers.
3. Decimal—Limits the user to entering a specified range of real numbers into a cell.
4. List—Requires the user to select a data value from a list of predefined values.
5. Date—Requires that data entered into a cell represent a valid date.
6. Time—Requires that data entered into a cell represent a valid time.
7. Text length—Places a limit on the number of text characters that can be entered into a cell.
8. Custom—Allows a developer to create custom criteria by specifying a formula that data entered into a cell must satisfy to be considered valid.

One limitation is that only a single validation criteria can be applied to a cell. For example, you cannot specify that a cell can contain an item from a list or that it can contain a whole number. Custom validation can be used to apply multiple validation criteria to a cell, but the formulas required can be very complex—as you will see later in this workshop.

Input Messages and Error Alert

Each of the validation criteria can be specified with an Input Message and/or an Error Alert. Although data validation certainly helps ensure that users correctly enter data into a worksheet, communication to the user regarding what constitutes valid data is a vital requirement. The Input Message and Error Alert are tools to assist you in communicating data validation constraints to the user. The Input Message appears when a user makes a validated cell active and prompts a user before data is entered with information about data constraints; the Error Message informs a user when entered data violates validation constraints.

List Validation

List validation presents the user with a list of data values that the user can choose from. Data for the list must be included as part of the workbook; it cannot be in an external workbook. Often Excel developers create a separate worksheet that includes list values as named ranges.

To Select an Option from a List

a. Click the **Source_Data worksheet tab**, select cell range **D2:D15**, type ProductList in the Name Box, and then press Enter.

b. Click the **Invoice worksheet tab**, and then select cell **B15**.

c. Click the **Data tab**, and then click **Data Validation** in the Data Tools group. The Data Validation dialog box will be displayed.

d. Click the **Settings tab** in the Data Validation dialog box, select **List** in the Allow box, and then make sure **In-cell dropdown** and **Ignore blank** are checked.

e. Type =ProductList in the Source box.

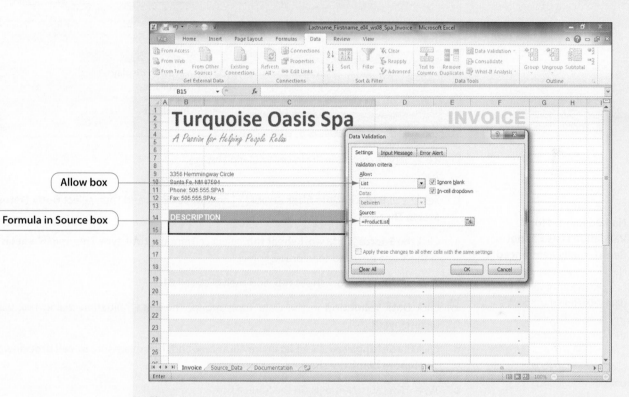

Allow box

Formula in Source box

Figure 1 Data Validation dialog box with List selected

f. Click the **Input Message tab** in the Data Validation dialog box, click in the **Title** box, and then type Service or Product Sold. Click in the **Input message** box, and then type Select a service or product from the list. Make sure **Show input message when cell is selected** is checked.

Figure 2 Data Validation Input Title and Message

g. Click **OK**.

h. Drag the **fill handle**, and fill the cell range **B16:B30**. Click **Auto Fill Options**, and then select **Fill Without Formatting** from the shortcut menu.

i. Click cell **B15**, click the **filter arrow** ▼ next to cell B15, and then select **Reflexology**—you may have to scroll down. Note that 150.00 will appear in cell D15. Click cell **D15**, and then examine the Formula box . This is the formula that contains an external reference to file e04_ws08_SpaSalon_Prices.

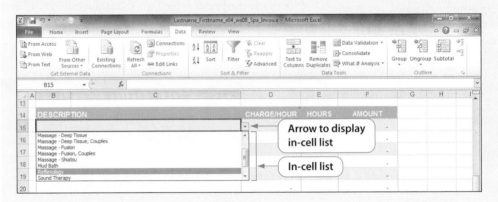

Figure 3 Service choices in the in-cell validation list

SIDE NOTE
Named Ranges for Validation Lists Cannot Be Externally Referenced
Named ranges that are to be used as lists of values for data validation must be in the same workbook where the validation is applied. External references are not allowed to identify source data for validation.

j. Select cell **B16**, click the **filter arrow** ▼ next to cell B16, and then select **Body Detox Steam Therapy**.

k. Click the **Source_Data worksheet tab**, select cell range **A2:A4**, type TherapistNameList in the Name box, and then press Enter.

l. Click the **Invoice worksheet tab**, and then click cell **E10**.

m. Click **Data Validation** in the Data Tools group. The Data Validation dialog box will be displayed.

n. Click the **Settings tab**, click **List** in the Allow box, and then make sure **In-cell dropdown** and **Ignore blank** are checked.

o. Type =TherapistNameList in the Source box.

p. In the Data Validation dialog box, click the **Input Message tab**. Type Therapist in the Title box, type Select the therapist that delivered these services in the Input message box, and then click **OK**.

q. Click the **filter arrow** ▼ next to cell **E10**, and then select **Niese, Jason**.

r. Press Ctrl+Home, and then click **Save** 💾.

Decimal Validation

Decimal validation restricts users to entering data that contains digits and a decimal point (.). Validation of this type requires the specification of upper and/or lower boundary values using standard relational operators such as equal to, not less than, greater than or equal to, and so on. A **relational operator** tests the relationship between two values and returns TRUE or FALSE. Data values that represent upper and/or lower boundaries can be explicitly specified in the validation criteria or through a cell or cell range address, or they can be derived from a formula.

For the clients' health, the Turquoise Oasis Spa recommends that individual therapies not exceed 2 hours in length. The invoice should question any line item billed for more than 2 hours.

To Limit HOURS to a Maximum of 2

a. Select cell **E15** in the Invoice worksheet.

b. Click **Data Validation** in the Data Tools group. The Data Validation dialog box is displayed.

c. Click the **Settings tab**, and then click **Decimal** in the Allow box.

d. Click the **Data** box, select **less than or equal to**, and then in the Maximum box type 2.

e. In the Data Validation dialog box, click the **Input Message tab**, click the **Title** box, type Hours, click the **Input message** box, and then type Enter the number of service hours.

f. In the Data Validation dialog box, click the **Error Alert tab**. Then
  Click the **Style** box, and then select Warning.
  Click the **Title** box, and then type WARNING!.
  Click the **Error Message** box, and then type The hours you entered exceed the maximum recommended for a service at the Turquoise Oasis Spa.

Figure 4 Error alerts

g. Click **OK**.

h. Drag the **fill handle** to fill the cell range **E16:E30**. Click **Auto Fill Options**, and then select **Fill Without Formatting** from the shortcut menu.

i. Select cell **E15**, type 3, and then press Ctrl + Enter.

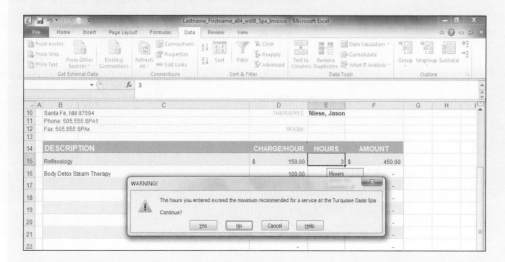

Figure 5 Error Alert displayed due to data validation rules

j. When the WARNING! dialog box displays, click **No**. Notice the questionable value is captured and the error message you specified is displayed.

k. Type 1.5, and press [Ctrl]+[Enter].

l. Select cell **E16**, type 0.5, and press [Ctrl]+[Enter].
    Notice that line item amounts in cells F15 and F16 are calculated from formulas that were in the template, as are tax and totals for the invoice in cells F31:F35.

m. Press [Ctrl]+[Home], and then click **Save** [💾].

Date Validation

Date validation works very much like decimal validation except the value entered must be a date that satisfies the specified criteria. As with decimal validation, Boolean operators can be used to specify a range of valid dates or a minimum or maximum date. Date constraint values can be explicitly entered, referenced via a cell address, or derived from a formula.

To Limit Data Entry to a Date

a. Select cell **E6**.

b. Click **Data Validation** in the Data Tools group. The Data Validation dialog box is displayed.

c. Click the **Settings tab**, and then select **Date** in the Allow box.

d. Click the **Data box**, and then select **less than or equal to**.

e. Click in the **End date** box, and then type =TODAY().

f. In the Data Validation dialog box, click the **Input Message tab**. Then
   - Click the **Title** box, and then type Invoice Date.
   - Click in the **Input message box**, and then type MM/DD/YYYY.

g. In the Data Validation dialog box, click the **Error Alert tab**, click in the **Title** box, and then type ERROR!.
   - Click the **Error message** box, and then type Future dates are not allowed. Please enter today's, or an earlier, date.
   - Click **OK**.

h. Type 01/01/2020, and then press [Ctrl]+[Enter]. Notice the error is captured and the error message you specified is displayed. Click **Retry** in the alert box that appears.

i. Press [Ctrl]+[;], and then press [Ctrl]+[Enter].

j. Press [Ctrl]+[Home], and then click **Save** [💾].

Time Validation

Time validation is the functional twin of date validation with the obvious difference that entered data must be a time value.

To Limit Data Entry to a Time Value

a. Select cell **E8**.

b. Click **Data Validation** in the Data Tools group. The Data Validation dialog box is displayed.

c. Click the **Settings tab**, select **Time** in the Allow box, if necessary click the **Data** box, and then select **between**. Click the **Start time** box, and then type =TIMEVALUE("8:00 AM"). Click the **End time** box, and then type =TIMEVALUE("4:30 PM").

Figure 6 Time data validation

d. In the Data Validation dialog box, click the **Input Message tab**, click the **Title** box, and then type Appointment Time. Click in the **Input message box**, and then type HH:MM AM/PM.

e. In the Data Validation dialog box, click the **Error Alert tab**, click the **Title** box, and then type ERROR!. Click the **Error message** box, type The time you enter must be between 8:00 AM and 4:30 PM, and then click **OK**.

f. Type 5:00 PM, press Ctrl+Enter, and then click **Retry** in the alert box that is displayed. Type 3:00 PM, and then press Ctrl+Enter.

g. Press Ctrl+Home, and then click **Save**.

Whole Number Validation

Whole number validation is functionally identical to decimal validation with the exception that only integer values are valid. A valid numerical range or a minimum or maximum value can be specified using standard Boolean operators.

The Painted Paradise Resort and Spa has 700 hotel rooms—140 rooms on each of five floors. Rooms are numbered in a manner generally referred to as codified. A **codified data value** is formed following a system of rules where the position of information is tied to its context. Turquoise Oasis room numbers are codified values: the first digit is the floor of the room, the next three digits uniquely identify the rooms in sequential order. For example, the 79th room on floor 3 is room 3079. The lowest room number is then 1001 and the highest room number is 5140.

To Limit Room Number to a Valid Minimum and Maximum

a. Select cell **E12**, and then click **Data Validation** in the Data Tools group. The Data Validation dialog box is displayed.

b. In the **Settings tab**, select **Whole number** in the Allow box, make sure the **Ignore blank** check box is checked. Then

- If necessary, click the **Data** box, and then select **between**.
- Click the **Minimum** box, type 1001.
- Click the **Maximum** box, and then type 5140.

c. In the Data Validation dialog box, click the **Input Message tab**. Then

- Click the **Title** box, and then type Room #.
- Click the **Input message** box, and then type Enter the room # to which this invoice is to be charged.

d. Click the **Error Alert tab** in the Data Validation dialog box.

- Click the **Title** box, and then type ERROR!.
- Click the **Error message** box, and then type Invalid room #.
- Click **OK**.

e. Type 5150, press Ctrl + Enter, and then click **Retry** in response to the ERROR! message box. Type 5125, and then press Ctrl + Enter.

f. Press Ctrl + Home, and then click **Save** 💾.

Custom Data Validation

Custom validation allows you to specify more complex criteria than allowed with the other validation types. Using custom validation, you can apply multiple criteria simultaneously—for example, you can specify a valid range of whole numbers if a number is entered and limit the length of a text value if a text value is entered.

In the previous exercise you used whole number validation to limit the value entered for room number to a range of numbers bounded by the lowest and highest room number values in the hotel. The problem is that there are many invalid values within that range. Each floor has 140 rooms. On floor 3, room numbers range from 3001 to 3140. There are no valid room numbers from 3141 to 3999; so the majority of values allowed by whole number validation criteria used in the previous exercise are invalid.

In this case, where a codified data value cannot be adequately validated within a single range of values, custom data validation can be used.

To Validate Room Number Based on the Codified Scheme

a. Select cell **E12**, type 3199, and then press Ctrl + Enter.

This is not a valid room number, but the data validation rule specified in the previous exercise does not indicate an error.

b. Click **Data Validation** in the Data Tools group. The Data Validation dialog box is displayed.

c. Click the **Settings tab**, select **Custom** in the Allow box, double-click in the **Formula** box, and then type:

=AND(LEFT(E12,1)<="5",LEFT(E12,1)>="1",RIGHT(E12,3)>="001",RIGHT(E12,3)<="140")

The custom formula above tests four individual criteria, all of which must evaluate to TRUE for a number in cell E12 to pass validation. According to the room codification scheme, floor number is the first digit: the 1 digit on the LEFT of E12 must be between 1 and 5—thus the criteria LEFT(E12,1)<="5" and LEFT(E12,1)>="1". The second LEFT( ) function is necessary because you cannot allow a zero. Further, the right three digits are

But What About Whole Number Validation?

You can extend the room number validation to only allow whole numbers by inserting the following before the last parenthesis: **,E12=INT(E12)**.

the unique number for each room on a floor. Those numbers must be between 1 and 140—thus the criteria RIGHT(E12,3)>="001" and RIGHT(E12,3)<="140". All four criteria must evaluate to TRUE, so they are combined in an AND( ) function. If any single criteria in an AND( ) function evaluates to FALSE, the entire function returns FALSE.

Troubleshooting

If you have trouble entering the data validation formula without making an error, open e04_ws08_Room#_Criteria, copy its contents to the clipboard, and paste it in the Formula box in the Data Validation dialog box.

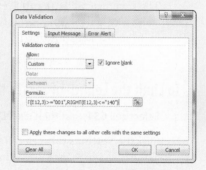

Figure 7   Custom data validation

d.   Click **OK**.

e.   Type 3199, press Ctrl+Enter, and then click **Retry** in response to the ERROR! message box. Type 3125, and then press Ctrl+Enter.

f.   Press Ctrl+Home, and then click **Save** 🖫.

Any Value Validation

Any value validation is a means of using the Input Message available through the data validation tools to communicate data entry rules and/or expectations to the user. The moment an Any value validated cell is made active, the Input Message is displayed as a prompt to the user.

To Use Data Validation to Display Data Entry Prompts

a.   Select cell **C31**, and then click **Data Validation** in the Data Tools group.

b.   Click the **Settings tab**, select **Any value** in the Allow box. Then
   •   Click the **Input Message tab** in the Data Validation dialog box.
   •   Click the **Title** box, and then type Client Comments.
   •   Click in the **Input message box**, and then type This comment section is for the client. Use for special instructions, reminders, thank-you notes and other correspondence.
   •   Click **OK**.
      Excel does not turn off the Error Alert tab for Any value validation, but it has no purpose given there is no way to indicate an error that would display an alert.

c.   Press Ctrl+Home, and then click **Save** 🖫.

Text Length Validation

Text length validation is generally used to limit the number of characters that can be entered into a cell. However, Boolean operators can be used to require the number of characters to fall within a valid range, to be less than or equal to a maximum, greater than or equal to a minimum, and so on.

Text length validation (for that matter, all types of data validation) can be very important when data entered into a worksheet will be imported into a database. Database fields are defined with specific attributes, one of which is length. Text data too long to be inserted into a database field is truncated—cut off on the right. Text length validation can be used in a worksheet to ensure that entered text will not be truncated when imported into a database.

Displaying a data entry prompt using the Any value data validation option is probably fine in situations where cell content is logically limited by convention or natural limits; for example, city, state, and postal code would likely never total more than approximately 30 characters.

The Comments box in cell C31 is free form, however. A lengthy comment could fill the available space and be truncated for display and printing purposes as well as for database importation. In such a case, limiting the amount of text that can be entered may be advisable.

To Limit the Length of Text in the Comments Box

a. Select cell **C31**, and then click **Data Validation** in the Data Tools group.

b. Click the **Settings tab**, select **Text length** in the Allow box, select **less than or equal to** in the Data box, click the **Maximum box**, and then type 180.

Figure 8 Text length validation

c. Click **OK**.

d. Type Jason is a fine therapist. I will stay in this resort again because the spa is wonderful!, and then press Ctrl + Enter .

e. Press Ctrl + Home , and then click **Save** .

Real World Advice   How Many Characters Can a Text Box Display without Being Truncated?

Fill a comment box like the one in cell C31 with a string of X's or other uppercase letters. Then in an unused cell of the worksheet, type =LEN(C31). The number returned from the formula is an approximation of how long a string of characters can be entered into the comment box.

Formulas Minimize Data Entry

New data is routinely generated using other data entered into worksheets. You have done this many times by calculating new values using formulas. Turquoise Oasis uses a codification scheme to number the rooms in its hotel. **Codification schemes** consist of rules that combine data values in specific formats and locations to generate a new data value. The spa uses a codification scheme to generate invoice numbers.

The invoice number is the combination of the appointment date in yyyymmdd format, appointment time in hhmm format, and employee number, all separated by single spaces. Certainly a user, with knowledge of the invoice number codification scheme, could enter invoice numbers manually, but this would be prone to errors and would require a user that fully understands the codification scheme. You, as the developer, can eliminate the need for manual entry of invoice numbers by using a formula to generate them from validated data in the worksheet.

To Generate the Invoice Number from Other Data in the Worksheet

a. Select cell **E4**, type =IF(E6>0,TEXT(E6,"YYYYMMDD"),""), and then press [Ctrl]+[Enter].
    This formats the invoice date as the first part of the invoice number but displays nothing if cell E6 is empty.

b. Click in the **Formula bar**. Place the insertion point at the end of the formula, type &" "&IF(E8>0,TEXT(E8,"HHMM"),""), and then press [Ctrl]+[Enter].
    This adds a space and the time of the appointment to the invoice number and separates the two items with a space but displays nothing if cell E8 is empty.

c. Click the **Source_Data worksheet tab**, and then select cell range **A2:B4**. Click the **Name** box, type TherapistData, and then press [Enter].

d. Click the **Invoice worksheet tab**, click cell **E4**, and then click in the **Formula bar**. Place the insertion point at the end of the formula, and then type &" "&IF(E10>0,VLOOKUP (E10,TherapistData,2),"").
    This adds a space and the employee number of the therapist selected in cell E10 to the end of the invoice number, but it displays nothing if cell E10 is empty. If you have entered the formulas correctly, you should see yyyymmdd 1500 5901 in cell E4, where yyyymmdd is today's date.

Troubleshooting

If you have trouble entering the data validation formula without making an error, open e04_ws08_Build_Invoice#.txt, copy its contents, and paste it into the Formula box in the Data Validation dialog box.

e. Press [Ctrl]+[Home], and then click **Save** 🖫.

Validation with Text-to-Speech

Data validation can never completely eliminate data entry errors. For example, text data might satisfy the criteria that it must be less than 100 characters in length, but data validation for length cannot ensure that the content is correct. In this case, and in many others, a human being must ensure that entered data actually represents the intended content.

Excel includes a Text-to-speech feature that can assist you, or a user, in manually validating data. Sir William Hamilton said, "The eye sees all but the mind shows us what we want to see." We interpret what we see based upon what we know should be there, so for example, we often do not recognize a misspelled word because we know how the word should be spelled. The ears are not as easily fooled as the eyes, so text-to-speech is a tool that can increase data proofing accuracy.

To Use Text-to-Speech for Data Proofing

a. In order to complete this exercise you must have a sound card and speakers or headphones. Click the **File tab**, click **Options** in the left pane of Backstage view, and then click **Customize Ribbon** in the Excel Options dialog box.

b. Select **Commands Not in the Ribbon** in the Choose commands from box, and then, if necessary, select **Main Tabs** in the Customize the Ribbon box.

c. In the Main Tabs list, right-click **Review**, and then select **Add New Group** from the shortcut menu. Right-click **New Group (Custom)**, and then select **Rename** from the shortcut menu. Type Text-to-Speech in the Display name box.

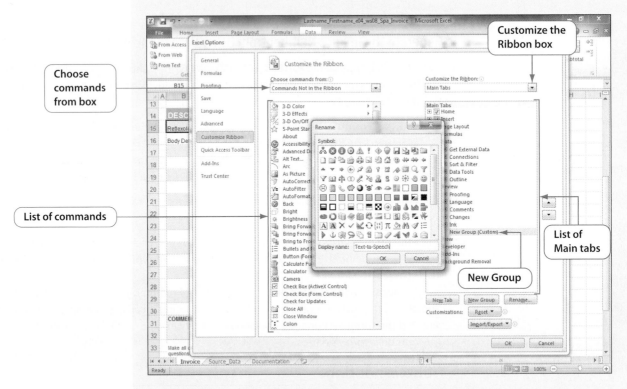

Figure 9 Add a new group to the Ribbon

d. Click **OK**, and then click **Text-to-Speech (Custom)** in the Main Tabs list box.

e. In the Commands list, scroll down until you see five commands that begin with Speak. Then
  - Select **Speak Cells**, and then click **Add >>**.
  - Select **Speak Cells – Stop Speaking Cells**, and then click **Add >>**.
  - Select **Speak Cells by Column**, and then click **Add >>**.
  - Select **Speak Cells by Row**, and then click **Add >>**.
  - Select **Speak Cells on Enter**, click **Add >>**.
  - Click **OK**.

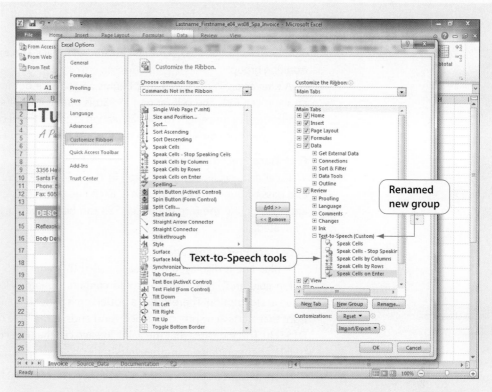

Figure 10 Add commands to a new group on the Ribbon

f. Click the **Review tab**, click the **Source_Data worksheet tab**, click the **Name box arrow** ▾, and then select **ProductList**. Click **Speak Cells** in the Text-to-Speech group. When several lines have been read, you may click **Stop Speaking** if you wish.

g. Click the **Name box arrow** ▾, and then select **TherapistData**. Click **By Columns** in the Text-to-Speech group, click **Speak Cells** in the Text-to-Speech group, and then let Excel read through both columns.

h. Click **By Rows** in the Text-to-Speech group, click **Speak Cells** in the Text-to-Speech group, and then let Excel read through both columns.

i. Click the **Invoice worksheet tab**, press Ctrl+Home, and then click **Save** 🖫.

Auditing Your Formulas

Formula auditing shows you which cells are used in a formula and how they are used. Whether you are working with a worksheet you developed or one developed by someone else, visual ties from a formula to the cells that are used in that formula help you understand the structure of the calculations and of the worksheet itself. Formula auditing includes several tools, such as the Trace Precedents, Trace Dependents, and Evaluate Formula tools.

Both tracing a formula and evaluating a formula are useful in understanding how a worksheet is structured and are particularly useful if a complex formula is not producing a correct result. In this section you will use formula-auditing tools to gain a clearer understanding of how the invoice worksheet is structured and to correct an error in an invoice formula.

Auditing Formulas with Trace Precedents and Trace Dependents

Tracing formulas draws lines from a formula to cells that supply source data (precedents) and to formulas that use the result of a formula (dependents). Tracing formulas presents a visual reference to the structure of a formula and to some extent a worksheet or workbook.

To Trace Precedents and Trace Dependents

a. Select cell **F31**, click the **Formulas tab**, and then click **Trace Precedents** in the Formula Auditing group.

A blue arrow is displayed that begins with a blue dot in cell F15 and ends with an arrow in cell F31. The cell range F15:F30 is outlined in blue. This shows that the outlined range is a precedent to the calculation in cell F31—all calculations in the cell range F15:F31 must be complete before the formula in F31 can be evaluated.

b. Click **Trace Precedents** again.

Excel displays lines to every cell in the cell range F15:F31 that start in column D and pass through a dot in column E. Each line represents an individual precedent. For example, before the formula in cell F23 can be evaluated, cells D23 and E23 must be evaluated.

c. Click **Trace Precedents** again.

A blue line is displayed from each cell in the range B15:B30 directly to its adjacent cell in column C. Any cell that could contain a Charge/Hour value must first have a value in Description. There is also a dotted green line that angles downward from left to right that starts at a spreadsheet icon and ends at the blue dot in each cell in the range D15:D30. This indicates that the value in each cell that can contain a Charge/Hour value is dependent on data in another workbook or worksheet.

d. Click **Trace Dependents**. An arrow is displayed from cell F31 to F33.

e. Click **Trace Dependents** again.

An arrow is displayed from cell F33 to F35. This indicates that cell F35 is dependent on cell F33—cell F33 must be evaluated before cell F35 can be evaluated.

SIDE NOTE
Where Is the Ribbon in Figure 11?
To make more of the worksheet visible, the Ribbon is hidden in Figure 11. Press Ctrl + F1 to minimize the Ribbon. Press the same keyboard shortcut to expand the Ribbon.

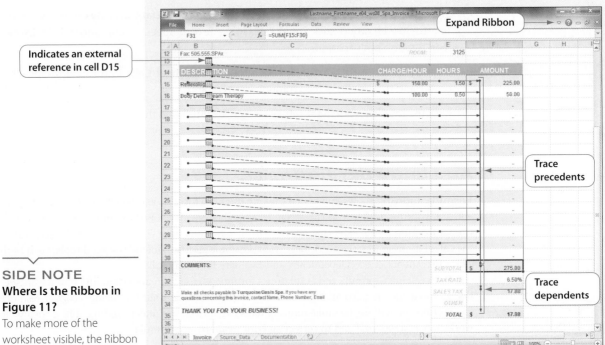

Figure 11 Trace precedents and trace dependents for cell F31

f. Click **Remove Arrows**, and then press Ctrl + Home.

Evaluating a Formula

Evaluating a formula walks you through the steps taken in calculating the result of a formula. The Evaluate Formula tool shows you exactly how a formula executes so that you can compare actual execution to the way you know (or think) the formula should work. When a formula contains an error and the Trace Dependents tool has not helped you correct the problem, using the Evaluate Formula tool is the next step.

Clearly, there is a problem with the calculation of the TOTAL in the invoice. For some reason the $275.00 SUBTOTAL is not being added into the TOTAL. You will use Evaluate Formula in the next exercise to determine what is wrong with the formula in cell F35.

To Check a Formula Using Evaluate Formula

a. Select cell **F35**, click the **Formulas tab**, and then click **Evaluate Formula** in the Formula Auditing group.

The Evaluate Formula dialog box is displayed. F34+F33+F30 is displayed in the Evaluation box.

b. Click **Step In** in the Evaluate Formula dialog box.

The Evaluation box is split. The value in F34 (no value actually) is shown in the bottom box.

c. Click **Step Out** to return to the formula in cell F35.

The contents of the Evaluation box have changed to reflect the evaluated value of cell F34, which you just stepped into. The Evaluation box now contains 0+F33+F30, the F33 in the formula is what will be evaluated next.

d. Click **Step In**. A second Evaluation box displays F31*F32, the formula in cell F33.

e. Click **Step In** again. A third Evaluation box displays SUM(F15:F30), the formula in cell F31.

SIDE NOTE

To Select All Cells That Contain a Formula

Press Ctrl+G, click Special, and then select Formulas. Notice the categories of formulas you can select. Click OK. This is a quick way to identify every cell in a worksheet that contains a formula.

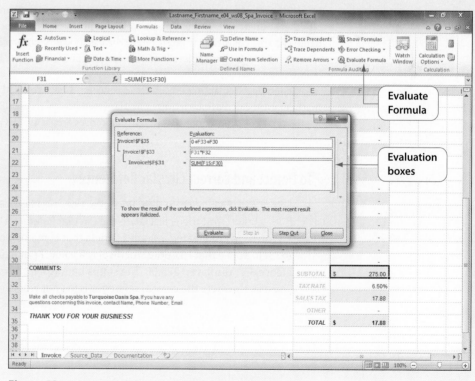

Figure 12 Stepping into a formula using Evaluate Formula

f. Click **Evaluate**. The third Evaluation box content changes to $275.00. F31 was evaluated and replaced with the result. Then

- Click **Step Out**. The third Evaluation box disappears, and the content in the second Evaluation box changes to 275*<u>F32</u>.
- Click **Step In**. The third Evaluation box reappears, and F32 is evaluated to 6.50%.
- Click **Step Out**. The third Evaluation box disappears, and <u>275*0.065</u> is displayed in the second Evaluation box.
- Click **Evaluate**. The formula 275*0.065 evaluates to 17.88.
- Click **Step Out**. The second Evaluation box closes, and 17.875 replaces F33 in the top Evaluation box formula, which now displays <u>0+17.875</u>+F30.
- Click **Evaluate**. The formula shown in the Evaluation box changes to 17.875+<u>F30</u>.
- Click **Step In**. The Evaluation box is split. The formula <u>D30</u>*E30 is shown in the bottom Evaluation box—the formula in cell F30.

  This is clearly in error. F30 is the total cell for the last line item in the invoice, not the subtotal. Notice that cell F30 is shown as the active cell in the worksheet as well, a visual indicator that the wrong cell is included in the formula in cell F35.

g. Click **Close**. You cannot edit a formula in evaluation mode. Select cell **F35**, click in the **Formula bar**, and then change F30 to **F31**. Press ⌨Ctrl+⌨Enter. The value in cell F35 should now be 292.88.

h. Press ⌨Ctrl+⌨Home, and then click **Save** 🖫.

Understanding Circular References

Excel uses the term **circular reference** to describe a single formula that references itself or multiple formulas that reference each other, such that each cannot evaluate until another in the circle is evaluated. Technically, the formulas are precedents and dependents of one another. In databases this condition is often referred to as a deadly embrace. Essentially it means action A requires action B to complete before it can execute, but action B requires action A to complete before it can execute.

Generally circular references are erroneous, but Excel only warns of them because some mathematical calculations require circular references. Circular calculations are outside the scope of this textbook, consequently circular references are treated as errors.

To Detect and Correct Circular References

a. Select cell **F31**, click in the **Formula bar**, highlight **30**, and then type 31. Press ⌨Ctrl+⌨Enter, and then click **OK** in the Circular Reference Warning alert.

  You have just created a single formula that contains a circular reference—a reference to itself. Notice that F31 does not display a value. Prior to introduction of the circular reference, F31 displayed 275.00. The status bar displays "Circular References: F31" to show you exactly where the circular reference is in your worksheet.

b. Click the **Error Checking arrow** in the Formula Auditing group, and then select **Circular References**. A list is displayed, indicating that you should check F31.

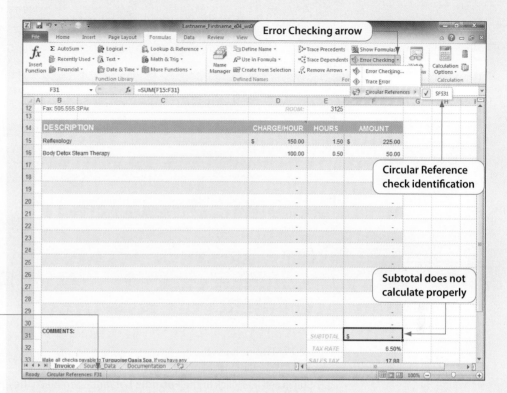

Figure 13 Circular reference identification

c. Click in the **Formula bar**, select **31**, and type **30**. Press Ctrl + Enter to correct the circular reference.

d. Select cell **F33**, click in the **Formula bar**, and then place the insertion point at the end of the formula.

e. Type **+F35**, press Ctrl + Enter , and then click **OK** in the Circular Reference Warning alert.

When a circular reference involves more than one formula, a blue arrow is automatically displayed that indicates the co-dependence of the two formulas. Notice it is a two-headed arrow—the indicant of a two-formula circular reference.

f. Click the **Error Checking arrow** in the Formula Auditing group, and then select **Circular References**. A menu is displayed, indicating that you should check F33 and F35.

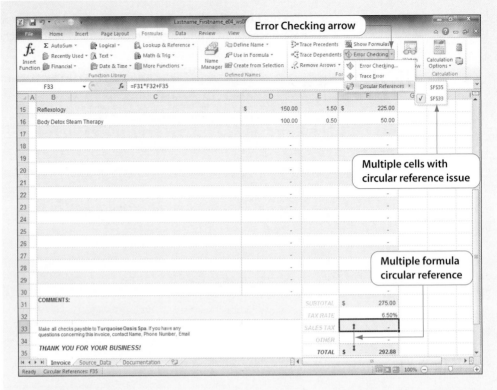

Figure 14 Two-formula circular reference identification

g. Still in cell F33, click in the **Formula bar**, and then place the insertion point at the end of the formula.

h. Highlight **+F35**, press ⌈Delete⌋, and then press ⌈Ctrl⌋+⌈Enter⌋.

i. Press ⌈Ctrl⌋+⌈Home⌋, and then click **Save** 🖫.

Using Watch Window

The Watch Window is an Excel feature that makes it possible to monitor cells the user considers important. The Watch Window is particularly useful when you are making changes in one worksheet or workbook and you want to monitor the effect of your changes to values in several other worksheets or workbooks.

To include a cell in the Watch Window, the workbook that contains the cell must be open and must remain open. The moment a workbook is closed, any cells in that workbook that are being watched are removed from the Watch Window.

To Track Worksheet Values Using the Watch Window

a. Click the **File tab**, click **Open** from the menu on the left, if necessary navigate to the location where your data files are stored, and then double-click **e04_ws08_SpaSalon_Prices**.

b. Press ⌈Ctrl⌋+⌈Tab⌋ to make Lastname_Firstname_e04_ws_08_Spa_Invoice the active workbook.

c. Click the **Formulas tab**. Then
   - Click **Watch Window** in the Formula Auditing group.
   - Click cell **B15**.

- Click **Add Watch** in the Watch Window, and then click **Add** in the Add Watch dialog box.
- Click cell **D15**. Press and hold Ctrl, and then select cells **F15**, **F31**, **F33** and **F35**.
- Click **Add Watch** in the Watch Window, and then click **Add** in the Add Watch dialog box.

d. Press Ctrl+Tab to make e04_ws_08_SpaSalon_Prices the active workbook. Click and hold the **Title bar** of the Watch Window—the mouse pointer will change to ✥—and then drag the Watch Window to locate its Title bar on row 22.

Real World Advice — Dock the Watch Window

Docking the Watch Window keeps it from floating on top of your worksheet where you may have to move it around. If you do not want to move the Watch Window around the application window, click and hold the Title bar of the Watch Window and drag it to the bottom of the worksheet application window. It will dock on the bottom and stay there. You can also dock the Watch Window on the top, left, or right of the Excel worksheet application window.

To undock the Watch Window, simply grab the Title bar and drag toward the middle of the application window.

e. Select cell **C23**, type 175, and then press Ctrl+Enter.

Notice that every monitored cell other than B15 in the Watch Window changed. Cell F35 changed from $292.88 to $332.81. You will have to scroll down to see cell F35 in the Watch Window, or resize the Watch Window by dragging the bottom border downward.

Figure 15 Monitor several workbook cells in the Watch Window

Troubleshooting

If the values in the watched cells were not updated when you changed the value in cell C23, there are two possible issues. The first is that you might need to manually refresh the links: click the Data tab and click Refresh All in the Connections group. If that does not work you probably have the wrong copy of e04_ws08_SpaSalon_Prices open—make sure it is the copy in the same folder as the Lastname_Firstname_e04_ws08_Spa_Invoice file.

f. Press Ctrl+Z to undo the change, and then notice the corresponding changes in the Watch Window.

g. Press Ctrl+Tab to make Lastname_Firstname_e04_ws_08_Spa_Invoice the active workbook.

h. Click and hold the **Title bar** of the Watch Window—the mouse pointer will change to ✥—and then drag the Watch Window up as until it docks below the Ribbon.

i. Click the **Source_Data worksheet tab**, click cell **D12**, type Reflexology Therapy, and then press Ctrl+Enter. Notice that cell B15 did not change in the Watch Window. Changing the value in a source cell does not change previously selected and validated values. Press Ctrl+Z to undo the change.

j. Click the **Invoice worksheet tab**, click cell **E15**, type 0.75, and then press Ctrl+Enter. Notice the changes to most of the watched values affected by this action in the Watch Window. Press Ctrl+Z to undo the change, and then notice the corresponding changes in the Watch Window. Clearly, cells can be monitored between and among worksheets and workbooks.

k. Click **Watch Window** in the Formula Auditing group to close the Watch Window.

l. Press Ctrl+Home, and then click **Save** 🖫. Press Ctrl+Tab to make e04_ws08_ SpaSalon_Prices the active workbook, click **Close** ✕ , and then click **Don't Save** if prompted.

Creating a Polished Excel Application

There are many characteristics that can be listed to describe a polished application, whether an Excel application or an application developed in a different technology:

- Easy-to-understand user interface
- User-entered data is validated as much as is possible
- Easy, guided navigation
- Unnecessary functionality hidden or disabled
- Offers protection from users inadvertently changing data that would break the application
- Only essential content is visible
- Good documentation exists

So far, in developing the invoice application, the worksheet is easy to understand—it is modeled after a standard invoice design and layout, and data validation has been applied to ensure correct data entry as much as can be programmatically determined. In this section you will modify the invoice workbook to make it a more polished and useable application.

Controlling Workbook Navigation

Workbook navigation is defined as moving from one cell to another in a worksheet and moving between worksheets. Assisting workbook users by adding navigation aids to a workbook and by hiding worksheets and features that are not needed by the user makes that workbook much more usable, easier to understand, and makes its appearance much cleaner and less intimidating.

Navigating with Hyperlinks

Hyperlinks are objects, such as a string of text, that when clicked with the mouse navigate to a predefined location within large worksheets, among worksheets in a workbook, among workbooks, to websites, to open documents and images, and to send e-mail. The inclusion of hyperlinks in a workbook can make navigation much more intuitive and self-explanatory and can make maintenance of workbook source data and other activities in a workbook that require the user to change locations much more efficient.

In the invoice workbook for the Turquoise Oasis Spa, the need to copy data from other workbooks to populate named ranges that are used in data validation is an opportunity to use hyperlinks to make maintenance of that data easier and less time consuming—generally more efficient and guided.

To Add Hyperlinks to the Workbook

a. Click the **Insert Tab**.

b. Click the **Source_Data worksheet tab**. Then

- Click cell **A8**.
- Click **Hyperlink** in the Links group, and the Insert Hyperlink dialog box is displayed. Make sure **Existing File or Web Page** is selected in the Link to menu.
- In the Text to display box, type Open Source Workbook for Employee Data.... If necessary, navigate to the location where you are storing your student data files, and then click **e04_ws08_Spa_Employees**.

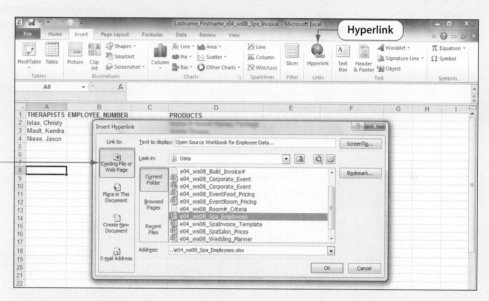

Figure 16 Insert hyperlink to an external file

c. Click **OK**, and then press Ctrl + B.

d. Click **Open Source Workbook for Employee Data** in cell A8. The e04_ws08_Spa_Employees workbook should open.

e. Click **Close** X.

f. Select cell **D19**, click **Hyperlink** in the Links group to display the the Insert Hyperlink dialog box. Type Open Source Workbook for Product Data... in the Text to display box. If necessary, navigate to the location where you are storing your student data files, and then click **e04_ws08_SpaSalon_Prices**, click **OK**, and then press Ctrl + B.

g. Click **Open Source Workbook for Product Data** in cell D19. The e04_ws08_SpaSalon_Prices workbook should open.

h. Click **Close** X.

i. Select cell **A16**. Then

- Click **Hyperlink** in the Links group to display the Insert Hyperlink dialog box.
- Click **Place in This Document** in the Link to menu, triple-click in the Text to Display box to select its contents, and then type Invoice Worksheet....
- Select **Invoice** in the Cell Reference branch of the Or select a place in this document box.

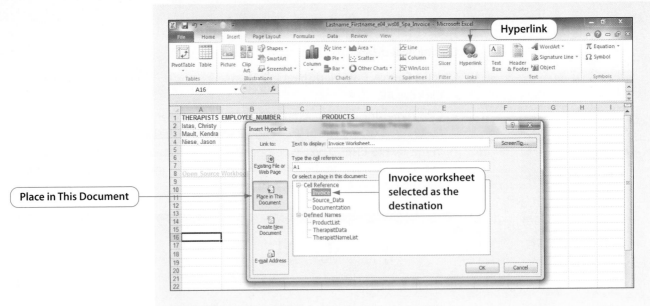

Figure 17 Insert hyperlink to a worksheet in the workbook

j. Click **OK**, and then press ⎡Ctrl⎤+⎡B⎤.

k. Click **Invoice Worksheet...** in cell A16. The Invoice worksheet should now be the active worksheet.

l. Select cell **B40** in the Invoice worksheet. Then

- Click **Hyperlink** in the Links group.
- Click **Place in This Document** in the Link to menu.
- Triple-click in the Text to display box to select its contents, and then type View Product Source Data....
- Click **ProductList** in the Defined Names branch of the Or select a place in this document box.
- Click **OK**, and then press ⎡Ctrl⎤+⎡B⎤.

m. Select cell **B42**. Then

- Click **Hyperlink** in the Links group.
- Triple-click in the Text to display box, and then type View Employee Source Data....
- Click **TherapistData** in the Defined Names branch of the Or select a place in this document box.
- Click **OK**, and then press ⎡Ctrl⎤+⎡B⎤.

n. Click **View Product Source Data** in cell B40. The Source_Data worksheet is made active and the ProductList named range is selected. Then

- Click **Invoice Worksheet** in cell A16.
- Click **View Employee Source Data** in cell B42. The Source_Data worksheet is made active and the TherapistData named range is selected.
- Click **Invoice Worksheet** in cell A16.

o. Press ⎡Ctrl⎤+⎡Home⎤. Click **Save** 🔲.

Hiding Worksheets

A workbook with a lot of source data, also called master data, stored in separate worksheets can seem cluttered and difficult to navigate. Additionally, there are situations where you would rather users not see source data or have access to background calculations and code that has been placed in a master data worksheet. To hide a worksheet, right-click the tab of the worksheet you want to hide and select Hide from the shortcut menu.

To Hide a Worksheet

a. Right-click the **Source_Data worksheet tab**, and then click **Hide** from the shortcut menu.

b. Click the **Invoice worksheet tab**, and then click **View Product Source Data** in cell B40, nothing happens—see Side Note.

c. Right-click the **Invoice worksheet tab**, select **Unhide** from the shortcut menu, and then click **OK** in the Unhide dialog box.

d. Click **Invoice Worksheet** in cell A16, and then click **View Product Source Data** in cell B40. Now hyperlinks to the Source_Data worksheet function.

e. Click **Invoice Worksheet** in cell A16.

SIDE NOTE
Hyperlinks and Hidden Worksheets
Once a worksheet is hidden, hyperlinks to the hidden worksheet will no longer work.

Hiding Worksheet Tabs

By hiding worksheet tabs, you can keep users from navigating to worksheets that contain master data you do not want them to edit. Unlike hiding worksheets, hiding worksheet tabs does not stop navigation to other worksheets in the workbook if hyperlinks have been created that allow the user to move from one sheet to another. If there are no hyperlinks between and among worksheets, hiding worksheet tabs yields basically the same result as hiding worksheets.

To Hide Worksheet Tabs

a. Click the **Invoice worksheet tab**.

b. Click the **File tab**, click **Options**, and then click **Advanced** in the Excel Options dialog box. Scroll down in the Excel Options dialog box until the Display options for this workbook group is visible.

c. Uncheck **Show sheet tabs**.

SIDE NOTE
Make the "User" Worksheet Active First!
Make sure the worksheet you want visible to users is active before hiding worksheet tabs, because you will not be able to move to another worksheet in the workbook without unhiding worksheet tabs, unless you already have hyperlinks created.

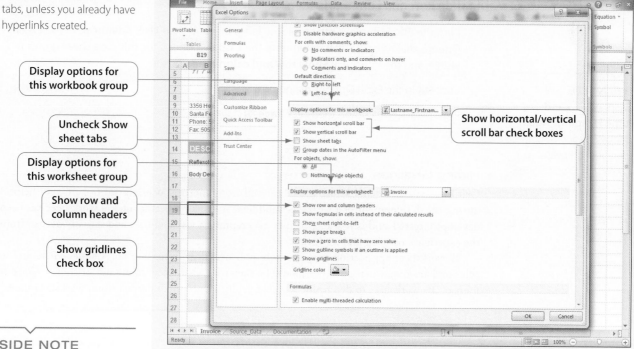

Figure 18 Workbook and worksheet display options

d. Click **OK**. Press $\boxed{\text{Ctrl}}+\boxed{\text{Home}}$, and then click **Save** 🖫.

SIDE NOTE
How Do I Display Worksheet Tabs Again?
To display worksheet tabs again, repeat step b, and then check Show sheet tabs.

Hiding Scroll Bars

Depending on the size of the worksheet and the resolution of users' monitors, vertical and/or horizontal scroll bars may or may not be unnecessary. The Turquoise Spa Invoice worksheet is small enough that neither horizontal nor vertical scroll bars are necessary for higher-resolution monitors; however, for lower-resolution monitors, the vertical scroll bar may be necessary.

To Hide Scroll Bars

a. Click the **File tab**, click **Options**, and then click **Advanced** in the Excel Options dialog box. Scroll down in the Excel Options dialog box until the Display options for this workbook group is visible. Uncheck **Show horizontal scroll bar**, uncheck **Show vertical scroll bar**, and then click **OK**.

   Notice that both scroll bars are gone from the application window. Some screen resolutions may not allow the entire invoice to be displayed vertically.

b. Click the **File tab**, click **Options**, and then click **Advanced** in the Excel Options dialog box. Scroll down until the Display options for this workbook group is visible. Check **Show vertical scroll bar**, and then click **OK**.

c. Press Ctrl+Home, and then click **Save** 🖫.

Hiding Row and Column Headings

In a well-designed worksheet, row and column headings may not be necessary. Users will be able to navigate and use the worksheet features without need of specific cell references as indicated by headings.

   For a form as ubiquitous as an invoice, users should be able to complete the activities required to build an invoice without row and column headings.

To Hide Row and Column Headers

a. Click the **File tab**, click **Options** in the left pane, and then click **Advanced** in the Excel Options dialog box. Scroll down until the Display options for this worksheet group is visible, and then uncheck **Show row and column headers**.

b. Click **OK** in the Excel Options dialog box.

c. Press Ctrl+Home, and then click **Save** 🖫.

SIDE NOTE

To Display Row and Column Headings Again

To display row and column headers again, repeat step a, and then click to select Show row and column headers in the Display options for this worksheet group.

Hiding Gridlines

Gridlines visually demark one worksheet cell from another. While gridlines are very helpful during the development of a worksheet and lend it visual structure, once a worksheet has been developed, tested, and is in use, gridlines may represent visual clutter and actually detract from the experience of using the worksheet.

   A worksheet application may be more polished if gridlines are not visible. There are no rules to determine when gridlines should be shown or when they should not be shown. Consult users of the worksheet to determine whether gridlines add to, or detract from, worksheet usage.

SIDE NOTE

How Do I Display Gridlines Again?

To display gridlines again, repeat step a, and then click Show gridlines in the Display options for this worksheet group. An alternative way to hide/unhide gridlines is to click the View tab, and then uncheck or check Gridlines in the Show group.

SIDE NOTE

Hiding Gridlines May Not Affect Printing

Gridlines may still print even if they are not displayed on the monitor. Whether or not gridlines are printed is set in the Sheet tab of the Page Setup dialog box. Either check or uncheck Gridlines in the Print group.

To Hide Gridlines

a. Click the **File tab**, click **Options**, and then click **Advanced**. Scroll down until the Display options for this worksheet group is visible.

b. Uncheck **Show gridlines**, and then click **OK**.

c. Press `Ctrl`+`Home`, and then click **Save** 🖫.

Automating with Macros

A **macro** is a form of computer program that automates activities such as mouse movements and clicks, menu selections, and data entry. At its most basic, a macro in Excel is just a recording of keystrokes and mouse clicks performed to complete a task. If a task is performed repeatedly in a worksheet, it is probably a candidate to be recorded as a macro, particularly if incorrectly performing the task could damage the worksheet.

Creating a Trusted Location

A **trusted location** is a folder that has been identified in the Microsoft Office Trust Center as a safe location from which to open files that contain active code such as macros, ActiveX controls, and so on. If a file, such as a workbook, is opened from a trusted location, macros contained in the document will be enabled; if the location where the file is stored is not known to the Trust Center as a trusted location, the Trust Center will block any macros, controls, scripts, and other items that could contain malicious code.

Trusted locations are specified in the Trust Center in Backstage view in the Excel Options dialog box.

To Create a Trusted Location

a. Click the **File tab**, and then click **Options**. Then
   - In the Excel Options dialog box click **Trust Center**.
   - Click **Trust Center Settings** under Microsoft Trust Center.
   - Click **Trusted Locations**, and then click **Add new location** in the right pane.
   - Click **Browse** in the Microsoft Office Trusted Location dialog box, navigate to the location where you store your files for this workshop, and then click **OK**.

b. If you have subfolders in the folder you selected in step b and you intend to store workbooks that contain macros in any of them, check **Subfolders of this location are also trusted**. Type Trusted Location for macro-enabled workbooks created in Your Office exercises for Workshop 8 in the Description box.

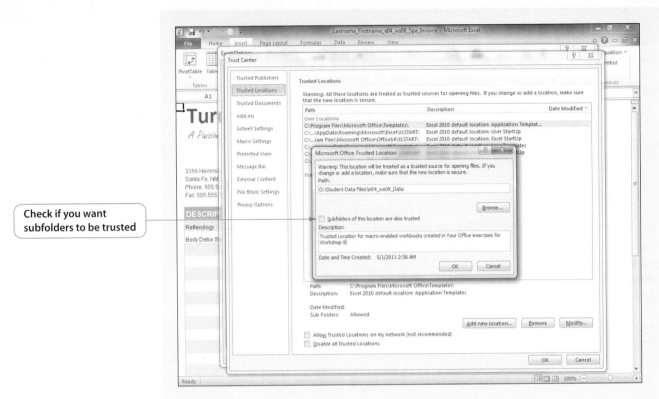

Check if you want subfolders to be trusted

Figure 19 Create a trusted location in the Microsoft Office Trust Center

c. Click **OK**, click **OK** in the Trust Center dialog box, and then in the Excel Options dialog box, click **OK** in the Excel Options dialog box.

d. Click **Save** 🖫.

Adding the Developer Tab to the Ribbon

Recording macros is generally considered an activity for worksheet developers. The Developer tab is not visible by default in Excel, so in order to record a macro, the Developer tab must be added to the Ribbon.

To Add the Developer Tab to the Ribbon

a. Click the **File tab**, click **Options**, and then click **Customize Ribbon**. If necessary, select **Main Tabs** in the Customize the Ribbon control, check **Developer** in the Main Tabs list, and then click **OK**.

b. Click **Save** 🖫.

Recording a Macro

Recording a macro is much like recording a speech or a musical performance with a sound or video recorder. Turn on the recorder, perform a planned series of mouse clicks and keystrokes, and then turn off the recorder. That is an oversimplification where Excel is concerned, but it is basically descriptive of the process.

The real work in recording a macro is in getting ready to record. Much like an artist recording a new song, you will spend much more time writing, arranging, and practicing your macro than you spend recording. Before hitting the record button, you must know exactly which mouse clicks and keystrokes form the macro. Make a plan:

1. Write—Determine what the macro is to do.

2. Arrange—Determine the exact mouse clicks and keystrokes and their order.

3. Practice—Go through the actions of the task prior to recording until you are sure the combination of keystrokes and mouse clicks will accomplish the task properly.

4. Record.

Absolute Macro References

As with cell references in formulas, cell references in macros can be absolute or relative. **Absolute macro references** affect exactly the same cell address every time the macro is run. Absolute macro references are set when the macro is recorded. The location of the active cell when the macro is run (think "played" like a recording) is irrelevant. Macros are recorded with absolute references by default.

To Record an Absolute Macro

a. Recording a macro will be easier and much more accurate if you first turn on the row and column headings. Click the **File tab**, click **Options**, and then click **Advanced**. Scroll down until the Display options for this worksheet group is visible. Check **Show row and column headers**, and then click **OK**.

b. Select cell range **B15:B30**. Then

- Type LineItemDescRange in the Name box, and then press ⏎Enter.
- Select cell range **E15:E30**, type LineItemHourRange in the Name box, and then press ⏎Enter.
- Select cell **C31**, type CommentText in the Name box and then press ⏎Enter.
- Press ⏎Ctrl+⏎Home.

c. Click the **Developer tab**, and then click **Record Macro** in the Code group. Type Macro_ClearInvoice in the Macro name box of the Record Macro dialog box. Press ⏎Tab. Press and hold ⏎Shift, and then type C in the Shortcut key box. Notice that Shift is added to the shortcut key combination. Type Clear all data entered into the invoice in the Description box.

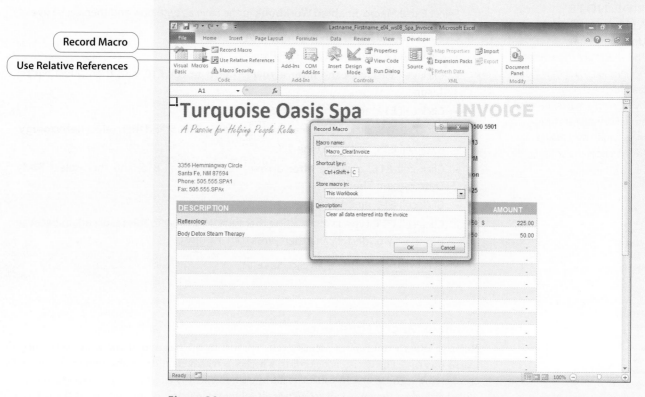

Record Macro

Use Relative References

Figure 20 Enter information to record a macro

d. Click **OK**. Everything you do from this point is recorded as part of the macro.

e. Select cell **E6** (the Invoice date). Then
   - Press and hold `Ctrl`, and then select cells **E8**, **E10**, and **E12**.
   - Press and hold `Ctrl`, click the **Name box arrow** `▾◖`, and then select **LineItemDescRange**.
   - Press and hold `Ctrl`, click the **Name box arrow** `▾◖`, and then select **LineItemHourRange**.
   - Press and hold `Ctrl`, click the **Name arrow** `▾`, and then select **CommentText**.
   - Press `Delete`, and then press `Ctrl`+`Home`.

f. Click **Stop Recording** in the Code group.

g. Press `Ctrl`+`Z` to Undo the effects of recording the Macro_ClearInvoice macro.

h. Press `Ctrl`+`Shift`+`C` to run Macro_ClearInvoice.

Troubleshooting

If Macro_ClearInvoice did not delete all user-entered data in the cells selected in step d above, you probably missed a step in recording the macro. Delete Macro_ClearInvoice (see Side Note), click Close Window, and then click Don't Save. Click the File tab, click Recent, and double-click Lastname_Firstname_e04_ws08_Spa_Invoice. Do not continue with this exercise; return to step a and repeat this exercise.

i. Press `Ctrl`+`Home`, and then click **Save** `💾`.
   The Microsoft Excel alert box that appears is warning you that you are trying to save a workbook that contains a macro as a macro-free workbook— with an .xlsx extension.

j. Click **No**. You do not want to save this workbook as a macro-free workbook.

k. Select **Excel Macro-Enabled Workbook** in the Save as type box, and then click **Save**.

l. Click cell **E6**, and then press `Ctrl`+`;`. Then
   - Click cell **E8**, and then type 3:00 PM.
   - Click cell **E10**, click the **filter arrow** `▾` next to cell E10, and then select **Niese, Jason**.
   - Click cell **E12**, and then type 3125.
   - Click cell **B15**, click the **filter arrow** `▾` next to cell B15, and then select **Reflexology**.
   - Click cell **E15**, and then type 1.5.
   - Click cell **B16**, click the **filter arrow** `▾` next to cell B16, and then select **Body DetoxSteam Therapy**.
   - Click cell **E16**, and then type 0.5.
   - Click cell **C31**, type Jason is a fine therapist. I will stay in this resort again because the spa is wonderful!, and then press `Ctrl`+`Enter`.

m. Press `Ctrl`+`Home`, and then click **Save** `💾`.

SIDE NOTE
To Delete a Macro
If you wish to delete a macro you have created, click Macro in the Code group of the Developer tab, select the macro you want to delete in the Macro name box, and then click Delete.

SIDE NOTE
A Macro Cannot Be Undone
The effects of a macro cannot be reversed using the Undo feature. The changes made by running a macro are not stored in the Undo history. In fact, running a macro in Excel deletes the entire Undo history.

Relative Macro References

Relative macro references identify cells relative to the location of the active cell when the macro was run. The decision regarding whether a macro should use absolute or relative references is simple. If the macro you are recording should always effect the same cells and those cells will always have the same cell references, absolute referencing is appropriate. If the macro you are recording should effect cells that are identified relative to the location of the active cell, or should effect cell references that change as worksheet rows or columns are inserted or deleted, relative macro references are appropriate.

To Record a Relative Macro

a. Select cell **B31**. Then

- Type CommentHeader in the Name box, press Enter, and then press Ctrl+ Home.
- Click the **Developer tab**.
- Click **Use Relative References** in the Code group.
- Click **Record Macro** in the Code group.
- In the Record Macro dialog box, type Macro_InsertInvoiceLine in the Macro name box.
- Press Tab. Press and hold Shift, and then type I in the Shortcut key box. Notice that Shift is added to the shortcut key combination.
- Type Insert a new line into the invoice in the Description box, and then click **OK**. Everything you do from this point is recorded as part of the macro.

b. Press Ctrl+G. Then

- In the Go To dialog box, select **CommentHeader** in the Go To box, and then click **OK**.
- Press ↑, right-click the active cell, and then select **Insert** from the shortcut menu.
- In the Insert dialog box, select **Entire row**, and then click **OK**.
- Press ↓, press and hold Shift, and then press → three times.
- Press Ctrl+C, press ↑, press Ctrl+V, press ↑, press and hold Shift, and then press → three times.
- Press Ctrl+C, press ↓ twice, press and hold Shift, and then press → three times.
- Right-click the selected cells, and then click **Paste Formatting** ⏚ from the short-cut menu.
- Press ←, and then press →.
- Press Delete, press End, and then press → twice.
- Press Delete, press Home, and then press →.

c. Click **Stop Recording** in the Code group.

d. Select cell **B31**, right-click the active cell, and then select **Delete** from the shortcut menu. In the Delete dialog box, select **Entire row**, and then click **OK**. Press Ctrl+Home.

e. Press Ctrl+Shift+I to run Macro_InsertInvoiceLine.

Troubleshooting

If Macro_InsertInvoiceLine did not insert a row in the invoice at row 31 or if the inserted row is not formatted properly, you probably missed a step in recording the macro. Delete Macro_InsertInvoiceLine (see Side Note), click Close Window and click Don't Save. Click the File tab, click Recent, and double-click Lastname_Firstname_ e04_ws08_Spa_Invoice (the macro-enabled version). Do not continue with this exercise; return to step a and repeat this exercise.

f. Select cell **B31**, right-click the active cell, and select **Delete** from the shortcut menu. In the Delete dialog box, click **Entire row**, and then click **OK**.

g. Press Ctrl+Home. Click **Save** ⊟.

Running a Macro

In the last two exercises you ran the macros you created using keyboard shortcuts. There are other ways to run a macro that require less specific knowledge of the macro's existence.

Macros can be run from the Developer tab, although most users will not have the Developer tab available. Macros can also be run from a button that you can add to a worksheet.

To Run a Macro from the Ribbon and from a Button

a. Click the **Developer tab**. Click **Macros** in the Code group to display the Macro dialog box. Click **Macro_ClearInvoice** in the select box—just below the Macro name box. Click **Run**.

   You just ran a macro from the Developer tab.

b. Click **Close Window** ⊠ , and then click **Don't Save**.

   You cannot undo the changes the macro made, so the most efficient way to put data back in the invoice is to not save it and open the workbook again.

c. Start Excel. Click the **File tab**, click **Recent** in the left pane, and then click **Lastname_ Firstname_e04_ws08_Spa_Invoice** to open the workbook. If prompted, click **Don't Update** in the alert box.

d. The next method you will learn to run a macro is to assign a macro to a button. Drawing buttons is a lot easier if gridlines are visible, so click the **View tab**, and then check **Gridlines** in the Show group.

e. Click the **Developer tab**, click **Insert** in the Controls group, and then click **Button (Form Control)** ▭ in the top row.

Figure 21 Insert a form control from the Developer tab

Troubleshooting

Be very careful once you create a button to run a macro. Even when editing the button and its properties, a left-click on the button will run the macro.

f. Move the mouse pointer to the bottom of the invoice below the Total line, and notice the pointer has changed to the Precision Select the pointer ✛. Drag to draw a button that covers cell F37 (you may have to scroll down a few lines first), and then release the mouse button. The Assign Macro dialog box is displayed. Select **Macro_InsertInvoiceLine** in the select box.

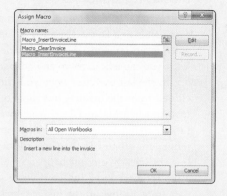

Figure 22 Insert a form control from the Developer tab

g. Click **OK**.

h. Right-click the button.

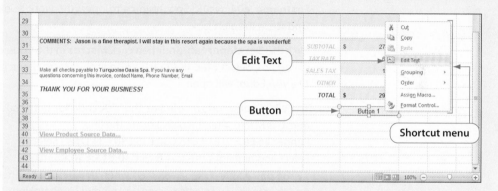

Figure 23 Edit button text

i. Click **Edit text** from the shortcut menu. The insertion point will be placed in the button. Select the text currently in the button, and then press Delete. Type Insert Invoice Line, and then click outside the button.

j. Click the **Insert Invoice Line button**.

   You just ran a macro from a button control.

k. Right-click the **Insert Invoice Line button**, click **Copy** from the shortcut menu, right-click just below the Insert Invoice Line button, and then click **Paste** from the shortcut menu.

l. Move the mouse pointer over the copy of the Insert Invoice Line button to a position where the mouse pointer changes to the Move Select pointer. Move the copied button so it is just below the original. You can refine its position using the arrow keys. Right-click the **copied button**, and then click **Edit text** from the shortcut menu. Select the text currently in the button, and then press Delete. Type Clear Invoice, and then click outside the button.

m. Right-click the **Clear Invoice button**, click **Assign Macro** from the shortcut menu, select **Macro_ClearInvoice** in the select box, and then click **OK**.

n. Select cell **B31**. Click the **filter arrow** ▼ next to cell B31, and then select **Massage - Fusion**. Select cell **E31**, type 1, and then press Ctrl+Enter.

o. Press Ctrl+Home, and then click **Save** 🖫.

p. Click the **Clear Invoice button**.

   Notice that Macro_ClearInvoice did not clear all the data in row 31! In the next exercise you will modify Macro_ClearInvoice to clear the data from all line items in the invoice.

q. Click **Close Window** ⊠ to close the workbook but not Excel, and then click **Don't Save**.

Modifying a Macro

When you record a macro, Excel is actually converting your keystrokes and mouse clicks to commands in a language called Visual Basic for Applications, or VBA. If you make a mistake when recording a macro, you can delete the macro and record a new one, or if you know a little VBA you can edit a macro and change the VBA that Excel produced.

In the last exercise, when you clicked the Clear Invoice button, the data above row 31 was cleared from the invoice, but some of the data in row 31 was not. Row 31 was not part of the invoice when Macro_ClearInvoice was recorded. Two named ranges, LineItemDescRange and LineItemHourRange, were created and used in the recording of Macro_ClearInvoice. Named ranges are supposed to expand to include new rows and columns that are inserted into them, but that clearly did not happen in Macro_ClearInvoice. In the next exercise you will edit the VBA code produced by Excel when you recorded Macro_ClearInvoice and modify it to delete data from all rows in the invoice, including any rows inserted using Macro_InsertInvoiceLine.

To Modify Macro_ClearInvoice to Affect All Line Items

a. Click the **File tab**, click **Recent** in the left menu pane, and then click **Lastname_Firstname_e04_ws08_Spa_Invoice** to open the work book. If prompted, click **Don't Update** in the alert box.

b. Click the **Developer tab**, and then click **Macros** in the Code group to display the Macro dialog box. Select **Macro_ClearInvoice** in the Macro name list box, and then click **Edit**. The VBA Editor will open.

c. The VBA Code window contains the VBA code for both macros you recorded. The first macro is Macro_ClearInvoice. Locate the line:
Range("E6,E8,E10,E12,B15:C30,E15:E30,C31:D32").Select
Select and highlight the text **B15:C30,E15:E30,C31:D32**.

B15:B30 was the range selected when you named LineItemDescRange, and E15:E30 was the range you selected when you named LineItemHourRange. C31:D32 is the range of merged cells you named CommentText. When you use the name box to select a named range while recording a macro, the range address is inserted into the VBA code, not the range name. Then, when you insert a row into the range with Macro_InsertInvoiceLine, Excel does not adjust the range address in Macro_ClearInvoice to reflect the inserted row as it would with formulas in a worksheet—the formula to create the subtotal of the invoice, for example. This can be corrected by replacing range addresses with range names.

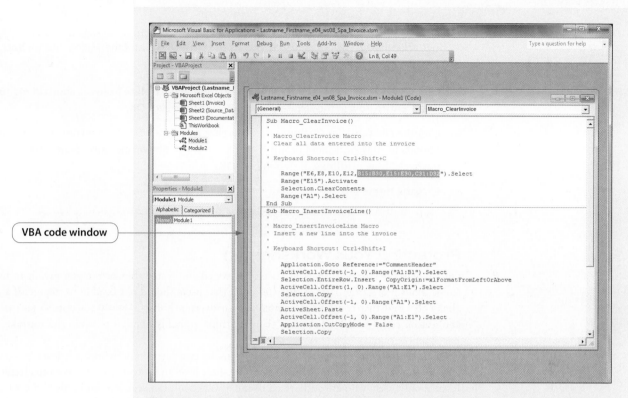

VBA code window

Figure 24 The Visual Basic for Applications Editor

Troubleshooting

The code you see in the VBA Code window may not exactly match the code shown in Figure 24. Excel converts every keystroke and mouse click to VBA code when recording a macro, so any deviation from the steps in the exercise where you created the macros, including keystrokes to correct deviations, are recorded.

d. Type **LineItemDescRange,LineItemHourRange,CommentText**. The line of VBA code should now read:

Range("E6,E8,E10,E12,LineItemDescRange,LineItemHourRange,CommentText").Select

e. Click **Save** 🖫, and then click **Close** ✕ to close the VBA Editor.

f. Click **Clear Invoice**.

Notice that all the data in row 31 was deleted by Macro_ClearInvoice. Because you modified the macro to select the named ranges, rather than the addresses of the ranges at the time the macro was recorded, the macro selects the named ranges at the time of execution, rather than the range address at the time of recording.

g. Enter the following data:
- Click cell **E6**, and then press Shift+;.
- Click cell **E8**, and then type 1:30 PM.
- Click cell **E10**, click the **filter arrow** ▾ next to cell E10, and then select **Mault, Kendra**.
- Click cell **E12**, and then type 2075.
- Click cell **B15**, click the **filter arrow** ▾ next to cell B15, and then select **Tibetan Reiki Therapy**.
- Click cell **E15**, and then type 1.
- Click cell **B16**, click the **filter arrow** ▾ next to cell B16, and then select **Aroma & Sound Therapy Package**.

- Click cell **E16**, and then type 0.5.
- Click cell **B17**, click the **filter arrow** ▾ next to cell B17, and then select **Steam Bath**.
- Click cell **E17**, and then type 0.5.

h. Click cell **B31**, right-click the active cell, and then select **Delete** from the shortcut menu. Select **Entire Row** in the Delete dialog box, and then click **OK**.

i. Click the **File tab**, click **Options**, and then click **Advanced**. Scroll down until the Display options for this worksheet group is visible. Uncheck **Show row and column headers**, uncheck **Show gridlines**, and then click **OK**.

j. Click the **Home tab**, press [Ctrl]+[Home], and then click **Save** 🖫.

Protecting Your Worksheet(s)

Once a workbook or worksheet has been developed and tested, but before you give it to users, think about protecting parts of the workbook that users should not be able to change. If a user clicks on a cell that contains a formula and inadvertently hits [Delete], a critical part of the application could be erased. Unless the user thinks quickly enough to undo the mistake, the Excel application could be broken.

Excel allows for protection of applications in two layers: the workbook level to control who has access to the workbook, and the worksheet level to protect worksheets from alteration. Ideally, only users who are authorized to use a workbook can access it, and only those who are authorized can change the contents of cells or change worksheet structures where appropriate.

Worksheet-level protection allows very finite control of how protection will affect the usability of a worksheet. Worksheet protection must be applied to individual worksheets; it cannot be applied to grouped worksheets. There are 15 activities that can be selectively restricted through worksheet protection; the most common are Select locked cells and Select unlocked cells. The other 13, such as Format row and Insert columns, are off by default when Protect Sheet is toggled on, but they can be turned on through the Protect Sheet dialog box. In a protected worksheet, many Ribbon commands are disabled and cannot be accessed unless Protected Sheet is toggled off.

Lock/Unlock Cells

By default, all cells in a worksheet are locked. This doesn't mean anything until you turn on worksheet protection. Once Protect Worksheet is toggled on, locked cells cannot be edited. Depending on the options you choose when you protect the worksheet, users may not be able to select locked cells.

The ability to toggle off worksheet protection is available to all Excel users; if you want to ensure users cannot unprotect a worksheet, add password protection through the Protect Sheet dialog box. Passwords are case sensitive, can be up to 256 characters in length, and can contain letters, numbers, and symbols such as #,$,!—basically any character than can be entered via the keyboard.

A worksheet in which all cells are locked and worksheet protection is turned on does not allow a user to modify worksheet contents. This may be desirable for master data worksheets and such, but for the Turquoise Oasis Spa invoice worksheet, cells in which users need to enter data must be unlocked prior to toggling on worksheet protection.

To Unlock Cells and Protect Locked Cells in a Worksheet

a. Click the **File tab**, select **Options**, and then click **Advanced**. Scroll down until the Display options for this worksheet group is visible. Check **Show row and column headers**, and then click **OK**.

   Visible row and column headers will make this procedure much easier.

b. Select cell **E6**, press and hold Ctrl, and then select cells **E8**, **E10**, **E12**, **C31**, **F32** and **F34**. Press Ctrl, and then select cell ranges **B15:B30** and **E15:E30**. Click the **Home tab**, and then click **Format** in the Cells group.

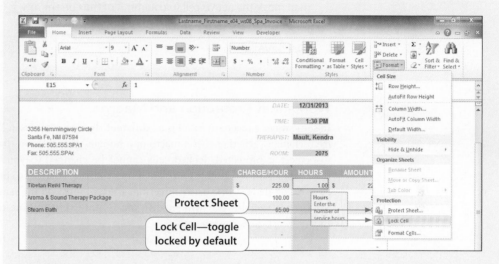

Figure 25 Unlock worksheet cells

c. Click **Lock Cell** in the Protection group of the menu. This toggles Lock Cell off. Press Ctrl + Home.

d. Click **Format** in the Cells group, and then click **Protect Sheet** in the Protection group of the menu to display the Protect Sheet dialog box. Uncheck the **Select locked cells** check box.

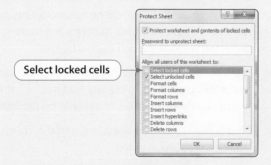

Figure 26 Protect Sheet dialog box

e. In the Protect Sheet dialog box, click **OK**.

f. Click **Format** in the Cells group. Notice that Protect Sheet in the Protection group of the menu is toggled to Unprotect Sheet.

g. Click cell **E4**. Cell E4 is locked, and because Protect Sheet is toggled on, you cannot select cell E4.

h. Click cell **B15**. Because cell B15 was unlocked in step b, you can select it even with Protect Sheet toggled on.

i. Click **Format** in the Cells group, click **Unprotect Sheet** in the Protection group of the menu, and then select cell **E4**. With Protect Sheet toggled off, you can now select cell E4.

j. Click **Format** in the Cells group, click **Protect Sheet** in the Protection group of the menu, and then click **OK** in the Protect Sheet dialog box.

k. Click cell **B20**, and then press ⎡Home⎤.

    Notice that the function of ⎡Home⎤ changes when Protect Sheet is toggled on. Rather than move the active cell to column A of the current row, it moves the active cell to the top-most and left-most unlocked cell in the worksheet.

l. Click **Save** 🖫.

Worksheet Protection and Macros

In some ways, a macro in Excel is no different than a human user. When a worksheet is protected from changes, whether it is a macro or a human user, making the changes is irrelevant—if the worksheet is protected, locked cells cannot be changed (beyond the activities allowed at the time protection was toggled on). For a user to make changes to protected cells, she or he would have to toggle off worksheet protection; a macro must do the same.

In this exercise you will modify Macro_InsertInvoiceLine to allow it to work when the Invoice worksheet is protected.

To Modify a Macro to Control Worksheet Protection

a. Click **Insert Invoice Line**. Notice the Microsoft Visual Basic error dialog that appears that indicates a run-time error.

b. Click **Debug**.

c. Click **Maximize** 🗖 in the top-right corner of the VBA Code window.

    Notice the highlighted line of code. Macro_InsertInvoiceLine cannot execute because it is trying to make CommentHeader the active cell. CommentHeader is a locked cell. One way to solve this would be to unlock CommentHeader, but that would only allow the macro to execute until it attempted to do something else that is not allowed in a protected worksheet, such as insert a line.

d. Use the mouse pointer to place the insertion point to the left of the yellow highlighted line of VBA code, next to the line that begins with *Application.Goto*. (If you recorded the macro exactly as specified, this should be the first line of executable VBA code.)

e. Press ⎡Enter⎤ to insert a blank line, and then press ⎡↑⎤ to move the insertion point to the blank line you just inserted.

f. Press ⎡Tab⎤, and then type ActiveSheet.Unprotect. Note: Do not type the period in your code.

g. Use the mouse pointer to move the insertion point to the left of *End Sub*—the last line of VBA code in the Macro_InsertInvoiceLine macro.

h. Press ⎡Enter⎤, press ⎡↑⎤, and then press ⎡Tab⎤.

i. Type ActiveSheet.Protect DrawingObjects:=True, Contents:=True, Scenarios:=True. Note: Do not type the period in your code.

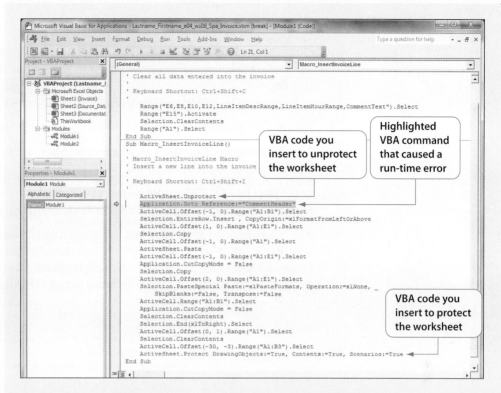

Figure 27 Macro_InsertInvoiceLine modified to control Worksheet Protection

j.   Click **Save** 🖫, and then click **Close** ✖ to close the VBA Editor.

k.   Click **Insert Invoice Line**. Macro_InsertInvoiceLine should execute properly.

l.   Press ⌂Home⌂, and then click **Save** 🖫.

Hiding Formulas

When Protect Sheet is toggled on, if Select Locked Cells in the Protect Sheet dialog box is unchecked, it is not possible to select a locked cell. Generally cells that contain formulas are locked, and because they cannot be selected, a user cannot view the formula in the Formula bar—proprietary formulas and methodologies are protected from inspection. There is another way that formulas can be examined even if cells that contain formulas are locked and Protect Sheet is toggled on—Show Formulas. Show Formulas is available in the Formula Auditing group of the Formulas tab, or via the Ctrl + ~ keyboard shortcut, even when Sheet Protection is toggled on.

To completely hide formulas in a worksheet is a three-step process:

1.   Select all cells in which you want to Hide formulas.

2.   Hide formulas by selecting Format in the Cells group of the Home tab, and then check Hidden in the Protection tab of the Format Cells dialog box.

3.   Leave all cells that contain formulas locked, and then toggle on Protect Sheet with Select locked cells unchecked.

The three steps above must be performed in that order, once Protect Sheet is toggled on, Format in the Cells group of the Home tab is not available.

To Hide Formulas

a. Click the **File tab**, click **Options**, and then click **Advanced**. Scroll down until the Display options for this workbook group is visible, check **Show horizontal scroll bar**, and then click **OK**.

You need to be able to scroll horizontally in the next step.

b. Press Ctrl+~ to toggle on Formula view. Scroll to the right to view the displayed formulas.

c. Click the **Review tab**, and then click **Unprotect Sheet** in the Changes group. This is an alternate way to toggle Protect Sheet on and off.

d. Click **Select All** ▦. Click the **Home tab**, click **Format** in the Cells group, and then click **Format Cells** in the Protection group of the menu to display the Format Cells dialog box.

e. If necessary, click the **Protection tab**, and then check **Hidden**.

In step b, you selected all cells in the worksheet. Only cells that are selected when Hidden is checked are protected from Show Formulas. Show Formulas is still available, that is, it will still toggle on and off, but it will not allow hidden cells to be shown.

Hidden check box

Figure 28 Protection tab of the Format Cells dialog box

f. Click **OK**. Press Ctrl+Home.

g. Click **Format** in the Cells group, click **Protect Sheet**, and then click **OK**.

Notice that formulas are no longer displayed. Formulas are hidden. All cells that contain formulas are locked so viewing formulas in the Formula box is not possible, and hiding formulas in this manner toggles off the ability to use the Ctrl+~ keystroke combination to view formulas as well.

h. Press Ctrl+~ to toggle off Formula view.

i. Click the **File tab**, click **Options**, and then click **Advanced**. Scroll down until the Display options for this workbook group is visible, and then uncheck the **Show horizontal scroll bar** check box. Scroll down until the Display options for this worksheet group is visible, uncheck the **Show row and column headers** check box, and then click **OK**.

j. Press Home, and then click **Save** 🖫.

Protecting Your Workbook

Protection at the workbook level is not nearly as flexible as is protection at the worksheet level. Worksheet protection allows many options for protection at the individual cell level, whereas workbook protection only allows you to require a password to open a worksheet, to lock down the structure of the workbook—prohibiting adding, deleting, or moving worksheets—and to mark a workbook as Final, which basically tells users the worksheet they are using is the final version intended for their use.

Encrypt with Password

The Info menu option of the File tab contains a Protect Workbook button. One of the options associated with the Protect Workbook button is Encrypt with Password. When a password is entered into the Encrypt Document dialog box, the workbook is encrypted when it is saved. **Encryption** uses a password to create a unique algorithm that is used to translate the saved Excel workbook into a stream of uninterpretable characters than can only be translated back using the password. For the user, the net result is that after a workbook has been saved with an encryption password, the password is required to open the workbook again.

If a password is lost, the workbook cannot be opened. It is very important that you remember your passwords. While many people write passwords down to remember them, it is better to use password management software available for computers, smart phones, and tablets—it is inexpensive, sometimes even free, and much safer than a sticky note under your keyboard.

To Encrypt a Workbook

a. Click the **File tab**, click **Protect Workbook**, and then select **Encrypt with Password** from the Protect Workbook menu.

Figure 29 Protect Workbook using encryption

Troubleshooting

> Back up your workbook. You are about to encrypt your workbook, which means it will require a password the next time you try to open it. If you make a typing mistake when entering your password, you may not be able to open your workbook again.

b. In the Encrypt Document dialog box type e04_ws08_Your_Office in the Password box. Excel matches case in passwords, so type very carefully.

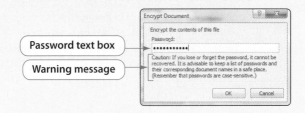

Password text box

Warning message

Figure 30 Password dialog box

c. Click **OK**, and then type e04_ws08_Your Office again. It is very important you enter a password correctly so Excel requires you to enter it twice. Click the **Home tab**. Click **OK**, click **Save** 🔲, and then click **Close** ⊠ to close Lastname_Firstname_e04_ws08_Spa_Invoice. Click the **File tab**, click **Recent** in the left menu pane, and then click **Lastname_Firstname_e04_ws08_Spa_Invoice.**

> The Password dialog box will appear. Opening Lastname_Firstname_eo4_ws08_Spa_Invoice now requires a password.

d. Type e04_ws08_Your_Office in the Password box of the Password dialog box.

e. Click **OK**, and then click **Don't Update**, if prompted.

Real World Advice   When Do You Use Encrypt with Password?

Encrypt with Password is a powerful form of workbook protection—powerful enough that you should use this option only when necessary. Encryption should be used in the following situations:

- The worksheet contains proprietary formulas or methodologies that you do not want users to be able to see (although worksheet-level protection is probably more important in this case).

- The worksheet contains data that is sensitive and should only be seen by users who have the password that allows the file to be opened.

When distributing an encrypted worksheet to users, it is considered a best practice to keep a pristine, unencrypted copy of the workbook stored in a safe location to ensure there is always a copy of the workbook that can be opened for maintenance and/or encryption and distribution.

Protect Current Sheet

Protect Current Sheet in the Protect Workbook menu is the same functionality already described and used in the exercises. The sequence of clicking the Review tab and Protect Sheet in the Changes group accesses the same functionality as does clicking the File tab, Format in the Cells group, and then Protect Sheet. This will not be covered again in an exercise. If you want to review using Protect Current Sheet, see the prior sections in this workshop on locking and unlocking cells and hiding formulas.

Protect Workbook Structure

Workbook structure protection stops users from adding, deleting, hiding, unhiding, and moving worksheets in a workbook. If a user accidentally deletes a formula from a cell, and if the user recognizes the error, Undo can be used to fix the problem. But Undo cannot undelete a worksheet that has been deleted.

Further, if a user decides to rename a worksheet, any unopened workbook that accesses data in the renamed worksheet will have its 3D references broken, and Undo will not fix it. If a worksheet in your workbook is accessed by other workbooks and you want to ensure that a user cannot delete or rename a critical worksheet, using Protect Workbook Structure will secure the worksheets and their names.

SIDE NOTE
Protect Windows?

Workbook structure protection includes an option to protect Windows. If you check that option, users cannot change the workbook window in the Excel application window—a workbook cannot be minimized if it is maximized.

SIDE NOTE
Turn Off Workbook Protection

All workbook protection options are essentially electronic toggle switches. To turn a workbook protection option off, simply navigate to it in Backstage view and click the option.

To Protect Workbook Structure

a. Click the **File tab**, click **Options**, and then click **Advanced**. Scroll down until the Display options for this workbook group is visible, click the **Show sheet tabs** check box, and then click **OK**.

   You'll need the worksheet tabs visible for the next steps.

b. Click the **File tab**, click **Protect Workbook**, and then select **Protect Workbook Structure** from the Protect Workbook menu. Verify the **Structure** check box is checked in the Protect Structure and Windows dialog box, and then do *not* enter a password. Click **OK**, and then click **Save** 🖫.

c. Right-click the **Invoice worksheet tab**.

   Notice menu items that could change the workbook structure are unavailable. Workbook structure is protected.

d. Click the **Invoice worksheet tab**. Try to move the Invoice worksheet to the right.

   Worksheets cannot be moved when workbook structure is protected.

e. Click the **File tab**, click **Options**, and then click **Advanced**. Scroll down the Advanced options for working with Excel pane until the Display options for this workbook group is visible, uncheck the **Show sheet tabs** check box, and then click **OK**.

f. Click **Save** 🖫.

Real World Advice   Don't Rely Solely on Workbook Protection

Workbook protection by itself does not lend much protection to your application. Even though a user cannot delete a worksheet, the user can still delete all the content in a worksheet unless worksheet protection is enabled. Protect your workbooks with both workbook-level and worksheet-level protection.

Mark as Final

Mark as Final is a workbook developer's way of notifying anyone who opens a workbook that development and testing are complete and that the workbook is ready for use. Mark as Final is a very weak form of protection, however. Even though a workbook has been marked as final, users are given the option to Edit Anyway. Mark as Final really represents a means of communicating the development status of a workbook. A workbook that has been marked as final, will display the Marked as Final 📄 icon in the status bar.

To Mark as Final

a. Click the **File tab**, click **Protect Workbook**, and then select **Mark as Final** from the Protect Workbook menu. Click **OK** in the alert box. You want the workbook to be marked as final and then saved. Click **OK** in the next alert box.

b. Click **Protect Workbook**.

Notice the other worksheet and workbook protection options are unavailable. Once Mark as Final is toggled on, other workbook protection functionality cannot be changed until such time as the Mark as Final is toggled off.

Mark as Final

Unavailable protection buttons because the workbook is Marked as Final

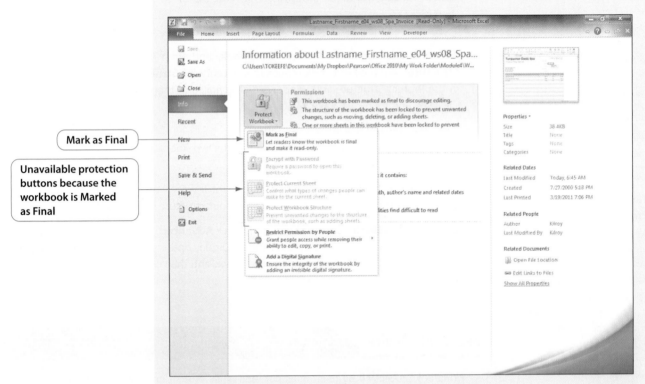

Figure 31 Mark as Final

c. Click the **Home tab**. The ⓘ information message below the menu bar indicates that the workbook is **Marked as Final**, and then it gives the user the option to Edit Anyway. Click **Close this message** ☒ at the right end of the information message.

Notice there is still a visible indicator that Mark as Final is toggled on. Mark as Final is displayed in the status bar in the bottom left of the application window.

d. Submit or print your project as directed by your instructor, and then **Close** ☒ Excel.

Concept Check

1. Excel makes several forms of data validation available on the Data tab. List five different types of data validation that can be applied to a cell, and describe a situation where you would use each. What are the relative advantages and disadvantages of custom data validation?

2. What is Formula Auditing? When is Formula Auditing useful? How does Formula Auditing differ from Show Formulas?

3. Macros are a powerful way to automate tasks in a workbook. Give an example of a macro you might record in a worksheet that would require absolute references. Give an example of a macro you might record in a worksheet that would require relative references. Can the inclusion of appropriate macros in a workbook improve worksheet protection? If so, give an example or two.

4. Several worksheet components can be hidden as a means of either protecting workbook content or making an Excel application appear more polished and professional. Both worksheets and worksheet tabs can be hidden. How does hiding these components improve the security of a workbook?

5. The concept of locked cells is fundamental to the effectiveness of worksheet-level protection. Discuss the nature of the relationship between Lock Cell and Protect Sheet. What must be done to ensure a user can select and change data values in cell range C10:C20 when Protect Sheet is toggled on? Compare worksheet-level protection and workbook-level protection, and discuss how they complement each other.

Key Terms

Absolute macro reference 405
Any value validation 387
Circular reference 394
Codification scheme 389
Codified data value 385
Custom validation 386
Data validation 380
Date validation 384

Decimal validation 382
Encryption 417
Formula auditing 391
Gridline 402
Hyperlink 398
List validation 380
Macro 403
Relational operator 382

Relative macro reference 406
Text length validation 388
Time validation 384
Trusted location 403
Validation criteria 380
Whole number validation 385

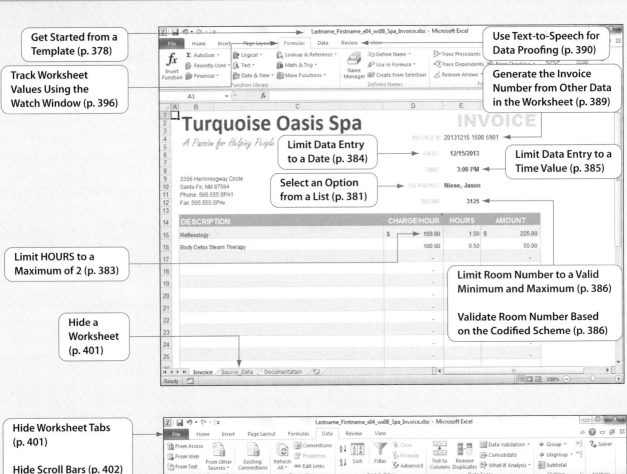

Get Started from a Template (p. 378)

Track Worksheet Values Using the Watch Window (p. 396)

Use Text-to-Speech for Data Proofing (p. 390)

Generate the Invoice Number from Other Data in the Worksheet (p. 389)

Limit Data Entry to a Date (p. 384)

Limit Data Entry to a Time Value (p. 385)

Select an Option from a List (p. 381)

Limit HOURS to a Maximum of 2 (p. 383)

Limit Room Number to a Valid Minimum and Maximum (p. 386)

Validate Room Number Based on the Codified Scheme (p. 386)

Hide a Worksheet (p. 401)

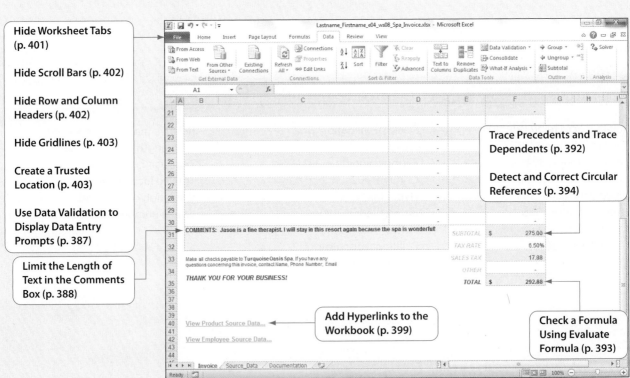

Hide Worksheet Tabs (p. 401)

Hide Scroll Bars (p. 402)

Hide Row and Column Headers (p. 402)

Hide Gridlines (p. 403)

Create a Trusted Location (p. 403)

Use Data Validation to Display Data Entry Prompts (p. 387)

Limit the Length of Text in the Comments Box (p. 388)

Trace Precedents and Trace Dependents (p. 392)

Detect and Correct Circular References (p. 394)

Add Hyperlinks to the Workbook (p. 399)

Check a Formula Using Evaluate Formula (p. 393)

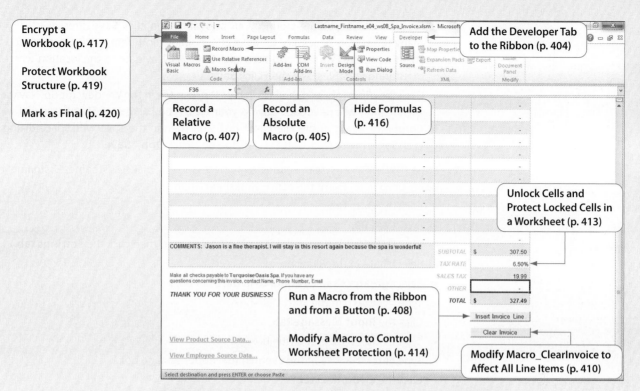

Encrypt a Workbook (p. 417)

Protect Workbook Structure (p. 419)

Mark as Final (p. 420)

Add the Developer Tab to the Ribbon (p. 404)

Record a Relative Macro (p. 407)

Record an Absolute Macro (p. 405)

Hide Formulas (p. 416)

Unlock Cells and Protect Locked Cells in a Worksheet (p. 413)

Run a Macro from the Ribbon and from a Button (p. 408)

Modify a Macro to Control Worksheet Protection (p. 414)

Modify Macro_ClearInvoice to Affect All Line Items (p. 410)

Figure 32 Turquoise Oasis Spa Invoice Generation final spreadsheets

---

Practice 1

Student data files needed:

e04_ws08_Corporate_Event
e04_ws08_Corporate_Event.xlw
e04_ws08_EventFood_Pricing
e04_ws08_EventRoom_Pricing

You will save your files as:

Lastname_Firstname_e04_ws08_Corporate_Event.xlsm
Lastname_Firstname_e04_ws08_Corporate_Event.xlw

Corporate Event Planning Revisited

Pattie Rochelle, the events manager, has decided that she would like some updates to the corporate event planning worksheet you developed for her. She would like to reduce the amount of typing required to use the worksheet, use it without the kind of user knowledge required by the current version, not worry about accidentally deleting any headings or formulas, and have the worksheet be easier to clear once an event has been planned and printed.

After visiting with Ms. Rochelle, you determined that the application of some data validation to the input fields, the use of a macro to reset the worksheet for a new event plan, and the application of worksheet and workbook protection will satisfy her requirements.

a. Start **Excel**, and then open **e04_ws08_Corporate_Event** workspace file. If you are asked if you would like to update links, click **Update**. If an alert box appears that indicates **one or more links…cannot be updated**, click **Continue**—the formula to calculate room rent uses an INDIRECT() function that cannot be updated unless a room has been selected to rent. Then

- Click the **File tab**, and then click **Save As**. In the Save As dialog box, navigate to the location where you are saving your files, and then in the File name box, type Lastname_Firstname_ e04_ws08_Corporate_Event in the File name box. Select **Excel Macro-Enabled Workbook** in the Save as type box, and then click **Save**.

- Press [Ctrl]+[Tab] as many times as is necessary to make e04_ws08_EventFood_ Pricing the active worksheet. Click the **File tab**, and then click **Save As**. Navigate to the location where you are storing your files, and then click **Save**. Press $\boxed{\text{Ctrl}}$+$\boxed{\text{Tab}}$ as many times as is necessary to make e04_ws08_EventRoom_Pricing the active worksheet. Click the **File tab**, and then click **Save As**. Navigate to the location where you are storing your files, and then click **Save**.

- Click the **View tab**, and then click **Save Workspace** in the Window group. Navigate to the location where you are saving your files, type Lastname_Firstname_e04_ws08_ Corporate_Event in the File name box, and then in the Save Workspace dialog box click **Save**. In the Microsoft Excel dialog box, click **Don't Save**.

b. Press $\boxed{\text{Ctrl}}$+$\boxed{\text{Tab}}$ as many times as is necessary to make Lastname_Firstname_e04_ ws08_Corporate_Event the active worksheet. Then
  - Click the **Data tab**.
  - Select cell **B9**.
  - Click **Data Validation** in the Data Tools group, and then click the **Settings tab**.
  - Select **Date** in the Allow box.
  - Select **greater than or equal to** in the Data box.
  - Type =TODAY() in the Start Date box.
  - Click the **Input Message tab**.
  - Type EVENT DATE in the Title box.
  - Type Enter the date of the event in the Input message box.
  - Click the **Error Alert tab**.
  - Type ERROR! in the Title box.
  - Type The date of the event cannot precede today's date in the Error message box.
  - Click **OK**.

c. Select cell **B10**. Then
  - Click **Data Validation** in the Data Tools group, and then click the **Settings tab**.
  - Select **Whole number** in the Allow box.
  - Verify that **between** is selected in the Data box.
  - Type 1 in the Minimum box, and then type 500 in the Maximum box.
  - Click the **Input Message tab**.
  - Type # OF GUESTS in the Title box.
  - Type Enter the number of guests expected in the Input message box.
  - Click the **Error Alert tab**.
  - Type ERROR! in the Title box.
  - Type The number of guests must be between 1 and 500 in the Error message box.
  - Click **OK**.

d. Select cell **B11**. Then
  - Click **Data Validation** in the Data Tools group, and then click the **Settings tab**.
  - Select **Whole number** in the Allow box.
  - Select **less than or equal to** in the Data box.
  - Type 150 in the Maximum box.
  - Click the **Input Message tab**.
  - Type # OF ROOMS in the Title box.
  - Type Enter the number of rooms reserved for guests in the Input message box.
  - Click the **Error Alert tab**.
  - Type ERROR! in the Title box.
  - Type The number of rooms must be 150 or less in the Error message box.
  - Click **OK**.

e. Select cell **B12**. Then

- Click **Data Validation** in the Data Tools group, and then click the **Settings tab**.
- Select **List** in the Allow box.
- Type Plate, Buffet in the Source box.
- Click the **Input Message tab**.
- Type DINING OPTION in the Title box.
- Type What style of dining is preferred? in the Input message box.
- Click **OK**.

f. Select cell **C15**. Then

- Click **Data Validation** in the Data Tools group, and then click the **Settings tab**.
- Select **List** in the Allow box.
- Type =RoomList in the Source box.
- Click the **Input Message tab**.
- Type ROOM in the Title box.
- Type Select the event room in the Input message box.
- Click **OK**.

g. Select cell **C17**. Then

- Click **Data Validation** in the Data Tools group, and then click the **Settings tab**.
- Select **List** in the Allow box.
- Type =MeatList in the Source box.
- Click the **Input Message tab**.
- Type MEAT COURSE in the Title box.
- Type Select the meat served with the meal in the Input message box.
- Click **OK**.

h. Select cell range **C18:C20**. Then

- Click **Data Validation** in the Data Tools group, and then click the **Settings tab**.
- Select **List** in the Allow box.
- Type =SideDishList in the Source box.
- Click the **Input Message tab**.
- Type SIDE in the Title box.
- Type Select a side dish in the Input message box.
- Click **OK**.

i. Select cell range **C21**. Then

- Click **Data Validation** in the Data Tools group, and then click the **Settings tab**.
- Select **List** in the Allow box.
- Type =SaladList in the Source box.
- Click the **Input Message tab**.
- Type SALAD in the Title box.
- Type Select a salad in the Input message box.
- Click **OK**.

j. Click the **Developer tab**. Then

- Click **Record Macro** in the Code group.
- Type Macro_ClearForm in the Macro name box.
- Click the **Shortcut key** box, press Shift+C.
- Type Clear all data from the form in the Description box.
- Click **OK**.

- Select cell range **B9:B12**. Press and hold ⌈Ctrl⌋ and select cell ranges **E9:E12** and **C17:C21** and cell **C15**.
- Press ⌈Delete⌋.
- Select cell **B9**.
- Click **Stop Recording** in the Code group.

    k. Click **Insert** in the Control group. Then

- Click **Button (Form Control)**.
- Draw a button that covers cell range **G15:H21**.
- Select **Macro_ClearForm** in the Macro name list box.
- Click **OK**.
- Right-click the button, select **Edit Text**, and then select the text shown in the button.
- Type CLEAR, press ⌈Enter⌋, and then type FORM.
- Select the text you just entered, and then press ⌈Ctrl⌋+⌈B⌋.
- Select cell **E9**, type Test, and then press ⌈Enter⌋.
- Click **Clear Form**. The text in cell E9 should have been cleared, and the active cell should be B9.

    l. Click the **Home tab**. Then

- Select cell range **B9:B12**, press and hold ⌈Ctrl⌋, and then select cell range **E9:E12**, cell **C15**, and cell range **C17:C21**.
- Click **Format** in the Cells group, and then select **Lock Cell** to unlock the selected cells.
- Click Format in the Cells group, and then select **Protect Sheet**.
- Uncheck **Select locked cells**.
- Click **OK**.

    m. Click the **File tab** and select **Options**. Then

- Click **Advanced** in the Excel Options dialog box.
- Scroll until both the Display options for this workbook and Display options for this worksheet sections are visible.
- Uncheck **Show horizontal scroll bar**, **Show vertical scroll bar**, **Show row and column headers**, and **Show gridlines**.
- Click **OK**.

    n. Click the **Data_Lists worksheet tab**. Then

- Click **Format** in the Cells group, select **Protect Sheet**.
- Click **OK**.

    o. Click the **File tab**. Then

- Click **Protect Workbook**.
- Select **Protect Workbook Structure** from the menu.
- Click **OK**.

    p. Click the **Event_Pricing worksheet tab**, press and hold ⌈Shift⌋, and then click the **Documentation worksheet tab**. Then

- Click the **Page Layout tab**.
- Click **Print Titles** in the Page Setup group.
- Click the **Header/Footer tab** in the Page Setup dialog box.
- Click **Custom Footer**, and then click the **Left section** box.
- Click **Insert File Name**.
- Click **OK**, and then click **OK** again.
- Right-click the **Event_Pricing worksheet tab**, and then select **Ungroup Sheets** from the shortcut menu.

q. Select cell **A1** (upper left-hand corner). You should not be able to select it. Then
  - Select the **Client cell**, type Warren Gates, and then press Enter.
  - Type 1 LottaMoneyWay and press Enter.
  - Type Omaha, WA 54321, and then press Enter.
  - Type 555.432.9900.
  - Select the **Event Date cell**, type 12/29/2013, and then press Enter.
  - Type 100, and then press Enter.
  - Type 40, and then press Enter.
  - Select **Plate** as the Dining Option, and then press Enter.
  - Select **Eldorado** as the room.
  - Select **Prime Rib – 16 oz.** as the Meat Selection and then press Enter.
  - Select **Shrimp Salad** as the first Side Dish, and then press Enter.
  - Select **Carrots – Baked**, as the second side dish, and then press Enter twice.
  - Select **Spinach** as the Salad, and then press Home.

r. Press **Clear Form**. The form should have been cleared of user entered data, and the active cell should be the Event Date.

s. Click the **Documentation worksheet tab**. Then
  - Select cell **A6**, and then press Ctrl + ;.
  - Select cell **B6**, enter your name in Lastname, Firstname format.
  - Select cell **C6**, and then type Added data validation for user-entered data.
  - Select cell **C7**, type Created a macro to clear user-entered data.
  - Select cell **C8**, and then type Added worksheet protection.
  - Click the **Event_Pricing worksheet tab**.

t. Repeat step q.

u. Click **Save**, and then submit or print your project as directed by your instructor.

v. Close Lastname_Firstname_e04_ws08_Corporate_Event. Close e04_ws08_EventFood_Pricing without saving it, close e04_ws08_EventRoom_Pricing without saving it, and then close Excel.

Practice 2

Student data file needed:	You will save your file as:
e04_ws08_Wedding_Planner	Lastname_Firstname_e04_ws08_Wedding_Planner.xlsm

Painted Paradise Resort Wedding Planner

Painted Paradise Resort has a wedding chapel and reception facilities capable of handling 300 people. Wedding guests stay in the hotel, dine in the restaurant, play golf, go to the spa, shop in the gift shop—often use a wedding as an opportunity to stay at the resort for a weekend. The resort is becoming a popular wedding destination, and Patti Rochelle, the events manager, has been trying to update a workbook she uses to generate wedding cost estimates for prospective clients.

She has an attractive and functional design developed. The calculations are pretty much handled, however her worksheet still requires a lot of hand data entry, and she would like a macro to clear data from the wedding planner after an estimate has been generated and printed.

a. Start **Excel**, and then open **e04_ws08_Wedding_Planner**. Click the **File tab**, and then click **Save As**. In the Save As dialog box, navigate to the location where you are saving your files, and then in the File name box, type Lastname_Firstname_ e04_ws08_ Wedding_Planner. Select **Excel Macro-Enabled Workbook** in the Save as type box, and then click **Save**.

b. Click the **Data tab**. Then
   - Select cell **C8**.
   - Click **Data Validation** in the Data Tools group.
   - Click the **Settings tab**.
   - Select **Whole number** in the Allow box.
   - Verify that **between** is selected in the Data box.
   - Type =GuestMin in the Minimum box.
   - Type =GuestMax in the Maximum box.
   - Click the **Input Message tab**.
   - Type Enter the estimated number of guests in the Input message box.
   - Click the **Error Alert tab**.
   - Type ERROR! in the Title box.
   - Type The number of guests is outside the required minimum or maximum in the Error message box.
   - Click **OK**.

c. Click cell **C10**.
   - Click **Data Validation** in the Data Tools group.
   - Click the **Settings tab**.
   - Select **Date** in the Allow box.
   - Select **Greater than or equal to** in the Data box.
   - Type =TODAY() in the Start date box.
   - Click the **Input Message tab**.
   - Type Enter the wedding date in the Input message box.
   - Click the **Error Alert tab**.
   - Type ERROR! in the Title box.
   - Type The wedding date must be today or later in the Error message box.
   - Click **OK**.

d. Click cell **C11**.
   - Click **Data Validation** in the Data Tools group.
   - Click the **Settings tab**.
   - Select **Time** in the Allow box.
   - Verify that **between** is selected in the Data box.
   - Type 10:00 AM in the Start time box.
   - Type 8:00 PM in the End time box.
   - Click the **Input Message tab**.
   - Type Enter the wedding start time in the Input message box.
   - Click the **Error Alert tab**.
   - Type ERROR! in the Title box.
   - Type The wedding must start between 10:00 AM and 8:00 PM in the Error message box.
   - Click **OK**.

e. Click cell **C12**.

- Click **Data Validation** in the Data Tools group.
- Click the **Settings tab**.
- Select **Time** in the Allow box.
- Select **Greater than** in the Data box.
- Type =C11 in the Start time box.
- Click the **Input Message tab**.
- Type Enter the wedding end time in the Input message box.
- Click the **Error Alert tab**.
- Type ERROR! in the Title box.
- Type End time must be later then start time in the Error message box.
- Click **OK**.

f. Click cell **F11**.

- Click **Data Validation** in the Data Tools group.
- Click the **Settings tab**.
- Select **Time** in the Allow box.
- Select **Greater than or equal to** in the Data box.
- Type =C12 in the Start time box.
- Click the **Input Message tab**.
- Type Enter the reception start time in the Input message box.
- Click the **Error Alert tab**.
- Type ERROR! in the Title box.
- Type The reception must start after the wedding ends in the Error message box.
- Click **OK**.

g. Click cell **F12**.

- Click **Data Validation** in the Data Tools group.
- Click the **Settings tab**.
- Select **Time** in the Allow box.
- Select **Greater than** in the Data box.
- Type =F11 in the Start time box.
- Click the **Input Message tab**.
- Type Enter the reception end time in the Input message box.
- Click the **Error Alert tab**.
- Type ERROR! in the Title box.
- Type The reception must end later than it starts in the Error message box.
- Click **OK**.

h. Select cell range **C24:C25**. Then

- Click **Data Validation** in the Data Tools group.
- Click the **Settings tab**.
- Select **List** in the Allow box.
- Click the **Source** box.
- Click the **Parameters worksheet tab,** and then select cell range **A9:A10**.
- Click **OK**.

i. Select cell range **C28:C29**, press and hold Ctrl, and then select cell **C32**. Then

- Click **Data Validation** in the Data Tools group.
- Click the **Settings tab**.
- Select **List** in the Allow box.

- Type Yes,No in the Source box.
- Click **OK**.

j. Select cell range **C35:C39**.
- Click **Data Validation** in the Data Tools group.
- Click the **Settings tab**.
- Select **List** in the Allow box.
- Click the **Source box**.
- Click the **Parameters worksheet tab**, and then select cell range **A14:A15**.
- Click **OK**.

k. Select cell **C5**, and then type MagPi. Then
- Select cell **C6**, and then type Amharach.
- Select cell **C8**, and then type 100.
- Select cell **C10**, and then type 12/28/2013.
- Select cell **C11**, and then type 4:00 PM.
- Select cell **C12**, and then type 5:00 PM.
- Select cell **F11**, and then type 6:00 PM.
- Select cell **F12**, and then type 11:00 PM.
- Select cell **C24**, click the **filter arrow** next to C24, and then select **Deluxe**.
- Select cell **C25**, click the **filter arrow** next to C25, and then select **Standard**.
- Select cell **C28**, click the **filter arrow** next to C28, and then select **Yes**.
- Select cell **C29**, click the **filter arrow** next to C29, and then select **Yes**.
- Select cell **C32**, click the **filter arrow** next to C32, and then select **No**.
- Select cell **C36**, click the **filter arrow** next to C36, and then select **Ceremony**.
- Select cell **C39**, click the **filter arrow** next to C39, and then select **Reception**.

l. Click the **Developer tab**. Then
- Click **Record Macro** in the Code group.
- Type Macro_DeleteEstimate in the Macro name box.
- Click the **Shortcut key** box, press [Shift]+[D].
- Type Delete all user-entered data from the wedding estimate worksheet.
- Click **OK**.
- Select cell range **C5:C6**.
- Press and hold [Ctrl], and then select cells and cell ranges **C8**, **C10:C12**, **F11:F12**, **C24:C25**, **C28:C29**, **C32**, and **C35:C39**.
- Press [Delete].
- Select cell **C5**.
- Click **Stop Recording** in the Code group.

m. Press [Ctrl]+[Z] to undo the changes you made recording the macro. Click **Save**. Press [Ctrl]+[Shift]+[D] to run Macro_DeleteEstimate.

n. Close the workbook without saving, but do not close Excel. Click the **File tab** and click **Recent**. Double-click **Lastname_Firstname_e04_ws08_Wedding_Planner**.

o. Click **Insert** in the Controls group. Then
- Click **Button (Form Control)** from the gallery menu.
- Draw a button that covers cell range **B48:F49**.
- Select Macro_DeleteEstimate in the Macro Name list box.
- Click **OK**.
- Right-click the button you just drew, and then select **Edit Text** from the shortcut menu.
- Select the **text** in the button, and then type **DELETE Estimate**.

- Select the **text** in the button, and press Ctrl+B.
- Click the **Home tab**, click the **Font size arrow** in the Font group, and then select **16**.
- Click a cell outside the button.

p. Click **Save**. Click **DELETE Estimate**. Close the workbook without saving, but do not close Excel. Click the **File tab** and click **Recent**. Click **Lastname_Firstname_e04_ws08_Wedding_Planner**.

q. Select cell range **C5:C6**. Then
- Press and hold Ctrl, and then select cells and cell ranges **C8**, **C10:C12**, **F11:F12**, **C24:C25**, **C28:C29**, **C32** and **C35:C39**.
- Click **Format** in the Cells group.
- Select **Lock Cell** to toggle off cell locking in the selected cells.

r. Click the **File tab**, click **Options**.
- In the File Options dialog box click **Advanced**.
- Scroll down in the File Options dialog box until Display options for this workbook and Display options for this worksheet are visible.
- Uncheck **Show horizontal scroll bar**, **Show row and column headers**, and **Show gridlines**.
- Click **OK**.

s. Click the **View tab**, and then uncheck **Formula Bar** in the Show group.

t. Click the **Home tab**. Then
- Click **Format** in the Cells group, select **Protect Sheet**.
- Uncheck **Select locked cells**, and then click **OK**.

u. Right-click the **Parameters worksheet tab**, and then select **Hide** from the shortcut menu.

v. Click the **Page Layout tab**. Then
- Click the **Wedding_Planner worksheet tab**, press and hold Shift, and then click the **Documentation worksheet tab**.
- Click **Print Titles** in the Page Setup group.
- In the Page Setup dialog box, click the **Header/Footer tab**.
- Click **Custom Footer**, and then click in the **Left section box**.
- Click **Insert File Name**.
- Click **OK**, and then click **OK** again.
- Right-click the **Wedding_Planner worksheet tab**, and then select **Ungroup Sheets** from the shortcut menu.

w. Click the **File tab**. Then
- Click **Protect Workbook**.
- Select **Protect Workbook Structure** from the menu.
- In the Protect Structure and Windows dialog box click **OK**.

x. Click the **Documentation worksheet tab**. Then
- Select cell **A6**, press Ctrl+;.
- Select cell **B6**, and then enter your name in Lastname, Firstname format.
- Select cell **C6**, and then type Added data validation for user-entered data.
- Select cell **C7**, and then type Created a macro to clear user-entered data.
- Select cell **C8**, and then type Added worksheet and workbook structure protection.
- Press Ctrl+Home.
- Click the **Wedding_Planner worksheet tab**. Press Home.

y. Click **Save**, submit or print your project as directed by your instructor.

z. Click the **View tab** and check **Formula Bar** in the View group. Close Excel.

Student data file needed:	You will save your file as:
e04_mp_Golf_Championship	Lastname_Firstname_e04_mp_Golf_Championship.xlsm

Red Bluff Golf Club Championship

The Red Bluff Golf Club holds an annual club championship in October. The 12 best golfers in the club are invited to play. The championship is a three-day event that begins on Friday and ends on Sunday.

One of the caddies, Woody Lugger, took it upon himself to record the scores for each golfer in a workbook, one worksheet for each day of the championship, and now he is having trouble completing the workbook.

Only a couple of golfers are left on the last day, and it is critically important that this workbook is completed to allow a rapid announcement of the club champion. You have been asked to step in and complete the workbook at the last minute.

a. Start **Excel**, and then open **e04_mp_Golf_Championship.xlsx**, click the **File tab**, and then click **Save As**. In the Save As dialog box, select **Excel Macro_Enabled Workbook** in the Save as type box, navigate to where you are saving your files, and then type Lastname_Firstname_e04_mp_Golf_Championship, replacing Lastname_Firstname with your own name, select **Excel Macro-Enabled Workbook** in the Save as type box, and then click **Save**.

b. Click the **Insert Worksheet tab**. Click and hold the **Sheet1 worksheet tab**, and then drag it to the left of the 2013_10_05 worksheet. Double-click the **Sheet1 worksheet tab**, type Results, and then press [Enter].

c. Column widths require adjustments in each of the worksheets.

   • Press and hold [Shift], click the **2013-10-07 worksheet tab**, release [Shift], and then click the **2013-10-05 worksheet tab**. The Results, 2013-10-05, 2013-10-06 and 2013-10-07 worksheets should be grouped.

   • Select cell range **A1:U5**, click **Fill** in the Editing group, select **Across Worksheets**, and then click **OK**.

   • Select column **A**, click **Format** in the Cells group, and then select **Column Width**. Type 18, and then click **OK**.

   • Select columns **B:S**. Click **Format** in the Cells group, select **Column Width**, type 3, and then click **OK**.

   • Select columns **T:U**. Click **Format** in the Cells group, select **Column Width**, type 5, and then click **OK**.

d. With the daily score worksheets still grouped, calculate round scores and net (par) score.

   • Press and hold [Ctrl], and then click the **Results worksheet tab**. The Results worksheet should no longer be grouped with the daily score worksheets.

   • Click cell **T6**, click **AutoSum** in the Editing group, and then press [Ctrl]+[Enter].

   • Click cell **U6**, type =T6-T$4, and then press [Ctrl]+[Enter].

   • Select cell range **T6:U6**, and then drag the fill handle to fill the formulas to the cell range **T6:U17**.

   • Right-click the **2013-10-05 worksheet** tab, and then select **Ungroup Sheets** in the shortcut menu.

e. Score in golf is related to par. Use conditional formatting to identify if a golfer's score on a hole is below or above par.

- Click cell **B6** in the 2013-10-05 worksheet. Click **Conditional Formatting** in the Styles group, point to **Highlight Cells Rules**, and then select **Greater Than**. Click cell **B4**. Edit the formula in the Format cell that are GREATER THAN box to =B$4. You want a mixed reference because you want the row reference to be absolute, but you want the column reference to be relative when copying this format.
- Ensure that **Light Red Fill with Dark Red Text** is selected in the with box, and then click **OK**.
- Click **Conditional Formatting** in the Styles group, point to **Highlight Cells Rules**, and then select **Less Than**.
- Click cell **B4**, and then edit the formula in the Format cell that are LESS THAN box to =B$4.
- Select **Green Fill with Dark Green Text** in the with box, and then click **OK**.
- Using the fill handle, fill the cell range **B7:B17**, click the **Auto Fill Options** button, and then select **Fill Formatting Only**.
- Using the fill handle, fill the cell range **C6:S17**, click the **Auto Fill Options** button, and then select **Fill Formatting Only**.

f. Total score is also considered relative to par. Use conditional formatting to highlight each golfer's score for the round relative to par.

- Click cell **T6**, click **Conditional Formatting** in the Styles group, point to **Highlight Cells Rules**, and then select **Greater Than**.
- Click cell **T4**, select **Red Text** in the with box, and then click **OK**.
- Click **Conditional Formatting** in the Styles group, point to **Highlight Cells Rules**, and then select **Less Than**.
- Click cell **T4**, select **Custom Format** in the with box. If necessary, click the **Font tab** in the Format Cells dialog box. Click the **Color arrow**, select **Green** under Standard Colors in the Palette menu, click **OK**, and then click **OK** again.
- Using the fill handle, fill the cell range **T7:T17**. Notice that you don't have to use Auto Fill to limit the fill to Formatting Only because cell T6 contains a formula that can be filled right along with the formatting.

g. Net score can also be highlighted using conditional formatting. In this case you want to highlight the lowest score (best score in golf) among all the day's scores.

- Select cell range **U6:U17**.
- Click **Conditional Formatting** in the Styles group, point to **Top/Bottom Rules**, and then select **Bottom 10 Items**.
- Replace the **10** in the box with 1.
- Select **Custom Format** in the with box.
- Click the **Border tab** in the Format Cells dialog box, and then make sure the **solid line** is selected in the Style box.
- Click the **Color arrow**, and then select **Green** under Standard Colors.
- Click the **Outline button** under Presets, click **OK**, and then click **OK** again.

h. Now copy the conditional formats to the other daily score worksheets.

- Select cell range **B6:U17**, press Ctrl+C, and then click the **Results worksheet tab**.
- Press and hold Ctrl, click the 2013-10-06 and 2013-10-07 worksheet tabs.
- Click cell **B6**, click the **Paste arrow** in the Clipboard group, and then click **Formatting** under Other Paste Options.
- Right-click the **Results worksheet tab**, and then select **Ungroup Sheets**.

i. This championship is won by the golfer who achieves the lowest total score over three days. Data consolidation will work perfectly to calculate total scores for each golfer.

- Click cell **A6** in the Results worksheet, click the **Data tab**, and then click **Consolidate** in the Data Tools group.
- Click the **Reference** box, click the **2013-10-05 worksheet tab**, select cell range **A6:U17**, and then click **Add**.
- Click the **2013-10-06 worksheet tab**, and then click **Add**.
- Click the **2013-10-07 worksheet tab**, and then click **Add**.
- Check **Left column** under Use labels in, and then click **OK**.

j. Total score on a hole for the tournament is the sum of the scores across the three days of play. You need to calculate this for the Results worksheet.

- Click cell **B4**, and then type =SUM(.
- Click the 2013-10-05 worksheet tab.
- Click cell **B4**, press and hold Shift, and then click the **2013-10-07 worksheet tab**.
- Press Ctrl+Enter.
- Using the fill handle, fill the cell range **B5:T4**.

k. The players should be ranked lowest score to highest score, with the lowest score the champion. Record a macro that will sort the golfers in the Results worksheet lowest to highest and highlight the champion.

- Click the **Developer tab**, and then click **Record Macro** in the Code group.
- Type FindChampion_Macro in the Macro name box.
- Press Tab, and then press Shift+F.
- Type Sort the tournament results by net score and highlight the champion in the Description text box, and then click **OK**.
- Click the **Home tab**.
- Select cell range **A6:U6**.
- Click the dialog box launcher in the bottom-right corner of the Font group to display the Format Cells dialog box. If necessary click the **Font tab**.
- In the Font style box, select **Regular**, and then click **OK**. This un-bolds the first line in case the macro has been run on the current data before.
- Click the **Data tab**.
- Select cell range **A5:U17**.
- Click the **Sort button** in the Sort & Filter group to reveal the Sort dialog box.
- Select **Net** in the Sort by box.
- Click **Add Level**.
- Select **Hole** in the Then by box (Hole is the heading above golfers' names. Selecting Hole actually will result in a second-level sort by golfer name).
- Click **OK**.
- Select cell range **A6:U6**, press Ctrl+B.
- Press Ctrl+Home.
- Click the **Developer tab**.
- Click **Stop Recording** in the Code group.
- Press Ctrl+Z two times to undo the effects of recording the macro.

l. Assign the macro to a button to make it easy to run.

- Click **Insert** in the Controls group, and then select **Button (Form Control)**.
- Draw a button that covers cell range **V1:W2**.

- Select **FindChampion_Macro** in the list in the Macro name box of the Assign Macro dialog box, and then click **OK**.
- Right-click the **button**, and then select **Edit Text** from the shortcut menu.
- Select all the **text** in the button, type Identify, and then press Enter.
- Press Ctrl+B, and then type Champion.
- Right-click the button, select **Exit Edit Text** from the shortcut menu, and then click a cell outside of the button.

m. The last two golfers' scores are in. Click the **2013-10-07 worksheet tab**. Enter the following data into the appropriate cells in the 2013-10-07 worksheet. Notice the effect of the conditional formatting as you enter the data.

Hole	1	2	3	4	5	6	7	8	9	10	11	12	13	14	15	16	17	18
Pully McDraw	4	3	5	3	4	4	3	4	4	4	4	4	4	6	4	5	4	3
Bogey Bruce	4	4	5	3	3	5	2	4	4	3	4	4	4	5	4	5	3	4

n. With new data in the 2013-10-07 worksheet, the consolidation needs to be refreshed.
- Click the **Results worksheet tab**, select cell range **A6:U17**, and then press Delete.
- Click cell **A6**.
- Click the **Data tab**, click **Consolidate** in the Data Tools group, make sure **Left column** under Use Labels in is checked, and then click **OK**.

o. Click the **Identify Champion** button.

p. Put the file name in the left section of the page footer.
- Click the **Page Layout tab**.
- Press and hold Shift, and then click the **Documentation worksheet tab**.
- Click **Print Titles** in the Page Setup group.
- Click the **Header/Footer tab** in the Page Setup dialog box.
- Click **Custom Footer**, and then click the **Left section** box.
- Click **Insert File Name**.
- Click **OK**, and then click **OK** again.
- Press Ctrl+Home.
- Right-click the **Results worksheet tab**, and then select **Ungroup Sheets** from the shortcut menu.

q. Complete your documentation.
- Click the **Documentation worksheet tab**.
- Click cell **A5**, and then press Ctrl+;.
- Click cell **B5**, and then type your name in Lastname, Firstname format.
- Click cell **C5**, and then type Completed round score calculations, used conditional formatting to identify non-par scores and to identify low round scores, summarized scores for the tournament, and included a macro button to identify the tournament champion.
- Press Ctrl+Home.

r. Click the **Results worksheet tab**, click **Save**, submit or print your work as directed by your instructor, and then close Excel.

Student data files needed:

e04_ps1_Custom_Clubs

You will save your files as:

Lastname_Firstname_e04_ps1_Custom_Clubs.xlsm

Pro Shop Custom Golf Club Order Worksheet

The Pro Shop at the Red Bluff Golf Club sells golf merchandise to club members and resort guests. The most expensive merchandise is custom-sized golf clubs. John Schilling is an expert golf club builder and specializes in fitting clients for his custom clubs.

Custom fitting clubs requires several items of data, some supplied by the client, some measurements of the client taken by John, and some data taken from tables after client data is collected. All this takes time and is prone to error, which, if left uncorrected can result in the manufacture of custom clubs that do not fit properly.

John has asked you to create a worksheet that will perform much of the complex work and eliminate data entry errors, where possible. You have started the worksheet and have it pretty well formatted, all of the necessary master data entered into a worksheet, and several cell ranges named to make formulas easier to enter, to understand, and to aid in self-documentation.

a. Start **Excel**, and then open **e04_ps1_Custom_Clubs**. Click the **File tab**, click **Save As**, and then in the Save as type box, select **Excel Macro_Enabled Workbook**. Type Lastname_Firstname_e04_ps1_Custom_Clubs, replacing Lastname_Firstname with your own name, in the File name box, and then click **Save**.

- Click the **Documentation worksheet tab**, click cell **A3**, and then press Ctrl+;. Press Ctrl+Enter. Press Ctrl+C, select cells **A5**, **B18**, and **B24**, right-click cell **B24**, and then click **Paste Values**.

- Click cell **B3**, and then type your Lastname, Firstname. Press Ctrl+Enter, and then press Ctrl+C. Select cells **B5**, **B17**, and **B23**, right-click cell **B23**, and then click **Paste Values**.

- Click cell **C3**, and then type Pro Shop Custom Golf Club SpecSheet.

- Click cell **C5**, and then type Added formulas, validation, a macro, and worksheet protection.

- Click cell **B19**, and then type Custom Club SpecSheet to be printed and used for club manufacture.

- Click cell **B25**, and then type Club fitment data and code conversion data and formulas.

- Press Ctrl+Home.

b. To validate gender.

- Click the **Custom_Clubs_Specsheet worksheet tab**.

- Click cell **C8**, click the **Data tab**, and then click **Data Validation** in the Data Tools group. If necessary, click the **Settings tab** in the Data Validation dialog box.

- Select **List** in the Allow box, type Male,Female in the Source box, and then click **OK**.

c. To validate wrist to floor length.

- Select cell **E8**, and then click **Data Validation** in the Data Tools group. If necessary, click the **Settings tab** in the Data Validation dialog box.

- Select **List** in the Allow box.

- Click the **Source** box, click the **Club_Fitment_Data worksheet tab**, and then select cell range **A4:A27**.

- Click the **Input Message tab**.

- Type Wrist to Floor Length in the Title box.

- For the Input Message type Measure in inches, standing in golf shoes, from where the hand meets the forearm to the floor.
- Click **OK**.

d. To validate the age.
- Click cell **C9**, and then click **Data Validation** in the Data Tools group. Click the **Settings tab** in the Data Validation dialog box.
- Select **Whole number** in the Allow box.
- Select **between** in the Data box, if necessary.
- Click the **Minimum** box, type 14, click the **Maximum** box, and then type 90.
- Click the **Input Message tab**, click the **Input message** box, and then type Age in years.
- Click the **Error Alert** tab, and then select **Warning** in the Style list.
- Click the **Title** box, and then type DOUBLE CHECK YOUR DATA....
- Click the **Error message** box, and then type Generally custom clubs are not made for golfers below 14 years of age, and there are few golfers over 90 years of age.
- Click **OK**.

e. To validate golfer skill level.
- Click cell **E9**, and then click **Data Validation** in the Data Tools group. Click the **Settings tab** in the Data Validation dialog box.
- Select **List** in the Allow box.
- Click the **Source** box, and then click the **Club_Fitment_Data worksheet tab**.
- Select cell range **R38:R40**, and then click the **Input Message tab**.
- Click the **Title** box, and then type Level of Expertise.
- Click the **Input message** box, and then type Pro Shop staff assessment of player ability and potential.
- Click **OK**.

f. To validate golfer height.
- Click cell **C10**, and then click **Data Validation** in the Data Tools group. Click the **Settings tab** in the Data Validation dialog box.
- Select **Whole number** in the Allow box.
- Select **between**, if necessary, in the Data box. Click the **Minimum** box, type 48.
- Click the **Maximum** box, and then type 81.
- Click the **Input Message tab**, click the **Input message** box, and then type Height in inches.
- Click the **Error Alert tab**, click the **Title** box, and then type ERROR!. Click the **Error message** box, type Height must be between 48 and 81 inches.
- Click **OK**.

g. To validate golfer glove size.
- Click cell **E10**, and then click **Data Validation** in the Data Tools group. Click the **Settings tab** in the Data Validation dialog box.
- Select **List** in the Allow box.
- Click the **Source** box, and then click the **Club_Fitment_Data worksheet** tab. Select cell range **O32:O39**.
- Click the **Input Message tab**.
- Click the **Input message** box, and then type Choose a golf glove size.
- Click **OK**.

h. To validate the date of the custom club order.

- Click cell **E19**, click the **Data tab**, and then click **Data Validation** in the Data Tools group. Click the **Settings tab** in the Data Validation dialog box.
- Select **Date** in the Allow box.
- Select **greater than or equal to** in the Data box.
- Click the **Start date** box and type =TODAY().
- Click the **Error Alert tab**, click the **Title** box, and then type ERROR!. Click the **Error message** box, type Date must be today or a future date.
- Click **OK**.

i. Enter some test data to check your validation processes.

- Click cell **C7**, and then type Sam Novice.
- Click cell **C8**, select **Female**.
- Click cell **C9**, and then type 37.
- Click cell **C10**, type 67.
- Click cell **E8**, select **34.5**.
- Click cell **E9**, and then select **Amateur**.
- Click cell **E10**, select **Small**.
- Click cell **E19**, press Ctrl+;, and then press Ctrl+Enter.

j. Now you need to enter formulas to calculate some codes and values from the golfer data you just entered.

- Click the **Club_Fitment_Data worksheet tab**.
- Click cell **D32** and type Height Code:. Click cell **E32**, and then type =VLOOKUP (Height,HeightRange,2).
- Click cell **D29** and type Club Length Adjustment:. Click cell **E29**, and then type =VLOOKUP(Wrist2Floor,ClubLengthAdjRange,HeightCode,FALSE).
- Click cell **D30** and type Player Level Code:. Click cell **E30**, and then type =IFERROR (VLOOKUP(PlayerLevelName,PlayLevelRange,2,FALSE),"Undefined").
- Click cell **D31** and type Club Code:. Click cell **E31**, and then type =IFERROR (VLOOKUP(IF(Gender="Male","Mens","Ladies")&" "&Shaft,ClubCodeRange,2," FALSE"),"Undefined"). Notice that the parameter FALSE is entered as "FALSE" in this formula. The result is the same, quotes are not required, but are included here to illustrate an alternative method you may see when maintaining others' workbooks.

k. The following formulas set codes that are used to determine club length, grip size and shaft recommendation.

- Click the **Custom_Clubs_SpecSheet worksheet tab**.
- Click cell **D12**, and then type =IFERROR(VLOOKUP(Age,INDIRECT(Gender&"Shaft Range"),PlayerLevelCode),"").
- Click cell **D13**, and then type =IFERROR(VLOOKUP(GloveSize,GripRange,2,FALSE),"").
- Click cell **C17**, type =IFERROR(VLOOKUP(B17,ClubLengthRange,ClubCode,"FALSE")+ ClubLengthAdj,""), and then press Ctrl+Enter.
- Using the fill handle, expand the active cell to encompass cell range **C17:C24**.
- Click cell **C7**.

l. Check your work using the following values in the above formulas:

Club Length Adjustment:	0	Recommended Shaft:	Graphite
Player Level Code:	3	Recommended Grip:	Small
Club Code:	5		
Height Code:	6		

If you are having trouble entering the formulas correctly, you can copy and paste them from the e04_ps1_Custom_Clubs.txt file.

m. Click the **Home tab** and complete the following steps:
- Select cell range **C8:C10**, press and hold Ctrl, and then select **E8:E10**, **B17:B24**, and cells **C7** and **E19**.
- Click **Format** in the Cells group, and then select **Lock Cell** in the Protection menu.
- Click **Format** in the Cells group, and then select **Protect Sheet** from the Protection Menu.
- In the Allow all users of this worksheet to box of the Protect Sheet dialog box, uncheck the **Select locked cells** check box. Worksheet protection is applied now so that it can be turned off during macro development in the next step. Recall that macros often perform actions that are not allowed in protected worksheets.
- Click **OK**.

n. Now record a macro to add a club to the order.
- Click the **Developer tab**.
- Select **Use Relative References** in the Code group.
- Click **Record Macro** in the Code group. In the Record Macro dialog box, type AddaClub_Macro in the Macro name box.
- Press Tab, and then press Shift+A.
- Click the **Description** box, type Add a club to the list of clubs to be manufactured.
- Click **OK**.
- Click the **Home tab**.
- Click **Format** in the Cells group, and then select **Unprotect Sheet** from the Protection menu.
- Press Ctrl+G to open the Go To dialog box.
- Select **ClubListBottom** in the Go to list box, and then click **OK**.
- Right-click cell **B25**, and then select **Insert** from the shortcut menu.
- Select **Entire row** in the Insert dialog box, and then click **OK**.
- Press →, press ↑, and then press Ctrl+C.
- Press ↓, press Ctrl+V, and then press ←. Press Esc.
- Click **Format** in the Cells group, select **Protect Sheet** from the Protection menu.
- Click **OK**.
- Click the **Developer tab**.
- Click **Stop Recording** in the Code group.
- Click the **Home tab**.
- Click **Format** in the Cells group, and then select **Unprotect Sheet** from the Protection menu.
- Right-click the **header** for row 25, and then select **Delete** from the shortcut menu to undo the results of recording the macro.
- Click **Format** in the Cells group, select **Protect Sheet** from the Protection menu, and then click **OK**.
- Press Ctrl+Shift+A to run the macro.

If the AddaClub_Macro executed and a line for a club was added at row 25, then you recorded the macro properly. Unprotect the worksheet, select row **25**, right-click the **row**, and then select **Delete** from the shortcut menu. DO NOT protect the worksheet. Otherwise, click **Macros** in the Code group, delete the AddaClub_Macro, and then repeat step n.

o. To add a button to run the macro.
- Click the **Developer tab**.
- Click **Insert** in the Control group, and then click **Button (Form Control)**.
- Draw a button along the approximate boundaries of cell **B26**.

- Select **AddaClub_Macro** from the list below the Macro name box in the Assign Macro dialog box, and then click **OK**.
- Right-click the **button** you just created, and select **Edit Text** from the shortcut menu.
- Delete the text in the button, type Add a Club, right-click the **button**, and then select **Exit Edit Text** from the shortcut menu.
- Click cell **C7**, and then click the **Home tab**. Click **Format** in the Cells group, select **Protect Sheet**, and then click **OK**.
- Click the **Add a Club** button.
- Select **Sand Wedge** in cell **B25**.
- Click the **Add a Club** button.

If a club was added above the Sand Wedge, you did not have Use Relative References selected when you recorded AddaClub_Macro. To correct this, delete rows 25:26 (remember to unprotect, delete the rows, and then protect the worksheet), click Macros in the Code group, delete AddaClub_Macro, and repeat step n.

- Select an **8 Iron** in cell **B26**.

p. To insert the file name into the page footer for documentation purposes.
- Click the **Page Layout tab**.
- Press and hold ⇧Shift, and then click the **Documentation worksheet tab**.
- Click **Print Titles** in the Page Setup group.
- Click the **Header/Footer tab** in the Page Setup dialog box.
- Click **Custom Footer**, and then click the **Left section** box.
- Click **Insert File Name**.
- Click **OK**, and then click **OK** again.
- Press Home.
- Right-click the **Custom_Clubs_SpecSheet worksheet tab**, and then select **Ungroup Sheets** from the shortcut menu.

q. To protect data against accidental damage by the user.
- Click the **Club_Fitment_Data worksheet tab**, press and hold Ctrl, and then click the **Documentation worksheet tab**.
- Right-click the **Documentation worksheet tab**, and then select **Hide** in the shortcut menu.
- Click the **File tab**.
- Click **Protect Workbook**, select **Protect Workbook Structure**, and then click **OK**.
- Click the **Home tab**.
- Click **Save**. Print—set page orientation to portrait or landscape as appropriate—or submit your file as directed by your instructor, and then close Excel.

r. To clear data from unlocked cells in the Custom_Clubs_SpecSheet and save this workbook as a template.
- Select cell range **C8:C10**, press and hold Ctrl, and then click cell range **E8:E10** and cells **C7** and **E19**. Press Delete.
- Click **Format** in the Cells Group, and then select **Unprotect Sheet**.
- Select rows **25:26**, right-click the selected rows, select **Delete** from the shortcut menu, and then click cell **C7**.
- Click **Format** in the Cells Group, select **Protect Sheet**, and then click **OK**.
- Click the **File tab**, and then click **Save As**.
- Select **Excel Macro-Enabled Template** in the Save as type box.
- Navigate to the location where you are storing your files, and then click **Save**.

s. Print—set page orientation to portrait or landscape as appropriate—or submit your file as directed by your instructor, and then close Excel.

Student data file needed:

e04_ps2_Championship_Schedule

You will save your files as:

Lastname_Firstname_e04_ps2_Championship_Schedule
Lastname_Firstname_e04_ps2_Championship_Schedule(Herriott)
Lastname_Firstname_e04_ps2_Championship_
Schedule(Dimas,Diaz)

Red Bluff Golf Club Championship Schedule

The Red Bluff Golf Club holds its championship tournament the first full weekend in October every year. The schedule for the three-day event is broken into three parts:

1. Golf schedule
2. Guest services schedule
3. Promotion schedule

Golf course manager Barry Cheney is responsible for the golf schedule and parts of the promotion schedule. Restaurant manager Alberto Dimas and Silver Moon Lounge manager Will Diaz are responsible for the guest services schedule, and Aleeta Herriott is responsible for parts of the promotion schedule.

Barry Cheney, who is ultimately responsible for the event, has asked you to help him find a better way to share the schedules among the responsible parties so that when the day of the championship arrives, he is certain he has the most up-to-date schedule possible.

You quickly realize that Excel's ability to share copies of a workbook and merge them into a single, updated master workbook is a good solution.

a. Start **Excel**, open **e04_ps2_Championship_Schedule.xlsx**, and then save the file as Lastname_Firstname_e04_ps2_Championship_Schedule.

b. To add a custom footer to each worksheet.
   - Click the **Page Layout tab**, and then if necessary, click the **Golfers worksheet tab**.
   - Press Shift, and then click the **Documentation worksheet tab**.
   - Click **Print Titles** in the Page Setup group.
   - Click the **Header/Footer tab** in the Page Setup dialog box.
   - Click **Custom Footer**, and then click the **Left section** box.
   - Click **Insert File Name**.
   - Click **OK**, and then click **OK** again.
   - Press Ctrl+Home.
   - Right-click the **Golfers worksheet tab**, and then select **Ungroup Sheets** from the shortcut menu.

c. To share the workbook and save copies for other managers.
   - Click the **Review tab**, and then click **Share Workbook** in the Changes group.
   - Click the **Editing tab** of the Share Workbook dialog box, check **Allow changes by more than one user at the same time**.
   - Click **OK**, and then click **OK** again—you want to continue.
   - Click the **File tab**, click **Save As**, in the File name box type Lastname_Firstname_e04_ps2_Championship_Schedule(Herriott), and then click **Save**.
   - Click the **File tab**, click **Save As**, in the File name box type Lastname_Firstname_e04_ps2_Championship_Schedule(Dimas,Diaz), and then click **Save**.

d. You will now play the role of Alberto Dimaz and Will Diaz. Barry agreed with a suggestion made by Alberto and Will that there should be 9th hole refreshments for players and guests, so 9th hole refreshments will be served from 12:00 noon to 3:00 PM. In the Guest Services worksheet, make an entry for 9th Hole Refreshments in each cell from 12:00 to 3:00 PM each day of the tournament—enter hard returns where necessary.

- Click the **Guest Services worksheet tab**.
- Double-click cell **B14**, and then place the insertion point after the word *Check*.
- Press ⎡Alt⎤+⎡Enter⎤, and then type 9th Hole Refreshments.
- Press ⎡Ctrl⎤+⎡Enter⎤, and then press ⎡Ctrl⎤+⎡C⎤.
- Click cell **B18**, press ⎡Ctrl⎤+⎡V⎤.
- Select cell range **B15:B17** and cell **B19**, and then type 9th Hole Refreshments.
- Press ⎡Ctrl⎤+⎡Enter⎤.
- Select cell range **B14:B19**, and then press ⎡Ctrl⎤+⎡C⎤.
- Select cell **D14** and cell **F14**, and then press ⎡Ctrl⎤+⎡V⎤.

e. Barry asked that you make the same note about 9th hole refreshments in the same manner in the Golfers worksheet. Be sure to insert hard returns before typing 9th Hole Refreshments where necessary.

f. Vendor booths are to close at 5:00 PM so select cells **B24** and **D24** in the Guest Services worksheet, type Vendor Booths Close, and then press ⎡Ctrl⎤+⎡Enter⎤. Double-click cell **F24** and place the insertion point after Reception. Type Vendor Booths Close.

g. Click **Save**, and then close this file.

h. You will now play the role of Aleeta Herriott.
- Click the **File tab**, click **Recent**, and then click **Lastname_Firstname_e04_ps2_ Championship_Schedule(Herriott)**.

i. Aleeta is in charge of Promotion and recognizes that the 9th hole refreshments represents a promotional opportunity. She is going to open a 9th hole pro shop during the same time.
- Click the **Promotion worksheet tab**.
- Double-click cell **B14**, and then place the insertion point after the word *Give-away*.
- Press ⎡Alt⎤+⎡Enter⎤, and then type 9th Hole Pro Shop.
- Press ⎡Ctrl⎤+⎡Enter⎤, and then press ⎡Ctrl⎤+⎡C⎤.
- Select cells **B18**, **D14**, **D18**, **F14**, and **F18**, and then press ⎡Ctrl⎤+⎡V⎤.
- Select cell ranges **B15:B17**, **D15:D17**, **F15:F17**, and cells **B19**, **D19**, and **F19**, and then type 9th Hole Pro Shop.
- Press ⎡Ctrl⎤+⎡Enter⎤.

j. From 5:00–6:00 on Friday and Saturday Aleeta wants to have staff standing at the clubhouse exit handing guests resort promotional materials and additional tickets for the next day's prize drawings to encourage guests to return the next day. On the last day, materials will be distributed that offer discounts at the resort and that attempt to drive guests to the resort website, Facebook page, or Twitter account.
- Double-click cell **B24**, and then place the insertion point after *set*.
- Press ⎡Alt⎤+⎡Enter⎤, and then type End of Day Promotion Distribution.

- Press ⌗Enter⌗, and then type End of Day Promotion Distribution.
- Press ⌗Ctrl⌗ +⌗Enter⌗, press ⌗Ctrl⌗+⌗C⌗.
- Click cell **D25**, and then press ⌗Ctrl⌗+⌗V⌗.
- Double-click cell **D24**, and then place the insertion point after **Weekend**.
- Press ⌗Alt⌗+⌗Enter⌗, and then type End of Day Promotion Distribution. Press ⌗Ctrl⌗+⌗Enter⌗.
- Double-click cell **F24**, and then place the insertion point after **Reception**.
- Press ⌗Alt⌗+⌗Enter⌗, and then type End of Day Promotion Distribution.
- Press ⌗Ctrl⌗+⌗Enter⌗, and then press ⌗Ctrl⌗+⌗C⌗.
- Click cell **F25**, and then press ⌗Ctrl⌗+⌗V⌗.
- Click **Save**, and then close the file.

k. You will now play the role of Barry Cheney.

- Click the **File tab**, and then click **Recent**.
- Click **Lastname_Firstname_e04_ps2_Championship_Schedule**.

l. Merging all the manager's updates into the master schedule requires the Compare and Merge Workbooks icon be available in the Quick Access Toolbar. If the Compare and Merge Workbooks icon is not in your Quick Access Toolbar, then right-click on the Quick Access Toolbar, select Customize Quick Access Toolbar, and add the Compare and Merge Workbooks icon using the Excel Options dialog box.

- Click **Compare and Merge Workbooks** on the Quick Access Toolbar, and then click **OK** in response to the warning dialog box.
- Select **Lastname_Firstname_e04_ps2_Championship_Schedule(Herriott)**, and then click **OK**.
- Click **Compare and Merge Workbooks** on the Quick Access Toolbar, and then if necessary, click **OK** in response to the warning dialog box.
- Select **Lastname_Firstname_e04_ps2_Championship_Schedule(Dimas,Diaz)**, and then click **OK**.

m. Barry now has a master copy of the schedule updated by the other managers. Barry does not have any additional changes to make himself. He wants to change the Shared status of his workbook before going any further.

- Click the **Review tab**, and then click **Share Workbook**.
- Uncheck **Allow changes by more than one user at the same time**, and then click **OK**.
- Click **Yes** in response to the Microsoft Excel alert box.

n. You have some documentation to complete.

- Click the **Documentation worksheet tab**.
- Click cell **A3**. press ⌗Ctrl⌗+ ⌗;⌗.
- Click cell **B3**. Type Barry Cheney.
- Click cell **C3**. Type Golf Championship Master Schedule.
- Click cell **A5**, press ⌗Ctrl⌗+⌗;⌗, and then press ⌗Tab⌗.
- Type your Lastname, Firstname. Press ⌗Ctrl⌗+⌗Enter⌗, and then press ⌗Tab⌗.
- Click cell **C5**, and then type Facilitate the joint maintenance of the championship event schedule among the managers responsible for different aspects of the event.
- Click cell **B16**. Type Golfers.
- Click cell **B22**. Type Guest Services.
- Click cell **B28**. Type Promotion.

- Copy cell **A3** to cells **B18, B24** and **B30**.
- Copy cell **B3** to cells **B17, B23** and **B29**.
- Click cell **B19**. Type Schedule for competing golfers.
- Click cell **B25**. Type Schedule for services offered to resort guests and competing golfers.
- Click cell **B31**. Type Schedule of promotions targeted to resort guests during the tournament.
- You have learned that it is common practice to reuse worksheets for efficiency. This is a reused documentation worksheet and there is a little cleanup to finish. Select rows **38:65**. Right-click in the selected rows and click **Delete** in the shortcut menu.
- Press Ctrl+Home.

o. Click the **Golfers worksheet tab**.

p. Click **Save**. Print—set page orientation to portrait or landscape as appropriate—or submit your project as directed by your instructor, and then close Excel.

Problem Solve 3

Student data file needed:	You will save your files as:
e04_ps3_Time_Window	Lastname_Firstname_e04_ps3_Time_Window.xltm
	Lastname_Firstname_e04_ps3_Time_Window.xlsm

Individual Employee Time Tracking

William Mattingly, CEO of Painted Paradise Resort and Spa, wants to better understand how he spends his time on the job. He would like a tool that can help others better understand their own time utilization and management. He has asked you to develop a worksheet that can be used to track time by category and to summarize time spent by day on a weekly basis.

You found a time-tracking template at Office.com and started a workbook several days ago. The time has come to finish this project.

a. Start **Excel**, and then open **e04_ps3_Time_Window**. Click the **File tab**, click **Save As**, and then select **Excel Macro_Enabled Template** in the Save as type box. Navigate to where you are storing your files, type Lastname_Firstname_e04_ps3_Time_Window, replacing Lastname_Firstname with your own name, in the File name box, and then click **Save**.

b. To validate that the date entered in cell D9 is a Sunday.
- Click cell **D9** in the Week_Template worksheet.
- Click the **Data tab**.
- Use Custom validation with the formula =WEEKDAY(D9)=1.
- Specify an Input Message of Enter the date of the Sunday that ends the work week.
- Specify an Error Alert title of ERROR! and an Error message of The date entered must be a Sunday. Click **OK**.

c. Select cell range **A13:A28**, and then apply data validation to allow the user to select from a list in the range TasksProjectsRange. Click cell **D9**.

d. Now, hide the template from users and record a macro to automatically create a schedule for a new week.
- Right-click the **Week_Template worksheet** tab, and then click **Hide**.
- Click the **Developer tab**. Make sure Use Relative References is NOT selected.
- Record a macro, NewWeek_Macro, invoked by Ctrl+Shift+W, with the Description Create a worksheet for a new work week to do the following:
  1. Right-click the **Master_Data worksheet tab**, and then click **Unhide**.
  2. Select **Week_Template**, and then click **OK**.
  3. Right-click the **Week_Template worksheet tab**, and then select **Move or Copy**.

4. Select **Master_Data** in the Before sheet box.

5. Check **Create a copy**, and then click **OK**.

6. Double-click the new worksheet's tab, and then type YYYY-MM-DD.

7. Right-click the **Week_Template worksheet tab**, and then select **Hide**.

8. Click the **YYYY-MM-DD worksheet tab**, and then click cell **D9**.

e. Stop recording the macro.

- To undo the effects of recording the macro, right-click the **YYYY-MM-DD worksheet tab**, and then select **Delete** from the shortcut menu.
- Click **Delete** in the Alert dialog box.
- Right-click the **Master_Data worksheet tab**, select **Unhide**, select **Week_Template**, and then click **OK**.

f. Unlock cells into which users will enter data.

- Select cells **D4:D5**, **D7**, **D9**, and **A13:H28**.
- Click the **Home tab**.
- Click **Format** in the Cells group, and then toggle off **Lock Cell**.
- Toggle on **Protect Sheet** with Select locked cells unchecked.
- Click cell **D9**.

g. Once a user has entered data for a week, she or he will want to protect it from accidental changes.

- Record a macro, ProtectWeek_Macro, invoked by Ctrl+Shift+P, with the Description Protect this week's data from being inadvertently changed.

1. Click the **Home tab**.

2. Click **Format** in the Cells group, and then click **Unprotect Sheet**.

3. Select cells **D4:D5**, **D7**, **D9**, and **A13:H28**.

4. Click **Format** in the Cells group, and then click **Lock Cell**.

5. Click **Format** in the Cells group, click **Protect Sheet**, and then click **OK**.

- Stop recording the macro.
- To undo the effects of recording the macro, click the **Home tab**.
- Click **Format** in the Cells group, and then click **Unprotect Sheet** (note that once you Unprotect Sheet the cells selected in step 3 above are still selected).
- Click **Format** in the Cells group, and then click **Lock Cell**.

h. Add buttons to execute the macros.

- Select cell range **B32:C33**, and then click **Bold**, **Merge Cells**, **Align Text Left**, and **Middle Align**.
- Type <-- Click this, and then press Enter.
- Click the **Developer tab**.
- Click **Insert** in the Controls group.
- Select **Button (Form Control)**, then draw a button that covers cell range **A32:A33**.
- Select **NewWeek_Macro** in the list below the Macro name box, and then click **OK**.
- Right-click the **button**, and then select **Edit Text** in the shortcut menu. Replace the button text with Add New Week Worksheet. Right-click the **button**, and then select **Exit Edit Text**.
- Click the **Home tab**.
- Click cell **A35** and type Then edit the YYYY-MM-DD worksheet name, Employee data, and Week Ending date as necessary.
- Click cell **A37**, and then type Then enter time utilization data throughout the week.
- Select cell range **B39:D40**, and then click **Bold**, **Merge Cells**, **Align Text Left**, and **Middle Align**.

- Type <-- **At the end of the week, click this.** Press $\boxed{\text{Enter}}$.
- Click the **Developer tab**.
- Click **Insert** in the Controls group.
- Select **Button (Form Control)**. Draw a button that covers cell range **A39:A40**.
- Select **ProtectWeek_Macro** in the list below the Macro name box, and then click **OK**.
- Right-click the **button**, and then select **Edit Text** in the shortcut menu. Replace the button text with Protect Time Data. Right-click the **button**, and then select **Exit Edit Text**.
- Click cell **D9**.
- Click the **Home tab**.
- Click **Format** in the Cells group, click **Protect Sheet**, and then click **OK**.

i. Create documentation to instruct the user how to create the first weekly timesheet.
- Click the **Master_Data worksheet tab**.
- Click the **Insert tab**.
- Click **Text Box** in the Text group.
- Draw a text box that covers cell range **C3:H10**.
- Click the **Home tab**.
- Click **Bold**, and then set Fill Color to White and Font Color to Dark Red. Set Font Size to 24, and then click **Center**.
- Type To create the first week's time tracking worksheet, Press Ctrl+Shift+W.
- Click a cell outside the text box.

j. Add the necessary footer documentation.
- Click the **Week_Template worksheet tab**.
- Press and hold $\boxed{\text{Shift}}$, and then click the **Documentation worksheet tab**.
- Add the filename to the left section of the print footer.
- Right-click the **Week_Template worksheet** tab, and then click **Ungroup Sheets**.

k. To finish development by hiding the worksheet and saving the workbook, right-click the **Week_Template worksheet tab**, click **Hide**, and then click **Save**.

l. Click the **File tab**, click **Save As**, and then select **Excel Macro_Enabled Workbook** in the Save as type box. Navigate to where you are storing your files, type Lastname_Firstname_e04_ps_Time_Window in the File name box, replacing Lastname_Firstname with your own name, and then click **Save**.

m. Now test with some data.
- Press $\boxed{\text{Ctrl}}+\boxed{\text{Shift}}+\boxed{\text{W}}$.
- Double-click the **YYYY-MM-DD worksheet tab**, and then type 2013-12-08.
- In cell **D9**, type 12/8/2013. Starting in cell **A13**, enter the following data:

Project/Task	Monday	Tuesday	Wednesday	Thursday	Friday
Admin	0.5	0.5	0.5	0.5	0.5
Email	1	1	3	1.5	2
Reading	1	1	1.5	0.5	0.5
Interviewing	2.5	3	2	3	
Interview Preparation	1	1.5	2	1.5	
Meetings	2.5	2.5	0.5	1.5	4
Telephone	1	0.5	1	1	2

- Click the **Protect Time Data** button.
- Click the **Add New Week Worksheet** button.
- Double-click the **YYYY-MM-DD worksheet tab**, and then type 2013-12-15.

- In cell D9, type 12/15/2013.
- Enter the following data:

Project/Task	Monday	Tuesday	Wednesday	Thursday	Friday
Admin	0.5	0.5	0.5	0.5	0.5
Email	2	1	2	2	2
Reading	1	1	0.5	0.5	1
Project A	3	1	1	2	2
Project B		2	2	1	1
Meetings	1	3	2	1	
Telephone	2.5	0.5	1	2	2

- Click the **Protect Time Data** button.

n. Click the **Documentation tab**.

- Select cells **A3** and **A5**. Press Ctrl+;. Press Ctrl + Enter.
- Select cells **B3** and **B5**. Type your name in Lastname, Firstname format. Press Ctrl + Enter.

o. Click **Save**. Print—set page orientation to portrait or landscape as appropriate—or submit your project as directed by your instructor. Close Excel.

Perform 1: Perform in Your Life

Student data file needed:

Blank Excel document

You will save your file as:

Lastname_Firstname_e04_pf1_Education_Costs

College Expense Tracking and Summary

Very few students keep track of what it actually costs to attend a college or university. The costs are usually higher than a person realizes and cross a staggering array of categories. For an example, see the list below, which is not nearly inclusive. It may be very helpful to have this type of information readily available for student aid applications, for decision-making associated with extending your education by a semester or two to add a major or minor, for seeking financing for a different car from a local bank, or maybe to help you decide whether or not you can really afford a different car.

Build a workbook that contains three worksheets and a documentation worksheet. Two of the worksheets are to be structured such that each tracks expenses for a single semester. The third worksheet is to consolidate the two semesters of data. At a minimum, your worksheets should address the following expenses:

- Tuition
- Fees
- Books
- Room
- Board

- Entertainment
- Clothing
- Utilities
- Groceries and personal care items
- Transportation

Structure your workbook as follows:

a. Start **Excel**. Save the blank document as Lastname_Firstname_e04_pf1_Education_Costs replacing Lastname_Firstname with your own name. The file should be saved as an Excel Macro_Enabled Template.

b. To build the structure of the workbook.

- Rename Sheet1 to Total Education Costs.

- Rename Sheet2 and Sheet3 to Fall, 20xx and Spring, 20yy—replacing xx and yy with the year of your most recent fall and spring semesters.

  If you have not attended a college or university for two semesters yet, reference the current semester and the prior semester, or the current semester and the next semester. In this case you will be predicting, or possibly budgeting, figures for the future.

c. Build two sections in your worksheets for the two semesters. The bottom part of the worksheet should include detailed expense information by expense category. The top section should summarize the bottom part of the worksheet. The top, or summary, section should be structured to make consolidation across multiple semesters of data in separate worksheets as simple as possible.

d. Enter data for each category of expenses. Include expenditure date, description, and amount. You do not need to enter actual figures that represent your personal costs, just reasonable estimates.

e. Copy the format of the summary section in a semester expense worksheet to the Total Education Costs worksheet. Use 3D cell references to calculate the expense totals across all other worksheets.

f. Use AutoSum to summarize detailed expenditures in the summary section of the semester worksheets.

g. Add the filename to the left section of the custom footer for each page, including the documentation worksheet.

h. Create a relative macro to add an expense line to any category in a semester worksheet. Include documentation that makes the user aware of how to properly run the macro.

i. Save your workbook, and then click **Save**. Print—set page orientation to portrait or landscape as appropriate—or submit your project as directed by your instructor, and then close Excel.

Perform 2: Perform in Your Career

Student data file needed:	You will save your file as:
e04_pf2_Expense_Reimbursement	Lastname_Firstname_e04_pf2_Expense_Reimbursement.xlsm

Biweekly Expense Reimbursement with Summary

Most professional positions require that employees track and report all job-related expenses for reimbursement and/or expense reconciliation. The organization you work for has used paper forms for years because employees could take the forms with them and fill them in "on the fly." Many employees now have smart phones, tablet computers, laptops, or other such devices. They want an officially approved digital solution for expense reporting, tracking, and reimbursement.

You have been asked by your supervisor to produce a workbook that can be used by individual employees to track expenses by pay period (every two weeks beginning on Monday for this organization). The workbook should contain one worksheet for every pay period for which an employee has expenses to report. In addition, there should be a summary worksheet where year-to-date totals for expenses are consolidated.

a. Start **Excel**. Navigate to where you have stored your student data files, and then open e04_pf2_Expense_Reimbursement. Save the template as a Macro-enabled workbook with the file name Lastame_Firstname_e04_pf2_Expense_Reimbursement replacing Lastname_Firstname with your own name.

b. Add a worksheet titled Parameters to the workbook. Add the following to the worksheet:

Parameter	Value	Account Code	Account
Name	Lastname, Firstname	100	Wilber Investments, Inc
Department	Information Systems	200	GeoScream.com
Position	Programmer/Analyst	300	Braathen Bridal
Manager	Eniac, Penny	400	ZenZuo, LLP
EmployeeID	JD135711	500	Lawson-Body Partners

c. Each cell that contains a value should be named as a range using the parameter. If Eniac Penny is typed into cell **B5**, cell B5 should be assigned the range name Manager.

 The column of numbers that represent account codes should be assigned the range name AccountCodeRange, and the two columns that contain both account codes and account names should be assigned the range name AccountDataRange. Make sure you do not include the column labels in the named ranges.

d. In the Expense Report worksheet, assign the parameter value for employee name to cell **C6**; for example, if you gave the parameter the range name "NAME", type =NAME in cell C6. Assign the appropriate parameter values to each of the data items in rows 6:7.

e. Apply data validation to cell L3 that ensures the date entered is a Monday. Use custom validation and the formula =WEEKDAY(L3)=2. Enter input and error messages that clearly explain that this date must be a Monday. In cell L4, enter a formula that adds 13 days to the value in L3. Type 12/2/2013 into cell L3.

f. Select cell range **B10:B24**. Apply data validation that limits the date values in this range to a start date of the value in cell L3 and an end date of the value in cell L4. Include an error alert that explains the date boundaries. When entering validation criteria for a range, Excel applies relative addresses, so be sure to make row references absolute, such as =L$3.

g. Select cell range **C10:C24**. Apply data validation that allows an employee to pick from the list of Account Codes.

h. Click cell **D10**. Type =IF(C10<>"",VLOOKUP(C10,AccountDataRange,2,FALSE),""). Fill without formatting the formula in cell D10 through the cell range D11:D24.

i. Type the following expenses into the worksheet:

Date	Account	Expense Type	Amount
12/2/2013	200	Hotel	120
12/2/2013	200	Meals	55.50
12/2/2013	200	Transport	40
12/4/2013	400	Hotel	199
12/4/2013	400	Meals	90
12/4/2013	400	Entertainment	50
12/15/2013	500	Misc	25
12/15/2013	200	Hotel	120
12/15/2013	200	Meals	67.50
12/15/2013	200	Fuel	25

j. Also reflect in the worksheet that you received a $500 advance for the pay period. Change the name of the Expense Report worksheet to match the date in cell L3, but type it in yyyy-mm-dd format.

k. Record a macro that selects the cell ranges B10:C24, E10:K24 and cells L27 and L3 and clears all contents. Assign the macro to a button titled Clear Expenses that covers cell D25. Be sure to undo the effects of the macro after you stop recording.

l. Right-click the **2013-12-02 worksheet tab**, and then select **Move or Copy**. Select **2013-12-02** in the Before sheet box, check **Create a copy**, and then click **OK**. Rename the 2013-12-02 (2) worksheet to 2013-12-16. Clear Expenses and then change the date to match the worksheet name in cell L3.

m. Enter the following expenses in to the 2013-12-16 worksheet:

Date	Account	Expense Type	Amount
12/19/2013	100	Hotel	139
12/19/2013	100	Meals	42
12/22/2013	400	Entertainment	189
12/23/2013	200	Hotel	219
12/23/2013	200	Meals	145
12/23/2013	200	Entertainment	300
12/27/2013	300	Misc	25
12/27/2013	300	Phone	10
12/27/2013	300	Fuel	49
12/29/2013	500	Entertainment	249

n. Create a copy of the 2013-12-16 worksheet, and then name it YTD Expenses. If necessary, move the YTD Expenses worksheet to the left of all other worksheets in the workbook.

   - Select cell ranges **J3:L4** and **B29:I31**, and then clear all content.
   - Select cell ranges **B10:L24**, **E25:L25**, and **L26:L28**, and then press Delete.
   - Select cell range **B9:D28**, right-click the selected range, and then select **Delete** in the shortcut menu. Select **Shift cells left** in the Delete dialog box, and then click **OK**.
   - Click cell **B10**.
   - Consolidate range E10:L28 in the 2013-12-16 and 2013-12-02 worksheets. Consolidate by position, so do not check Top row or Left column.

o. Group all the worksheets in the workbook together.

   - Press Ctrl+Home.
   - Insert the filename into the left section of the print footer.
   - Ungroup the worksheets.

p. Unlock cells that the user will enter data into and protect each worksheet, including the Parameters worksheet. Do not do this for the YTD Expenses worksheet.

q. In the YTD Expenses worksheet, select cell ranges **B2:I2**, **B5:I5**, **C6:E6**, **C7:E7**, **G6:I6**, and **G7:I7**.

   - Merge the selected cell ranges.
   - Use AutoFit Colum Width for columns B:I.

r. Create a documentation worksheet and document your work.

s. Save the workbook. Print—set page orientation to portrait or landscape as appropriate— or submit your project as directed by your instructor. Close Excel.

Student data file needed:	You will save your file as:
e04_pf3_Time_Billing	Lastname_Firstname_ e04_pf3_Time_Billing

Law Firm Time Billing Summary

Professionals often generate revenue by billing clients for their time. This is certainly true of attorneys. Attorneys need to keep an accurate log of the time they spend working on each client's account or case.

Assume you are an attorney working in an intellectual property firm and your specialty is patents, trademarks, and copyrights. The e04_pf3_Time_Billing file contains billing information for two weeks of your time, but you need to somehow compile a quick summary of the billable hours dedicated to each client.

Create a summary of your billable time by client that includes detailed information that contributed to the total billable hours.

a. Open the **e04_pf3_Time_Billing** file, and then save the file as Lastname_Firstname_ e04_pf3_Time_Billing.

b. Consolidate the billing data by client in worksheets 2013-12-08 – 2013-12-14 and 2013-12-01 – 2013-12-07. The consolidation will have to be by category because billable events for clients are not in a specific location; they are entered in the order of event occurrence.

  • Click cell **A2** in the Time_Summary worksheet.

  • Click the **Data tab**, and then click **Consolidate**.

  • Add cell range **A3:E24** in the 2013-12-08 – 2013-12-14 worksheet and cell range **A3:E22** in the 2013-12-01 – 2013-12-07 worksheet to the consolidation.

  • Consolidate by the categories in the left column of the ranges.

  • Create links back to the source data.

c. Delete columns B and G from the consolidation results, as they are not informative in this analysis. Column B references the source workbook for linked source data. Since all of the consolidated data came from this workbook, column B contains the same value for every detail entry. Column G is a description that is not even copied to hidden detail rows.

d. Format the consolidation to better match source formatting.

  • Select cell range **A2:E2** in the 2013-12-08 – 2013-12-14 worksheet, and then copy it to the clipboard.

  • Select cell range **A1:E1** in the Time_Summary worksheet, right-click the **selected range**, and then select **Keep Source Column Widths** in the Paste Special menu, Paste group.

e. Click the **expand button** for row 30. Notice that individual date, start time, and end time values are part of the source data detail—B25:D29. You do not want to lose that detail data, but the summary data in B30, as well as in all other summary cells in columns B:D, is nonsensical—notice the year value in the dates. To delete the summary values and not lose the detail, you could select each summary range noncontiguously, meaning press and hold Ctrl and select **B6:D6**, select **B12:D12**, select **B20:D20**, and so on, until you have selected columns B:D in all summary rows, and then press Delete. A better method would be to: Click the **Level 1 button** to hide all detail rows. Select cell range B6:B54 and Press Alt + ;—this selects only the visible cells, and then press Delete.

f. Click the **Level 2** button to expand the consolidation. All detail data in columns B:D should be visible, but there should be no summary data for those columns in the consolidation.

g. Select rows **2:5**. Set the background fill color of these rows to No Fill. Click ⌐Ctrl⌐+ ⌐B⌐.

h. Click the **Level 1 button**.
   - Select cell range **A6:E54**.
   - Press ⌐Alt⌐+ ⌐;⌐ to select only the visible cells and set the fill color to **Olive Green, Accent 3, Lighter 80%**. Press ⌐Ctrl⌐+⌐Home⌐.
   - Click the **Level 2 button**—detail data cells should not have a background fill color.
   - Click the **Level 1 button**.

i. Add the file name to the left section of the page footer on all worksheets. For all but the Master_Data and Documentation worksheets, replace "Lastname" with your last name in the company name in the Print Titles header.

j. Complete a documentation worksheet for this exercise. Assume you built this worksheet in its entirety.

k. Save the file. Print or submit your project as directed by your instructor—set page orientation to portrait or landscape as appropriate, and close Excel.

Perform 4: How Others Perform

Student data file needed:	You will save your file as:
e04_pf4_Burnt_Ashes	Lastname_Firstname_e04_pf4_Burnt_Ashes

Rising Ashes Culinary Celebrations Event Planner

Carbonita Burnt owns and operate Rising Ashes Culinary Celebrations. She contracts with a local hotel to rent their ballrooms—The Gargoyle Room, The Phoenix Room, and The Dragon Room—for events. This works well for the hotel because they block out a number of rooms for event guests. Carbonita has developed a worksheet that accurately calculates the price of events based on manually entered data. The data entry process is prone to error and requires a bit more knowledge of how the worksheet operates than is optimal.

Improve the pricing worksheet by doing the following:

a. Open **e04_pf4_Burnt_Ashes**, and then save a copy with the file name Lastname_Firstname_e04_pf4_Burnt_Ashes, replacing Lastname and Firstname with your name.

b. Review the Master_Data worksheet and determine what named ranges exist that may be of use.

c. Apply data validation to cells in which data are entered.
   - Event Date, cell B9, must be greater than today.
   - # of Guests, cell B10, can't exceed 500.
   - Room Block, cell B11, can't exceed the # of Guests / 3.
   - Dining Option, cell B12, limit to either "Plate" or "Buffet".
   - Room Rent, cell C15, only allow the selection of a room that has the capacity to hold the # of Guests. See step d.
   - Food selections, cells C17:C21 should be tied to the appropriate lists in the Master_Data worksheet.

d. In the Master_Data worksheet:

- Name cell C10 PhoenixRoomCapacity.
- Name cell C18 GargoyleRoomCapacity.
- Type Rooms for # of Guests in cell C34.
- **Align Text Right** in cell C34.
- Name call range D34:D36 RoomList.
- In cell D34, type Dragon.
- In cell D35 type =IF(GuestNumber <= PhoenixRoomCapacity,"Phoenix","")
- In cell D36, type =IF(GuestNumber <= GargoyleRoomCapacity,"Gargoyle","")
- Apply data validation to cell C15 in the Event_Pricing worksheet that allows selection from the list in the RoomList named range.

e. Include the file name in the left section of the custom footer of all worksheets in the workbook.

f. Remove any content that is unnecessary from the worksheet once data validation has been applied to data entry cells.

g. Increase the space available to display information in cells C15:21 by merging columns C and D. Be careful not to lose any information and also merge any other cells that will keep the appropriate look and feel of the ESTIMATE OF COSTS section of the worksheet.

h. Protect the Event_Pricing worksheet such that only data entry cells can be selected.

i. Add any other protection you feel may be warranted, for example, if you protect all cells in the Master_Data worksheet and you check Select locked cells, then you cannot change the data, but you can still select ranges and find range names.

j. Create workbook documentation.

k. Print or submit your file as directed by your instructor, set page orientation to portrait or landscape as appropriate. Close Excel.

WORKSHOP 9

Objectives

1. Understand the importance of connecting to external data sets.   p. 456

2. Create, edit, and save a web query.   p. 456

3. Import XML data. p. 462

4. Import a text file. p. 465

5. Connect to an Access database and query with Microsoft Query.   p. 468

6. Clean and standardize data including data containing dates. p. 472

7. Use Text and Date functions for data manipulation.   p. 472

Manipulating Data Sets for Business Analytics

PREPARE CASE
Red Bluff Golf Club Pro Shop Data Integration

The Red Bluff Golf Club Pro Shop manager, Ed Stokes, has asked you to create a report showing the pro shop sales from the last quarter. In the past, they had to manually reenter data from different sources in order to create this report, because no one at the resort knew how to import the data. As a result, they rarely completed the report. Ed worries about the accuracy of the reports that were compiled because of the manual data entry. However, he did keep all the original files.

Courtesy of www.Shutterstock.com

Recently, a new Golf database was created to track sales and allow for easy export to Excel for analysis. However, Ed wants you to design a spreadsheet that will help them automate the process of gathering and standardizing the data from the past for analysis.

Student data files needed for this workshop:

 e05_ws09_Data_Import

 e05_ws09_Data_Cleanse

 e05_ws09_Documentation_Template

 e05_ws09_Maintenance

 e05_ws09_Customers

 e05_ws09_Northwind

You will save your files as:

 Lastname_Firstname_e05_ws09_Data_Import

 Lastname_Firstname_e05_ws09_Data_Cleanse

Working with Data Sets

One reason that spreadsheets are so popular is their ability to combine data and information from a wide variety of sources. Once you have advanced beyond the novice level to become a more advanced user, you will very likely need to integrate data from multiple sources. Most organizations have their data spread throughout the organization in a wide variety of devices and formats. They may collect data on websites or in word-processing programs, databases, network servers, or even in paper reports. In this section you will learn about external data sets and how to connect to them. You will also work with web queries and import data.

Understanding External Data Sets

Anything that is not stored in an Excel format (.xls or .xlsx) or not stored locally is considered to be **external data**. Spreadsheets such as Excel offer a wide variety of tools to help the user extract external data and integrate it into reports so that it can be actively used to make better decisions. By using the import tools, you can avoid a lot of extra typing. Microsoft has continued to expand the file types that can be easily imported, and this feature has improved considerably in recent years. Common file formats include HTML, XML, text, and .accdb files from Microsoft Access.

One of the reasons that spreadsheets are such powerful tools is that they have evolved into the de facto means of consolidating diverse types of data. For example, someone may want you to work on an analysis or report, but they are not able to grant you access to their databases. In this case, one solution would be for them to export their data to a text format, which you can then easily import into Excel.

Source	Description
Microsoft Access (.mdb, .accdb)	Import data from relational database tables created in Access (.mdb, .accdb) formats.
HTML (.html)	Link to data stored in tabular form on websites.
Comma separated (.csv)	Convert data stored in a comma-delimited format, .csv files. Even though this is a separate file type, you cannot choose it when importing data into Excel. Excel will automatically open a .csv file.
XML (.xml)	Import data stored in .xml format.
Text (.txt)	Exchange data between mainframes and other systems using the (.txt) format.
dBase (.dbf)	Data stored in a popular PC database program. Converts from .dbf files.
SQL Server	A popular relational database server for corporate web servers.
Analysis Services	Designed to import data formatted as a data cube in SQL Server Analysis Services.
Microsoft Query	A query wizard to help in importing data from less common or unlisted sources using ODBC (standard data conversion drivers).
Data Connection Wizard	Another query wizard for creating and maintaining connections with unlisted data sources; uses OLEDB drivers.

Figure 1 Common data sources for Excel

Using a Web Query

One popular way to integrate information from web pages is to use a web query. A **query** is a question that you would ask a database such as Access. Access allows users to formulate queries in a variety of tools or languages to search for information in the database. You might think of a web query as something you could type into a search engine such as Google or Yahoo in order to search the web. However, in Excel, a **web query** is just a way of importing data into a spreadsheet directly from a web page. This could be financial data such as stock prices from a financial web site such as **http://money.msn.com** or it could be sales data from a company web server.

More and more, companies are using websites to make their data available to users. Financial, governmental, and even college-related data is uploaded and refreshed daily. By linking this data to a spreadsheet via a web query, users can automatically update the data for use in their spreadsheet applications. You could just copy and paste this data, but by using a web query you will know that it is accurate and up to date.

Web queries are tied to specific URLs; when the URL changes, the web query will no longer be able to access the data. So before you start, be sure you have the exact URL address you need.

To Import Web Data

a. Start **Excel**, click the **File tab**, and then click **Open**. In the Open dialog box, navigate to where your student data files are located, and then double-click **e05_ws09_Data_Import**.

b. Click the **File tab**, click **Save As**, and then in the Save As dialog box, navigate to the location where you are saving your files. In the File name box, type Lastname_Firstname_ e05_ws09_Data_Import replacing Lastname and Firstname with your own name. Click **Save**.

c. To insert your filename as a footer, click the **Insert tab**, and then click **Header & Footer** in the Text group.

d. Click the **Design tab**, and then click **Go to Footer** in the Navigation group. If necessary, click the **left section** of the footer, and then click **File Name** in the Header & Footer Elements group.

e. Click any cell on the spreadsheet to move out of the footer, press Ctrl+Home, click the **View tab**, click **Normal** in the Workbook Views group, and then click the **Home tab**.

f. Make sure the Cust_Web worksheet is displayed, and then click the **Data tab**.

g. Click **From Web** in the Get External Data group.

h. In the New Web Query dialog box, click in the **Address** input box, and delete any text. Type the following URL: http://www.paintedparadiseresort.com/Red_Bluff_Web.htm. If you get a security warning message, select **No**, and continue.

i. Click **GO**. The New Web Query window now displays the target website.

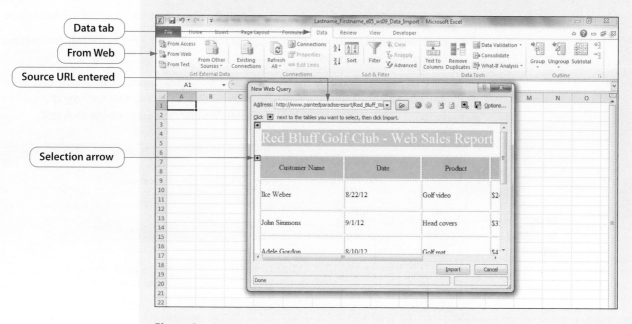

Figure 2 Creating a web query

j. Click the second black **Selection arrow** to select the table.

k. Click **Import**, accept the default location of cell A1, and then click **OK**. You should see the data from the table on your worksheet.

l. **Save** 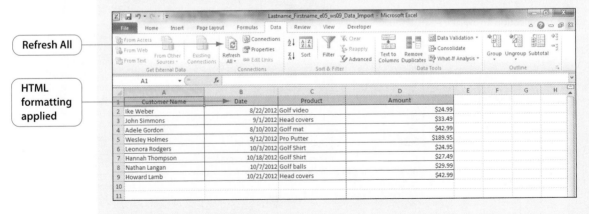 your work.

Troubleshooting

Due to the variable speed of connections and the amount of data being downloaded from the targeted website, it may take several minutes for the data to download.

Editing a Web Query

You may have noticed that the data you pulled into your spreadsheet from the web page with your original web query retained some, but not all, of the web page formatting. Web queries can be modified so that they are set to retain all the formatting from the target HTML tables. Excel gives you several options for formatting your web query. The default None option retrieves the text with some basic formatting. The RTF (Rich Text Format) option retains most of the text formatting. The Full HTML formatting option allows you to import more advanced features like tables and hyperlinks.

Now you want to print out the Sales data report just as it is formatted on the website for your upcoming meeting. Go back and edit your web query to allow for Full HTML formatting.

To Modify Web Queries

a. With the same worksheet displayed, click **Connections** in the Connections group.

b. In the Workbook Connections dialog box, click **Properties**.

c. Accept the default Connection name in the Connection name text box, and in the Description text box type Web sales data for Pro Shop site. Click to check the **Refresh data when opening the file** check box, if necessary.

d. Click the **Definition tab**, and then click **Edit Query** at the bottom left of the dialog box.

e. Click the **Options** button in the top right of the window. Click the **Full HTML formatting** option, and then click **OK**.

f. Click **Import**, click **OK**, and then close the Workbook Connections dialog box. Click **Refresh All** in the Connections group. You should see that the data has now changed to include the blue colors in the table field headers and borders to divide each cell.

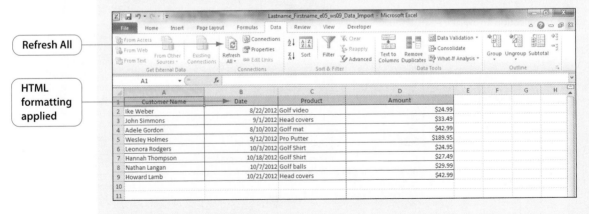

Figure 3 Modified web query

CONSIDER THIS | **Beyond Spreadsheets**

The amount of data in the business world is growing at a huge rate—faster, in fact, than at any time in previous recorded history. Companies and governments store massive amounts of data. Facebook alone stores over 40 billion photos. What kinds of data could a company like Facebook be collecting that you might not have considered, and how could the information be used (both on a positive level and a negative level)?

Saving a Web Query

At times, you will want to share your completed web query with other users. By saving a copy of your web query, you create a permanent file along with the connection file. This file can then be used in any Microsoft Office application, including Microsoft Word.

To Save a Web Query

a. On the Cust_Web worksheet tab, click **Connections** in the Connections group.

b. In the Workbook Connections dialog box, click **Properties** for the Connection web query you just created.

c. In the Connections Properties dialog box, click the **Definition tab**, and then click **Edit Query**. The same web page you saw before is displayed.

d. Click the **Save Query** button 🖫, located next to the Options button. The Save Workspace dialog box defaults to a special Queries folder that is displayed as the default location for saving queries.

Connections

Save Workspace dialog box

Figure 4 Saving a web query

e. Navigate to where you stored your student data files. Accept the default file name, click **Save**, and then click **Cancel** and close the remaining dialog boxes.

f. Recall that it is good practice to document all your work in Excel. To make it easy, use the document template you have used in previous workshops. From your student data folder, open **e05_ws09_Documentation_Template**.

g. To copy the documentation worksheet, right-click the **Documentation worksheet tab**, and then click **Move or Copy**.

h. In the Move or Copy dialog box, under **To book**, select **Lastname_Firstname_e05_ ws09_Data_Import**, and then under **Before sheet**, click **(move to end)**. Remember to click the **Create a copy** check box, and then click **OK**.

i. Close the **e05_ws09_Documentation_Template** workbook without saving changes if prompted.

j. In the Lastname_Firstname_e05_ws09_Data_Import workbook, verify the Documentation worksheet was copied over. Click cell **A3** under the Create Date field, and then press Ctrl + ; to enter the current date. Press Tab, and then in cell B3 under the By Whom field enter your name in Firstname Lastname format. Press Ctrl + Home.

k. **Save** your work.

Real World Advice   How is Connecting to Web Data Different than Copy and Pasting?

It may seem simpler to just copy the web data and then paste it into your worksheet. In fact, you can copy and paste for the occasional import of web data. With a newer browser, you can right-click a web table and copy it to Excel with the Export to Microsoft Excel option. However, when you use the copy-and-paste method, you will have to spend time reformatting the data to use it in your formulas in Excel. More importantly, web queries provide a great advantage when you are creating an application that needs to be updated frequently. The web query will create a connection to the web page and automatically update the data in your Excel file.

Using Web Queries to Retrieve Stock Quotes

There are a number of prewritten web queries that come with Excel. One of the most popular is the MSN Money site for stock ticker data. This site can add stock price data to any reports. The data provided includes information about the stock's high and low price for that day, its closing price, and its closing price on the previous day. This data is necessary to calculate the current value of your portfolio or to track companies of special interest. The site also includes a useful News link to breaking financial news. To access this data and build it into a report, you need the stock's ticker symbol. The ticker symbol is just a short abbreviation that uniquely identifies a company's stock—for example, VZ for Verizon.

When you explained this to your boss, he said that this would be a perfect way to track key companies in the golf resort industry. He has given you a list of golf equipment manufacturers and resort operators and wants you to create a stock-tracking report for them that will allow him to monitor the overall industry better. The list of key golf resort companies include Adidas (symbol: ADDDF), Calloway Golf Company (symbol: ELY), Nike Inc. (symbol: NKE), Marriot International Inc. (symbol: MAR), Starwood Hotels and Resorts (symbol: HOT) and Great Wolf Resorts Inc. (symbol: WOLF).

To Create a Stock Report Using a Web Query

a. Click the **Sheet2 worksheet tab** to display a blank worksheet, double-click the tab to edit the name, and then type ResortStocks to rename the worksheet. Press Ctrl+Enter.

b. Click cell **A1**, and then type in Stock Tracking Report. Press Ctrl+Enter. If necessary, click the **Home tab**, and then click the **Font Size arrow** and change the size to **22** point. Select **A1:H1**, and then click **Merge & Center** in the Alignment group.

c. Click cell **A2**, and then type in Key Golf Resort Industry Companies. Press Ctrl+Enter, click the **Font Size arrow** and change the size to **20** point. Select **A2:H2**, and then click **Merge & Center**.

d. Click cell **A4**, click the **Data tab**, and then click **Existing Connections** in the Get External Data group. The Existing Connections dialog box displays a list of existing connections for the current workbook and also a list of preconfigured connections.

e. Click **MSN MoneyCentral Investor Stock Quotes**, and then click **Open**.

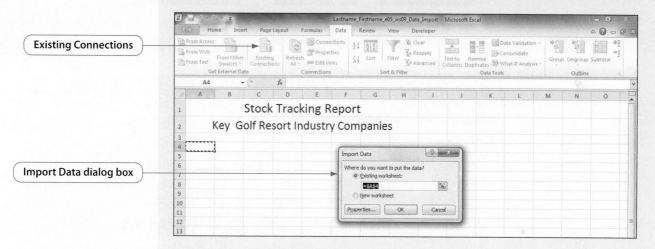

Existing Connections

Import Data dialog box

Figure 5 Stock-tracking web query

f. Confirm that the Existing worksheet cell location for the data is A4 in the Import Data dialog box, and then click **OK**.

g. In the **Enter Parameter Value** dialog box type the following stock symbols separated by commas (not case sensitive): ADDDF, ELY, NKE, MAR, HOT, WOLF. Click the **Use this value/reference for future refreshes** check box, and then click **OK**. The web query populates the worksheet with current stock data. This data can now be used in other calculations, charts, dashboards, and so on.

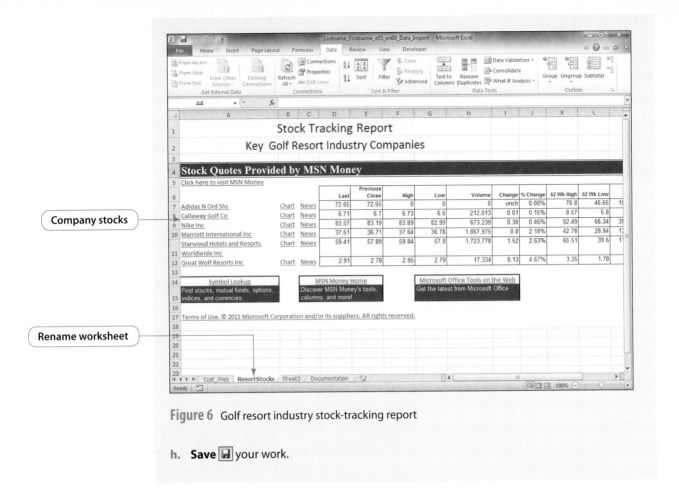

Company stocks

Rename worksheet

Figure 6 Golf resort industry stock-tracking report

h. **Save** 💾 your work.

Working with XML Data and Text Files

Two of the most common data formats for importing data into Excel are XML data and text files. In the following section you will learn how to import data in these two formats into Excel.

Importing XML Data

XML, or Extensible Markup Language, is an increasingly popular tool working behind the scenes in Excel. A little knowledge of how it is used shows that you are well beyond the usual beginner's knowledge of spreadsheets. In an earlier exercise, you imported data that was stored in a table on a web page. This made it easier to import the data into Excel without reformatting it. However, in most cases, data on web pages is not stored in an organized manner. That is to say, it is usually just a bunch of text that has been formatted to fit the page. **XML** was created to help give structure to web page data so that it can be searched and processed more efficiently. XML allows users to define their own tags in order to define the content of the document.

Most web pages are programmed in **HTML** or Hypertext Markup Language. Both XML and HTML are examples of markup languages. **Markup languages** use special sequences of characters or "markups" inserted in the document to indicate how the document should look when it is displayed or printed. The markup indicators are often called "tags" and are enclosed in angle brackets (< >).These tags tell the processor of the document what to do with it. HTML is used to format and display the web data, whereas XML was developed to help convert web data into a tabular structure so it could be easily stored and transported. Unlike HTML, the tags in XML actually describe the content of the data between the tags. So, HTML uses tags such as <H1></H1> to help describe the formatting of the document. XML uses tags to describe the actual content between the tags <revenue></revenue>. Because of this, XML capabilities were soon extended to databases, spreadsheets, and word processors and became the de facto standard for transmitting data between systems and different applications.

One of the most powerful aspects of XML is that you can define custom tags for content specific to a particular industry. In HTML, all the tags are prespecified so the browser knows how to interpret them. XML is different in that as long as the rules for creating XML tags and documents are followed, you can define the tags any way you like.

The goal of XML is to allow users to automate the storage, transmission, and processing of content. To accomplish this, XML separates the content from the format and structure of the document. To understand how to process an XML document, it is crucial to understand its structure. The structure of an XML document is described in the XML schema or data map. The **XML schema** describes the structure of an XML document in terms of what XML elements it will contain and their sequence. In Excel, the term **XML map** is synonymous with XML schema. **XML element** includes the start and stop tags and everything in between, such as <revenue>$345,678</revenue>. The document structure is separate from the actual content of the document itself and uses a completely separate file with an .xsd extension. It is similar in concept to the idea of a mail merge. The content is contained in the .xml file, the formatting is described in an .xsl file, and the structure of all the data elements is laid out in the schema or .xsd file. All of these files are merged in the resulting XML document, just as a list of names and addresses is merged with a form letter in Word, as illustrated in Figure 7.

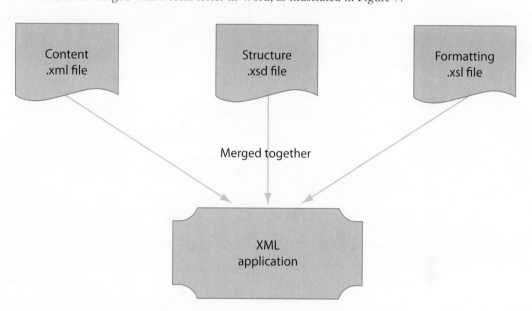

Figure 7 XML document files

Determining the structure of any document may not be obvious. If you were to look at a book index or a table of contents, you would know just by glancing at them what these two different documents were. This is because over the years publishers have defined what the structure of an index or table of contents should look like. It is the same way with schemas. You can define the structure of a sales order document to contain the customer number, name, date, productID, cost, and total cost. All of these would be represented as elements within the XML schema. So when Excel processes an XML file, it looks for an existing XML schema to check whether it has received a valid XML document. This way it can automate the processing of XML files since it knows what to expect because it is defined by the schema.

In this exercise, you will be working with an XML file, in which no schema has been specified. This XML file replicates a maintenance list for the Red Bluff Golf Pro Shop. By saving the data in this XML document, it can be electronically transmitted, queried, and stored. When Excel imports the maintenance list data into a worksheet, it automatically creates an XML schema, or XML map as it is called in Excel. When viewing an XML file in Internet Explorer 6.0 and above, you can also export an XML file into Excel by right-clicking anywhere in the browser screen, selecting Export to Microsoft Excel, and following the directions. Both methods give the same results. When you drag the XML elements from the XML Source pane into your spreadsheet, you are binding your data to the cell in which you placed the element. So, whenever you refresh the data by clicking on the Refresh button, it should automatically connect to the source to import the changes and update the data on your worksheet.

To Import XML Data

a. First, open your web browser, click **File**, and then click **Open**.

Troubleshooting

Depending on the browser you are using and your browser settings, you may not see a file menu at the top. To show the file menu in Internet Explorer, press Alt and this will take you directly to the file menu. If you are using Chrome you will not see any file menu.

b. In the Open dialog box, click **Browse**, and then navigate to where the data files are stored. In the File type box near the File name, click the **arrow**, and then click as necessary to display the **All Files** option as the File type in order to display the available .xml files. Select **e05_ws09_Maintenance.xml**, and then click **Open**. If necessary, click **OK** in the Open dialog box. If an ActiveX security warning displays at the top of your browser, you can simply ignore it and proceed.

c. View the different parts of the maintenance document, then close the browser.

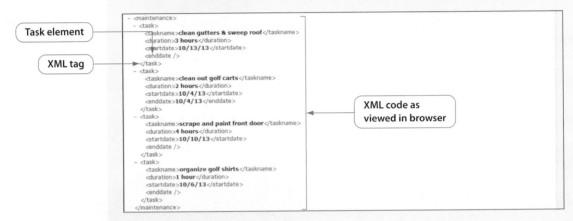

Figure 8 XML document structure

d. Click **Lastname_Firstname_e05_ws09_Data_Import** to make it the active file, click the **Sheet3 worksheet tab**, and then using the technique previously learned, rename the worksheet XML_Data.

e. If you do not see the Developer tab in the Excel ribbon, click the **File tab**, and then click **Options**.

f. In the Excel Options dialog box, click **Customize Ribbon** in the left pane. Under Customize the Ribbon, a list of Main Tabs should be visible. Click to select **Developer** in the list of Main Tabs.

g. Click **OK** to close the Excel Options dialog box.

h. Click the **Developer tab**, and then click anywhere on the worksheet to activate the buttons. Click **Source** in the XML group. The XML Source pane is displayed on the right side of your worksheet.

i. Click **XML Maps** in the bottom right of the XML Source pane. A list of XML Maps attached to the current workbook is displayed. In this instance, no maps are attached yet so you will not see any displayed in the pane.

j. In the XML Maps dialog box, click **Add**. In the Select XML Source dialog box, navigate to where your data files are stored, click **e05_ws09_Maintenance**, and then click **Open**. A dialog box opens stating that no schema exists for this file. Click **OK** two times to close the dialog boxes.

k. Drag the **task** element with all of its child elements from the XML Source pane to cell **A4**.

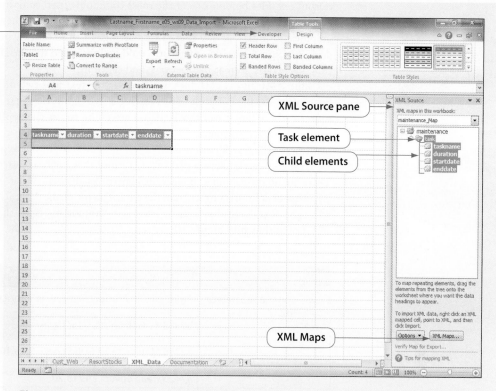

Figure 9 XML document imported into Excel

l. Click the **Developer tab**, and then click **Refresh Data** in the XML group. This is raw data from an XML source so the headings are taken from the XML element names and will not necessarily be properly formatted.

m. To make a change in the original .xml file, click **Start**, click **All Programs**, click **Accessories**, and then click **Notepad** (Note: The location of your Notepad editor may vary from computer to computer). Notepad is a basic text editor for Microsoft Windows.

n. In Notepad, click **File**, and then click **Open**. Navigate to where your data files are stored, change the File type to **All Files (*.*)**, and then select **e05_ws09_Maintenance**. Click **Open**, click the **Format** menu, and then ensure **Word Wrap** is selected.

SIDE NOTE
XML Code Looks Different
No, the &amp you see in step o is not a typographical error. This is XML code for an ampersand.

o. On the first task element, click to place the insertion point after golf, and then replace clean golf clubs & sweep roof with clean golf club storage area.

p. Click **File**, click **Save**, and then close Notepad.

q. In Excel, on the Developer tab, click **Refresh Data** in the XML group. You should see the changes you just made in the source .xml file reflected in your data.

r. Close the XML Source pane, and then save your work.

Importing Text Files

Text data files used to be called flat files because they were structured as simple lines of data separated by delimiters. **Text data** consists of any grouping of characters, numbers or dates. A **text file** is just a simple container of text data that is structured by the use of delimiters. A **delimiter** is just a way of indicating the beginning and end of a text data segment. As a container of data, a text file can transmit virtually any kind of data. They are simple to understand and transmit, but are not as efficient as binary files because they take up more space in memory. Many different computer systems share data by transmitting text files back and forth. For that reason, text files become one of the most commonly used computer file formats. Text files (also called ASCII files) have no metadata associated with them, so they are not used for transmitting graphics, formulas, or any special formatting. In this context, **metadata** is simply data about data. For digital graphics, metadata could include when the image was created, source information, key words, format instructions, and captions.

Like XML and HTML files, you can import text files two different ways: one file at a time by opening the file in Excel, or by creating a live connection that is maintained between the file source and the target workbook. If you are going to use the application often and the external data will change frequently, you will want to maintain a live connection. Otherwise you can just import the text files as needed. Both methods are similar and easy to accomplish in Excel.

Text files are known as plain text because they contain just text, without any formatting. There are no special fonts, images, or hyperlinks allowed. What makes the text understandable is the use of delimiters to separate the data. The use of the delimiter tells the receiving computer when the next data value begins. The most common file types that use delimiters are .csv, .txt, and .prn as shown in Figure 10.

File Type	Sample			
.csv—comma separated	ProductNum,ProductName,DateShipped,Quantity Shipped 59313,XL Golf Shirts,3/15/13,35 72316,Men's size 12 Golf Shoe,2/5/13,10 47423,Head covers,3/6/13,20			
.txt—tab delimited	PNum	PName	Shipped	Quantity
	59313	XL Golf Shirts	3/15/13	35
	72316	Men's Shoe	2/5/13	10
	47423	Head covers	3/6/13	20
.prn—space delimited	PNum PName Shipped Quantity 59313 XL_Golf_Shirts 3_15_13 35 72316 Mens_size_12_Golf_Shoe 2_5_13 10 47423 Head_covers 3_6_/13 20			

Figure 10 Common delimited text file formats

You can import a text file by simply clicking the File tab to open Backstage view and clicking Open. Navigate to the file, and then click Open. This is a quick way to view the data, and it often works well enough for your immediate needs. However, if you want to take advantage of all the text import features, you can use the Text Import Wizard that can be initiated by clicking the From Text button on the Data tab in Excel.

Real World Advice More Advanced Features of the Text Import Wizard

If you do not want to include all the headings or if there is a comment at the beginning of the file, you can tell Excel to start in any row below a target row so it will omit extraneous text. Sometimes Excel will incorrectly identify the language used in the text file, and this may throw the import wizard off. You can manually change this by clicking the File tab, click Options, and then click Language. Also, occasionally you will get a text file that is too big to import into Excel. By previewing the data in the Import Wizard you can see exactly how much it will import and then split the file into two or more files using one of the free file-splitting utilities such as GSplit.

Red Bluff's web developer has exported some customer data from the new Red Bluff website and saved it as a text file. He has sent it to your boss who has asked you to integrate it into some Excel applications. To start with, you need to import it into Excel.

To Import Text Data

a. Click the **Insert Worksheet tab** 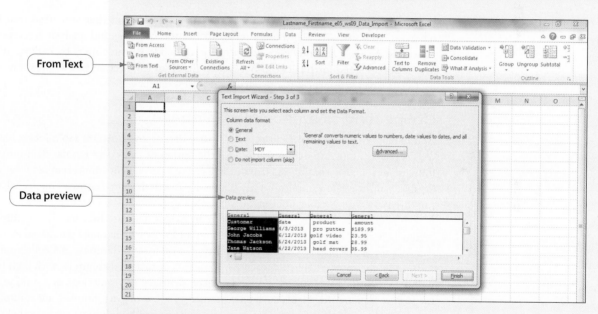 at the bottom of the Excel workbook, rename the new sheet Text_Data, and then press [Enter].

b. If necessary, click cell **A1**, click the **Data tab**, and then click **From Text** in the Get External Data group.

c. In the Import Text File dialog box, navigate to the folder where your data files are stored, and select **e05_ws09_Customers**.

d. Click **Import**. The Text Import Wizard recognizes that the file is delimited and has this option selected. Click **Next**.

e. Notice the sample data from the file is separated by commas. Under delimiters, select the **Comma** option, and click as needed to deselect any other options that may be selected already. Excel shows you a preview of how the data will be separated into cells when imported. Click **Next**.

From Text

Data preview

Figure 11 Importing a comma-delimited file

f. Click **Finish**, and then in the Import Data dialog box, click **OK** to accept cell A1 as the cell where you want the insertion point for the data to start.

g. Click **Start**, click **All Programs**, click **Accessories-Utilities**, and then click **Notepad**.

h. In Notepad, click **File**, click **Open**, navigate to where your data files are stored, and then change the File type to **All Files (*.*)**. Double-click the **e05_ws09_Customers** file to open it in Notepad.

i. Go to the last record for Andrew Clifton and change golf balls to golf clubs. Click **File**, save your changes, and then close Notepad.

j. In Excel, click the **Data tab**, and then click **Refresh All** in the Connections group. The Import Text File dialog box reopens.

k. Select **e05_ws09_Customers**, and then click **Import**.

SIDE NOTE
Problems with Raw Data

When you import data from external sources using XML or comma-delimited text files, it is common to have extra spaces or improperly formatted entries. Before being used in other reports and analyses it is necessary to clean and reformat the data.

l. Check to make sure that you can see the changed data reflected in your imported comma-separated text file, and then **save** [💾] your file.

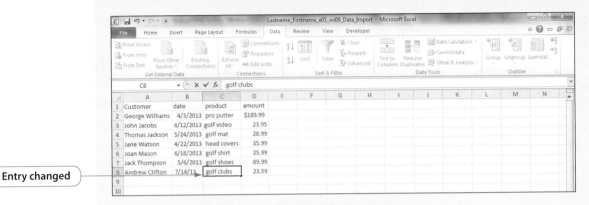

Figure 12 Results of editing a comma-separated text file

Interacting with Access

Long-term data may be held in a database such as Access and then imported into Excel for reporting and analysis. Many users prefer to use the charting and analysis features of Excel instead of Access. Over the years, Excel has accommodated these users by making it easier to move data back and forth between Access and Excel. In this section you will learn how to connect your Excel spreadsheet to the data in an Access database.

Connecting to an Access Database

At the most basic level, you can copy and paste data from an Access table into a blank Excel worksheet. Within Access, users also have the option of exporting tabular data into an Excel format. For longer-term projects one can also create a permanent connection between an Access database and the Excel application by using the Access Import feature. This live data can be imported as a simple table, or even a PivotTable Report and PivotChart.

To understand how to import data from an Access database into Excel, it is important to review how the data is stored in Access. As a tool for using relational databases, Access stores data as a set of one or more tables. By definition, a **relational database** is a collection of tables linked together by shared fields. Each table consists of rows and columns, with each row being uniquely identified by a primary key field. The **primary key** functions as a unique identifier for each row or record. Fields such as customer_number or part_number are commonly used as primary keys. Multiple tables are designed to be linked by joining a common field. In some cases the primary key field of one table is connected to match a common field of another table in which the field for the other table is not a primary key. This field is then known as a **foreign key** field when linked to a primary key field in another table.

With a little background, you can quickly understand the basics of relational databases like Access. Figure 13 shows a sample view of a table with product data for a company called Northwind Traders. The company supplies specialty food items to the resort and the pro shop snack bar. Across the top you can see all the field labels, and each row represents a single product record. The Product ID field is the unique identifier for each product Northwind Traders carries, and this field functions as the primary key field. This is automatically generated by the system. Important data for Northwind Traders is kept in other tables for customers, suppliers, shippers, orders, and employees. Information in each of these different tables is linked through the primary key in one table being shared as the foreign key in another table.

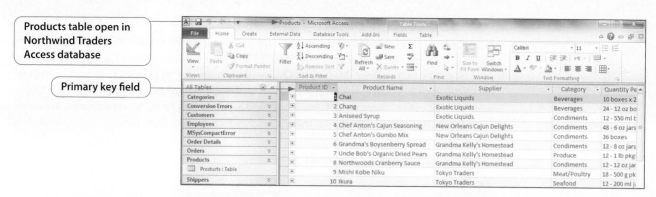

Products table open in Northwind Traders Access database

Primary key field

Figure 13 Product data table in Access for Northwind Traders

SIDE NOTE

Drag Access Data into Excel

You can also import tables and queries from Access into Excel by dragging the table or query object from the Access Navigator Pane and laying it directly in the desired starting cell of your Excel worksheet.

From Access

Select Table dialog box

List of available tables

To Connect to an Access Database

a. With the Excel file still open, click the **Insert Worksheet tab** at the bottom of the Excel workbook, rename the new worksheet Access_Data, and then press Enter.

b. Click the **Data tab**, and then click **From Access** in the Get External Data group. This will display the Select Data Source dialog box. Navigate to the folder where your data files are stored, select **e05_ws09_Northwind.accdb**, and then click **Open**.

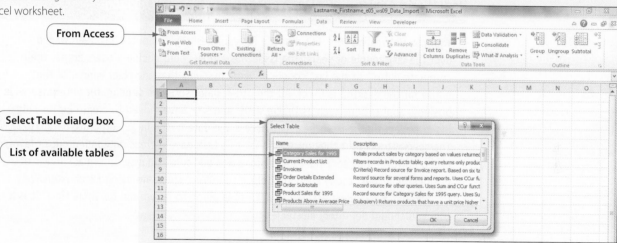

Figure 14 Connecting to an Access database

c. In the Select Table dialog box, a long list of tables and queries is displayed. Scroll down, click the **Products** table, and then click **OK**.

d. The Import Data dialog box provides the option to import this as a table, PivotTable report, or PivotChart and PivotTable report. Make sure the default option **Table** is checked, and then verify the **Existing worksheet** option is selected and the input box displays **=$A$1** to indicate the data will import into cell A1. Click **OK**, and then click **Save**.

SIDE NOTE

Importing Zip Codes

When zip codes are entered or imported into Excel, sometimes the leading zero gets dropped. A zip code such as 06383 is displayed 6383. Avoid this by formatting your worksheet cells as General or Text, or use the Special cell formatting Category option with a type of Zip Code or Zip Code + 4.

Using Microsoft Query to Query an Access Database

Sometimes, instead of pulling a complete table into an Excel worksheet from Access, users prefer to pick and choose specific fields. Perhaps you want to create a PivotTable report showing sales by region and country. **Microsoft Query** is a special tool to help users import individual data fields into their Excel applications. Excel has a query wizard built into its Microsoft Query function that can be a very powerful aid for linking a worksheet to an Access database. Microsoft Query now has built in drivers that make it easy to retrieve data from these common databases:

- Access
- SQL Server
- Paradox
- Oracle
- dBase
- Text files
- FoxPro

This list can be further expanded by loading drivers for almost all the major database packages out there. It is now very common for business users to use Excel to routinely access a wide variety of data sources in the course of their work. By using Microsoft Query to access external data, users do not have to redo the query, but can simply refresh their connection to the source data so that the Excel application will reflect any changes.

Real World Advice   Winning the Battle for the Desktop

You may not realize this, but a battle for your desktop computer has been waged over the last couple of years. The issue was, "How could business users access their corporate data?" In the last couple of years it seems that the clear winner of the battle for the desktop is Excel. All the other major software vendors for enterprise-wide business applications such as Oracle, IBM, and SAP have moved to create better plug-ins or drivers that make it easier to access the data in the large corporate databases. The special tools that they once sold for this task have increasingly fallen out of favor. Excel, however, has continued to improve and add functionality. Informal surveys of business managers today show that close to 90% of them are using Excel extensively on a regular basis. Rest assured that Excel is going to be around for some time. It is a tool you should definitely master.

To Import Data from an Access Database Using Microsoft Query

a. Click the **Insert Worksheet tab** at the bottom of the Excel workbook, rename the new worksheet MS_Query, and then press Enter.

b. Click the **Data tab**, if necessary. In the Get External Data group, instead of using From Access, click **From Other Sources**, and then click **From Microsoft Query** from the gallery menu.

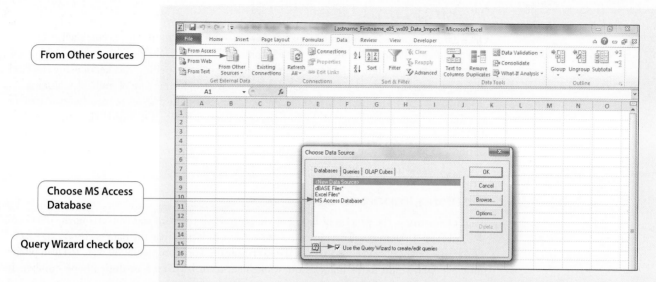

From Other Sources

Choose MS Access Database

Query Wizard check box

Figure 15 Connecting to an Access database with Microsoft Query

c. In the Choose Data Source dialog box, click **MS Access Database**, make sure **Use the Query Wizard to create/edit queries** is checked, and then click **OK**.

d. In the Select Database dialog box, under **Directories**, locate where your data files are stored, and then under **Database Name**, select **e05_ws09_Northwind**. Click **OK**.

e. In the Query Wizard – Choose Columns dialog box, scroll through the list of tables and columns until you see the **Sales by Category** query, and then click **Expand Button** ⊞ to see the available fields.

f. Double-click to select and move **CategoryName** to the Columns in your query box (alternately select an item from the tables list and click the Move button). Using the technique just used, double-click the **ProductName** and **ProductSales** fields to move them into the Columns in your query list.

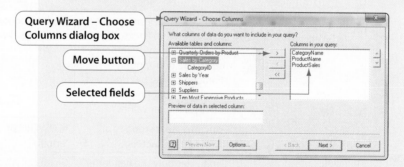

Query Wizard – Choose Columns dialog box

Move button

Selected fields

Figure 16 Selecting fields for Microsoft Query

g. Click **Next**, click to select the **ProductSales** field, click the first **Filter arrow**, and then click **is greater than**. In the input box to the right, type **3000**.

h. Click **Next**, click the **Sort by arrow**, click **CategoryName**, and then accept the default **Ascending** order. Click in the input box under **Then by**, click **ProductName**, and then keep the **Ascending** option. Click **Next**.

i. Click **Finish**, verify **Existing worksheet** is selected and the input box displays **=$A$1**, and then click **OK**. The Access data is imported and displayed starting in cell A1.

j. **Save** 🖫 your file, print or submit your documents as directed by your instructor, and then **close** ☒ Excel.

Making Data Useful

Once data is imported into Excel, it may require manipulation to fit your needs, such as formatting it differently and cleaning the data before it can be used for decision-making purposes. Sometimes this is straightforward and entails simply using the spelling checker or using the Find and Replace feature. Other times it may require extensive reformatting of multiple columns.

This can be a major problem for corporations. The cost to businesses in man-hours to correct and find bad data is estimated to be billions of dollars each year. Of course, the impact of bad data can also cost companies unnecessary problems in bad decisions based on the data. In this section you will learn some efficient methods to save time when cleaning data so that it is ready to be used in your Excel applications.

Cleaning Imported Data

Data cleansing is the process of fixing obvious errors in the data and converting the data into a useful format. **Data verification** is the process of validating that the data is correct and accurate. Importantly, data cleansing is not data verification. For example, if you were to clean phone numbers, you would fix or mark as questionable a record with a four-digit phone number. If you were to verify a phone number, you would call the phone number and verify that it dialed the person it purported to call. Data verification is very costly both in time and money. Thus, for the majority of data, most companies will only conduct data cleansing and not necessarily data verification.

Using Text Functions to Clean Data

Previously you imported text data into Excel with some of the built in tools. Recall that text data refers to strings of characters. Do not be confused by this term since it can include special characters, spaces, and numbers too. Text is a very generic data type. Often, data from external sources might easily be cleaned up with proper formatting, for example, formatting number values into currency values. **Text functions** also offer a range of functions that help manage text data as shown in Figure 17. Excel text functions help to manipulate and standardize data and can offer additional tools to automate the process.

Function Name	Description	Example
CLEAN =CLEAN(text)	Removes any nonprinting characters from a text string. The CLEAN function removes the first 32 nonprinting character codes, but does not remove nonprinting character codes for higher values.	If cell A2 contains =CHAR(6)&"text", =CLEAN(A2) will leave only "text".
LOWER =LOWER(text)	Converts a text string to all lowercase characters.	=LOWER(Apt. 4B) will result in "apt.4b"
PROPER =PROPER(text)	Capitalizes only the first letter in each word of a text string with remaining characters in lowercase.	Given cell A2 contains the string "this is a TITLE", =PROPER(A2) returns "This Is A Title".
TRIM =TRIM(text)	Removes all spaces from text except for single spaces between words (this includes extra spaces at the beginning or at the end of the string).	Given cell A2 contains the string " profit margin ", =TRIM(A2) would remove the extra spaces to yield "profit margin".
UPPER =UPPER(text)	Converts all the characters in a text string to uppercase.	=UPPER("total") will result in the word "TOTAL".

Figure 17 Text functions for cleaning data

Have you ever received mail in which your name or address was misspelled? This is just one small example of how bad data is propagated. At some point, your name was entered into a database incorrectly, and then that list of names is sold to others. If you multiply this by the millions of times it occurs, you will start to get an idea of the scale of this problem. And this is just one example. Studies indicate that the total cost to businesses from bad data is well into the billions of dollars. How else does bad data get into the system? What are some basic steps you could take to prevent or minimize the problem when entering or importing data, and evaluating for errors?

Using Text Functions

Text functions help users extract and standardize their data in ways that make life easier; a little knowledge of these advanced functions can reap big rewards. For example, your manager has received a file from a golf club manufacturer listing all the customers who bought their brand of golf clubs in your club shop. The customers filled out warranty cards and the information was entered into a database. Now your manager wants you to import this data into a spreadsheet for the pro shop's own record keeping.

When looking over the data, you see that some cells were entered in all caps and extra spaces are apparent in other cells. Text functions like **LOWER** can be used to change the uppercase characters to lowercase (the opposite of the **UPPER** function). The **PROPER** function will capitalize the first letter of each word in the text string. The formulas you use in other spreadsheet applications will malfunction when they encounter the irregular spacing.

To Clean Your Data File

a. Start **Excel**, click the **File tab**, and then click **Open**. In the Open dialog box, navigate to the where your data files are located, and double-click **e05_ws09_Data_Cleanse**.

b. Click the **File tab**, click **Save As**, and then in the Save As dialog box, navigate to the location where you are saving your student files. In the File name box, type Lastname_Firstname_e05_ws09_Data_Cleanse replacing Lastname and Firstname with your own name. Click **Save**.

c. Click the **CustNames worksheet tab** to make it active. This worksheet contains a list of customer names that you received from one of the major golf club manufacturers whose products Red Bluff sells. To insert a filename as a footer, click the **Insert tab**, and then click **Header & Footer** in the Text group.

d. On the **Design tab**, and then click **Go to Footer** in the Navigation group. If necessary, click the **left section** of the footer, and then click **File Name** in the Header & Footer Elements group.

e. Click any cell on the spreadsheet to move out of the footer, press Ctrl+Home, click the **View tab**, click **Normal** in the Workbook Views group, and then click the **Home tab**.

f. Click cell **B1**, and then type Lower. Click cell **B3**, type =LOWER(A3), and then press Ctrl+Enter. Double-click the **AutoFill** handle to copy this formula down to cell **B27**. It is not necessary to type these text functions in uppercase in order for them to work.

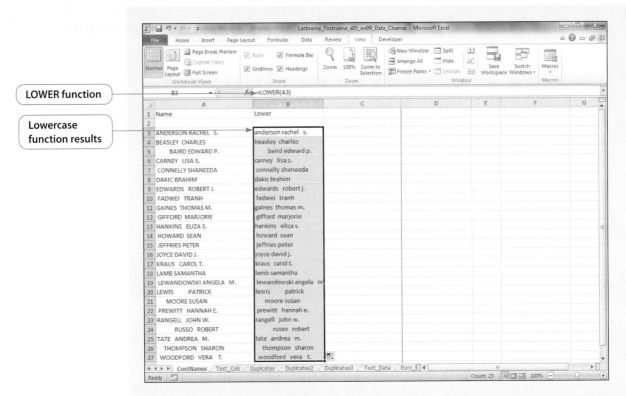

LOWER function

Lowercase function results

Figure 18 Using the LOWER text function

g. Click cell **C1**, and then type Proper. Click cell **C3**, type =PROPER(A3), and then press ⌈Ctrl⌉+⌈Enter⌉. Double-click the **AutoFill** handle to copy cell C3 down to **C27**. This function will capitalize the first letter of each name and leave the rest in lowercase.

h. The next function will demonstrate how to remove any extra spaces before or after the names as well as extra spaces between names. Click cell **D1**, and then type Trim. Click cell **D3**, type =TRIM(C3), and then press ⌈Ctrl⌉+⌈Enter⌉.

   The name from C3 is displayed in D3 without the extra spaces at the beginning. The TRIM function removes extra spaces before and after and leaves single spaces between the words. Notice that the cell reference was C3 (the Proper results) rather than cell A3 (all caps). This was to display the trim results in combination with the proper results. However, you could nest these formulas and achieve the same combination effect for target cell A3 by adjusting the formula to nest as follows: =PROPER(TRIM(A3)).

i. Double-click the **AutoFill** handle to copy the D3 TRIM function down to **D27**. Resize the columns to show all the names if necessary. Now all extra spaces in the names have been removed and the data results have been cleaned up significantly but there are still more Text functions to learn about.

j. Select **D3:D27**, right-click anywhere in the selected cells, and then click **Copy**. Right-click again in the selected cells, and then under the Paste Options on the displayed menu, click the **Values** option ⌷. This action converts all your TRIM functions in column D to their new text values and removes the underlying formula. Press ⌈Esc⌉, and then click **Save** ⌷.

Real World Advice | Cleaning Nonprintable Characters

Cleaning extra spaces is only half the problem. Many times there are nonprinting characters that are not easily visible—such as a hard return or other unseen characters that are often transferred from Internet data. This can be quite frustrating when performing a logical test on that data or when using one of the LOOKUP functions. If you do not have clean data, with all the extra spaces or unprintable characters removed, you will get an error message. This is another reason why the TRIM function is so useful because it addresses the extra spaces problem. **TRIM** removes all spaces from text except for single spaces between words.

Another Text function to keep in your arsenal is the CLEAN function. Recall, the **CLEAN** function removes any nonprinting characters, such as spaces and carriage returns, from a text string, but unfortunately it will not remove them all. To remove the remaining six characters (values 127, 129, 141, 143, 144, and 157 in the Unicode set), the SUBSTITUTE function can help in the cleansing process to find each of these remaining characters and replace them with a code that the CLEAN function will remove. A sample formula might be written as follows:
=SUBSTITUTE(text,CHAR(141),CHAR(6)).

The arguments for the above example formula include the *text* argument, which can be a text string or a cell reference (to text). The *old_text* would be the next argument that would be the problem character to search for, and the *new_text* argument is the character to use as a replacement—such as typing " " to indicate replacing odd characters with a normal space so the TRIM function can then be applied. The instance_num argument is optional. If omitted, then the formula will search and replace every instance in the text or cell reference, but if a number is provided, it will only change the first number of instances specified. The syntax appears as follows: =SUBSTITUTE(text, old_text, new_text, [instance_num])

To be complete, run this for all six of the missing characters and then run the TRIM or CLEAN function as needed.

Using Text Functions to Separate String Data

In the CustNames worksheet example, the goal is to actually manipulate the content within each of the cells so that a comma can be added between the last and first names, and then finally, to move the first and last names to their own separate cells. Be observant when analyzing the data. Notice any patterns that help to define the best functions to use when preparing the text for the company's specific needs. Additional functions to consider along with a description to explain how each can be applied are shown in Figure 19.

Function Name	Description	Example
CONCATENATE =CONCATENATE(Text1, [Text2], …Textn)	This function is used to join up to 255 text strings into one text string.	=CONCATENATE(A1&" "&B1) will return the value of A1, a space, and the value of B1 in one text string.
FIND =FIND(find_text, within_text, [start_num])	Locates a particular string of data within a second text string, and returns the number of the starting position of the first text string from the starting position of the second text string. The "start_num" is an optional parameter giving a position within the string where to start the search. If omitted, the position is assumed to be 1.	=FIND(" ","ABC corp.") will return the value of 4 since the space is the fourth character.
REPLACE =REPLACE(old_text, start_num, num_chars, new_text).	Replaces part of a text string, based on the number of characters you specify, with a different text string. *Old_text* is the original string, *start_num* is the position to start replacing text, *num_chars* the number of characters to replace, and *new_text* is what string to replace in that position.	If cell A2 contains "2007", then =REPLACE(A2,3,2,"12") results in "2012" by starting at the third position and replacing 2 characters with "12".
SEARCH =SEARCH(find_text, within_text, [start_num])	Locates one text string within a second text string, and returns the number of the starting position of the first text string from the starting character of the second text string. Is not case sensitive.	Given cell A2 contains the string "revenue" =SEARCH("e",A2,6) returns "7" as the position of the next "e" after the starting position of 6 characters. If the start_num argument value of 6 is omitted, the formula would return 2.
SUBSTITUTE =SUBSTITUTE(text, old_text, new_text [instance_num]).	Similar to REPLACE. This function substitutes *new_text* for *old_text* in a text string. *Text* is the text string or the cell reference to text data.	If cell A2 contains "sales data" then =SUBSTITUTE(A2,"sales","cost") results in "cost data".

Figure 19 Text functions for separating and combining data

SIDE NOTE
Care in Use of Spaces
In step a of this exercise be careful to put a space between the double quotes to indicate the character to search for is a space character. This function will return a number telling you how many characters there are before encountering the character specified as the first function argument—in this case—a space. As can be expected, the number of characters the function will return will vary for the names in each cell.

To Separate the Last Name and First Name

a. On the CustNames worksheet tab, click **E1**, and then type Find. Click cell **E3**, type =FIND(" ",D3), and then press Ctrl+Enter. Double-click the **AutoFill** handle for cell E3 to copy the function down to cell **E27**.

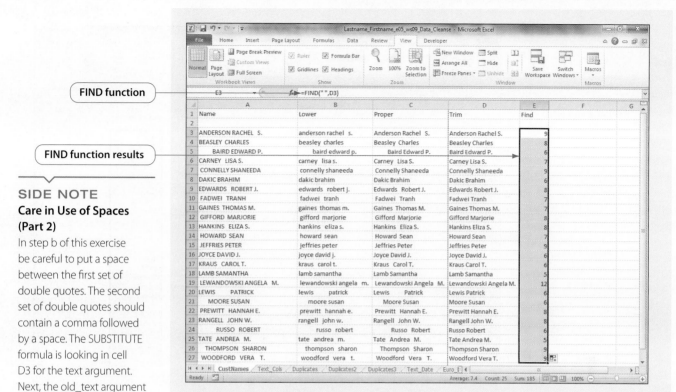

FIND function

FIND function results

Figure 20 Using the FIND function

b. Click cell **F1**, and then type Substitute Comma. Click cell **F3**, type =SUBSTITUTE(D3, " ",", ",1), and then press Ctrl + Enter. Double-click the **AutoFill** handle to copy cell F3 down to **F27**.

c. Click cell **G1**, and then type Replace and Find. Click cell **G3**, type =REPLACE(D3,1,E3,""), and then press Ctrl + Enter. Double-click the **AutoFill** handle to copy cell G3 down to **G27**, and double-click the column G **right border edge** to have the column G width automatically fit the contents.

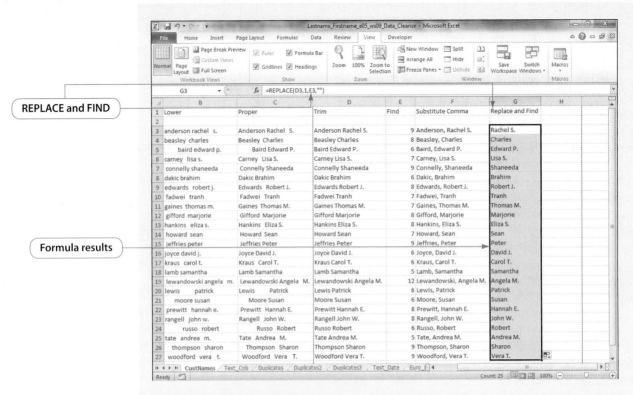

Figure 21 Results of using REPLACE with a FIND

d. Click cell **H1**, type Left and Find, and then click cell **H3**.

e. Type =LEFT(D3,E3), and then press Ctrl + Enter.

f. Double-click the **AutoFill** handle to copy cell H3 down to **H27**, resize the column if necessary, and then **Save**.

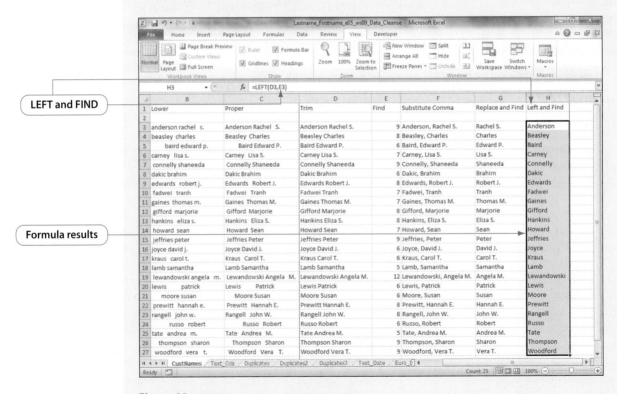

Figure 22 Results of using a LEFT with a FIND

SIDE NOTE

Making Use of the Find Results Calculated Previously

FIND is used to locate one text string within a second text string, and returns the number of the starting position of the first text string from the starting character of the second text string. Recall that the FIND formula had already been calculated for cell E3 to determine the character location of the first space encountered for cell D3 text. In step c of this exercise, the first REPLACE argument (old_text) uses the same D3 text, and the next argument (start_num) is 1, which tells Excel to start counting at the beginning of the string. The next argument is num_chars—how many characters to count—a value provided in cell E3—where the FIND formula has done the needed calculation. The final argument is new_text, which you replaced with no characters signaled by empty double quotes (no space this time). The result is to display all characters following the replacement text—which is a null character replacement in this example.

Concatenating Data

Concatenating data refers to combining or joining multiple strings of data to form a single string. Using the current worksheet data example, the goal is to change the name order from the original version of last name, first name, and middle initial to a result of first name, middle initial, followed by last name. It would be useful to show it all together in a single field. The previous exercise separated the name data; all that is needed is to string it together in the desired order. There are a variety of ways to accomplish this in Excel. You could manually string together data using the ampersand (&), or you can use the CONCATENATE function to string together data to join into one cell.

CONCATENATE is a text function used to join up to 255 text strings into one text string. One of the advantages of using this function is that it also allows users to do some formatting of the data at the same time if needed, such as nesting the function in combination with the PROPER function to have the first character in each word capitalized.

In this case, the first name (plus middle initial) appears in column G and the last name is stored in column H. Column I will be used to join the data using the ampersand. Column J will join the data using the CONCATENATE function. Keep in mind that spaces (entered between a set of double quotes) will need to be added at the appropriate points when joining strings of text together.

To Join Columns

a. Click cell **I1**, and then type Join with &. Click cell **I3**, and then type =G3&" "&H3. Be sure to include a space between the quotes. Press Ctrl+Enter, and then double-click the **AutoFill** handle to copy the formula down to cell **I27**.

b. Click cell **J1**, and then type Concatenate. Click cell **J3**, and then type =CONCATENATE(G3, " ",H3). Press Ctrl+Enter, and then double-click the **AutoFill** handle to copy the formula down to cell **J27**.

Troubleshooting

Missing Spaces

Are spaces missing between the names in the final result? Check to see if a space was typed between the double quotes. Recall that in addition to text from a cell reference, quotes can be used to string together additional characters—in this case a space between the words.

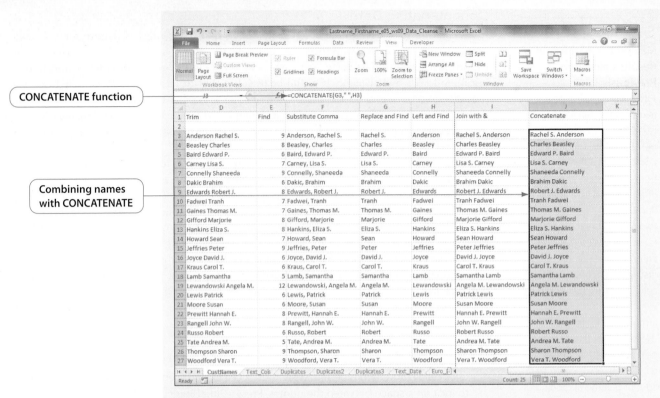

Figure 23 Functions for joining columns

Using the CONCATENATE function allows you to link as many items as you like up to a limit of 255. You can link multiple cells or even add your own phrases. In this example you are using the CONCATENATE function to link text in two cells, an added space, and an extra phrase. This can be a useful tool in customizing Excel applications.

To Join Multiple Columns Using the CONCATENATE Function

a. Click cell **K1**, and then type Concatenate Multiple. Click cell **K3**, and then type =CONCATENATE(G3," ",H3," ","scored a hole in one.").

b. Press Ctrl + Enter. Double-click the **AutoFill** handle to copy down to **K27**, resize the column to fit as needed.

c. **Save** and continue.

Real World Advice — Recognizing Data Patterns is Important!

The secret to understanding how to clean your data is realizing that there are character patterns in the data. Little things like commas and spaces in between words can become crucial signposts that the resourceful Excel user can exploit with Text functions. When you see a character pattern in your data, you can use the FIND operator to find just about anything, especially commas and spaces. Once you start looking for character patterns you will be amazed at how many there are.

Using the LEN and the FIND Functions to Separate Data

The LEN function is a useful way to calculate the length of a specified string of values. The basic syntax of this function is

=LEN(text).

So if you typed =LEN("Red Bluff") the function would return the result of 9, which includes counting the space character. This can help when you want to tell Excel how to find the data you want to extract. However, beware of spaces at the front or end of a cell entry, LEN will count these, and you may not even know it! To avoid this problem, you can always nest the TRIM function or apply TRIM before applying the LEN operator to your data.

The goal for the next exercise is to extract the customer's first name using the RIGHT function in conjunction with the nested LEN and FIND functions as shown in Figure 24. The RIGHT function tells Excel to start counting from the right side of the string. Then the **LEN** function counts all the characters for the complete string. The FIND function locates the comma and space combination between the names in D3, and these characters are subtracted from the total via the LEN results minus the FIND results.

Function Name	Description	Example
LEFT =LEFT(text, [num_chars]).	This function returns the characters in a text string based on the number of characters you specify starting with the far left character in the string. The *text* argument is a string of text or a cell reference to text data, and the *num_chars* argument specifies the characters to extract.	If cell A2 contains the text string "sale price" then =LEFT(A2,4) will return the word "sale".
LEN =LEN(text)	This function returns the number of characters (including spaces) in a text string.	If cell A2 contains the string "Excel 2010" then =LEN(A2) will return the number "10".
MID =MID(text, start_num, num_chars)	Returns a specific number of characters from a text string starting at the position you specify, and based on the number of characters you specify.	If cell A2 contains the string "purchase price" then =MID(A2,10,10) yields "price". Takes 10 characters starting at 10th position. If num_chars exceed the remaining string length, MID returns to the end of the string.
RIGHT =RIGHT(text, [num_chars])	Returns the characters in a text string based on the number of characters you specify starting with starting from the far-right character position.	If cell A2 contains the string "item price" then =RIGHT(A2,5) will result in "price".

Figure 24 Text functions for extracting data

To Extract the Customer's First Name from the List of Names

a. On the CustNames worksheet tab, click cell **L1**, and then type Right with LEN.

b. Click cell **L3**, and then enter the formula =RIGHT(D3,LEN(D3)-E3). Press Ctrl+Enter, and then double-click the **AutoFill** handle to copy down to **L27**. Resize the column as needed.

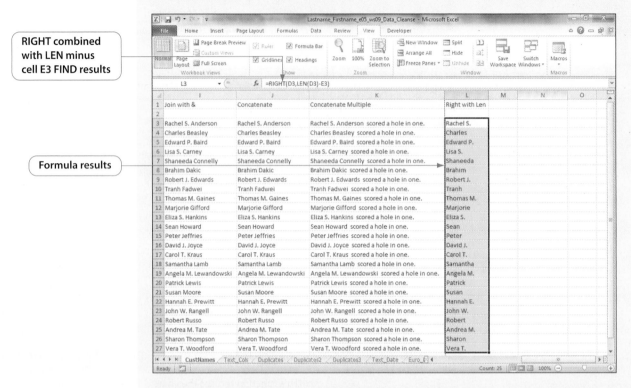

RIGHT combined with LEN minus cell E3 FIND results

Formula results

Figure 25 Results of RIGHT, LEN, and FIND functions

c. Before saving this file, document your work. Using the technique previously practiced, or opening a file, navigate to your data files, and then open **e05_ws09_Documentation_ Template**.

d. Right-click the **Documentation worksheet tab**, and then click **Move or Copy**.

e. In the Move or Copy dialog box, under To book, select **Lastname_Firstname_e05_ ws09_Data_Cleanse**, and then under Before sheet, select (**move to end**). Remember to click the check box next to **Create a copy**. Click **OK**.

f. Close the e05_ws09_Documentation_Template workbook without saving changes if prompted. On the Documentation worksheet tab, click cell **A3**, and then press Ctrl+[;]. Press Tab, and then in cell B3 type Firstname Lastname using your name. Press Ctrl+Home.

g. Save and continue.

Using the MID Function to Extract Data

You have seen how to use the LEFT function to extract data working from the left side of a string, and the RIGHT function to extract data counting from the right side. The MID function is yet another option to choose from when extracting a string of data from within another string (or text cell reference). An example of when this might be useful is if you need to extract the middle two digits of a product code that indicate what warehouse the item is stored in; for example, GVR-25-86409 is stored in cell A1. To extract these two middle numbers for the warehouse, use the MID function.

=MID(A1,5,2)

This example will return a result of 25. The first argument is the location of the text string. The second argument is the starting character location, character 5 (the hyphen counts as a character). And the third argument is how many characters to extract—2 in this example.

Quick Reference — Which Function to Use?

So how do you know which of these three formulas to use if they all work in a similar manner?

1. If the desired text starts on the left side of the cell, use the LEFT function.

2. If the desired text starts from the right side of the cell, use the RIGHT function.

3. And if the desired text is in the middle of a text string, use the MID function.

One of the common questions when confronted with name data is what to do with the middle initial. Some customer names include a middle initial and some do not. Recall, that one of the problems encountered when multiple people enter data, is that the data is not always consistent. Many customers might offer a middle initial or name, while others may not. What is important is knowing how the information can be extracted and stored for future use. With a focus on extraction, also recall that character patterns help, yet you have one problem already in assessing patterns in that an initial is not consistently included. What is even worse is that sometimes you might even encounter data where some middle initials are followed by a period while others are not. Fortunately, this is not a problem in our data, but this could present additional challenges when evaluating a character pattern in order to extract the data. The period along with a space or any other character that is not typically used in a name itself are helpful characters to use as important pattern indicators to test for when extracting data.

CONSIDER THIS | Variations in Data Entry

It is clear that data entry is not consistently uniform. As a result, extracting data can become a challenge if you are depending on a character pattern to evaluate through the use of a formula(s) to help automate the extraction process. Given the sample name data in the CustNames worksheet exercises, what formula or formulas could be used to extract the middle initial data if a period is not always available after the middle initial? What if some of the data even supplied a full middle name—what formula(s) could be used to take into account this variation in data?

The first thing to understand in this case is that because some of the names have a middle initial and some do not, you need to perform a logical test to see which names have one and which do not. In Excel functions such as the IF function, the logical test has three parts to it. The first part is the test, the second is what result to return if the test is true, and the final argument is what result to return if the test is false. The trick is how to specify the logical part.

For this scenario, you need to extract the middle initial data string from your list of customer names because it is more beneficial to break up the name data into separate field columns when doing a mail merge.

Because all of the middle initials are followed by a period, the logical test in this case will be to search the string for a period. The **ISERROR** function is used to check for error values and returns TRUE if an error is found, and FALSE if no error is encountered. When the ISERROR function is used in conjunction with the IF function, a different action result can be defined if an error occurs. The ISERROR will test for a period character, and keep in mind if *no* period is found, an ERROR result of TRUE is returned. Therefore, if the ISERROR test is true then the IF formula result should display the cell content (which assumes no middle initial data). If the ISERROR test is false then the IF formula uses the LEFT, RIGHT, SEARCH, and LEN functions to extract the first name, subtract two characters (to get rid of the period and middle initial but leave the space), and join (&) with the last name; less one character to get rid of the space—since you have a space from the LEFT function and do not want an extra space from the RIGHT function.

To Remove the Middle Initial from a List of Names

a. Click the **CustNames worksheet tab** to make this the active worksheet.

b. Click cell **M1**, and then type Remove Middle Initial. Click cell **M3**, type =LEFT(I3, SEARCH(".",I3)-2), and then press [Ctrl]+[Enter]. Notice that the formula returns the first name "Rachel" followed by a space (even though the space is not apparent).

c. Click cell **M3**, click in the formula bar to place the insertion point at the end of the current formula, and then type &RIGHT(I3,LEN(I3)-SEARCH(".",I3)-1). Press [Ctrl]+[Enter]. Notice that the formula returns the full name Rachel Anderson.

d. Double-click the **AutoFill** handle to copy the formula down to **M27**. Notice, that the formula returns a #VALUE! error for any name that does not contain a middle initial. For example, click cell **M4** and note the result in M4 when compared to the data in target cell I4 (referenced in the formula bar). Recall that the fix for this problem will be to use the IF function in combination with the ISERROR function to test for errors and return the cell contents if an error exist.

e. Click cell **M3**, click in the formula bar to place the insertion point after the equal (=) sign and before the "L" in LEFT, and then type the following: IF(ISERROR(SEARCH(".",I3)),I3,. Notice the visual clues of color parenthesis. However, the formula starts with a black color parenthesis, but no ending black parenthesis. Click to place the insertion point at the very end of the formula, and then type). Press [Ctrl]+[Enter], and then double-click the **AutoFill** handle to copy the formula down to **M27**.

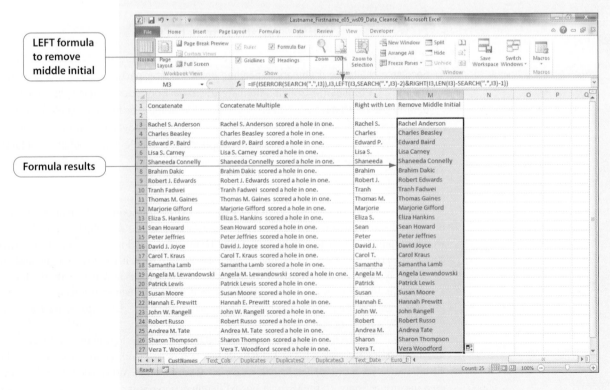

Figure 26 Removing a middle initial from names

f. Resize column M to show all the names. Press Ctrl+Home. **Save** 🖫 your work and continue.

Troubleshooting

Formula Problems?

Concatenate is a very long and strange sounding word. Even the most careful typist will make errors in entering data and formulas. It is a good practice to let Excel enter the function names whenever the AutoComplete feature offers a list. So start typing a function name like CONCATENATE, and when you see the name pop up in the AutoComplete list, double-click it and let Excel finish the typing for you. This method not only avoids typing errors but Excel will also insert the first parenthesis, which also helps to save typing time.

Using Wizards for Separating Data

You have already separated data using the REPLACE and FIND functions. However, Excel provides a special wizard called the **Text to Columns Wizard** for separating simple data cell content. This wizard can often provide another option to consider whenever it can be applicable. This is a very handy Excel feature because it walks you through the whole process of separating your data and gives you control over a variety of formatting options.

Your manager has given you a list of names that he managed to download from the resort's membership database. These are new members of the Resort who have not yet purchased anything at the pro shop. So the pro shop would like to target them in a new promotion to offer them a 10% discount. To help accomplish this, your boss would like you to separate the name data into two separate fields.

To Separate Name Data

a. Click the **Text_Cols worksheet tab** to make it the active worksheet.

b. Select cells **A3:A27**.

c. Click the **Data tab**, and then in the Data Tools group, click **Text to Columns**.

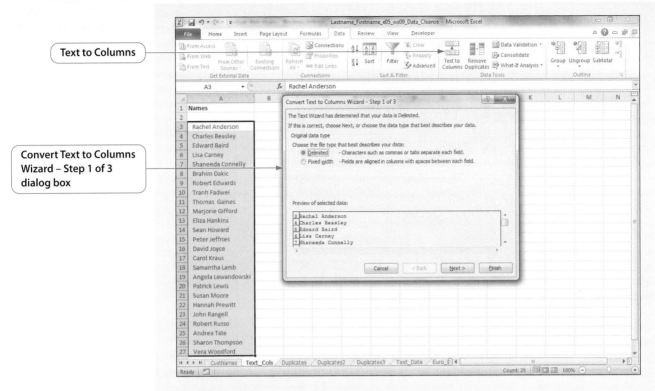

Text to Columns

Convert Text to Columns Wizard – Step 1 of 3 dialog box

Figure 27 Using Text to Columns to separate name data

d. On the Convert Text to Columns Wizard dialog box, under Choose the file type that best describes your data, make sure **Delimited** is selected, and then click **Next**.

e. Under Delimiters, click to check the check box next to **Space**, and then click to uncheck the check box next to **Tab**. Click **Next**.

f. Click in the **Destination** input box, change the destination cell reference to $B$3, and then click **Finish**. Press Ctrl + Home .

g. **Save** and continue.

Real World Advice   Wizard vs. Manual?

In Excel, there are many tools available, thus, there are typically many ways to accomplish the same task. Obviously, the main goal is always to reach for the tool that fulfills the needs at hand in the most efficient manner. So now that you have seen how to separate data via Text functions or through the simple automated wizard process using the Text to Columns button, when do you know which one to choose over the other? The wizard is designed for simple cell content, so if you are separating text data once in a while, and the data fits the requirements of the wizard, the Text to Columns Wizard will be the easiest and most efficient to use. On the other hand, if you will be converting data repetitively, or the data consistently comes from an external source in which it needs to be cleaned up, the Text functions are the way to go. Creating the function on the front end can be more time consuming, but in the bigger picture, it can be infinitely faster and more efficient in automating the process.

Removing Duplicates

It is easy to enter a customer contact more than once or to have multiple customer entries when merging customer data from multiple sources. This is one of the most common data entry errors. Even when steps are taken to minimize redundant data, there is a chance that duplicate entries will still result.

Excel provides an easy tool for removing duplicate entries—the Remove Duplicates button found on the Data tab in the Data Tools group. In the Remove Duplicates dialog box, you specify which columns you want the wizard to check. Excel searches whichever columns you have selected and prompts you to remove any duplicates that it finds. However, use this tool with caution, since it will not show what Excel is about to delete. Click OK to delete the duplicates.

To Remove Duplicates

a. Click the **Duplicates worksheet tab** to make this worksheet active. The fictional last names are set up so you can easily spot the duplicates by the duplicate numeric value attached to the Lname.

b. Select the names in cells **A3:A29**.

c. Click the Data tab, and then click **Remove Duplicates** in the Data Tools group.

Remove Duplicates

Remove Duplicates dialog box

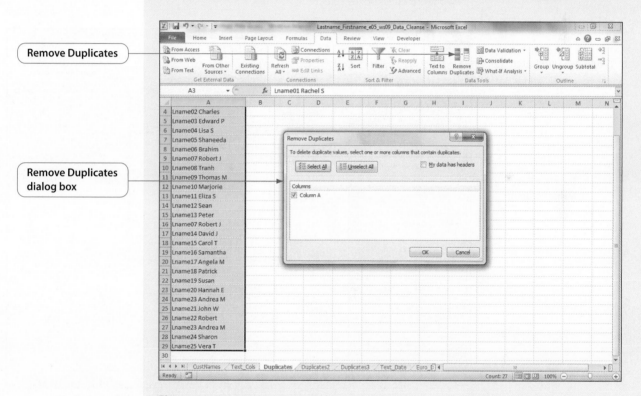

Figure 28 Removing duplicates

d. Make sure Column A is selected in the Remove Duplicates dialog box, and then click **OK**. Excel returns a message saying that *2 duplicate values found and removed; 25 unique values remain*. Press Ctrl+Home.

e. Click **OK**, and then **Save** your file.

Workshop 9

Removing Partial Duplicates

The above exercise offers an example in which the duplicate data is exact wherever it occurs. However, it is often the case that one entry is only slightly different than another. Maybe a golf instructor entered a customer's name using a nickname instead of their given name. By selecting all the other columns in the dialog box you are able to test for other duplicate indicators such as an address field. You can then check to see if all but one of the fields match, which would be an indicator of a possible duplicate record. By default, the wizard will leave the first duplicate it encounters and delete the second duplicate record.

To Remove Partial Duplicates

a. Click the **Duplicates2 worksheet tab**. You will find and remove records that may be very close but not exactly the same.

b. Select **A1:C29**.

c. Click the Data tab, click **Remove Duplicates**.

d. In the Remove Duplicates dialog box, click to check the **My data has headers** check box, and then click to deselect the **First Name** check box, leaving the Last Name and Sale Amount checkboxes selected.

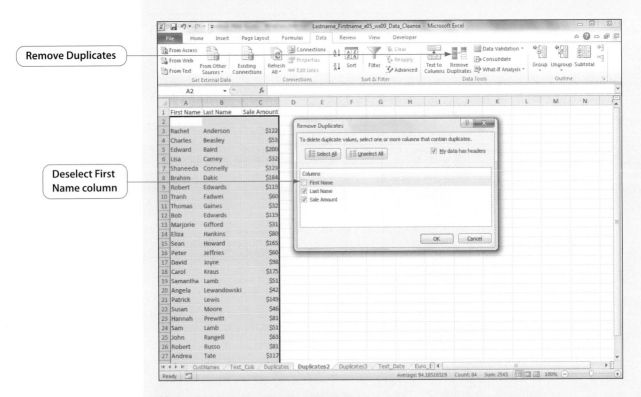

Figure 29 Removing partial duplicates

e. Click **OK**. Excel returns a message saying *2 duplicate values found and removed; 26 unique values remain*. Click **OK**, press Ctrl+Home, and then **Save** your file.

Using Conditional Formatting to Remove Duplicates

In the previous methods for removing duplicates, Excel will automatically delete the records once it finds them and you click OK without reviewing which records were deleted. You can also remove duplicates by using advanced filtering techniques to find and delete them. If it is necessary to look at the duplicate records first, an alternate method is to create a rule in the Conditional Formatting feature that will display the duplicates in a different color so you can review them and decide what to do. Prior to Excel 2007 you had to write a complex logical test formula with conditional formatting to achieve the same result. Recent versions of Excel have made this concept much easier to perform. With the Conditional Formatting feature, Excel now has a special predefined rule for identifying duplicate values.

The accounts manager at Red Bluff has asked you to go through a list of invoices in order to identify if there are any duplicates among them. The manager has instructed you not to delete any without first showing him the duplicate information. In viewing the long list of numbers, it is apparent that the most efficient and simplest method would be to create a rule in Excel to highlight any duplicate invoices.

To Find and Highlight Duplicates without Deleting Them

a.   Click the **Duplicates3 worksheet tab**.

b.   Select **A3:A278**.

c.   Click the **Home tab**, in the Editing group, click **Sort & Filter**, and then click **Sort Smallest to Largest**.

d.   In the Styles group, click **Conditional Formatting**.

e.   In the gallery menu, select to **Highlight Cells Rules**, and then click **Duplicate Values**.

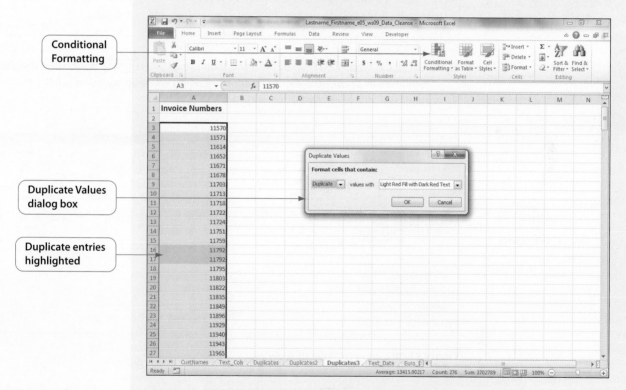

Figure 30 Using Conditional Formatting to remove duplicates

f.   Accept the default entries in the Duplicate Values dialog box, click **OK**, and then press Ctrl + Home . The duplicate values are now highlighted.

g.   **Save** 💾 your file.

Cleaning Date-Related Data

One of the biggest problems in combining data from a variety of sources is coming up with a standard date format. Some users include a full, four-digit year, whereas others use two digits. Some include a zero with single-numbered months, whereas others do not. In fact, different countries change the order of the date components around completely.

Another problem with dates is that sometimes when you import web data into Excel or you paste it in as text from an external source, the default format for the dates is a text format. These text dates are usually left aligned instead of right aligned, and they may also be marked with an error indicator icon (if error checking is turned on). This creates problems when the date field is used in other calculations, such as when you create a PivotTable and want to group the data by date. The **DATEVALUE** function converts a date in a text format into a serial value. In Excel, dates are actually a real number where the value is calculated as the number of days since December 31, 1899. So January 1, 1900, is equivalent to a value of 1 in this system. Converting dates into serial values is what allows you to use dates in mathematical calculations.

To Convert Text Using DATEVALUE

a. Click the **Text_Date worksheet tab**.

Troubleshooting

> How can you tell if your date field is in a text or date format? By default, dates are right justified and text is left justified. So if your dates end up on the left side of their cells, it is likely that they are formatted as text and not dates.

b. Click cell **C2**, type =DATEVALUE(A2), and then press Ctrl+Enter. Notice that the data is formatted as a table, therefore a Column1 heading will be assigned to cell C1, and the formula will automatically fill down to C11.

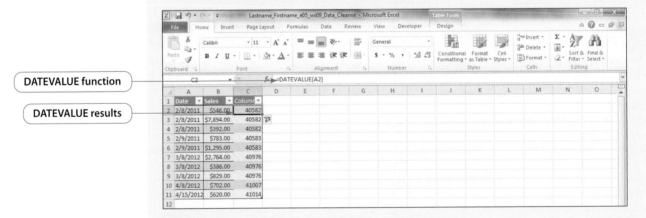

Figure 31 Results of DATEVALUE function

c. Select the range **C2:C11**, right-click the selected cell range, and then click **Copy**. Right-click the selected cell range again, and under the Paste Options on the displayed menu, click **Values** 123.

d. Right-click the range of serial dates, and then click **Format Cells**. In the Format Cells dialog box, on the Number tab, click **Date** in the Category list box, click OK, and then press Ctrl+Home. Notice the dates in column A are left-justified, while the dates in column C are right-justified.

e. **Save** your work.

Reconstructing Dates

Because there are many different date formats as shown in Figure 32, dates can be very tricky. For example, the standard European format for dates is DD/MM/YY, whereas in the United States the standard is MM/DD/YY. Recent improvements in Excel have made the conversion of dates much easier. The **DATE** function returns the sequential serial number that represents a particular date. You can make the conversion quickly by using the Text to Columns feature and changing the date format.

Function Name	Description
DATE =DATE(year, month, day)	Returns the sequential serial number that represents a particular date.
DATEVALUE =DATEVALUE(date_text)	Returns the serial number of the date represented by date_text. Use DATEVALUE to convert a date represented by text to a serial number.
DAY =DAY(serial_number)	Returns the day of the month from a date entry. The serial_number argument has to be a serial date or cell reference to a date formatted cell. The DATE function can be used to determine the serial number if needed.
MONTH =MONTH(serial_number)	Returns the month (i.e., 1–12) of the date entry.
YEAR =YEAR(serial_number)	Returns the year corresponding to a date. This works for years from 1900 to 9999.
WORKDAY =WORKDAY(start_date, days, [holidays])	Given a starting date, this function calculates the number of standard working days (less weekends and holidays) there are before or after that date. Date must be in serial or Date format.
NETWORKDAYS =NETWORKDAYS(start_date, end_date, [holidays])	Returns the number of whole working days between two given dates.
WEEKDAY =WEEKDAY(serial_number, [return_type])	Returns the day of the week corresponding to a date (1–7). The optional return_type argument allows you to change how days are counted.

Figure 32 Commonly used date functions

To Convert a European Date to a U.S. Standard

a. Click the **Euro_Date worksheet tab**.

b. Select cells **A2:A11**, click the **Data tab**, and then click **Text to Columns** in the Data Tools group.

c. On the Text to Columns Wizard dialog box, under Choose the file type that best describes your data, select **Fixed Width**, and then click **Next**.

d. There are no column breaks to add, remove, or move, so click **Next**.

e. Under Column data format, click **Date**, click the **Date arrow**, and then click **DMY**. Click the **Destination** input box, and adjust the cell reference by typing $B$2 for cell B2. Click **Finish**.

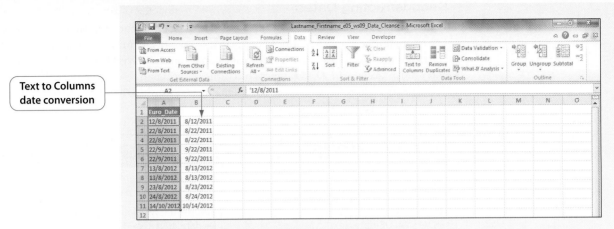

Text to Columns
date conversion

Figure 33 Converting a European date to a U.S. date

f. Resize the columns if necessary to show all the dates. Click cell **B1**, and then type the header US Date. Select **A1:A11**, click the **Home tab**, and then click **Format Painter** in the Clipboard group. Select **B1:B11** to copy the formatting to column B cells. Press Ctrl+Home, and then click **Save**.

Troubleshooting

Before attempting to rearrange dates by using the LEFT, RIGHT, and MID text functions, keep in mind that Excel stores dates as a serial number, and it is the cell formatting that displays this serial number in a date format. The **LEFT** function extracts a specified number of characters from a text string starting from the far-left character. The **RIGHT** function does the same starting from the far-right character. And the **MID** function extracts characters starting in the middle of the text string. So applying the LEFT function to a date will only return the specified numbers beginning on the left of the serial number for that date. You can extract the day, month, and year from a date field by using Text to Columns or applying the DAY, MONTH, YEAR functions.

Combining Dates

You have seen that there are many functions in Excel to help you process date-related data. It might seem that working with dates in Excel is a confusing process. But any business person can tell you that doing calculations with dates and manipulating them is something that you are sure to encounter. Knowing how to apply some of the more sophisticated functions will heighten your value to any company.

In fact, your manager, Ed, at Red Bluff, has been so impressed with your work that he has asked for help in sorting out some data sent from the main office. The data has already been imported from the .csv file for a summary sales report and converted into an Excel format. But it still has some strange looking date fields that are preventing Ed from running his own Excel formulas. When the raw data was first imported, it looked as if the source system put the name of the day (such as Tuesday) in front of the standard date format for the Ord_Date field. In addition, the data imported the standard date format into Excel as three separate fields with the headings Ord_Year, Ord_Day, and Ord_Month. Technically, there is nothing wrong with the data itself, but with several hundred thousand transactions in the report, it makes doing any date-related calculations challenging.

You have a quick solution in mind to the second problem example. Making use of the DATE function allows a quick conversion of the data in the three separate fields since you can find the serial date with the following arguments:

=Date(year, month, day)

By simply putting in the correct cells for the three arguments, you should be able to recreate the dates in a standard date format.

To Combine Multicolumn Dates into a Single Column

a. Click the **DateConv1 worksheet tab**, and then right-click **column E**.

b. Click **Insert**. A new blank column is inserted to the right of column D.

c. Click cell **E1**, type Complete_Date, and then press Ctrl+Enter. Resize column E to fit if necessary.

d. Click cell **E2**, and then type =DATE(B2,D2,C2). Press Ctrl+Enter. Double-click the **AutoFill** handle to copy down to cell **E15**. With cell range E2:E15 still selected, click the Home tab, click the **Number Format arrow** [General] in the Number group, and then click **Short Date** to format the column data as a date. Click **Save**.

Date function

Date function and formatting results

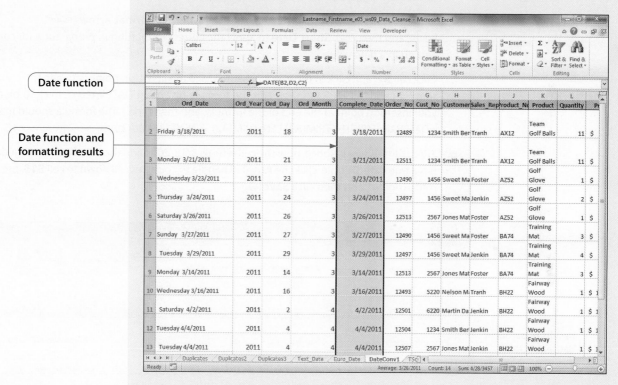

Figure 34 Combining data to make a complete date

Extracting Partial Dates

The problem is solved, but what if the date data was not easy to extract? The next exercise tackles extracting the date when data is a little more complicated. Column A of this data set contains a complex date. The goal is the same—to extract the standard numeric date out of the cell data. When you look at column A for any character patterns that might need to be factored into the task at hand, you notice the dates have an odd variety of spacing in front, behind, and in between. This can easily be removed using the TRIM function. Once the cell spacing is standardized, the RIGHT function can be used to extract the far-right part of the date entry. FIND and LEN functions will also aid in the extraction to locate the length of characters up to the space that separates the two parts of the data entry. All of this will need to be nested into the DATEVALUE function to extract the numbers needed to convert to a serial date. As can be expected, the serial number can then be formatted in a standard date format to make it more readable.

To Extract a Date from Another Column

a. On the DateConv1 worksheet tab, right-click column **B**, and then click **Insert** from the displayed menu to add a new blank column.

b. Click cell **B1**, type Standard_Date, and then press Enter.

c. In cell **B2**, type the formula =RIGHT(TRIM(A2),LEN(TRIM(A2))-FIND(" ",TRIM(A2))). Press Ctrl+Enter, and then double-click the **AutoFill** handle to copy down to cell **B15**. Note that the extracted date results in column B are left-justified.

d. With the range B2:B15 still selected, click the **Home tab**, click the **Number Format arrow** General in the Number group, and then click **General**.

   Notice, cell B2 (for example) still returns 3/18/2011. If this result were in true date format, the General format would reveal the serial number for the date. In the case of cell B2, it should display 40620. Because you created this date with text functions, Excel cannot format the cell like a date. So, while B2 looks like a date, it is still text.

e. With the range B2:B15 still selected, click the **Number Format arrow** General again, and then click **Short Date** to apply the correct formatting in preparation for converting to a date value.

f. Click cell **B2**, and click in the formula bar to place the insertion point between the equal sign (=) and "RIGHT", and then edit the formula by typing DATEVALUE(. Click to place your insertion point at the end of the formula, and then type). The formula should read =DATEVALUE(RIGHT(TRIM(A2),LEN(TRIM(A2))-FIND(" ",TRIM(A2)))).

g. Press Ctrl+Enter. Notice, now the cell returns 3/18/2011 and the value is right-aligned. It is a true date. Double-click the **AutoFill** handle to copy this cell down to cell **B15**, press Ctrl+Home, and then click **Save**.

Results of partial date extraction

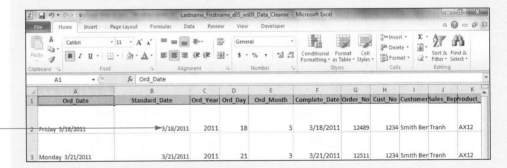

Figure 35 Extracting a partial date

More Date Functions

Because Red Bluff Golf Course is famous for its competitive layout and challenging greens, it is often asked to host golf tournaments. They currently host several major and minor tournaments. Their most popular event is the Senior Legends tournament, which they host in December. Golf tournaments have to be scheduled years in advance, and members have to be alerted about them so they learn to expect times when the course is unavailable to them. It is also important for the maintenance staff to schedule enough workdays to keep everything looking nice and for the inventory in the pro shop to be restocked in time for each event.

   With this in mind, the Red Bluff golf course manager has asked you to help him build a long-term tournament schedule report. In talking with him, you found out that he would really like to keep track of the number of working days he has between events so he can give members and staff plenty of notice prior to an event.

With a little research you discovered a function called NETWORKDAYS that can be used to calculate the number of available work days between two given dates. Its syntax looks like this: =NETWORKDAYS(start_date, end_date, [holidays]).

The optional holidays argument at the end even allows users to factor in how specific holidays might reduce the number of available work days. Additional research shows that the Text function can be used to display the name of the day by using the dddd format as one of the arguments.

To Create the Tournament Schedule Report

a. Click the **TSchedule worksheet tab**. This has a list of all the tournaments scheduled at Red Bluff Golf Course for 2012 and 2013.

b. Click cell **G5**, and then type =NETWORKDAYS(F5,E6,$I$5:$I$12). Press Ctrl+Enter. Double-click the **AutoFill** handle to copy down to cell **G9**. This function automatically calculates the total number of work days that are available between each of the given dates. Notice that cell G9 shows a negative number. This is because the formula in G9 does not refer to the correct end date for the next golf tournament.

c. To correct the error click cell **G9**, click in the **formula bar** to edit the E10 cell reference, and then type **E13** in place of E10. Press Enter and the negative number should change to a positive 60.

d. Click cell **G13**, and then type =NETWORKDAYS(F13,E14,$J$5:$J$12) to do the same for the 2013 Season tournament schedule. Press Ctrl+Enter, and then click the **AutoFill** handle and drag to copy down to cell **G16**. Notice you do not need to copy down to G17 this time, the end date, argument is unavailable for the last entry, thus you cannot calculate the available workdays between the 2013 Senior Legends Event and the next event since the schedule for 2014 is unknown at this time.

e. Click cell **H5**. Type =TEXT(E5,"dddd"). Press Ctrl+Enter, click the **AutoFill** handle, and then drag down to cell **H9**. This allows you to determine the day of the week each event will start.

Figure 36 Calculating the number of workdays with NETWORKDAYS

f. Click cell **H5**, and then press Ctrl+C to copy the formula in H5. Click cell **H13**, and then press Ctrl+V. Double-click the **AutoFill** handle to copy down to **H17**, and then press Ctrl+Home.

g. **Save** your file. Adjust the print orientation as necessary to ensure the best view of your work and resave as necessary. Then, print or submit your documents as directed by your instructor, and then **close** ✕ Excel.

1. What are the different types of external data? How can you import this data into Excel?

2. What is a web query? How is it used to import data into Excel?

3. What is the difference between data cleansing and data verification?

4. What are Text functions? How are they used for cleaning data?

5. How are character patterns in data used to help clean and manipulate data within a cell?

Key Terms

CLEAN   475
Comma separated   456
CONCATENATE   479
Data cleansing   472
Data verification   472
DATE   491
DATEVALUE   490
Delimiter   465
External data   456
FIND   479
Foreign key   468
HTML   462
ISERROR   483

LEFT   492
LEN   481
LOWER   473
Markup language   462
Metadata   466
Microsoft Query   470
MID   492
Primary key   468
PROPER   473
Query   456
Relational database   468
REPLACE   476
RIGHT   492

SEARCH   476
SUBSTITUTE   476
Text data   465
Text file   465
Text functions   472
Text to Columns Wizard   485
TRIM   475
UPPER   473
Web query   456
XML   462
XML element   463
XML map   463
XML schema   463

Visual Workshop

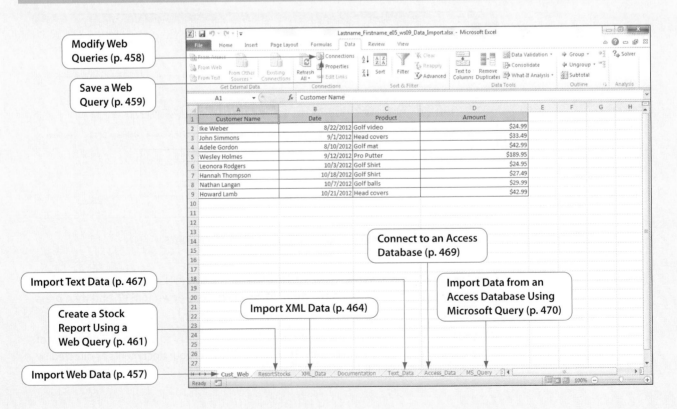

Modify Web Queries (p. 458)

Save a Web Query (p. 459)

Connect to an Access Database (p. 469)

Import Text Data (p. 467)

Import Data from an Access Database Using Microsoft Query (p. 470)

Create a Stock Report Using a Web Query (p. 461)

Import XML Data (p. 464)

Import Web Data (p. 457)

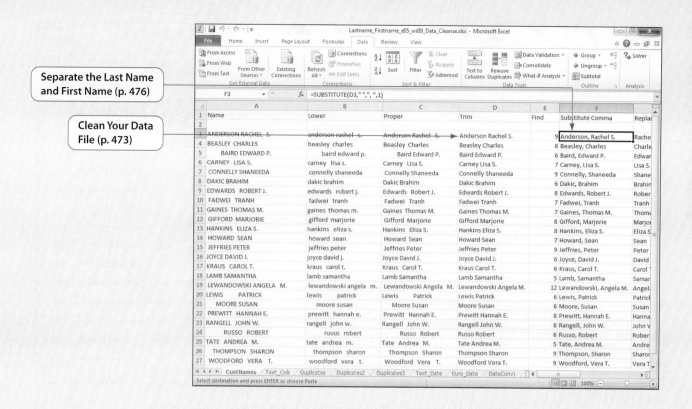

Separate the Last Name and First Name (p. 476)

Clean Your Data File (p. 473)

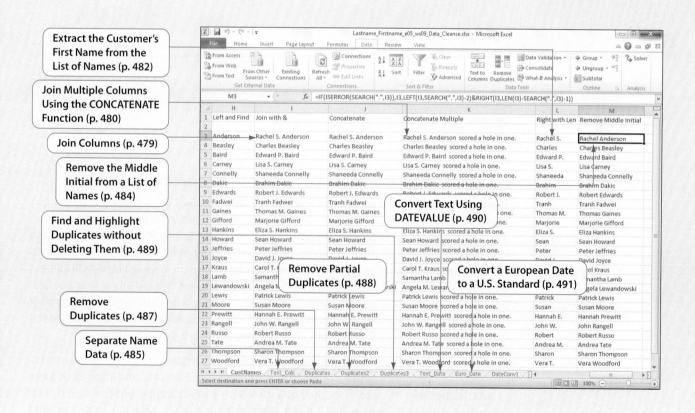

Extract the Customer's First Name from the List of Names (p. 482)

Join Multiple Columns Using the CONCATENATE Function (p. 480)

Join Columns (p. 479)

Remove the Middle Initial from a List of Names (p. 484)

Find and Highlight Duplicates without Deleting Them (p. 489)

Convert Text Using DATEVALUE (p. 490)

Remove Partial Duplicates (p. 488)

Convert a European Date to a U.S. Standard (p. 491)

Remove Duplicates (p. 487)

Separate Name Data (p. 485)

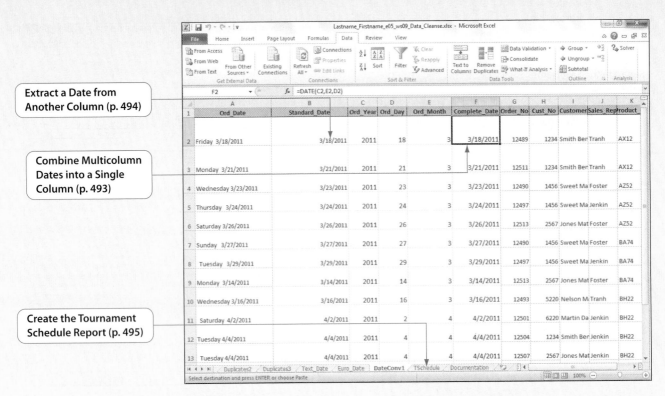

Extract a Date from Another Column (p. 494)

Combine Multicolumn Dates into a Single Column (p. 493)

Create the Tournament Schedule Report (p. 495)

Figure 37 Red Bluff Golf Club Pro Shop Data Integration final worksheets

---

Practice 1

Student data files needed:

e05_ws09_Newsletter_List
e05_ws09_Customer_Web
e05_ws09_ProShop_Customer

You will save your file as:

Lastname_Firstname_e05_ws09_Newsletter_List

Golf Pro Shop Special Promotions Spreadsheet

The Golf Pro Shop at Painted Resort and Spa regularly runs special promotions to sell golf equipment and clothing. When customers visit the pro shop website, they can opt to receive electronic copies of the pro shop newsletter via e-mail. The website administrator then e-mails your boss an XML file with this information at the end of every week. Customers who walk into the pro shop can also opt to receive the newsletter by writing their name and e-mail address on a signup sheet. At the end of each day, these names are then entered into an Access database. Your boss has asked you to take the XML file from the website customers and integrate it with the customer data from the Access database. Then it also needs to be sorted and cleaned up so it can then be used to send out e-mail versions of the pro shop newsletter.

a. Open **Excel**, click the **File tab**, click **Open**, navigate to where your data files are stored, and then open **e05_ws09_Newsletter_List**. Click the **File tab**, and then click **Save As**. In the Save As dialog box, navigate to where you are saving your files, and then type Lastname_Firstname_e05_ws09_Newsletter_List and replacing Lastname and Firstname with your own name. Click **Save**.

b. To insert a filename footer, click the **Insert tab**, and then click **Header & Footer** in the Text group.

c. Click the **Design tab**, and then click **Go to Footer** in the Navigation group. If necessary, click the **left section** of the footer, and then click **File Name** in the Header & Footer Elements group.

d. Click any cell on the spreadsheet to move out of the footer, press Ctrl+Home, click the **View tab**, click **Normal** in the Workbook Views group, and then click the **Home tab**.

e. If necessary, click the **Newsletter worksheet tab** to make it the active worksheet, then click the **Data tab**.

f. Click **A3**, and then click **From Other Sources** in the Get External Data group.

g. In the gallery menu list, click the **From XML Data Import** option.

h. In the Select Data Source dialog box, navigate to where the student data files are stored, and click to select **e05_ws09_Customer_Web**. Click **Open**, and then click **OK** if you get a warning message stating there is no XML schema for this file. In the Import Data dialog box, verify that XML table in existing worksheet is checked and that the location is set to $A$3 so the import starts at cell A3, and then click **OK**.

i. Click the **Access worksheet tab**. If necessary, click cell **A1**, and then click the **Data tab**. Click **From Access** in the Get External Data group.

j. In the Select Data Source dialog box, navigate to where the student data files are stored, click **e05_ws09_Proshop_Customer**, and then click **Open**. In the Import Data dialog box, verify the location in the Existing worksheet input box is set to =$A$1 so the import starts at cell A1, and then click **OK**.

k. Select the cell range **A2:B9**, and then press Ctrl+C to copy the range. Click the **Newsletter worksheet tab**, click cell **A11**, and then press Ctrl+V to paste the range in. Resize the columns as needed to fit the contents.

l. Click cell **C3**, type Cleaned Names, and then press Enter. In cell **A4** type =CLEAN(A4), and then press Enter. This will copy the formula down to C18. Edit the column headings in cells **A3** and **B3** so that the first letters are capitalized. Resize column C to show the whole name.

m. Click cell **D3**, type Trimmed Names, and then press Enter. In cell **D4**, type =TRIM(C4), and then press Enter. This will copy the formula down to D18. Resize the column to show the whole name.

n. Click cell **E3**, type Proper Names, and then press Enter. In cell **E4**, type =PROPER(D4), and then press Enter. This will copy the formula down to E18. Resize the column to show the whole name.

o. Select the range **E4:E18**, right-click any of the selected cells, and then click **Copy** from the displayed menu. Right-click any of the selected cells again, and then on the displayed menu, under Paste Options, click **Values**.

p. Click cell **F3**, type Last Names, and then press Tab. In cell **G3**, type First Names, and then press Enter. Select the range **E4:E18**, and then click the **Data tab**.

q. In the Data Tools group, click **Text to Columns**. In the step 1 of the Convert Text to Columns Wizard dialog box, click **Next**. Click the check box next to **Comma**, check to deselect the check box next to **Tab**, and then click **Next**.

r. Click the **Destination input** box, adjust the cell reference from $E$4 to $F$4 so the results start in cell F4, and then click **Finish**. Resize the last two columns as necessary. Press Ctrl+Home.

s. Save 💾 your file. Adjust the print orientation as necessary to ensure the best view of your work and resave as necessary. Then, print or submit your documents as directed by your instructor, and then close Excel.

Student data files needed:

e05_ws09_Inv_Report

e05_ws09_Inventory

You will save your file as:

Lastname_Firstname_e05_ws09_Inv_Report

Gift Shop Inventory Tracking Spreadsheet

The gift shop is having a difficult time keeping track of its inventory. The resort receiving department uses scanners to scan in product codes as they arrive at the resort. Whenever an order arrives at Painted Paradise Resort, it is immediately given an internal inventory number, which is coded with a prefix of either R (resort), G (Gift Shop), or M (Maintenance) to show which division of the resort is responsible for it. The inventory number also has a suffix of S1, S2, or S3 to indicate its storage location. This raw data is stored in an Access database. The gift shop would like both the division and storage location information separated from the inventory number so they can analyze the data more easily.

Your job is to import the source data and reformat it so that further analysis can be done.

a. Open **Excel**, click the **File tab**, click **Open**, navigate to where your data files are stored, and then open **e05_ws09_Inv_Report**. Click the **File tab**, and then click **Save As**. In the Save As dialog box, navigate to where you are saving your files, and then type Lastname_Firstname_e05_ws09_Inv_Report replacing Lastname and Firstname with your own name. Click **Save**.

b. To insert a filename footer, click the **Insert tab**, and then click **Header & Footer** in the Text group.

c. Click the **Design tab**, and then click **Go to Footer** in the Navigation group. If necessary, click the **left section** of the footer, and then click **File Name** in the Header & Footer Elements group.

d. Click any cell on the spreadsheet to move out of the footer, press [Ctrl]+[Home], click the **View tab**, click **Normal** in the Workbook Views group, and then click the **Home tab**.

e. Click the **Data tab**, click **From Access** in the Get External Data group.

f. In the Select Data Source dialog box, navigate to where the data files are stored, select **e05_ws09_Inventory**, and then click **Open**. In the Import Data dialog box, verify the **Table** option is selected. Under Where do you want to put the data?, verify the **Existing worksheet** is selected, and then click the **Existing worksheet input** box and change the location from =$A$1 to =$A$2. Click **OK**.

You should see a two-column list with the field headings of Inv_Num and Inv_Name. Now, you need to separate out the division code, inventory code, and the storage location from the Inv_Num field.

g. Click cell **C2**, type Division_Code, and then press [Enter].

h. In cell C3, type =LEFT(A3,1), and then press [Enter]. This extracts the first character in cell A3. Resize the column as necessary.

i. Click cell **D2**, type Inventory_Code, and then press [Enter].

j. In cell **D3**, type =MID(A3,2,LEN(A3)-3), and then press ⎡Enter⎤. This extracts the middle piece of the Inv_Num. Resize the column as necessary.

k. Click cell **E2**, type Storage_Location, and then press ⎡Enter⎤.

l. In cell **E3**, type =RIGHT(A3,2), and then press ⎡Enter⎤. This extracts the far-right characters of Inv_Num. Resize the column as necessary. Press ⎡Ctrl⎤+⎡Home⎤.

m. **Save** ⊟. Adjust the print orientation as necessary to ensure the best view of your work and resave as necessary. Then, print or submit your documents as directed by your instructor, and then close Excel.

Objectives

1. Understand the basics of dashboard design. p. 504

2. Build the analysis layer. p. 508

3. Create the presentation layer. p. 516

4. Understand the components of VBA. p. 526

5. Improve readability of VBA with formatting and structure. p. 532

6. Enhance functionality and usability with VBA. p. 533

7. Troubleshoot VBA. p. 538

8. Prepare a dashboard for production. p. 539

Dashboards and Visual Basic for Applications

PREPARE CASE

The Red Bluff Golf Club Pro Shop Digital Dashboard

Management at the Red Bluff Golf Club Pro Shop have been collecting data on their business for three years now and are looking for ways to extract information from that data to make important, strategic decisions about the future of Red Bluff. You have been given access to a set of sales data from 2008–2010 and have been asked to create a digital dashboard using Microsoft Excel that will provide management with a multiperspective view of the business.

Courtesy of www.Shutterstock.com

Student data files needed for this workshop:

 e05_ws10_ProShop_Dashboard

 e05_ws10_ProShopSales

You will save your file as:

 Lastname_Firstname_e05_ws10_ProShop_Dashboard

The Importance of Business Intelligence and Dashboards

Business intelligence is more than just a buzzword. **Business intelligence (BI)** refers to a variety of software applications that are used to analyze an organization's data in order to provide management with the tools necessary to improve decision making, cut costs, and identify new opportunities. The role of BI has increased over the last decade because the amount of data being collected by businesses continues to grow.

This increasing dependence on BI has manifested itself in many forms in the business community over the past few years. The most recent trend, which shows no signs of slowing, is the desire for digital dashboards. **Digital dashboards** are mechanisms that deliver business intelligence in graphical form. Dashboards provide management with a "big picture" view of the business, usually from multiple perspectives using various charts and other graphical representations. There are many factors that are driving businesses to use the power of dashboards. Figure 1 shows the top pressures that are driving these dashboard initiatives according to Aberdeen Group, Inc., a provider of fact-based research helping organizations and individuals make better business decisions. In this section you will learn about the dashboard design concepts, conduct some analysis, and create a dashboard.

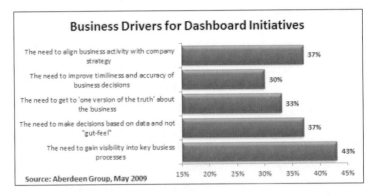

Figure 1 Top pressures driving dashboard initiatives

CONSIDER THIS | **Decisions, Decisions, Decisions...**

Studies have shown that a typical manager engages in over 300 different tasks and decisions each day. These often involve interacting with many different people in the organization using a variety of different channels and technologies. Some of them are very brief and quick decisions, whereas others may require research. Certainly the number of channels and media a manager must master and use (phone, Internet, e-mail, texting, and so on) is growing. From your perspective, do you think technology increases, decreases, or holds neutral the volume and speed of decision making today?

Understanding the Basics of Dashboard Design

Dashboards are becoming more and more important today as a tool for helping managers run their businesses. They are no longer just for executives and are being integrated at all levels of the business and in many different industries. You will likely encounter them in other classes as you discuss management techniques such as Balanced Scorecards and Six Sigma. Both of these management initiatives involve generating key performance indicators and dashboard reports for all levels of the organization. Using dashboards, everyone from the CEO to the delivery truck driver can have a personalized view of information to quickly and easily see how well they are performing.

How a dashboard is designed has just as much of an impact on its effectiveness as the data displayed. Think of the dashboard in a car. The gauges and layout of the dashboard are designed to help the driver make better decisions and interpret important things like relative speed, gas consumption, and critical malfunctions in a very immediate and effective way. The driver of the car has to monitor the situation constantly and make crucial decisions about what to do with the car. An effective dashboard supports effective decision making.

This analogy holds true for the "driver" of a company as well. A manager must be able to quickly review and monitor the current health of the company and make decisions in a timely manner to correct problems. A dashboard can be a huge help to a manager, because it is specifically organized to provide alerts and monitor the business as a whole. Typically, dashboards are also oriented around specific business activities, such as sales analysis, cash flow, employee productivity, customer service, and so on. Some typical features of a dashboard might include:

- A single-screen, visually oriented user interface that is intuitive and easy to navigate
- Interactive controls that allow the user to customize the data display
- Integration of multiple types of data from a variety of sources
- Data that is frequently updated so it reflects the current situation
- Information oriented around a specific problem or decision
- An easy-to-use layout that is intuitive and does not require a lot of extra training to use effectively

Dashboard components typically consist of tables, PivotTables, PivotCharts, conditional formatting, and other features available in Excel. There are also some basic design concepts that you need to take into consideration when creating a dashboard.

Keep It Simple

Adding more and more data and charts is tempting. However, you must always keep in mind the basic principle: When it comes to dashboards *less is more*. If users cannot easily interpret your dashboard, then you may have made it too complicated. An overly complicated dashboard is not usable as a management tool. Remember, one of the primary goals is to help the user navigate and interpret a large quantity of data at a glance.

Make Sure It Is Well Defined

Stay focused on a specific business problem. A company can track product sales, employee productivity, customer complaints, revenue, portfolio value, machine defects, and so on. However, doing all of these in the same dashboard is ill advised. As a general rule, the more defined you can make your dashboard theme, the more useful your users will find it.

Know Your Users

Not all users are alike. They can have different decision-making styles. You can increase the success of your dashboard by taking personal preferences into account whenever possible. You should interview the main users of the dashboard to see what they would find most useful. The earlier you can let them see your dashboard design, the fewer headaches you will have later in the project. Changes are easier to make early in development rather than when you are almost done.

Define Crucial KPIs

A **key performance indicator (KPI)** is a measure that is very important for the design of dashboards in that it helps managers track and interpret data. Some KPIs are year-to-date (YTD) sales growth, customer satisfaction, call resolution rates, and percent of market share as shown in Figure 2. In fact, every functional area of business has its own set of commonly used KPIs. Often, many firms in the same industry will all focus on similar KPIs because they are so critical to the nature of their business—for example, profit margin.

Quick Reference — Commonly Used Business KPIs

Business Area	KPI
Accounting	• Gross profit • Operating margin • Cumulative annual growth rate • ROI (Return on investment) • Cost of goods sold
Finance/Accounting	• Gross yield • Price-to-earnings ratio (P/E) • Earnings before interest, taxes, depreciation and amortization (EBITDA) • Earnings per share (EPS) • Budget ratio
Marketing/Sales	• Market share by segment • Customer churn rate • Customer lifetime value • Cost per lead • Productivity by channel
Personnel	• Productivity ratios • Turnover rates • % overtime • Employee satisfaction rates • % absenteeism
Operations	• Out of stock % • Defect rate • Production cycle time • On-time delivery • % downtime
Customer Service	• Customer satisfaction • First call resolution rate • Average wait time • % of dropped calls • Time per call
IT	• Access speed • Site click-through • System availability • Service satisfaction levels • Project success rates

Figure 2 Common key performance indicators in business

Strategic Placement

Successful dashboards should help summarize complex data so users can interpret the information at a glance. The dashboard needs to make it as easy as possible for users to read and understand the data. The layout of the dashboard can have a big impact on its usability. Figure 3 illustrates the particular regions of a screen that a user's eyes tend to pay attention to based on research conducted by the Poynter Institute.

Figure 3 Design layout priority zones

Regions with the number 1 appear to have prominence over the other regions. This means that eyes tend to spend more time in that part of the screen than others. This research can be useful in strategically placing components of a dashboard to maximize its effectiveness.

White Space

Empty space on the screen that gives eyes a place to rest is called **white space**. White space is not necessarily white, just void of content. White space helps keep a design simple, accessible, and visually pleasing to users. There is no rule for how much white space to include in your design. Generally speaking, you should include more white space than you initially think is necessary. However, including too much white space may mean you are wasting valuable real estate. Including the right amount of white space can give an elegant feel to your dashboard and make it easier for the user to read.

Getting Started

a. Start **Excel**.

b. Click the **File tab**, and then click **Open**.

c. In the Open dialog box, navigate to where the student data files are located, and then double-click **e05_ws10_ProShop_Dashboard** to open the file.

d. Click the **File tab**, click **Save As**, and then in the Save As dialog box, navigate to the location where you are saving your files. In the File name box type Lastname_Firstname_e05_ws10_ProShop_Dashboard, replacing Lastname_Firstname with your own name. Select **Excel Macro-Enabled Workbook (*.xlsm)** from the **Save as type** list, and then click **Save**.

e. Click the **Documentation worksheet tab** if it is not the active worksheet, click cell **A6**, and then press Ctrl+; to input the current date. Click cell **B6**, and type Lastname, Firstname using your own first name and last name.

There are several commercially available products that exist with the aim of making it easy to create complex dashboards. Some examples include:

- Cognos
- Hyperion
- Dundas
- Corda
- SQL Server Analysis Services
- Oracle Business Intelligence

While these programs may be powerful and effective, they all suffer from two significant drawbacks. First, they require a software purchase; although some tools are nominally "free," the free or trial versions may be limited in functionality and/or may not be legal to use for your company. Second, off-the-shelf software nearly always requires that its users have that particular software installed on their computers.

There are many benefits to using Microsoft Excel to create digital dashboards:

- Minimal costs: Not every business is a multibillion dollar business that can afford to purchase top-of-the-line BI software. Leveraging the capabilities of Microsoft Excel is a very cost-effective solution without compromising too much on usability and functionality.

- Broad familiarity: From the entry-level sales representative to the CEO, familiarity with Excel is widespread. People will spend less time learning how to use the dashboard and more time getting value from what is displayed.

- Flexibility: With the appropriate know-how, Excel can be much more flexible in the variety of analytics it can provide in a dashboard than many off-the-shelf solutions. Such features as PivotTables, AutoFilters, and Form controls allow you to create mechanisms that provide the audience multiple perspectives of the data.

- Rapid development: Having the capability of creating your own reporting mechanisms in Excel can reduce your reliance on the IT department's resources. With Excel, not only can you develop reporting mechanisms faster, but you have the flexibility to adapt more quickly to changing requirements.

Real World Advice — Dashboard Design and the SDLC

Creating dashboards requires far more preparation than a standard Excel model. It requires closer communication with business leaders, stricter data modeling techniques, and following certain best practices. The systems development life cycle (SDLC) provides a structure for managing complex IT projects. One of the SDLC models is broken into six stages: analysis, design, develop, implement, test, and maintain. Following this SDLC model can provide the necessary guidance to creating an effective dashboard.

Building the Analysis Layer

The most effective dashboards are driven from three layers of design: the data layer, the analysis layer, and the presentation layer. The **data layer** consists of the raw data that will not be directly modified. Best practice dictates that the data layer is linked to an external source—though it can exist in the spreadsheet. The **analysis layer** consists primarily of formulas that analyze or extract data from the data layer into formatted tables. The **presentation layer** consists of graphics and charts that are based on the tables in the analysis layer. Together, these three layers can help you navigate your way to a clean, elegant, and informative dashboard, regardless of the various other factors you have to work with. It is often a good idea to separate the layers of the data model into separate worksheets in a workbook, but this is not a requirement.

Connecting to an External Source

The key to an effective dashboard is timeliness. The data that make up dashboards needs to be able to be updated quickly and easily when new data becomes available. Excel can link to external data sources such as an Access database, a SharePoint site, a text file, or a web page, and as new data are collected in the external source, the dashboard can be updated with the click of a button. In this exercise you will connect to a query in an Access database that contains all the data you will use to create a dashboard.

To Connect to an External Data Source

a. Click the **SalesData worksheet tab**, click cell **A2**, click the **Data tab**, and then click **From Access** in the Get External Data group.

b. In the Select Data Source dialog box, navigate to where the student data files are located, double click **e05_ws10_ProShopSales**, and then double-click **qrySalesData** from the list of database objects in the Select Table dialog box.

c. In the Import Data dialog box click **OK**. The data being imported is automatically placed into a dynamic Excel table starting in cell A2 and will expand automatically when new data are added.

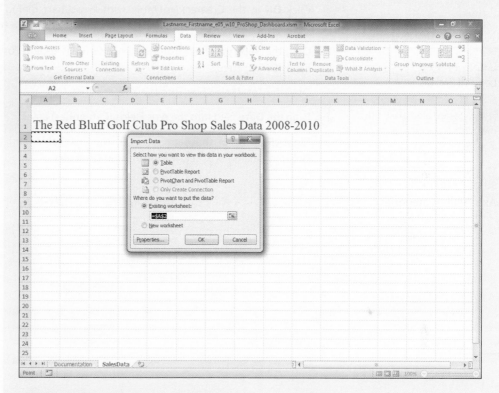

Figure 4 Import Data dialog box

d. Save 🖫 the workbook.

Troubleshooting

Excel will automatically disable connections to external data sources if the directory in which the file is saved is not a designated Trusted Location. To avoid having to continuously enable the connection you must create a Trusted Location for the directory that contains the workbook.

Creating PivotCharts for Analysis

Now that you have created the data layer by linking to e05_ws10_ProShopSales, you can begin work on the analysis layer. The PivotChart is commonly used in Excel for creating dashboards. A **PivotChart** is a built-in analysis tool that allows for graphical representations of a PivotTable. As the user pivots the data in the PivotTable, the chart shifts accordingly to represent the filtered data.

Management at the Red Bluff Golf Course Pro Shop is interested in getting a better understanding of their sales data over the past three years. You have been asked to conduct some analysis on the raw data in the SalesData worksheet to provide management with some high-level information.

To Create a Pivot Line Chart

a. Select any cell on the **SalesData** worksheet that contains data.

b. Click the **Insert tab**, click the **PivotTable button arrow** in the Tables group, and then select **PivotChart**.

c. Click **OK** in the Create PivotTable with PivotChart dialog box. A new worksheet is inserted to the left of the SalesData worksheet containing the PivotTable Field List.

d. Drag the **SaleType** field from the Choose fields to add to report area to the Legend Fields(Series) area.

e. Drag the **TotalSales** field into the Σ Values area.

f. Drag the **Date** field into the Axis Fields (Categories) area.

g. Right-click one of the date values in the PivotTable, and then select **Group**. In the Grouping dialog box, select **Months** and **Quarters**.

SIDE NOTE
Legend Entries
Fields placed in the Legend Entries(Series) area make up the vertical axis (y-axis) of a chart.

SIDE NOTE
Axis Fields (Categories)
Fields placed in the Axis Fields area make up the horizontal axis (x-axis) of a chart.

Figure 5 Grouping dialog box

h. Click **OK**.

Troubleshooting

When the PivotTable was selected in order to group the dates, the Field List areas automatically changed from Legend Fields and Axis Fields (Categories) to Column Labels and Row Labels, respectively. Because the areas are synonymous with each other, it does not matter if you have the PivotChart or the PivotTable selected to complete the next steps.

i. Drag the **Year** field to the Report Filter area.

j. Clear the check box next to the **Date** field in the Field List so that it no longer appears in the Row Labels area. The PivotTable now consists of Year for a Report Filter, SaleType for Column Labels, Quarters for Row Labels, and Sum of TotalSales for Σ Values.

k. Right-click any of the sales figures in the PivotTable, and in the right-click menu click **Number Format**. In the Format Cells dialog box, select **Accounting** with 2 decimal places, and then click **OK**.

l. Right-click the **PivotChart**, and then click **Change Chart Type**. In the Change Chart Type dialog box, click **Line with Markers** in the Line chart group, and then click **OK**. Line charts are more effective in illustrating trends over time.

m. Right-click the **vertical axis** on the PivotChart, and then click **Format Axis**. In the Format Axis dialog box, click the **Logarithmic Scale** check box, and then click **Close**.

Because the scale is dramatically different for the amount of sales generated by the purchase of accessories and the amount of sales generated by the purchase of golf rounds, it will be easier to compare trends using the logarithmic scale.

n. Click the **PivotChart Tools Layout tab**, click **Chart Title** in the Labels group, and then click **Above Chart**. Type Quarterly Sales Trend by Type as the chart title, and press Enter.

o. Notice the PivotTable filters are also part of the chart. Test the PivotChart by selecting **2009** from the **PivotChart Year** filter, and then click **OK**. Observe how the chart shifts to reflect the change in data for that year.

p. Reposition the line chart so that it is just below the PivotTable.

q. Click the **PivotTable**, and then click the **PivotTable Tools Options tab**. Click the **PivotTableName** text box in the PivotTable group, and then type SaletypeTrend ByQuarter to rename the PivotTable. Press Enter.

r. Right-click the **Sheet1 worksheet tab**, and then click **Rename**. Type Analysis-SalesData, and then press Enter.

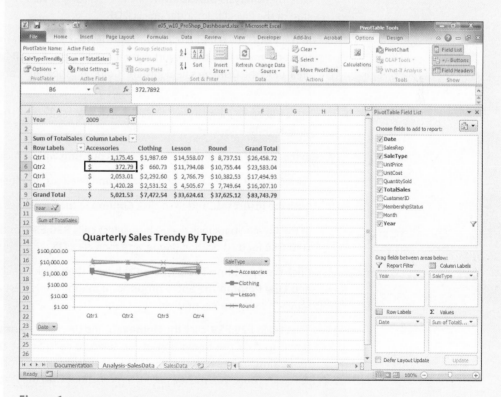

Figure 6 Total Sales by Quarter PivotTable/PivotChart

s. **Save** the workbook.

Creating PivotTables with Sparklines

Another common method of representing data graphically for dashboards created in Excel is to use sparklines. **Sparklines**, or miniature charts, are new to Excel 2010 and provide a way to graphically summarize a row or column of data in a single cell. There are three different types of sparklines: line, column, and win/loss. Management at the Red Bluff Golf Pro Shop feels that it would benefit from comparing trends in sales revenue from each sales representative. In this exercise you will create a PivotTable adding sparklines that illustrate the trend over four quarters for each sales representative.

Real World Advice   Creating Dashboards That Work for Everyone

The new features available in Excel 2010 allow for a much better user experience; however, they are not compatible with earlier versions. When gathering requirements for a dashboard, be sure to take software version into consideration to avoid creating tools that cannot be used because of the end user's software.

To Create a PivotTable and Add Sparklines

a. Click the **SalesData worksheet tab**, and then select any cell that contains data.

b. Click the **Insert tab**, and click **PivotTable** in the Tables group.

c. In the Create PivotTable dialog box, click **Existing Worksheet**, click in the **Location** box under the Choose where you want the PivotTable report to be placed header, and then click the **Analysis-SalesData** worksheet. Click cell **A28** to make the selected cell the start of the PivotTable, and then click **OK**.

d. In the PivotTable Field List pane, drag the **Year** field from the Choose fields to add to the report area into the Report Filter area, drag the **SalesRep** field into the Row Labels area, drag the **Quarters** field into the Column Labels area, and drag **TotalSales** into the Σ Values area.

e. Right-click any one of the sales values in the PivotTable, and then in the right-click menu, click **Number Format**.

f. In the Format Cells dialog box, select **Accounting** with 2 decimal places.

g. Click cell **G29**, type Chart for a new column heading, and then press Enter.

h. Click the **Insert tab**, and then click **Column** in the Sparklines group.

i. In the Create Sparklines dialog box, select cells **B30:E34** for the Data Range, select cells **G30:G34** for the Location Range, and then click **OK**.

j. Click the **Sparkline Tools Design tab**, and then click the check boxes for **High Point** and **Low Point** in the Show group to highlight the lowest and highest quarter sales for each sales representative.

k. Select cells **F28:F29**, click the **Home tab**, and then click **Format Painter** in the Clipboard group to copy the formatting of the selected cells. Select cells **G28:G29** to paste the formatting to the selected cells. Do the same to apply the formatting of cell **F35** to **G35**. This will ensure that the formatting is consistent with the PivotTable.

l. Click cell **A28**, type Total_Sales, and then press Enter. Type Sales Reps in cell **A29**, and then press Enter. Click cell **B28**, type Quarters, and then press Enter.

m. If necessary, double-click between each of the column headings **A:F** to adjust the width of the columns in the PivotTable so that all values are visible.

n. Click the **PivotTable Tools Options tab**, and type QuarterSalesByRep in the PivotTableName text box in the PivotTable group to rename the PivotTable. Press Enter.

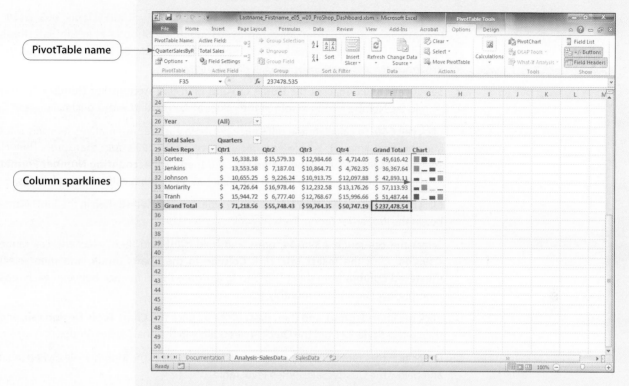

PivotTable name

Column sparklines

Figure 7 Sales by Rep PivotTable with sparklines

o. Test the PivotTable and sparklines by modifying the Year report filter to display the values for different years.

p. **Save** the workbook.

Creating an Excel Table for Analysis

Management would like to be able to compare each sales representative's monthly sales revenue against a monthly target in order to measure performance. In this exercise, you will create an Excel table that will calculate the total sales revenue for each representative. You will also allow for the user to enter a particular year and month to evaluate performance.

To Create an Excel Table

a. Click cell **A37**, type Year, press Tab, and then type Month in cell **B37**. Press Tab, type Monthly Goal per Rep in cell **C37**, and then press Enter.

b. Type 2008 in cell **A38**, press Tab, and then type Jan in cell **B38**. Press Tab, type 975 in cell **C38**, and then press Enter.

c. Type Sales Rep in cell **A39**, press Tab, and then type Monthly Revenue in cell **B39**. Press Tab, type Above/Below Goal in cell **C39**, and then press Enter.

d. Select cells **A39:C39**, click the **Insert tab**, and click **Table** in the Tables group. In the Create Table dialog box, check the **My table has headers** check box, and then click **OK**.

e. Click cell **A40**, type Cortez, and press [Enter]. Type Jenkins in cell **A41**, press [Enter], type Johnson in cell **A42**, and then press [Enter]. Type Moriarity in cell **A43**, press [Enter], type Tranh in cell **A44**, and then press [Enter].

f. Click cell **B40**, and then type the following SUMIFS function: =SUMIFS(Table_e05_ws10_ProShopSales.accdb[TotalSales],Table_e05_ws10_ProShopSales.accdb[SalesRep], [@[Sales Rep]],Table_e05_ws10_ProShopSales.accdb[Year],$A$38,Table_e05_ws10_ProShopSales.accdb[Month],$B$38). Press [Enter].

g. Select cells **B40:B44**, click the **Home tab** and then click **Accounting Number Format** [$ ▾] in the Number group to format the values as Accounting with 2 decimal places.

h. Click cell **C40**. To calculate the difference between each representative's monthly sales and the goal amount, type =[@[Monthly Revenue]]-$C$38, and then press [Enter]. Select cells **C40:C44**, click the **Home tab**, and then click **Accounting Number Format** [$ ▾] in the Number group to format the values as Accounting with 2 decimal places.

i. Click the **Table Tools Design tab**, and then type MonthlySalesByRep in the Table Name box in the Properties group. Press [Enter].

j. Select the cell range **A39:A44**, press and hold [Ctrl], and then select the cell range **C39:C44**. Click the **Insert tab**, click **Column** in the Charts group, and then select **Clustered Column** from the 2-D group to illustrate the difference between each rep's monthly revenue and the monthly goal.

k. Click the **chart legend**, and then press [Delete]. Click the **Chart Tools Design tab**, and then select **Style 32** from the Quick Styles Gallery in the Chart Styles group.

l. Reposition the column chart so that it is just to the right of the MonthlySalesByRep table and below the QuarterSalesByRep PivotTable.

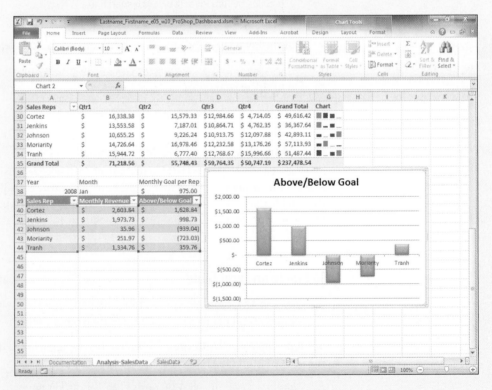

Figure 8 Column chart with Excel table

m. Test the interactivity of the chart by changing the Year, Month, and Monthly Goal values.

n. **Save** [💾] the workbook.

Enhancing Analysis with Conditional Formatting

Dashboards are much more than just charts and tables. Using simple tools, a dashboard can become more effective by directing users to important information in a visually arresting manner. Conditional formatting is the easiest way to do this.

Consider a case where a user has a sales dashboard. While the charts, tables, and graphs may be useful, even the most well-intentioned executives can sometimes overlook critical trends and changes in the data they are reviewing. Calling attention to changes that are out of the ordinary—in a good or bad way—can make things nearly impossible to ignore.

Management at the Pro Shop would like to be able to tell at a glance if each sales rep is selling above or below the average annual sales for all sales reps. In this exercise you will apply conditional formatting that will provide a visual indicator to illustrate if the annual sales of each rep are above or below the average.

To Apply Conditional Formatting

a. On the **Analysis-SalesData worksheet tab**, click cell **H29**. Type Above/Below Avg, and then press Enter.

b. In cell **H30**, type = F30, and then press Enter. Type =F31 in cell **H31**, and then press Enter. Repeat the same process for cells **H32**, **H33**, and **H34** referencing cells F32, F33, and F34.

   Applying conditional formatting directly in a cell that contains an important value like a grand total can make it difficult for users to see the amount. By referencing the grand total cells in column F the conditional formatting can now be applied to column H and avoid any visual hindrance of important data.

c. Select the range of cells **H30:H34**. Click the **Home tab**, click **Conditional Formatting** in the Styles group, and then click **New Rule**.

d. Click the **Format Style arrow** in the New Formatting Rule dialog box under Edit the Rule Description, and then select **Icon Sets**.

e. Click the **Icon Style arrow**, scroll to the top, and select the **3 Arrows (Colored)** icons set.

f. Click the **Show Icon Only** check box.

g. Click both of the **Type arrows** under Display each icon according to these rules, and then select **Formula** for both.

h. Click the **first box** under Value, and then type =AVERAGE($F$30:$F$34).

i. Click the **second box** below Value, and again type =AVERAGE($F$30:$F$34).

j. Click **OK**.

k. Select cells **G28:G29**, click **Format Painter** in the Clipboard group, and then select **H28:H29** to apply the same formatting.

l. Click cell **G35**, click **Format Painter**, and then click **H35** to copy the formatting.

m. Select cells **H30:H34**, and then click the **Center** button in the Alignment group to center the arrows. Double-click the **right edge** of the column header H to expand the column so that all of H29 is visible.

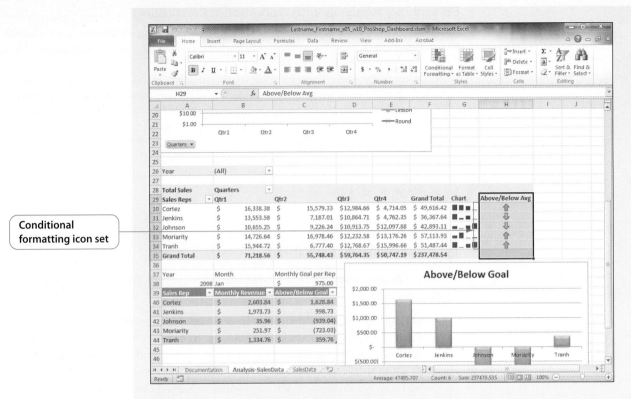

Conditional formatting icon set

Figure 9 Conditional formatting icon sets added

n. **Save** 🖫 the workbook.

All of the data, charts, and PivotTables on the Analysis-SalesData worksheet can give some insight into the Red Bluff Golf Course Pro Shop sales data from 2008 to 2010. Each can be filtered on various fields to view the data from multiple perspectives. However, placing charts and PivotTables with some sparklines and conditional formatting on a worksheet does not constitute a dashboard.

Creating the Presentation Layer

It is important to maintain separation between the analysis and presentation layers when creating a dashboard. The analysis layer in the e05_ws10_ProShop_Dashboard workbook now contains several different views of the overall sales data for the Pro Shop.

To effectively utilize the space on the dashboard it is helpful to plan the layout on paper first by creating a wireframe, similar to what designers do when creating web pages. Figure 10 shows an example of how each area of the dashboard can help answer a specific question about the pro shop's sales.

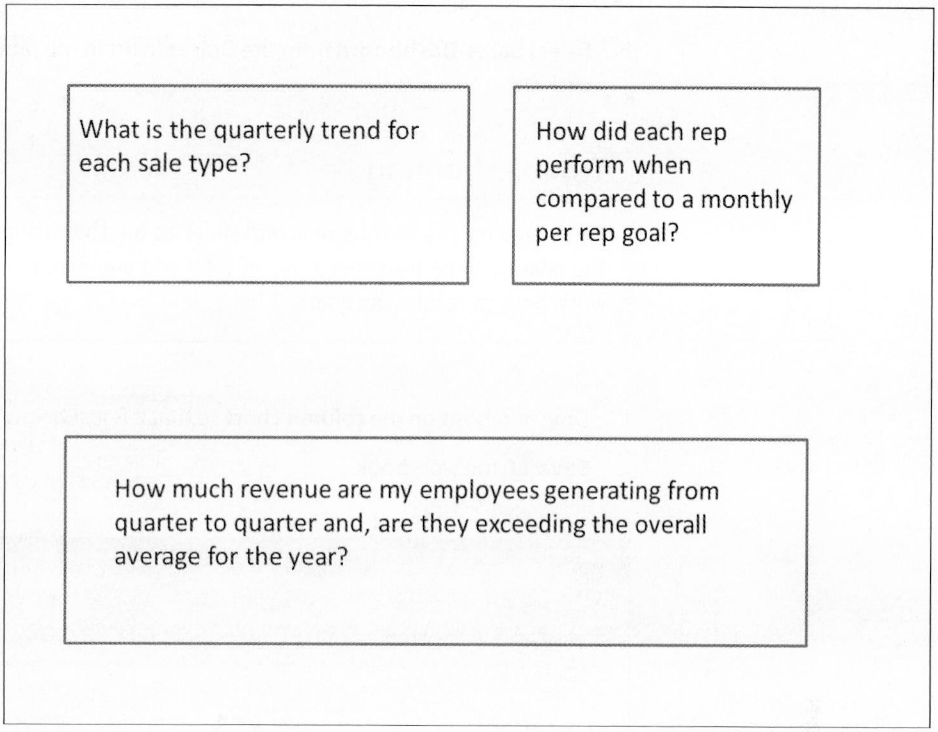

What is the quarterly trend for each sale type?	How did each rep perform when compared to a monthly per rep goal?

How much revenue are my employees generating from quarter to quarter and, are they exceeding the overall average for the year?

Figure 10 Dashboard layout wireframe

Creating the Dashboard

Now that the analysis layer has been completed, it is time to begin work on putting the dashboard together. In this exercise you will begin by transferring some of the objects from the analysis layer to a new worksheet.

To Create the Dashboard

a. Click the **Insert Worksheet** button 📋 located to the right of the SalesData worksheet. Right-click the **Sheet2 worksheet tab**, and then click **Rename**. Type Sales-Dashboard as the name, and then press Enter. Drag the **Sales-Dashboard** worksheet to the left of the **Analysis-Sales worksheet**.

b. Click the **Analysis-SalesData worksheet tab**, and then select the line chart. Click the **PivotChart Tools Design tab**, and then click **Move Chart** in the Location group.

c. Select **Sales-Dashboard** from the Object in list in the Move Chart dialog box, and then click **OK**.

d. Drag to reposition the line chart so that it is in the top-left corner of the worksheet. The width of the chart should span across columns **A:H**. Resize the chart by using the bottom right sizing handle. Be sure to keep the chart in row 15.

e. Click the **Analysis–SalesData worksheet tab**, select cells **A37:C44**, and press Ctrl+X to cut the contents of the cells to the clipboard. Click the **Sales-Dashboard worksheet tab**, click cell **I1**, and then press Ctrl+V to paste the contents from the clipboard.

f. Double-click between each of the column headings **I:K** to adjust the width of the data table columns to ensure all values are visible.

g. Click the **Analysis-SalesData worksheet tab**, and then select the **column chart**. Click the **Chart Tools Design tab**, and then then click **Move Chart** in the Location group.

h. Select **Sales-Dashboard** from the Object in list in the Move Chart dialog box, and then click **OK**.

Troubleshooting

When moving charts from one worksheet to another using the Move Chart command, the chart may be positioned out of view and you may need to scroll down the worksheet to locate the chart.

i. Drag to reposition the **column chart** so that it is just below the MonthlySalesByRep table.

j. **Save** 🖫 the workbook.

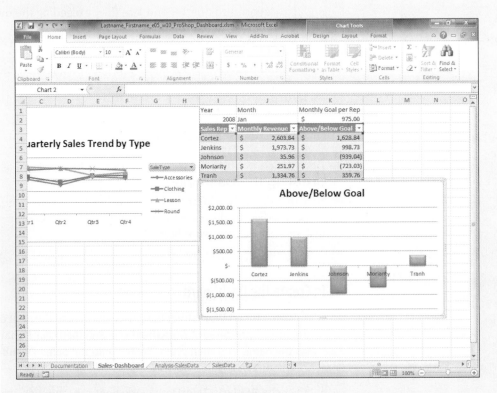

Figure 11 Partial dashboard placement

Using the Camera Tool

To make the dashboard user friendly, it is best to not have PivotTables directly accessed in the presentation layer. The **Camera tool** in Excel can be used to take a live image of a range of cells and display it in the dashboard. In this exercise you will add the Camera tool to the Quick Access Toolbar and use it to create a live image of the QuarterSalesByRep PivotTable, sparklines, and conditional formatting to place on the dashboard.

To Use the Camera Tool

a. Right-click the **Quick Access Toolbar**, and then in the right-click menu, click **Customize Quick Access Toolbar**.

b. In the Excel Options dialog box, click the **Choose Commands from arrow**, and then select **Commands Not in the Ribbon**.

c. Select **Camera** from the list of commands, click **Add**, and then click **OK**.

Commands Not in the Ribbon

Camera tool

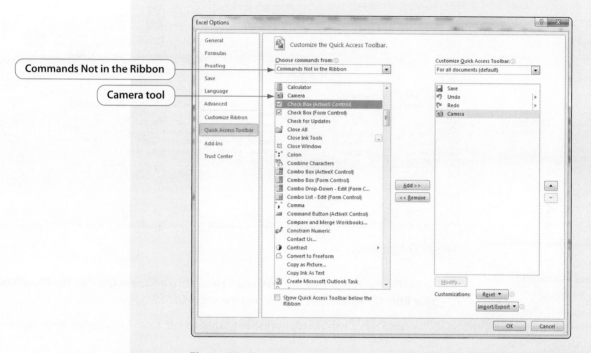

Figure 12 Customize the Quick Access Toolbar in the Excel Options dialog box

d. Click the **Analysis-SalesData worksheet tab**, select the range **A28:H35**, and then click the **Camera tool** in the Quick Access Toolbar.

Troubleshooting

Camera images can become distorted if the size is changed. Before taking an image with the Camera tool, make sure the range of cells that is selected is displaying all the data you want displayed by adjusting the columns and rows.

e. Click the **Sales-Dashboard worksheet tab**, and then click cell **A24** to paste the image.

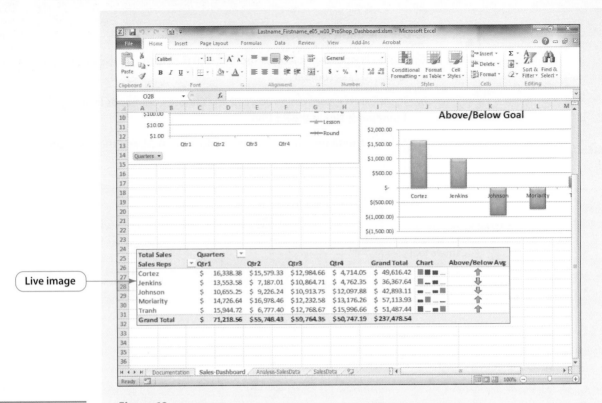

Figure 13 Live image

f. To test the live image, click the **Analysis-SalesData worksheet tab**, click the **PivotTable Year filter** in cell B26, select **2009**, and then click **OK**.

g. Click the **Sales-Dashboard worksheet tab**, and notice the image has been updated automatically.

h. **Save** the workbook.

Enhancing Dashboards with Slicers

The current mixture of charts and PivotTables in the dashboard is lacking an easy and efficient way to filter all of the components to view, such as by individual years. Slicers, a new feature in Excel 2010, can enhance a dashboard and create a more user-friendly experience. **Slicers** are visual controls that allow you to quickly and easily filter your data in an interactive way. They can be used to replace the filter icons in the PivotCharts. However, slicers are not compatible with earlier versions of Excel. In this exercise you will create slicers and begin to alter the overall look and function of the dashboard.

To Create Slicers

a. On the **Analysis-SalesData worksheet tab**, select the **SaleTypeTrendByQuarter** PivotTable, click the **Insert tab**, and then click **Slicer** in the Filter Group.

b. Check **SaleType** and **Year** in the Insert Slicers dialog box, and then click **OK**. Notice the two slicer menus each containing individual filters that can be used to filter the SaleTypeTrendByQuarter PivotTable.

c. Test the slicers by clicking on the various filters, and observe the changes being made to the SalesTypeTrendByQuarter PivotTable. Click **Clear Filter** on each of the slicers to remove all filters.

d. Select the **QuarterSalesByRep** PivotTable. Click the **PivotTable Tools Options tab**, click the **Insert Slicer button arrow** in the Sort & Filter group, and then click **Slicer Connections**. In the Slicer Connections dialog box, check the **Year** and **SaleType** check boxes, and then click **OK**.

e. Press and hold Ctrl, and then click each of the slicers.

f. Press Ctrl+X to cut the slicers from the worksheet.

g. Click the **Sales-Dashboard worksheet tab**, click cell **A16**, and press Ctrl+V to paste the slicers.

h. Click any cell in the worksheet to unselect the slicers.

i. Right-click the **SaleType slicer**, and then click **Size and Properties**. Click **Position and Layout** on the left side of the Size and Properties dialog box. In the Layout area, change Number of columns to **2**, and then click **Close**.

j. If necessary, drag the edges of the **SaleType slicer** to adjust the width and height so that all four sale types are visible.

k. Right-click the **Year slicer**, and then click **Size and Properties**. Click **Position and Layout** on the left side of the Size and Properties dialog box. In the Layout area, change Number of columns to **3**, and then click **Close**.

l. Drag the edges of the **Year slicer** to adjust the width and height so that only years 2008-2010 are visible across the top row.

m. Reposition the slicers so that they are in the space between the Quarterly Sales Trend by Type line chart and the image of the QuarterSalesByRep PivotTable.

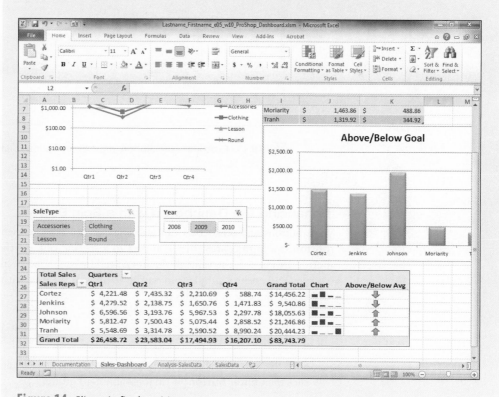

Figure 14 Slicers in final position

n. Click the **Quarterly Sales Trend by Type line chart** and click **PivotChart Tools Analyze tab** and click **Field Buttons** in the Show/Hide group to hide them.

o. **Save** the workbook.

Enhancing the Dashboard with Form Controls

Adding form controls like spin buttons and scroll bars to a dashboard can increase its interactivity and enrich the user's experience. To access the form controls available in Excel you must first add the Developer tab to the Ribbon.

To Add the Developer Tab

a. If you do not already have access to the Developer tab in the Ribbon, click the **File tab**, and then click **Options**.

b. In the Excel Options dialog box, click **Customize Ribbon** in the left pane.

c. Click the check box next to **Developer** in the Main tabs list, and then click **OK**.

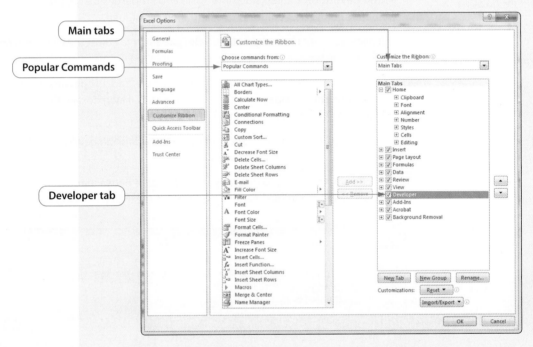

Figure 15 Customize the Ribbon in the Excel Options dialog box

Enhancing the Dashboard with a Spin Button

Spin buttons and scroll bars can also enhance a user's experience with a dashboard. A **spin button** is a form control that is linked to a specific cell. As the up and down arrows on the button are clicked, the value in the linked cell increases and decreases accordingly. In this exercise you will create a simple spin button to provide the user with an easy way of increasing and decreasing the year of the sales data.

To Create Spin Buttons

a. Click the **Sales-Dashboard worksheet tab**, click cell **I2**, click the **Home tab**, and then click the **Center button** in the Alignment group.

b. Right-click the **row header** for row 2, in the right-click menu click **Row Height**, in the Row Height dialog box, type **27**, and then click **OK**.

c. Click the **Developer tab**, click **Insert** in the Controls group, and then click the **Spin Button (Form Control)** .

d. Drag a vertical rectangle in cell **I2** to the right of the centered year value.

e. Right-click the **spin button**, and then in the right-click menu click **Format Control**.

f. In the Format Control dialog box, on the Control tab type 2008 for the Current value and for the Minimum value.

g. Type 2010 for the **Maximum value** and ensure 1 is selected for the **Incremental change**.

h. Click the **Cell link** box, click cell **I2**, and then click **OK**.

i. Click cell **I2** to deselect the spin button, and then test the added functionality of the spin button by clicking the up and down arrows to increase and decrease the year and observe the changes in the chart.

j. **Save** 🖫 the workbook.

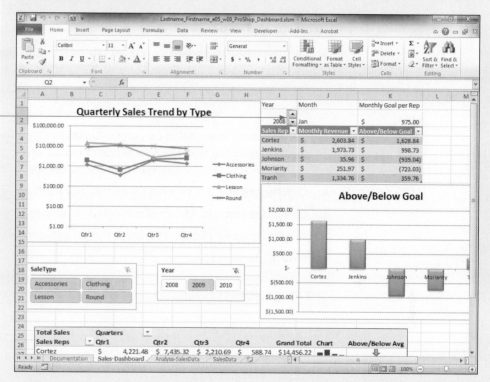

Figure 16 Spin button for year

Creating a Lookup Table to Use with Form Controls

Creating a lookup table and using the VLOOKUP function in Excel is a common approach to linking values to form controls. In this exercise you will create a lookup table for the months to use with a scroll bar control.

To Create a Lookup Table of Months

a. Click the **Analysis-SalesData worksheet tab**, and then click cell **J1**. Type the values 1 through 12 down column J.

b. Click cell **K1**, and then type the months Jan through Dec down column K next to the numbers.

c. Select the range **J1:K12**, type Month_Range in the **Name box**, and then press Enter to name the range.

d. Click the **Sales-Dashboard worksheet tab**, click cell **L1**, and then type the number 1.

e. Click cell **J2**, and then type the following VLOOKUP function to retrieve the month abbreviation from the Month_Range named range based on the number entered in cell L1: =VLOOKUP(L1,Month_Range,2,FALSE). Press Enter.

f. **Save** the workbook.

Enhancing the Dashboard with a Scroll Bar

A **scroll bar** has a very similar function as the spin button. However, with a scroll bar, the value of the linked cell is increased or decreased by sliding the scroll bar to the left or right. In this exercise you will create a scroll bar so that the user can easily scroll through different months.

To Create a Scroll Bar

a. Click the **Sales-Dashboard worksheet tab**, click the **Developer tab**, click **Insert**, and then click the **Scroll Bar (Form Control)**.

b. Drag a horizontal rectangle inside cell **J2** to the right of the month displayed.

c. Right-click the **scroll bar**, and then in the right-click menu click **Format Control**.

d. In the Format Control dialog box, on the Control tab type 1 for the Current value and for the Minimum value, type 12 for the **Maximum value**, ensure **1** is selected for **Incremental change**, and then ensure **10** is selected for **Pace change**.

e. Click the **Cell link** box, click cell **L1**, and then click **OK**.

f. Change the font color of the value in cell **L1** to white so that it is not visible in the model.

g. Test the added functionality by sliding the bar back and forth.

h. **Save** the workbook.

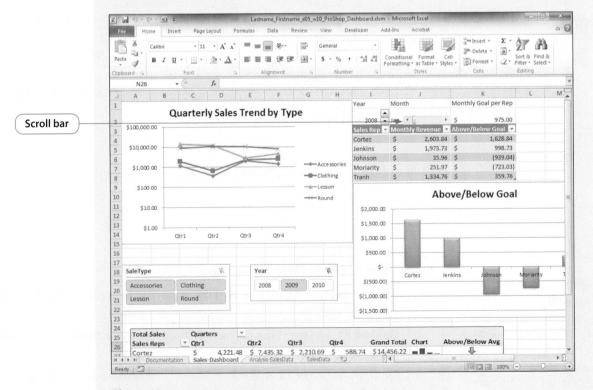

Figure 17 Scroll bar for month

Creating Dynamic Labels

Labels are critical to dashboard design and can add clarity to the graphics being displayed. Dynamic labels can add additional clarity in PivotCharts by displaying the year and/or month that is being displayed when filtered.

To Create Dynamic Chart Labels

a. On the Sales-Dashboard worksheet tab, select the **line chart**, click the **Insert tab**, and then click **Text Box** 🔲 in the Text group.

b. Drag to create a text box in the top-right corner of the line chart.

c. Click in the **formula bar**, type =, and then click the **Analysis-SalesData worksheet tab**. Click cell **B1**, and then press Enter.

d. Click the **Home tab**. Using the skills you have developed in previous workshops, change the font size to **16** and apply a bold style to the text in the text box. Click the **Drawing Tools Format tab**, click the **Shape Outline button arrow** in the Shape Styles group, and then click **No Outline**. Adjust the size of the text box by dragging the edges, if necessary, to be able to display the value.

e. Test this new label by clicking different years in the Year slicer.

f. Click the **column chart** on the Sales-Dashboard worksheet tab. Click the **Insert tab**, and then click **Text Box** in the Text group. Drag to create a text box in the top-left corner of the chart.

g. Click in the **formula bar**, type =, and then click cell **I2**. Press Enter.

h. Click the **Home tab**. Using the skills you have practiced, change the font size to **16** and apply a bold style. Click the **Drawing Tools Format tab**, click the **Shape Outline button arrow** in the Shape Styles group, and then click **No Outline**. Adjust the size of the text box by dragging the edges, if necessary, to be able to display the value.

i. Click the **Insert tab**, and then click **Text Box** in the Text group. Drag to create a text box in the top-right corner of the chart. Click in the **formula bar**, type =, click cell **J2**, and then press Enter.

j. Using the skills you have practiced, change the font size to **16** and apply bold as the font style. Click the **Drawing Tools Format tab**, click the **Shape Outline button arrow** in the Shape Styles group, and then click **No Outline**. Adjust the size of the text box by dragging the edges, if necessary, to be able to display the value.

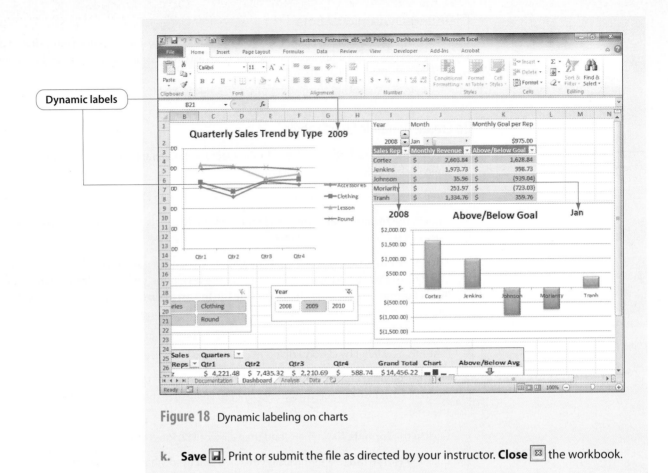

Dynamic labels

Figure 18 Dynamic labeling on charts

k. **Save** 🖫. Print or submit the file as directed by your instructor. **Close** ⊠ the workbook.

Leveraging the Power of Visual Basic for Applications (VBA) in Excel

VBA (Visual Basic for Applications) is a powerful programming language that is part of most of the Microsoft Office applications—Word, Access, Excel, and PowerPoint. VBA can allow for a wide variety of enhancements to any of these Microsoft Office applications. It is particularly valuable in automating repetitive tasks similar to macros, but it also provides additional tools that can enhance functionality and usability of an Excel application. VBA is considered a very basic form of object-oriented programming. **Object-oriented programming (OOP)** uses a hierarchy of objects—also called classes—as the focus of the programming. VBA manipulates objects by using the methods and properties associated with them. In this section you will learn about using Visual Basic for Applications (VBA) and create additional functionality in a dashboard.

Understanding the Components of VBA

The key to effectively using VBA to enhance your dashboard or other Excel applications is to understand Excel's object model. An **object model** consists of a hierarchical collection of objects that can be manipulated using VBA. Excel is made up of several dozen objects. **Objects** are combinations of data and code that are treated as a single unit including workbooks, worksheets, charts, PivotTables—and even Excel itself is an object. Objects can also serve as containers for other objects. For example, Excel is an object called an application. This application object contains workbook objects, workbook objects contain worksheet objects, and worksheet objects contain cell range objects. Figure 20 shows a partial object model for Excel.

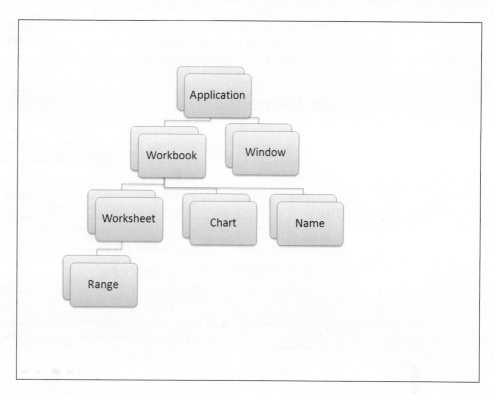

Figure 19 Partial Excel object model

Objects are often grouped together into what are called **object collections**, which are also objects. For example a worksheet is an object in a workbook, and all worksheets in a workbook are also an object. A particular object can be referenced inside a collection by referring to the object collection and then the name or number that represents that specific member of that collection. For example Sheets("Sheet2") is a reference to a worksheet with the name Sheet2 that is a member of the Sheets object collection. Figure 20 shows some common object collections and their descriptions.

Quick Reference — Object Collections

Object Collection	Description
Workbooks("Book1")	Refers to a workbook named Book1.xlsx
Sheets("Sheet1")	Refers to a worksheet named Sheet1
Range("A2:C23")	Refers to a collection of cells A2:C23
Charts(2)	Refers to the second chart in a workbook
ChartObjects(3)	Refers to the third embedded chart in a worksheet
Windows(3)	Refers to the third open Excel workbook window

Figure 20 Common object collections

To refer to a particular object using VBA, the objects needs to be referred to in their hierarchical structure. For example, to refer to cell A1 in a specific worksheet, the following code would be necessary:

Application.Workbook(workbookname.xlsx).Sheets("sheet1").Range("A1")

The periods in between each object are referred to as separators. **Separators** indicate the distinction between the object container and the member of that container. Having to type the entire hierarchy each time a particular object is used can be really tedious. Because of this,

VBA provides special object names that can be used to refer to specific objects. For example, ActiveCell refers to the specific cell that is currently selected in the workbook. Figure 21 contains a list of some of the most frequently used special object names.

Quick Reference — VBA Special Object Names

Property	Description
ActiveCell	The active cell
ActiveChart	The active chart sheet or chart contained in a ChartObject on a worksheet. This property is Nothing if a chart is not active.
ActiveSheet	The active sheet (worksheet or chart)
ActiveWindow	The active window
ActiveWorkbook	The active workbook
Selection	The object selected. It could be a Range object, Shape, ChartObject, and so on.
ThisWorkbook	The workbook that contains the VBA procedure being executed. This object may or may not be the same as the ActiveWorkbook object.

Figure 21 Special object names

Every Excel object has properties. **Properties** are attributes of an object that can be referred to or manipulated using VBA. For example, the cell range object has properties such as value and address. Figure 22 lists some common properties.

Quick Reference — Properties of Common Objects

Object	Properties	Description
Workbooks	Name	The name of the workbook
	Path	The directory in which the workbook resides
	Saved	Whether or not the workbook has been saved
	HasPassword	Whether or not the workbook has a password
Worksheets	Name	The name of the worksheet
	Visible	Whether or not the worksheet is visible
Range	Address	The cell reference of the range
	Comment	A comment attached to the cell
	Formula	The formula entered in the cell
	Value	The value entered in the cell
Chart	ChartTitle	The text of the chart's title
	ChartType	The type of chart e.g., bar, column, line
	HasLegend	Whether or not the chart has a legend

Figure 22 Properties of common objects

An object's properties can be easily modified with a simple expression: *Object.Property = expression*. For example, to rename a worksheet that is currently selected using VBA you would type the following expression: *ActiveSheet.Name = "NewSheetName"*.

Excel objects also have methods. A **method** is an action Excel performs with an object. For example, one of the methods for a Range object is ClearContents. When this method is called, values would be cleared from the range. The basic syntax required to call an object's method is:

ObjectName.Method

For example, to clear the values in the cell range A1:A5 you would type Range("A1:A5").ClearContents.

Figure 23 lists some common methods and their descriptions.

Quick Reference — Common Methods and Descriptions

Object	Methods	Descriptions
Workbook	Close	Closes the workbook
	Protect	Protects the workbook
	SaveAs	Saves the workbook with a specified file name
Worksheet	Delete	Deletes the worksheet
	Select	Selects and displays the worksheet
Range	Clear	Clears all content in the range
	Copy	Copies the vales in the range to the clipboard
	Merge	Merges the cells in the range
Chart	Copy	Copies the chart to the clipboard
	Select	Selects the chart
	Delete	Deletes the chart
Worksheets	Select	Selects all the worksheets in the workbook
Charts	Select	Selects all chart sheets in the workbook

Figure 23 Common methods and descriptions

Methods often have parameters that must be included to use the method on the object. A **parameter** is a special kind of variable used to refer to one of the pieces of data provided in a method. For example, the Workbook object has a SaveAs method that requires the file name as a parameter. Most methods contain required an optional parameters. The basic syntax for providing parameters in a method is:

object.method parameter1: = value, parameter2:= value2.

For example

ActiveWorkbook.SaveAs Filename:="NewWorkbookName", FileFormat:=52 saves the active workbook as NewWorkbookName.xlsm. Figure 24 shows some common FileFormat values.

Quick Reference — Common FileFormat Values

FileFormat Value	File Extension
51	.xlsx
52	.xlsm
6	.csv
-4158	.txt

Figure 24 Common FileFormat values

The Visual Basic Editor

The **Visual Basic Editor (VBE)** is the tool built into Microsoft Office that is used for creating and editing VBA. At the top of the VBE screen is the title of the workbook that is currently open and being edited. Directly under the application title are the File menu and Standard toolbars, which are visible by default. On the left side of the Visual Basic Editor is the Project Explorer. The **Project Explorer window** contains a hierarchical list of all the objects in the workbook, including macros, modules, and worksheets. VBA in an Excel workbook can be contained either in a specific worksheet, the specific workbook, or within a module. Below the Project Explorer window is the Properties window. The **Properties window** contains a list of all the properties of a selected object such as name, size, and color. Depending on your system settings, the Property window may not be displayed by default when the VBE is opened. The larger window on the right of the Visual Basic Editor is the Code window. The **Code window** is where all the VBA code is typed and also where VBA generated by a recorded macro can be viewed and edited.

SIDE NOTE

Display the VBE

Alternatively, you can press Alt+F11 to access the VBE. This key combination works as a toggle between the workbook and editor environments.

SIDE NOTE

Show/Hide VBE Windows

The Project Explorer and Properties windows can be shown or hidden by clicking View on the menu bar, or they can be viewed by pressing Ctrl+R or F4.

To Open the Visual Basic Editor

a. Open the **Lastname_Firstname_e05_ws10_ProShop_Dashboard** workbook.

b. Click the **Developer tab**, and then click **Visual Basic** in the Code group.

c. Click **Insert**, and then click **Module**.

d. Press F4 to display the Properties window for Module 1 if it is not already displayed.

e. Click the **Name** property, rename Module 1 with Firstname_Lastname_Module1, replacing Firstname and Lastname with your own first and last name, and then press Enter.

f. Examine the various components that make up the VBE.

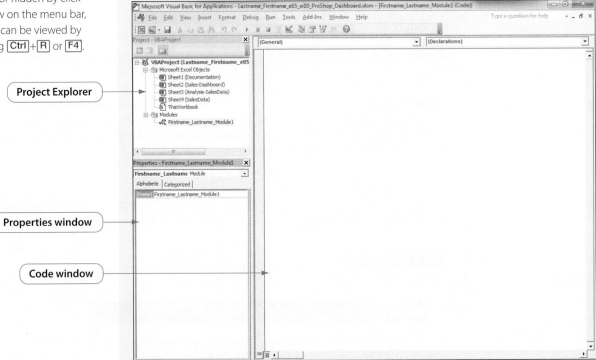

Project Explorer

Properties window

Code window

Figure 25 Visual Basic Editor windows

A **module** is simply a container for code. You can have zero or hundreds of Sub procedures and functions written within a single module. Modules are just for organization, and for the most part, you should not have to deal with them that much. Just know that when you are writing VBA code, you are doing so in a module that is contained in your workbook.

The two primary types of procedures that are supported by VBA are Sub procedures and function procedures. A **Sub procedure** performs an action on your project or workbook, such as renaming a worksheet or clearing filtered values from PivotTables. A **function procedure** is a group of VBA statements that performs a calculation and returns a single value. Function procedures are often used to create custom functions that can be entered in worksheet cells.

CONSIDER THIS | **Public vs. Private Sub Procedures**

There are both public and private Sub procedures. By default, Excel makes all Sub procedures public, which means they are available to be accessed in the Macro window. If the Sub procedure is created as private, then the code is only viewable inside the editor window. What are the advantages and disadvantages of creating public and private Sub procedures?

Renaming Worksheets Using VBA

Pro shop managers are already talking about all the benefits they expect to get from this sales dashboard, and other areas of the resort are expected to request dashboards of their own once this one is officially in production. In this exercise, you will create a subroutine to rename the worksheets in the workbook. This simple routine can be useful to developers who will be creating the other dashboards.

To Rename Worksheets Using VBA

a. Click the **Code window**, type the following line: Private Sub renameWorksheets (), and then press Enter.

   The word "Sub" is required and states that a Sub procedure is being created. The name of the Sub procedure is next followed by a pair of empty parenthesis. If this function required parameters, then the logic would be contained within the parenthesis.

b. Enter the following text above the End Sub command: 'Created by Firstname Lastname. This code will rename the worksheets in this workbook. Replace Firstname and Lastname with your own first and last name.

   The apostrophe is required to create a comment in the code. Comments are an excellent way to document and provide clarification of what the VBA code is to accomplish.

c. Press Enter, and then notice that the VBA editor turns the previous line of code a green color to indicate that it is a comment.

d. Type the following line of code to refer to a specific sheet inside the object collection Sheets, refer to its name property, and assign it a new name value: Sheets("Sales-Dashboard").Name = "Dashboard". Press Enter.

e. Type the following code to rename the Analysis-SalesData worksheet tab to Analysis: Sheets("Analysis-SalesData").Name = "Analysis". Press Enter.

f. Type the following code to rename the SalesData worksheet tab to Data: Sheets("SalesData").Name = "Data". Press Enter.

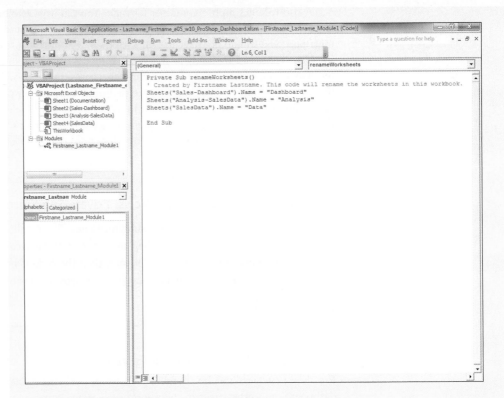

Figure 26 Rename Worksheets sub procedure

SIDE NOTE
Displaying the Project Explorer Window

If the Project Explorer window is no longer visible, press Ctrl+R to view it.

g. **Save** 💾 the code and workbook, and then press F5 to run the renameWorksheets Sub procedure. Notice the new worksheet names in the Project Explorer window.

Real World Advice   Using the Macro Recorder to Learn VBA

An easy way to gain a better understanding of how VBA works is to use the Macro Recorder to generate VBA code for an action you want to complete. See Workshop 8 for information about recording macros. The code generated can be useful in identifying the key elements of the language and how the objects, properties, and methods work together to accomplish specific tasks.

Improving Readability of VBA with Formatting and Structure

An important aspect of writing VBA is making sure the code is easy to read so that you and others can interpret what is happening. This means using indentation, comments, and line breaks often. This is especially true when working with more complex code.

You need to take extra steps to keep the code legible and to document what steps you are taking and why. This will make it easier on you and others who may need to edit, analyze, or troubleshoot the code. One of these extra steps will be using the tab key to create indentations in the code.

Commenting code in VBA is an excellent way of explaining the purpose and the intention of a procedure. This way, you can add straightforward documentation as to what the procedure is doing and what steps to take next. If you are developing more complicated procedures you might want to leave yourself notes about what still needs to be completed or what statements are not working as expected. Adding comments in the Code window is as simple as typing an apostrophe. The (') symbol tells the VBE to ignore any text following the apostrophe on a line of the code.

Also, the VBE interprets code on a line-by-line basis, which means that if you type part of a statement on a line and press Enter before the end of the statement, it will create a syntax error. This means that lengthy statements become difficult to read, because without pressing Enter, they will extend continuously to the right. To break a line of code across two lines, a space followed by an underscore character can be used. This tells the VBE that the two lines of code should be treated as one.

Enhancing Functionality and Usability with VBA

VBA procedures can be used to enhance a dashboard by providing an easy way to clear filters, prompt users for values, and display informative message boxes. All of these can enhance the user experience and transform an Excel spreadsheet into a truly interactive dashboard.

Using VBA to Clear Filters

The dashboard worksheet contains two slicers used for filtering on year and sale type. You have been asked to write VBA code that will clear the filters from both of the slicers. You will be calling the clearManualFilter method for the SlicerCache object for the ActiveWorkbook.

To Clear Slicer Filters with VBA

a. In the VBE, click the line below the **End Sub** command of the renameWorksheets Sub procedure.

b. Create a new Sub procedure by typing Sub clearSlicers(), and then press Enter.

c. Type the following comment 'Created by Firstname Lastname. This code will clear the filters on the slicers on the dashboard. Replace Firstname and Lastname with your own first and last name. Press Enter.

d. Type ActiveWorkbook.SlicerCaches("Slicer_SaleType").ClearManualFilter, and then press Enter. This line of code will clear the filter from the SaleType slicer.

e. Type ActiveWorkbook.SlicerCaches("Slicer_Year").ClearManualFilter, and then press Enter. This line of code will clear the filter from the Year slicer.

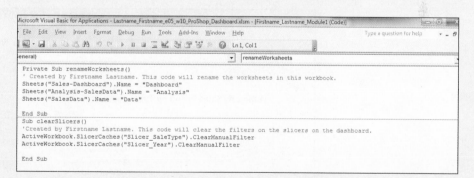

Figure 27 Clear Slicers sub procedure

f. **Save** 💾 the VBA and the workbook.

Real World Advice — Even Simple VBA Code Can Add Value

Many Excel users are hesitant to enter into the VBA realm. However, as the above Sub procedure illustrates, even a couple of lines of VBA code can enhance the user experience and improve the overall functionality of a dashboard.

Providing End Users with an Easy Way to Run VBA Code

The clearSlicers subroutine is not very useful without giving the end user a way of running the code from the dashboard. Sub procedures can be added to command buttons for easy access.

To Add a Sub Procedure to a Button Control

a.   Press ⎇Alt+F11 to go back to the Workbook view.

b.   Click the **Dashboard worksheet tab**, click the **Developer tab**, and then click **Insert** ▦ in the Controls group.

c.   Click the **Button (Form Control)** ▭ .

d.   Drag to create a rectangular button above the Year Slicer stretching across columns G and H.

e.   In the Macro name area, select **clearSlicers** in the Assign Macro dialog box, and then click **OK**.

f.   Click the **button**, and then rename it to read Clear Filters. Resize the button if necessary so that all the text is visible.

g.   Right-click the **Year slicer**, and then in the right-click menu click **Slicer Settings**. In the Slicer Settings dialog box, in the header area, clear the check box next to Display header to hide the header, and then click **OK**.

h.   Resize the **Year slicer** so that only the 2008-2010 years are visible in the top row of the slicer.

i.   Right-click the **SaleType slicer**, and then in the right-click menu click **Slicer Settings**. In the Slicer Settings dialog box, in the header area, clear the check box next to Display header to hide the header, and then click **OK**.

j.   Resize the **SaleType slicer** by dragging the edges so that all sale types are visible and there is no scroll bar on the right side of the slicer.

k.   Test the clearSlicers macro by selecting a year and sale type from the slicers, and then click **Clear Filters**.

l.   **Save** 🖫 the workbook.

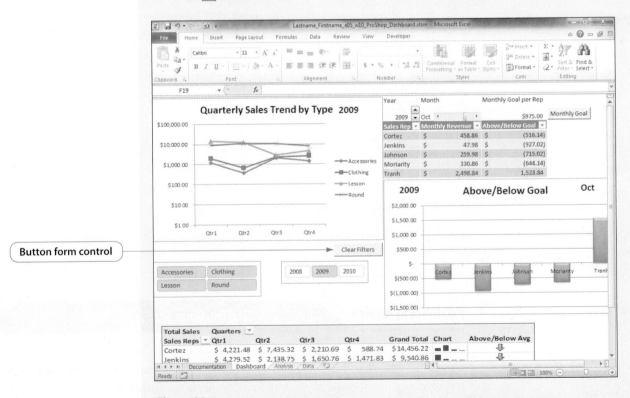

Figure 28   Clear Filters macro button

Dimensioning a Variable

VBA can also enhance a dashboard by prompting a user for input, storing that value in a variable, and then doing something with it. A **variable** is space in a computer's memory that is given a name and is used to store a value. To create a variable, the space needs to be allocated in the computer's memory. This is known as dimensioning a variable. VBA abbreviates this as Dim, and is a required command before a variable can be created. In this exercise, you will create a Sub procedure that is more complex than the last and will be broken up into several sections.

Quick Reference — Restrictions to Naming Variables:

1. Variable names must start with a letter and not a number.
2. Variable names cannot have more than 250 characters.
3. Variable names cannot be the same as any one of Excel's key words, for example a variable cannot be named "Sheet" or "Workbook".
4. Spaces are not allowed in variable names. You can separate words by either capitalizing the first letter of each word, or by using the underscore character.

SIDE NOTE
Comment/Uncomment Blocks

The VBE allows for large blocks of code to be commented out by using the comment block/uncomment block options. Click View on the menu bar, click Toolbars, and click Edit to access these options.

SIDE NOTE
Variables

Assigning a type to a variable is not necessarily required in VBA. If no type is specified the VBA will determine the type based on the value entered by the user.

To Dim a Variable

a. Press Alt+F11 to toggle back to the VBE.

b. Click inside the Code window just under the **End Sub** command of the clearSlicers Sub procedure, type Sub inputGoal (), and then press Enter.

c. Type the following comment text:
'Created by Firstname Lastname. This code will generate an input box that will prompt the user for a Total monthly goal, divide that value by 4, enter that value into cell K2 and then compare the total value to the sum of all reps and determine if the overall monthly goal was met. Replace Firstname and Lastname with your own first and last name, and then press Enter.

d. Break up the lengthy comment by pressing Enter where you need a line break and type ' at the beginning of each line. The comment block should resemble the way the comment is laid out in step c.

e. Type Dim mGoal As Currency, and then press Enter.

f. Type Dim repGoal As Currency, and then press Enter.

Creating an Input Box

An **input box** is an effective way of using VBA code to increase the interactivity of a dashboard by prompting the user for information and storing that information in a variable to be used later. In this exercise, you will create an input box prompting the use for a monthly sales revenue goal amount. That value will be stored in the mGoal variable and will be divided by four to calculate the goal for each of the four sales representatives. The calculated value will be stored in the repGoal variable and entered into cell K2 on the dashboard.

SIDE NOTE

Extracting Values from Cells

If the code in step c were written in reverse—repGoal=Range("K2").Value—then the repGoal variable would store the value that had been entered in cell K2.

a. Type mGoal = InputBox("Enter the monthly goal", "Monthly Goal"), and then press Enter.

    This line of code creates an input box object with a message text and title. The value entered will be stored in the mGoal variable as a currency.

b. Type repGoal = mGoal / 4, and then press Enter. This line divides the mGoal value by 4 and stores it in the repGoal variable.

c. Next type Range("K2").Value = repGoal, and then press Enter to assign the value stored in the repGoal variable to the cell K2.

CONSIDER THIS | **Planning for Future Growth**

As a business grows it will need additional sales representatives to meet demand. How would you account for five, six, or ten additional sales representatives? Could you dim another variable and prompt for the number of sales reps? Or, could you calculate in a cell the number of sales reps, then grab that value, store it in a variable, and use that value? What other ways could you account for a changing number of sales representatives?

Incorporating Conditional Statements

The most basic method of running VBA commands in response to a specific condition is the If statement. A VBA IF statement is very similar to the Excel IF function. The main difference is that with the Excel IF function you are limited to only one outcome if the condition is true and one outcome if the condition is false. With the VBA If-Then-Else control structure there is virtually no limit to the commands and logic that can be applied. The basic syntax of the If-Then-Else structure is:

    If Condition Then

        Command if condition is true

    Else

        Commands if condition is false

    End If

The condition portion of the structure is an expression that is resolved to either true or false. If it is true, then the first set of commands is run; otherwise, the second set of commands is run. In this next exercise you will create an If-Then-Else statement in which the condition is to check whether the sum of the total monthly sales is greater than or equal to the value entered in the input box. You will then create two different commands that will run based on the result of that condition. The commands will make use of message boxes. A **message box** is a dialog box object that is created using the MsgBox command. The message box is used to display an informative message to the user and includes buttons for the user to interact with. The MsgBox syntax is:

    MsgBox Prompt:="Message Text", Buttons, Title:="Title Text"

The only required argument is the Prompt argument. Due to the more complex nature, you will also be including comments and adding indentations to make the code easier to understand.

To Create an If-Then-Else Statement

a. Type the following comment on the next line in the inputGoal Sub procedure: 'Check if the sum of cells J4:J8 is greater than or equal to the value stored in the mGoal variable. Press [Enter] two times for better spacing.

b. Type If WorksheetFunction.Sum(Range("J4:J8")) >= mGoal Then, press [Enter] two times, and then press [Tab] to create an indentation.

c. Type the following comment that explains what happens if the outcome of the condition is true: 'Display a message box informing user that goal was met. Press [Enter] two times.

d. Type MsgBox Prompt:="The monthly goal was met", Title:="Congratulations!". Press [Enter] two times.

e. Type the following comment that explains what happens if the outcome of the condition is false: 'Display a message box that informs the user that the goal was not met for that month. Press [Enter] two times.

f. Type Else: MsgBox Prompt:="The monthly goal was not met", Title:="Goal Not Met". Press [Enter] two times, and then press [Backspace] to end the indentation.

g. Type End If, and then press [Enter].

```
End Sub
Sub inputGoal()
'Created by Firstname Lastname. This code will generate an input box that
'will prompt the user for a Total monthly goal, divide that value by 4,
'enter that value into cell K2 and then compare the total value to the sum
'of all reps and determine if the overall monthly goal was met.
Dim mGoal As Currency
Dim repGoal As Currency
mGoal = InputBox("Enter the monthly goal", "Monthly Goal")
repGoal = mGoal / 4
Range("K2").Value = repGoal
'Check if the sum of cells J4:J8 is greater than or equal to the value stored in the mGoal variable.

If WorksheetFunction.Sum(Range("J4:J8")) >= mGoal Then

    'Display a message box informing user that the goal was met.

    MsgBox Prmpt:="The monthly goal was met", Title:="Congratulations!"

    'Display a message box that informs the user that the goal was not met for that month.

    Else: MsgBox Prompt:="The monthly goal was not met", Title:="Goal Not Met"

End If

End Sub
```

Figure 29 Completed Input Goal sub procedure

h. **Save** the VBA and workbook, and then test the VBA code. Press [Alt]+[F11] to switch back to the spreadsheet, and then use the spin buttons so that 2009 is the year in cell I2. Use the scroll bar to view the month of Feb.

i. Press [Alt]+[F11] again to switch back to the VBE, and then click inside the inputGoal Sub procedure. Press [F5] to run the code. In the Monthly Goal dialog box, type 10000, and then click **OK**.

j. When the Goal Not Met dialog box appears, click **OK**. Press [Alt]+[F11] to switch back to the spreadsheet. Notice that *2500* is now the value in cell K2, which is 10000/4.

k. Press [Alt]+[F11] to switch back to the VBE and run the code by pressing [F5]. In the Monthly Goal dialog box, type 5000, click **OK**. The Congratulations dialog box displays. Click **OK**.

l. **Save** the VBA code.

m. Assign the inputGoal Sub procedure to a button on the dashboard.

- Press ⎡Alt⎤+⎡F11⎤ to switch back to the spreadsheet, click the **Developer tab**, click **Insert** in the Controls group, and then click the **Button (Form Control)** ▭.
- Drag a rectangle-shaped button inside cell L2. In the Macro name area, select the **inputGoal** macro in the Assign Macro dialog box, and then click **OK**.
- Right-click the **button**, and then in the right-click menu, click **Edit Text** to rename the text to Monthly Goal.
- If necessary, drag the bottom right sizing handle to the right so that all text is visible.

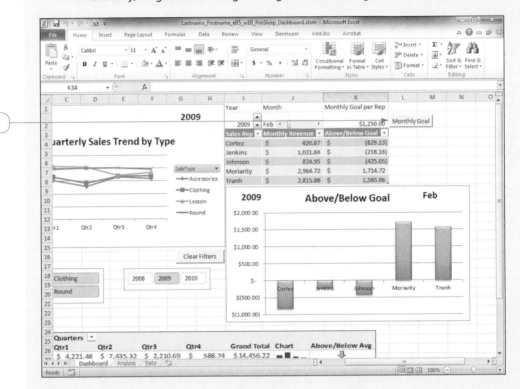

Button form control

Figure 30 Monthly Goal macro button

n. Test the VBA code again using the button and enter a monthly goal of your choosing.

o. **Save** 🖫 the workbook.

CONSIDER THIS | **A Dashboard Free from Errors**

The inputGoal Sub procedure is an excellent example of how VBA can increase the interactivity of a dashboard. However, if the user were to press Cancel when the input box prompts for a monthly goal value an error occurs. What is the cause of this error? What could be done in the code to prevent this from happening? What other kinds of errors might you want to check for when testing your code?

Troubleshooting VBA

You may have encountered some errors when attempting to write VBA code. Some of the errors may have been caused by pressing ⎡Enter⎤ to break up a line of code without inserting an underscore, or some other syntax error. With those types of errors, the VBA code cannot be executed until the problem is corrected. The other common VBA error is called run-time error. A **run-time error** occurs when the code is executed, displaying a description of the error. The VBE includes a tool called the debugger to help troubleshoot run-time errors. When using the debugger, the code is executed one line at a time to make it easier to identify the exact point that the run-time error occurs.

In this exercise, you will create a new module and enter a simple Sub procedure with a fairly obvious error in order to learn how to use the VBE debugger.

To Debug VBA

a. Press Alt + F11 to switch to the VBE. Click **Insert** in the menu, and then click **Module**.

b. In the Project Explorer Window, click **Module1**, and then press F4, if necessary, to display the Properties window. Click the **Name property**, delete the existing name, type Firstname_Lastname_Troubleshoot replacing Firstname and Lastname with your own first and last name. Press Enter.

c. Any spelling errors in this code are intentional for the purposes of this exercise. Please type this code exactly as follows:

Private Sub troubleShootingExample() Press Enter.

Sheets("Dashboard").Range("O1").Value = "Red Bluff" Press Enter.

Sheets("Dashboard").Range("P1").Valu = "Pro Shop" Press Enter.

d. Place your pointer at the top of the code to the left of **Private**, and then press F8 to enter debugging mode.

e. Notice the first line of code is highlighted in yellow. Press F8 again to execute that line of code. No warnings or errors are displayed, and the next line of code is now highlighted yellow.

f. Press F8 again to execute the second line of code. Again, no warnings or errors are displayed, and the next line of code is now highlighted yellow.

g. Press F8 again to execute the third line of code. A run-time error is displayed, indicating that the object does not support this property or method.

h. Click **Debug** in the Microsoft Visual Basic dialog box, and the third line of code is highlighted. Notice the line of code is trying to call the Valu property for the Range object, which is not a valid property name.

i. Correct the property name by adding an e to **Valu**, and then press F8 again to execute the line with the corrected property name. No warnings or errors are displayed and the last line of code is now highlighted yellow.

j. Press F5 to exit the debugger.

k. Save the VBA code, and then press Alt + F11 to switch back to the spreadsheet. Notice the text Red Bluff in cell O1 and **Pro Shop** in cell P1.

l. Select **O1:P1**, and then press Delete.

SIDE NOTE
VBA Debugging Mode
Alternately, to enter debugging mode, click Debug in the menu bar, and then click Step Into.

Troubleshooting

Other macros and VBA code cannot be executed while the debugger is still active. Press F5 or close the VBE completely and press OK when notified that "This command will stop the debugger" to enable the code.

Preparing a Dashboard for Production

Once a dashboard has been designed to meet the business requirements, there are several steps you need to take to get it ready for use. This process may include protecting various worksheets and cells from accidental mistakes, hiding various elements from the user that are not necessary for the dashboard, as well as making some simple design modifications to enhance the user experience.

Protecting Excel Worksheets

To prevent a user from intentionally or unintentionally modifying content in any of the layers of a dashboard, the entire workbook can be protected. Individual cells can be unprotected from a worksheet to allow for user input if desired.

SIDE NOTE

Linked Cells to Spinners and Scroll Bars

The value in cell L1 is linked to the scroll bar and needs to be unlocked so when the worksheet is protected it is allowed to change.

SIDE NOTE

Modifying Slicers on a Protected Sheet

Slicers are considered objects, and in order to use the feature on a protected sheet the Edit objects box must be checked.

To Protect a Worksheet

a. Right-click cell **I2**, and then in the right-click menu click **Format Cells**. In the Format Cells dialog box, click the **Protection tab**, clear the **Locked** check box, and then click **OK**.

b. Right-click cell **K2**, and then in the right-click menu click **Format Cells**. In the Format Cells dialog box, click the **Protection tab**, clear the **Locked** check box, and then click **OK**.

c. Right-click cell **L1**, and then in the right-click menu click **Format Cells**. In the Format Cells dialog box, click the **Protection tab**, clear the **Locked** check box, and then click **OK**.

d. Click the **Review tab**, and then click **Protect Sheet** in the Changes group.

e. In the Protect Sheet dialog box scroll down, click the **Edit objects** check box, and then click **OK**.

f. Test the protected worksheet by trying to delete columns and/or rows or trying to enter values in any cell that has not been unlocked.

g. **Save** the workbook.

Hiding Unnecessary Screen Elements

Many of the interactive elements of Microsoft Excel can be hidden from users. Normally controls such as the Ribbon and scroll bars are useful and necessary parts of working with Excel. However, when a dashboard is presented to a user, it is preferable to hide any unnecessary objects that may distract the user from the dashboard's intent.

To Hide Excel Screen Elements

a. Click the **File tab**, and then in the Excel Options dialog box, click **Options**.

b. Click **Advanced** in the left pane.

c. Scroll down to the Display options for this workbook section, and then clear the check box for **Show Sheet tabs**.

d. Scroll down to the Display options for this worksheet section. This section's controls apply only to the currently-selected worksheet. Make sure **Dashboard** is selected, and then clear the check boxes for the following options: **Show row** and **column headers** and **Show gridlines**. Click **OK**.

e. Right-click anywhere on the Ribbon, and then in the right-click menu, click **Minimize Ribbon** to maximize the amount of dashboard space.

f. **Save** the workbook.

Real World Advice | Dashboards and SharePoint

The information contained in dashboards often needs to be shared with many members of management across an organization. This can be easily done with a Microsoft SharePoint site. The dashboard can be published to a SharePoint site, and it can be viewed by anyone with access via a web browser. Not only does this mean that many people can view the information at the same time, but because it is being displayed in a web browser, there are no compatibility issues with earlier versions of Microsoft Excel. Further, if the external data source is a SharePoint list, the dashboard is automatically updated in real time.

Adding Additional Security to Protect the Dashboard

Although the other worksheets containing the data and analysis layers are hidden from the user, they can easily be made visible by anyone who knows where to go in the Excel Options menu. With access to these worksheets, someone could potentially alter the data. Adding a simple Sub procedure that alters the visible property of the worksheets ensures that the worksheets cannot be made visible via the options menu.

To Make Worksheets Very Hidden

a. Press Alt + F11 to switch to the VBE.

b. Double-click the **Firstname_Lastname_Module1** in the Project Explorer window, and then click the Code window just below the End Sub command of the inputGoal Sub procedure. Type **Private Sub hideSheets()**, and then press Enter.

c. Type the following comment: **'Created by Firstname Lastname. Specified worksheets cannot be made visible even if the Show Sheet tabs box is selected.** Replace Firstname and Lastname with your own first and last name. Press Enter.

d. Type **Sheets("Analysis").Visible = xlVeryHidden**, and then press Enter.

e. Type **Sheets("Data").Visible = xlVeryHidden**, and then press Enter.

```
    End Sub
    Private Sub hideSheets()
    'Created by Firstname Lastname. Specified worksheets cannot be made visible even if the Show Sheet tabs box is selected.
    Sheets("Analysis").Visible = xlVeryHidden
    Sheets("Data").Visible = xlVeryHidden

    End Sub
```

Figure 31 Hide Sheets sub procedure

f. Press F5 to run the code, and then **Save** the workbook.

g. Press Alt + F11 to switch back to the spreadsheet. Click the **File tab**, click **Options**, and then in the Excel Options dialog box, click **Advanced**. Scroll down to the Display options for this workbook section, check the **Show Sheet tabs** box, click **OK**, and then verify that the Data and Analysis worksheet tabs are still not visible.

h. Hide the sheet tabs again, and then **Save** the workbook.

SIDE NOTE
Making Hidden Worksheets Visible

The sheets can only be made visible by checking the Show sheet tabs box and by running another VBA procedure. Refer to the following example, if necessary: *Sheets("SheetName").Visible = TRUE.*

Password Protect VBA Code to Prevent Unauthorized Access

Management is concerned about unauthorized access to the VBA code and would like to require a password to be able to view the code. Password protecting the VBA code is a very simple process.

To Password Protect VBA Code

a. Press Alt + F11 to switch to the VBE.

b. Click **Tools** on the menu bar, and then click **VBAProject Properties**.

c. In the VBAProject - Project Properties dialog box, click the **Protection tab**, and then in the Lock project area, click the **Lock project for viewing** box.

d. Type password2011 in the Password and Confirm password boxes, and then click **OK**.

e. **Save** and **Close** the VBE and workbook.

f. Reopen the workbook, press Alt + F11 to switch to the VBE, and then double-click **VBAProject** in the Project Explorer. You will now be prompted for the password in order to view any of the VBA code.

g. In the VBProject Password dialog box, type password2011 as the password. Print or submit the workbook as directed by your instructor. **Close** the VBE and the workbook and exit Excel.

Concept Check

1. Define business intelligence, and explain the role that dashboards play in BI.

2. Explain why Microsoft Excel would be a good choice for dashboard creation.

3. Discuss some of the things to consider when building a dashboard.

4. Describe the Excel object model.

5. Discuss ways that VBA can be used to enhance a dashboard.

Key Terms

Analysis layer 508
Business intelligence (BI) 504
Camera tool 518
Code window 530
Data layer 508
Digital dashboards 504
Function procedure 531
Input box 535
Key performance indicator (KPI) 505
Message box 536
Method 529
Module 531

Object collections 527
Object model 526
Object-oriented programming (OOP) 526
Objects 526
Parameter 529
PivotChart 509
Presentation layer 508
Project Explorer window 530
Properties 528
Properties window 530
Run-time error 538

Scroll bar 524
Separators 527
Slicers 520
Sparklines 512
Spin button 522
Sub procedure 531
Variable 535
VBA (Visual Basic for Applications) 526
Visual Basic Editor (VBE) 530
White space 507

Visual Summary

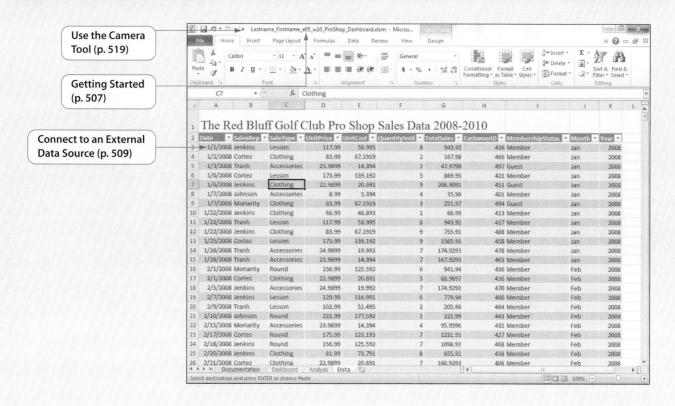

Use the Camera Tool (p. 519)

Getting Started (p. 507)

Connect to an External Data Source (p. 509)

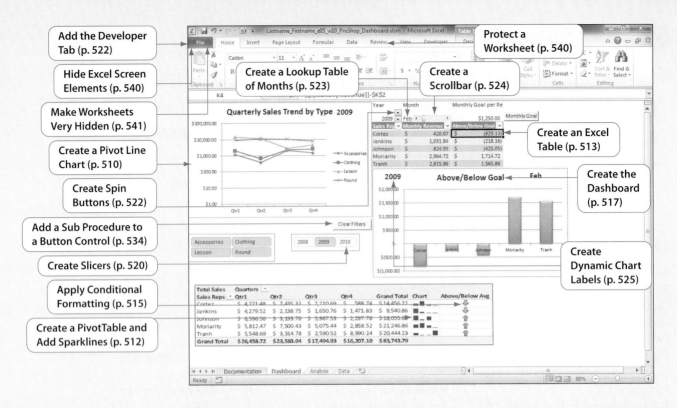

Add the Developer Tab (p. 522)

Hide Excel Screen Elements (p. 540)

Make Worksheets Very Hidden (p. 541)

Create a Pivot Line Chart (p. 510)

Create Spin Buttons (p. 522)

Add a Sub Procedure to a Button Control (p. 534)

Create Slicers (p. 520)

Apply Conditional Formatting (p. 515)

Create a PivotTable and Add Sparklines (p. 512)

Create a Lookup Table of Months (p. 523)

Create a Scrollbar (p. 524)

Protect a Worksheet (p. 540)

Create an Excel Table (p. 513)

Create the Dashboard (p. 517)

Create Dynamic Chart Labels (p. 525)

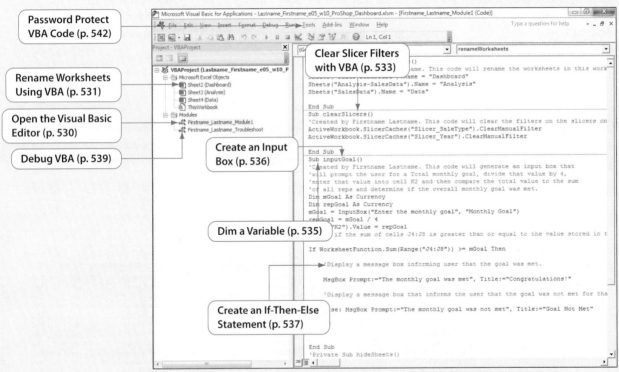

Password Protect VBA Code (p. 542)

Rename Worksheets Using VBA (p. 531)

Open the Visual Basic Editor (p. 530)

Debug VBA (p. 539)

Clear Slicer Filters with VBA (p. 533)

Create an Input Box (p. 536)

Dim a Variable (p. 535)

Create an If-Then-Else Statement (p. 537)

Figure 32 The Red Bluff Golf Club Pro Shop Digital Dashboard final spreadsheet and VBA code

Student data file needed:

e05_ws10_ProShop_Metrics

You will save your file as:

Lastname_Firstname_e05_ws10_ProShop_Metrics

Additional Pro Shop Metrics

Management at the Red Bluff Golf Course Pro Shop now understands the benefits that come from using dashboards to monitor the business. They would like another dashboard and have asked you to start the process with some analysis of their sales data. Management would like to know how much of the annual sales revenue is generated by the top ten customers each month, the percentage of total monthly revenue generated by members and nonmembers, as well as a way of visually representing the 12-month trend of each month's sales revenue in relation to that month's sales goal for each year.

a. Start **Excel**. Click the **File tab**, click **Open**, and then browse to your student data files. Locate and open **e05_ws10_ProShop_Metrics**.

b. Using the skills you have practiced, add a filename footer to the left section of the footer for all worksheets. Click the **File tab**, click **Save As**, and then rename the workbook Lastname_Firstname_e05_ws10_ProShop_Metrics.

c. Click the **Documentation worksheet tab** if it is not the active worksheet, click cell **A6**, and then press Ctrl+; to input the current date. Click cell **B6**, and type Firstname Lastname using your own first name and last name.

d. Click the **Data-Sales worksheet tab**. Select the range of cells **A2:K470**, click the **Formulas tab**, and then click **Create from Selection** in the Defined Names group. Clear the check box next to **Left column**, leave **Top row** selected, and then click **OK** to create a named range for each of the columns to be used later.

e. Click the **Data-RevenueGoals worksheet tab**, and then click cell **D5**. Type the following formula to calculate the difference between the January actual revenue and the January goal for 2008: =B5-C5. Press Ctrl+Enter. Double-click the **AutoFill** handle in cell B5 to copy the formula down the column. Enter similar formulas in cells **I5:I16** and **D21:D32**.

f. Right-click the **Sheet1 worksheet tab**, click **Rename**, and then type Analysis as the new sheet name.

g. Click the **Data-Sales worksheet tab**, and then select any cell that contains data. Click the **Insert tab**, click the **PivotTable arrow**, and then click **PivotChart**. Click **Existing Worksheet**, click the **Location** box, and then click the Analysis worksheet cell **A3**. Click **OK**.

h. Drag the **Year** and **Month** fields into the Report Filter area, **Customer ID** into the Axis Fields (Categories) area, and **TotalSales** into the Σ Values area.

i. Right-click one of the Customer ID values (Row Labels) in the PivotTable, point to **Filter**, and then click **Top 10**. Keep the default values to show the Top 10 Items by Sum of TotalSales, and then click **OK**.

j. Right-click any of the **Sum of TotalSales** values in the PivotTable, and then click **Number Format**. Format the values as **Accounting** with 2 decimal places, and then click **OK**.

k. Select the chart, click the **Analyze tab**, and then click **Field Buttons** to hide the filters on the chart. Click the **chart legend**, and then click Delete. Click the **chart title**, and then rename the chart Top 10 Customers' Monthly Revenue.

l. Click the **Design tab**, and then select **Style 30** from the Chart Styles gallery. Right-click the **data series**, click **Format Data Series**, and then reduce the Gap Width to 25%. Reposition the chart so that is to the right of the PivotTable and expands across columns C:K.

m. Click cell **A18**, type Year, click cell **B18**, and then type TotalSalesActual. Click cell **C18**, type TotalSalesGoal, click cell **D18**, and then type 12 Month Win/Loss.

n. Click cell **A19**, type 2008, and then press Enter. Click cell **A20**, type 2009, press Enter, type 2010, and then press Enter.

o. Click cell **B19**, and then type the following formula to calculate the total actual sales revenue for all of 2008: =SUM('Data-RevenueGoals'!B5:B16). Press Enter. Enter similar formulas in cells **B20:B21** making sure to reference the appropriate cell references for 2009 and 2010 actual sales.

p. Click cell **C19**, and then type the following formula to calculate the total revenue goal for all of 2008: =SUM('Data-RevenueGoals'!C5:C16). Press Enter. Type similar formulas in cells **C20:C21** making sure to reference the appropriate cell references for 2009 and 2010 goals. Widen the columns as needed to accommodate the column headings and data.

q. Click cell **D19**, click the **Insert tab**, and then click **Win/Loss** in the Sparklines group. Select **'Data-RevenueGoals'!D5:D16** to produce the sparkline chart based on the Above/Below Goal amounts for 2008, and then click **OK**. Create similar Win/Loss sparklines in cell **D20:D21**, making sure to reference the appropriate cell references for the Above/Below Goals for 2009 and 2010. Adjust the column widths as necessary to accommodate all values.

r. Click cell **A24**, type Year, press Tab, type Month, and then press Enter. Click cell **A25**, type 2008, press Tab, type Jan, and then press Enter.

s. Click cell **A26**, type Membership Status, press Tab, type Monthly Sales, press Tab, type % of Total, and then press Enter. Click cell **A27**, type Member, press Delete to reject the AutoFill value, and then press Enter. Type Guest in cell A28, and then press Enter.

t. Click cell **B27**, and then type the following formula to calculate the total sales revenue for members for January 2008: =SUMIFS(TotalSales,MembershipStatus,A27,Year,$A$25, Month,$B$25). Press Ctrl+Enter. Double-click the **AutoFill** handle in cell **B27** to copy the formula to **B28** in order to calculate the same for Guests. Format **B27:B28** as **Accounting** with 2 decimal places.

u. Click cell **C27**, and then type the following formula to calculate the percentage of total revenue is made up of member sales: =B27/SUM($B$27:$B$28). Press Ctrl+Enter. Double-click the **AutoFill** handle in cell **C27** to copy the formula to **C28**. Format **C27:C28** as a **Percent** with 2 decimal places.

v. Select cells **A26:C28**, click the **Insert Tab**, click **Table**, and then click **OK**. Click the **Table Tools Design tab**, and then type PercentOfMonthlySales for the table name in the Properties group.

w. With cells A26:C28 selected, click the **Insert tab**, click **Pie** in the Charts group, and then click **pie in 3-D**. Click the Design tab select **Style 32** from the Chart Styles gallery. Click the **chart title**, and then type % of Monthly Sales. Right-click the **data series**, and then click **Add Data Labels**. Format the Data labels so that Percentage shows and leader lines do not show.

x. Reposition the pie chart over the range **D26:J40**.

y. Save your file. Print or submit your file as directed by your instructor. Close the workbook.

Student data files needed:

e05_ws10_PaintedTreasures_Dashboard

e05_ws10_Painted_Treasures

You will save your file as:

Lastname_Firstname_e05_ws10_PaintedTreasures_Dashboard

Enhancing the Painted Treasures Gift Shop Dashboard

Management at the Painted Treasures Gift Shop have had some analysis done on some sample data from their 2008 and 2009 sales and have put together a worksheet with PivotTables, charts, and Excel tables. You have been asked to enhance the spreadsheet into an interactive dashboard. You will create the dashboard using conditional formatting, sparklines, the Camera tool, slicers, spin buttons, scroll bars, and VBA. You will also hide unnecessary elements that distract from the dashboard.

a. Start **Excel**. Click the **File tab**, click **Open**, and then navigate to your student data files. Locate and open **e05_ws10_PaintedTreasures_Dashboard**. Click **Enable Content**.

b. Add a filename footer to the left section of the footer for all worksheets. Click the **File tab**, click **Save As**, and then rename the workbook Lastname_Firstname_e05_ws10_ PaintedTreasures_Dashboard. Select **Excel Macro-Enabled Workbook (*.xlsm)** from the Save as type list, and then click **Save**.

c. Click the **Documentation worksheet tab** if it is not the active worksheet, click cell **A6**, and then press [Ctrl]+[;] to input the current date. Click cell **B6**, and type Lastname, Firstname using your first name and last name.

d. Click the **Analysis worksheet tab**, and then click the **PivotTable** located in the top-left corner. Click the **Pivot Table Tools Options tab**, and then click **Insert Slicer** in the Sort & Filter group to add slicers to the PivotTable.

e. Click the **Month**, **Year**, and **Quarters** check boxes in the Insert Slicers dialog box, and then click **OK**.

f. Click the other **PivotTable** located to the bottom left, click the **Insert Slicer button arrow** in the Sort & Filter group, and then click **Slicer Connections**. In the Slicer Connections dialog box, click the check boxes next to the **Month**, **Quarters**, and **Year** field names, and then click **OK**.

g. Press and hold [Ctrl], and then click each of the slicers so that all are selected. Press [Ctrl]+[X] to cut the slicers from the worksheet. Click the **Dashboard worksheet**, click cell **K18**, and then press [Ctrl]+[V] to paste the slicers. Click any cell in the worksheet to unselect the slicers.

h. Right-click the **Year** slicer, and then in the right-click menu, click **Size and Properties**. Click **Position and Layout** in the Size and Properties dialog box. Change Number of columns to 2, and then click **Close**. Adjust the width and height of the Year slicer so that only 2008 and 2009 are visible in the two columns. Move the Year slicer in between the two charts at the top of the dashboard; position them approximately within the cell range H1:J4.

i. Using the method in the above step, change the Number of columns to 2 for the **Quarters** slicer and the number of columns to 4 for the Month slicer. Resize the Month slicer to so that only the month abbreviations are visible (no extra white space at the bottom), and then move it just below the Year slicer in between the two charts; position it approximately within the cell range H5:K11. Resize the Quarters slicer so that only Q1, Q2, Q3, and Q4 are viewable, and then move it so it is just below the Month slicer; position it approximately within the cell range H12:K16.

j. To hide the field buttons on the charts, click the **Total Monthly Sales Revenue** column chart, click the **PivotChart Tools Analyze tab**, and then click **Field Buttons** in the Show/Hide group. Click the **Top Products by Volume** pie chart, and then click **Field Buttons** in the Show/Hide group.

k. Click the **Analysis worksheet tab**, select **D13:E26**, and then press Ctrl+X to cut. Click the **Dashboard worksheet** tab, click cell **I17**, and then press Ctrl+V to paste. Widen the columns if necessary to accommodate the values in the table.

l. To add conditional formatting, click cell **K20**, type =J20, and then press Ctrl+Enter. Double-click the **AutoFill** handle in cell **K20** to copy the formula down the column. With cells **K20:K30** selected, click the **Home tab**, in the Styles group click **Conditional Formatting**, and then click **New Rule**.

m. In the New Formatting Rule dialog box, click the **Format Style arrow**, and then select **Icon Sets**. Click the **Icon Style arrow**, and then scroll up to select the **3Arrows (Colored)** style. Click the **Show Icon Only** check box. Click the **Type arrow** under the Display each icon according to these rules heading, and then select **Formula** in both the first and second boxes. Click the first box under **Value**, and then type =AVERAGE($K$20:$K$30). Click the second box below **Value**, and then type =AVERAGE($K$20:$K$30). Click **OK**.

n. Click cell **K19**, and then type Above/Below Avg. Select **K19:K30**, and then center the text of the column. Use the Format Painter to copy the formatting of cell J19 to K19. Widen the columns as necessary so that all data are displayed.

o. To add a spin button to easily change the year for the data in the table.

- Click the **Developer tab**, click the **Insert button**, and then click the **Spin Button (Form Control)**.
- Drag the vertical **spin button** in cell **I18** next to **2008**. Change the row height if necessary to be able to see and use the button.
- Right-click the **spin button**, and then in the right-click menu, click **Format Control**. In the Format Control dialog box, type 2008 as the Current value and Minimum value. Type 2009 as the **Maximum value**, and then ensure 1 is selected for **Incremental change**. Click the **Cell link** box, select cell **I18**, and then click **OK**.

p. To add a scroll bar to easily change the month for the data in the table.

- Click the **Developer tab**, click **Insert**, and then click the **Scroll Bar (Form Control)**. Drag to create a horizontal scroll bar in cell J18 to the right of Jan.
- Click cell **K18**, and then type 1 (K18 will be the linked cell to the scroll bar control).
- Click cell **J18**, and then type the formula =VLOOKUP(K18,MonthLookup,2,FALSE). Press Enter.
- Right-click the **scroll bar**, and then in the right-click menu, click **Format Control**. In the Format Control dialog box, type 1 for the Current value and Minimum value. Type 12 for the **Maximum value**, and then keep the default values for Incremental change and Pace change. Click the **Cell link** box, select cell **K18**, and then click **OK**.
- Click cell **K18**, click the **Home tab**, and then change the font color to white so that it is not visible.

q. To create a sparkline line chart, click the **Analysis worksheet tab**, and then in the Create Sparklines dialog box select cells **Q4:Q7** in the data range box. Click the **Insert tab**, and then click **Line** in the Sparklines group. Select range **E4:P7**, and then click **OK**.

r. To use the Camera tool.

- Select the range **D1:D2**, press Ctrl+X to cut. Click the **Dashboard** worksheet, click cell **A31**, and then press Ctrl+V to paste.
- Click the **Analysis worksheet tab**, select the range **D3:Q7**, and then click the **Camera** tool from the **Quick Access toolbar**.
- Click the **Dashboard worksheet tab**, and then click cell **A34** to paste the image.

s. Click anywhere on the worksheet to deselect the image. Click the **Developer tab**, click **Insert** in the Controls group, and then click the **Spin Button (Form Control)**. Drag a **spin button** to cell A32 next to **2008**. Change the row height if necessary to be able to see and use the button. Right-click the **spin button**, and then in the right-click menu click **Format Control**. In the Format Control dialog box, type 2008 as the Current value and Minimum value. Type 2009 as the **Maximum value**, and then ensure 1 is selected for **Incremental change**. Click the **Cell link** box, select cell **A32**, and then click **OK**.

t. Press Alt + F11 to switch to the Visual Basic Editor, and then double-click **ThisWorkbook** in the Project Explorer window. Type Public Sub clearSlicers(), and then press Enter. Type the following comment: 'Created by Firstname Lastname. This VBA will automatically clear all 3 slicer filters on the Dashboard replacing Firstname and Lastname with your first and last name. Press Enter. Type ActiveWorkbook.SlicerCaches("Slicer_Year"). ClearManualFilter, and then press Enter. On the next two lines type:

ActiveWorkbook.SlicerCaches("Slicer_Month").ClearManualFilter. Press Enter

ActiveWorkbook.SlicerCaches("Slicer_Quarters").ClearManualFilter. Press Enter

u. Press Alt + F11 to switch back to the workbook. Right-click the **Year** slicer, and then click **Slicer Settings**. In the Slicer Settings dialog box, in the header area, clear the check box next to Display header to hide the header, and then click **OK**. Adjust the width and height of the **Year slicer** so that only the years 2008 and 2009 are visible in the top row of the slicer. Do the same for the **Month slicer** and the **Quarters slicer**. Adjust the width and height of both slicers so that only the filters you need are visible.

v. **Save** the workbook and close the VBE. Click the **Dashboard worksheet tab**, click the **Developer tab**, in the Controls group click **Insert**, and then click the **Button (Form Control)**. Drag to create a button to the right of the Year slicer. In the Macro name section, select the **ThisWorkbook.clearSlicers** macro in the Assign Macro dialog box, and then click **OK**. Right-click the **button**, in the right-click menu, click **Edit Text** and then rename it Clear Filters. Adjust the size of the button to accommodate the text. Click the button to test the macro. Debug if necessary.

w. Right-click cell **I18**, in the right-click menu click **Format Cells**, in the Format Cells dialog box click the **Protection tab**, and then clear the check box next to **Locked**. Click **OK**. Do the same for cells **K18** and **A32**. Click the **Review tab**, and then in the Changes group click **Protect Sheet**. In the Protect Sheet dialog box scroll down and click the check box next to **Edit objects**, and then click **OK**.

x. Click the **File tab**, and then click **Options.** In the Excel Options dialog box, click **Advanced**, scroll down to the Display options for this workbook section, and then clear the **Show sheet tabs** check box. Scroll down to the Display options for this worksheet section, and then clear the check boxes for the following options: **Show row and column headers** and **Show gridlines**. Click **OK**. Right-click anywhere on the Ribbon, and then click **Minimize Ribbon** to maximize the amount of dashboard space.

y. Save the workbook, and then test out all the new features created. Print or submit your file to your instructor as directed. Close the workbook, and then exit Excel.

MODULE CAPSTONE

Student data file needed:	You will save your file as:
e05_mp_Indigo5_Data	Lastname_Firstname_e05_mp_Indigo5_Data

Indigo5 Restaurant

Management at Indigo 5, a five-star restaurant that caters to local patrons in addition to clients of the resort and spa, has outsourced its data collection processes to a new firm in town. The data collected is in the e05_mp_Indigo5_Data workbook and is not compatible in its current form with the database that Indigo 5 currently uses to store this data. You will need to use your knowledge of Excel functions to clean the data so that it can be imported into the database.

a. Start **Excel** and then open **e05_mp_Indigo5_Data**.

b. Click the **File tab**, click **Save As**, and then save the workbook with the name Lastname_Firstname_e05_mp_Indigo5_Data replacing Lastname_Firstname with your own name. Insert a filename footer in the left section of the footer on all worksheets.

c. Click the **Documentation worksheet tab** if it is not the active worksheet, click cell **A6**, and then press [Ctrl]+[;] to input the current date, press [Enter]. Click cell **B6**, and type Lastname, Firstname using your own first name and last name.

d. Click the **FoodCategories worksheet tab**. Click cell **B1**, type CategoryCode, and then press [Tab]. Type Description in cell **C1**, and then press [Enter].

e. In cell **B2**, type the following function to parse out the category number from the value in cell A2: =LEFT(A2,FIND("-",A2)-1), and then press [Ctrl]+[Enter]. Double-click the **AutoFill** handle in cell **B2** to copy the formula down the column.

f. Click cell **C2**, type the following function to parse out the description of the category from the value in cell A2: =RIGHT(A2,LEN(A2)-FIND("-",A2)), and then press [Ctrl]+[Enter]. Double-click the **AutoFill** handle in cell **C2** to copy the formula down the column.

g. Click the **Reviews worksheet tab**, and then click cell **E1**, type ProperReviewer, and then press [Tab]. Type Date in cell **F1**, and then press [Enter].

h. Type the following function in cell **E2** to convert the text in cell A2 to proper case: =PROPER(A2), and then press [Ctrl]+[Enter]. Double-click the **AutoFill handle** in cell **E2** to copy the formula down the column. Use AutoFit on the column so that all contents are viewable.

i. Click cell **F2**, type the following formula to return the number that represents the date in cell B2: =DATE(LEFT(B2,4),MID(B2,5,2),RIGHT(B2,2)), and then press [Ctrl]+[Enter]. Double-click the **AutoFill** handle in cell **F2** to copy the formula down the column. If necessary, double-click the **column headings** for column F to fit the contents of the cells to the column.

j. Click the **Customers worksheet tab**, and then click cell **E1**. Type StreetAddress, press [Tab], type City in cell F1, and then press [Tab]. Type State in cell G1, press [Tab], type Zip in cell H1, and then press [Enter].

k. Type the following function in cell E2 to parse out the street address from cell C2: =LEFT(C2,FIND(" ",C2)-1), and then press Ctrl+Enter. Double-click the **AutoFill handle** in cell E2 to copy the formula down the column. Use AutoFit on the column so that all contents are viewable.

l. Click cell **F2**, type the following function to parse out the city name from cell C2: =MID(C2,LEN(E2)+3,FIND(" ",C2,LEN(E2)+2)-FIND(" ",C2)-2), and then press Ctrl+Enter. Double-click the **AutoFill** handle in cell F2 to copy the formula down the column. Use AutoFit on the column so that all contents are viewable.

m. Click cell **G2**, type the following function to parse out the state abbreviation from cell C2: =RIGHT(C2,2), and then press Ctrl+Enter. Double-click the **AutoFill handle** in cell G2 to copy the formula down the column.

n. Click cell **H2**, type the following formula to add a 0 before any zip code in column D that has fewer than 5 characters: =IF(LEN(D2)<5,"0"&D2,D2), and then press Ctrl+Enter. Double-click the **AutoFill** handle in cell H2 to copy the formula down the column. Click the **Home tab**, click the **Align Text Right** button.

o. Save the workbook. If your instructor requests a printout of the modified data use the default settings for the FoodCategories and Review worksheets. Modify the orientation to **Landscape** if printing the Customers worksheet. Submit your file as directed by your instructor, and then close the workbook. Exit Excel.

Problem Solve 1

Student data file needed:	You will save your file as:
e05_ps1_Hotel_Dashboard	Lastname_Firstname_e05_ps1_Hotel_Dashboard

Hotel Reservations Dashboard

Management of the hotel would like to get a better idea of how well they are meeting their goals in terms of number and types of reservations booked at the hotel. The e05_ps1_Hotel_Dashboard workbook contains sample data from 2009 and 2010. You have been asked to conduct some analysis and create a functional, interactive dashboard. Once approved, the entire data set will be integrated.

a. Start **Excel** and then open **e05_ps1_Hotel_Dashboard**.

b. Click the **File tab**, click **Save As**, and then save the workbook as Lastname_Firstname_e05_ps1_Hotel_Dashboard replacing Lastname_Firstname with your own name. Insert a filename footer in the left section of the footer on all worksheets.

c. Click the **Documentation worksheet tab** if it is not the active worksheet, click cell **A6**, and then press Ctrl+; to input the current date, press Enter. Click cell **B6**, and type Lastname, Firstname using your own first name and last name.

d. Rename the Sheet2 worksheet Analysis, and then rename the Sheet3 worksheet Dashboard.

e. Click the **Data worksheet tab**, click cell **I1**, and then type Month. Click **I2**, use the TEXT function to return the month abbreviation for each CheckInDate, and then automatically fill the function down the column.

f. In cell **J1** type Year. In cell **J2** enter a formula that returns the year each CheckInDate occurs, and then automatically fill the formula down the column.

g. Click the **Analysis worksheet tab** and create a column PivotChart in cell **A3** that shows the top three customers based on the sum of total room charges for each month.
  - Make the **Year** field the report filter.
  - Format the sum of total room charges as **Currency** with 2 decimal places.
  - Use **a 2-D Clustered Column chart** with **Style 19** applied.
  - Give the chart a title of Top Customers per Month.
  - Hide the legend and field buttons from the chart.
  - Reposition the PivotChart to the right of the PivotTable.

h. Create a PivotChart in cell **D19** of the Analysis worksheet that shows the total number of nights booked for any month.
  - Make the **Year** field the report filter.
  - Choose a **Line with Markers line chart** with **Style 20** applied.
  - Hide the legend and field buttons.
  - Give the line chart a title of Total Nights Booked.
  - Reposition the PivotChart to the right of the PivotTable.

i. Create an Excel table that calculates the total revenue for each month for each year.
  - Use the top row of column labels on the Data worksheet to create 10 named ranges to use in formulas.
  - Click cell **D35** on the Analysis worksheet, and then type Year. Click cell **E35**, and then type Jan. Automatically fill months through Dec across row 35.
  - Type 2009 in cell **D36** and 2010 in **D37**. Click cell **E36**, calculate the sum of total room charges based on the check-in date year and month, and then automatically fill the formula across and down.
  - Format the values as **Currency** with 2 decimal places, and then automatically fit the columns to their content.
  - Select **D35:P37** and then format the range as a table with a **Medium Style 7** applied.
  - Type TotalRevenueByMonth as the table name.
  - Click cell **Q35**, and then type Chart. Enter a **Sparkline column chart** that will compare monthly revenue for each year in cell Q36:Q37. Adjust the column width so that the column chart is easily viewable.

j. Move the column and line charts from the **Analysis worksheet** to the **Dashboard worksheet**.
  - Rearrange the charts so that the column chart is on top and is positioned approximately within the cell range **A1:M12**. Place the line chart underneath the column chart positioned approximately within the cell range **A13:M26**.
  - Create a slicer for the Year field, and then connect both PivotTables to it. Move the slicer to the **Dashboard worksheet** to the right of the charts, and then position it approximately within the cell range **N1:O5**.
  - Add a dynamic label to each chart to the right of the chart title that displays the year that is currently being viewed.
  - Use the Camera tool to take a picture of the TotalRevenueByMonth table, and then place the image on the Dashboard underneath the charts starting in cell **A27**.
  - Protect the Dashboard worksheet so that the slicer object can still be used.

k. Hide unnecessary elements from end users by not showing row or column headings, worksheets, or gridlines.

l. Save the workbook. If instructor requests a printout of the dashboard adjust the print layout settings to fit to 1 page wide and 1 page tall. Submit your file as directed by your instructor, and then close the workbook. Exit Excel.

Student data file needed:

e05_ps2_Reservation_Data

You will save your file as:

Lastname_Firstname_e05_ps2_Reservation_Data

Cleaning Online Reservation Data

Corporate has purchased a new online reservation system to help meet the demand for the hotel. It is currently being pilot tested, and there are a few issues with how the data is exported from the website. You will need to clean the data in the e05_ps2_Reservation_Data workbook so that it can be imported to the database.

a. Start **Excel** and then open **e05_ps2_Reservation_Data**.

b. Click the **File tab**, click **Save As**, and then save the workbook with the name Lastname_Firstname_e05_ps2_Reservation_Data replacing Lastname_Firstname with your own name. Insert a filename footer in the left section of the footer on all worksheets.

c. Click the **Documentation worksheet tab** if it is not the active worksheet, click cell **A6**, and then press Ctrl+; to input the current date, press Enter. Click cell **B6**, and type Lastname, Firstname using your own first name and last name.

d. Click the **Guests worksheet tab**, insert three columns to the right of the **Name** column, and then label the new columns LastName, MiddleInitial, and FirstName.

e. Parse the name in column **B** so that each part of the name is separated into the appropriate columns using various text functions, and then automatically fill the formulas down the columns.

f. Insert a column to the right of **Gender**, and then name the column GenderDescription.

g. In the GenderDescription column, enter the appropriate function so that Male will appear if the Gender is "M" in column F and Female if the gender is "F", and then automatically fill the formula down the column. Auto fit the columns to the data.

h. Insert four additional columns after the Address column. Name the first StreetAddress, the second City, the third State, and the fourth ZipCode.

i. Parse the contents of column H so that each portion of the address is in the appropriately named column using a combination of text functions. Automatically fill the formulas down each of the columns.

j. Name the column to the right of the Phone column, FormattedPhone.

k. In the FormattedPhone column combine the data from the Phone column using the standard telephone number formatting symbols and spaces. The formatted phone number should resemble (702) 555-6627 and should be done using a combination of the LEFT, RIGHT, and MID functions. Automatically fill the formula down the column.

l. Fit all of the columns to the data.

m. Click the **Reservations worksheet tab**, insert two columns to the right of the Reservation column, and then name them GuestID and ReservationID.

n. The data in the Reservation column needs to be parsed to separate the guest ID and the reservation ID. The guest ID begins with "RBH", and the reservation ID begins with "RES". Use text functions to separate each of these files into the appropriate columns, and then automatically fill the formulas down the columns.

o. Insert a new column after the Discount Type column, and then name it DiscountDescription. Use IF functions to return the appropriate discount descriptions based on the following information:

- Discount Type 1 = None
- Discount Type 2 = AAA
- Discount Type 3 = AARP
- Discount Type 4 = Military

Automatically fill the formula down the column, and then fit the column to accommodate the text.

p. Insert a new column to the right of the Date column, and then name it CheckInDate. Use the DATE function to return the number that corresponds to the date in the Date column (MM/DD/YYYY). Automatically fill the function down the column, and then fit the column if necessary. Format the column as **Short Date**.

q. Name the column to the right of NumNights, CheckOutDate. Calculate the check-out date based on the check-in date and the number of nights. Automatically fill down the column, and fit the column if necessary. Format the column as **Short Date**.

r. Save the workbook. If your instructor requests a printout of the worksheets, adjust the print layout settings for the Guests worksheet to fit to 2 wide and 1 tall. Adjust the print layout settings for the Reservations worksheet to **Landscape** orientation and to fit to 1 wide and 2 tall. Submit your file as directed by your instructor, and then close the workbook. Exit Excel.

Problem Solve 3

Student data file needed:	You will save your file as:
e05_ps3_Advanced_Dashboard	Lastname_Firstname_e05_ps3_Advanced_Dashboard

Enhancing Reservation Dashboard with VBA

Management at the Hotel has been realizing the benefits of using a dashboard to help make decisions. The dashboard is very basic and provides management with the data they need to monitor the business. However, the dashboard could be enhanced with some conditional formatting, slicers, and VBA.

a. Start **Excel** and then open **e05_ps3_Advanced_Dashboard**.

b. Click the **File tab**, click **Save As**, and then save the workbook with the name Lastname_Firstname_e05_ps3_Advanced_Dashboard replacing Lastname_Firstname with your own actual name. Select **Excel Macro-Enabled Workbook (*.xlsm)** from the **Save as type** list, and then click **Save**. Insert a filename footer in the left section of the footer on all worksheets.

c. Click the **Documentation worksheet tab** if it is not the active worksheet, click cell **A6**, and then press Ctrl+: to input the current date, press Enter. Click cell **B6**, and type Lastname, Firstname using your own first name and last name.

d. Hide the field buttons from the charts on the Dashboard worksheet.

e. Add slicers to the dashboard to allow the user to filter on discount type, year, and month. Be sure to connect the slicers to all three pivot tables. Adjust the number of columns and the size of the slicers according to the table on the next page:

Slicer Name	Columns	Height × Width
Year	1	1" × 1.27"
Month	3	1.75" × 2"
DiscountType	2	.98" × 2"

Align the slicer objects along the bottom of the Total Reservations by Discount bar chart, between columns **H:L**.

f. Use the **Format as Table** Style on the cell range **H21:I43**, apply a **Table Style Medium 3** style, and check the box indicating that the table has headers. Name the table TotalRevenueByMonth. If necessary, fit the columns so that all values are viewable in the table.

g. Add a spin button form control to cell **H30** so that the year 2009-2010 can be selected using the button.

h. Add conditional formatting to the Total Revenue column with the **3 Triangles icon** sets. The green triangle should appear if the monthly revenue is above the overall average revenue, and the red triangle should appear if the monthly revenue is below the overall average.

i. Create a new module in the VBE, and then name it Lastname_Firstname_Module1 replacing Lastname and Firstname with your own name.

j. Create a public Sub procedure called clearSlicers, and then add a comment that states: 'Created by Firstname Lastname. Clears all slicer filters in workbook. Replace Firstname and Lastname with your own name. The clearSlicers Sub procedure needs to clear the filters from all three slicers. Assign the clearSlicers Sub procedure to a form control button with the label of Clear Filters. Position the button below the Year slicer on the Dashboard worksheet within the cell range **H24:I25**.

k. Create a private Sub procedure named hideSheets, and then add a comment that states: 'Created by Firstname Lastname. Specified worksheets cannot be made visible even if the Show Sheet tabs box is selected. This Sub procedure needs to make the Analysis and Data worksheets hidden regardless of whether or not the Show Sheet tabs box is checked. Run the VBA code from the VBE. Click the **Dashboard worksheet tab** and type the following label in cell **D34**: Total Discounts.

l. Create a public Sub procedure called totalDiscounts, insert the following comment: 'Created by Firstname Lastname. Prompts the user for a discount type and then calculates the total amount discounted.

  • Create two variables, one called discountType of type String and the other totalDiscount of type Currency.

  • Create an input box that prompts the user with the following text: Enter a discount type, and then type Discount Type for the title of the input box. Store the result in the discountType variable.

  • If the discount type is "AAA", calculate the sum of TotalRevenueByMonth[Total Revenue] by .10, and then store the calculation in the totalDiscount variable. Set the value of cell **C35** as discountType and the value of cell **D35** as totalDiscount.

  • If the discount type is "AARP", calculate the sum of TotalRevenueByMonth[Total Revenue] by .15, and then store the calculation in the totalDiscount variable. Set the value of cell **C35** as discountType and the value of cell **D35** as totalDiscount.

  • If the discount type is "Military", calculate the sum of TotalRevenueByMonth[Total Revenue] by .20, and then store the calculation in the totalDiscount variable. Set the value of cell **C35** as discountType and the value of cell **D35** as totalDiscount.

  • If none of the above types are entered, display a message box that states That discount type does not exist, and then set the value of **C35:D35** to null.

- Assign the totalDiscounts Sub procedure to a form button, and then place it approximately within the cell range **B34:B35**. Name the button Calculate Discounts.
- Test the VBA using the button and entering in the various discount types.

m. Protect the dashboard worksheet making sure to unlock any cells that need to be modified either by the spin button or the VBA. Modify the settings to hide the row and column headers, gridlines, and sheet tabs.

n. Password protect the VBA code with the password admin.

o. Save the workbook, and if the instructor requests a printout of the dashboard set the print layout settings to a **Landscape** orientation and to fit 1 wide and 1 tall. Submit your file as directed by your instructor, and then close the workbook.

Perform 1: Perform in Your Life

Student data file needed:	You will save your file as:
Blank workbook	Lastname_Firstname_e05_pf1_Expenses_Dashboard

College Expenses Analysis and Dashboard

The first step in learning how to effectively manage your money is to keep track of your monthly expenditures. Understanding what you spend your money on will allow you to identify areas in which you can cut spending, if necessary, in order to free up enough cash to make a car payment or pay off your student loans. Some banks provide members with an option to export bank statements as a text file that can be imported into Excel. If your bank provides you with this option, you may wish to export an entire statement, or partial statement to begin with. If your bank does not offer this option, then you will need to think back and hand enter expenditures for at least a week. Include expenses from the following categories if applicable: Rent, Food, Entertainment, Clothing, Utilities, Groceries, Transportation, and any other categories that you see fit.

a. Start **Excel**. Click the **File tab**, click **Save as**, browse to your student files, and then save the workbook as Lastname_Firstname_e05_pf1_Expenses_Dashboard. Replace Lastname and Firstname with your own name. Rename Sheet1 as ExpenseData. If you were able to export your bank statement then import the data into the ExpenseData worksheet. If you need to hand enter your expenditures then do so, on the ExpenseData worksheet.

b. First you need to manipulate some of the data.
- Create categories for your expenses. This may require you to create a lookup table of such categories as Food, Transportation, Entertainment, and Rent. Then create a column that lists the category of each expense.
- Create a column that displays the month abbreviation that each transaction took place. You may choose to use the TEXT function or a VLOOKUP function.
- Format the list of expenses as a table, and then name it Expenses.

c. Create or rename two worksheets in your workbook.
- Name one of the worksheets Analysis and the other worksheet Dashboard.
- Insert a filename footer in the left section of the footer on all worksheets.

d. Create a PivotChart from the expense data, using cell **A3** on the **Analysis worksheet** as the destination cell.
- Create a line chart with markers that will show the trend of total expenses.
- Place month and transaction date in the Axis Fields (Categories) area.

- Apply **Style 44** to the chart.
- Move the line chart to the **Dashboard worksheet**, and then place it within the cell range **F20:N36**. Hide the field buttons and chart legend.

e. Click the **Dashboard worksheet tab** and calculate the total expenses for each category in an Excel table. Enter the column label Category in cell **C4** and Monthly Expenses in cell **D4**. List your expense categories starting in cell **C5**, and then starting in cell **D5** enter a formula that will calculate the total expenses within each category for any month entered in cell D3. Name the table ExpensesByCategory.

- Create a 3-D column chart based on the data in the ExpensesByCategory table, and then apply **Style 40** to the chart. Position the chart within the cell range **F2:N18**.
- Insert a horizontal scroll bar to control the month in cell **D3**. Change the font color of the cell linked to the scroll bar to white.
- Add a month and category slicer to the line chart so that you are able to see trends for different months and different spending categories, and then place the slicers to the left of the line chart.

f. Hide the sheet tabs and gridlines as well as the row and column headers.

g. Save the workbook. Print or submit your file as directed by your instructor. Close the workbook. Exit Excel.

Perform 2: Perform in Your Career

Student data files needed:

S&P_Sample_Data
Blank workbook

You will save your file as:

Lastname_Firstname_e05_pf2_Stock_Trader

Stock Trader

You have been hired by a local firm that specializes in stock trading. You have been given a comma-delimited text file consisting of sample data from some of the stocks that make up the S&P 500. You will import the data into an Excel workbook, clean the data using your knowledge of Excel functions, conduct some analysis, and create a simple dashboard.

a. Start **Excel**. Click the **File tab**, click **Save as**, browse to your student files, and then save the workbook as Lastname_Firstname_e05_pf2_Stock_Trader. Replace Lastname and Firstname with your own name.

b. Import the data from the **Sample_S&P_Data** CSV file into cell **A1** of the Sheet2 worksheet, and then rename the Sheet2 worksheet StockData.

- Type DateValue as the heading for column **H**, and then use the DATE function to return the number that represents the date in column **A**. Fill the formula down the column, and then fit the column to the data.
- Type Month as the heading for column **I**, and then use the TEXT function to format the data in the DateValue column as a 3-character month abbreviation. Copy the formula down the column.
- Create named ranges using the top row on the StockData worksheet for cells **A1:I453**.

c. Rename Sheet3 S&P_Analysis.

d. Create a Line with Markers PivotChart, using cell **A3** on the **S&P_Analysis worksheet** as the destination cell.

- Place the **Ticker** and **Month** fields in the Axis Fields (Categories) area.
- Place the **Volume** field in the Σ Values area, and then calculate the average volume.

- Format the average of volume values to a number with 0 decimal places and with a 1000 separator.
- Modify the vertical axis of the line chart to be on a logarithmic scale with a default base of 10.
- Apply **Style 41** to the chart.
- Hide the field buttons and legend from the line chart.
- Add or modify the chart title to be S&P Average Volume.
- Create a Ticker slicer for the PivotTable.

e. Insert a new worksheet, and then name it S&P_Dashboard.

f. Create an Excel table starting in cell **B2** on the S&P_Dashboard worksheet with column labels of Month, Average Open, Average Close, and Average Change. Type Jun, Jul, and Aug in cells **B3:B5**.
- In cell **C3**, calculate the average opening amount for AAPL in the month of June, taking advantage of the named ranges created in the StockData worksheet.
- In cell **D3**, calculate the average closing amount.
- In cell **E3**, calculate the difference between the average open and average closing amounts.
- Format **C3:E5** as **Accounting** with 2 decimal places. Fit the columns as necessary.
- Name the Excel table StockAnalysis.
- Type Stock Symbol in cell **C1**, and then type AAPL in cell **D1**.

g. Create three 3-D clustered column charts based on the data in the StockAnalysis table. One chart needs to compare the average opening amounts for all three months:
- Hide the chart legend.
- Apply **Style 35** to the chart.

h. One chart needs to compare the average closing amounts for all three months:
- Hide the chart legend.
- Apply **Style 36** to the chart.

i. One chart needs to compare the average change from open to closing amounts for all three months:
- Hide the chart legend.
- Apply **Style 37** to the chart.

j. All three charts should be positioned within the cell range **A6:N19**, horizontally in the order they were created from left to right.

k. Move the line chart from the S&P_Analysis worksheet to the S&P_Dashboard worksheet, and then position it within the cell range **C20:N34**.

l. Cut and paste the Ticker slicer from the StockAnalysis worksheet to the S&P Dashboard worksheet, and then position it to the left of the line chart.

m. Add a scroll bar to the dashboard that will allow the user to easily view the data for any of the stock symbols by sliding the scroll bar from left to right.
- This will require a LOOKUP table and a linked cell. Create the lookup table on the S&P_ Analysis worksheet using cells **D1:D8**.
- Change the font color of the linked cell to white so that it is not visible.

n. Create a dynamic label to the right of the chart title for each of the 3-D column charts that display the stock symbol in cell D1.

o. Modify the workbook properties to ready the dashboard for production:
- Hide the sheet tabs.
- Hide the row and column headings.
- Hide the gridlines.

p. Insert a filename footer in the left section of the footer on all worksheets. Save the workbook. Print or submit your file as directed by your instructor. Close the workbook, and then exit Excel.

Perform 3: Perform in Your Career

Student data file needed:

e05_pf3_Inventory_Data

You will save your file as:

Lastname_Firstname_e05_pf3_Inventory_Data

Cleaning Data

You have been contacted by corporate headquarters of the grocery store you currently work for because word of your expertise in Excel has reached upper management. The database used for keeping track of inventory has been corrupted, causing some issues with the inventory data. You have been asked to use your knowledge of Excel to clean the inventory data.

a. Start **Excel**. Open the **e05_pf3_Inventory_Data** workbook, and then save it as Lastname_Firstname_e05_pf3_Inventory_Data, replacing Lastname_Firstname with your own name. Insert a filename footer in the left section of the footer on all worksheets.

b. Remove any duplicates that exist in the Inventory worksheet. Duplicate records are any record with the same item number and stock code.

c. The word dairy was misspelled as dariy throughout the inventory list. Replace all spellings of dariy with dairy.

d. The stock code should consist of all uppercase letters. Create a new column next to the StockCode column with the appropriate function to display the stock code correctly.

e. Insert a new column after the ItemNumber field, and then label it ItemCode. The item code needs to combine the stock code with the item number.

f. The data in the Category/Brand column has been corrupted the most. There are several spaces before and after the data that need to be removed. There are also symbols that need to be removed from the data. The category and brand should be in two separate columns to the right of the Category/Brand column. Display the corrected values in their own columns labeled Category and Brand. The category data should be in proper case. Use as many columns to the right of the Inventory data that you need to accomplish these tasks.

g. Use the appropriate function for the SellingPrice and WholeSale data that will convert the numbers to a text with a currency. Place the converted SellingPrice data to the right of the SellingPrice column. Place the converted WholeSale data to the right of the WholeSale column.

h. Parse the units and measurement into two separate columns. Use the appropriate function to convert the unit value to a number. Place the parsed unit data to the right of the Unit/Measurement column and the parsed measurement data to the right of the unit column.

i. Save the workbook. Print or submit your file as directed by your instructor. Close the workbook, and then exit Excel.

Student data file needed:

e05_pf4_Sales_Dashboard

You will save your file as:

Lastname_Firstname_e05_pf4_Sales_Dashboard

Troubleshooting a Dashboard

An intern has attempted to create a simple dashboard for management to get a big picture view of how well the company is doing in terms of sales. The intern left out some key features and has made a few critical errors, preventing the dashboard from being used. You have been asked to take a look at the dashboard, determine the cause of the errors, and make some changes to improve the overall functionality. You will also create a Word document to answer some questions below.

a. Open the **e05_pf4_Sales_Dashboard** workbook, and then save it as Lastname_Firstname_e05_pf4_Sales_Dashboard. Note that this file should be saved as an **Excel Macro-Enabled Workbook (*.xlsm)**. If prompted, click **Enable Content** at the top. Insert a filename footer in the left section of the footer on all worksheets.

b. Open **Word**, create a new blank document, and then save it as Lastname_Firstname_e05_pf4_Sales_Dashboard. This will be used to answer any questions.

c. Attempt to operate the dashboard and make note of any issues in the Word document that you observed when trying to use the dashboard. Limit your analysis to the Dashboard worksheet.

d. Take the appropriate steps to correct the errors, and then explain what you did to correct them.

e. The Excel table at the bottom of the dashboard is not an actual table. Describe what it is and how it was created.

f. Make a note of any screen or chart elements you believe could be hidden or removed to maximize the space on the dashboard, and then remove or hide them.

g. Save the workbook. Print or submit your files as directed by your instructor. Close and exit Word and Excel.

Objectives

1. Construct a loan analysis using the PMT, IPMT, PPMT, RATE, and NPER functions.   p. 562

2. Create an amortization table.   p. 571

3. Calculate cumulative interest and principal using the CUMIPMT and CUMPRINC functions.   p. 572

4. Analyze annuities and investments using the PV, FV, NPV, XNPV, IRR, and XIRR functions.   p. 576

5. Calculate the depreciation of an asset using the SLN, DB, and DDB functions.   p. 583

Making Financial Decisions with Help from Excel

PREPARE CASE

The Turquoise Oasis Spa Financial Analysis

Painted Paradise Golf Resort and Spa CEO William Mattingly recently announced that Genisys Corporation—a large technology company—will soon break ground on their new corporate headquarters about three miles from the resort. In addition, Genisys has proposed a partnership with the resort to provide lodging, recreation conferences, and other services to Genisys Corporation staff, executives, and VIP guests.

Courtesy of www.Shutterstock.com

Turquoise Oasis managers Irene Kai and Meda Rodate believe that the new relationship with Genisys Corporation has the potential to double the Spa revenue. To handle the increased business, they plan several upgrades and improvements. The Spa will have to handle more simultaneous clients while maintaining high-quality service.

The managers would like you to prepare an analysis of several options to finance these improvements and eventual expansion. In addition, they will need to be able to make a sound financial proposal to Mr. Mattingly with appropriate documentation supporting the recommendations.

Student data file needed for this workshop:

 e06_ws11_Financial_Analysis

You will save your file as:

Lastname_Firstname_e06_ws11_Financial_Analysis

Constructing a Financial Analysis

Businesses need to have cash flow in order to survive. **Cash flow** is the movement of cash in and out of a business. The measurement of cash flow can be used to determine a company's value and financial situation. As an analytical tool, the statement of cash flows is useful in determining the viability and solvency of a company. The statement of cash flows is particularly helpful in assessing a company's short-term viability, which includes its ability to collect cash from customers and to pay bills. The longer a company stays profitable and the better it manages its cash flow, the better its viability. Once a company's value and financial situation are determined, banks can use that information to determine its eligibility for business loans.

From a personal perspective, individuals deal with managing money on a regular basis. People need to understand not only how to successfully invest their money, but also how loans work—such as a car, student, or home loan, known as a mortgage. Personal finance is similar to managing an organization's cash flow, except it relates to the individual's or family's monetary choices. It addresses the ways in which individuals or families obtain, budget, save, and spend money, taking various economic risks and future life events—such as getting married or having a family—into account.

An **economic risk** occurs when there is a concern that a chosen act or activity will not generate sufficient revenues to cover operating costs and repay debt obligations. This notion suggests that a choice has an effect on the outcome. Potential losses themselves may also be called risks. Almost any human endeavor, whether personal or professional, carries some type of risk, but some are more risky than others. For example, the Turquoise Oasis Spa may decide to obtain a bank loan to fund an expansion. Before the bank agrees to finance the loan, they will need to consider many factors, including the spa's cash flow and short-term viability. This will help the bank determine the level of risk—whether the spa will be able to repay the loan on time and in full.

Excel includes financial functions that are used for business and personal analysis and financial management. It is important to understand the purpose and features of each function so you can apply them to a specific task or problem. These financial functions are designed to calculate the monthly payment and other components of a loan, determine the future value of an investment, compare and contrast different investment opportunities, and calculate the depreciation of assets over time. In this section, you will analyze loans using the PMT, IPMT, PPMT, RATE and NPER functions.

Constructing a Loan Analysis with PMT, IPMT, and PPMT

Many businesses and individuals need to borrow money—it is a fact of life. And if you need to apply for a loan, you will want to know the monthly payment, which is dependent on such factors as the loan terms—particularly the interest rate—and the length of the loan.

Using the PMT Function

The Payment function, or **PMT function**, can be used to calculate a payment amount based on constant payments and a constant interest rate—payments on business loans, mortgages, car loans, or student loans can be calculated. For example, if the Turquoise Oasis Spa determined that they need to borrow $200,000 to help fund the spa's expansion, and the bank is charging 6.75% interest over a 10-year period, the spa managers could use the PMT function to determine what the monthly payment would be.

To use the PMT function for the Turquoise Oasis Spa's loan, you have to understand the structure of the function and what each function argument is determining. The PMT function calculates payments for a loan for a fixed amount with a fixed interest rate and for a fixed period of time. The PMT function syntax uses five arguments, the first three are required, and the last two are optional: (1) interest rate per period (rate); (2) number of periods (nper); (3) present value (pv); (4) future value (fv); and (5) type (type). Notice that the optional arguments are placed in square brackets.

=PMT(rate, nper, pv, [fv], [type])

The **rate** is the periodic interest rate—the interest rate of the loan. For example, if the annual percentage rate (APR) is 12% and you make monthly payments, the periodic rate—the rate charged per period and in this case, per month—is 1%. This is calculated by dividing the APR by 12, the number of months in a year.

CONSIDER THIS | Determining What to Divide the Rate By

The key to determining what to divide the rate by is looking at the total number of payments and/or how frequently the payments are made each year. If they are monthly payments, then you need to divide the rate argument by 12. What would you divide the rate by if the payments were made quarterly? What if they were made yearly?

The **nper** argument is the total number of payments that will be made in order to pay the loan in full. The term of the loan is generally specified in years; however, payments are made several times a year. If the loan is for five years, and you make 12 monthly payments, you would calculate the nper by multiplying the number of years by the number of payments in one year. Thus, five years times 12 monthly payments equals 60, which is the number to use in the formula.

The **pv** argument is the present value of the loan. Usually the loan amount is used as the present value. The PMT( ) function in Excel returns a negative number by default. This is due to the nature of cash flow when viewed from a business perspective. Incoming cash flows are "positive," whereas outgoing flows are "negative." It pays to keep this in mind when working with financial functions to avoid receiving a wildly incorrect answer. To avoid receiving a negative answer, you can type a minus sign in front of the present value. This will help ensure that your payment result is positive.

The **fv** argument—future value of the loan—is the balance you want to reach after the last payment is made. Consider any type of loan that you may have. The ultimate goal is to pay off the loan, meaning that the future value would be zero. If fv is omitted (because it is an optional argument), Excel assumes that the future value is zero. To avoid receiving a negative answer, you can type a minus sign in front of the future value. This will help ensure that your payment result is positive.

Real World Advice — When Would You Use the Fv Argument?

Sometimes when you have a loan and make regular payments, you may have a lump sum payment at the end of the loan. Consider a lease. You may lease a car or a business may lease office equipment—copy machines, printers, or computers—and then make regular payments during the term of the lease. At the end of the lease, you can return the car to the dealership or the business can return the equipment to the supplier. You also have the option of purchasing the vehicle or the business could purchase the equipment for a specific price that was determined at the time you signed the lease. This lump sum payment would be entered into the fv argument of the PMT function.

The **type** argument indicates when the payments are due—either at the beginning (1) or the end (0) of a period—such as the end of a month, quarter, or year. If type is omitted (because it is an optional argument), Excel assumes that the value is zero.

The Turquoise Oasis Spa can use the PMT function to calculate the monthly payment on a $200,000 loan if the bank is charging 6.75% interest over a 10-year period. Thus, the PMT function arguments would be:

- Rate: 6.75% divided by 12 months = .5625%
- Nper: 10 years * 12 months = 120 months
- Pv: –$200,000—recall that this argument is negative because it represents an outflow of money.

Because the future value and type arguments are not given, you would end the PMT function after entering the present value and calculate the monthly payment as $2,296.48. If you do not have a future value and the payment is made at the end of period, you can stop at principal—the pv argument—and just type your ending parenthesis.

$$=\text{PMT}(.0675/12,10*12,-200000)$$

The amount of the payment can change based on when the payment needs to be made—either at the beginning or the end of a period—because of how interest is calculated. If the payments are made at the beginning of a period, the total interest that will be paid on the loan is lower because you are paying down the principal faster. The **principal** is the unpaid balance amount of the loan. Because the future value is not given and you want to enter 1 in the type argument, you would type two commas after the present value argument to indicate that you want to skip the future value argument. The PMT function calculates the monthly payment as $2,283.64 and would be entered as follows:

$$=\text{PMT}(.0675/12,10*12,-200000,1)$$

CONSIDER THIS | **Payments and Playing What-If Analysis**

It is important to mention that when you create your Excel model to calculate a payment, you would format the model so that you can reference cells that hold the interest rate, loan amount, and terms. How could referencing cells with these values allow you to perform what-if analysis? **What-if analysis** is when you use several different values in one or more formulas to explore all the various results. What if you decided that you could not afford the loan payments? How could you modify the interest rate, loan amount, and terms to find a payment that you can afford?

To Calculate Payments Using the PMT Function

a. Open **Microsoft Excel 2010**.

b. Click the **File tab**, click **Open**, and then browse to your student data files. Locate and select **e06_ws11_Financial_Analysis**, and then click **Open**.

c. Click the **File tab**, and then click **Save As**. Browse to your student files. In the File name box, type Lastname_Firstname_e06_ws11_Financial_Analysis, replacing Lastname_Firstname with your actual name, and then click **Save**.

d. Click the **Insert tab**, and then click **Header & Footer** in the Text group to insert a footer with the file name.

e. Click the **Design tab**, and then click **Go to Footer** in the Navigation group. If necessary, click on the left section of the footer, and then click **File Name** in the Header & Footer Elements group.

f. Click the **View tab**, click **Normal** in the Workbook views group, and then click the **Home tab**.

g. This workbook includes information for some of the financing options collected by the managers. If necessary, click the **Loan Analysis worksheet tab**. Click cell **B6**, type 200000, press Enter, and then press ↑. Click the **Home tab**, and then click the **Format Cells: Number** dialog box launcher in the Number group. In the Format Cells dialog box, on the Number tab, click **Currency**, set Decimal places to 0, and then click the last option to show Negative numbers in red with parenthesis format. Click **OK**. This is the amount that the Turquoise Oasis Spa thinks they may have to borrow from the bank.

h. Click cell **B7**, type .0675 as the rate, and then format the cell as Percentage with two decimal places.

i. Click cell **B8**, and then type 10 as the term of the loan.

j. Click cell **B9**, and then type 12 because the payments will be made monthly.

k. To calculate a monthly payment that is made at the end of the period, click cell **B10**, and then type =PMT(B7/B9,B8*B9,-B6). Press Enter, and then format the cell as Currency, if necessary.

l. To calculate a monthly payment that is made at the beginning of the period, click cell **B11**, and then type =PMT(B7/B9,B8*B9,-B6,,1). Press Enter, and then format the cell as **Currency**, if necessary. Notice the difference between the payments is dependent upon when the payment is made.

Monthly payment using 0 in type argument

Monthly payment using 1 in type argument

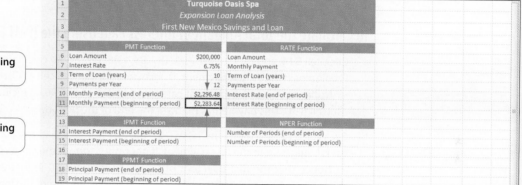

	Turquoise Oasis Spa			
1				
2	*Expansion Loan Analysis*			
3	First New Mexico Savings and Loan			
4				
5	PMT Function		RATE Function	
6	Loan Amount	$200,000	Loan Amount	
7	Interest Rate	6.75%	Monthly Payment	
8	Term of Loan (years)	10	Term of Loan (years)	
9	Payments per Year	12	Payments per Year	
10	Monthly Payment (end of period)	$2,296.48	Interest Rate (end of period)	
11	Monthly Payment (beginning of period)	$2,283.64	Interest Rate (beginning of period)	
12				
13	IPMT Function		NPER Function	
14	Interest Payment (end of period)		Number of Periods (end of period)	
15	Interest Payment (beginning of period)		Number of Periods (beginning of period)	
16				
17	PPMT Function			
18	Principal Payment (end of period)			
19	Principal Payment (beginning of period)			

Figure 1 Loan analysis using PMT function

m. **Save** 💾 your changes.

Quick Reference Understanding the PMT Function Syntax

The PMT function syntax has the following arguments:

rate	The interest rate per period for the loan. This argument is required.
nper	The total number of payments for the loan. This argument is required.
Pv	The present value or the total amount that a series of future payments is worth now; also known as the loan amount. This argument is required.
Fv	The future value or a cash balance you want to attain after the last payment is made. If fv is omitted, it is assumed to be 0 (zero), that is, the future value of a loan is 0. This argument is optional.
type	The number 0 (zero) or 1 and indicates when payments are due. This argument is optional. Set type equal to 0 (or omit) if payments are due at the end of the period. Set type equal to 1 if payments are due at the beginning of the period.

Figure 2 Example of the PMT function syntax

Using the IPMT Function

When a payment is made on a loan, a portion of the funds is applied to interest and the rest is applied to the loan principal. As the total loan balance decreases, a smaller proportion is applied to interest and a greater proportion is applied to principal. Excel has two functions to determine these values: IPMT for the interest portion and PPMT for the principal. The sum of the IPMT and PPMT results should equal the PMT.

The Interest Payment function, or **IPMT function**, is a financial function that calculates the amount of interest paid for a fixed term or fixed rate loan or investment. The syntax is similar to the PMT function, with one addition—the period, or per argument. The **per** argument is the period for which you want to find the interest and must be a value within the range of 1 to nper.

=IPMT(rate, per, nper, pv, [fv], [type])

To Calculate the Total Amount of Interest Paid Using the IPMT Function

a. Click cell **B14**, and then type =IPMT(B7/B9,1,B8*B9,-B6) to calculate how much interest is being paid in the first payment. If necessary, format the cell as **Currency**.

Notice that the first payment calculated in B10 of $2,296.48 includes $1,125 in interest (cell B14). This payment is made at the end of the period.

b. Click cell **B15**, and then type =IPMT(B7/B9,1,B8*B9,-B6,,1) to calculate how much interest is being paid in the first payment. If necessary, format the cell as **Currency**.

Notice that the first payment of $2,283.64 includes $0 in interest. This payment is made at the beginning of the period and at the beginning of the loan; thus, no interest has been added—accrued—yet.

c. Modify the formula in **B15** to adjust the period argument value to 2. Type =IPMT(B7/B9,2,B8*B9,-B6,,1) to calculate how much interest is being paid in the second payment.

Notice that the second payment (cell B11) of $2,283.64 includes $1,112.15 in interest (cell B15). This payment is made at the beginning of the second period, and interest has had time to accumulate.

Interest payment using 0 in type argument

Interest payment using 1 in type argument

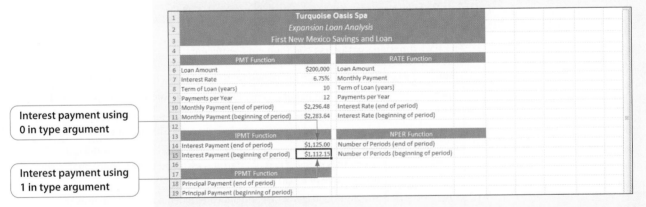

Figure 3 Loan analysis using IPMT function

d. **Save** 💾 your changes.

Using the PPMT Function

The Principal Payment function, or **PPMT function**, is a financial function that calculates the amount of principal paid for a fixed term or fixed rate loan or investment. Where you just calculated how much interest is included in the payment, this function calculates how much of the payment goes toward paying off the principal balance of the loan. The syntax is the same as the IPMT function.

=PPMT(rate, per, nper, pv, [fv], [type])

To Calculate the Total Amount of Principal Paid Using the PPMT Function

a. Click cell **B18**, and then type =PPMT(B7/B9,1,B8*B9,-B6) to calculate how much of the principal is being paid in the first payment. Notice that in the first payment, $1,171.48 is being applied to the loan principal. If necessary, format the cell as **Currency**.

b. Click cell **B19**, and then type =PPMT(B7/B9,1,B8*B9,-B6,,1) to calculate how much of the principal is being paid in the first payment if the first payment is due at the end of the period.

Notice that the first payment of $2,283.64 is all going toward the loan principal. This payment is made at the beginning of the period at the beginning of the loan, and no interest has been added—accrued—yet; thus, no interest needs to be paid.

c. Modify the function in **B19** to adjust the period argument value to 2. Type =PPMT(B7/B9,2,B8*B9,-B6,,1) to calculate how much of the principal is being paid in the second payment.

Notice that the second payment, $1,171.48 is being applied to the loan principal. This payment is made at the beginning of the second period, and interest has had time to accrue.

SIDE NOTE
Do the Math!
You can easily double-check your calculation by adding the result in B18 to the Interest Payment in B14. The total should equal the Monthly Payment in B10.

SIDE NOTE
Edit in the Formula Bar
Alternatively, you could edit the formula in the formula bar if you feel more comfortable doing so.

SIDE NOTE
When You Pay Matters
Notice, the principal payment is much higher in the first period as compared to the second. Since you make a payment on the first day of the loan, the entire amount goes to principal.

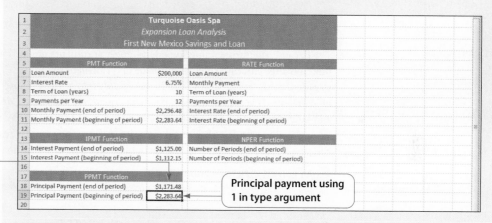

Principal payment using 0 in type argument

Principal payment using 1 in type argument

Figure 4 Loan analysis using PPMT function

d. Save your changes.

CONSIDER THIS | **Why Are the Principal Payments the Same?**

The amount of the loan payment is the same when using IPMT + PPMT versus using the PMT function. The principal payment would be the same because the loan amount, interest rate, and terms are the same. The interest and principal proportions are what vary within the payment. This is due to the fact that as you pay down the balance of the loan, the remaining principal (balance) becomes smaller each period and less interest is owed. Does the period play a role in the amount of the interest payment?

Using RATE and NPER to Find the Missing Pieces

There are times when you do not have all the information needed to calculate PMT functions, such as the rate (RATE) or number of periods (NPER). However, you may know the payment, and Excel includes functions to help you calculate the missing information.

Using the RATE Function

The **RATE function** calculates the interest rate per period for an investment or loan, given that you know the loan or present value, payment, and number of payment periods. The RATE function syntax uses six arguments. The first three are required, and the last three are optional: (1) number of periods (nper); (2) payment (pmt); (3) present value (pv); (4) future value (fv); (5) type (type); and (6) interest rate guess (guess).

=RATE(nper, pmt, pv, [fv], [type], [guess])

The difference between the RATE function arguments and previous functions' arguments is the addition of the guess argument. The **guess** argument is used when you want to guess what the interest rate will be. RATE usually calculates if you enter a guess between zero and one. If nothing is entered, Excel assumes that the guess is 10%. If RATE does not calculate, you can try different values for the guess argument.

The Turquoise Oasis Spa can use the RATE function to calculate the interest rate on a 10-year, $200,000 loan if the monthly payment is $2,853. Thus, the RATE function arguments would be:

- Nper: 10 years * 12 months = 120 months
- Pmt: $2,853
- Pv: $200,000

=RATE(10*12, 2853,−200000)

Because the future value, type, and guess arguments are optional, you would end the RATE function after entering the present value and calculate the interest rate as 0.988%. It is important to note that the result in this case is the *monthly interest rate* because you used 12 times the number of loan years. If you were making payments quarterly and used 4 times the number of loan years or annually, the number of loan years only, Excel would calculate the rate as quarterly or annually. If you wanted to calculate the annual interest rate from the monthly result, you could simply multiply the rate by 12. As a result, the bank would be charging the Turquoise Oasis Spa 11.858% annually.

=RATE(10*12,2853,−200000)*12

To Calculate the Interest Rate Using the RATE Function

a. Click cell **E6**, type 200000, and then format the cell as **Currency** (Hint: Use Format Painter to copy formatting from cell B6). If necessary, resize your column to see all the data. This is the amount that the Turquoise Oasis Spa thinks they may have to borrow from the bank.

b. Click cell **E7**, type 2853 as the monthly payment, and then format the cell as **Currency**.

c. Click cell **E8**, and then type 10 as the term of the loan.

d. Click cell **E9**, and then type 12 because the payments will be made monthly.

e. Click cell **E10**, and then type =RATE(E8*E9,E7,-E6)*12 to calculate the annual interest rate for a loan where the payment is made at the end of the period. Format the cell as **Percentage** with **3** decimal places. Notice that the annual interest rate is 11.858% when the payment is made at the end of the period.

f. Click cell **E11**, and then type =RATE(E8*E9,E7,-E6,,1)*12 to calculate the annual interest rate for a loan where the payment is made at the beginning of the period. Format the cell as **Percentage** with **3** decimal places. Notice that the annual interest rate is 12.107% when the payment is made at the beginning of the period.

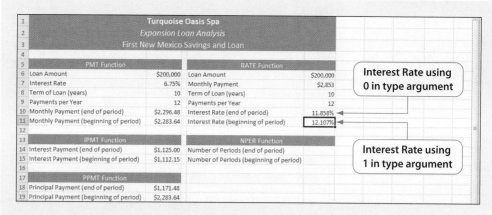

Figure 5 Loan analysis using RATE function

g. **Save** 💾 your changes.

Using the NPER Function

The Number of Periods function, or **NPER function**, calculates the number of payment periods for an investment or loan if you know the loan amount, interest rate, and payment amount. The NPER function syntax uses five arguments. The first three are required, and last two are optional: (1) rate (rate); (2) payment (pmt); (3) present value (pv); (4) future value (fv); and (5) type (type).

=NPER(rate, pmt, pv, [fv], [type])

The Turquoise Oasis Spa can use the NPER function to calculate the number of periods on a $200,000 loan with an annual rate of 11.858% if the monthly payment is $2,853. Thus, the RATE function arguments would be as follows:

- Rate: 11.858%
- Pmt: $2,853
- Pv: $200,000

=NPER(.11858/12, 2853, −200000)

Because the future value and type arguments are optional, you would end the NPER function after entering the present value and calculate the number of periods as 120.

To Calculate the Number of Periods Using the NPER Function

a. Click cell **E14**, and then type =NPER(E10/E9,E7,-E6) to calculate the number of periods for a loan where the payment is made at the end of the period. Format the cell as **Number** with **0** decimal places. Notice that the number of periods is 120 when the payment is made at the end of the period.

b. Click cell **E15**, and then type =NPER(E10/E9,E7,-E6,,1) to calculate the number of periods for a loan where the payment is made at the beginning of the period and using the beginning of period interest rate of 12.107%. Format the cell as **Number** with **0** decimal places. Notice that the number of periods is 118 when the payment is made at the beginning of the period.

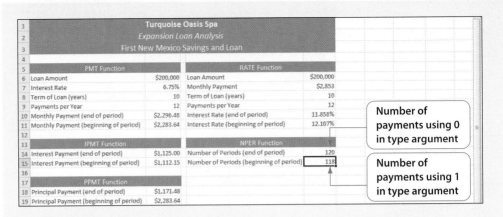

1			Turquoise Oasis Spa			
2			*Expansion Loan Analysis*			
3			First New Mexico Savings and Loan			
4						
5	PMT Function			RATE Function		
6	Loan Amount	$200,000	Loan Amount		$200,000	
7	Interest Rate	6.75%	Monthly Payment		$2,853	
8	Term of Loan (years)	10	Term of Loan (years)		10	
9	Payments per Year	12	Payments per Year		12	
10	Monthly Payment (end of period)	$2,296.48	Interest Rate (end of period)		11.858%	
11	Monthly Payment (beginning of period)	$2,283.64	Interest Rate (beginning of period)		12.107%	Number of payments using 0 in type argument
12						
13	IPMT Function			NPER Function		
14	Interest Payment (end of period)	$1,125.00	Number of Periods (end of period)		120	
15	Interest Payment (beginning of period)	$1,112.15	Number of Periods (beginning of period)		118	Number of payments using 1 in type argument
16						
17	PPMT Function					
18	Principal Payment (end of period)	$1,171.48				
19	Principal Payment (beginning of period)	$2,283.64				

Figure 6 Loan analysis using NPER function

c. **Save** 💾 your changes.

Using Amortization Tables and Analyzing Loans

The PMT function is helpful when you are calculating the payments of your loan. However, when conducting an analysis of a loan, amortizing can provide detailed information about the loan balances and payments made for principal and interest, which can aid you in managing the loan. Now that you have learned how to calculate payment, principal, and interest amounts, you have the tools needed to create an amortization table. **Amortize** with respect to loan balances, refers to repaying the balance of a loan over a period of time in multiple installments (payments). An **amortization table** is a schedule that calculates the interest and principal payments along with the remaining balance of the loan. When you repay a loan, the beginning payments focus on paying off the interest. As you make payments, the amount of each payment that is applied to repaying interest decreases because the interest that is accrued is based on the amount of principal left to repay. The last few payments are almost entirely applied towards the principal.

Turquoise Oasis Spa could use an amortization table to analyze a loan for improvements. For example, Irene Kai would like to borrow $25,000 for new equipment and pay this loan off in one year. By creating an amortization table showing the date of each payment, she can see how much will be applied to the interest and principal as well as the balance of the loan. After creating the amortization table, she finds that the payment would be $2,160.29 per month, and the salon would end up paying $923.46 in interest over the life of the loan. In this section, you will create an amortization table that helps Irene Kai analyze the repayment schedule to see if the payments are within the salon's budget. You will also calculate cumulative interest and principal using the CUMIPMT and CUMPRINC functions.

Real World Advice — Four Things to Check in an Amortization Table

There are four things that you can do to ensure you have accurately constructed your amortization table:

- The last value in your table will be exactly zero.
- A given monthly payment (PMT) will equal the sum of the interest(IPMT) and principal(PPMT).
- The sum of the principal payments (PPMT) will always equal the loan amount. If you add interest it will be everything paid over the course of the loan period, both in interest and principal.
- All interest and principal paid should equal the sum of all the payments made.

You can check your calculations in one easy step. Highlight a range of cells—such as the IPMT and PPMT calculations for the first period, then Excel puts the Average, Count, and Sum in the status bar located at the bottom-left of the Excel window (to the right of the navigation and view buttons).

Creating an Amortization Table

When you create an amortization table, start with the simplest configuration. Initially you should calculate the payment number, payment amount, interest and principal portions, and an ending balance for each payment. You can always add more details and complexity later.

To Create an Amortization Table

a. Click the **Amortize1 worksheet tab**.

b. Click cell **G5**, and then type =C7*C8 to calculate the number of payments.

c. Click cell **G6**, type =PMT(C6/C8,G5,-C5) to calculate the payments that will be made at the end of the period, and then format the cell as **Currency** with **2** decimals, if necessary. Notice that the monthly payment will be $2,160.29.

d. Click cell **G7**, type =G5*G6 to calculate the total amount that will be paid, and then format the cell as **Currency**, if necessary. Notice that the total amount that will be paid on the loan is $25,923.46.

e. Click cell **G8**, and then type =G7-C5 to calculate the total interest that will be paid on the loan. Notice that the total interest that will be paid on the loan is $923.46.

f. Click cell **C12**, and then type =C5 to begin creating your amortization table. If necessary, format as **Currency** with **2** decimal places.

g. Click cell **D12**, type =$G$6 to enter your payment, and then copy the formula down to cell **D23** using the AutoFill handle.

h. Click cell **E12**, type =IPMT($C$6/$C$8,A12,$G$5,-$C$5) to calculate how much of the monthly payment is being applied to the interest portion of the loan, format as **Currency** with **2** decimal places, and then copy the formula down to cell **E23** using the **AutoFill** handle. Notice how the interest portion of the payment decreases as the loan is paid off, with $140.63 total interest being paid in the first payment and $12.08 total interest being paid in the last payment.

i. Click cell **F12**, type =PPMT($C$6/$C$8,A12,$G$5,-$C$5) to calculate how much of the monthly payment is being applied to the principal portion of the loan, and then copy the formula down to cell **F23** using the **AutoFill** handle. Notice how the principal portion of the payment increases as the loan is paid off, with $2,019.66 total principal being paid in the first payment and $2,148.20 total principal being paid in the last payment.

j. Click cell **G12**, type =C12-F12 to calculate the remaining balance after each payment, and then copy the formula down to cell **G23** using the **AutoFill** handle. The calculations will be negative until you fill in the beginning balance.

k. Your beginning balance for the next payment will be the same as the ending balance after the previous payment. Click cell **C13**, and then type =G12 to calculate the beginning balance for the second period. Then copy the formula down to cell **C23** using the **AutoFill** handle to supply the beginning balance for the remaining periods.

l. To use the SUM function in cells D24:F24 to check your calculations, click cell **D24**, type =SUM(D12:D23), and then use AutoFill to copy the formula over to cell **F24**. The results in D24 and E24 should equal your results in cells G7 and G8, respectively, and the total principal in F24 should equal the loan amount in C5.

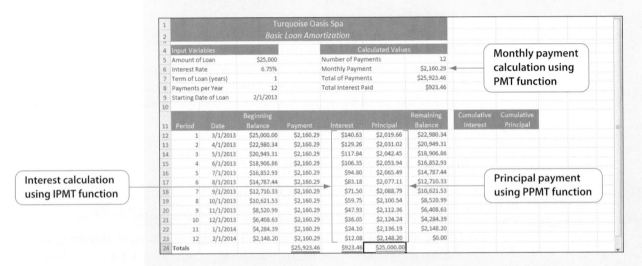

Figure 7 Amortization table

m. **Save** your changes.

Calculating Cumulative Interest and Principal Using CUMIPMT and CUMPRINC

The amortization table contains the IPMT and PPMT functions so you can view the specific amount of interest and principal that are being paid in each payment. However, there may be times that you want to know the total interest or principal being paid over a given period of time. Consider a mortgage. If someone is paying a mortgage, they can use the mortgage interest paid throughout the year as a deduction on their federal income taxes. Thus, knowing the amount of cumulative interest paid can make it easier to complete this section on a tax return.

Using the CUMIPMT Function

The Cumulative Interest function, or **CUMIPMT function**, can be used to calculate the amount of interest paid over a specific number of periods, such as quarterly or annually. Thus, if you do not want to calculate a running total of the interest paid, you can total the payments between two payment periods. The CUMIPMT function syntax uses six arguments, all of which are required: (1) rate (rate); (2) number of periods (nper); (3) present value (pv); (4) start period (start_period); (5) end period (end_period); and (6) type (type).

=CUMIPMT(rate, nper, pv, start_period, end_period, type)

The two new arguments are start_period and end_period; they indicate the period numbers during the life of the loan. Start_period defines the start of the payment period for the interval you want to sum. The end_period defines the end of the payment period. With this function, Excel does not allow you to place a negative sign in front of the pv argument. Thus, to display numbers as a positive result, you can nest the CUMIPMT function within the Absolute Value (ABS) function. The **ABS function** will return the absolute value of a number—the number without its negative sign.

=ABS(CUMIPMT(rate, nper, pv, start_period, end_period, type))

Using the CUMPRINC Function

Similar to the CUMIPMT function, the Cumulative Principal function, or **CUMPRINC function**, can be used to calculate the amount of principal paid over a specific number of periods, such as quarterly or annually. Thus, if you do not want to calculate a running total of the principal paid, you can total the payments between two payment periods. The CUMPRINC function syntax uses the same six arguments that the CUMIPMT uses, all of which are required. Like the CUMIPMT function, you are unable to place a negative sign in front of the pv argument. Thus, to display positive numbers, you can nest the CUMPRINC function within the Absolute Value function.

=ABS(CUMPRINC(rate, nper, pv, start_period, end_period, type))

To Calculate Cumulative Interest and Principal

a. Click cell **I12**, type =ABS(CUMIPMT($C$6/$C$8,$G$5,$C$5,$A$12,A12,0)) to calculate the cumulative interest payment for the life of the loan, and then format the cell as **Currency** with **2** decimals. This will calculate the first interest payment.

b. Use the **AutoFill** handle to copy the formula down to cell **I23**. Notice that the value in cell I23 is the same as your total interest payment in cell G8.

c. Click cell **J12**, type =ABS(CUMPRINC($C$6/$C$8,$G$5,$C$5,$A$12,A12,0)) to calculate the cumulative principal payment for the life of the loan, and then format the cell as **Currency** with **2** decimal places. This will calculate the first principal payment.

d. Use the **AutoFill** handle to copy the formula down to cell **J23**. Notice that the value in cell J23 is the same as your total loan amount.

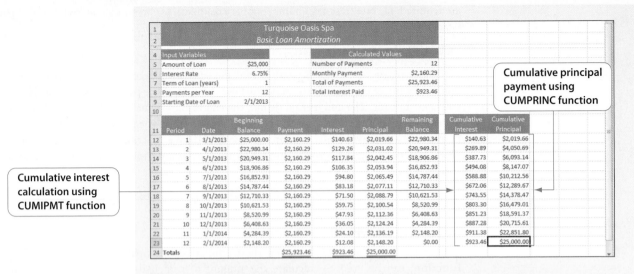

Cumulative principal payment using CUMPRINC function

Cumulative interest calculation using CUMIPMT function

Figure 8 Amortization table

e. **Save** 💾 your changes.

CONSIDER THIS | **Be Careful When Comparing Two Loans**

Time plays a role in calculating interest. Because of the time value of money, this is not an apples-to-apples comparison. The faster you pay off a loan, the less time there is to accumulate interest. Consider a credit card. If you make the minimum payments each month it will take you longer to pay off the balance because you are accumulating additional interest each month. This interest is being accumulated on both the principal balance of the credit card *and* any interest from previous months that you have accumulated but have not yet paid. This means that most, if not all, of your minimum payment is being applied to the interest. However, if you make a larger payment each month, you will pay the balance off faster because you are paying the principal as well as the interest. What do you think about comparing the CUMIPMT of two loans when the term is different? Are you comparing the same thing when you do this?

Alternatives to Monthly Payments

When businesses plan the budget, it is generally created on an annual basis. Because of this, you may want to create an amortization table that calculates quarterly or yearly payments on a loan instead of monthly payments, depending on the terms of your loan. Additionally, many businesses and individuals pay estimated quarterly taxes—federal, state, and local—if they believe they may owe taxes at the end of the year. For example, if you are self-employed or contract out services, your pay generally does not have taxes deducted. Therefore, you may want to create a quarterly amortization table to estimate your tax payments.

To Calculate the Yearly Cumulative Interest and Principal

a. Click the **Amortize2 worksheet tab**.

b. Click cell **J12**, type =ABS(CUMIPMT(C6/C8,G5,C5,A12,A15,0)) to calculate the cumulative interest payment for the first year of the loan, and then format the cell as **Currency** with **2** decimal places.

c. Click cell **J13**, type =ABS(CUMIPMT(C6/C8,G5,C5,A16,A19,0)) to calculate the cumulative interest payment for the second year of the loan, and then format the cell as **Currency** with **2** decimal places.

d. Click cell **J14**, type =ABS(CUMIPMT(C6/C8,G5,C5,A20,A23,0)) to calculate the cumulative interest payment for the third year of the loan, and then format the cell as **Currency** with **2** decimal places.

e. Click cell **K12**, type =ABS(CUMPRINC(C6/C8,G5,C5,A12,A15,0)) to calculate the cumulative principal payment for the first year of the loan, and then format the cell as **Currency** with **2** decimal places.

f. Click cell **K13**, type =ABS(CUMPRINC(C6/C8,G5,C5,A16,A19,0)) to calculate the cumulative principal payment for the second year of the loan, and then format the cell as **Currency** with **2** decimal places.

g. Click cell **K14**, type =ABS(CUMPRINC(C6/C8,G5,C5,A20,A23,0)) to calculate the cumulative principal payment for the third year of the loan, and then format the cell as **Currency** with **2** decimal places.

h. Use the SUM function in cells J24 and K24 to check your calculations. Click cell **J24**, type =SUM(J12:J14), and then AutoFill the formula over to cell **K24**. The results in J24 and K24 should equal your results in cells G8 and C5 respectively.

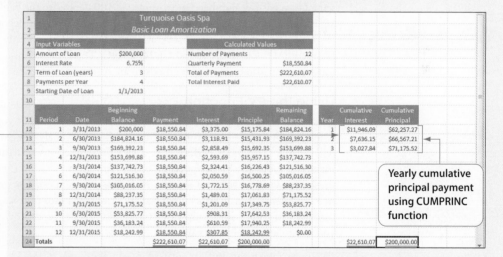

Yearly cumulative interest calculation using CUMIPMT function

Yearly cumulative principal payment using CUMPRINC function

Figure 9 Amortization table

i. **Save** your changes.

Predicting Future Values and Handling Depreciation

Another important task of business and personal financial management includes analyzing investments and depreciating assets. Many businesses do not generate revenue just by selling goods or services, they also invest money. Additionally, businesses are required for tax and reporting purposes to show that the original cost of the property they purchase such as buildings, vehicles, and equipment is reduced (depreciated) over time as they utilize these assets. In this section, you will learn how to calculate the present value and future value of an investment, you will work with annuity functions and rates of return functions, and you will calculate the depreciation of assets.

Analyzing Annuities and Investments with the PV, FV, NPV, and XNPV Functions

Whether you are a business or individual investing money, analyzing how the investments are performing is a critical part of the investment process. There are many methods in which money can be invested—stocks, bonds, certificates of deposit, Treasury bills, and mutual funds are just a few examples.

Understanding Annuity Functions

One way an individual can invest money is in an annuity. An **annuity** is a recurring amount paid or received at specified intervals, for instance, a cash payment of $100 made to an investment account every month for five years is an example of an annuity. Another example of a type of annuity is an agreement between an individual and an insurance company. The individual pays the insurance company money, either in a lump sum or regularly over time, and then the money is invested. Upon retirement, the individual begins receiving regular payments from the insurance company for the rest of the individual's life. These regular payments are an example of an annuity.

In annuity functions, cash you pay, such as depositing money into a savings account, is represented by a negative number. Cash you receive, such as interest earned on a savings account, is represented by a positive number. For example, a $100 deposit to the bank would be represented by the argument: −100—negative 100—if you are the one making the deposit and 100 if you are the bank.

You have already learned several of the functions that apply to annuities—RATE, PMT, IPMT, PPMT, CUMIPMT, and CUMPRINC. The Present Value (PV) and Future Value (FV) functions can also be used as methods to analyzing investments.

Using the PV Function

Regardless of how you decide to invest your money—whether you are saving for a home, college, or retirement—if you understand the basics of analyzing your investment portfolio, you will be able to assess its performance. One of the functions that can help you analyze an investment is the Present Value function, or **PV function**. The PV function is used to calculate the present or current value of a series of future payments on an investment and uses the same five arguments seen in other financial functions: (1) rate (rate); (2) number of periods (nper); (3) payment (pmt); (4) future value (fv); and (5) type (type). If you do not know the payment, you must enter the future value.

=PV(rate, nper, pmt, [fv], [type])

For example, you might decide to retire at age 65 and want to use the PV function to compare which situation would be better: withdrawing all of the $500,000 you saved now or withdrawing $50,000 over the next 10 years. By using the PV function, you can determine that investing the yearly payments at 5% interest results in a lower present value—$386,086.75—than the lump-sum payment of $500,000.

=PV(.05,10, −50000)

Turquoise Oasis Spa managers are considering a different option for financing the expansion—withdrawing money from an investment account that they have and reinvest it in a higher yield investment. The spa can either take the total amount of $200,000 in one lump-sum payment or withdraw $100,000 each year for the next two years.

To Calculate the Present Value of an Investment

a. Click the **PV and FV worksheet tab**.

b. Click cell **B5**, type **200000**, and then format your cell as **Currency** with **2** decimal points.

c. Click cell **B6**, type **100000**, and then format your cell as **Currency** with **2** decimal points.

d. Click cell **B7**, and then type **2**.

e. One of the opportunities that the spa has is to invest the money for two years at 12% interest, compounded annually. Click cell **B8**, type **.12**, and then format your cell as **Percentage** with **0** decimal points.

f. Click cell **B9**, and then type **=PV(B8,B7,-B6)** to calculate the present value. Notice that the spa would lose money if they took the annual withdrawal and invested in this option because they have not left the money in the account long enough to earn the money they expected to earn.

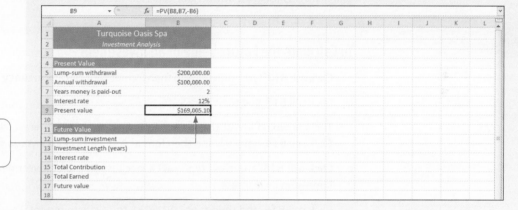

Present value calculation using the PV function

Figure 10 Present value of an investment

g. The other opportunity that the spa has is to invest the money at 6% interest, compounded monthly. Click cell **B8**, type **6**.

h. Click cell **B9**, type **=PV(B8/12,B7,-B6)** to calculate the present value. Notice that the spa would essentially break-even if they invested in this option.

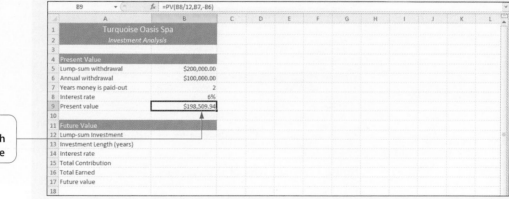

Present value calculation with 6% interest rate

Figure 11 Present value of an investment

i. **Save** 💾 your changes.

Using the FV Function

The Future Value function, or **FV function**, is used to calculate the value of an investment with a fixed interest rate and term, and periodic payments over a specific period of time. The FV function syntax uses five arguments, the first three are required, and the last two are optional: (1) rate (rate); (2) number of periods (nper); (3) payment (pmt); (4) present value (pv); and (5) type (type). If you do not know the payment, you must enter the present value.

=FV(rate, nper, pmt, [pv], [type])

For example, you might decide to start saving for retirement and want to use the FV function to calculate how much you would have by the age of 65. By using the FV function, you can determine how much your Individual Retirement Account (IRA) would be worth when you retire. If you contributed $2,500 per year to your IRA for 40 years—a total of $100,000—with an interest rate of 8% annually, you would have nearly $650,000.

=FV(.08,40, −2500)

Turquoise Oasis Spa managers are considering investing money that would be provided by private investors. This would require them to wait for five years to allow the investment to grow. The managers use the Future Value function to help them make their decision.

To Calculate the Future Value of an Investment

a. Click cell **B12**, type 400000, and then format your cell as **Currency** with **2** decimal points.

b. Click cell **B13**, and then type 5.

c. The spa would invest the money for five years at 4% interest, compounded annually. Click cell **B14**, type .04, and then format your cell as **Percentage** with **0** decimal points.

d. Click cell **B15**, and then type =B12, because the total investment will be a one time, lump-sum investment.

e. Click cell **B16**, and then type =B17-B15 to calculate the total earned. The value will be −$400,000.00 until you enter your Future Value function.

f. Click cell **B17**, and then type =FV(B14,B13,0,-B12) to calculate the future value of this investment. Notice that the spa would earn $86,661.16 if they invested in this option.

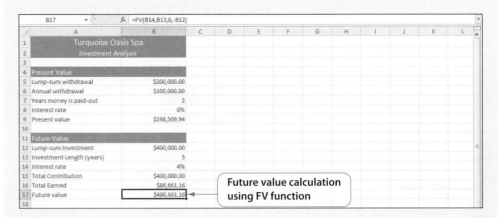

Figure 12 Future value of an investment

g. **Save** your changes.

> **CONSIDER THIS** | **Should Turquoise Oasis Spa Wait Until It Makes Money?**
>
> Turquoise Oasis Spa could earn more than enough money to complete the upgrades and expansion if they accepted the money from the private investors and invested it. Would this be a wise decision to wait five years? What repercussions could the managers face if they do wait? Could it affect the amount of revenue that is generated?

Using the NPV Function

The Net Present Value function, or **NPV function**, is used to determine the value of an investment or business by analyzing a series of future incoming and outgoing cash flows, expected to occur over the life of the investment. The NPV function sums the present values of these individual cash flows. This function is used for capital budgeting and measures the surplus or deficit of cash flows, in present value terms, once financing charges are met. **Capital budgeting** is the planning procedure used to evaluate whether an organization's long-term investments—such as acquiring a business or starting a new business, purchasing new machinery and new buildings, or performing the research and development of new products—are worth pursuing.

Many businesses use a net present value analysis to gauge the quality of an investment. The NPV function syntax is a little different from other financial functions and includes rate and value arguments. The value1 argument is required, and subsequent value arguments are optional. The ellipse indicates that additional arguments can be entered and Excel allows for 1 to 254 values entered (implied by the ellipses). The NPV function uses the order of the value arguments to interpret the order of cash flows. Be sure to enter your payment and income values in the correct sequence where the value1 argument is the amount of the loan. Subsequent values are the net income values from the capital budget, which are based on future cash flows.

=NPV(rate, value1, [value2],...)

The management at Turquoise Oasis Spa can use the NPV function to see if it benefits them financially to take out a loan for new equipment. Given a capital budget, they can add input values for the loan and then use the projected cash inflows from the business operations to calculate whether the purchase of new equipment produces positive financial benefits. If the spa borrows $125,000 at 8% interest and the return or projected cash inflows over three years were $8,000 from first year, $9,200 from second year, and $10,000 from third year, the net present value would result in a loss of $68,645. Thus, this would not be a good investment for Turquoise Oasis.

=NPV(.08,8000,9200,10000,−125000)

Turquoise Oasis Spa managers are considering the equipment—such as massage tables, salon chairs, and sinks—that they want to purchase to complete the improvements and expansion. You have been given the spa's capital budget to use for your net present value analysis.

To Calculate the Net Present Value of a Loan

a. Click the **NPV worksheet tab**.

b. Click cell **B5**, type **.0765** as the rate, and then format your cell as **Percentage** with **2** decimal places.

c. An investment of $125,000 will be required to purchase the new equipment. Click cell **B6**, type **125000**, and then format your cell as **Currency** with **0** decimal places.

d. The goal is to have the loan paid off in three years. Click cell **B7**, type **3**.

e. Click cell **B20**, type **=NPV(B5,B18:D18,-B6)** to calculate the net present value, and then if necessary, format the cell as **Currency** with **0** decimal places.

Notice in your formula bar that your loan amount is entered last and that a negative sign is placed in front of it. This is because you have to repay the loan, and the value has to be deducted from the overall net present value.

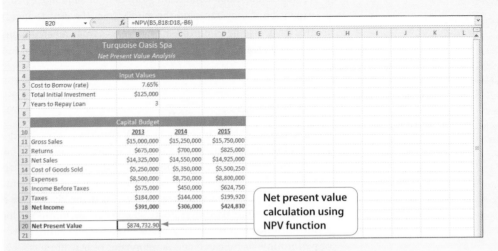

Figure 13 Net present value analysis

f. **Save** 🖫 your changes.

Using the XNPV Function

Similar to NPV, the Irregular Net Present Value function, or **XNPV function**, determines the value of an investment or business by analyzing an irregular time series of incoming and outgoing cash flows. The XNPV function syntax is a little different from the NPV function and includes rate, values, and dates arguments, all of which are required. The values argument corresponds to payments, and one of these values must be a negative value, which will most likely represent the initial loan disbursement. The series of values must contain at least one positive value and one negative value. The dates argument corresponds with when the payments were made, including the loan disbursement date. The first payment date indicates the beginning of the schedule of payments. All subsequent dates must be after the first payment date, but they may be listed in any order.

=XNPV(rate, values, dates)

To Calculate an Irregular Net Present Value of a Loan

a. Click the **XNPV worksheet tab**.

b. Click cell **B17**, type =XNPV(B5,B9:B15,A9:A15) to calculate the net present value, and then format the cell as **Currency** with **0** decimal places and negative numbers displayed in red parenthesis format.

    Notice that your loan amount is entered in cell B9 and a negative sign is placed in front of it. This is because you have to repay the loan and the value has to be deducted from the overall net present value.

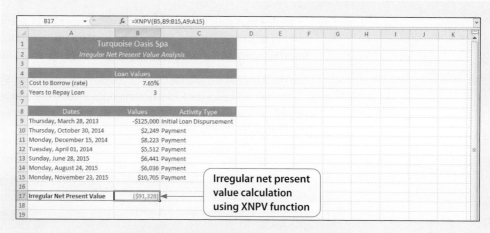

Irregular net present value calculation using XNPV function

Figure 14 Irregular net present value of a loan

c. **Save** 🖫 your changes.

Analyzing Rates of Return on Investments with the IRR and XIRR Functions

Investing money can be a profitable venture. Whether you are investing in an annuity, or purchasing stocks, bonds, certificates of deposit, Treasury bills, or mutual funds, you can invest your money sensibly and meet your savings goals. Another way for businesses to ensure that they are making wise investing decisions is to analyze the rate of return. One way this can be completed is to use the Internal Rate of Return function, or IRR function.

Using the IRR Function

The **IRR function** indicates the profitability of an investment and is commonly used in business when choosing between investments. This function is generally used in capital budgeting to measure and compare how profitable a potential investment is. The IRR of an investment is the rate that makes the net present value of both positive and negative cash flows equal to zero. Internal rates of return are commonly used to evaluate how suitable an investment is. The higher the internal rate of return, the more desirable the investment is. If you are comparing multiple investment options, the investment with the highest IRR would be considered the best and should be chosen first—assuming all investments have the same amount of initial investment. The IRR function has two arguments, which you have seen in previous financial functions—values and guess—and returns a percentage.

=IRR(values, [guess])

Turquoise Oasis Spa can use the IRR function to see which investment would be the best option. For example, if the spa were to borrow $125,000 at 7.65% interest and they are uncertain if they should pay the loan back in three, four, or five years, they could analyze how much additional money would be lost if the loan were spread over four or five years versus three years. By analyzing the net cash flows over a five-year period, they can make a more educated decision.

To Calculate an Internal Rate of Return

a. Click the **IRR worksheet tab**.

b. Click cell **E13**, and then type =IRR($B$11:E11) to calculate the internal rate of return for 2015—the third year of the loan.

Notice that your loan amount is entered in cell B11 and a negative sign is placed in front of it. This is because you have to repay the loan and the value has to be deducted from the overall internal rate of return. This cell reference will be absolute.

c.   Use the **AutoFill** handle for cell E13 to copy the formula to **F13:G13**.

The IRR function for F13 calculates the internal rate of return for 2016—the fourth year of the loan. The IRR function for G13 calculates the internal rate of return for 2017— the fifth year of the loan.

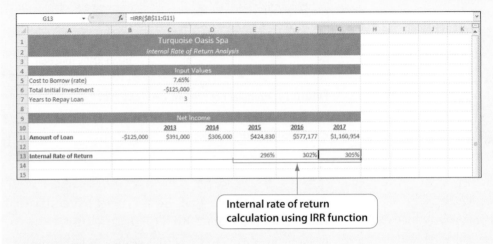

Internal rate of return calculation using IRR function

Figure 15 Internal rate of return analysis

d.   **Save** 💾 your changes.

Using the XIRR Function

Another way you can analyze the rate of return is to use the Irregular Internal Rate of Return function, or XIRR function. The difference between the IRR function and the XIRR function is that the IRR function assumes that the cash flows are periodic, whereas the **XIRR function** analyzes a series of cash flows that are irregular or not periodic. The syntax of the XIRR function is similar to the IRR function with the addition of the dates argument. Additionally, like the XNPV function, the series of values must contain at least one positive value and one negative value. The dates argument corresponds with when the payments were made, including the loan disbursement date. The first payment date indicates the beginning of the schedule of payments. All subsequent dates must be after the first payment date, but they may be listed in any order.

=XIRR(values, dates, [guess])

To Calculate an Irregular Internal Rate of Return

a. Click the **XIRR worksheet tab**.

b. Click cell **B14**, type =XIRR(B6:B12,A6:A12) to calculate the irregular internal rate of return, and then format the cell as **Percentage** with **1** decimal place. Notice that your loan amount is entered in cell B6 and a negative sign is placed in front of it.

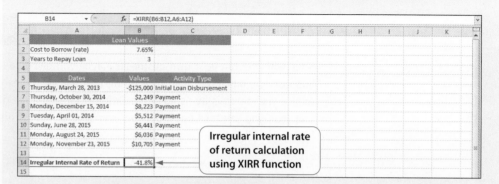

Figure 16 Irregular internal rate of return analysis

c. **Save** 💾 your changes.

CONSIDER THIS | **What Should Turquoise Oasis Do?**

The result of the XIRR function was -41.8%. Does it benefit Turquoise Oasis Spa to make irregular payments? What if they made irregular payments, but the payments were higher? Would this then be a viable option?

Calculating the Depreciation of Assets Using the SLN, DB, and DDB Functions

As you learned, an amortization table can be used to analyze loan balances and repayments. A company can also use amortization tables to show the appropriate accounting or "net book value" of its tangible assets such as machinery, equipment, buildings, vehicles, or property for tax or reporting purposes. To do so, you would use functions that allow you to calculate the present value, future value, and depreciation of the asset over its useful life. When you depreciate the original cost of tangible assets, you first need to know the rules for depreciating the particular assets, because there are different rules for different types of assets. Depreciation represents a reduction in the amount of original cost of a fixed asset that is used to reduce income as an expense for accounting and tax purposes. The idea is that because the item generates income over time, you should be able to deduct from that income the amount of the resource (asset) used.

To calculate the depreciated value, you need to know the original cost of the asset, the asset's useful life, the asset's salvage value—what the asset is worth at the end of its useful life—and the rate at which the asset depreciates over time. It is assumed that over time, these assets decline in value because of deterioration and obsolescence and therefore should be depreciated. Depreciation functions provide a method that matches the decline in value with the income that results from using the assets. In addition, you have to know what depreciation method the IRS expects you to apply to particular types of assets. The IRS, Generally Accepted Accounting Principles and International Financial Reporting Standards all have specific requirements for depreciating assets and reporting depreciation based on the type of asset being depreciated.

In order to report the "net book value" tangible assets, a depreciation schedule must be maintained. A **depreciation schedule** records the date that the asset was placed into service, a calculation for each year's depreciation, and the accumulated depreciation. An asset remains on the depreciation schedule until the asset becomes fully depreciated or is taken out of service—sold or discarded. Finally, the depreciation schedule should be evaluated on an annual basis to ensure accuracy. With a growing business and increased inventory, the Turquoise Oasis Spa must prepare a depreciation schedule for its tangible assets.

Real World Advice — Have You Thought About Depreciating Your Assets?

Have you ever run your own business? Maybe you owned a lawn mowing service. Suppose you purchased your own riding lawn mower. Come tax time, one method to reduce your taxes is by using depreciation. Rather than taking the full cost out in one year, you can take out a portion over several years. This is particularly useful for high-priced items.

Using the SLN Function

One way that you can calculate depreciation is using the Straight-Line Depreciation function, or SLN function. The **SLN function** calculates the depreciation of an asset for a specified period using the fixed-declining balance method. This means that the amount of money that is depreciated is the same for each year of the life of the asset. This is the easiest type of depreciation to calculate and is the depreciation method used by the majority of small businesses. The SLN function syntax uses three arguments, all of which are required: (1) initial cost of asset (cost); (2) salvage value (salvage); and (3) useful life (life). The salvage value can be set to zero if that is what the expected salvage value is.

=SLN(cost, salvage, life)

Turquoise Oasis Spa managers need to track the tangible assets—such as massage tables, salon chairs, and sinks—that they previously purchased. You have been given the cost of the asset, salvage value, and useful life to create a straight-line depreciation table.

To Create a Straight-Line Depreciation Schedule

a. Click the **SLN worksheet tab**.

b. Click cell **B8**, type =SLN($B$3,$B$4,$B$5), format your cell as **Currency** with **0** decimal places, and then copy the function down to **B12** using the **AutoFill** handle.

c. To calculate the accumulated depreciation for the first year, click cell **C8**, type =B8, and then format your cell as **Currency** with **0** decimal places.

d. To calculate the accumulated depreciation for years two through five, click cell **C9**, type =C8+B9, format your cell as **Currency** with **0** decimal places, and then copy the function down to **C12** using the **AutoFill** handle.

e. To calculate the salvage value at year end, click cell **D8**, type =$B$3-C8, format your cell as **Currency** with **0** decimal places, and then copy the function down to **D12** using the **AutoFill** handle. Notice that the salvage value at the end of year five is $1,750—the same salvage value you started with.

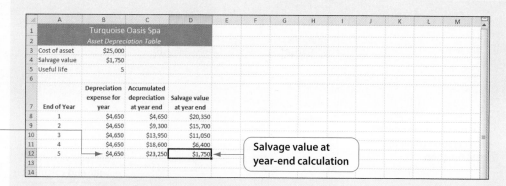

Depreciation expense calculation using the SLN function

Salvage value at year-end calculation

Figure 17 Straight-line asset depreciation table

f. **Save** 💾 your changes.

Using the DB Function

Another way that you can calculate depreciation is using the Declining Balance function, or DB function. The **DB function** calculates the depreciation of an asset for a specified period using the fixed-declining balance method. The difference between the DB function and SLN function is that when you use the DB function, you can specify the period and month that the asset was placed into service. Thus, instead of spreading the cost of the asset evenly over its life as you did with the SLN function, the DB function calculates the depreciation of the asset at an accelerated rate, which results in higher depreciation in earlier periods and progressively declining depreciation each succeeding period. Because the month argument is optional, Excel assumes the value as 12 if a value is omitted.

=DB(cost, salvage, life, period, [month])

Turquoise OasisSpa managers have asked you to calculate depreciation using the Declining Balance function.

To Create a Declining Balance Depreciation Schedule

a. Click the **DB worksheet tab**.

b. The equipment was placed into service at the beginning of May of the first year. Therefore, the period for the first year will be eight—May through December is eight months. Click cell **B8**, type =DB(B3,B4,B5,A8,8) to begin calculating the declining balance depreciation, and then format the cell as **Currency** with **2** decimal places, if necessary.

c. Click cell **B9**, and then type =DB($B$3,$B$4,$B$5,A9) to continue calculating the declining balance depreciation. Format your cell as **Currency** with **2** decimal places, and then copy the function down to **B12** using the **AutoFill** handle. Notice that the depreciation is declining as the periods increase with a depreciation value of $1,231.25 in year five.

d. To calculate the accumulated depreciation for the first year, click cell **C8**, type =B8, and then format your cell as **Currency** with **2** decimal places, if necessary.

e. To calculate the accumulated depreciation for the years two through five, click cell **C9**, type =C8+B9, format your cell as **Currency** with **2** decimal places, if necessary. Copy the function down to **C12** using the **AutoFill** handle.

f. To calculate the salvage value at year end, click cell **D8**, type =$B$3-C8, format your cell as **Currency** with **2** decimal places, if necessary. Copy the function down to **D12** using the **AutoFill** handle.

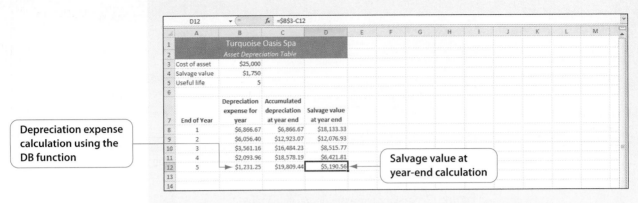

Depreciation expense calculation using the DB function

Salvage value at year-end calculation

Figure 18 Declining balance asset depreciation table

g. **Save** 🖫 your changes.

Real World Advice ┃ **The Salvage Values Do Not Match**

The Declining Balance method assumes that depreciation is more rapid earlier in the asset's life. Notice the salvage value at year end in year 5 is greater than the salvage value. Even if the salvage value in B4 were greater than $1,750, the final salvage value at year end would not change. Remember that instead of spreading the cost of the asset evenly over its life as you did with the SLN function, the DB function calculates the depreciation of the asset at an accelerated rate, which results in decreasing depreciation charges each succeeding period. The salvage value is never considered in the calculation—even though Excel has you reference the value in the DB function. Thus, there is no way for the original salvage value to force the depreciation to assume its final salvage value.

Using the DDB Function

Still another way that you can calculate depreciation is using the Double Declining Balance function, or DDB function. The **DDB function** calculates the depreciation of an asset for a specified period using the double-declining balance method. With the straight-line depreciation method, the useful life of the asset is divided into the total cost to arrive at an equal annual amount per year. The DDB function permits twice the straight-line annual percentage rate to be applied each year. For example, if you have a straight-line depreciation that is depreciating assets over a five-year period, the annual depreciation amount would be 20%. If the initial cost is $1,000, the depreciation would be 20% × $1,000 = $200 each year until the asset reaches a net book value of zero. With the Double Declining Balance method, the depreciation amount would be 40% each year—40% × $1,000 = $400 in the first year, 40% × $600 = $240 in the second year, and so on.

The DDB function syntax uses five arguments, four of which are required: (1) initial cost of asset (cost); (2) salvage value (salvage); (3) useful life (life); (4) period for which you want to calculate the depreciation (period); and (5) rate at which the balance declines (factor). The **factor** argument is optional and is the rate at which the balance declines. If factor is omitted, Excel assumes the value to be 2 (the double declining balance method). The salvage value can be set to zero if that is what the expected salvage value is.

=DDB(cost, salvage, life, period, [factor])

Turquoise Oasis Spa managers have asked you to calculate depreciation using the Double Declining Balance function.

To Calculate the Double Declining Balance Depreciation

a. Click the **DDB worksheet tab**.

b. Click cell **B8**, type =DDB($B$3,$B$4,$B$5,A8), format your cell as **Currency** with **2** decimal places if necessary, and then copy the function down to **B12** using the **AutoFill** handle.

  Notice that you would be able to deduct higher depreciation on your taxes. However, your salvage value at the end of the five years would be less than it would when using the Double Declining Balance function.

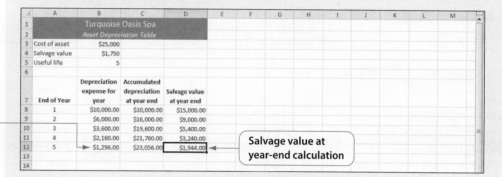

Figure 19 Double declining balance asset depreciation table

c. Click the **Documentation Worksheet tab**. Review and update the worksheet information as necessary.

d. **Save** 💾 your changes Print or submit your file as directed by your instructor. **Close** your file, and then exit **Excel**.

Real World Advice — Choosing a Depreciation Method

Accountants use depreciation as a method to approximate the value that assets lose over time. As property ages and wears out or becomes obsolete, you can calculate the depreciation and use the depreciation as a potential tax write-off. You learned three different methods to calculate depreciation of assets. All of the depreciation methods in effect according to the IRS and other authoritative accounting bodies should be considered before making a final decision as to how you depreciate an asset.

1. What is short-term viability, and how does cash flow contribute to the viability of a business?

2. How are Excel's financial functions used for business and personal analysis and financial management?

3. What is the difference between an amortization table and a depreciation schedule?

4. What is an economic risk, and how can using some of Excel's functions help you analyze data to ensure that the economic risk is low?

5. Explain the difference between the three depreciation functions—SLN, DB, and DDB—and how you would decide which function is the best one to use.

Key Terms

Visual Summary

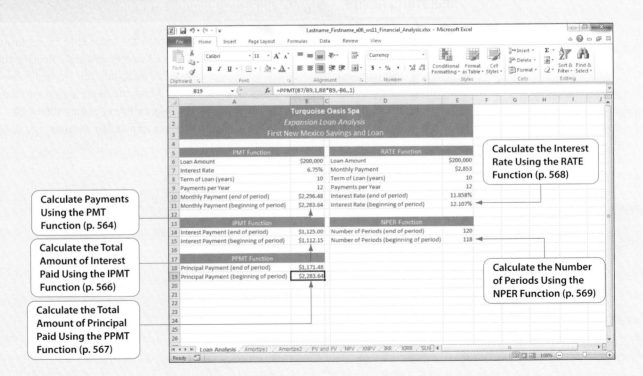

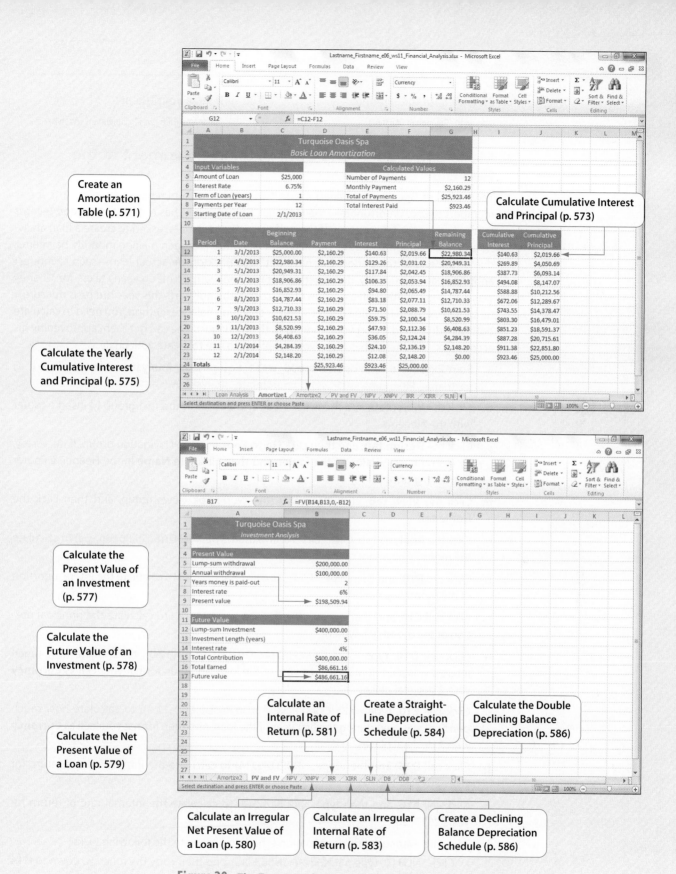

Figure 20 The Turquoise Oasis Spa Financial Analysis final workbook

Student data file needed:

e06_ws11_Equipment_Analysis

You will save your file as:

Lastname_Firstname_e06_ws11_Equipment_Analysis

Managing a Loan and Depreciating Equipment at the Red Bluff Golf Club

The Red Bluff Golf Club obtained a loan two years ago to purchase new golf carts for its members to use. Unfortunately, the manager, Barry Cheney, has not kept very good records for the loan or for depreciation of the golf carts. You have been asked to create a loan analysis and depreciation schedule. The Red Bluff Golf Club has been making monthly payments, due at the end of the period, but have not kept track of the actual loan—such as interest andprincipal. Additionally, depreciation has not been written off on yearly taxes. Mr. Cheney wants to begin writing off a portion of the cost of the golf carts this year, but he is not sure if he should use a straight-line depreciation or declining balance method. You need to calculate both schedules and report your findings to the manager so he can get them approved by his accountant. Mr. Cheney has given you templates to use to create your analysis.

a. Start **Excel**, and then open the **e06_ws11_Equipment_Analysis** workbook. Save it as Lastname_Firstname_e06_ws11_Equipment_Analysis.

b. Click the **Insert tab**, and then click **Header & Footer** in the Text group to insert a footer with the filename.

c. Click the **Design tab**, and then click **Go to Footer** in the Navigation group. If necessary, click on the left section of the footer, and then click **File Name** in the Header & Footer Elements group.

d. Click the **View tab**, click **Normal** in the Workbook views group, and then click the **Home tab**.

e. Click the **Analysis tab**. Click cell **A10**, and then type =PMT(A6/D6,B6*D6,-C6) to calculate the monthly payment of the loan.

f. Click cell **B10**, and then type =IPMT(A6/D6,1,B6*D6,-C6) to calculate the interest portion of the monthly payment.

g. Click cell **C10**, and then type =PPMT(A6/D6,1,B6*D6,-C6) to calculate the principal portion of the monthly payment.

h. Click cell **D10**, type =ABS(CUMIPMT(A6/D6,B6*D6,C6,1,12,0)) to calculate how much interest was paid during the first year of the loan, and then format your cell as **Currency** with **2** decimal places.

i. Click cell **E10**, type =ABS(CUMPRINC(A6/D6,B6*D6,C6,1,12,0)) to calculate how much principal was paid during the first year of the loan, and then format your cell as **Currency** with **2** decimal places.

j. Click cell **D16**, and then type =IRR(B14:D14) to calculate the internal rate of return for years 2013 and 2014.

k. Click cell **E16**, and then type =IRR(B14:E14) to calculate the internal rate of return for years 2013–2015.

l. To create a straight-line depreciation schedule, complete the following tasks:
   - Click cell **H10**, type =SLN($G$6,$H$6,$I$6), and then copy the function down to **H14** using the **AutoFill** handle. Click the **Border arrow** in the Font group, and then click **Bottom Border**.
   - To calculate the accumulated depreciation for the first year, click cell **I10**, and then type =H10.
   - To calculate the accumulated depreciation for the years two through five, click cell **I11**, type =I10+H11, and then copy the function down to **I14** using the AutoFill handle.

- To calculate the salvage value at year end, click cell **J10**, type =$G$6-I10, and then copy the function down to **J14** using the **AutoFill** handle. Select cells **H14:J14**, click the **Border arrow** in the Font group, and then click **Bottom Border**.

m. To create a declining balance depreciation schedule, complete the following tasks:

- Click cell **H17**, type =DB($G$6,$H$6,$I$6,G17), and then copy the function down to **H21** using the **AutoFill** handle. Click the **Border arrow** in the Font group, and then click **Bottom Border**.
- To calculate the accumulated depreciation for the first year, click cell **I17**, and then type =H17.
- To calculate the accumulated depreciation for the years two through five, click cell **I18**, type =I17+H18, and then copy the function down to **I21** using the **AutoFill** handle.
- To calculate the salvage value at year end, click cell **J17**, type =$G$6-I17, and then copy the function down to **J21** using the **AutoFill** handle. Select cells **H21:J21**, click **Border arrow** in the Font group, and then click **Bottom Border**.

n. To create a double declining balance depreciation schedule, complete the following tasks:

- Click cell **H24**, type =DDB($G$6,$H$6,$I$6,G24), and then copy the function down to **H28** using the **AutoFill** handle.
- To calculate the accumulated depreciation for the first year, click cell **I24**, and then type =H24.
- To calculate the accumulated depreciation for the years two through five, click cell **I25**, type =I24+H25, and then copy the function down to **I28** using the **AutoFill** handle.
- To calculate the salvage value at year end, click cell **J24**, type =$G$6-I24, and then copy the function down to **J28** using the AutoFill handle. Select cells **H28:J28**, click the **Border arrow** in the Font group, and then click **Thick Bottom Border**.

o. Click the **Documentation Worksheet** tab. Review and update the worksheet information as necessary.

p. Save your changes and print or submit your file as directed by your instructor. Close yourfile, and exit Excel.

Practice 2

Student data file needed:

e06_ws11_GiftShop_Analysis

You will save your file as:

Lastname_Firstname_e06_ws11_GiftShop_Analysis

Loan Amortization at the Painted Treasures Gift Shop

Three years ago the gift shop manager, Susan Brock, acquired a seven-year loan to add new fixtures and new inventory to the store. These fixtures are used to house the new products from the resort's restaurant—Indigo 5 house dressing, specialty foods by Chef Sanchez such as his famous salsa, and so on. While Ms. Brock has done a fair job paying the loan back, the payments have not been made on a regular schedule. You have been asked to create a loan amortization table and calculate the irregular net present value as well as the irregular internal rate of return. Ms. Brock also is considering borrowing some money from an investment to upgrade some of her existing fixtures and should be able to pay it back within five years. You have been asked to calculate some of the loan's missing pieces. Ms. Brock has given you templates to use to create your analysis.

a. Start **Excel**, and then open the **e06_ws11_Gift_Shop_Analysis** workbook. Save it as Lastname_Firstname_e06_ws11_Gift_Shop_Analysis, and then click the **Amortize worksheet tab**.

b. Click the **Insert tab**, and then click **Header & Footer** in the Text group to insert a footer with the filename.

c. Click the **Design tab**, and then click **Go to Footer** in the Navigation group. If necessary, click on the left section of the footer, and then click **File Name** in the Header & Footer Elements group.

d. Click the **View tab**, click **Normal** in the Workbook views group, and then click the **Home tab**.

e. Click cell **G5**, and then type =C7*C8 to calculate the number of payments.

f. Click cell **G6**, type =PMT(C6/C8,G5,-C5) to calculate the payments that will be made at the end of the period, and then format the cell as **Currency**, if necessary.

g. Click cell **G7**, type =G5*G6 to calculate the total amount that will be paid, and then format the cell as **Currency**, if necessary.

h. Click cell **G8**, and then type =G7-C5 to calculate the total interest that will be paid on the loan.

i. Complete the following tasks to create your amortization schedule:

   - Click cell **C12**, and then type =C5.
   - Click cell **C13**, type =G12 to calculate the beginning balance for periods 2–24, and then copy the formula down to cell **C35** using the **AutoFill** handle. (Hint: Your cells will display zeros until you complete the rest of the worksheet.)
   - Click cell **D12**, type =$G$6 to enter your payment, and then copy the formula down to cell **D35** using the **AutoFill** handle.
   - Click cell **E12**, type =IPMT($C$6/$C$8,A12,$G$5,-$C$5) to calculate how much of the monthly payment is being applied to the interest portion of the loan, and then copy the formula down to cell **E35** using the **AutoFill** handle.
   - Click cell **F12**, type =PPMT($C$6/$C$8,A12,$G$5,-$C$5) to calculate how much of the monthly payment is being applied to the principal portion of the loan, and then copy the formula down to cell **F35** using the **AutoFill** handle.
   - Click cell **G12**, type =C12-F12 to calculate the remaining balance after each payment, and then copy the formula down to cell **G35** using the **AutoFill** handle.
   - Click cell **D36**, type =SUM(D12:D35), and then use the **AutoFill** handle to copy the formula over to cell **F36**. Use the calculated values to check your calculations.

j. Complete the following tasks to calculate cumulative interest and principal:

   - Click cell **I12**, type =ABS(CUMIPMT($C$6/$C$8,$G$5,$C$5,$A$12,A12,0)) to calculate the cumulative interest payments for the life of the loan, and then copy the formula down to cell **I35** using the **AutoFill** handle.
   - Click cell **J12**, type =ABS(CUMPRINC($C$6/$C$8,$G$5,$C$5,$A$12,A12,0)) to calculate the cumulative principal payments for the life of the loan, and then copy the formula down to cell **J35** using the **AutoFill** handle.
   - Click cell **M12**, and then type =ABS(CUMIPMT(C6/C8,G5,C5,A12,A23,0)) to calculate the cumulative interest payment for the first year of the loan.
   - Click cell **M13**, and then type =ABS(CUMIPMT(C6/C8,G5,C5,A24,A35,0)) to calculate the cumulative interest payment for the second year of the loan.
   - Click cell **N12**, and then type =ABS(CUMPRINC(C6/C8,G5,C5,A12,A23,0)) to calculate the cumulative principal payment for the first year of the loan.
   - Click cell **N13**, and then type =ABS(CUMPRINC(C6/C8,G5,C5,A24,A35,0)) to calculate the cumulative principal payment for the second year of the loan.

k. Click the **Values** worksheet tab, click cell **B9**, and then type =PV(B8/12,B7,-B6).

   - Click cell **B17**, and then type =FV(B14,B13,-B12) to calculate the future value.

l. Click the **Loan Analysis** worksheet tab. Click cell **B20**, type =NPV(B5,D6:F6,B9) to calculate the net present value, and then format the cell as **Currency** with **0** decimal places.

m. Click cell **B21**, and then type =XNPV(B5,B9:B18,A9:A18) to calculate the irregular net present value.

n. Click cell **B22**, and then type =XIRR(B9:B18,A9:A18) to calculate the irregular internal rate of return.

o. Click the **Documentation Worksheet tab**. Review and update the worksheet information as necessary.

p. Save your changes and print or submit your file as directed by your instructor. Close your file, and then exit Excel.

Objectives

1. Perform break-even analysis.   p. 594

2. Analyze variables in formulas through the use of data tables.   p. 601

3. Use Goal Seek.   p. 606

4. Use the Scenario Manager to create scenarios.   p. 609

5. Create scenario reports.   p. 612

6. Solve complex problems using Solver.   p. 615

7. Generate and interpret Solver answer reports.   p. 620

8. Save and restore a Solver model.   p. 622

Decision Making with Excel

PREPARE CASE

The Turquoise Oasis Spa Business Planning Analysis

Turquoise Oasis managers Irene Kai and Meda Rodate believe that the expansion has the potential to double the spa and salon revenue. However, they need to provide detailed analysis of past sales along with sales forecasts to ensure Mr. Mattingly, the resort's CEO, that the money spent on the improvements and expansion will have positive financial benefits for Turquoise Oasis.

To increase management's understanding of the current capacity of the Turquoise Oasis Spa, Meda Rodate has collected data about their traffic, sales, and product mix. Meda has asked you to analyze this data using Excel's What-If Analysis tools.

Courtesy of www.Shutterstock.com

Student data file needed for this workshop:

 e06_ws12_Spa_WhatIf

You will save your file as:

 Lastname_Firstname_e06_ws12_Spa_WhatIf

Examining Cost-Volume-Profit Relationships

Managers need to analyze business data in order to help them plan and monitor the organization's day-to-day operations. **Cost-volume-profit (CVP) analysis** is the study of how certain costs react to changes in business activities such as costs, selling prices, revenues, profits, and production volume—if you manufacture products. Management relies on the accounting department to provide the data needed to perform CVP analysis. This data allows management to not only perform CVP analysis, but also examine operational risks as a suitable cost structure is chosen.

Consider the Turquoise Oasis Spa. Organizations such as the spa do not simply decide to renovate or expand operation based on an impulse. Nor do they decide to acquire an existing business or open a new location this way either. Managers spend a great deal of time analyzing past sales data along with future or projected sales data to determine if every strategy from beginning to end has the desired results in mind—increased profit or greater market share.

For example, if the spa does expand or renovate its business, in what ways will it expand or renovate? Will the expansion include more massage rooms, hair styling stations, or spa treatment areas? Will it be for housing more of the retail products sold? Or will the spa simply upgrade the existing equipment? Management needs to know what the most popular services are before making any decisions about the types of areas to add. What about revenue? If the spa takes out a loan and its costs rise because of the interest on the loan, what sales volume or revenue does the spa need to generate in order to afford the increased costs? CVP analysis is a way of evaluating the relationships among the fixed and variable costs, the sales volume—either in terms of units or dollars—and the profits. In this section, you will create a break-even analysis, work with conditional and custom formatting, use Goal Seek, and create data tables to analyze data.

Performing Break-Even Analysis

CVP analysis is used to help understand how changing volumes of sales or revenue affect profits. One of the main CVP analysis tools is break-even analysis and can help managers understand the relationships among cost, volume, and profit. Managers can use **break-even analysis** to calculate the break-even point in sales volume or dollars, estimate profit or loss at any level of sales volume, and help in setting prices. The **break-even point** is the sales level at which revenue equals total costs—there is neither a profit nor a loss. Understanding how profit of an item or service is affected by other variables requires an analysis of the costs. This analysis helps identify the items or services that change as sales volume changes and those that do not.

When calculating the break-even point, you need to consider the fixed, variable, and mixed costs. **Fixed costs** are expenses that never change regardless of how much product is sold or how many services are rendered. For example, when the spa is open for business, they have to pay management salaries, insurance, depreciation of building and equipment, and so on, regardless of how many customers they have during the day. **Variable costs**, however, do change based on how many products are sold or services are rendered. For example, when the salon cuts and styles a client's hair, they use two pumps of shampoo and one pump of conditioner to cleanse the hair. How many cut and styles they perform in a given day determines how much they spend on shampoo and conditioner. Thus, the cost of the supplies used varies depending on the services rendered. **Mixed costs** are costs that contain a variable component and a fixed component. Consider utilities such as electricity and water. Utility companies charge a specific amount—electric companies charge per kilowatt hour used and water companies charge a base fee and then per gallon used, but the bill will vary depending on the usage per billing cycle.

To determine the break-even point, the spa would need to consider all costs before it can determine its profit. For example, consider the Turquoise Spa's House Brand shampoo. The manufacturer charges $4.59—a variable cost—to produce one 16-ounce bottle. The total variable cost would be the variable cost per bottle multiplied by the number of bottles produced. The manufacturer also charges $10,000 per production run—a fixed cost—regardless of how many bottles are manufactured. This fee covers the costs that the manufacturer incurs to set up the production line. The spa sells the bottle of shampoo of $16.95 and would need to sell approximately 812 bottles to break-even (see Figure 1).

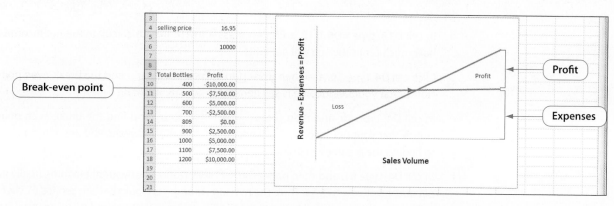

Break-even point

3		
4	selling price	16.95
5		
6		10000
7		
8		
9	Total Bottles	Profit
10	400	-$10,000.00
11	500	-$7,500.00
12	600	-$5,000.00
13	700	-$2,500.00
14	809	$0.00
15	900	$2,500.00
16	1000	$5,000.00
17	1100	$7,500.00
18	1200	$10,000.00
19		
20		
21		

Figure 1 Break-even analysis chart

The spa manager is considering raising the current price of massages. She has given you a workbook that includes information for some of the business activities such as costs, selling prices, revenues, and profits as provided by the accounting department. The price is dependent on client demand, and you need to determine the break-even point for the price.

To Create a Break-Even Analysis

a. Start **Excel**.

b. Click the **File tab**, click **Open**, and then navigate to your student data files. Locate and click to select **e06_ws12_Spa_WhatIf**, and then click **Open**.

c. Click the **File tab**, and then click **Save As**. Navigate to where your student files are stored. In the File name box, type Lastname_Firstname_e06_ws12_Spa_WhatIf, replacing Lastname_Firstname with your own name. Click **Save**.

d. Click the **Insert tab**, and then click **Header & Footer** in the Text group to insert a footer with the file name.

e. Click the **Design tab**, and then click **Go to Footer** in the Navigation group. If necessary, click the **left section** of the footer, and then click **File Name** in the Header & Footer Elements group.

f. Click any cell on the spreadsheet to move out of the footer, press Ctrl+Home, click the **View tab**, click **Normal** in the Workbook Views group, and then click the **Home tab**.

g. Click the **Documentation worksheet tab**, click cell **A6**, type today's date, click cell **B6**, and then type your first and last name.

h. Click the **Breakeven Analysis worksheet tab**.

i. Click cell **D6**, type =D4*D5, and then press Enter to calculate the gross revenue—the amount of money generated by servicing clients.

j. Click cell **D13**, type =SUM(D9:D12), and then press Ctrl+Enter to calculate the total fixed costs.

k. Click cell **D15**, type =D6*C15, and then press Enter to calculate the total commission the massage therapists will earn.

l. In cell **D16**, type =C16*D4, and then press Enter to calculate the cost of supplies.

m. In cell **D17**, type =D15+D16, and then press Enter to calculate the total variable costs.

n. In cell **D18**, type =D13+D17, and then press Enter to calculate the total expenses.

SIDE NOTE
No Value Displays in Cell D6

You are setting up the spreadsheet to perform a break-even analysis. Once you enter a value in D4, all the zeros will be replaced with values.

o. In cell **D19**, type =D6-D18, and then press Ctrl+Enter to calculate the net income— how much profit the spa will generate.

p. Click cell **D4**, type 50, and then press Ctrl+Enter to try and find the break-even point. Notice that your net income is still negative (−$1,118.50).

q. In cell **D4**, type 60, and then press Ctrl+Enter to try and find the break-even point. Notice that your net income is still negative (−$33.00). However, you are getting closer to finding the break-even point.

r. In cell **D4**, type 61, and then press Ctrl+Enter. Notice that your net income finally has become positive—$75.55. Thus, the massage therapists would have to service 61 clients before the spa starts making a profit. All clients above and beyond 61 will continue to generate a profit.

Point where spa begins making a profit

Positive net income when total clients exceed 60

			Client Demand	Expenses	Revenue	Net Income
1	**Turquoise Oasis Spa**					
2	Break-even Analysis for Massages					
3	**Revenue**					
4	Total Clients		61			
5	Massage Fee		$125.00	10		
6	Gross Revenue		$7,625.00	20		
7	**Expenses**			30		
8	*Fixed Costs*			40		
9	Manager Salaries		$4,669.00	50		
10	Utilities		$427.00	60		
11	Equipment Depreciation		$1,122.00	70		
12	Insurance		$328.00	80		
13	**Total Fixed Costs**		$6,546.00	90		
14	*Variable Costs*			100		
15	Massage Therapist Commission	10%	$762.50			
16	Supplies per Client	$3.95	$240.95			
17	**Total Variable Costs**		$1,003.45			
18	**Total Expenses**		$7,549.45			
19	Net Income		$75.55			
20						

Figure 2 Working with a break-even analysis

s. **Save** 💾 your changes.

> **CONSIDER THIS** | How Do You Contribute to Costs?
>
> Have you ever thought about the costs you add to or experience on a daily basis? Think about how the money you spend contributes to the business or organization you are paying. What about paying tuition? Buying lunch? Making a car payment? Paying student organization dues? Can you determine which of these would be fixed, variable, or mixed costs?

Using the Scroll Bar to Perform Break-Even Analysis

Managers use break-even analysis to determine the minimum volume the business needs to make and sell if it is a manufacturer, or buy and sell if it is a retail business, to be sustainable. Once you know a variable cost per unit and total fixed costs, you can calculate the break-even point. By knowing the break-even point, you can set sales goals, prices, and employee hours. When you entered various numbers in the previous exercise, you were performing what-if analysis. **What-if analysis** is when you use several different values in one or more formulas to explore all the various results. These different values are called variables. A **variable** is a value that you can change to see how the change affects other values. Throughout your career, your day will consist of what-if questions. For example, "What if you sell more massages at a lower price? Would you generate more net revenue than if you sold fewer at a higher price?"

Real World Advice — The Operative Word Is "Tool"

The operative word in what-if analysis tools is "tools." It is important to understand that these tools help managers analyze data so the manager can make the best decision based on the information he or she has. Analyzing data is only one component of decision making. Managers make decisions through exploring different options as well as reviewing documents, personal knowledge, or business models to identify and solve problems and make decisions. The fact is that these tools support organizational decision-making activities and are a method of analyzing and interpreting data.

Another way you can determine the break-even point is by using a scroll bar. The **scroll bar** is a form control that allows you to change a number in a target cell location in single-unit increments. The scroll bar is a type of **scenario tool** because of the ability to calculate numerous outputs in other cells by referencing the target cell in formulas and functions. When you use scenario tools to aid in decision making, you are performing what-if analysis. For example, Turquoise Oasis Spa managers can use the scroll bar to change the number of clients and price of each massage to determine when the business will meet and exceed its goal. This can be a challenge to determine if you were to perform this analysis manually—by entering random numbers into cells—because it is extremely time consuming and you do not want users to make physical changes to your spreadsheet model. Additionally, in many cases, when the price increases, the total number of items that can be sold will decrease. In this example, the higher the price of a massage, the fewer clients the spa will have booking the service.

Real World Advice — The Scroll Bar Can Be Used with the VLOOKUP Function

If you are given a table of data, such as quantity and price information, you can use a VLOOKUP function to help connect values. For example, when the massage fee is changed in cell D5, the VLOOKUP function will display a new value—Total Clients—in cell D4. When the values in cells D4 and D5 change, the results in Gross Revenue, Massage Therapist Commission, Supplies per Client, Total Variable Costs, Total Expenses, Taxes, and Net Income also change.

Quick Reference — Adding the Developer Tab

Before you are able to add a scroll bar, you first need to add the Developer tab. Click the File tab, click Options, and then click Customize Ribbon. On the right side of the window, under Customize the Ribbon, click to check the check box next to Developer under the Main Tabs list.

To Create a Break-Even Analysis Using a Scroll Bar

a. Click the **Developer tab**, and then click **Insert** in the Controls group.

b. Click **Scroll Bar (Form Control)** 🔲, and then draw the scroll bar in the area of cells E4 through E17. Be careful **not** to select the ActiveX Scroll Bar.

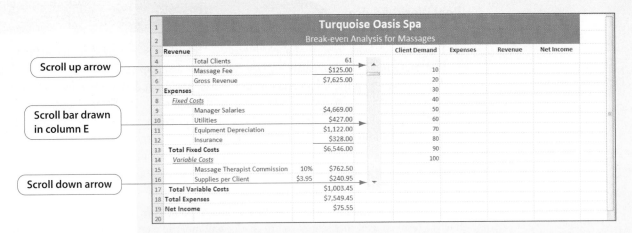

Figure 3 Break-even analysis using the scroll bar

c. Click the Developer tab, and then click **Properties** in the Controls group. In the Format Control dialog box, click the **Control** tab, if necessary. Because you want to analyze the net income from one client to 100 clients, you need to type the following criteria in the Format Control dialog box.

    Current value: type **61**

    Minimum value: type **60**

    Maximum value: type **100**

    Incremental change: Leave at the default value of **1**

    Page change: Leave at the default value of **10**

    Cell link: type **$D$4**

SIDE NOTE

Right-Click Works Too

You can also right-click the scroll bar, and then click Format Control to enter the scroll bar properties.

Scroll bar properties

Figure 4 Format Control dialog box

SIDE NOTE

White Dots and Squares around the Edge

The white dots and squares around the edge mean that the scroll bar is active. To deactivate the scroll bar, click a blank area away from the scroll bar. To make the scroll bar object active again, right-click the scroll bar, and click Format Control from the displayed menu, or click Properties in the Controls group on the Developer tab.

d. Click **OK**, click a cell away from the scroll bar to deactivate the scroll bar, and then click the **up arrow** on the scroll bar. You will notice that the value decreases. Analyze the net income for 60 to 100 clients.

e. Scroll down to the maximum value of 100 by clicking the **down arrow** on the scroll bar. Notice that with 100 clients the spa would make a profit of $4,309.

f. Scroll up until you have a net income that is at the break-even point. Notice that the spa would have to service 61 clients in order to make a profit.

g. **Save** your changes.

Using the scroll bar can be a quick and easy method to find the break-even point once the spreadsheet is formulated. How could you find the break-even point if you wanted higher pricing? Would it be easier to type values into the price and clients cells? Would you rather change the data on the Scroll Bar Data worksheet? Which would be more efficient?

Using Conditional Formatting

When you format font, borders, alignment, fill colors, and so on, you are making the spreadsheet easier for you to use and read. The same is true about conditional formatting. **Conditional formatting** applies custom formatting to highlight or emphasize values that meet specific criteria (see Figure 5). This kind of formatting is called conditional because the formatting occurs when a particular condition is met. For example, a manager may want to highlight cells for employees who exceeded monthly sales quotas or products that are selling below cost.

Quick Reference / Conditional Formatting Options

Conditional formatting makes the data easier to read and understand because it adds a visual or graphical element to the cells or values.

Conditional Formatting	Description
Highlight Cells Rules	Highlights cells with a fill color, font color, or border if values are greater than, less than, between two values, equal to a value, or duplicate values
Top/Bottom Rules	Formats cells with values in the top 10 items, top 10%, bottom 10 items, bottom 10%, above average, or below average
Data Bars	Applies a color gradient or solid fill bar; the width of a solid fill bar symbolizes the current cell's value as compared to other cells' values
Color Scales	Formats different cells with different colors; one color is assigned to the lowest group of values, another color is assigned to the highest group of values, and gradient colors are assigned to other values
Icon Sets	Inserts an icon from the icon palette in each cell to point out values as compared to each other

Figure 5 Conditional formatting options

To Create Conditional Formatting

a. Click cell **D19**, click the **Home tab**, click **Conditional Formatting** in the Styles group, select **Highlight Cells Rules**, and then click **Less Than** to open the Less Than dialog box.

b. Click the **Format cells that are LESS THAN** box, and type 0. Click the **with arrow** on the right side of the dialog box, click to select the **Red Text** option, and then click **OK**.

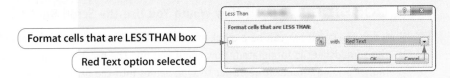

Format cells that are LESS THAN box

Red Text option selected

Figure 6 Less than dialog box

c. Click **Conditional Formatting** in the Styles group. Click the **Format cells that are GREATER THAN** box, and type 0. Click the **with arrow** on the right side of the dialog box, click to select the **Green Fill with Dark Green text** option, and then click **OK**.

d. Click the **up arrow** ▲ on the scroll bar.

Notice when the net income becomes a negative number that the font changes to red. This makes it easier for users to identify when the spa has not reached the break-even point.

e. **Save** 🖫 your changes.

Quick Reference · Custom Formatting Can Be Created

Not only can you apply preset conditional formatting within Excel, but you can also create your own formatting properties for fill colors, font colors, border colors, and so on. There are three ways to create custom formatting in Excel. Begin each option by clicking the Conditional Formatting button.

1. Select a Highlight Cells Rule, click the arrow to choose a color, and click Custom Format.
2. Click New Rule.
3. Click Manage Rules to open the Conditional Formatting Rules Manager dialog box where you can then click the New Rule button.
4. The color can be changed for an existing rule by choosing Edit Rule.
5. Select a rule category—such as Icon Sets—and then click More Rules.

Real World Advice · How Much Is Too Much?

Have you ever seen a document or web page that is so busy with colors and graphics that it is too difficult to read? Where do you draw the line when using conditional formatting or custom formatting? Not only can too much formatting make worksheets difficult for your audience to read, but it can make the worksheets difficult for you to maintain. Although formatting gives you more control over styles and icons, improved data bars, and the ability to highlight specific items and display data bars for negative values to more accurately illustrate your data visuals, consider what the repercussions can be if you format too much. Think about someone who is visually impaired or color blind. What is appealing to you may not be easy for someone else to read.

Using Data Tables

Excel contains three types of what-if analysis tools—Goal Seek, Data Table, and Scenario Manager. A **data table** takes sets of input values, determines possible results, and displays all the results in one table on one worksheet. Because data tables only focus on one or two variables, the results are easy to read and share in tabular form. Although it is limited to only one or two variables, a data table can include as many different variable values as needed.

One-Variable Data Table

A one-variable data table has input values that are listed either down a column—referred to as column-oriented—or across a row—referred to as row-oriented. A **one-variable data table** can help you analyze how different values of one variable in one or more formulas will change the results of those formulas. The formulas that are used in a one-variable data table must refer to only one input cell. For example, you can use a one-variable data table to see how different interest rates affect a monthly car payment by using the PMT function. In this case, the interest rate cell would be the input cell of the one-variable data table. The results display all possible interest rates provided in a data table after Excel performs a what-if analysis on these variables, as shown in Figure 7.

Figure 7 Analyzing data with a one-variable data table

The spa manager would like you to determine how much the monthly payment on a loan would be based on varying interest rates. Additionally, the spa manager also wants to avoid a profit of less than $1,000 and know when the target profit is greater than $7,500. Applying custom formatting will make the data easier to read. Finally, the spa manager would like you to build a traditional cost-volume-profit chart off the one-variable data table that will further analyze the break-even point for massage pricing.

To Create a One-Variable Data Table

a. Click the **One-Variable worksheet tab**, click cell **D4**, and then type 4. Press [Enter], in cell D5 type 5, select the range **D4:D5**, and then drag the **AutoFill** handle down to cell **D10**. Click cell **E3**, type =B6, and then press [Ctrl]+[Enter].

b. Right-click cell **E3**, and then click **Format Cells**. In the Format Cells dialog box, if necessary, click the **Number tab**. Under Category, click **Custom**, and then click the **Type** box. Delete any existing text, and then type ;;; to hide the results of the PMT function. Click **OK**, and then select the range **D3:E10** to select the data for your data table.

c. Click the **Data tab**, click **What-If Analysis** in the Data Tools group, and then click **Data Table** to open the Data Table dialog box.

d. Press [Tab] to move your pointer to the Column input cell box, type $B$4, and then click **OK**. Notice that Excel calculated the monthly payment for each interest rate.

SIDE NOTE

Typing $B$4 into the Column Input Cell

Notice that the interest rates being used are listed in a column. This is why you entered the interest rate cell—$B$4—into the column input cell box.

e. Select the range **E4:E10**, click the **Home tab**, click **Conditional Formatting**, select **Data Bars**, and then click **Green Data Bar** under Gradient Fill. Click **OK**.

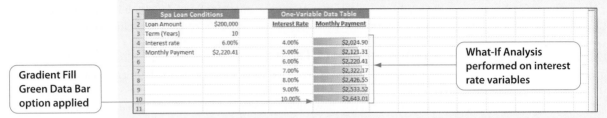

Gradient Fill Green Data Bar option applied

What-If Analysis performed on interest rate variables

Figure 8 One-variable data table with conditional formatting

SIDE NOTE
Your Data Table Will Be Automatically Updated
If you entered incorrect data such as the wrong loan amount or wrong down payment, the data table will be automatically updated as you update your data.

f. Click the **Break-even Analysis worksheet tab**, click cell **F4**, and then type =D4. Press [Tab]. Type =D18, and then press [Tab]. Type =D6, and then press [Tab]. In cell **I4**, type =D19, and then press [Enter].

g. Select the range **F4:I4**, right-click any of the selected cells, and then click **Format Cells**. On the Number tab, under Category, click **Custom**, and then scroll to the bottom of the list under **Type**, and then click the **;;;** option. Click **OK**.

h. Select the range **F4:I14** to select the data for your data table. Click the **Data tab**, click **What-If Analysis**, and then click **Data Table** to open the Data Table dialog box.

i. Press [Tab] to move your pointer to the Column input cell box, type **$D$4**, and then click **OK**. Notice that Excel calculated the expenses, revenue, and profit based on client demand.

j. Select the range **G5:I14**, click the **Home tab**, click **Conditional Formatting**, select **Highlight Cells Rules**, and then click **Less Than** to open the Less Than dialog box. Click the **Format cells that are LESS THAN** box, type **3000**, click the **with arrow** in the box to the right, and then if necessary, click the **Light Red Fill with Dark Red Text** option. Click **OK**.

k. Click **Conditional Formatting** again, select **Highlight Cells Rules**, and then click **Greater Than** to open the Greater Than dialog box. Click the **Format cells that are GREATER THAN** box, type **7500**, click the **with arrow** in the box to the right, and then click the **Green Fill with Dark Green Text** option. Click **OK**.

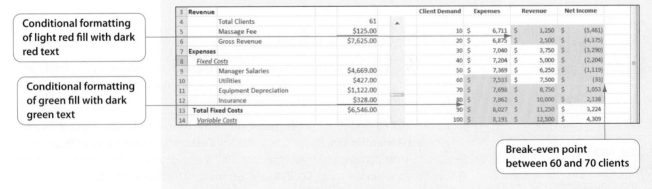

Conditional formatting of light red fill with dark red text

Conditional formatting of green fill with dark green text

Break-even point between 60 and 70 clients

Figure 9 One-variable data table of break-even analysis

l. Select the range **F3:H3**, hold down [Ctrl], and then select the range **F5:H14**. Click the **Insert tab**, click **Line** in the Charts group, and then select **Line** in the 2-D Line category. Click the **border edge** of the Line chart, and then drag to move it until the upper-left corner is in cell **F16**.

m. Click the **Design tab**, and then click **Select Data**. Under Legend Entries (Series) click **Client Demand**, under Horizontal (Category) Axis Labels click **Edit**, and then with the insertion point in the Axis label range box, select the range **F5:F14**.

n. Click **OK** two times to close the dialog boxes, click the **Blue data line** to select it, and then press Delete.

o. Click the **Layout tab**, click **Axis Titles**, select **Primary Horizontal Axis Title**, click **Title Below Axis**, and then type Client Demand. Press Enter to apply the changes to the axis title chart object.

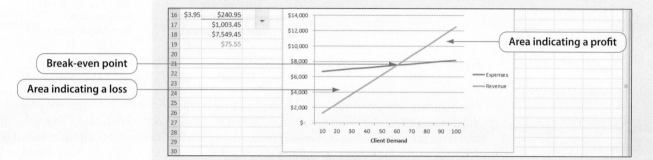

Figure 10 Traditional cost-volume-profit chart

p. Click any cell outside the chart to deselect it. Press Ctrl + Home.

q. **Save** 💾 your changes.

CONSIDER THIS | **What Does the Chart Tell You?**

Have you ever heard that a picture is worth a thousand words? Look at the chart you just created. Can you tell where the break-even point is? Is it easier to look at the chart and tell instantly, or is it easier to look at the data table?

Two-Variable Data Table

A two-variable data table has input values that are listed both down a column and across a row. A **two-variable data table** can help you analyze how different values of two variables in one or more formulas change the results of those formulas. For example, you can use a two-variable data table to see how different interest rates and loan amounts affect a monthly car payment by using the PMT function. In this case, the interest rate and loan amount cells would be the input cells. The results display all possible payment variations in a data table after Excel performs a what-if analysis using the interest rate cell as one variable (row input cell) and loan amounts as the other variable (column input cell) in calculating the payment variations (see Figure 11).

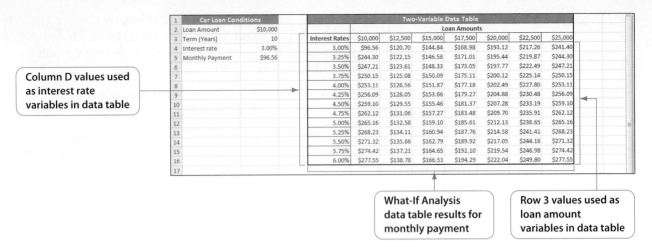

Column D values used as interest rate variables in data table

	Car Loan Conditions		Two-Variable Data Table						
1						Loan Amounts			
2	Loan Amount	$10,000							
3	Term (Years)	10	Interest Rates	$10,000	$12,500	$15,000	$17,500	$20,000	$22,500	$25,000
4	Interest rate	3.00%	3.00%	$96.56	$120.70	$144.84	$168.98	$193.12	$217.26	$241.40
5	Monthly Payment	$96.56	3.25%	$244.30	$122.15	$146.58	$171.01	$195.44	$219.87	$244.30
6			3.50%	$247.21	$123.61	$148.33	$173.05	$197.77	$222.49	$247.21
7			3.75%	$250.15	$125.08	$150.09	$175.11	$200.12	$225.14	$250.15
8			4.00%	$253.11	$126.56	$151.87	$177.18	$202.49	$227.80	$253.11
9			4.25%	$256.09	$128.05	$153.66	$179.27	$204.88	$230.48	$256.09
10			4.50%	$259.10	$129.55	$155.46	$181.37	$207.28	$233.19	$259.10
11			4.75%	$262.12	$131.06	$157.27	$183.48	$209.70	$235.91	$262.12
12			5.00%	$265.16	$132.58	$159.10	$185.61	$212.13	$238.65	$265.16
13			5.25%	$268.23	$134.11	$160.94	$187.76	$214.58	$241.41	$268.23
14			5.50%	$271.32	$135.66	$162.79	$189.92	$217.05	$244.18	$271.32
15			5.75%	$274.42	$137.21	$164.65	$192.10	$219.54	$246.98	$274.42
16			6.00%	$277.55	$138.78	$166.53	$194.29	$222.04	$249.80	$277.55
17										

What-If Analysis data table results for monthly payment

Row 3 values used as loan amount variables in data table

Figure 11 Two-variable data table for car loan

One way that a two-variable data table can be useful is when you want to analyze the relationships among cost, sales volume, and profit. When doing so, you need to consider how demand affects the price of a product or service. The analyses you have performed thus far have assisted in determining the break-even point for products and services. Additionally, you have considered the quantity of products that may be sold or the number of clients that may be serviced. The bottom line is that these analyses have clearly indicated how this relationship between the price and revenue affects demand.

A product or service is **elastic**—or responsive to change—if a small change in price is accompanied by a large change in the quantity demanded. The opposite is also true. A product is **inelastic**—or not responsive to change—if a large change in price is accompanied by a small amount of change in demand. This effect is known as the price elasticity of demand and can be calculated by dividing the change in quantity demanded by the change in price. When calculating the elasticity as shown in Figure 12, some assumptions do need to be made about your business and how any changes in price will affect demand. The quotient is conveyed as an absolute value because it is assumed that demand will never increase when prices increase.

Elasticity = [% change in quantity demanded ÷ % change in price]

Figure 12 Elasticity formula

For example, the spa manager may assume that if she increases the price of a massage by 15%, that demand will decrease by 20%. When calculating the elasticity, you are calculating the price elasticity of demand. Thus, if Ms. Rodate wanted to calculate the elasticity of demand, the equation would be as shown in Figure 13.

Elasticity = [–20% ÷ 15%] = [–133] = 1.33

Figure 13 Elasticity calculation of price increase at the spa

However, instead of having to calculate and interpret elasticity, you can use a two-way data table to view how the price of a product or service responds to change. The spa manager would like you to determine how much net income would be generated for massages based on varying prices and client demand.

Real World Advice

A Two-Variable Data Table Is *NOT* Calculating Elasticity

The two-variable data table you are creating does not actually tell you about the elasticity of price versus demand. It calculates the outcomes of varying prices of massages and client demand. When determining selling prices or financing a project, the risk is that the yield will not generate adequate revenue to cover operating costs and to repay debt obligations. A two-variable data table gives you another way of assessing the risk associated with pricing a product or service at a certain level or anticipating a specific level of demand.

To Create a Two-Variable Data Table

a. Click the **Two-Variable worksheet tab**, click cell **D3**, type =B7 to reference the Net Income formula that Excel will use to calculate your data table, and then press Ctrl + Enter.

b. Right-click cell **D3**, and then click **Format Cells**. On the Number tab, under Category, click **Custom**, click the **Type** box, delete any text, and then type "Client Demand" with the quotation marks.

c. Click **OK**, press Ctrl + B, and then resize column D width to fit the text as necessary. Select the range **D3:L15** to select the data for your data table.

d. Click the **Data tab**, click **What-If Analysis**, and then select **Data Table** to open the Data Table dialog box.

e. With the insertion point in the **Row input cell** box, type $B$3, and then press Tab to move to the Column input cell box. Type $B$2, and then click **OK**. Notice that Excel calculated the net income for the combination of client demand and massage pricing.

f. Select the range **E4:L15**, click the **Home tab**, click the **Number Format arrow** General in the Number group, and then click **Currency** with 2 decimal points.

g. Click the **Home tab**, click **Conditional Formatting** in the Styles group, select **Highlight Cells Rules**, and then click **Less Than** to open the Less Than dialog box. Click the **Format cells that are LESS THAN** box, and then type 0. If necessary, click the **with arrow**, click to select the **Light Red Fill with Dark Red Text** option, and then click **OK**.

h. Click **Conditional Formatting** again, select **Highlight Cells Rules**, and then click **Greater Than** to open the Greater Than dialog box. Type 3500 in the Format cells that are GREATER THAN box, click the **with arrow**, click to select the **Green Fill with Dark Green Text** option, and then click **OK**. Press Ctrl + Home. Format the cell to display negative numbers with a negative sign and no parentheses.

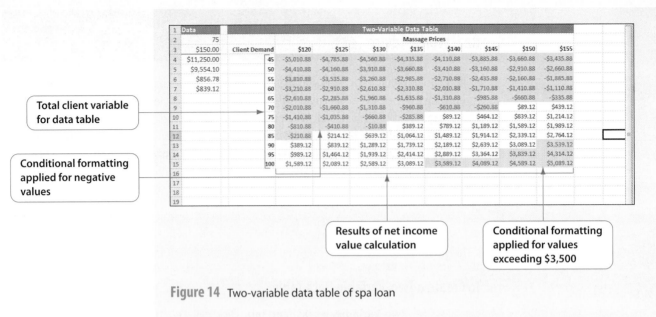

Total client variable for data table

Conditional formatting applied for negative values

Results of net income value calculation

Conditional formatting applied for values exceeding $3,500

Figure 14 Two-variable data table of spa loan

i. **Save** 💾 your changes.

Quick Reference / Interpreting Elasticity

Products and services are often evaluated by their elasticity. When interpreting elasticity, consider the following:

1. **Relatively elastic:** If the elasticity is greater than one, demand is very responsive to changes in price.

2. **Relatively inelastic:** If the elasticity is less than one, large changes in price will cause small changes in demand.

3. **Perfectly elastic:** For high elasticity values, any change in price causes a vast change in demand.

4. **Perfectly inelastic:** For elasticity values of zero, a change in price has no influence on demand.

5. **Unit elastic:** For elasticity values of one, any change in price results in an equal and opposite change in demand.

Using Goal Seek

Goal Seek is another scenario tool that maximizes Excel's cell-referencing capabilities and enables you to find the input values needed to achieve a goal or objective. To use Goal Seek, you select the cell—variable cell—containing the formula that will return the result you are seeking. Once you have selected the cell, indicate the target value you want the formula to return. Then, finally, select the location of the input value that Excel can change to reach the target. In simpler terms, when you perform Goal Seek, Excel is manipulating the data much like you would in an algebraic equation that requires you to solve for x.

Through a process called **iteration**, Goal Seek repeatedly enters new values in the variable cell to find a solution to the problem. Iteration continues until Excel has run the problem 100 times or has found an answer within .001 of the target value you specified. Because Goal Seek calculates so quickly, you save significant time and effort. Without Goal Seek, you would have to manually type one number after another in the formula or a related cell to attempt to find the solution.

You will use the data given to you by the spa manager to forecast quantities and prices of the less-popular selling items. This will ensure that the management and employees are striving to meet the sales goals for the items that currently are not selling very well.

To Forecast Using Goal Seek

a. Click the **Goal Seek worksheet tab**, and then click cell **E5**.

b. Click the **Data tab**, click **What-If Analysis**, and then click **Goal Seek** to open the Goal Seek dialog box. Excel automatically selects the active cell as the Set cell value; in this case, cell E5.

c. The spa wants to set a sales goal of $25,000 for a shampoo and conditioner package. Because you know the selling price and target goal of the shampoo and conditioner package, you can calculate the quantity the spa needs to sell to meet the sales goal. Click the **To value** box, type 25000, press Tab, and then in the By changing cell box, type $C$5.

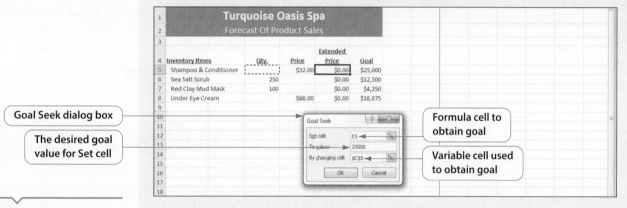

Goal Seek dialog box

The desired goal value for Set cell

Formula cell to obtain goal

Variable cell used to obtain goal

Figure 15 What-if analysis using Goal Seek

SIDE NOTE

What Exactly Is Excel Doing?

Excel will display the iteration process in the Goal Seek Status dialog box as it searches for a result. Excel will also confirm when it finds a solution.

d. Click **OK** two times. Notice that in order for the spa to reach its $25,000 sales goal for shampoo and conditioner, the spa would need to sell 781.25 bottles. Click cell **C5**. Click the **Home tab**. In the Number group, click the **Number Format arrow** General ▾ , click **Number**, and then click the **Decrease Decimal** button twice to format with no decimal places because the spa cannot sell part of a bottle of shampoo or conditioner.

Troubleshooting

If Excel displays in the Goal Seek Status dialog box that it could not find a viable solution, click Cancel, and then ensure that you have entered the correct values in the Goal Seek dialog box. Some rules to keep in mind: Verify the Set cell box contains a formula, the To value box contains the result desired for the formula, and the By changing cell box contains a cell reference from the formula that can be adjusted to achieve the goal.

e. Click the **Data tab**, click **What-If Analysis**, and then click **Goal Seek** to open the Goal Seek dialog box.

f. The spa wants to set a sales goal of $12,500 for sea salt scrub. Because you know the quantity and target goal, you can calculate the price the spa needs to charge to meet the sales goal. In the **Set cell** box, replace any text by typing $E$6, press [Tab], and then in the **To value** box, type 12500. Press [Tab], and then in the **By changing cell** box, type $D$6.

g. Click **OK** two times, and then format D6 as **Currency** with 2 decimal points.

    Notice that the spa should charge $50 to meet its sales goal volume of 250 jars of sea salt scrub. Additionally, if 250 jars are sold, the spa will meet the sales revenue goal of $12,500.

h. Click the **Data tab**. Click **What-If Analysis**, and then click **Goal Seek** to open the Goal Seek dialog box.

i. The spa wants to set a sales goal of $4,250 for the red clay mud mask. Because you know the quantity and target goal, you can calculate the price the spa needs to charge to meet the sales goal. In the **Set cell** box, type $E$7 to replace the text, press [Tab], and then in the **To value** box, type 4250. Press [Tab], and then in the **By changing** cell box, type $D$7.

j. Click **OK** two times. Format D7 as **Currency** with 2 decimal points. Notice that the spa should charge $42.50 to meet its sales goal volume of 100 jars of red clay mud mask. Additionally, if 100 jars are sold, the spa will meet the sales revenue goal of $4,250.

k. Click the **Data tab**. Click **What-If Analysis**, and then click **Goal Seek** to open the Goal Seek dialog box.

l. The spa wants to set a sales goal of $18,675 for under eye cream. You can calculate the quantity the spa needs to sell to meet the sales goal. In the **Set cell** box, type $E$8 to replace any text, press [Tab], and then in the **To value** box, type 18675. Press [Tab], and then in the **By changing cell** box, type $C$8.

m. Click **OK** two times. If 275 tubes of under eye cream are sold, the spa will meet the sales revenue goal of $18,675. Click cell **D5**. Click the **Home tab**, click **Format Painter** ✂ in the Clipboard group, and then select the cell range **D6:D7** to copy the Currency format settings to these cells. Click cell **C5**, click **Format Painter** ✂ in the Clipboard group, and then select the cell range **C6:C8** to copy the Number format settings to these cells. Press [Ctrl]+[Home].

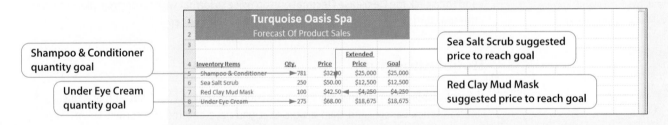

Figure 16 Results of Goal Seek analysis

n. **Save** 🖫 your changes.

Real World Advice — Goal Seek Can Be Used For Basic Forecasting

When managers forecast, they are estimating or predicting future occurrence of sales, manufacturing needs, inventory, and so on, by looking at past data—such as the past three years of sales trends. Goal Seek determines the unknown value that produces a desired result, such as the number of $16 bottles of shampoo and conditioner the spa must sell to reach its goal of $10,000. Goal Seek is simple because it is streamlined, can calculate only one unknown value, and can be helpful in a variety of forecasting efforts.

Quick Reference — Changing Excel's Iteration Settings

Excel's default iteration settings can be changed by completing the following steps:

1. Open Excel, and then click the File tab.
2. Click Options.
3. Click Formulas in the left pane.
4. Under Calculation options, click Enable iterative calculation.
5. Select the Maximum Iterations and Maximum Change you would like Excel to perform.
6. Click OK.

Using Scenario Manager

A **scenario** allows you to build a what-if analysis model that includes variable cells linked by one or more formulas or functions. By running the scenarios, you have the ability to compare multiple variables and their combined effects on the various calculated outcomes. Managers can use scenarios to view best-case, worst-case, and most-likely scenarios in order to make decisions and solve problems. For example, the spa manager might want to compare best-case, most-likely, and worst-case scenarios for sales based on the number of clients they see in a week.

Scenarios can be most beneficial because they can use multiple variables. Through the use of Goal Seek and data tables, you learned that you could use what-if analysis tools when you want to analyze the effects on various calculations when inputting one or two variables. Scenarios can evaluate one, two, or many variables. For example, the spa manager may want to view best-case, worst-case, and most-likely scenarios of the spa's total net income based on variable costs, fixed costs, and gross revenue of both retail products and spa services rendered. In this section, you will learn how to use the **Scenario Manager**, the third type of what-if analysis tool, to manage scenarios by adding, deleting, editing, and viewing scenarios, and to create scenario reports.

Creating Scenarios

You can use scenarios to predict the outcome of different situations in your spreadsheet. Before creating a scenario, you need to design your worksheet to contain at least one formula or function. This formula or function will rely on other cells and can have different values inserted into it. The significant step in creating the various scenarios is identifying the various data cells whose values can differ in each scenario. You can then select these cells—known as **changing cells**—in the worksheet before you open the Scenario Manager dialog box. Once the Scenario Manager dialog box is open, you can enter and define the different scenarios. Each scenario includes a scenario name, input or changing cells, and the values for each input cell.

The spa manager would like you to determine how much net income—profit—the spa is forecasted to generate based on varying retail sales, revenue from services rendered, and variable costs. You have been given the forecasted amounts and need to enter the formulas that will help calculate each scenario.

To Design a Worksheet Used for Scenarios

a. Click the **Scenario worksheet tab**.

b. Click cell **D6**, type =SUM(D4:D5) to calculate the forecasted total or gross revenue, and then press Enter.

c. Click cell **D13**, type =SUM(D9:D12) to calculate the total forecasted fixed costs, and then press Enter.

d. Click cell **D15**, type =D6*C15 to calculate the forecasted employee commissions, and then press Enter.

e. In cell **D16**, type =D13+D15 to calculate the forecasted total expenses, and then press Enter.

f. In cell **D17**, type =D6-D16 to calculate the forecasted net income, and then press Ctrl+Home.

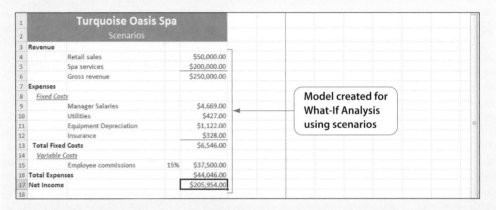

Figure 17 Forecasting model

g. **Save** 💾 your changes.

Adding, Deleting, and Editing Scenarios

Once you identify the changing cells—which can be anywhere on your worksheet—you can then select these cells in the worksheet before you open the Scenario Manager dialog box, or you can enter the target cells directly into the Scenario Manager dialog box as well as enter and define the different scenarios. Each scenario represents different what-if conditions to evaluate the spreadsheet model. Once scenarios are added, they are stored under the name you assigned to them. The number of scenarios you can create is limitless.

To Add, Delete, and Edit Scenarios

a. Select the range **D4:D5**. These will be your changing cells.

b. Click the **Data tab**, click **What-If Analysis**, and then click **Scenario Manager** to open the Scenario Manager dialog box.

c. In the Scenario Manager dialog box, click **Add** to begin creating your first scenario. In the Add Scenario dialog box, type Most Likely Scenario in the Scenario name box.

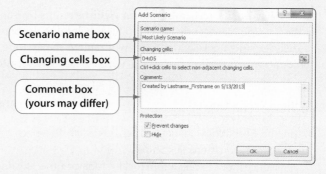

Scenario name box

Changing cells box

Comment box (yours may differ)

Figure 18 Add Scenario dialog box

d. The values that are entered in cells D4 and D5 are the most likely scenario values. Click **OK**.

e. In the Scenario Values dialog box, click **Add** to begin creating your second scenario. In the Add Scenario dialog box, type Best-case Scenario in the Scenario name box, and then click **OK**. The Scenario Values dialog box will open.

f. The spa manager believes that the best-case scenario would result in revenue of $100,000 in Retail sales and $325,000 in Spa services. Type 100000 in the $D$4 box, and then type 325000 in the $D$5 box.

Row 1 referencing Retail sales revenue in D4

Row 2 referencing the Spa services revenue in D5

Figure 19 Scenario Values dialog box

g. Click **OK**, and then in the Scenario Manager dialog box, click **Add**.

h. In the Add Scenario dialog box, type Worst-case Scenario in the Scenario name box, and then click **OK**. The Scenario Values dialog box will open.

i. The spa manager believes that the worst-case scenario would result in revenue of $25,000 in Retail sales and $75,000 in Spa services. Type 25000 in the $D$4 box, type 75000 in the $D$5 box, and then click **OK**.

j. Because the spa manager already created a forecast with the most likely scenario values entered, she decided that she does not need this scenario and e-mails you to let you know. In the Scenario Manager dialog box, click to select the **Most Likely Scenario** under Scenarios, and then click **Delete** to delete the Most Likely Scenario.

k. The spa manager also informed you that the worst-case scenario would have retail sales forecasted at $20,000. In the Scenario Manager dialog box, click to select the **Worst-case Scenario** under Scenarios, click **Edit**, and in the Edit Scenario dialog box, click **OK**.

l. In the $D$4 box of the Scenario Values dialog box, change 25000 to 20000, and then click **OK**.

Viewing Scenarios

After you create the scenarios, you can view the results by using the Show button at the bottom of the Scenario Manager dialog box. This is helpful to double-check whether the values entered in each scenario are accurate. Excel will replace the existing values in your spreadsheet with those entered into each scenario.

To View Scenarios

a. In the Scenario Manager dialog box, click to select the **Best-case Scenario** under Scenarios, and then click **Show**.

   Notice how Excel automatically replaces the existing values in D4 and D5 with $100,000 for Retail sales and $325,000 for Spa services. The Net Income result is $354,704.

b. Click to select the **Worst-case Scenario** under Scenarios, and then click **Show**.

   Notice how Excel automatically replaces the existing values in D4 and D5 with $20,000 for Retail sales and $75,000 for Spa services. The Net Income result is $74,204.

Generating a Scenario Summary Report

Although you can view your scenarios while the Scenario Manager dialog box is open, you will probably want to view them side by side to compare the results. Additionally, it is not possible to print and distribute them very easily this way. You can create a scenario summary report automatically by clicking the Summary button in the Scenario Manager dialog box. The Summary button opens the Scenario Summary dialog box where you can choose the type of report you would like to create. By selecting the **Scenario Summary** option, you can create a worksheet that includes subtotals and the results of the scenarios.

To Generate a Scenario Summary Report

a. In the Scenario Manager dialog box, click **Summary** to open the Scenario Summary dialog box.

b. Leave the Report type at the default selection of Scenario summary, verify the Result cell as **D17**, and then click **OK**. Notice that Excel adds a new worksheet named Scenario Summary to your workbook.

c. Format the scenario summary report so it is easier to read. Click the **Home tab**, select cells **B6:C6**, click **Merge & Center** in the Alignment group, and replace $D$4 text by typing Retail Sales.

d. Select cells **B7:C7**, click **Merge & Center**, and replace $D$5 text by typing Spa Services.

e. Select cells **B9:C9**, click **Merge & Center**, and replace $D$17 text by typing Net Income. Press Ctrl + Home.

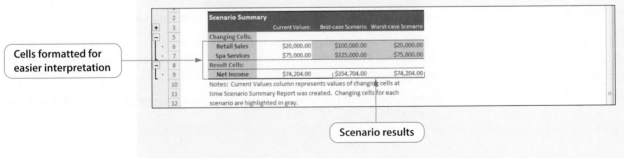

Figure 20 Scenario summary report

f. **Save** 💾 your changes.

Generating a Scenario PivotTable Report

A scenario PivotTable report can also be created automatically by clicking the Summary button in the Scenario Manager dialog box. The Summary button opens the Scenario Summary dialog box where you can choose the **Scenario PivotTable report** option. You can create a worksheet that includes a summary of the scenarios in PivotTable format. PivotTables allow even more manipulation of data because of the two-dimensional view they provide.

To Generate a Scenario PivotTable Report

a. Click the **Scenario worksheet tab**.

b. Click the **Data tab**, click **What-If Analysis**, and then click **Scenario Manager** to open the Scenario Manager dialog box.

c. In the Scenario Manager dialog box, click to select the **Best-case Scenario**, and then click **Edit**.

d. The spa manager wants to see if the spa could still be profitable if the employees earn different commissions based on sales. In the Edit Scenario dialog box, click the **Changing cells** box to place the insertion point after the range D4:D5, and type ,C15. Click **OK**.

e. In the Scenario Values dialog box, in the $C$15 box, verify the value displays 0.15 to reflect the commission of 15%, and then click **OK**.

f. In the Scenario Manager dialog box, click to select the **Worst-case Scenario**, and then click **Edit**.

g. In the Edit Scenario dialog box, click the **Changing cells** box to place the insertion point after the range D4:D5, and then type ,C15. Click **OK**.

h. In the Scenario Values dialog box, click the row 3 **$C$15** box, delete the 0.15 value, type .075 to change the commission to 7.5%, and then click **OK**.

i. The spa manager wants you to re-create the most-likely scenario. In the Scenario Manager dialog box, click **Add**, type Most Likely Scenario in the Scenario name box, and then click **OK**. Your D4:D5,C15 changing cells will automatically be entered into the Changing cells box.

j. Type the following values for each changing cell in each box of the Scenario Values dialog box. Type 25000 in box 1, type 162500 in box 2, and then type 0.10 in box 3.

k. Click **OK**, and then click **Summary** in the Scenario Manager dialog box to open the Scenario Summary dialog box.

l. The spa manager wants to view the ending values for gross revenue, commission, taxes, and net income. Click to change the Report type to **Scenario PivotTable report**, click the **Result cells** box, delete any existing text, type =D6,C15,D17, and then click **OK**. Notice that Excel added a new worksheet named Scenario PivotTable to your workbook.

m. Format your PivotTable report so it is easier to read the data. Click cell **A1**, replace the existing $D$4:$D$5,$C$15 by text by typing Retail Sales and Spa Services, and then press [Ctrl]+[Enter]. Click the **Home tab**, click **Format** in the Cells group, and click **Column Width**. In the **Column width** box, set the width of column A to 26. Click **OK**.

n. Click cell **A2**, type Scenario PivotTable Report, press [Ctrl]+[Enter], select the range **A2:D2**, and click **Merge & Center**. Click the **Bold** button, click the **Font Size arrow**, and then click **16**.

o. Click cell **A3**, type Scenarios, and then press [Tab].

p. Add headings to your data. Click cell **B3**, type Gross Revenue, and then press Tab. In cell C3, type Commission, and then press Tab. In cell D3, type Net Income, and then press Ctrl+Enter.

q. Select the range **B3:D3**, click **Center** in the Alignment group to center the text, and then click **Format**. Click **Column Width**, in the Column width box type 14, and then click **OK**.

r. Select the range **B4:B6**, hold down Ctrl, select the range **D4:D6**, click the **Number Format arrow**, and then click **Currency**. Click the **Decrease Decimal** button two times to format with no decimal places.

s. Select the range **C4:C6**, click the **Number Format arrow**, and then click **Percentage**. Click the **Decrease Decimal** button once to format with one decimal place, and then press Ctrl+Home.

Scenario results in PivotTable format ⟶

	Gross Revenue	Commission	Net Income
1 Retail Sales and Spa Services (All)			
2 Scenario PivotTable Report			
3 Scenarios	Gross Revenue	Commission	Net Income
4 Best-case Scenario	$425,000	15.0%	$354,704
5 Most Likely Scenario	$187,500	10.0%	$162,204
6 Worst-case Scenario	$95,000	7.5%	$81,329
7			

Figure 21 Scenario PivotTable report

t. **Save** 💾 your changes.

Using Solver

An important item to note is that there is no true or right answer on how to raise prices. The answer relies, in part, on the business person's notion of how much demand he or she believes to be likely at the various prices and what that relationship is for that particular business. It may be risky to raise the price very high because it will lower demand, which means fewer units will be sold at the higher price. If the belief is wrong and the demand stays the same or is higher than expected, the profit potential is also higher. This is when a tool such as Solver can help give a business person enough information to make an educated decision.

Excel's **Solver** is an add-in that helps optimize a problem by manipulating the values for several variables with constraints that you determine. A **constraint** is a rule you establish when formulating your Solver model. You can use Solver to find the highest, lowest, or exact value for a specific outcome by adjusting values for selected variables. Business managers can use Solver to minimize or maximize the output based on the constraints. For example, the spa manager could use Solver to determine a sales strategy that will help the spa maximize its profit given a specific mix of services given to clients. In this section, you will learn how to load the Solver add-in; find optimal solutions by setting objectives, changing variable cells, and defining constraints; generate a Solver answer report; and save and restore a Solver model.

Loading the Solver Add-in

To use the Solver, you need to activate the add-in. An **add-in** is an application with specific functionality geared toward accomplishing a specific goal. Because companies other than Microsoft develop the add-ins, they are not automatically activated when Excel is installed.

To Load the Solver Add-In

a. Click the **File tab**.

b. Click **Options**, and then click **Add-Ins**.

c. At the bottom of the View and manage Microsoft Office Add-ins pane, if necessary, click the **Manage arrow**, click **Excel Add-ins**, and then click **Go**.

d. In the Add-Ins dialog box, click the **Solver Add-in** check box, and then click **OK**.

e. To verify the Solver Add-in was added properly, click the **Data tab**, and then check to see that the Solver button is displayed in the Analysis group (on the right side of the Ribbon).

SIDE NOTE

The Menu Option Was Already Selected

The default selection in the menu is Excel Add-ins so it may already be selected for you.

Solving Complex Problems and Finding Optimal Solutions

The purpose of using Solver is to perform what-if analysis to solve more complex problems and to optimize the outcome. When you **optimize**, you are finding the best way to do something. For example, the spa manager may want to find the best product mix of its retail products to maximize profitability. The manager could use Excel's Solver to find the values of certain cells in a spreadsheet that optimize—maximize or minimize—a certain objective. Thus, Solver helps answer this type of optimization problem.

Prior to configuring the Solver constraints, you need to ensure that you create a spreadsheet model that can be used to manipulate the values for your variables. This involves creating a target cell, which defines the goal of your problem. For example, the spa manager may create a formula that calculates total revenue. Additionally, you need to select one or more variable cells that the Solver can change to reach the goal. You should evaluate your spreadsheet as you define your goal, identify one or more variables that can change when attaining the chosen goal, and then determine the limitations of the spreadsheet model. These variable cells are used to formulate the three Solver parameters—objective cell, changing cells, and constraints.

Your worksheet can also contain other values, formulas, and functions that use the target cell and the variable cells to reach the goal. For the Solver to work properly, the formula in the target cell must reference and depend on the variable cells for part of its calculation. If you do not construct your Solver model in this format, you will get an error message that states, "The Set Target Cell values do not converge."

Real World Advice — Solver Can Be Used For Many Analyses

The Excel Solver add-in can be a powerful tool for analyzing data. In many financial planning problems, an amount such as the unpaid balance on a loan or the amount saved in a retirement fund changes over time. Consider a situation in which a business borrows money. Because only the principal of the monthly payment reduces the unpaid loan balance, the business may want to determine how it can minimize the total interest paid on the loan if it pays more than the minimum payment each month.

Setting the Objective Cell and Variable Cells

The **objective cell** contains the formula that creates a value that you want to optimize— maximize, minimize, or set to a specific value. For example, the spa manager may want to maximize the gross revenue of massage therapists by analyzing the number of customers per day in relation to the total number of therapists employed by the spa. The spa manager would have to consider many factors; however, deciding the actual goal of using Solver is the first step to creating a Solver analysis.

Solver works with a group of cells, called variable cells, which take part in calculating the formulas in the objective and constraint cells. Solver adjusts the values in the variable cells to satisfy the limits on constraint cells and return the result you want for the objective cell.

The spa manager wants you to find the number of massages the massage therapists can give to maximize net income. The worksheet you were given was previously set up with functions to calculate the net income.

To Set the Objective Cell and Variable Cells

a. Click the **Solver worksheet tab**.

b. Click the **Data tab**, if necessary, and then click **Solver** in the **Analysis** group.

c. Because the spa manager wants to maximize the net income, the cell that holds the net income will become the objective cell. In the Solver Parameters dialog box, click the **Set Objective** box, and then type $D$21.

d. Because you need to maximize the net income, set the objective to **Max**, which is Excel's default value.

e. Several input variables will be considered in order to maximize the spa's net income. Click the **By Changing Variable Cells** box, and then type $D$4:$D$6,$C$18.

Defining Constraints

Constraints are the rules or restrictions that your variable cells must follow when the Solver performs its analysis. For example, if the spa manager wants to maximize the net income based on how many massages are given per day, the spa manager would have to consider how many hours the spa is open per day, how many massage therapists work per day, and how long it takes to give a massage. In addition, the cost of supplies can vary depending on how many clients the massage therapists have.

To Define Constraints

a. In the Solver Parameters dialog box, click **Add** to enter the first constraint. The Add Constraint dialog box will open.

b. The spa manager always has four massage therapists scheduled at any given time. In the Add Constraint dialog box, type $D$6 in the Cell Reference box, click the **arrow**, click to select = in the mathematical operands box, and then type 4 in the Constraint box.

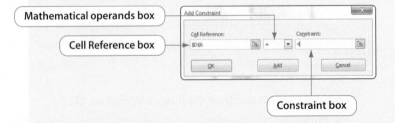

Figure 22 Add Constraint dialog box

c. Click **OK**, and then in the Solver Parameters dialog box, click **Add** to enter the next constraint.

d. The spa is open from 8AM to 7PM daily. In the Add Constraint dialog box, type **$D$5** in the Cell Reference box, click the **arrow**, click to select **=** in the mathematical operands box, and then type **11** in the Constraint box. Click **OK**, and then click **Add** to enter the next constraint.

e. Massages can last from 45 minutes to 90 minutes, meaning that massage therapists can give anywhere from 7 to 14 massages per day. Communicating this requires you to enter two constraints. In the Add Constraint dialog box, type **$D$4** in the Cell Reference box, click to select **>=** in the mathematical operands box, and then type **7** in the Constraint box.

f. Click **Add**, and then in the Add Constraint dialog box, type **$D$4** in the Cell Reference box. Select **<=** in the mathematical operands box, and then type **14** in the Constraint box.

g. In the Add Constraint dialog box, click **Add**. Because the therapists cannot service part of a client, you have to add a constraint that will ensure the value returned for cell D4 is a whole number. In the Add Constraint dialog box, type **$D$4** in the Cell Reference box, and then click to select **int** in the mathematical operands box. Excel will enter the word "integer" in the Constraint box. Click **Add**.

h. Because the spa cannot have part of a therapist working, you have to add a constraint that will ensure the value returned for cell D6 is a whole number. In the Add Constraint dialog box, type **$D$6** in the Cell Reference box, and then click to select **int** in the mathematical operands box.

i. Click **OK**. Notice that the six constraints you entered appear under the Subject to the Constraints list of the Solver Parameters dialog box.

SIDE NOTE
You Can Use Either Add Button
Either Add button works—either from within the Solver Parameters dialog box or the Add Constraint dialog box.

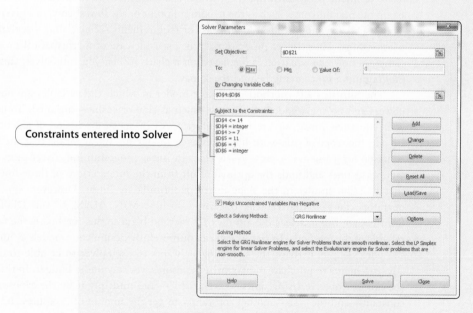

Constraints entered into Solver

Figure 23 Solver Parameters dialog box

The integer constraint—int—mandates that the variable cells remain a whole number. For example, the manufacturers of the spa's retail products—such as shampoo and conditioner—will not produce partial bottles of product. Thus, to guarantee that the variable cell values remain a whole number, you need to create integer constraints for them.

The greater than or equal to zero constraint requires the variable cell values remain greater than or equal to zero when you run Solver. For example, the manufacturers of the spa's retail products will not produce negative bottles of product. However, a negative value in a changing variable cell could possibly produce higher results in the objective cell. By default, the Make Unconstrained Variables Non-Negative check box is selected to guarantee that the variable cells remain greater than or equal to zero. If you want to let a variable cell be negative, you can uncheck the Make Unconstrained Variables Non-Negative check box and create a constraint that allows this to occur—such as D7>=–50.

One item to note: If Solver takes too long to solve, you can press Esc to break Solver and stop running the analysis.

Selecting a Solving Method

Three solving methods are available within the Solver Parameters dialog box—Simplex LP, Evolutionary, and Generalized Reduced Gradient (GRG) Nonlinear. These solving methods relate to **linear programming** (LP), which is a mathematical method for determining how to attain the best outcome, such as the maximum profit or the lowest cost, in a given mathematical model such as your spreadsheet for a list of requirements—constraints—represented as linear relationships. Thus, linear programming is a specific case of mathematical programming and compares how the equation is displayed on a chart. When you run Solver, this mathematical programming is occurring behind the scenes.

The **Simplex LP method** is a linear model in which the variables are not raised to any powers and no transcendent functions—such as sine or cosine—are used. To use Simplex LP, your equations must not break the linearity. An in-depth discussion of algebraic linearity is beyond the scope of this workshop. However, in algebra, linear means that the slope-intercept equation for a line—$y = mx + b$—is true. In linear programming, Excel plots all of the constraints as lines and finds the optimal result from the intersections of those lines. So, formulas that function similar to the slope-intercept formula are linear. However, some functions and operators can potentially break linearity—such as MIN, MAX, IF and DIVISION. If your formulas are linear, select the Simplex LP method because this method is the fastest and most reliable of the methods. In fact, if you can purposefully design your models as linear, it is better.

For example, perhaps the spa manager wants to use Solver to be able to determine what advertisements to purchase to maximize exposures, yet stay under budget. In this case, you take the number of advertising units—the variable—and multiply it by the exposures per unit—a constant—and the cost—another constant—to get the amount of exposures and cost per advertisement type, such as television, Internet, and radio. Then, you add all of those together and constrain it by the maximum amount you can spend—along with any other constraints. Then, you optimize for maximum exposures. Notice, you multiplied the variable cells by a constant and then added them together similar to the slope-intercept formula. Thus, if the constraints were plotted on a chart, the lines would be linear, as illustrated in Figure 24.

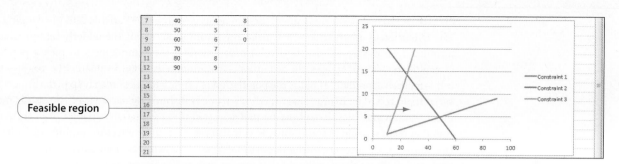

7	40	4	8
8	50	5	4
9	60	6	0
10	70	7	
11	80	8	
12	90	9	

Feasible region

Figure 24 Linear chart with three linear constraints

The **GRG Nonlinear method** is used for more complex models that are nonlinear and smooth. It is also the default method that Excel's Solver uses. Smooth means that when the constraints are graphed, a curve of some kind exists: concave, convex, a wave, and so on. Generally, the model is smooth when it uses trigonometric functions, exponentials, multiplies the variables together, and so on. A nonlinear model is one in which just one of the constraint lines breaks the linearity of the model. You may have several constraints that are linear, but one line that turns into a relationship that has any curves breaks the linearity of the model, as shown in Figure 25.

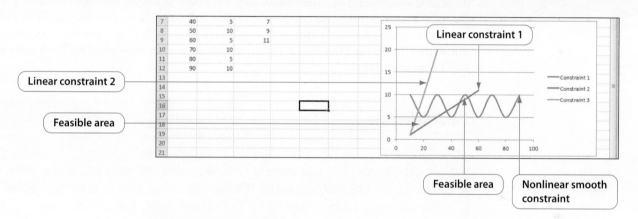

Linear constraint 2
Feasible area
Linear constraint 1
Feasible area
Nonlinear smooth constraint

Figure 25 Nonlinear chart with two feasible areas

In the GRG Nonlinear method, Excel uses an iterative process and starting point. You tell Excel where to start, and it starts moving along the constraint lines—linear and nonlinear. The starting point is typically zero, unless specific individualized business knowledge would indicate otherwise. As it moves along the graph lines, Excel is looking for peaks—when maximizing—and valleys—when minimizing. When it finds a significant enough peak or valley, Excel finds an optimal answer. If you give Excel a different starting point, Excel may find a different locally optimal answer, particularly if a higher peak or lower valley exists far away from the starting point used the first time. Thus, GRG Nonlinear is less reliable than the Simplex LP method. However, the Simplex LP method is limited to what can be modeled because linearity must be maintained.

There is a setting in GRG Nonlinear to help resolve this potential issue. You can take advantage of the Multistart method. This allows Excel to have multiple start points to compare all of the locally optimal answers. By way of this comparison, Excel can potentially find a probabilistically global optimal answer.

Finally, integer constraints break the linearity of a model even if you set it to use Simplex LP. Thus, integer constraints force GRG Nonlinear and a special branching method that takes longer. Also, if the model is actually linear, setting the method to GRG Nonlinear will force a linear model to be solved with GRG Nonlinear.

The **Evolutionary method** is used when a worksheet model is nonlinear and nonsmooth and thus the most complex model. Nonsmooth means that the line takes sharp bends or has no slope at all. Typically, these are models that use functions—such as VLOOKUP, PMT, IF,

SUMIF and so on—to derive values based on or derived from the variable cells or changing cells. The Evolutionary method does not make any assumptions about the underlying functions and formulas relationship. Thus, the Evolutionary method uses randomness to pick a population of candidates. Then, it uses the variables—changing cells—and evaluates the result—target cell—for each candidate. It holds the population of candidate answers to help pick the next set of variables to test. The Evolutionary method's name is inspired by nature itself. So, as the method picks random variables, it will use natural selection to reuse certain variables from the population that seem to yield better results. It will also use a crossover effect to combine variables from two known good answers in the population. Further, it will also randomly "mutate" to create new candidates for the population that may or may not be better than the other candidates.

Importantly, this means that the Evolutionary method cannot guarantee the most optimal result, but only the best result it found. Thus, every time you run the Evolutionary method, you might get a different answer. Evolutionary takes more processing power and time than the other methods. The only way the Evolutionary method knows to stop is based on the user-defined setting for length of time, number of iterations, or number of candidates. Therefore, the Evolutionary method is best only in situations that cannot be adequately modeled with an optimal answer method—Simplex LP or GRG Nonlinear. Using the Evolutionary method is beyond the scope of this workshop.

With all three methods, scalability can be an issue. If there is a wide scale for the object or constraint values, then it can cause issues in Solver. If you are dealing with numbers that differ in several magnitudes, consider revising the model to express the values differently. For example, instead of listing the number to purchase as 2,000,000, express the number as 2,000 in units of thousands. While there is an automatic scaling setting, best practice is to uncheck this setting. At the time this book was written, this setting can cause problems when using the GRG Nonlinear method.

Quick Reference / Selecting a Solving Method When You Are Not Sure Where to Begin

Start with Simplex LP. If your model is nonlinear, Solver will notify you. At that point, you can try the GRG Nonlinear model. If Solver still cannot seem to converge—gather or develop—on a solution, then try the Evolutionary model. One of these three models will eventually give you an optimal or good solution.

Generating and Interpreting Solver Answer Reports

When you run Solver, an answer report in a new worksheet is created and named "Answer Report." Other items to be considered when producing a Solver Answer Report include the type of report you want to generate—Answer, Sensitivity, Limits, or Population—as well as deciding how you want your worksheet to look after you run the Solver. When the Evolutionary Solving method is used, the Population report is also available. If Solver finds an optimal solution, and there are no integer constraints, two additional reports are available: the sensitivity report and the limits report.

Generating a Solver Answer Report

After you define the objective, variable cells, constraints, and solving method, you are ready to generate a Solver answer report. After you run Solver, you have several options before the report is generated. Once Solver displays a message that states it found a solution, you can choose the type of report that you want—answer, sensitivity, limits, or population. The **Solver answer report** lists the target cell and the changing cells with their corresponding original and final values for the problem, input variables, and constraints. In addition, the formulas, binding status, and slacks are given for each constraint. The **Solver sensitivity report** provides information about how sensitive the solution is to small changes in the formula for the target cell. This report displays the shadow prices for the constraint—the amount the objective function value changes per unit change in the constraint. Because constraints are often determined by resources, a comparison of the shadow prices of each constraint provides valuable information about the most effective place to apply additional resources in order to achieve the best improvement. This report can only be created if your Excel model does not contain integer or Boolean—the values 0 and 1—constraints. The **Solver limits report** displays the achieved optimal value and all the input variables of the model with the optimal values. Additionally, the report displays the upper and lower bounds for the optimal value. A variable cell could vary without changing the optimal solution. Finally, the **Solver population report** displays various statistical characteristics about the given model, such as how many variables and rows it contains.

You can also choose how you want your Excel model to behave—either restoring it to the original values or keeping the Solver solution. If you restore the original values, the original values that were entered into the variable cells prior to running Solver are restored. This can be helpful in case you have to run Solver again because it keeps you from having to manually change the values back to what they were when you began. If you choose to keep the Solver solution, you will be able to see the final outcome on both the answer report and the Excel model. Regardless of which option you choose, you will still be able to run Solver over and over again as needed.

To Generate a Solver Report

a. In the Solver Parameters dialog box, if necessary, click the **Select a Solving Method arrow**, and then click to select **GRG Nonlinear** solving method because the changing cells are being multiplied together.

b. Click **Options**, click the **All Methods tab**, if necessary, and verify the **Use Automatic Scaling** check box is unchecked.

c. Click the **GRG Nonlinear tab**, click to check the **Use Multistart** check box, and then click **OK**.

d. Click **Solve** at the bottom of the Solver Parameters dialog box.

e. In the Solver Results dialog box, verify the **Keep Solver Solution** option is selected. This will display your optimal results on the spreadsheet as well as your report.

f. Under the Reports options, on the right side of the Solver Results dialog box, click to select **Answer**, and then click **OK**. Notice that a worksheet tab named Answer Report 1 now exists in the workbook.

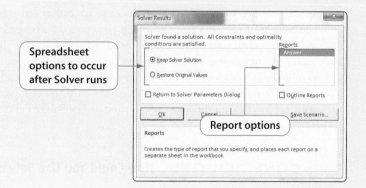

Figure 26 Solver Results dialog box

g. Click the **Answer Report 1 worksheet tab**, and then **Save** 🖫 your changes.

Interpreting a Solver Answer Report

The Solver answer report is divided into four sections—report details, objective cell information, variable cell information, and constraints information. The report details section displays information about the Solver report—report type, file name, and worksheet that contains the Excel model, date, and time the report was created; Solver Engine details; and Solver Options that you set at the time you created the report.

The second section reports information about the objective cells—cell references; changing cell names; whether you searched for the minimum, maximum, or a specific value; as well as the original and final objective cell values. For example, in the Solver report you just created, you were trying to maximize the net income. Before running Solver, the net income value was –$1,701.50; however, once Solver ran, the net income was maximized. The result indicated that the spa could make $8,172.20 in profit.

The third section displays information about the variable cells—cell references, variable cell names, original cell values, and final cell values. In your report, you can see that if the spa is open 11 hours per day, each of the four therapists can see 14 clients. This mix will create the profit of $8,172.20 per day.

The fourth section displays information about the constraints you entered—cell references, descriptions, new cell values, formulas, status, and slack—for each constraint. In your report, notice that the total clients slack is seven, the difference between the lower constraint of 7 and the upper constraint value of 14 for cell D4. A constraint is considered to be a **binding constraint** if changing it also changes the optimal solution. A less severe constraint that does not affect the optimal solution is known as a **nonbinding constraint**.

One item to note is that if you change your Excel model or Solver parameters, you must run Solver again to create an updated report. The names of new reports will be "Answer Report" followed by consecutive numbering—1, 2, 3, and so on. Simply delete the reports you no longer need.

CONSIDER THIS | **Why Is It Important to Know How to Read Reports?**

You have spent a considerable amount of time creating your Solver answer report. Why do you think it is so important to be able to understand what the output data for the answer report is telling you? How would analyzing the data and interpreting the output affect management decisions? What factors would you consider when setting the variable constraints for any adjustments to the Solver model?

Saving and Restoring a Solver Model

When you save your workbook, the most recent Solver settings are automatically saved, even if you have multiple worksheets in which you created Solver parameters. For example, if you have made changes to your Solver constraints, the previous ones will not be saved. You can save your Solver settings as you work—that way, you can apply previous settings again in the future. By saving the Solver model, the objective cells, variable cells, and constraints are saved, and Excel places this information in a few cells on the worksheet. Solver models can be easily saved and reloaded by clicking the Load/Save button on the Solver Parameters dialog box.

CONSIDER THIS | **How Could You Use Solver?**

Have you ever wondered what you need to get on your outstanding assignments and final exam to earn a specific grade in a course? Or wondered how much of a salary increase you would need to budget for a specific purchase or adjustment to household expenses? Or how much money you could use to invest, what types of investments to choose, and how to meet certain goals for retirement? How could you configure Solver to determine the optimal solution? Which Solver model would you use to solve your problem? Which type of report would you choose? How would you format your report?

To Save and Reload a Solver Model

a. Click the **Solver worksheet tab**, restore the original values, click cell **D4**, type **1**, repeat typing the same value in cells **D5** and **D6**, click cell **C18**, and then type **3.95**. Click the **Data tab**, and click **Solver** in the Analysis group.

b. In the Solver Parameters dialog box, click **Load/Save** to open the Load/Save Model dialog box.

c. Excel guides you through the process. Because you are saving this model, Excel prompts you to select a specific number of cells. In this case, Excel needs ten cells to write the objective cell, variable cell, and constraint data. Type **$A$24** in the box for the Load/Save Model dialog box, and then click **Save**. Notice how Solver placed data in 10 cells beginning with A24. Once the Solver model was saved, the Solver Parameters dialog box reopened.

d. Add a new constraint by clicking **Add**. The spa manager is thinking about being open for more hours during the day—possibly being open for up to 16 hours per day. The spa must be open at least 12 hours per day.

e. In the Add Constraint dialog box, type **$D$5** in the Cell Reference box, click to select <= in the mathematical operands box, type **16** in the Constraint box, and then click **OK**.

f. In the Solver Parameters dialog box, under Subject to the Constraints, click to select the **$D$5 = 11** constraint, and then click **Change**. In the Change Constraint dialog box, click to select >= in the mathematical operands box, replace any text, and then type **12** in the Constraint box. Click **Add**.

g. If the spa manager extends the spa's operating hours, she will need to schedule more massage therapists each day. The spa manager knows that a minimum of four therapists will need to work; however, there could be up to seven scheduled in a given day. In the Add Constraint dialog box, type **$D$6** in the Cell Reference box, click to select <= in the mathematical operands box, and then type **7** in the Constraint box.

h. Click **OK**. Notice under Subject to the Constraints that the two new constraints you entered appear in the list of the Solver Parameters dialog box.

i. Click to select **$D$4 <= 14** from the list of constraints, and then click **Change**.

j. In the Change Constraint dialog box, in the Constraint box, change the value of 14 to **25**. By adding additional hours and 15-minute massages, the spa can service more clients. Click **OK**.

k. In the Solver Parameters dialog box, click to select the **$D$6 = 4** constraint, click **Change**, and then click to select >= in the mathematical operands box. Click **OK**.

l. Click **Load/Save** to open the Load/Save Model dialog box, type **$B$24** in the box, and then click **Save**.

m. In the Solver Parameters dialog box, click **Solve** to open the Solver Results dialog box.

n. Click to select the **Restore Original Values** option, and then under Reports on the right side of the Solver Results dialog box, click to select **Answer**.

o. Click **OK**. Notice that a worksheet tab named Answer Report 2 now exists, and on the Solver worksheet tab, the value of 1 was reset in cells D4, D5, and D6, and cell C18 reflects $3.95.

p. Click the **Answer Report 2 worksheet tab**. Notice that the spa can maximize the massage therapists' schedule and realize a net income of $29,526.75 per day.

q. **Save** 🖫 your changes. Print or submit your work as directed by your instructor. Close your file, and then exit Excel.

Quick Reference / Saving Solver Parameters

You can save the last selections in the Solver Parameters dialog box with a worksheet by saving the workbook. Each worksheet in a workbook may have its own Solver selections, and all of them are saved. You can also define more than one problem for a worksheet by clicking Load/Save to save problems individually.

When you save a model, enter the reference for the first cell of a vertical range of empty cells in which you want to place the problem model. When you load a model, enter the reference for the entire range of cells that contains the problem model.

Concept Check

1. Why do managers use CVP analysis, and what does it help them learn about their business?

2. What is a break-even point? Explain the two types of costs that need to be considered when performing a break-even analysis.

3. Give three examples of how you could use Goal Seek. Describe how Goal Seek uses iteration to find the solution.

4. What are scenarios used for, and how can analyzing scenarios assist managers in decision making?

5. What is Solver? What can Solver help managers determine?

Key Terms

Add-in   614
Binding constraint   622
Break-even analysis   594
Break-even point   594
Changing cell   609
Conditional formatting   599
Constraint   614
Cost-volume-profit (CVP) analysis   594
Data table   601
Elastic   604
Evolutionary method   619
Fixed cost   594
Goal seek   606

GRG Nonlinear method   619
Inelastic   604
Iteration   606
Linear programming   618
Mixed cost   594
Nonbinding constraint   622
Objective cell   615
One-variable data table   601
Optimize   615
Scenario   609
Scenario Manager   609
Scenario PivotTable report   613
Scenario summary   612

Scenario tool   597
Scroll bar   597
Simplex LP method   618
Solver   614
Solver answer report   620
Solver limits report   621
Solver population report   621
Solver sensitivity report   620
Two-variable data table   603
Variable   596
Variable cost   594
What-if analysis   596

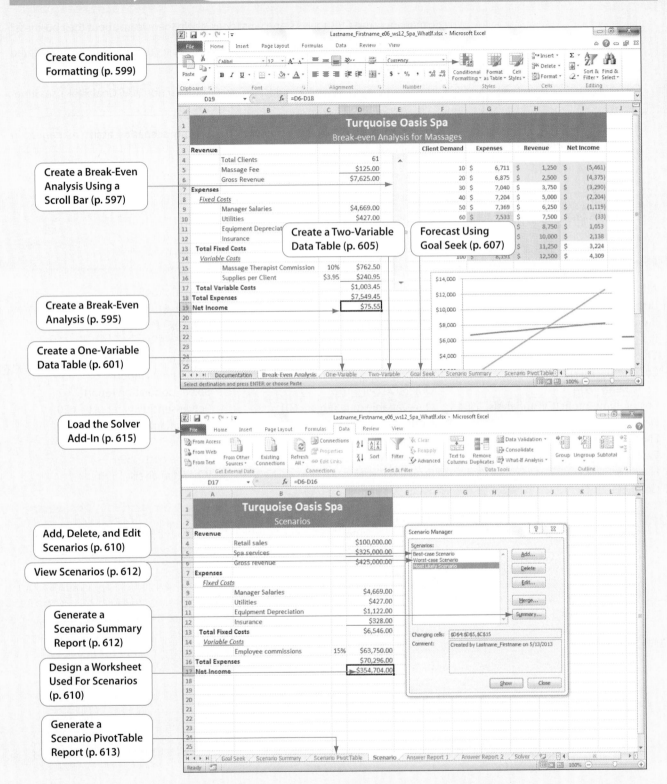

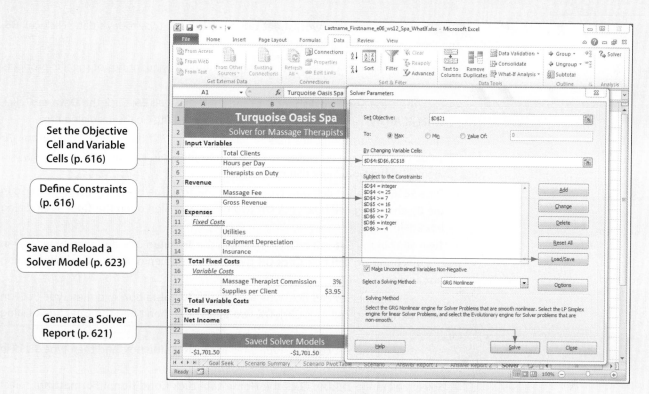

Set the Objective Cell and Variable Cells (p. 616)

Define Constraints (p. 616)

Save and Reload a Solver Model (p. 623)

Generate a Solver Report (p. 621)

Figure 27 The Turquoise Oasis Spa Business Planning Analysis final worksheets

Practice 1

Student data file needed:

e06_ws12_Golf_Forecasting

You will save your file as:

Lastname_Firstname_e06_ws12_Golf_Forecasting

Forecasting at the Red Bluff Golf Club Pro Shop

The Red Bluff Golf Club Pro Shop needs to analyze current sales trends and forecast prices for the upcoming year to ensure they are maximizing profit. Barry Cheney, the manager, is not certain if the prices he is currently charging are going to help him reach his sales goals. Additionally, he needs some guidance about how many hours a day he should open for business as well as how many employees he should schedule during operating hours to maximize the pro shop's net income. Mr. Cheney has asked you to perform what-if analyses through the use of a break-even analysis, data tables, Goal Seek, scenarios, and Solver. He has given you templates and data to use to create your analysis. Upon completion, you will need to present your findings to Mr. Cheney.

a. Start **Excel**, navigate to the student data files, and then open **e06_ws12_Golf_ Forecasting**. Save the workbook to your student files as Lastname_Firstname_e06_ ws12_Golf_Forecasting.

b. Click the **Insert tab**, and then click **Header & Footer** in the Text group to insert a footer with the file name.

c. Click the **Design tab**, and then click **Go to Footer** in the Navigation group. If necessary, click the **left section** of the footer, and then click **File Name** in the Header & Footer Elements group.

d. Click any cell on the spreadsheet to move out of the footer, press [Ctrl]+[Home], click the **View tab**, click **Normal** in the Workbook Views group, and then click the **Home tab**.

e. Click the **Documentation worksheet tab**. Click cell **A6**, type today's date, click cell **B6**, and then type your first and last name.

f. Complete the following tasks to forecast prices and sales quantities of specific products using Goal Seek.

- Click the **Goal Seek worksheet tab**, and then click cell **E5**. Click the **Data tab**, click **What-If Analysis**, and then click **Goal Seek** to open the Goal Seek dialog box.

- The spa wants to set a sales goal of $27,500 for its golf balls. Type 27500 in the **To value** box, and then type $C$5 in the **By changing cell** box. Click **OK** two times, and then open the **Goal Seek** dialog box again.

- Type $E$6 in the **Set cell** box, type 9000 in the **To value** box, and then type $D$6 in the **By changing cell** box. Click **OK** two times, and then open the **Goal Seek** dialog box again.

- Type $E$7 in the **Set cell** box, type 7500 in the **To value** box, and then type $C$7 in the **By changing cell** box. Click **OK** two times, and then open the **Goal Seek** dialog box again.

- Type $E$8 in the **Set cell** box, type 9250 in the **To value** box, and then type $C$8 in the **By changing cell** box. Click **OK** two times, and then open the **Goal Seek** dialog box again.

- Type $E$9 in the **Set cell** box, type 2495 in the **To value** box, and then type $D$9 in the **By changing cell** box. Click **OK** two times.

- Select cell range **D5:D9**. Click the **Home tab**, click **Conditional Formatting**, select **Highlight Cell Rules**, and then click **Greater Than**. In the Format cells that are GREATER THAN box, type 100. Click the **with arrow**, and then click **Custom Format**. Under Font style click **Bold**, and then click **OK** two times to apply bold to the font of the product prices, where the price is greater than $100. Press [Ctrl]+[Home].

g. Complete the following tasks to forecast the best-case, worst-case, and most-likely case scenarios using Scenario Manager.

- Click the **Scenario worksheet tab**. Click the **Data tab**, click **What-If Analysis**, and then click **Scenario Manager** to open the Scenario Manager dialog box.

- Click **Add**, type Most Likely Scenario in the Scenario name box, and press [Tab]. In the Changing cells box, type D4:D5,C15. The values that are currently on the spreadsheet are the values for the Most Likely Scenario. Click **OK** two times.

- Click **Add** to begin creating your second scenario, type Worst-case Scenario in the Scenario name box, and then click **OK**. Type 75000 in row 1, type 125000 in row 2, type 0.09 in row 3, and then click **OK**.

- Click **Add** to begin creating your third scenario, type Best-case Scenario in the Scenario name box, and then click **OK**. Type 200000 in row 1, type 350000 in row 2, type 0.05 in row 3, and then click **OK**.

- In the Scenario Manager dialog box, view each of your scenarios by clicking each Scenario's name in the listing box, and then click **Show**. Click **Summary** to create a Scenario summary report, type D18 in the Result cells box, and then click **OK**.

- Click the **Scenario Summary worksheet tab**, if necessary. To add headings to your data, delete the cell reference headings in cells in **C6**, **C7**, **C8**, and **C10**. Click cell **B6**, type Retail sales, click cell **B7**, type Equipment sales, click cell **B8**, type Commission, click cell **B10**, and then type Net income. Format the font as bold.

- Click the **Scenario worksheet tab**. Click **What-If Analysis**, click **Scenario Manager** to open the Scenario Manager dialog box, and then click **Summary**. Select the **Scenario PivotTable report** option. Click the **Result cells** box, type D18, and then click **OK**.

- Click the **Scenario PivotTable worksheet tab** to format the report to make it easier to read. Click cell **A1**, type Monthly Forecasting Solution, press [Ctrl]+[Enter], and then set the width of column A to 27. Click cell **A2**, type Scenario PivotTable Report, press [Ctrl]+[Enter], merge and center the range **A2:B2**, and then change the Font Size to

16 point and apply **Bold**. Click cell **A3**, and then type Scenarios. Press Tab, in cell B3 type Net Income, press Ctrl+Enter, and then resize the width of column B as needed. Select the range **B4:B6**, and then format the cells as Currency with 2 decimal places.

h. Complete the following tasks to create a Solver answer report that determines the maximum net income that can be generated.

- Click the **Solver worksheet tab**, click the **Data tab**, and then click **Solver** in the Analysis group.

- In the Solver Parameters dialog box, click the **Set Objective** box, type D23, and then type $D$4:$D$5 in the By Changing Variable Cells box. Click **Add** to begin entering your constraints.

- The pro shop can be open from 12 to 18 hours per day, depending on what Mr. Cheney decides. Using the techniques you have practiced, type $D$4>=12 in the appropriate boxes as your first constraint, click **Add**, and then type $D$4<=18 as your second constraint.

- Click **Add**. The pro shop can have three to seven employees working per day, depending on the day and time of year. Using the techniques you have practiced, type $D$5>=3 as your next constraint, click **Add**, and then type $D$5<=7 as your next constraint.

- Click **Add**. The hours and employees must be integers. Using the techniques you have practiced, type $D$4=integer as your next constraint (*Hint*: Click **int** as the mathematical operand option and Excel will add the word "integer" for you), click **Add**, and then type $D$5=integer as your last constraint.

- Click **OK**. To save your Solver model, click **Load/Save**, type $A$25 into the box in the Load/Save Model dialog box, click **Save**, and then click **Solve** to create a Solver answer report. Be sure to click **Restore Original Values**, and then click **Answer** before you click **OK**.

i. Complete the following tasks to create a two-variable data table with conditional formatting that will help analyze the break-even point.

- Click the **Data Table worksheet tab**, click cell **F5**, type =D19, and press Ctrl+Enter. To format cell F5 to hide the results of the function, right-click cell **F5**, and then click **Format Cells**.

- Click the **Number tab**, click to select the **Custom** category, and then click the **Type** box. Delete any existing text and type "Total Golfers". Click **OK**, and then press Ctrl+B to apply bold. Select the range **F5:Q21** to select the data for your data table.

- Click the **Data tab**, click **What-If Analysis**, and then click **Data Table** to open the Data Table dialog box. Type $D$5 in the Row input cell box, type $D$4 in the Column input cell box, and then click **OK**.

- Select the range **G6:Q21**, and then format the cells as **Currency** with 2 decimal places. To view all the data, widen the columns if necessary.

- Click the **Home tab**, click **Conditional Formatting**, select **Highlight Cells Rules**, click **Less Than** to open the Less Than dialog box, type 0 in the Format cells that are LESS THAN box, if necessary click to select the **Light Red Fill with Dark Red Text** option, and then click **OK**.

- Click **Conditional Formatting** again, select **Highlight Cells Rules**, click **Greater Than** to open the Greater Than dialog box, type 3500 in the Format cells that are GREATER THAN box, click to select the **Green Fill with Dark Green Text** option, and then click **OK**. Press Ctrl+Home.

j. Format the page layout to the orientation that works best for each new worksheet you created.

k. Save your changes, and then print or submit your file as directed by your instructor. Close your file, and then exit **Excel**.

Student data file needed:

e06_ws12_GiftShop_Analysis

You will save your file as:

Lastname_Firstname_e06_ws12_GiftShop_Analysis

Break-Even Analysis and Product Pricing at the Painted Treasures Gift Shop

The gift shop manager, Susan Brock, needs an easy way to price new and existing products in the gift shop. She has asked you to develop a break-even analysis and data tables to ensure she is pricing some of her gift items properly. She would also like you to create a scenario summary report to forecast the net income generated from Painted Paradise items. Ms. Brock has given you templates to use to create your analysis. Upon completion, you will need to present your findings to Ms. Brock.

a. Start **Excel**, navigate to the student data files, and then open the **e06_ws12_GiftShop_Analysis** workbook. Save the workbook to your student files as Lastname_Firstname_e06_ws12_GiftShop_Analysis.

b. Click the **Insert tab**, and then click **Header & Footer** in the Text group to insert a footer with the file name.

c. Click the **Design tab**, and then click **Go to Footer** in the Navigation group. If necessary, click the **left section** of the footer, and then click **File Name** in the Header & Footer Elements group.

d. Click any cell on the spreadsheet to move out of the footer, press Ctrl+Home, click the **View tab**, click **Normal** in the Workbook Views group, and then click the **Home tab**.

e. Click the **Documentation worksheet** tab. Click cell **A6**, type today's date, click cell **B6**, and then type your first and last name.

f. Click the **Break-even Analysis worksheet tab**. Complete the following tasks to create your break-even analysis using a scroll bar, and build a traditional cost-volume-profit chart off a one-variable data table that will help analyze the break-even point.

   - Click cell **D5**, and then type =VLOOKUP(D4,'Scroll Bar Data'!A3:B43,2,FALSE). Press Ctrl+Enter.

   - Click the **Developer tab**, click **Insert**, click **Scroll Bar (Form Control)**, and then drag to draw the scroll bar in the area of cells E4 through E14.

   - Right-click the selected **scroll bar**, and then click **Format Control**. Type the following criteria in the Format Control dialog box.

   Current value: type 75

   Minimum value: type 60

   Maximum value: type 100

   Incremental change: Leave as the default value of 1

   Page change: Leave as the default value of 10

   Cell link: type $D$4

   - Click **OK**. Click a blank cell away from the scroll bar to deselect. Click the **Home tab**, and then use conditional formatting to format cell D14 so numbers that are less than zero display in red text, and then scroll until you find the break-even point.

   - Click cell **F4**, type =D4, press Tab, in cell G4 type =D13. Press Tab, in cell H4 type =D6, press Tab, and then in cell I4 type =D14. Press Ctrl+Enter.

   - Select the range **F4:I4** to hide the results of the function you just referenced. Right-click any cell in the selected range F4:I4, and then click **Format Cells**. Click the **Number**

tab, and then click to select the **Custom** category. Click the **Type** box, delete any existing text, and then type ;;;, and then click **OK**.

- Select the range **F4:I13** to select the cells for your data table. Click the **Data tab**, click **What-If Analysis**, and then click **Data Table** to open the Data Table dialog box. Press Tab to move to the Column input cell box, type $D$4 in the Column input cell box, and then click **OK**.

- Click the **Home tab**, select the range **G5:I13**, and then format the cells as **Currency** with 2 decimal places.

- Select the range **I5:I13**, click the **Home tab**, click **Conditional Formatting**, select **Data Bars**, and then under Gradient Fill click **Green Data Bar**.

- Select the range **F3:H3**, hold down Ctrl, and then select the range **F5:H13**. Click the **Insert tab**, click **Line** in the Charts group, and then select **Line** in the 2-D Line category. Click the **border edge** of the chart, and then drag to move the chart until the top-left corner is in cell F15.

- Click the **Design tab**, click **Select Data**, click **Quantity Sold** under Legend Entries (Series), and under Horizontal (Category) Axis Labels, click **Edit**. In the Axis Labels dialog box, click the **Axis label range** box, and then select the range **F5:F13**. Click **OK** two times. Click the **Layout tab**, click the **Chart Elements arrow** in the Current Selection group, click **Series "Quantity Sold"** to select the blue data line, and then press Delete.

- Click the **Layout tab**, click **Axis Titles**, select **Primary Horizontal Axis Title**, click **Title Below Axis**, type Quantity in the formula bar, and then delete any remaining AutoComplete text. Press Enter to apply the change to the axis title object. Click a cell away from the chart to deselect the chart, and press Ctrl+Home.

g. Click the **Home tab**, click the **Scroll Bar Data worksheet** tab, select the range **A3:A43**, and then click **Conditional Formatting** to format the cells with **Data Bars**, **Gradient Fill**, the **Blue Data Bar** option. Select the range **B3:B43**, and then click **Conditional Formatting** to the cells with Icon Sets that have the 3 Flags under Indicators. Press Ctrl+Home.

h. Click the **Two-Variable worksheet tab**, and then complete the following tasks to create a two-variable data table.

- Click cell **D4**, type =B2 to reference the input cells, and then press Enter. In cell D5, type 150, press Enter, in cell D6 type 200, select the range **D5:D6**, and then drag the **AutoFill** handle down to cell **D19**. Click the **AutoFill Options arrow**, and then click the **Fill Without Formatting** option.

- Click cell **E3**, type 10.95, and then press Tab. In cell F3 type 11.95, select the range **E3:F3**, and then drag the **AutoFill** handle across to cell **L3**. Click the **Auto Fill Options arrow**, and then click the **Fill Without Formatting** option.

- Click cell **D3**, type =B4, and then press Ctrl+Enter to reference the formula that Excel will use to calculate your data table. Right-click cell **D3**, and then click **Format Cells**. Click the **Number tab**, click to select the **Custom** Category, click the **Type** box, delete any existing text, and then type "Quantity" to hide the results of the formula you just referenced and display. Click **OK**.

- Select **D3:L19**. Click the **Data tab**, click **What-If Analysis**, and then click **Data Table** to insert a two-variable data table. Type $B$3 in the Row input cell box, type $B$2 in the Column input cell box, and then click **OK**.

- Click the **Home tab**, and then apply **Conditional Formatting** to the range **E4:L19** so values that are Less Than $5,000 have Light Red Fill with Dark Red Text. Apply another Conditional Formatting for values Greater Than $10,000 to display a Green Fill with Dark Green Text. Add a third conditional format that displays values between $5,000 and $10,000 in Yellow Fill with Dark Yellow Text. Press Ctrl+Home.

i. Click the **Scenarios worksheet tab**, and then complete the following tasks to create a Scenario summary report.

- Click cell **E4**, type =C4*D4, press Ctrl+Enter, and then drag the **AutoFill** handle down to cell **E8** to calculate the forecasted extended prices. Click the **Auto Fill Options arrow**, and then click the **Fill Without Formatting** option.

- Click cell **E9**, type =SUM(E4:E8), press Enter. Click cell **E16**, type =SUM(E12:E15), and then press Enter to calculate the total forecasted fixed costs. Click cell **E17**, type =IF(E9-E16>0,(E9-E16)*0.28,0), and then press Enter to calculate the forecasted taxes paid to the Internal Revenue Service. Click cell **E18**, type =E9-E16 to calculate the forecasted net income. Press Enter, and then press Ctrl+Home.

- Click the **Data tab**, click **What-If Analysis**, click **Scenario Manager**, and then click **Add**. Type Most Likely in the Scenario name box, and then type $C$4:$C$8 in the Changing cells box. The current values on the worksheet will be your Most Likely scenario values. Click **OK** twice.

- Click **Add** to add a new scenario. Type Best-case in the Scenario name box, and then click **OK**. Click **row 1**, type 250, press Tab. In row 2 type 75, press Tab, in row 3 type 40, press Tab, in row 4, type 55, press Tab, and then in row 5 type 75. Click **OK**.

- Click **Add** to add a new scenario. Type Worst-case in the Scenario name box, and then click **OK**. Click **row 1**, type 75, and then press Tab. In row 2 type 25, press Tab, in row 3 type 10, press Tab, in row 4 type 25, press Tab, and then in row 5, type 25. Click **OK**.

- Click **Summary** to create a Scenario summary report, and then type E18 in the Result cells box. Click **OK**. Click the **Scenario Summary worksheet tab**, and then click the **Home tab**. Select range **C6:C10**, and then press Delete. Click cell **C12**, and then press Delete. Click cell **B6**, type T-shirt, and then press Enter. In cell **B7**, type Sweatshirt, and then press Enter. In cell **B8**, type Beach Towel, and then press Enter. In cell **B9**, type Coffee Cup, and then press Enter. In cell **B10**, type Sweatshirt, and then press Enter. Click cell **B12**, type Net Income, and then press Enter. Select the range **D6:G10**, and then format as Currency with 2 decimal places. Select cells **B6:B10**, hold down Ctrl, and then click cell **B12**. Click **Increase Indent** in the Alignment group one time. Press Ctrl+Enter.

j. Format the page layout to the orientation that works best for each new worksheet you created.

k. Save your changes, and then print or submit your file as directed by your instructor. Close your file, and then exit Excel.

MODULE CAPSTONE

Student data file needed:	You will save your file as:
e06_mp_Indigo5_Analysis	Lastname_Firstname_e06_mp_Indigo5_Analysis

Forecasting Product Pricing at the Indigo5 Restaurant

The Painted Paradise Golf Resort and Spa is home to a world-class restaurant with a top chef, Robin Sanchez. Robin is regularly updating data in his database to make certain he has all the ingredients and recipes needed to offer the high-quality food for which the restaurant is known. You have been asked to build a spreadsheet model that will assist managers in answering what-if questions about product pricing when Chef Sanchez wants to add a new menu item. Additionally, Ms. Vargas, the server manager, wants you to set up a model that will help her analyze a loan for front-of-house improvements—such as new uniforms for the servers, a new computer system for order entry, and a dining room renovation. Mr. Dimas, the restaurant manager, gave you an Excel workbook and some data to use while building your spreadsheets. Upon completion, you will present your model to Chef Robin Sanchez, Alberto Dimas, and Krishna Vargas.

a. Start **Excel**, and then open the **e06_mp_Indigo5_Analysis** workbook from the student data files. Save the file as Lastname_Firstname_e06_mp_Indigo5_Analysis.

b. Using previously learned skills, insert a file name footer in the left section of the footer.

c. Click the **Documentation worksheet tab**. Click cell **A6**, type today's date, click cell **B6**, and then type your first and last name.

d. Complete the following tasks to perform a break-even analysis for a new menu item. Fixed expenses have been spread evenly among all menu items.

- Click the **Break-even Analysis worksheet tab**, if necessary. Click cell **D6**, type =D4*D5, and then press Enter to calculate the gross revenue—the amount of money generated from selling the new menu item.

- Click cell **D13**, type =SUM(D9:D12), and then press Enter to calculate the total fixed costs. Click cell **D15**, type =D4*C15, and then press Enter to calculate the total food cost based on how many items were sold.

- In cell **D16**, type =D13+D15, and then press Enter to calculate the total expenses. In cell **D17**, type =D6-D16, and then press Enter to calculate the net income—how much profit the restaurant will generate from the new menu item.

- Apply Conditional Formatting to cell D17 so numbers that are less than zero are displayed in red text font and numbers that are greater than zero are displayed in green font from the Custom Format option, and then enter quantities in cell D4 until you find the break-even point.

- Click cell **F4**, type =D4, and then press Tab. In cell G4, type =D16, and then press Tab. In cell H4, type =D6, and then press Tab. In cell I4, type =D17, and then press Ctrl+Enter. Select cells **F4:I4** to format with the formula results hidden. Right-click any of the cells in the selected range **F4:I4**, and then click **Format Cells**. On the Number tab, click to select the **Custom** Category, click in the **Type** box, remove any existing text, and then type ;;;. Click **OK**.

- Select the range **F4:I18** for your data table. Click the **Data tab**, click **What-If Analysis**, and then click **Data Table** to open the Data Table dialog box. Press [Tab] to move to the Column input cell box, type $D$4, and then click **OK**.

- Select the range **I5:I18**, click the **Home tab**, click **Conditional Formatting button**, select **Color Scales**, and then click **Green - White - Red Color Scale**.

- Select the range **F3:H3**, hold down [Ctrl], and then select the range **F5:H18**. Click the **Insert tab**, click **Line** in the Charts group, and then click **Line** in the 2-D Line category. Click the **border edge** of the chart, and then drag to reposition the top-left corner into cell F20.

- Click the **Design tab**, click **Select Data**, click **Total Ordered** under Legend Entries (Series), and then under Horizontal (Category) Axis Labels click **Edit**. With the insertion point in the Axis label range box, select the range **F5:F18**. Click **OK** two times. Click the **Layout tab**, in the Current Selection group, click the **Chart Elements arrow**, and then click **Series "Total Ordered"** to select the blue data line. Press [Delete].

- On the Layout tab, click **Axis Titles**, select **Primary Horizontal Axis Title**, and then click **Title Below Axis**. In the formula bar, type Total Ordered, and then press [Enter] to apply the new title in the text box. Click an empty cell to deselect the chart. Press [Ctrl]+[Home].

e. Complete the following tasks to build a loan amortization table for Front-of-House Improvements.

- Click the **Loan Amortize worksheet tab**. Click cell **G5**, type =C7*C8, and then press [Enter] to calculate the number of payments.

- In cell **G6**, type =PMT(C6/C8,G5,-C5), and then press [Enter] to calculate the payments that will be made at the end of the period. In cell G7, type =G5*G6, and then press [Enter] to calculate the total amount that will be paid. In cell G8, type =G7-C5, and then press [Enter] to calculate the total interest that will be paid on the loan.

- Click cell **C12**, type =C5, and then press [Enter]. In cell **C13**, type =G12, and then press [Ctrl]+[Enter] to calculate the beginning balance for periods 2–36. Copy the formula down to cell **C47** using the **AutoFill** handle.

- Click cell **D12**, type =$G$6, and then press [Ctrl]+[Enter] to enter your payment. Copy the formula down to cell **D47** using the **AutoFill** handle.

- Click cell **E12**, type =IPMT($C$6/$C$8,A12,$G$5,-$C$5), and then press [Ctrl]+[Enter] to calculate how much of the monthly payment is being applied to the interest portion of the loan. Copy the formula down to cell **E47** using the **AutoFill** handle.

- Click cell **F12**, type =PPMT($C$6/$C$8,A12,$G$5,-$C$5), and then press [Ctrl]+[Enter] to calculate how much of the monthly payment is being applied to the principal portion of the loan. Copy the formula down to cell **F47** using the **AutoFill** handle.

- Click cell **G12**, type =C12-F12, and then press [Ctrl]+[Enter] to calculate the remaining balance after each payment. Copy the formula down to cell **G47** using the **AutoFill** handle.

- Click cell **D48**, type =SUM(D12:D47), and then press [Ctrl]+[Enter]. Use the **AutoFill** handle to copy the formula over to cell **F48**. Use the calculated values displayed in cells G7, G8, and C5 to check your total calculations.

- Click cell **I12**, type =ABS(CUMIPMT($C$6/$C$8,$G$5,$C$5,$A$12,A12,0)), and then press [Ctrl]+[Enter] to calculate the cumulative interest payments for the life of the loan. Copy the formula down to cell **I47** using the **AutoFill** handle.

- Click cell **J12**, type =ABS(CUMPRINC($C$6/$C$8,$G$5,$C$5,$A$12,A12,0)), and then press [Ctrl]+[Enter] to calculate the cumulative principal payments for the life of the loan. Copy the formula down to cell **J47** using the **AutoFill** handle, and then press [Ctrl]+[Home].

f. Format the page layout to the orientation that works best for each worksheet.

g. Save your changes, and then print or submit your file as directed by your instructor. Close your file, and then exit Excel.

Student data file needed:

e06_ps1_Hotel1_WhatIf

You will save your file as:

Lastname_Firstname_e06_ps1_Hotel1_WhatIf

Analyzing Room Rates at the Painted Paradise Resort and Spa

The hotel area has asked you to develop a spreadsheet model that will assist in determining room rates and the break-even point for specific types of rooms—such as the Grand Villa Suite. Currently, William Mattingly is not certain whether the pricing helps cover expenses such as housekeeping costs or whether the price even generates a profit for the resort. He would also like you to generate a Scenario summary report that will illustrate the net income based on best-case, worst-case, and most-likely scenarios. Mr. Mattingly gave you an Excel workbook with a partial model already built and some data to use while building your model. Upon completion, you will present your model to Mr. Mattingly before the spreadsheet model is implemented.

a.   Start **Excel**, and then open the **e06_ps1_Hotel1_WhatIf** workbook from the student data files. Save the file as Lastname_Firstname_e06_ps1_Hotel1_WhatIf, and then insert a file name footer in the left section of the footer.

b.   Click the **Documentation worksheet tab**. Click cell **A6**, type today's date, click cell **B6**, and then type your first and last name.

c.   Click the **Break-even Analysis worksheet tab**, if necessary, install the Developer tab as explained in Workshop 12. Insert a scroll bar in the area of cells E4 through E14, and then complete the following tasks to create a weekly break-even analysis for the Grand Villa Suite.

   • In the Format Control dialog box, type the following criteria:

   Current value: type 1

   Minimum value: type 1

   Maximum value: type 50

   Incremental change: Leave as the default value of 1

   Page change: Leave as the default value of 10

   Cell link: type $D$4, and then click **OK**.

   • Format cell **D17**, apply Conditional Formatting so numbers that are less than zero are displayed in red text, and then use the scroll bar to scroll until you find the break-even point.

   • Click cell **G4**, and then type =D16. In cell **H4**, type =D6, and then in cell **I4**, type =D17. Format the range **G4:I4** to hide the results of the functions you just referenced by right-clicking any of the selected cells, clicking **Format Cells**, and then using the ;;; Custom Category format.

   • Select the range **F4:I14**. Click the **Data tab**, click **What-If Analysis**, and then insert a one-variable data table. Type $D$4 in the Column input cell box, and click **OK**. Select the range **G5:I14**, and then format the cells as **Currency** with 2 decimal places.

   • Select the range **I5:I14**, click the **Home tab**, click **Conditional Formatting**, select **Data Bars**, and then click **Green Data Bar** under Gradient Fill.

   • Select the range **F3:H3**, hold down Ctrl, and then select the range **F5:H14**. Insert a line chart in the 2-D Line category. Use the range F5:F14 as the Horizontal (Category) Axis Labels. Delete the Blue data line. Add a horizontal axis title that is below the axis. Type Rooms Booked in the Title text box, and then move your chart below the one-variable data table. Click cell **A1** to deselect the chart.

d. Click the **Scenarios worksheet tab**, and then complete the following tasks to create a Scenario summary report.

- Click the **Data tab**, click **What-If Analysis**, and then click **Scenario Manager**. Add a Most-Likely scenario, and then use $C$4:$C$7 as the Changing cells. The current values on the worksheet will be your Most Likely scenario values.

- Add a new scenario named Best-case scenario. In the Scenario Values dialog box, in row 1, type 400. In row 2, type 200, click row **3**, type 250, click row **4**, and then type 125.

- Add a new scenario named Worst-case scenario. In the Scenario Values dialog box in row 1, type 170, click row **2**, type 100, click row **3**, type 150, click row **4**, and then type 50.

- Create a Scenario Summary report using E17 as your Result cells. Format your report with the appropriate row headings. Resize column B to 23.57.

e. Format the page layout to the orientation that works best for each worksheet.

f. Save your changes, and then print or submit your file as directed by your instructor. Close your file, and then exit Excel.

Problem Solve 2

Student data file needed:

Blank Excel Workbook

You will save your file as:

Lastname_Firstname_e06_ps2_Hotel2_WhatIf

Break-Even Analysis for Vacation Packages at the Painted Paradise Resort and Spa

The hotel area has asked you to develop a spreadsheet model that helps determine its break-even point when a vacation package—such as the spa special or golf weekend—is booked. Currently, William Mattingly is not certain whether the pricing helps cover expenses such as marketing costs or whether the price even generates a profit for the resort. He would also like you to generate a Solver answer report that will optimize the price of a few of the vacation packages. Upon completion, you will present your model to Mr. Mattingly before the spreadsheet model is implemented.

a. Start **Excel**, and then create a new workbook. Save it as Lastname_Firstname_e06_ps2_Hotel2_WhatIf, and then insert a file name footer in the left section of the footer.

b. Click the **Sheet1 worksheet tab**, if necessary, and then rename it Break-even Analysis. Complete the following tasks to create your monthly break-even analysis, and then build a two-variable data table that will help analyze the break-even point of the Golf & Spa Special.

- Add the following categories and items to your spreadsheet. Revenue will list the quantity, price, and extended price for the Golf Weekend along with the gross revenue. Use $1,245 as the Golf Weekend price. Expenses will list fixed costs of the marketing manager salary—type $4,669—and office equipment depreciation—type $865.31. Variable costs include advertising costs—which are 10% of the gross revenue—and miscellaneous overhead per package—type $14.82. Finally, calculate your net income.

- Apply Conditional Formatting to the Net Income value so numbers that are less than zero are displayed in red text font, and then enter values in quantity until you find the break-even point.

- In cell range G3:L15, build a two-variable data table with the title Golf & Spa Special Pricing merged and centered in H3:L3 that lists the pricing along with the quantity booked. Use the following pricing data column headings for H4:L4: $2,425, $2,668, $2,934, $3,228, and $3,550. Using the range G5:G15 add headings between 50 to 100 in increments of five for quantity. Hide the results of the G4 formula referencing the Net Income value using the ;;; custom format.

- Insert a two-variable data table using price as the Row input cell and quantity as the Column input cell text box. Format the cells as **Currency** with 2 decimal places. Resize your columns to see all the data, if necessary. Create Conditional Formatting for cell range H5:L15 that uses the **Highlight Cells Rules** to format the cells with the **Light Red Fill with Dark Red Text** option for values less than $155,000, the **Green Fill with Dark Green Text** option for values greater than $200,000, and the **Yellow Fill with Dark Yellow Text** option for values between $155,000 and $200,000.

c. Click the **Sheet2 worksheet tab**, and then rename it Goal Seek. Complete the following tasks to create next year's forecast of vacation packages.

Use the following data to create your Goal Seek model:

Packages	This Year
Golf Weekend	583
Spa Special	247
Golf and Spa Special	331

- Create a column named Next Year, and then type a formula that calculates the forecasted totals for next year. Management anticipates having a 15% increase over this year's sales. Add a column named Extended Price that calculates the total revenue forecasted for next year's sales.

- Open the Goal Seek dialog box. The resort wants to set a sales goal of $1,000,000 for its Golf Weekend package, a sales goal of $750,000 for its Spa Special package, and a sales goal of $1,250,000 for its Golf and Spa Special package.

d. Click the **Sheet3 worksheet tab**, and then rename it Solver. Complete the following tasks to create a Solver Answer report that determines the maximum net income that can be generated next year.

- Add the following categories and items to your spreadsheet. Revenue will list the quantity, price, and extended price for all three vacation packages along with the gross revenue. Use $1,245 as the Golf Weekend price, $1,445 as the Spa Special price, and $2,425 as the Golf and Spa Special price. Expenses will list fixed costs of the marketing manager salary—type $146,375—and office equipment depreciation—type $10,383.72. Variable costs include advertising costs—which are 10% of the gross revenue—and miscellaneous overhead per package—type $14.82. Finally, calculate your net income.

- Click the **Data tab**, open the **Solver Parameters** dialog box, use Net Income as the Set Objective cell, and then use the Qty. cells and Misc. overhead per package cell as the By Changing Variable Cells.

- Add the following Solver constraints. The resort wants to book at least 100 of each Revenue vacation package. The resort only has the resources to book at most 300 of each vacation package. Each vacation package must be whole numbers—integers—because the resort cannot sell part of a package. Create three constraints that define the quantities as integers. The minimum that management wants to spend on Misc. overhead per package is $15, and the maximum that management wants to spend on Misc. overhead per package is $20.

- Create a Saved Solver Models section, and then save your Solver model. Create a Solver answer report using the GRG Nonlinear solving method. Be sure to restore original values. (*Hint*: Click **Answer** under Reports. Do not forget to check **Options** and **Use Multistart** and not **Use Automatic Scaling**.)

e. Format your spreadsheet so users can easily read it—such as Number or Currency format—and then delete any worksheets that were not used.

f. Format the page layout to the orientation that works best for each worksheet.

g. Save your changes, and then print or submit your file as directed by your instructor. Close your file, and then exit Excel.

Student data file needed:

e06_ps3_Hotel3_Analysis

You will save your file as:

Lastname_Firstname_e06_ps3_Hotel3_Analysis

Financial Analysis for the Painted Paradise Resort and Spa

The hotel area is considering some upgrades to hotel rooms and the lobby—such as adding a business center with computers, a fax machine, and a printer. Management has asked you to develop a spreadsheet model that performs a loan and investment analysis. Currently, William Mattingly is not certain if spending money on upgrades will result in a return on the investment. Mr. Mattingly gave you an Excel workbook with a partial model already built and some data to use while building your model. Upon completion, you will present your model to Mr. Mattingly before the spreadsheet model is implemented.

a. Start **Excel**, and then open the **e06_ps3_Hotel3_Analysis** workbook. Save it as Lastname_Firstname_e06_ps3_Hotel3_Analysis, and then insert a file name footer in the left section of the footer. Click the **Documentation worksheet tab**. Click cell **A6**, type today's date, click cell **B6**, and then type your first and last name.

b. Click the **Loan Analysis worksheet tab**. Complete the following tasks to build a loan analysis model. Assume all payments will be made at the end of the period.

- Click cell **B10**, and then use the PMT function to calculate the monthly payment of the loan.

- Click cell **B13**, use the IPMT function to calculate the interest portion of the monthly payment, and then click cell **B16** and use the PPMT function to calculate the principal portion of the monthly payment.

- Click cell **E10**, use the RATE function to calculate the rate of the loan based on the data in the range E6:E9, and then then click cell **E13** and use the NPER function to calculate the number of periods based on the data in the range E6:E10.

- Click cell **E14**, use the ABS and CUMPRINC functions to calculate how much principal was paid during the life of the loan, and then click cell **E15** and use the ABS and CUMIPMT functions to calculate how much interest was paid during the life of the loan. You will need to type 1 in the start_period, 120 in the end_period arguments, and 0 for the type argument.

- Click cell **B34**, and then use the NPV function to calculate the net present value of the loan. Click cell **B35**, use the XNPV function to calculate the irregular net present value, and then click cell **B36** and use the XIRR function to calculate the irregular internal rate of return. (*Hint*: Use the data located under the Loan Values section of the spreadsheet to calculate these values.)

c. Click the **Values worksheet tab**. Click cell **B9**, use the PV function to calculate the present value of the loan, and then click in cell **B17** and use the FV function to calculate the future value. Assume all payments will be made at the end of the period.

d. Click the **Depreciation worksheet tab**. Use this worksheet to build an asset depreciation table for new office equipment.

- Select the range **B8:B12**, create a straight-line depreciation schedule using the SLN function. To calculate the accumulated depreciation for the first year, click cell **C8**, type =B8, and then calculate the accumulated depreciation for the years 2 through 5 by adding the depreciation expense for year and previous accumulated depreciation at year end. Copy the function down to **C12** using the AutoFill handle.

- Click cell **D8**, calculate the salvage value at year end by subtracting accumulated depreciation at year end from the cost of asset, and then copy the function down to **D12** using the AutoFill handle.

- Select the range **F8:F12**, and then create a declining balance depreciation schedule using the DB function. Calculate the accumulated depreciation in G8:G12, and then salvage value at year end for years 1 through 5 in H8:H12. (*Hint*: Use the range A8:A12 as the values for the period argument for F8:F12 formulas.)

- Select the range **J8:J12**, and then create a declining balance depreciation schedule using the DDB function. Calculate the accumulated depreciation in K8:K12, and then salvage value at year end for years 1 through 5 in L8:L12. (*Hint*: Use the range A8:A12 as the values for the period argument for J8:J12 formulas.)

e. Format the page layout to the orientation that works best for each worksheet.

f. Save your changes, and then print or submit your file as directed by your instructor. Close your file, and then exit Excel.

Perform 1: Perform in Your Life

Student data file needed:

e06_pf1_Syllabus

You will save your file as:

Lastname_Firstname_e06_pf1_Grade_WhatIf

Using Solver and Goal Seek to Help Calculate Your Grade

This spreadsheet model will help you use Solver to calculate a grade based on a weighted average. The Solver model will allow you to enter multiple grade categories and determine how you can maximize your current grade. This could answer a question such as "what grades do I need to earn on my research paper and final exam to earn an A in the course?" Additionally, this model will allow you to use Goal Seek to determine the grade you will need to earn on an assignment or exam to earn a specific grade in the course. For example, you may currently have a B and want to calculate what grade you need to earn on a final exam to earn an A in the course. You need to set up Solver and Goal Seek based on the grading information from your course syllabus.

a. Start **Excel**, and then create a new blank workbook. Save it as Lastname_Firstname_e06_pf1_Grade_WhatIf, and then insert a file name footer in the left section of the footer.

b. Open the **e06_pf1_Syllabus** or the syllabus for your course if directed by your instructor. Use the information within the grading section of your syllabus to create your Solver model.

c. Click the **Sheet1 worksheet tab**, if necessary, and then rename it Weighted Grade. Complete the following tasks to build a Solver Answer report.

- Create a model that lists your grade categories and specific assignments under each one. For example, you may have five assignments. Create a heading for assignments and then list the specific assignments such as Assignment 1, Assignment 2, and so on.

- Type a formula that calculates the weighted grade of each category. To do so, you would add what you earned on all items in the category, divide by the total points possible, and multiply by the weighted percent. The result will be a decimal. The sum of the results would then be multiplied by 100 to convert it to a percent—which is your grade. Format your spreadsheet so users can easily read it—such as Number or Percent format.

- Use the Final Grade Total calculation as your objective cell and the outstanding measurement items—the items that have no grade entered—as your changing cells.

- Add constraints that set outstanding assignments to specific values. For example, if you want to earn an A in your class, you would add a constraint that limits the result of the objective cell to the lowest and highest values within the grade range—such as 92 percent to 100 percent.

- Create a Saved Solver Models section, and then save your Solver model. Create a Solver answer report using the GRG Nonlinear solving method. Be sure to restore original values.

d. Create a table that will be used for a Goal Seek analysis next to your Solver model. Enter each category, type a formula that calculates the weighted grade of each category, and then enter your grades with the exception of a final grade. Determine what grade you need on the final exam to earn a B in the course by using Goal Seek.

e. Click the **Sheet2 worksheet tab**, and then rename it Straight Percent. Complete the following tasks to create a Solver answer report and Goal Seek model based on a straight percent grading structure.

- Recreate the Solver model you created on the Weighted Grade worksheet. Modify the formulas on the worksheet as well as the Solver constraints to calculate your grade based on a straight percent calculation. Determine what you will need to earn on outstanding measurement items to earn an A in the course. Create a Solver answer report using the GRG Nonlinear solving method. Format your numbers appropriately.

- Create a Saved Solver Models section, and then save your Solver model. Create a Solver Answer report using the GRG Nonlinear solving method. Be sure to Restore Original Values.

- Recreate the Goal Seek model from the Weighted Grade worksheet to determine what grade you would need to earn on the final exam to earn a B+ in the course. Use the same grades that you entered on the Weighted Grade worksheet.

f. Format your spreadsheet so users can easily read it—such as Number format—and then delete any worksheets that were not used—such as Sheet3.

g. Format the page layout to the orientation that works best for each worksheet.

h. Save your changes, and then print or submit your file as directed by your instructor. Close your file, and then exit Excel.

Perform 2: Perform in Your Career

Student data file needed:
e06_pf2_Charity_Analysis

You will save your file as:
Lastname_Firstname_e06_pf2_Charity_Analysis

Managing Finances for a Charity Fundraising Event

This spreadsheet model will help you use What-If analysis tools to determine how much of the monies raised at a charity event will actually be donated to the charity. When a charity event is held, there are costs associated with setting it up and running it. Jonas Lamar, the event coordinator, has asked you to create a break-even analysis, a one-variable data table, and a two-variable data table to determine the break-even point. Additionally, you need to perform a financial analysis to determine how much money the charity can make if the fundraising profits are invested. You also want to analyze the finances to determine how much a loan would cost if you needed to take out a loan for startup costs. Mr. Lamar has given you an Excel workbook and the appropriate information to get started.

a. Start **Excel**, and then open **e06_pf2_Charity_Analysis**. Save it as Lastname_Firstname_e06_pf2_Charity_Analysis, and then insert a file name footer in the left section of the footer. Click the **Documentation worksheet tab**. Click cell **A6**, type today's date, click cell **B6**, and then type your first and last name.

b. Click the **Break-even Analysis worksheet tab**, if necessary. Complete the following tasks to build a break-even analysis, a one-variable data table, and build a traditional cost volume profit chart off the one-variable data table that will help analyze the break-even point.

- Insert the appropriate formulas to cells D6, D11, D13, D14, D15, D16, D17, D18, and underline D15.
- Insert a scroll bar in the area of cells E4 through E16. Type the following criteria in the Format Controls dialog box.

  Current value: 10

  Minimum value: 10

  Maximum value: 5000

  Incremental change: 1

  Page change: 10

  Cell link: type $D$4
- Format cell D18 with conditional formatting so numbers that are less than zero are displayed in red text, and then scroll until you find the break-even point.
- Click cell **G4**, reference the total expenses cell, click cell **H4**, reference the gross revenue cell, click cell **I4**, and then reference the net income cell. Format the range G4:I4 to hide the results of the functions you just referenced.
- Select the range **F4:I19**, and then insert a one-variable data table using Total attendees for the Column input cell. Select the range **G5:I19**, and then format the cells as Currency with no decimal places.
- Select the range **I5:I19**, and then format the cells using the Green - Yellow - Red Color Scale.
- Select the range **F3:H3**, and then select the range **F5:H19**. Insert a line chart in the 2-D Line category. Use the range **F5:F19** as the Horizontal (Category) Axis Labels. Delete the blue data line. Add a horizontal axis title that is below the axis with Attendees in the title text box. Reposition the chart below the one-variable data table.

c. Click the **Financial Analysis worksheet tab**. Complete the following tasks to build a financial analysis and two-variable data table. The event manager believes that the total donation will be $250,000.

- Click cell **B8**, and then use the PMT function to calculate the monthly payment of the loan. Assume the payment will be made at the end of the period.
- Click cell **B14**, and then type a formula that calculates the total money earned on the investment.
- Click cell **B15**, and then use the FV function to calculate the future value of the investment. Assume the lump sum payout will be made at the end of the period.
- Click cell **D5**, and then reference the loan payment. Format the cell so it displays **Rate** instead of the payment.
- Click the range **D5:J15**, and then create a two-variable data table based on Interest Rate for the Row input cell and the Payment for the Column input cell. Apply Conditional Formatting for payments in range **E6:J15** that are less than $1,050 in Green Fill with **Dark Green Text** and payments that are greater than $1,350 in Light Red Fill with **Dark Red Text**. Apply Conditional Formatting for values that fall between $1,050 and $1,350 in Yellow Fill with **Dark Yellow Text**.

d. Format the page layout to the orientation that works best for each worksheet.

e. Save your changes, and then print or submit your file as directed by your instructor. Close your file, and then exit Excel.

Student data file needed:	You will save your file as:
e06_pf3_Roadhouse_WhatIf	Lastname_Firstname_e06_pf3_Roadhouse_WhatIf

Managing Beverage Pricing at The Roadhouse Bar and Grill

You are the bar manager at the Roadhouse Bar and Grill, a local restaurant that specializes in home-cooked meals for breakfast, lunch, and dinner. The general manager has given you an Excel workbook that contains data about the beverages offered and sold. You need to manage the inventory of beverage items to ensure you have enough beverages for each day you are open for business as well as to determine pricing for special drink items.

a. Start **Excel**, and then open the **e06_pf3_Roadhouse_WhatIf**. Save it as Lastname_Firstname_e06_pf3_Roadhouse_WhatIf, and then insert a file name footer in the left section of the footer. Click the **Documentation worksheet tab**. Click cell **A6**, type today's date, click cell **B6**, and then type your first and last name.

b. Click the **Goal Seek worksheet tab**, if necessary. Complete the following tasks to forecast prices for drink specials.

   • Select the range **D5:D9**, type a formula that increases this year's quantity sold by 20%. Select the range **F5:F9**, and then type a formula that calculates the extended price for next year's forecast.

   • The current prices are located in range E5:E9. Use Goal Seek to determine new prices based on the revenue goals for next year, located in range G5:G9.

c. Click the **Scenarios worksheet tab**. Complete the following tasks to create a Scenario Summary report.

   • Select range **E4:E8**, type a formula that calculates the extended price for next year's forecast. Click cell **E9**, and then type a formula that calculates the gross revenue.

   • Click cell **E18**, and then type a formula that calculates the variable cost for all drinks sold.

   • Open the Scenario Manager. Add a Worst-case scenario, and then use the Qty cells as the changing cells. The current values on the worksheet will be your Worst-case scenario values.

   • Add a new scenario named Best-case scenario. Use the following values as your Scenario values:

   Mojito: 175

   Fuzzy Navel: 60

   Strawberry Daiquiri: 45

   Pina Colada: 30

   Roadhouse Special: 200

   • Add a new scenario named Most Likely scenario. Use the following values as your Scenario values:

   Mojito: 150

   Fuzzy Navel: 45

   Strawberry Daiquiri: 30

   Pina Colada: 20

   Roadhouse Special: 150

   • Create a Scenario Summary report using the net income cell as your result cell. Format your report with the appropriate row headings, and then resize columns if necessary.

d. Click the **Scenarios worksheet tab**. Complete the following tasks to create a Scenario PivotTable report.

- Modify your result cells to include gross revenue, variable costs, taxes, and net income, and then create a Scenario PivotTable report.

- Format your report with the appropriate row headings, cell formats, and resize columns if necessary.

e. Format the page layout to the orientation that works best for each worksheet.

f. Save your changes, and then print or submit your file as directed by your instructor. Close your file, and then exit Excel.

Perform 4: How Others Perform

Student data file needed:	You will save your file as:
e06_pf4_Cappys_Analysis	Lastname_Firstname_e06_pf4_Cappys_Analysis

Being an Entrepreneur, Cappy's Car Rental

You are the owner of a small rental car company—Cappy's Car Rental. Your intern created a spreadsheet model for you to use when analyzing financial information about your fleet of cars and the loans you have taken out to purchase cars. Additionally, the spreadsheet model will allow you to determine which type of depreciation will be the best to use. Finally, you notice that the lack of formatting of numbers makes the information difficult to read, several formulas are missing, and formulas that do exist should be evaluated to ensure they are correct. Although your intern made the spreadsheet visually appealing, you realize that once you begin analyzing the workbook, quite a few changes need to be made.

a. Start **Excel**, and then open the **e06_pf4_Cappys_Analysis** workbook from the student data files. Save the file as Lastname_Firstname_e06_pf4_Cappys_Analysis, and then insert a file name footer in the left section of the footer. Click the **Documentation worksheet tab**. Click cell **A6**, type today's date, click cell **B6**, and then type your first and last name.

b. Click the **Analysis worksheet tab**, if necessary. Complete the following tasks to correct the mistakes. Assume that all payments will be made at the end of the period.

- Apply appropriate formatting to all numbers.
- Check all existing formulas to ensure they are correct and correct them as needed.
- Enter any missing formulas.

c. Format the page layout to the orientation that works best for each worksheet.

d. Save your changes, and then print or submit your file as directed by your instructor. Close your file, and then exit Excel.

Glossary

3-D named range References the same cell or range of cells across multiple worksheets in a workbook. 3-D named ranges can be used in formulas as a replacement for 3-D cell references.

3-D reference Has the following structure: Sheetname!ColumnRow. It includes a reference to the worksheet, a third dimension, that allows access to cell contents in other worksheets.

A

ABS function A function that returns the absolute value of a number—the number without its negative sign.

Absolute cell reference The exact address of a cell, when both the column and row need to remain a constant regardless of the position of the cell when the formula is copied to other cells.

Absolute macro reference Affects exactly the same cell address every time the referencing macro is run. Absolute macro references are set when the macro is recorded.

Active cell Identifiable as the cell with the thick black border. Only the active cell can have data entered into it.

Active worksheet The worksheet that is visible in the Excel application window. The active worksheet tab has a white background.

Add-in An application with specific functionality geared toward accomplishing a specific goal.

Aggregate To consolidate or summarize data with functions like SUM, COUNT, or AVERAGEIF.

Alignment The positioning of content in a cell, either horizontally left, centered, or horizontally right; vertically bottom, middle, or top.

Amortization table A schedule that calculates the interest and principal payments along with the remaining balance of the loan.

Amortize Paying off debt in payments over a period of time.

Analysis layer Consists primarily of formulas that analyze or extract data from the data layer into formatted tables.

Annuity A fixed sum payable at specified intervals such as a series of cash payments made over a continuous period of time.

Any Value validation A form of validation that does not restrict data entry in any way, but makes the prompts available.

Area chart Emphasizes magnitude of change over time and depict trends.

Argument Variables or values the function requires in order to calculate a solution. A value passed to a function, either as a constant or a variable.

AutoFill Copies information from one cell, or a series in adjacent cells, into adjacent cells in the direction the fill handle is dragged.

AutoSum function Shortcuts to using the SUM functions.

AVERAGE function A function that returns a weighted average from a specified range of cells.

B

Backstage view Provides access to the file-level features, such as saving a file, creating a new file, opening an existing file, printing a file, and closing a file, as well as program options.

Banding Alternating the background color of rows and/or columns to assist in tracking information.

Bar chart Displays data horizontally and is used for comparisons among individual items.

Binding constraint A constraint is binding if changing it also changes the optimal solution.

Break-even analysis Used to calculate the break-even point in sales volume or dollars, estimate profit or loss at any level of sales volume, and help in setting prices.

Break-even point The sales level at which revenue equals total costs—there is neither a profit nor a loss.

Built-in cell style Predefined and named combination of cell and content formatting properties.

Built-in function A function included in the Excel application that can be categorized as financial, statistical, mathematical, date and time, text, etc.

Built-in templates Provided with an installation of Microsoft Office and are stored in the \Program Files\Microsoft Office\ Templates\1033 folder.

Business intelligence (BI) Refers to a variety of software applications that are used to analyze an organization's data in order to provide management with the tools necessary to improve decision making, cut costs, and identify new opportunities.

C

Camera tool A tool in Excel used to take a live image of a range of cells.

Capital budgeting The planning procedure used to evaluate whether an organization's long-term investments are worth pursuing.

Cascade view Overlaps all open Excel workbooks in such a way that all workbook title bars are visible and switching between workbooks can be accomplished by clicking the title bar of the workbook you want to make active.

Cash flow The movement of cash in and out of a business.

Cell The intersection of a row and a column in a worksheet.

Cell reference 1. The combination of a cell's column and row addresses. 2. Refers to a particular cell or range of cells within a formula or function instead of a value.

Changing cell The cell or cells used to identify the various data cells whose values can differ in each scenario.

Chart sheet A tabbed sheet that only holds a chart.

Circular reference A condition where a formula references itself.

CLEAN Removes any nonprinting characters from a text string.

Code window Where VBA code is typed and also where VBA generated by a recorded macro can be viewed and edited.

Codification scheme Consists of rules that combine data values in specific formats and locations to generate a new data value.

Codified data value Formed following a system of rules where the position of information is tied to its context.

Column Part of a spreadsheet that is lettered in ascending sequence from left to right.

Column chart Used to compare across categories, show change, sometimes over time.

Comma separated Is a format for text files (.csv) that uses commas to separate data elements.

Complex function A function that combines multiple functions within a formula.

CONCATENATE A text function used to join up to 255 text strings into one text string.

Conditional aggregate function A function that aggregates a subset of data that has been filtered based upon one or more criteria.

Conditional formatting Applies custom formatting to highlight or emphasize values that meet specific criteria and is called conditional because the formatting occurs when a particular condition is met.

Conjunction function A function that enables linking or joining of functions and formulas.

Consolidate by category Aggregates data in cells with matching row and or column labels.

Consolidate by position Aggregates data in the same position in multiple worksheets.

Constant A value that does not change.

Constraint A rule that you establish when formulating your Solver model.

Contextual tab A Ribbon tab that contains commands related to selected objects so you can manipulate, edit, and format the objects.

Cost-volume-profit analysis The study of how certain costs react to changes in business activities such as costs, selling prices, revenues, profits, and production volume—if you manufacture products.

COUNT function A function that returns the number of cells in a range of cells that contain numbers.

CUMIPMT function A function used to calculate the amount of interest paid over a specific number of periods, such as quarterly or annually.

CUMPRINC function A function used to calculate the amount of principal paid over a specific number of periods, such as quarterly or annually.

Custom validation A form of validation that restricts data entry through a user-entered formula.

D

Data bars Graphical display of data that is overlaid on the data in the cells of the worksheet.

Data cleansing The process of fixing obvious errors in the data and converting the data into a useful format.

Data layer Consists of the raw data that will not be directly modified.

Data point An individual piece of data being graphed.

Data series A set or subset of data that is graphed.

Data set Organized data, includes fields and data that have context and meaning.

Data table A what-if analysis tool that takes sets of input values, determines possible results, and displays all the results in one table on one worksheet.

Data validation Any means of increasing the probability of correct data entry through programmatic tools and behavioral modifications.

Data verification The process of validating that the data is correct and accurate.

DATE Returns the sequential serial number that represents a particular date.

Date validation A form of validation that restricts data entry into a cell to valid date values.

DATEVALUE A function that converts a date in a text format into a serial number.

DB function A function used to calculate the depreciation of an asset for a specified period using the fixed-declining balance method.

DDB function A function used to calculate the depreciation of an asset for a specified period using the double-declining balance method.

Decimal validation A form of validation that restricts entered data to real numbers within a specified range.

Default A setting that is in place unless you specify otherwise.

Delimiter A way of separating text data segments or elements in text files.

Depreciation schedule Records the date that the asset was placed into service, a calculation for each year's depreciation, and the accumulated depreciation.

Dialog box A window that provides more options or settings beyond those provided on the Ribbon.

Dialog Box Launcher Opens a corresponding dialog box or task pane.

Digital dashboard Mechanisms that deliver business intelligence in graphical form.

Document Depending on the application, a document can be a letter, memo, report, brochure, resume, or flyer.

Drilling down A method for accessing the detailed records used in a PivotTable to get some aggregated data.

E

Economic risk When there is a risk that a chosen act or activity will not generate sufficient revenues to cover operating costs and to repay debt obligations.

Elastic A product or service is *elastic*—or responsive to change—if a small change in price is accompanied by a large change in the quantity demanded.

Emphasis Adds any group of features to characters in a font that includes bold, italics, and underline.

Encryption A process that uses a password to create a unique algorithm that is used to translate the saved Excel workbook into a stream of uninterpretable characters than can only be translated back using the password.

Evolutionary method The method used when a worksheet model is nonlinear and nonsmooth and uses functions—such as VLOOKUP, PMT, IF, and so on—to calculate the values of the variable cells or constraint cells.

External data Any data that is not stored locally or not in an Excel format (.xls or .xlsx).

F

Factor An argument for the rate at which the balance declines. If factor is omitted, Excel assumes the value to be 2.

Field An item of information associated with something of interest. A collection of fields about an item of interest form a record.

Fill Across Worksheets Can be used to copy cell contents, formats, or contents and formats (All) to worksheets in a group.

Fill color The background color of a cell.

Filtering A process of hiding records that do not meet specified criteria in a data set.

FIND Locates one text string within a second text string, and returns the number of the starting position of the first text string from the starting character of the second text string.

Fixed cost An expense that never changes regardless of how much product is sold or how many services are rendered.

Font A style of displaying characters, numbers, punctuation, and special characters.

Foreign key In the context of relational databases, the foreign key is a shared field that is not a primary key but serves to link to a table in which the same field is a primary key of the other table.

Format Painter A tool that facilitates rapid application of formats between one cell to another cell or a range of cells.

Formula An equation that performs a mathematical calculation (or calculations) using information in the worksheets to calculate new values and can contain cell references, constants, functions, numbers, mathematical operators, and text.

Formula auditing A process that shows you which cells are used in a formula and how they are used.

Function A small program that performs operations against data based on a set of inputs and returns a value. Some functions, null functions, do not require arguments.

Function procedure A group of VBA statements that performs a calculation and returns a single value.

Fv An argument used for the future value of the loan—the balance you reach after the last payment is made.

FV function A function used to calculate the value of an investment with a fixed interest rate, term, and periodic payment over a specific period of time.

G

Goal seek A scenario tool that maximizes Excel's cell-referencing capabilities and enables you to find the input values needed to achieve a goal or objective.

Graphic Pictures, clip art, SmartArt, shapes, and charts that can enhance the look of your documents.

Graphical format The presentation of information in charts, graphs, and pictures.

GRG nonlinear method A method used when the worksheet model is nonlinear and smooth and is the default method that Excel's Solver uses. A nonlinear and smooth model is one in which a graph of the equation used would not show sharp edges or breaks if you were to plot the equation on a graph.

Gridline Lines that demarcate the boundaries of individual cells in a worksheet.

Grouping Allows you to perform certain tasks once and have those tasks affect all worksheets in the group.

Grouping variable A field that could be used to categorize or group for the purpose of comparison.

Guess An argument used when you want to guess what the interest rate will be. If nothing is entered, Excel assumes that the guess is 10 percent.

H

Hard-coding Including actual data in formulas, making it necessary to edit the formula whenever the number needs to be changed.

HTML Short for Hypertext Markup Language, this language defines how web page content is displayed in a browser.

Hyperlink An object, such as a string of text, that when clicked on navigates to a predefined location within large worksheets, among worksheets in a workbook, among workbooks, opens websites, opens documents and images, or sends e-mail.

I

Inelastic A product is *inelastic*—or not responsive to change—if a large change in price is accompanied by a small amount of change in demand.

Information Data that has context, meaning, and relevance and thus value to the user.

Information management program Gives you the ability to keep track and print schedules, task lists, phone directories, and other documents.

Input box A way of using VBA code to increase the interactivity of a dashboard by prompting the user for information and storing that information in a variable to be used later.

IPMT function A financial function that calculates the amount of interest paid for a fixed term or fixed rate loan or investment.

IRR function A function used to indicate the profitability of an investment. It is commonly used in business when choosing between investments.

ISERROR A function used to check for error values. It returns TRUE if an error is found, and FALSE if no error is encountered. When the ISERROR function is used in conjunction with the IF function, a different action result can be defined if an error occurs.

Iteration A process that repeatedly enters new values in the variable cell to find a solution to the problem.

K

Key performance indicator (KPI) A measure that is very important for the design of dashboards in that it helps managers track and interpret data.

Key tip A form of keyboard shortcut. Pressing Alt will display Key Tips (or keyboard shortcuts) for items on the Ribbon and Quick Access Toolbar.

Keyboard shortcut Keyboard equivalents for software commands that allow you to keep your hands on the keyboard instead of reaching for the mouse to make Ribbon selections.

L

Landscape Orientation For page layout and printing purposes, landscape indicates the longer dimension of the page is on the horizontal axis.

LEFT Returns the characters in a text string based on the number of characters you specify starting with the far-left character in the string.

LEN Returns the number of characters in a text string.

Line chart Used to show continuous data over time, great for showing trends.

List validation A form of validation that restricts the user to selecting from a list of predefined values.

Live preview Lets you see the effects of menu selections on your document file or selected item before making a commitment to a particular menu choice.

Logical function A function that returns a result based on evaluation of a logical test.

Logical test Also known as logical expression, an equation with comparison operators that can be evaluated to either true of false.

LOWER Converts all uppercase characters in a text string to lowercase.

M

Macro A form of computer program that automates activities such as mouse movements and clicks, menu selections, and data entry.

Markup language Uses special sequences of characters or "markup" indicators called "tags" inserted in the document to indicate how the document should look when it is displayed or printed.

Mathematical operators Parentheses (), exponentiation ^, division /, multiplication *, addition +, subtraction –.

MAX function A function that examines all numeric values in a specified range and returns the maximum value.

Maximize The button located in the top-right corner of the title bar that, when clicked, offers the largest workspace.

Message box A dialog box used to display informative messages to the user and includes buttons for the user to interact with.

Metadata Data about data. It describes the content and context of the data.

Method An action Excel performs with an object.

Microsoft Query A query wizard used to connect to external data sources, select data from those external sources, import that data into a worksheet, and refresh the data as needed to keep the worksheet data synchronized with the data in the external sources.

MID Returns a specific number of characters from a text string, starting at the position you specify, based on the number of characters you specify.

MIN function A function that examines all numeric values in a specified range and returns the minimum value.

Mini toolbar Appears after text is selected and contains buttons for the most commonly used formatting commands, such as font, font size, font color, center alignment, indents, bold, italic, and underline.

Minimize Hides the application on the taskbar.

Mixed cell reference Using a combination of absolute cell referencing and relative cell referencing for a cell address within a formula by preceding either the column letter or the row value with a dollar sign to "lock" as absolute while leaving the other portion of the cell address as a relative reference.

Mixed cost A cost that contains a variable component and a fixed component.

Module A container for code.

N

Named range A set of cells that has been given a name, other than the default column and row cell address name, that can then be used within a formula or function.

Nested IF An equation using one or more IF function within another IF function.

Nonbinding constraint Less severe constraints that do not affect the optimum solution.

Nper An argument used for the total number of payments that will be made in order to pay the loan in full.

NPER function A function used to calculate the number of payment periods for an investment or loan if you know the loan amount, interest rate, and payment amount.

NPV function A function used to determine the value of an investment or business by analyzing a time series of incoming and outgoing cash flows.

O

Object collection A group of objects that are also considered objects themselves.

Object model Consists of a hierarchical collection of objects that can be manipulated using VBA.

Object-oriented programming (OOP) Uses a hierarchy of objects also called classes as the focus of the programming.

Objective cell A cell that contains the formula that creates a value that you want to optimize—maximize, minimize, or set to a specific value.

Objects Combinations of data and code that are treated as a single unit including workbooks, worksheets, charts, PivotTables, and even Excel itself.

One-variable data table A data table that can help you analyze how different values of one variable in one or more formulas will change the results of those formulas.

Optimize To obtain a solution and find the best way to do something.

Order of operations The order in which Excel processes calculations in a formula that contains more than one operator.

P

Parameter 1. A special form of variable included in a worksheet for the sole purpose of inclusion in formulas and functions. 2. A special kind of variable used to refer to one of the pieces of data provided in a method.

Per An argument used as the period for which you want to find the interest and must be a value within the range of 1 to nper.

Pie chart Displays a comparison of each value to a total.

PivotChart A built-in analysis tool that allows for graphical representations of a PivotTable.

PivotTable Interactive tables that extract, organize, and summarize source data.

PMT function A function used to calculate a payment amount based on constant payments and a constant interest rate.

Portable Document Format (PDF) A file format developed by Adobe Systems in 1993 that has become a standard for storing files.

Portrait Orientation For page layout and printing purposes, portrait indicates the longer dimension of the page is on the vertical axis.

PPMT function A financial function that calculates the amount of principal paid for a fixed term or fixed rate loan or investment.

Presentation layer Consists of graphics and chart that are based on the tables in the analysis layer.

Primary key In the context of relational database, this is a unique field that functions as a unique identifier for each row or record.

Principal The unpaid balance amount of the loan.

Print Preview View that allows you to preview how your document will print on the monitor before actually printing to paper or to a file.

Project Explorer window Contains a hierarchical list of all the objects in the workbook including macros, modules, and worksheets.

PROPER Capitalizes the first letter in each word of a text string with remaining characters for each word in lowercase.

Properties The attributes of an object that can be referred to or manipulated using VBA.

Properties window Contains a list of all the properties of a selected object such as name, size, and color.

Protected view A view in which the file contents can be seen and read, but you are not able to edit, save, or print the contents until you enable editing.

Pseudocode The rough draft of a formula or code. It is intended to help you understand the logic and determine the structure of a problem before you develop the actual formula.

Pv An argument used as the present value of the loan, and usually the loan amount is used as the present value.

PV The present value of an investment or loan.

PV function A function used to calculate the present or current value of a series of future payments on an investment.

Q

Query In the database context a query is just a way of structuring a question so that the computer can retrieve data.

Quick Access Toolbar Located at the top left of the Office window, it can be customized to offer commonly used buttons.

R

Range A group of cells in a worksheet that have been selected or highlighted. Commands performed while the group is selected will affect the entire range.

Rate 1. An argument in several financial functions that notes the periodic interest rate—the interest rate of the loan. 2. The periodic interest rate used for calculating interest accrued.

RATE function A function used to calculate the interest rate for an investment or loan, given that you know the loan or present value, payment, and number of payment periods.

Raw data Elements or raw facts—numeric or text—that may or may not have meaning or relevance.

Record Dataset that generally takes the form of a collection of fields.

Relational database A 3-dimensional database able to connect data in separate tables to form a relationship when common fields exist—to offer reassembled information from multiple tables.

Relational operator Tests the relationship between two values and returns a TRUE or FALSE response.

Relative cell reference Default cell reference in a formula to a cell reference position that will automatically adjust when the formula is copied or extended to other cells, the cell being referenced changes relative to the placement of the formula.

Relative macro reference Identifies cells relative to the location of the active cell when the macro was run. The actual cells relative macro references will affect are not determined until the macro is run.

REPLACE Replaces part of a text string, based on the number of characters you specify, with a different text string.

Restore Down Allows the user to arrange and view several windows at a time when multiple applications are open.

Ribbon Where you will find most of the commands for the application. The Ribbon differs from program to program, but each program has two tabs in common: the File tab and the Home tab.

Ribbon button Located just below the Minimize and Close buttons in the top-right corner of the window (and directly next to the Help button, which looks like a question mark), it can hide or show the Ribbon.

RIGHT Returns the characters in a text string based on the number of characters you specify starting from the far-right character position.

Row Part of a spreadsheet that is numbered in ascending sequence from top to bottom.

Run-time error Occurs when the code is executed, displaying a description of the error.

S

Scatter chart Shows the relationship between numeric variables.

Scenario Allows you to build a what-if analysis model that includes variable cells linked by one or more formulas or functions.

Scenario Manager Allows you to manage scenarios by adding, deleting, editing, and viewing scenarios and to create scenario reports.

Scenario PivotTable report The report you can create that includes the summary results of the scenarios in PivotTable format.

Scenario summary The report you can create that includes subtotals and the results of the scenarios.

Scenario tool A tool that enables a user to calculate numerous outputs in other cells by referencing the target cell in formulas and functions.

ScreenTip Small windows that display descriptive text when you rest the mouse pointer over an object or button.

Scroll bar 1. A form control that is linked to a specific cell. As the scrollbar slides left to right or up and down the value in the linked cell increases and decreases accordingly. 2. A form control used in what-if analyses that allows you to change a number in a target cell location in single-unit increments.

SEARCH Locates one text string within another text string and returns the number of the starting position of the first text string from the starting character of the second text string.

Separator Indicates the distinction between the object container and the member of that container.

Shortcut menu A list of commands related to a selection that appears when you right-click (click the right mouse button).

Show Formulas view Displays a toggle feature that allows for viewing the formula(s) in the spreadsheet cells instead of the output, or value, of the formula(s).

Simplex LP method A linear model in which the variables are not raised to any powers and no transcendent functions—such as sine or cosine—are used. A linear model can be charted as straight lines.

SkyDrive An online workspace provided by Microsoft. SkyDrive's online filing cabinet is a free Windows Live Service.

Slicer 1. A dialog window used for quickly filtering data in a PivotTable. 2. A visual control that allows you to quickly and easily filter your data in an interactive way to replace filter icons in PivotCharts.

SLN function A function used to calculate the depreciation of an asset for a specified period using the fixed-declining balance method.

Solver An add-in that helps you optimize a problem by manipulating the values for several variables with rules that you determine.

Solver answer report This report lists the target cell and the changing cells with their corresponding original and final values for the problem, input variables, and constraints. In addition, the formulas, binding status, and slacks are given for each constraint.

Solver limits report This report displays the achieved optimal value and all the input variables of the model with the optimal values. Additionally, the report displays the upper and lower bounds for the optimal value.

Solver population report This report displays various statistical characteristics about the given model like how many variables and rows it contains.

Solver sensitivity report This report provides information about how sensitive the solution is to small changes in the formula for the target cell. This report displays the shadow prices for the constraint—the amount that the objective function value changes per unit change in the constraint. This report can only be created if your Excel model does not contain integer or Boolean—the values 0 and 1—constraints.

Sparkline Small charts embedded into cells on a spreadsheet.

Sparklines New to Excel 2010, they provide for a way to graphically summarize a row or column of data in a single cell with a mini chart.

Spin button A form control that is linked to a specific cell. As the up and down arrows on the button are clicked, the value in the linked cell increases and decreases accordingly.

Spreadsheet A software application that organizes data in a row and column format and supports manipulation of data to support decision making.

Sub procedure Performs an action on your project or workbook.

SUBSTITUTE Substitutes new_text for old_text in a text string.

Summary variable Data that is not categorical in nature and would likely be used for summarization.

Syntax The structure and order of the function and the arguments needed to run the function.

T

Table A tabular data formatting tool that facilitates data sorting, filtering, and calculations by organizing data into rows and columns.

Table style A predefined set of formatting properties that determine the appearance of a table.

Tabular format The presentation of information such as text and numbers in tables.

Task pane A smaller window pane that often appears to the side of the program window and offers options or helps you to navigate through completing a task or feature.

Template A workbook saved as a template to facilitate its reuse. Generally usage-specific data are removed. Templates have a special file extension of .xltx.

Text data Any grouping of characters, numbers or dates.

Text file A file structured as a simple container of text data and sometimes structured by the use of delimiters to separate text.

Text functions A range of functions in Excel that help manage text data.

Text length validation A form of validation that restricts data entry to a string less than or equal to a specified limit.

Text to Columns Wizard A step-by-step guide used to separate simple data cell content such as dates or first and last names into separate columns.

Thumbnail A small picture of the open program file displayed.

Time validation A form of validation that restricts data entry into a cell to valid time values.

Trendline Graphing the trend in the data with the intent of helping predict the future.

TRIM Removes all spaces from text except for single spaces between words. Use TRIM on text that you have received from another application that may have irregular spacing.

Trusted location A folder that has been identified in the Microsoft Office Trust Center as a safe location from which to download executable code such as macros, ActiveX controls, and so on.

Two-variable data table A data table that can help you analyze how different values of two variables in one or more formulas will change the results of those formulas.

Type An argument to indicate when the payments are due—either at the beginning (1) or the end of a period (0). If type is omitted (because it is an optional argument), Excel assumes that the value is zero.

U

UPPER Converts text in a text string to uppercase.

V

Validation criteria A limitation that constrains what worksheet users are allowed to enter into a particular cell.

Variable 1. Space in a computer's memory that is given a name and is used to store a value. 2. A value that you can change to see how the change affects other values. 3. A value stored in a cell and used in a formula or function.

Variable cost A cost that changes based on how many products are sold or services rendered.

VBA (Visual Basic for Applications) A powerful programming language that is part of most Microsoft Office products that allows for a wide variety of enhancements to Microsoft Office applications.

Visual Basic Editor (VBE) The tool built into Microsoft Office that is used for creating and editing VBA.

W

Web query A tool for importing data into a spreadsheet directly from a web page.

What-if analysis Changes values in spreadsheet cells to investigate the effects on calculated values of interest, and allows you to examine the outcome of the changes to values in an worksheet.

White space Empty space on the screen or document that gives eyes a place to rest.

Whole number validation A form of validation that restricts data entry to whole numbers within a specified range.

Workbook A file that contains at least one worksheet.

Workbook theme A collection of built-in cell styles all associated with a theme name.

Worksheet Traditionally referred to as a spreadsheet.

Workspace A special file type that identifies multiple workbooks and remembers the manner in which you want them arranged.

X

XIRR function A function used to analyze a series of cash flows that are irregular or not periodic.

XML Short for Extensible Markup Language. XML allows users to define their own tags in order to define the content of the document. Used for web documents and transmitting data between systems.

XML element Includes the start and stop tags and everything in between them.

XML map The same as an XML schema in that it describes the structure of an XML document. Excel creates an XML map either based on an existing schema or creates a default map.

XML schema Also called a data map, describes the structure of XML document in terms of what XML elements it will contain and their sequence.

XNPV function A function to determine the value of an investment or business by analyzing an irregular time series of incoming and outgoing cash flows.

Index